Handbook of EMDR and Family Therapy Processes

Handbook of EMDR and Family Therapy Processes

Edited by

Francine Shapiro • Florence W. Kaslow • Louise Maxfield

John Wiley & Sons, Inc.

Library of Congress Cataloging-in-Publication Data:

Handbook of EMDR and family therapy processes / Francine Shapiro,
    Florence W. Kaslow, Louise Maxfield, editors.
      p.   cm.
    Includes bibliographical references and index.
    ISBN 978-0-471-70947-3 (cloth : alk. paper)
    1. Eye movement desensitization and reprocessing.   2. Family psycho-
therapy.   I. Shapiro, Francine.   II. Kaslow, Florence Whiteman.
III. Maxfield, Louise.   IV. Title: Handbook of eye movement desensitization and reprocessing and family therapy processes.
    [DNLM: 1. Desensitization, Psychologic—methods.   2. Family Thera-
py—methods.   3. Eye Movements.   WM 430.5.F2 H23548 2007]
    RC489.E98H36 2007
    616.89′156—dc22
                                                              2006015620
Printed in the United States of America.

10   9   8   7   6   5   4

To

ROBBIE DUNTON

who nurtured the development of EMDR
child treatment and laid the groundwork
for all those who followed.

To put the world right in order, we must first put the nation in order; to put the nation in order, we must first put the family in order; to put the family in order, we must first cultivate our personal life; we must first set our hearts right.

—Confucius

If you cannot get rid of the family skeleton, you may as well make it dance.

—George Bernard Shaw

Contents

PART V
Community Disasters

PART VI
Conclusion

APPENDIXES

Foreword

I was extremely pleased to be invited to write the Foreword for this book, which I believe is so important that it should rapidly become essential reading for those in our field. In the past 2 decades, Eye Movement Desensitization and Reprocessing (EMDR) has become one of the most important methods for treating trauma. It has recently been recognized by the American Psychiatric Association as well as lauded by countries as diverse as Turkey and Ireland, where it has been used by professionals with populations beset by both natural disasters and people-made civil strife. The idea of the three editors to bring together EMDR and family systems theories is indeed a brilliant one, and I am honored to have this opportunity to be part of this groundbreaking endeavor.

The focus of this book on attachment, family relationships, and intrapersonal functioning is very similar to my own professional focus on interpersonal neurobiology. This multidisciplinary perspective (Siegel, 1999) enables us to build on the wisdom of many scientific disciplines in defining the mind and mental health. The integrative focus is extremely useful in understanding the mechanisms underlying trauma's effects and an effective means to facilitate healing (Solomon & Siegel, 2003). In this book, EMDR and family system approaches are integrated in a unique fashion to reinforce the ways in which the treatment of individuals and families suffering from trauma's wake can be brought into well-being.

Our brains are the social organs of our bodies. In the early years of our lives, interactions with others shape the important connections in our brains that in turn influence our internal sense of self and our capacity for healthy relationships with others. The internal and the interpersonal are woven together during these early years, and these domains of our experience continue to weave a tapestry of our ways of living throughout our lives. In clinical terms, "self-regulation" is the way we manage and balance such things as our emotions, our bodily functions, our thinking, and even our communication patterns with others. The term *self* can be misleading: An individual is continually shaped by relationships with others throughout the life span. This view is reinforced by new findings that the brain continually restructures itself in response to life experiences.

The synaptic connections among neurons create the fundamental structure of the brain. Genes are important for determining the overall architecture of the brain, but the conditions in the womb can also influence these connections, contributing to the temperament with which one is born. Temperament is the constitutional makeup of the nervous system, one's sensitivities, proclivities to react intensely or subtly, overall mood, regularity, and capacity to engage with novel situations. When a baby is born, his or her communication patterns with others, especially caregivers, play a fundamental role in molding the continuing development of the brain. Research in attachment has revealed that it is these patterns of communication between caregiver and child that influence the development of the child's capacity for self-regulation: balancing emotions, interpersonal intimacy, and even how he or she develops self-reflection (Sroufe, Egeland, Carlson, & Collins, 2005),

ATTACHMENT

When a child is fortunate enough to have interactions that are caring, attuned, and mutually regulating with the caregiver, he or she usually develops a *secure* attachment relationship. This attachment experience results in healthy development across a wide array of domains, including social, emotional, and cognitive (Cassidy & Shaver, 1999). Children less fortunate, who have suboptimal experiences with their caregivers, often develop insecure attachment types. If parents are emotionally distant, the child's attachment can become *avoidant,* and the child may become prematurely independent (Sroufe et al., 2005). These children ultimately may experience a distancing of their own awareness from their internal state as well as the internal worlds of others (Siegel, 1999). When caregivers are inconsistent and intrusive, the child's attachment relationship tends to be *ambivalent,* and the child may grow up with a great deal of uncertainty and anxiety about having his or her needs met or relying on others. In both of these situations, children adapt the best they can, finding a solution to their situation and coping in a way that enables them to survive and move on in life.

When the parent is terrifying to the child, a *disorganized* form of attachment can develop. In this situation, unlike the secure and first two insecure forms, the child has "fear without solution" and lives with the biological paradox of two simultaneously activated brain circuits: When children are placed in a state of terror, their brain activates the reflex "Go to my parent for soothing and safety"; simultaneously, the brain also has the activated circuit "Go away from the source of terror." There is no organized adaptation to these conflicting experiences. Some theorists (Hesse, Main, Yost-Abrams, & Rifkin, 2003) have hypothesized that the result is a fragmentation in the child's state, one that ultimately leads to clinical forms of dissociation. This situation is not the same as the "double bind," which has been alluded to in the family literature (Watzlawick, 1963), but is a form of biological paradox in which two circuits are simultaneously activated in the child's brain, leading to the fragmentation of a coherent response.

Attachment researchers (Hesse et al., 2003) found that the best predictor of each of these four categories of children's attachment—secure, insecure-avoidant, insecure-ambivalent, and disorganized—was the nature of the parents' adult attachment category:

Child's Attachment Category	Parent's Attachment State of Mind
Secure	Secure-autonomous
Insecure-avoidant	Dismissing
Insecure-ambivalent	Preoccupied
Disorganized	Unresolved-disorganized

The parents' adult attachment state of mind was measured by assessing their *narrative coherence.* A coherent narrative indicates that a parent has made sense of his or her early life and understands and is open to the impact of past relationships on present experiences. Even if parents had a frightening upbringing, the research suggests that if they have come to terms with their early life experience, their children will develop a secure attachment relationship. It is never too late to develop a coherent life story. Processes that aid the integration of the brain and facilitate the development of coherent narratives of one's life, such as EMDR, can be very effective in assisting parents to explore the nature of their own attachment, so that they can "earn" security in their own lives (Siegel & Hartzell, 2003). Family systems therapy can help them change their parenting behaviors so that their children can thrive.

If parents' communication with their child is distant, they may have developed a "dismissing" style of attachment. Their narrative will reveal a kind of incoherence—if they have not yet created a coherent life story—that is characterized by a dismissing of the importance of relationships in the past and in the present. There is often an insistence on not recalling prior family experiences. It is likely that this lack of recall is not due to "repression" of trauma per se, but rather to a lack of encoding of emotionally barren interactions. Sometimes self-reflection, new forms of relationships, and therapeutic interactions can help individuals get in touch with the nonverbal, visceral, and emotional senses of their inner life; this enables them to progress toward an adult form of secure attachment and a coherent narrative of their life.

When parents' behaviors are inconsistent and intrusive, their narrative often contains "leftover" issues, in which themes from the past intrude into current life reflections. This adult form of "preoccupied" attachment often reveals painful needs that were not met in a confusing childhood family situation. With the adult's mind still mired in emotionally unsettled past experiences, it is probable that these may intrude into interactions with the child. Relationships, including those of psychotherapy, that help parents examine these concerns and find an inner sense of understanding and peace can help them progress to a freer form of coherent, secure attachment narrative.

For parents who experience states in which they unintentionally terrify their child, the narrative often has elements of unresolved trauma or grief. As they tell their early life story, moments of disorganization and disorientation are apparent in both verbal and nonverbal communication. These unresolved states of mind seem to increase the risk that they will enter into states of irrational behavior, filled with fear, anger, or sadness. These overwhelm the parents' capacity to parent in that moment and create a state of terror in the child. Individual therapy, such as EMDR, can help parents identify and address these painful past losses and traumas and profoundly change their attachment state of mind. With the assistance of family systems therapy, they can alter the quality and nature of their relationships, thus shifting the child's developmental pathway from disorganized to secure.

BRAIN DEVELOPMENT

Our state of knowledge about the independent fields of brain science and attachment research point to the likelihood that each of these four patterns of communication shape the ongoing development of circuits in the brain (Cozolino, 2006; Schore, 2003a, 2003b; Siegel 1999, 2001). A multidisciplinary view of the brain, family relationships, and cognitive development leads to the idea that experiences within families directly influence the development of the self-regulatory circuits of the brain. From this perspective, healthy secure attachment likely promotes the development of integrative regions of the brain, especially in the prefrontal regions responsible for self-regulation.

The brain develops from a predominant genetic influence in the womb, beginning with the lower brain stem and moving upward to the limbic areas regulating emotion and attachment, and then to the top of the brain at the level of the cortex. Much of the cortex's interconnections develop after birth, influenced both by genetics and then by experiences as the child interacts with his or her environment. It appears likely that attachment experiences early in life directly shape the cortical processes involved in bodily regulation, capacity for communication with others, emotional balance, flexibility, empathy, self-understanding, and the capacity to self-soothe states of fear. Brain research (Siegel, 2007b) has revealed that this diverse set of regulatory processes is carried out by the functions of the middle aspect of the front-most part of the cortex, called the middle prefrontal cortex.

Recent explorations of the impact of psychotherapy on the resolution of trauma suggest that this area of the brain plays an important role in the process of healing, becoming more engaged after effective psychotherapy than in the unresolved state (van der Kolk, 2006). Mindfulness meditation may also promote the development of this region and prevent its natural thinning as one ages (Lazar et al., 2005). What these separate studies suggest is that secure attachment, effective psychotherapy, and mindful practices may each involve the development and activity of the middle prefrontal cortex (Siegel, 2007b).

In the next section of this Foreword, I present a condensed overview as a template for thinking about these intricate issues. It focuses on various elements at the heart of how therapy draws on these fundamental notions of mind, relationships, brain, and well-being.

EMDR and family systems therapy can be described as a powerful approach to facilitating integration within and among individuals. It is hypothesized that the brains of individuals with traumatic histories may have impairments in the capacity to develop integrative patterns of firing. These patterns may be associated with unresolved issues and the disorganizing states of mind following painful loss and trauma. Using EMDR within a couples and family context catalyzes and integrates this neurobiological information and helps the client move toward states of security. Freeing an individual from these small and large "t" traumas (Shapiro, 2001) allows the family or couple to interact in new ways, thus reinforcing an integrated, secure state of attachment. In many ways, EMDR enables individuals to make sense of their inner worlds so that they can participate in a loving and mutually beneficial way within their families.

INTERPERSONAL NEUROBIOLOGY

To understand the inner workings of mind, brain, and human relationships at the heart of psychotherapy, a wide array of scientific disciplines have been brought together in an integrated perspective called "interpersonal neurobiology" (Cozolino, 2001, 2006; Schore 2003a, 2003b; Siegel, 1999, 2001). By examining the parallel findings from independent efforts to understand reality, from anthropology to genetics, and psychology to complexity theory, this interdisciplinary view weaves a picture of the larger whole of human development.

From an interpersonal neurobiology perspective, the mind is defined as a process that regulates the flow of energy and information. The mind can be seen as *emerging* moment to moment, as energy and information flow between neurons and among people; this can be understood as a transaction between the domains of the neurobiological and the interpersonal. The mind's *development* is determined both by its genetic program and ongoing experience. It is thought that, during psychotherapy, when clients focus attention on the elements of their mental experience, novel states of neural firing are initiated, which directly shape the growth of new synaptic connections within the brain. These connections are the product of neural plasticity, and they can alter the future functioning of the individual's mind and his or her interpersonal communication patterns.

Interpersonal neurobiology posits that the field of mental health can offer a working *definition of mental well-being*. In my own experience of lecturing to more than 60,000 mental health practitioners in the first 6 years of this millennium, I have found that an average of only 5% had received formal education defining the mind or mental health. Naturally, the vast majority had studied disorder, disease, and symptom-focused interventions. However, it is striking that each of the fields in the larger domain of mental health has lacked a definition of what we are practicing.

Interpersonal neurobiology offers a working definition of mental health that emerges from various scientific disciplines. It states that a system that moves toward well-being is one that flows toward a flexible, adaptive, coherent, energized, and stable (FACES) state (Siegel, 2007b). This FACES state travels a river of well-being that is flanked on one side by rigidity and on the other by chaos. An examination of the *Diagnostic and Statistical Manual of Mental Disorders* (American Psychiatric Association, 2000) reveals that most of the symptoms listed in that text are examples of either rigidity or chaos. This working definition of mental health offers each of our disciplines a neutral lens through which we can define our personal and professional goal of mental well-being.

The FACES state of well-being has at its core the quality of COHERENCE (the word itself is the acronym): connected, open, harmonious, engaged, receptive, emergent (a feeling of newness moment to moment), noetic (knowing with a sense of clarity), compassionate, and empathic. These characteristics of a coherent mind are an articulation of the qualities of a FACES state of well-being from the interpersonal neurobiology viewpoint.

How does one achieve a coherent mind and a FACES state of well-being? Having examined a range of disciplines, we propose that well-being emerges when a system is *integrated*. When differentiated components of a system become connected, that system moves toward an integrated state. Integration is defined as the linkage of separate elements into a functional whole. Integration itself is a process, an ever-moving state of being, and thus well-being is a dynamic process in a continual state of emergence.

Well-being can be seen to involve at least three elements, visualized as the three sides of a triangle composed of mind, brain, and relationships. In this perspective, a coherent mind, an integrated brain, and attuned, empathic relationships mutually reinforce and create each other.

EMDR's powerful efficacy can be understood from an interpersonal neurobiology perspective. During EMDR, both the protocol and the bilateral stimulation contribute to the simultaneous activation of previously disconnected elements of neural, mental, and interpersonal processes. This simultaneous activation then primes the system to achieve new levels of integration.

In the example of Posttraumatic Stress Disorder, various impairments to the integration of memory and affective regulation can be seen as the fundamental blockage to well-being (Siegel, 2003). In parents who have not "made sense" of past trauma or loss, there is a direct negative impact on the outcome of attachment for their children (Hesse et al., 2003). These findings suggest that when parents make sense of their early life experiences through the creation of a coherent narrative, there may be a corresponding change in their interpersonal style and an increase in their children's security (Siegel & Hartzell, 2003). The combination of EMDR and family therapy offers a powerful strategy through which to alter familial patterns of suboptimal interactions; it also helps parents make sense of the confusion in their past and present lives emanating from unresolved trauma, loss, and other issues. Such a movement from an incoherent (non-sense-making) to a coherent (making-sense) narrative has been shown to help families transform from insecure attachment styles in both parent and child to a more resilient form of secure attachment and improved patterns of communication in the parent-child relationship (see Sroufe et al., 2005).

In this *Handbook of EMDR and Family Therapy Processes,* the authors describe a number of contexts in which families and couples have been impaired in their capacity to move toward states of relational well-being. In each of these examples, it is useful to consider how these impairments resulted in chaotic or rigid patterns of interaction and internal experience. These are the two banks of the river of coherent well-being. EMDR and family systems therapy effectively pull the relational difficulties out of the nonintegrated state and into a coherent level of functioning. Such facilitation can move a couple or family from the banks of chaos and rigidity into the harmonious flow of integration and well-being.

Parents and children are hardwired to connect to each other from birth (Cozolino, 2006; Schore, 2003a, 2003b; Siegel, 1999). The neural circuitry that regulates affective states, bodily balance of the autonomic nervous system, self-knowing awareness, and empathy is directly impacted by relational experiences early in life (Schore, 2003a, 2003b; Siegel, 2001). These socially shaped regulatory processes appear to be open to continued development throughout the life span. Consequently, it appears that deficits from early childhood can be remedied with adequate experiences later in life. It may be possible to stimulate the growth of new and compensatory—if not reparative—neural connectivity that could bring an individual to a more neurally integrated state of well-being. EMDR with family therapy may catalyze these changes in the brains of treated individuals. It is anticipated that one outcome will be a more robust activation of areas in the brain, such as the middle aspect of the prefrontal cortex, which contributes to both self-regulation and various forms of neural integration. Within the social settings of family and couple life, individual neural integration may be greatly amplified by the collective experiences that are inspired in these therapeutic endeavors and then reinforced at home. Partners and family members who share their lives with each other can reinforce integrative interactions beyond the therapeutic session.

There are a number of relational features that seem to enhance this amplification of therapeutic efficacy and that contribute to the "integrative" quality of interpersonal communication (Siegel & Hartzell, 2003). These include attunement, collaboration and compassion, and connection and cooperation. *Attunement* is at the heart of secure attachment and can be described as the resonance of two individuals to create a mutually regulating set of reverberant states. With interpersonal attunement, an integrated state is created within the mind/brain/body of both the interactive members.

Clinicians can promote interpersonal and intrapersonal attunement. Intrapersonal attunement is the capacity to become intimate with the inner workings of one's own mind and is central to our innate potential for *mindsight*. This is the ability to see our own minds compassionately with insight and to envision the minds of others with caring and empathy, and it yields the inner resources for well-being (Siegel, 2007a). EMDR may enhance mindsight by facilitating the integration of the brain that provides these mind-maps with clarity and fluidity in their construction. Promoting mindsight in family and couples therapy enables clinicians to harness the power of integration so that it is naturally reinforced in caring relationships.

As the drive toward integration moves couples and families into more coherent states of functioning, the natural drive toward well-being is liberated. This innate drive toward health (Shapiro, 2001) is the therapist's ally. Our task is not so much to do something *to* those with whom we work, but to work *with* them so that their own innate drive toward well-being will be released. Finding creative ways to liberate this human drive toward health and well-being is both the joy and the challenge of our profession. This excellent, thoughtful, integrative book offers a window into that creative journey that I believe you will find useful and inspiring in your own professional endeavors.

DANIEL J. SIEGEL, MD

REFERENCES

American Psychiatric Association. (2000). *Diagnostic and statistical manual of mental disorders.* Arlington, VA: Author.

Cassidy, J., & Shaver, R. (1999). *The handbook of attachment.* New York: Guilford Press.

Cozolino, L. (2001). *The neuroscience of psychotherapy.* New York: Norton.

Cozolino, L. (2006). *The neuroscience of relationships.* New York: Norton.

Hesse, E., Main, M., Yost-Abrams, K., & Rifkin, A. (2003). Unresolved states regarding loss or abuse have "second generation" effects: Disorganization, role-inversion, and frightening ideation in the off-spring of traumatized, non-maltreated parents. In M. Solomon & D. J. Siegel (Eds.), *Healing trauma* (pp. 57–106). New York: Norton.

Lazar, S., Kerr, C. E., Wasserman, R. H., Gray, J. R., Greve, D. N., Treadway, M. T., et al. (2005). Meditation experience is associated with increased cortical thickness. *NeuroReport, 16,* 1893–1897.

Schore, A. N. (2003a). *Affect dysregulation and the disorders of the self.* New York: Norton.

Schore, A. N. (2003b). *Affect regulation and the repair of the self.* New York: Norton.

Shapiro, F. (2001). *Eye movement desensitization and reprocessing (EMDR): Basic principles, protocols, and procedures* (2nd ed.). New York: Guilford Press.

Siegel, D. J. (1999). *The developing mind: Toward a neurobiology of interpersonal experience.* New York: Guilford Press.

Siegel, D. J. (2001). Toward an interpersonal neurobiology of the developing mind: Attachment, "mindsight" and neural integration. *Infant Mental Health Journal, 22,* 67–94.

Siegel, D. J. (2003). An interpersonal neurobiology of psychotherapy: The developing mind and the resolution of trauma. In M. Solomon & D. J. Siegel (Eds.), *Healing trauma* (pp. 1–56). New York: Norton.

Siegel, D. J. (2007a). *The mindful brain in psychotherapy: How neural plasticity and mirror neurons contribute to emotional well-being.* New York: Norton.

Siegel, D. J. (2007b). *Mindsight.* New York: Bantam/Random House.

Siegel, D. J., & Hartzell, M. (2003). *Parenting from the inside out: How a deeper self-understanding can help you raise children who thrive.* New York: Penguin Putnam.

Solomon, M., & Siegel, D. J. (Eds.). (2003). *Healing trauma.* New York: Norton.

Sroufe, L. A., Egeland, B., Carlson, E. A., & Collins, W. A. (2005). *The development of the person: The Minnesota Study of Risk and Adaptation from Birth to Adulthood.* New York: Guilford Press.

van der Kolk, B. (2006, March 5). *When you stop moving you are dead.* Paper presented at the fifth annual UCLA Attachment Conference: The Embodied Mind, Skirball Center, Los Angeles, CA.

Watzlawick, P. (1963). A review of the double bind theory. *Family Process, 2,* 132–153.

Preface

While baby boomers were raised on a weekly diet of *Father Knows Best* and *Leave It to Beaver,* clearly this reflection of optimism was a source of great pain to many who come into therapy saying, "Why wasn't my family like that?" The answer is, "Few are." Looking back at the very first family, biblical iconography paints a very different picture of fallible parents whose children must suffer for their disastrous errors and sibling rivalry resulting in mayhem and violence. Most families come out somewhere in the middle, but it is all too often a truism that the "sins" of the parents are visited on the children through multiple generations. Our clients come into therapy reflecting their family of origin in many ways. Those who were raised in loving, supportive environments with secure attachments have very different intrapsychic and interactional patterns from those who were raised in demeaning or assaultive households. Not only do they see themselves differently, but their upbringing influences their views of life's possibilities, the partners they choose, and, in turn, their own parenting styles. There are thousands of ways to undercut a child's developing psyche. So, indeed, the harm done in one generation is frequently transmitted through succeeding generations.

Although Eye Movement Desensitization and Reprocessing (EMDR) was developed originally as an individual psychotherapy, it should be clear that all psychotherapy must be practiced in the context of interlocking systems. No person exists outside of relationships. Even gurus who meditate for decades on a mountaintop are in a relationship with the Divine, and with those who leave food outside their cave. In any therapeutic evaluation there must be sensitivity to those who have influenced the growth of the client's psyche and those who continue to impact for good or ill. Friends', colleagues', and most of all family members' interactions must be assessed to enable the therapist to thoroughly understand the nature of the external forces that continue to shape the client's sense of self and other. Fortunately, the family system therapies have focused on just these interactional and transactional patterns and can help inform individual psychotherapists, thus providing them with a broader and richer understanding of the clinical picture. At the same time, EMDR therapists have enjoyed the luxury of watching a rapid and rich unfolding of intrapsychic patterns as processing opens the doorway to the mind in the manner of time-lapse photography. Both disciplines have much to learn from each other.

This book is envisioned as a bridge for both individual psychotherapists and family systems therapists. Whether or not one practices EMDR, the individual therapist is engaged in a journey with clients to liberate them from the bonds of previous experiences that have chained them to unfulfilling repetitive patterns of emotions, thoughts, and behaviors. The family therapist similarly is attempting to help the system resolve destructive patterns of dislocation, chaos, or stagnation and develop healthier interaction and coping patterns. Various forms of family systems therapy (FST) have identified the subtle patterns of past and present family experiences that can be investigated to formulate targets for therapeutic attention. The EMDR processing can then liberate the client from these experiences, as well as address therapeutic impasses that have prevented current healthy familial interactions from taking place. When EMDR has prepared the client to relate to family members without the burden of reactive emotional baggage, FST can help teach family members how to interact with each other more positively and provide new models for healthy interpersonal communication. In turn, EMDR processing can help accelerate the learning process by incorporating templates for positive future functioning.

In sum, knowledge of how and when to use both EMDR and FST in a complementary fashion can prove enormously beneficial to both clinicians and clients. Consequently, the purpose of this book is to offer the knowledge and procedures that will encourage immediate integrative clinical application. To accomplish this goal, the initial chapters offer an overview of EMDR and FST, plus instructions on how to construct a genogram and an "inside" view of the client's healing process written by a former client. After this groundwork, each subsequent chapter author presents a comprehensive review of the current theory and knowledge base regarding a distinct form of FST utilized along with EMDR in his or her clinical work, as well as of a ubiquitous clinical issue or complaint. Extensive case examples are then given, along with specific FST and EMDR procedures to guide the practicing clinician. It should be noted that names, ages, occupations, and other data about individuals discussed in cases have been changed to protect their identity. Often two or more similar cases have been combined to make any recognition less possible.

The book ends with an overview to highlight commonalities and differences among the various forms of treatment. Appendixes include an overview of EMDR trauma research and additional readings, a history of FST, and additional EMDR and FST resources.

Clearly, a family is composed of individual members who are best served by therapies that foster actualization and individuation as well as connectedness and healthful interactions. Likewise, individuals are the product of their family of origin and current experiences, which may include their family of creation. It is vital that those in the diverse fields of psychotherapy seek knowledge regarding the rich and myriad robust procedures of alternative approaches and remain curious and open to new information and ideas. This book is an attempt to communicate that kind of knowledge and forge a needed bond between individual and family therapies. Although EMDR and FST are distinct forms of psychotherapy, each with rich and strong sets of procedures, they strengthen and reinforce each other when used appropriately in combination, concurrently, or sequentially, to treat the comprehensive clinical picture. The field of psychotherapy can be viewed as a huge family in its own right, with many factions and tributaries or tribes. Boundaries should not be impermeable, and functioning is best improved by fruitful and healthy communication that respects different identities and points of view.

Authors were carefully selected to convey the wide range of populations and settings in which EMDR is being utilized and also the variety of models of family therapy with which practitioners are using it in tandem, as it pairs well with a number of theories. We learned a great deal from our interchanges with one another as we crafted this book and shared our different lineages and heritages, finding that they often dovetailed and enriched one another, and at other times needed to stand separately. We hope the reader will also find his or her journey in pursuit of greater therapeutic skill and wisdom illuminated by this integrative volume.

FRANCINE SHAPIRO
Palo Alto, California

FLORENCE W. KASLOW
Palm Beach Gardens, Florida

LOUISE MAXFIELD
London, Ontario, Canada

April 2006

Acknowledgments

Writing a book can be a lonely endeavor, whereas editing a book puts you in constant interpersonal contact as myriad lives converge, all hoping to meet a deadline that was based initially on the best of all possible worlds. Unfortunately, Life (with a capital "L") too often intervenes. For that reason, the editors want to express their appreciation to all of the authors for their perseverance in the face of the exigencies that arise when one is trying to write while also juggling the needs of family and full-time clinical practice or academic responsibilities. For many, this was compounded by having to face personal and family illness, death, and many global tragedies that propelled them into emergency humanitarian service. Their willingness to continue the writing process despite many challenges is a testimony to their commitment to offering the world an enhanced road to healing. We also wish to thank the many clients who were willing to share their stories so that others might be helped.

We thank Peggy Alexander and David Bernstein of Wiley for their support and assistance in these trying times, as well as Nancy Marcus Land and Pamela Blackmon of Publications Development Company for carefully shepherding the book through the final publication process. An undertaking of this magnitude also takes a personal toll, emphasizing the importance of having relationships with significant others you can trust and rely on.

Dr. Shapiro wishes to thank her husband, Bob Welch, for always being her oasis and peerless helpmate in sickness and in health. Profound gratitude also to Susan Sandoval, whose sisterly support and many kindnesses during this period epitomize true friendship. Many thanks as well to Robin Robbins and Susan Sandoval for their editorial assistance.

Dr. Kaslow expresses her sincere gratitude to her patient, supportive husband, Sol Kaslow, who always encourages her endeavors, and to her loyal and gracious secretary, Gladys Adams, whose excellent skills and positive attitude make having her assistance in producing this book so valuable.

Dr. Maxfield would like to thank her friends and family for their patience with her lack of availability during this extended process, with special appreciation to her son, Isaac Maxfield, for his invaluable assistance, friend Andrea Kohan for her unwavering support and kindness, and mentor Bill Melnyk for his confidence and encouragement.

About the Editors

Francine Shapiro, PhD, is the originator and developer of EMDR, which has been so well researched that it is now recommended as a frontline treatment for trauma in the *Practice Guidelines* of the American Psychiatric Association and those of the Departments of Defense and Veterans Affairs. Dr. Shapiro is a Senior Research Fellow at the Mental Research Institute, Palo Alto, California, Executive Director of the EMDR Institute, Watsonville, California; and Founder and President Emeritus of the EMDR Humanitarian Assistance Programs, a nonprofit organization that coordinates disaster response and pro bono trainings worldwide. She is a recipient of the International Sigmund Freud Award of the City of Vienna for distinguished contribution to psychotherapy and the Distinguished Scientific Achievement in Psychology Award presented by the California Psychological Association. Dr. Shapiro was designated one of the Cadre of Experts of the American Psychological Association and Canadian Psychological Association Joint Initiative on Ethnopolitical Warfare and has served as advisor to a wide variety of trauma treatment and outreach organizations and journals. She has been an invited speaker at psychology conferences worldwide and has written and coauthored more than 60 articles, chapters, and books about EMDR, including *Eye Movement Desensitization and Reprocessing: Basic Principles, Protocols and Procedures* (New York: Guilford Press, 2001); *EMDR: The Breakthrough Therapy for Overcoming Anxiety, Stress and Trauma* (New York: Basic Books, 1997); and *EMDR as an Integrative Psychotherapy Approach* (Washington, DC: American Psychological Association, 2002).

Florence W. Kaslow, PhD, ABPP, is Director of the Florida Couples and Family Institute; President of Kaslow Associates, a family business consulting firm; and Visiting Professor of Psychology at Florida Institute of Technology. She was President of the American Board of Family Psychology (1996 to 2000), the first President of the American Board of Forensic Psychology (1977 to 1980), and the American Academy of Forensic Psychologists, and a President of the International Academy of Family Psychology (1998 to 2002) and APA's Divisions of Family Psychology and Media Psychology. She was the first President of the International Family Therapy Association (1987 to 1990) and remained on its Board until 2004. Currently, she serves on the ABPP Board of Trustees, the Board of the Division of Family Psychology, and the APA Council of Representatives and is active in a Female Doctors Group in North Palm Beach. She is a past Editor-in-Chief of the *Journal of Marital and Family Therapy* and currently serves on numerous editorial boards of U.S. and foreign journals. She has edited, authored, or coauthored 30 books and has contributed chapters to more than 50 others. More than 180 of her articles have been published in professional journals. Dr. Kaslow has received numerous honors, including APA's Distinguished Contribution to Applied Psychology Award, AAMFT's Outstanding Contribution to the Field of Family Therapy Award, ABPP's Award for Outstanding Contribution and Distinguished Service to the Profession, and APA's Award for Distinguished Contributions to the International Advancement of Psychology. Her most recently published book is *Handbook of Family Business and Family Business Consultation: A Global Perspective* (International Business Press, 2006).

Louise Maxfield, PhD, is a psychologist with the Mental Health Care Program at the London Health Sciences Center and has a private counseling practice in London, Ontario. She is an Assistant Professor in the Department of Psychiatry at the University of Western Ontario and an Adjunct Professor in the Department of Psychology at Lakehead University. She has many years of clinical experience working with trauma and abuse survivors in Ontario and British Columbia and was contracted for 3 years by the BC provincial government to train counselors working with abuse victims and their families. Dr. Maxfield has presented hundreds of educational workshops for professionals and the community at regional, national, and international conferences. She has been an investigator in four EMDR research studies, has been a research consultant on many international projects, and has written about 20 scientific articles and chapters on the treatment of trauma and EMDR. The recipient of numerous awards, including two for her research from the EMDR International Association and the EMDR Association of Canada, Dr. Maxfield is the Founding Editor of the journal of the EMDR International Association, *Journal of EMDR Practice and Research.*

About the Foreword Author

Daniel J. Siegel, MD, is an Associate Clinical Professor of Psychiatry at the UCLA School of Medicine, where he is Co-Investigator at the Center for Culture, Brain, and Development and Co-Director of the Mindful Awareness Research Center. He is also the Director of the Mindsight Institute, an educational organization that focuses on how the development of insight and empathy within individuals, families, and communities can be enhanced by examining the interface of human relationships and basic biological processes. He formerly directed the training program in child psychiatry at UCLA and is the recipient of teaching awards, honorary fellowships, and professorships including the Distinguished Fellowship of the American Psychiatric Association, the Soule Lectureship of the University of Washington, the Edna Reiss-Sophie Chair of Vista Del Mar, and the Outstanding Mentor Award of the American Academy of Child and Adolescent Psychiatry. Dr. Siegel is the Founding Editor of the Norton Series on Interpersonal Neurobiology and the author of *The Developing Mind* and coauthor of *Parenting from the Inside Out*. His upcoming texts include *Mindsight, Our Seventh Sense,* and *The Mindful Brain,* which expand the applications of interpersonal neurobiology in understanding the mind and the cultivation of well-being.

Contributing Authors

Anita Bardin, MS, is an accredited family therapy supervisor and past Director of the Shiluv Institute for Family and Couple Therapy in Jerusalem, Israel. She currently works in the Shiluv Trauma Treatment Unit and in private practice in Jerusalem.

Joel Comet, PhD, is a licensed clinical psychologist and family therapist. He is the Director of the Trauma Treatment Unit, Shiluv Institute for Family and Couple Therapy, and is in private practice in Jerusalem, Israel.

Katherine E. B. Davis, MSW, is a licensed clinical social worker in private practice in New Haven, Connecticut. She is the former Clinical Director of the Hamden Mental Health Service, a coauthor of Connecticut's first child abuse law, and a coauthor of the EMDR Humanitarian Assistance Program's workshops on *Traumatology, Stabilization,* and *Trauma and Addiction.*

Nancy Errebo, PhD, is a clinical psychologist at the Readjustment Counseling Service of the Department of Veterans Affairs, Missoula, Montana. She is in private practice in Missoula and trains military therapists internationally.

Robert A. Gelbach, PhD, is Executive Director of EMDR Humanitarian Assistance Programs in Hamden, Connecticut, Emeritus Professor of Political Science at Southern Connecticut State University, and former Director of its Quality Management Institute. In 2 years at HAP he has overseen disaster response projects in seven countries involving more than 100 volunteers.

Frances (Frankie) R. Klaff, PhD, is a licensed psychologist in private practice in Elkton, Maryland, and Wilmington, Delaware. She has presented training programs for the University of Delaware, Delaware Council for Drug Abuse, Delaware Hospice Program, the Red Cross, and many others.

Nancy Knudsen, MEd, is a licensed marriage and family therapist in private practice in Northampton, Massachusetts. She is also an Adjunct Faculty member at the Smith College School for Social Work and has presented at local and international conferences on the integration of EMDR and Bowen Theory.

Wilhelmina S. Koedam, PhD, has authored articles on the Federal Witness Protection Program and book chapters on such topics as Dissociative Identity

Disorders, sexual harassment, and stalking. She is a licensed psychologist in private practice in North Miami Beach, and Davie, Florida.

Barry Litt, MFT, is a licensed marriage and family therapist in private practice with Human Dynamics Associates in Concord, New Hampshire. He is an AAMFT-Approved Supervisor and has taught in the family therapy programs of Antioch University and the University of New Hampshire.

Antonio Madrid, PhD, is a licensed psychologist, a part-time Professor of Counseling at the University of San Francisco, and the Director of Russian River Counselors in Monte Rio, California.

Marcelle Manon (pseudonym) is a former nonprofit executive and teacher working in commercial real estate in the southeastern United States.

Margaret (Peggy) V. Moore, MSW, is a licensed independent social worker in private practice in Albuquerque, New Mexico. Prior to retirement from the University of New Mexico School of Medicine, she worked in the Department of Pediatrics in the Interpersonal Skills program for Pediatric Residents.

Mark D. Moses, PhD, is Clinical Assistant Professor in the MFT Graduate program at the University of New Hampshire and an AAMFT Approved Supervisor. Dr. Moses is also Director, Portsmouth Family Institute and a psychologist maintaining a practice of psychotherapy and supervision in Portsmouth, New Hampshire.

Deborah Porten, MSW, MA, is an accredited family therapy supervisor and Clinical Director of the Shiluv Institute for Family and Couple Therapy. She is a member of the Shiluv Trauma Treatment Unit and is in private practice in Jerusalem, Israel.

Sylvia Shellenberger, PhD, is a psychologist and Professor at Mercer University School of Medicine in Macon, Georgia, where she directs the behavioral science program for family medicine residents. She is coauthor of *Genograms: Assessment and Intervention* (New York: Norton, 1999) and was awarded the 2005 Kaslow International Family Psychology Award from APA's Division of Family Psychology.

Rita Sommers-Flanagan, PhD, is a Professor of Counselor Education at the University of Montana. Trained as a clinical psychologist, she also serves as a clinical mental health consultant to the Missoula Vet Center and to Trapper Creek Job Corps.

Julie E. Stowasser, MS, is in private practice as a licensed marriage and family therapist in San Luis Obispo and Atascadero, California. She worked for a number of years as a therapist at the Central Coast Violence Intervention Programs in San Luis Obispo.

Beverly S. Talan, PhD, is a licensed clinical psychologist and a licensed marriage and family therapist who teaches workshops on Imago Relationship Therapy. Dr. Talan is a consultant in business environments and is in private practice in Birmingham, Michigan.

Laura Rocchietta Tofani, PhD, was trained in psychology at the University of Rome and certified as a family therapist at the Milan School of Family Therapy. She is employed as a family therapist in the Italian National Health Service and is in private practice as a Psychotherapist and Supervisor in Ivrea (To), Italy.

Debra Wesselmann, MS, is in private practice as a licensed professional counselor in Omaha, Nebraska. She is a consultant and research co-investigator with the YWCA Omaha and author of *The Whole Parent: How to Become a Terrific Parent Even If You Didn't Have One* (Perseus, 1998).

PART I

Foundations

CHAPTER 1

EMDR and Case Conceptualization from an Adaptive Information Processing Perspective

Francine Shapiro

Just as "beauty is in the eye of the beholder," so is clinical dysfunction. Although certain symptom patterns are consistently recognized as constituting diagnosable disorders, each psychological modality is grounded in a specific paradigm that guides the clinician into a different way of conceptualizing clinical complaints. These theoretical paradigms provide explanations of pathology and recommend related interventions to eliminate symptoms and assist the client.

Eye Movement Desensitization and Reprocessing (EMDR) is no exception. In its 20-year history, it has evolved from a simple technique into an integrative psychotherapy approach with a theoretical model that emphasizes the brain's information processing system and memories of disturbing experiences as the basis of pathology. The eight-phase treatment comprehensively addresses the experiences that contribute to clinical conditions and those that are needed to bring the client to a robust state of psychological health.

HISTORY OF EMDR

EMDR was introduced in 1989 with a published randomized controlled study (Shapiro, 1989) that evaluated one-session treatment effects with traumatized individuals. At that time, it was called Eye Movement Desensitization, or EMD, because it was informed by a behavioral orientation and it was thought that eye movements were unique in causing an effective desensitization. From this vantage point, the treatment effects were viewed primarily as a reduction in the fear and anxiety resulting from the traumatization.

Over subsequent years, it was discovered that other forms of bilateral stimulation* (i.e., taps, tones) were also effective (Shapiro, 1991b, 1994a). Further, it was realized that changes in anxiety and fear, in fact, the whole process of desensitization, were only by-products of a comprehensive reprocessing of the experience. During treatment, negative emotions were replaced with positive ones, insights surfaced, body sensations changed, and new behaviors spontaneously

---

* Also described as dual attention stimulation.

emerged, along with a new sense of self. In short, the traumas were transformed into learning experiences that rapidly unfolded and strengthened the victim into a survivor and then into a thriver. EMD then became EMDR, with the addition of the word "reprocessing" (Shapiro, 1991a, 1994b) to signify these changes. This concept of the transformation of the stored experience through a rapid learning process is the key to understanding the basis and application of EMDR and its guiding Adaptive Information Processing model (Shapiro, 1995, 2001, 2002). The purpose of this chapter is to provide an overview of both theory and practice.

CONTROLLED RESEARCH

As with any form of psychotherapy, the neurobiological underpinnings of EMDR's treatment effects are currently unknown. Although the bilateral stimulation is only one procedural element of the treatment, because of its uniqueness it has attracted the most attention. The component analyses of the eye movements with clinical populations have shown only marginally significant effects (Davidson & Parker, 2001) but are flawed by the inclusion of inappropriate populations and limited amounts of treatment (Chemtob, Tolin, van der Kolk, & Pitman, 2000; Department of Veterans Affairs and Department of Defense, 2004; Perkins & Rouanzoin, 2002). However, laboratory studies have identified distinct effects of the eye movements in regard to memory retrieval, reduction of negative emotions, imagery vividness, and attentional flexibility (e.g., Andrade, Kavanagh, & Baddeley, 1997; Barrowcliff, Gray, Freeman, & MacCulloch, 2004; Christman Garvey, Propper, & Phaneuf, 2003; Kavanagh, Freese, Andrade, & May, 2001; Kuiken, Bears, Miall, & Smith, 2001–2002; Van den Hout, Muris, Salemink, & Kindt, 2001; see Appendix B).

The efficacy of EMDR's application to trauma treatment has been demonstrated in approximately 20 controlled studies in which it was compared to pharmaceuticals (van der Kolk et al., in press) and various forms of psychotherapy (e.g., Carlson, Chemtob, Rusnak, Hedlund, & Muraoka, 1998; Edmond, Rubin, & Wambach, 1999; Ironson, Freund, Strauss, & Williams, 2002; Jaberghaderi, Greenwald, Rubin, Dolatabadim, & Zand, 2004; Lee, Gavriel, Drummond, Richards, & Greenwald, 2002; Marcus, Marquis, & Sakai, 1997, 2004; Power et al., 2002; Rothbaum, Astin, & Marsteller, 2005; Scheck, Schaeffer, & Gillette, 1998; Taylor et al., 2003; Vaughan et al., 1994). Consequently, both the practice guidelines of the American Psychiatric Association (2004) and the Departments of Veterans Affairs and Defense (2004) have placed EMDR in the highest category of effectiveness and research support. This status is also reflected in numerous international guidelines (e.g., Bleich, Kotler, Kutz, & Shalev, 2002; Dutch National Steering Committee, 2003; National Institute for Clinical Excellence, 2005; Sjöblom et al., 2003). A number of neurobiological studies also have demonstrated pre- to post-EMDR processing changes in conjunction with the remediation of trauma symptoms (Lamprecht et al., 2004; Lansing, Amen, Hanks, & Rudy, 2005; P. Levin, Lazrove, & van der Kolk, 1999). Evaluations of EMDR studies have found that degree of adherence to treatment procedures and protocols is positively correlated with the size of the treatment effects (Maxfield & Hyer, 2002; Shapiro, 1999).

The aforementioned practice guidelines and a number of published meta-analyses (e.g., Bradley, Greene, Russ, Dutra, & Westen, 2005; Van Etten & Taylor, 1998) have documented that EMDR is as effective and long lasting as the most researched cognitive-behavioral therapy (CBT) methods. However, unlike the other forms of trauma therapy that include 30 to 100 hours of prescribed homework, EMDR's effects are accomplished with only in-session treatment and with less exposure to the trauma. This difference in exposure time and homework was noted by the investigators of a controlled study funded by the National Institute of Mental Health comparing EMDR (Shapiro, 2001) and prolonged exposure (Foa & Rothbaum, 1998); the investigators commented, "It will be important for future research to explore these issues" (Rothbaum et al., 2005, p. 614).

The pattern of recovery in EMDR treatment sessions allows clinicians to view a rapid progression of intrapsychic connections as emotions, insights, sensations, and memories surface and change with each new set of bilateral stimulation. Process studies and qualitative analyses have identified distinct treatment effects (including a rapid reduction of subjective distress) that differentiate EMDR from other trauma therapies (Edmond, Sloan, & McCarty, 2004; Lee, Taylor, & Drummond, 2006; McCullough, 2002; Rogers & Silver, 2002; Rogers et al., 1999). In addition to the reduction of emotional disturbance and overt symptoms, EMDR clients experience a variety of responses indicating the emergence of comprehensive reorganization that may be reflected in changes in affect regulation and personality characteristics (Brown & Shapiro, 2006; Korn & Leeds, 2002; Zabukovec, Lazrove, & Shapiro, 2000), cessation of chronic pain and other dysfunctional somatic reactions (Grant & Threlfo, 2002; Gupta & Gupta, 2002; Ray & Zbik, 2001; Schneider, Hofmann, Rost, & Shapiro, 2006), and shifts in cognitive organization reflected in the number of positive memories that can be recalled posttreatment (Sprang, 2001). Although EMDR may be used to eliminate overt symptoms attendant on various clinical conditions (see Shapiro, 2001), as a psychotherapy approach its primary goal is to address the entire clinical picture to bring about the most comprehensive treatment effects.

ADAPTIVE INFORMATION PROCESSING MODEL

EMDR's wide range of therapeutic applications is grounded in the Adaptive Information Processing (AIP) model that guides its clinical practice. Basically, EMDR is used to address the experiential contributors of dysfunction and health. Initially used for the treatment of Posttraumatic Stress Disorder (PTSD), it became apparent over time that the Criterion A events (e.g., an immediate threat to one's life or loved one, such as a car accident or physical or sexual assault; American Psychiatric Association, 2000) officially required to diagnose the condition were too limiting a conceptualization. For instance, if the sudden death of a man's wife of 30 years results in intrusive thoughts, depression, and sleep disturbance that last over a period of years, the event may be recognized as a trauma, and he can be diagnosed with PTSD. However, if the man has exactly the same symptoms subsequent to his wife running off with her dance instructor, the event is not given the same stature, and a diagnosis of PTSD is precluded because the precipitating event does not meet the designated criteria.

Clearly, people are haunted for years by a variety of experiences that do not rise to the level of Criterion A events. In the AIP model, these are designated small "t" trauma, not because they are less traumatic or indelible, but because they are more ubiquitous. A recent study by Mol et al. (2005) supports this conceptualization. A survey of 832 people indicated that there were more PTSD symptoms related to life events than to Criterion A events. The conclusion of Mol et al. was, "Life events can generate at least as many PTSD symptoms as traumatic events" (p. 494). The recognition of this fact has extremely important implications for treatment.

The AIP model is used to explain clinical phenomena, predict successful treatment effects, and guide clinical practice. Consistent with neurobiological findings, it is posited that to make sense of incoming stimuli, new experiences are assimilated into already existing memory networks. For instance, when handed a cup, one needs previous "cup" experiences to know what to do with it. Likewise, a failed love experience is assimilated into memory networks associated with relationships and adds to one's knowledge base regarding such things as expectations and potential warning signs.

In a healthy individual, as new experiences are processed, they are "metabolized" or "digested," and what is useful is learned, is stored with appropriate emotions, and guides the person in the future. For instance, a child may fall off a bicycle and cry, but with appropriate comforting and nurturing the fear passes and she learns what is necessary for a more successful ride in the future. However, some children become anxious about bike riding, and the distress does not abate. This persistent anxiety suggests that the information processing system has stored the experience without adequately processing it to an adaptive resolution. Instead of remembering the earlier, enjoyable rides or that the physical pain went away, when they think of bike riding all they remember is the fall. The event is essentially frozen in time in the moment of fear and pain. This lays the foundation for future inappropriate (dysfunctional) responses to similar events: It becomes a touchstone event for any associated experience.

Pathology According to the Adaptive Information Processing Model

The AIP model posits that pathology results when unprocessed experiences are stored in their own neural network, unable to link up naturally with anything more adaptive. Therefore, a person may observe myriad counterexamples or be in therapy for years, offered constant reframes, alternatives, and examples of success, without changing the emotions involving distressing personal failures. The new information, positive experiences, and affects are unable to link into the network where the unprocessed material is stored.

For example, a person with a diagnosis of Borderline Personality Disorder may feel positively about a therapist (or lover) one moment and fly into a rage the next. The AIP model conceptualizes this dichotomy as follows: The positive experiences are stored in one memory network, but the disturbing experiences of early abandonment or abuse are in another and can get triggered by anything reminiscent of those events. The same is true, to a greater or lesser degree, for most volatile couples. Whether the earlier events have incorrect information or information that was once correct but is no longer valid in the adult (such as the powerlessness and lack of choices of a child), adaptive learning cannot take place because of the dysfunctional storage.

Childhood phobias are another example of disorders that are considered to result from experiences that have not been adaptively processed. The stored memory experiences (whether a product of direct confrontation, parental modeling, or vicarious traumatization from a story or TV) contain within them the emotions and physical sensations of the frightening events. When a current similar event occurs, it automatically links into the memory network containing the earlier unprocessed experience, and the previously stored physical sensations and negative affects arise involuntarily. Regardless of how many positive examples may exist all around them, the earlier disturbing event remains unchanged.

According to the AIP model, the inherent disturbance also serves to block access to other positive events that may already exist in the memory networks. For instance, the death of a loved one may cause distressing images of unresolved pain and suffering to emerge and prevent pleasant memories from being accessed. Completing the processing of the events allows positive recall to increase (Sprang, 2001). Failing to do so leaves the negative memories "hot" and liable to be triggered at any time. Consequently, regardless of the numbers of subsequent positive experiences that may exist in the person's life, earlier unprocessed events can set the groundwork for an impoverished sense of identity and self-efficacy.

Neurobiological investigators believe these experiences are stored improperly in memory (Siegel, 2002; Stickgold, 2002; van der Kolk, 1996, 2002). For instance, the implicit system is the one that allows a person to ride a bicycle after a 10-year hiatus because the physical sensations are stored in the memory. However, physical sensations are not useful when they retain the pain and fear from a rape, accident, or assault. These problems are not limited to exceptional trauma. Being bullied in school or demeaned by a teacher is a common childhood event. However, when people bring up that memory decades later, many still feel the heat of the emotions and sense their bodies cringe. This indicates that the memory has not been processed and that it may be at the root of a variety of psychosocial issues the person has in the present. Basically, the emotions, sensations, and perspectives of these childhood events arise and color the person's perception of the past. In short, the past is present.

The AIP model distinguishes EMDR from other forms of psychotherapy by viewing the present situation producing distress simply as a trigger for a past, unprocessed incident. It is thought that the current event stimulates the memory network, causing stored negative emotions, physical sensations, and perspectives to emerge. As previously noted, a current situation that is similar in any way to an earlier event will automatically link into the memory network in which the earlier event is stored. These associational linkups are necessary to make sense of the world, and they typically occur without conscious control. So, whether or not the person is aware of the earlier unprocessed experience, and whether or not he* can recognize the similarity to the present situation, the dysfunctionally stored

---

*Pronouns are alternated throughout the chapter to avoid the awkwardness of "he or she."

emotions, physical sensations, and perspectives are the reflexive responses to current events and drive the person's behaviors. Someone may be anxious when entering a room with many people and not know why. People may have trouble with authority and not be able to explain their fear response. In the AIP model, most clinical complaints are considered to be experientially based, but with a genesis below conscious awareness.

Although these experiences may be below the level of consciousness, they are ultimately responsible for the behaviors that bring a person into therapy. Most clients do not come into therapy because they "had a bad childhood." Rather, they are there because life has become unmanageable. They are propelled into doing things they do not want to do or are prevented from doing the things they want to do. They are distraught, feeling out of control, unhappy at home or work or in social relationships. Certain problems may be purely situational, such as a dysfunctional work environment; most others emanate from clients' patterns of thinking and behavior with those of the people around them. The AIP model conceptualizes these patterns of dysfunctional emotions, physical sensations, and perspectives as symptoms, not causes. The cause is understood to be the unprocessed memories of earlier experiences that are pushing the client into inappropriate responses in the present. For example, the person who feels "not good enough" will act in ways that reflect this belief in the present—in ways that can cause others to view him in that way as well. He may interpret even innocent distraction on another's part as dismissive and demeaning, which reinforces his own negative self-perspective. The belief "I'm not good enough" is not the cause—it is the symptom. The cause is the unprocessed earlier life experience that contains that affect and perspective.

EMDR's procedures have been developed to access the dysfunctionally stored experience and stimulate the innate processing system, allowing it to transmute the information to an adaptive resolution, shifting the information to the appropriate memory systems (Siegel, 2002; Stickgold, 2002). When fully processed, the necessary information is assimilated and the memory structures have accommodated to the new information. Although the event and what has been learned can be verbalized, the inappropriate negative affects and physical sensations have been discarded and can no longer be felt. This processing, or rapid learning, is at the heart of every EMDR treatment. The clinician works to ascertain which current situations are triggering the disturbance, which experiences have laid the groundwork for the dysfunction, and what positive experiences are needed to overcome any lack of knowledge or skill.

EIGHT-PHASE TREATMENT APPROACH

EMDR is a psychotherapy approach that employs an eight-phase model of treatment to address the full range of clinical complaints caused or exacerbated by prior negative experiences. Therefore, if a problem is organically based, as in certain learning or processing disabilities subsequent to a car accident, EMDR would not be a frontline treatment. However, EMDR would be used to address the psychological ramifications of that type of event, to assist the person to come to grips with new limitations and address the potential struggle with a new sense of identity and existential or spiritual issues that may arise. The eight phases of EMDR (see Table 1.1) provide a systematic way to explore and process the negative experiences that are contributing to dysfunction and the positive experiences that are needed to bring a client to full health. To illustrate the methodology, we use the case of a 15-year-old female client presented by a clinician in consultation.

―――――――――――――――――――― **Case Example** ――――――――――――――――――――

Tara is brought into therapy by her mother because of her excessive anxiety, panic attacks, and pronounced school phobia. The family is composed of Tara (15 years old), and her parents. She presents with very low self-esteem, social anxiety, extreme self-consciousness (her body is even hunched over in a constricted way), and suicidal thoughts. She sees herself as a "constant burden" to her parents, even though they deny feeling this way.

Tara was born quite prematurely, weighing only 2 pounds. She was in a pediatric inpatient care unit for 4 months on a respirator. While hospitalized, she experienced daily traumas involving cardiac and respiratory distress. When she finally came home, she remained on oxygen for several weeks. Mother would spend 8 hours a day watching over her, and Father would come home after work and spend hours with her as well. As a result, of this, Mother was very overprotective. At the time she brought Tara for treatment, Mother was still very traumatized by the experience; when Mother attempted to complete a homework assignment to write down a narrative of the events, she sobbed all night.

When Tara was 5 years old the family moved. Tara reported that this was traumatic for her, as were memories of her parents fighting. Mother and Father used to fight a great deal but have gotten along fairly well in the past several years. Tara further disclosed that she had never felt comfortable in class and had vomited before school. She was no longer doing this, but she remained anxious and uncomfortable and had occasional panic attacks. She described having a couple of friends, but she rarely engaged in social activities outside school. She appeared to have no internal sense of security.

Phase 1: Client History

This rudimentary case history opens a number of case management suggestions. The overall goal of EMDR is to achieve the most profound and comprehensive treatment effects possible while maintaining a stable client in a balanced social system. Therefore, it is important to assess the case systemically as well as individually to identify the appropriate targets for processing.

Conceptually, the individual is shaped by an interaction of genetics and experiences. Prenatal conditions, which include the hormonal flooding from the mother's emotional states, can impact the developing fetus. Sometimes physical conditions are called into play, including fatigue levels and physical development. Some information processing systems may be constitutionally predisposed to be

Table 1.1 Overview of EMDR Treatment

Phase	Purpose	Procedures
Client History	• Obtain background information. • Identify suitability for EMDR treatment. • Identify processing targets from positive and negative events in client's life.	• Administer standard history-taking questionnaires and diagnostic psychometrics. • Review criteria and resources. • Ask questions regarding (1) past events that have laid the groundwork for the pathology, (2) current triggers, and (3) future needs.
Preparation	• Prepare appropriate clients for EMDR processing of targets. • Stabilize and increase access to positive affects.	• Educate regarding the symptom picture. • Teach metaphors and techniques that foster stabilization and a sense of personal self-mastery and control.
Assessment	• Access the target for EMDR processing by stimulating primary aspects of the memory.	• Elicit the image, negative belief currently held, desired positive belief, current emotion, and physical sensation, and baseline measures.
Desensitization	• Process experiences and triggers toward an adaptive resolution (0 SUD level). • Fully process all channels to allow a complete assimilation of memories. • Incorporate templates for positive experiences.	• Process past, present, future. • Use standardized EMDR protocols that allow the spontaneous emergence of insights, emotions, physical sensations, and other memories. • Use Cognitive Interweave to open blocked processing by elicitation of more adaptive information.
Installation	• Increase connections to positive cognitive networks. • Increase generalization effects within associated memories.	• Identify the best Positive Cognition (initial or emergent). • Enhance the validity of the desired positive belief to a 7 VOC.
Body Scan	• Complete processing of any residual disturbance associated with the target.	• Concentrate on and process any residual physical sensations.
Closure	• Ensure client stability at the completion of an EMDR session and between sessions.	• Use guided imagery or self-control techniques if needed. • Brief regarding expectations and behavioral reports between sessions.
Reevaluation	• Evaluate treatment effects. • Ensure comprehensive processing over time.	• Explore what has emerged since last session. • Reaccess memory from last session. • Evaluate integration within larger social system.

Source: Eye Movement Desensitization and Reprocessing (EMDR) Training Manual, by F. Shapiro, 2005, Watsonville, CA: EMDR Institute.

weaker or stronger, just like cardiac and respiratory systems. This may explain why some events impact some children more than others. Other factors include the child's earliest interactions, which forge the very sense of self through which the rest of the world is interpreted. These early experiences are stored in memory and become the basis of the networks into which other experiences link. The child raised in a family that engendered a sense of inadequacy will interact with friends and at school with a very different set of behaviors and emotions than one raised to believe she is worthwhile and valued. These early experiences set the groundwork for either further traumatization or resilience.

Given the case history so far, we see a 15-year-old girl with severe anxiety and low self-esteem. Extensive neonatal distress had traumatized the mother into extreme overprotectiveness. Tara correctly felt that she was physically "substandard" and that her condition was distressing to Mother. From an AIP perspective, this resulted in an internalized inappropriate sense of defectiveness, undue responsibility for her mother's distress (including the perception of being a "constant burden"), and lack of physical safety. These feelings were reinforced by her parents' reflexive fear and anxiety responses to a variety of Tara's childhood circumstances. Parental fights during her childhood increased her sense of instability and potentially exacerbated the pivotal issues of inappropriate responsibility, lack of safety, and powerlessness (see Shapiro, 2001).

Tara's consequent low self-esteem and heightened anxiety, with the physical manifestations such as her hunched posture, resulted in a paucity of appropriate socialization and interpersonal behaviors. The anxiety undoubtedly was intensified in school through interaction with her peers, causing additional social problems, teasing, and humiliations. This in turn fostered and maintained her lack of self-worth. The resulting panic attacks further exacerbated Tara's sense of defectiveness and powerlessness. Basically, she was locked into home and school environments that amplified the problems through arousing repetitive feelings of defectiveness, lack of safety, and absence of power or choice.

In information processing terms, children grow up in an environment of accumulated experiences that set the foundation for a sense of self. Each experience is a discrete event, but the memory network is expanded with each new addition. When raised in an adaptive environment, one's sense of self is flexible as new experiences occur and new information is incorporated into the existing memory networks. A healthy individual is one who can take in both positive and negative experiences and learn from them. However, even loving parents (such as Tara's) can provide an upbringing that results in a self-defining core of dysfunctionally stored unprocessed memories. In this case, the many times Tara's overprotective mother reacted with fear and anxiety around her had a negative effect. The pervasiveness of her mother's responses to myriad behaviors, including Tara's attempts at differentiation and achieving some autonomy (which are intrinsic and hardwired), set the groundwork for her perception "I am defective."

Once this type of core identity network has been forged, it may be reinforced by negative experiences but is generally unable to link up naturally with other, more adaptive information. Alternatives and positive experiences occur, but they are stored in separate networks. For example, Tara may have seen a friend bullied and felt protectiveness and anger on his behalf because she knew it was unfair, unjust, and inappropriate for others to be cruel. However, if Tara was personally bullied, she may have been unable to defend herself because that experience would link into a central core of memories of being inadequate and not good enough. These feelings would rise automatically in her body and mind. It would be difficult for her to comfort or defend herself as she could a friend. Similar dynamics are seen with a combat veteran with unprocessed war memories who cannot forgive himself for things he can forgive in his comrades.

It is important to remember that, according to the AIP model, dysfunctional reactions in the present are based on stored memories that are triggered by current life conditions. Reprocessing involves the accessing of dysfunctionally stored memories (which contain the negative emotions, physical sensations, and beliefs) and forging their subsequent connection to more adaptive networks. During the Client History Phase it is important to ascertain if there are adaptive networks. In other words, did Tara have undiluted success experiences in any area of her life? Did she have any memories of times where she felt safe, or times when she felt good about herself? If not, these types of incidents will have to be constructed therapeutically during the Preparation Phase.

During the Client History Phase the clinician uses a variety of techniques to identify the large and small "t" traumas and the triggers that need to be processed. Adult clients are asked to describe the 10 most disturbing memories they have from childhood, or a time line may be used that visually charts the most salient events from birth to the present. They may be asked to bring in photos of their family of origin and different significant figures and to discuss them with the therapist. The therapist may also construct a genogram (Kitchur, 2005; McGoldrick, Gerson, & Shellenberger, 1999; see Shellenberger, Chapter 3) to help identify the systemic issues and familial contributions. It is important to supplement this with questions regarding peers and other significant figures, as these types of interactions also have a major impact on the developing psyche. Specific targets are then selected, particularly when highlighted by indicators of abuse.

Present situations are evaluated for levels of distress, as well as the influences of previous experiences. The specific difficulties and symptoms that the client has in the present are listed, and she is asked to recall the first time that something similar occurred. If she is unable to do so, she is asked to remember the last time it happened, notice where she feels it in her body, and let her mind drift back to the earliest time she remembers feeling that way (Shapiro, 1995). This is sometimes called an "Affect Scan" (Shapiro, 2005) or "Affect Bridge" (Watkins & Watkins, 1997) but does not contain the hypnotic or reliving element associated with the latter technique. The goal at this point in EMDR therapy is simply to identify the salient memories contributing to the dysfunction that are in need of processing.

It is also useful to delineate the specific aspects of current situations that precede a negative response. The CBT technique of behavioral analysis can be used for that purpose (Smyth & Poole, 2002). Then, for EMDR, the experiences, affects, and thoughts are investigated to identify the earlier events that set their foundation. Another useful procedure is to give clients a list of negative beliefs and ask them to check off the ones that feel like theirs (see Table 1.2). It appears that most salient beliefs can be divided into those involving *responsibility* ("I am [or did] something wrong"), *safety,* and *choices* (see Shapiro, 2001). As these negative beliefs are manifestations of the stored experiences and are verbalizations of the stored affects, clients are then asked to identify the earliest event they

Table 1.2   Examples of Negative Beliefs

Responsibility (I am defective)	I don't deserve love.
	I am a bad person.
	I am terrible.
	I am worthless (inadequate).
	I am shameful.
	I am not lovable.
	I am not good enough.
	I deserve only bad things.
	I am permanently damaged.
	I am ugly (my body is hateful).
	I do not deserve . . . .
	I am stupid (not smart enough).
	I am insignificant (unimportant).
	I am a disappointment.
	I deserve to die.
	I deserve to be miserable.
	I am different (don't belong).
Responsibility (I did something wrong)	I should have done something.*
	I did something wrong.*
	I should have known better.*
Safety/Vulnerability	I cannot be trusted.
	I cannot trust myself.
	I cannot trust my judgment.
	I cannot trust anyone.
	I cannot protect myself.
	I am in danger.
	It's not OK to feel (show) my emotions.
	I cannot stand up for myself.
	I cannot let it out.
Control/Choices	I am not in control.
	I am powerless (helpless).
	I am weak.
	I cannot get what I want.
	I am a failure (will fail).
	I cannot succeed.
	I have to be perfect (please everyone).
	I cannot stand it.
	I cannot trust anyone.
	I cannot do . . . .*

* What does this say about you (e.g., does it make you feel: I am shameful/I am stupid/I am a bad person/I am not good enough)?

Source: Eye Movement Desensitization and Reprocessing: Basic Principles, Protocols, and Procedures, second edition, by F. Shapiro, 2001, New York: Guilford Press.

can remember when they felt that way. If they cannot remember an experience consciously, then they may be asked to perform a "Floatback" (Browning, 1999), which uses the negative belief to perform a variation of the previously described Affect Scan (see Shapiro, 2001). Although the negative belief (or *Negative Cognition*) is considered the symptom rather than the cause of the dysfunction, it is extremely useful in verbalizing the problem and identifying the earlier etiological event (Shapiro, 1995, 1998).

In Tara's case, she could easily identify a number of experiences from childhood that made her feel inadequate and a burden to her parents. These included many instances when her father seemed to ignore her and occasions when her mother rushed to pick her up or seemed stressed out over something she did. At various times during Tara's therapy, when preparing to address a specific issue, various techniques were used. For example, an Affect Scan was used to identify a good target for addressing her bad posture. Remembered incidents and floatbacks elicited the memories salient to her panic attacks, including her feelings of "I'm not good enough" and "I can't defend myself" in school situations. The Client History Phase is also the first opportunity to begin to sketch out what Tara will need to be taught to overcome any developmental deficits resulting from her traumatization and lack of adequate socialization.

Phase 2: Preparation

EMDR emphasizes coparticipation between client and clinician. Therefore, especially when working with children, it is critical to educate both child and parents about the entire clinical picture. It is essential to a successful course of therapy that everyone understand where the problems came from (including the panic attacks), what is reinforcing them in the present, what the choices are, what the therapy can achieve, and the importance of actively engaging in the treatment by identifying memories and triggers.

For therapy to proceed, Tara was taught self-control techniques that she could use to eliminate any fear of the processing, to terminate distress during sessions, and to cope between sessions. The ability to use self-control techniques outside of the therapist's office introduced an element of self-mastery that bolstered her self-esteem and reduced the impact of occasional ongoing social problems at school. Such state change techniques (see Shapiro, 2001, 2002) allow life to become more manageable while the processing work is done. The goal of EMDR therapy is trait change so that the negative emotions and sensations will no longer habitually arise. However, until the genesis events and current situations are processed, the self-control techniques are useful to decrease the current triggering. This helps to prevent new negative experience from becoming stored in turn and enlarging the trauma memory network.

A wide variety of self-control techniques may be used (see Shapiro, 2001). The *Safe Place* technique, in which clients are able to bring back at will a feeling of safety, calm, or courage, is generally sufficient to give them a feeling of self-control. However, when feelings of helplessness or hopelessness emerge from unprocessed memories, the client may be helpless at that moment and incapable of using the techniques. The processing of the memories may be needed to dissipate the power of the affects so that it is not such a struggle to self-monitor and use the self-help tools and so that present situations lose their power.

During information processing, the disturbing memory links up with more adaptive information so that learning can take place. If an individual does not have sufficient positive experiences and counterexamples stored in memory networks, EMDR processing cannot happen. The AIP model posits that in such situations, it is important to establish adaptive networks of positive experiences through the therapeutic relationship and resource work that includes the incorporation of mastery experiences before attempting comprehensive processing. The Safe Place technique, *Resource Development and Installation* (RDI; Korn & Leeds, 2002), and other imagery techniques supplemented Tara's positive experiences with her friends to enable successful processing to occur. Particularly when clients are locked in a dysfunctional home environment, it is crucial to make sure that a sufficient number of positive experiences are available from other sources. In their absence, attempts to process will be premature and very likely to fail.

Client stabilization and empowerment and the building of a solid therapeutic relationship are the basic elements of the Preparation Phase. The importance for clients of the therapeutic relationship cannot be overemphasized (Dworkin, 2005; Norcross, 2002). In AIP terms, transference reactions are clearly the interaction of present situations and the client's unprocessed material, and countertransference occurs when the therapist's personal unprocessed memories are stimulated. The ability to be attuned and sensitive to the client's needs and nonverbal cues, offer unconditional positive regard, and model positive relational values is contingent on the therapist's ability to be present, attentive, and optimally interactive. A variety of specific techniques and questionnaires have been devised to assist therapists in identifying their own problem areas and memories that may benefit from processing (Dworkin, 2005).

Dissociative and some personality-disordered clients may need an extended Preparation Phase, but in most cases it is not useful to wait until clients are capable of controlling their environment through techniques. These techniques serve only to make life more tolerable while the processing completes the therapy. If the client can use the techniques in the clinician's office to remove "fear of fear" and stop processing at will, it is usually safe to begin processing (Korn, van der Kolk, Weir, & Rozelle, 2004).

Phase 3: Assessment

During this phase the designated target is elicited in a controlled fashion and the components are delineated and measured.

Tara's anxiety, fear, stooped posture, and other presenting symptoms were conceptualized as the result of the disturbing experiences dysfunctionally stored in her memory networks. These included the many parental and peer responses that did not support her psychic development. Accessing and processing these events should result in a transmutation of the stored information and a release of the negative attributes. Fortunately, although a large number of events contributed to Tara's dysfunction, it was not necessary to access each one.

Rather, in such cases, similar events are grouped in clusters, and one representative event is chosen for each type; because all the events are connected through the associative memory networks, the positive treatment effects will generalize to the others in the cluster. When possible, targets should be accessed chronologically, with the earliest events processed first, as they set the foundation for the remaining ones. In all cases, EMDR treatment entails processing the past events that have set the groundwork for current dysfunction, the present situations that bring up the disturbance, and templates for appropriate future action.

For Tara, it was clear that her premature birth and her parents' reactions to that extreme situation set the groundwork for many of her problems. However, it was not necessary to specifically target precognitive memories because, as all experiences are aggregated in connected memory networks, they are linked somatically to the later events. Therefore, preverbal memories such as those in her infancy can be accessed through remembered targets and will be generally processed in an associative channel. These precognitive experiences may manifest themselves during processing as primarily somatic shifts without verbalizations. *If,* after all remembered targets, triggers, and templates have been addressed, there is still somatic dysfunction and if there is a known neonatal trauma, it can be addressed by having Tara imagine the scenes as described by her parents (Lovett, 1999). However, undifferentiated somatic processing is not a first-line strategy.

Any remembered experience can be an entry point into the memory network for comprehensive processing (Shapiro, 2001). Present situations can be used to help the accessing. Tara had many current situations that were upsetting, and each was explored for the genesis of the negative response. For instance, she reported being insulted by a classmate earlier in the week and being extremely upset by it. She was asked to bring to mind the disturbing event from school. Then she was asked to focus on whatever feelings were most prevalent, such as humiliation, fear, anxiety, or lack of safety, and let her mind take her back to the earliest time she remembered feeling that way. In this way, in addition to the specific events identified during the History Taking, the present triggers were used to identify the precursor events that can be accessed for initial processing.

The event to be processed was carefully accessed in a structured manner to elicit the pertinent aspects of the stored information, contain the reactions, and guide the client to a full assessment. Tara was asked to identify (a) an image that represented the target experience (being humiliated at school); (b) the negative belief, termed the *Negative Cognition,* that verbalized how she felt about herself (e.g., "I'm worthless"); (c) the desired positive belief, termed the *Positive Cognition* ("I'm worthwhile"); (d) how true that positive belief felt on the Validity of Cognition (VOC) scale (1 = Completely false to 7 = Completely true; Shapiro, 1989); (e) the emotion that arose when the memory and negative belief were combined; (f) how disturbing it felt as measured on the Subjective Units of Disturbance (SUD) scale (0 = No disturbance to 10 = The most disturbance possible; Shapiro, 1989; Wolpe, 1958); and (g) the location of the physical sensations that were experienced.

As another example, one of Tara's problems was her anxiety about going to school. Tracing the anxiety back to her earliest memory revealed the primary target of throwing up, every morning, in the third grade.

Altogether, The Assessment Phase included:

- *Image:* Throwing up before going to school.

- *Negative Cognition (irrational belief):* "I can't do this."

  Generally, the clinician searches for a belief that underlies a statement such as this, which would indicate a feeling of defectiveness (see Table 1.2). However, given Tara's level of distress, the statement was accepted.

- *Positive Cognition (desired belief):* "I can do this."

  Likewise, this simplified version was accepted, as it was exactly opposite the Negative Cognition and encapsulated Tara's feelings.

- *Validity of Cognition:* 2.

  Because 1 = Completely false and 7 = Completely true, the number 2 indicates a low level of believability that she will be able to go to school without anxiety. However, it was sufficient to begin processing.

- *Emotions:* Terror, helplessness.

- *Subjective Units of Disturbance:* 10.

  Tara rated the target event at 10 out of 10 in anxiety. It is important to note the high SUD level even though not a big "T" trauma, and even though the incidents of throwing up had occurred over 7 years ago.

- *Physical sensations:* In the stomach and head.

  These sensations were the somatic memories that were part of the stored event. Once processing has successfully occurred, they should no longer be present.

Phase 4: Desensitization

During this phase, the reprocessing is conducted according to structured procedures that engage the associative processes of the brain and stimulate memory networks to ensure that all salient information has been addressed. Insights emerge, new memories may surface, negative emotions are replaced with positive ones, and the entire memory becomes adaptively assimilated within the larger memory networks.

In AIP terms, each personality trait is a constellation of habitual or consistent responses that arise under particular circumstances. Each set of responses emerges from memory networks that are stimulated by current situations. Each of these networks is composed of the earlier stored experiences. When a clinician diagnoses a personality disorder, or any other type of clinical syndrome, it is because there are certain responses that are maladaptive. These responses and personality characteristics are fed by unprocessed events that result in thoughts, emotions, and physical sensations that inappropriately color the person's perceptions of the present and result in dysfunctional responses and behaviors. To liberate the client to move toward a state of improved mental health, it is vital to identify and process the earlier experiences that set the groundwork for these responses. Personality is not an immutable monolith but an accumulation of memory-based reactions that can be processed.

The standard EMDR procedures used to process the disturbing experiences are geared to access the memories as they are currently stored, stimulate the information processing system, and monitor the transmutation of the information to an adaptive resolution. Each set of bilateral stimulation seems to allow new connections to be made among the memory networks. The client is asked initially to concentrate on the target memory (image, negative belief, sensation) while simultaneously attending to the bilateral stimulation. At the end of each set of stimulation, which is customized to the client response (see Shapiro, 2001), the client reports any new associations that may have emerged. Depending on the response, the clinician may direct the client to concentrate on the new information that has arisen or return to the target. The various channels of association are addressed until the client can return to the targeted experience with no distress (0 SUD). Unlike exposure therapies that compel the client to maintain a concentration on the targeted event for extended periods of time (Foa & Rothbaum, 1998), EMDR incorporates an associative process that often leads to a far-ranging exploration of memories and topics (Rogers & Silver, 2002; for detailed client transcripts, see Shapiro, 2001, 2002).

For example, to process Tara's memory of vomiting in school, she was asked to hold together the image, negative belief, and physical sensations in her mind while simultaneously following the clinician's fingers with her eyes. She was instructed, "Just let whatever happens happen." At the end of each set she was told, "Let it go. Take a deep breath," and asked, "What do you get now?"

After the first set of eye movements Tara reported, "I'm different, everyone hates me." This revealed the feeling underlying "I can't," which was "There is something wrong with me." After being asked to concentrate on that statement and receiving a second set of eye movements, she stated, "I want to stay home and be taken care of." Concentrating on this, after the third set she declared, "My mother doesn't understand." We can see from this statement that the memory was becoming assimilated into the larger context. Even though she wanted to stay home, she did not receive what she needed there. After still another set, while concentrating on that statement, Tara said, "Once I'm at school, I'm okay; it's just that initial walking in." From this we see that the positive experiences she had stored were now becoming accessible. With further processing Tara was able to say, "I enjoy seeing my friends and most of the teachers." A return to the initial target found the SUD level reduced, and further processing produced the realization that there were people at school more attuned to her needs than her parents were. Going back again to the memory at the end of the Desensitization Phase, once processing was completed, Tara viewed it as in the past, with a SUD of 0.

The transmutation of the stored memory experience into a more adaptive form occurs through a reprocessing that brings together the relevant information stored in the client's own memory networks. Whereas many forms of therapy depend on the clinician to suggest alternative perspectives, direct action, or reframe the interpretation of an inherent belief, EMDR uses procedures that allow the client's own history and knowledge to reshape the targeted experience. Additional memories that need to be addressed or that offer counterexamples generally emerge spontaneously during processing. For instance, in Tara's case, the memories of positive experiences with friends at school automatically arose into consciousness without clinician prompting. The observed changes in imagery, sensation, belief, and perspective are the result of the forging of new connections among the memory networks.

EMDR clinicians are trained to stay out of the way as much as possible, because the therapist does not know what the best unconscious connections are that need to be made. When change has not occurred after consecutive sets of dual attention stimulation, then the clinician may use a *Cognitive Interweave* and ask a question, offer a statement for consideration, or suggest an action that is geared to elicit the next bit of information needed to continue the learning experience. For instance, if Tara's processing had stopped when she contemplated going to school (which would be indicated by the lack of cognitive, emotional, or sensory change after consecutive sets of eye movements), the clinician might have said, "I'm confused. Didn't you tell me that you had some friends there that you liked?" Then, if Tara had replied in the affirmative, she would have been asked to think about that during another set. Likewise, if a rape victim were stuck in the sense of shame and blame, the clinician might ask, "Do you mean if your niece had been raped it would be her fault?" When the rape victim says no, she is asked to think about that during another set of stimulation. All that is needed is a tentative, even hesitant agreement or willingness to consider it. This serves to access the adaptive information stored in the brain in a separate memory network. If the information is relevant, it will become assimilated during the next set of eye movements. A short set of eye movements is used so the client can report on whether the information feels right.

Conceptually, the Cognitive Interweave simulates spontaneous processing by accessing the needed memory network; then the clinician gets out of the way so that the appropriate neurological connections can take place (for detailed transcripts, see Shapiro, 2001, 2002). The emphasis is on allowing processing to occur that will result in trait change, not simply the elicitation of a temporary state change. A variety of ways to stimulate blocked processing may be used (for detailed parameters, see Shapiro, 2001). However, the eliciting of positive information is only a starting point, as a superficial intellectual understanding of lack of blame or potential resources is not the goal of EMDR therapy. It is important to return to the undistorted target to complete processing so that all the relevant connections can be made.

Tara's initial treatment included processing all the large and small "t" remembered traumas, including the family interactions that contributed to her feeling defective and unsafe (e.g., her mother running to agitatedly question her when Tara tripped or came home out of breath after playing; her cousins making fun of her; her parents fighting), as well as the move that had disturbed her, and any demeaning peer responses (e.g., teasing, fights, snubs).

Phase 5: Installation

This phase strengthens positive cognitive connections. After processing a given target to a 0 SUD level, the clinician checks to see whether the desired positive belief identified at the beginning of the session is still appropriate, or if a better one has emerged. It is not unusual for a new Positive Cognition (PC) to be more applicable once processing has cleared away the confusion and brought more positive information to light. In Tara's case, "I can do it" was no longer applicable as she realized that she already had positive connections with people in school who made her comfortable. Her more appropriate PC was found to be "I'm a good person." Tara was then asked to hold together the thought of vomiting in third grade and the words "I'm a good person," and rate it on the VOC scale to assess the felt believability of the statement. She reported feeling it at a 5 (of 7) level. She was then asked to hold the image and statement in mind and follow the therapist's fingers. After each subsequent set she was asked to rate the VOC again and report anything else that came up. Consecutive sets brought the VOC to a 6.5. After a set with no change, she was asked, "What prevents it from being a 7?" Tara responded, "I'll have to see how I feel tomorrow." This desire for a test drive of her newfound confidence was considered ecologically valid (i.e., realistic and practical, given the circumstances), and she was encouraged to report back the following week. If she had said, "I'm not okay outside this office," then more targeting and processing would have been indicated.

Phase 6: Body Scan

Once a 0 SUD and 7 VOC (or 1 and 6, respectively, if ecologically valid) are achieved, the Body Scan Phase identifies any residual physical sensation. The client is asked to think of the target memory, along with the PC, and mentally scan the body from head to feet looking for sensation. Any sensation is then focused on and processed in consecutive sets until the sensation dissipates. At times, a sensation may prove to be linked to further dysfunctional information and another memory may arise. If that is the case, it is targeted and processed. At times, the client may identify a pleasurable sensation. These are generally linked to positive affects and are enhanced by the bilateral stimulation. This phase is completed when the client has a clean body scan, devoid of any negative sensation.

Phase 7: Closure

This phase ensures that the client is in an appropriate state of equilibrium at the end of the session and is able to maintain this stability between sessions. If the processing is incomplete and the client is in any distress, one of the self-control or guided imagery techniques is used to eliminate it. For clients such as Tara, who has a pronounced lack of positive self-worth, it is useful to end each session with positive, reinforcing imagery that includes a reinforcement of her self-love, sense of safety, and sense of control.

In this phase of treatment, clients are briefed on what to expect between sessions and reminded to use their *Trigger, Image, Cognition, Emotion, Sensation (TICES)/SUD Log.* The Log is a telescoped journal used to identify any positive or negative experiences in a form that allows the client to give an accurate report to the clinician. If Tara were disturbed by a teacher's remark in the following week, she would indicate it in the following way:

Trigger	Image	Cognition	Emotion	Sensation/SUD
Teacher said I wasn't paying attention	Her face	I'm stupid	Shame	Knot in stomach 7 SUD

Tara's experience with the teacher would trigger a high level of negative affect because it linked into previous experiences she had of feeling defective and not good enough. The Log report would allow Tara and the clinician to observe patterns of response and the information needed to process the triggers and etiological events. After she wrote down what occurred, she was to use one of the self-control techniques to get rid of the negative emotions and physical sensations that might have surfaced. The ability to self-monitor and use an "aspirin" (a technique to temporarily relieve pain) is important, as indicated by numerous studies on self-mastery (Bandura, 1977, 2000; Peterson, Maier, & Seligman, 1993; Seligman, 1972). However, the ultimate goal of EMDR is to liberate clients from these automatic responses and allow them to evolve to a state of freedom and well-being consistent with their chronological age.

Tara might come into the session with 10 things on her Log list during the early weeks of therapy. Over time, the processing of the etiological memories should cause the triggering situations to decline. Eventually, there should be few habitual negative responses because the earlier events that contain the dysfunctional emotions, sensations, and perspectives have been processed. While Tara is an adolescent, and therefore unable to fully individuate because of her age and position in the family power hierarchy, she can nevertheless achieve a level of self-worth that will allow her to acquire a realistic self-concept, a sense of resilience, and the ability to socialize appropriately.

In addition to the earlier events, current conditions that still consistently trigger disturbance are processed, as they may be the result of second-order conditioning. That is, if one walks into a room 100 times and is anxious, that response can condition numerous stimuli in the room to elicit anxiety. Processing the past events that set the groundwork for the dysfunction, as well as current events that elicit disturbance, frees the individual from the forced negative responses. Once Tara is liberated from these experiences, the self-control techniques can be used occasionally, as anyone might, because life is messy, with occasional unpleasant surprises. Some things appropriately cause a certain amount of distress; even in these cases, self-mastery is important, and the self-control techniques can allow people to feel in control and make better decisions.

Phase 8:   Reevaluation

This phase opens each session subsequent to initial processing. It is important to ensure that treatment effects have been maintained and to determine if any new issues need to be explored. If a memory has been successfully processed, it has been transformed in meaning and affect. However, perhaps a new perspective has emerged that needs to be addressed. For instance, Tara may have come to terms with her memories of vomiting in third grade, but now remembers an un-supportive teacher that added to her difficulties. If so, that memory would be processed in turn. If processing was incomplete in the previous session, the memory is elicited and completed. Other manifestations of the stored dysfunction are also addressed. Perhaps the client reports a troubling nightmare; this is likely to be a useful target, because dream states are periods during which unresolved experiences are processed, and nightmares indicate a distressing memory in need of attention (see Shapiro, 2001). The nightmare image is identified along with the Negative Cognition, the Positive Cognition, and the rest of the aspects discussed during the Assessment Phase and processed to completion. Often, the client derives considerable insight and understanding during processing as the symbolic veil is removed and the underlying issue revealed (Shapiro, 2001; Wachtel, 2002).

One purpose of the Reevaluation Phase is to determine how the client is now functioning in the relevant interpersonal systems. As the targeted experiences are processed, the client's automatic reactions and behaviors also transmute. Therapists must be attuned to whether the client has processed the dysfunctional, increased the positive, and been offered sufficient education and support to overcome previous deficits. Regardless of within-session observations, this can be ascertained only with progress reports after real-world experiences.

As Tara continued to process the etiological events, not only had her negative self-concept become replaced with a more affirmative one, but also many new behaviors and positive attitudes automatically emerged as her self-esteem increased. However, her extreme level of anxiety and agitation during her formative years had not allowed a variety of interpersonal skills to be learned. As she reported back to her therapist weekly, it became clear which social skills and interactional behaviors would need to be taught. The clinician could use modeling, role-play, group instruction, videotapes—basically any means necessary to give the instruction didactically. Then, to aid in the process, Tara would be asked to imagine engaging in the new behaviors in the future while they are targeted with successive sets of eye movements. For instance, Tara's first experience of going to a school dance was preceded by her receiving dance instruction and participating in role-plays of different interactions, starting from entering the gymnasium to dancing with friends and ways of responding if asked to dance by one of the boys. The entire evening would be reviewed imaginally with a variety of scenarios while simultaneously engaging in eye movements to infuse a *future template* of appropriate responses and behaviors. This procedure allowed her to incorporate appropriate responses and to explore any hesitancies, cognitive distortions, or concerns.

On a weekly basis, it was important to reinforce the self-control techniques and, after the etiological memories were completed, to process the triggers revealed in Tara's Log. In addition, processing was used to incorporate templates for appropriate future action based on the situations revealed in her journal, as well as to inoculate and buffer her against potential failure ("It's okay to make a mistake"). For instance, after etiological events had been processed, a humiliating remark by a teacher was targeted. Because Tara was at a loss about how to respond if such a thing should happen again, processing was followed by role-play on how to respond and then a future template. If Tara was hesitant to join a school club, that would be targeted, including through role-play on how to proceed.

After templates are processed it is useful to suggest taking action with achievable social tasks for the following week. It is also important to assess the need for additional aids, such as assertiveness training, makeup, clothing, dance classes, and other ways to foster additional physical, recreational, and social interests. The goal is to have a happy, self-assured young woman able to bond and connect and who is comfortable in her own body. These procedures would be the same whether treating an adolescent or an adult.

Given Tara's age, however, it is crucial to remember that she is embedded in familial and school social systems. A certain amount of her anxiety and avoidance was reality based, born both of her parents' reactivity and of humiliations at school. To cope with family and school systems that she cannot leave or control, she was taught self-control techniques to deal with parental and peer responses that were unfair. After processing potential triggers, the clinician suggested specific behaviors to deal with difficult situations and helped Tara learn them by processing and incorporating future templates. The clinician-client relationship was extremely important as it not only offered Tara emotional support, but served as a model of a good and healthy relationship. It was important that she have caring and reinforcing interactions with the clinician about the previous week to debrief interactional issues and to underscore her progress and potential.

Tara made personal progress with her EMDR therapy, losing both her social and school phobia. After a processing session directed toward her posture, she realized that she was shrinking to garner sympathy from others, but did not need to use that defense. Her appearance and demeanor improved to the point that teachers and school staff commented on it. She went from having few social supports to having many friends, who even gave her a surprise party for her birthday.

The importance of family systems therapy (FST) is sadly underscored in this case, as treatment was stopped prematurely. In working with children and adolescents, it is important to help the parents anticipate and support changes in the child's behavior. Usually the parents are stuck in maladaptive responses to the child's attitudes and actions. As would be expected, the traumas Tara's parents experienced over her initial fragility strongly impacted their feelings, actions, and attitude toward her. Optimally, to allow the most comprehensive treatment, her parents' traumatization would be processed, along with the attendant triggers, and their familial interactions with Tara would benefit from education and adjustment. For instance, her parents could be taught more supportive ways to communicate concerns to Tara and self-control techniques to deal with their own anxiety, including increasing their ability to allow Tara to individuate. The psychoeducational approach discussed in Chapter 2 might be particularly useful with parents in a case such as this.

Unfortunately, the father believed strongly in a patriarchal arrangement and remained detached from the parenting and therapy process. He was preoccupied with business affairs and rarely home. When he was present, his primary interactions with Tara were dismissive and derogatory. Tara's mother had given up trying to involve her husband more in family life. In the face of her husband's absence she devoted herself completely to her children. She reported a history of anxiety and depression but refused personal therapy. Not surprisingly, as Tara became more assertive, Mother appeared unable to allow her to differentiate. When Tara wanted to cut her hair, Mother would not allow it, saying, "I like it that way." When Tara wanted to take on more responsibility as she approached college age, Mother would not permit it and began sabotaging the treatment. Finally, despite Tara's objections, therapy was terminated. The poignancy of the unresolved issues, as well as the insight Tara gained during the course of therapy, were verbalized when she mused about her future: "If I leave for college, who will hold the family together?" (For additional discussion of differentiation difficulties from an FST perspective, see Tofani, Chapter 13). The concluding chapter of this book picks up on Tara's case and makes suggestions from a variety of FST perspectives on how these issues might be addressed.

THREE-PRONGED PROTOCOL
(PAST, PRESENT, FUTURE)

Each form of psychotherapy is differentiated by specific sets of procedures and the underlying paradigm that guides their applications. Although EMDR originated from a behavioral tradition (Shapiro, 1989), a recent panel (Barlow, Shapiro, & White, 2005) emphasized how the intervening years have changed it to a very different treatment approach. Cognitive and behavioral therapies attempt to handle the current problems directly by trying to change the client's thinking or behavior in the here and now. In contrast, the AIP model that guides EMDR practice views the negative beliefs and emotions, such as fear and anxiety, not as the cause of the problem, but as the effect. The cause is viewed as specific memories of earlier events that have been inappropriately stored and contain the perspective and affects that are manifested currently through verbalized beliefs, inappropriate emotions, and behaviors.* Whereas most therapies view pathologies as having an experiential component, as previously discussed, in EMDR the experiences are viewed as information stored in the brain in memory networks that are stimulated by current situations. Except in cases of defined organic deficits, the lack of adequate processing of these earlier memories is the primary cause of the current dysfunctional responses.

The specific paradigm of various psychotherapies provides the heuristic for clinical practice. Therefore, in EMDR treatment, phobias (or panic attacks such as Tara's) are not dealt with by forcing the client to remain exposed to situations in the present that cause the distress, as one would do in CBT (e.g., Emmelkamp, Bouman, & Scholing, 1992). Rather, in EMDR the earliest, worst, and most recent memories of the feared object or event are accessed and

---

* It is possible to directly target current situations (which often results in earlier events surfacing in memory), but it is generally more efficient and successful to first target the earlier precursor memories (for detailed explanation, see Shapiro, 2001).

processed (De Jongh, Ten Broeke, & Renssen, 1999; Fernandez & Faretta, in press; Shapiro, 1995, 1999). Once this is done, to handle any remnants of second-order conditioning the client imagines and processes the current situations that might have triggered the fear, for example, a claustrophobic being stuck in traffic or in an elevator. When the client no longer feels fear while imagining the situation, a future template is processed so he can imagine engaging with the previously feared event calmly. As this is done, the imaginal scene is stored in memory and forms the neural configuration that will be tapped into when the client leaves the office and encounters a real-life situation. Only then, when clients are no longer afraid, are they asked to expose themselves in real life to the event or object. At that point, the real-world interaction can be used for feedback to identify anything else that might need to be processed.

This use of past targets (earliest, worst), present (most recent, triggers), and future (template) characterizes the generic protocol that underlies all the EMDR specialty protocols, such as those for pain and addiction (see Shapiro, 2001). It is also the framework used to assess the clinical picture in determining treatment for any clinical complaint. Had Tara entered therapy when she was 30 years old instead of 15, her symptoms likely would include a social phobia, low self-esteem, and collapsed posture. The EMDR treatment would involve identifying the childhood memories that set the foundation for the pathology, the current situations that triggered the disturbance, and what was necessary to fill the deficits caused by her anxiety-ridden childhood so that she would be able to excel in her current social systems. The same memories that caused her inability to interact appropriately at school would be responsible for her social problems as an adult. The memories causing her collapsed posture in school would be the same ones that contain the physical sensations causing her to slouch as an adult. These memories cause the past to be present.

Fortunately, no matter how long the memories have resided in the brain, they can still be processed. The older the client, the more memories will need to be addressed and the more potential comorbid conditions may exist to be treated. However, the function of the EMDR treatment is the same: to liberate the client from the dysfunctionally stored memories that contain the affects and perspectives driving the current pathology. It is much easier for clients to enhance their social skills if they do not have unprocessed earlier memories that are causing them to feel defective and unsafe. Consequently, EMDR treatment proceeds from the inside out and attends to the inner world before using the excellent CBT tool of modeling or the experiential technique of role-play to incorporate the skill sets that help define a healthy adult.

ADAPTIVE INFORMATION PROCESSING AND FAMILY DYNAMICS

Although EMDR was originally developed as an individual therapy, the AIP model helps to inform family system therapists of the contribution of previous experiences to their clients' current pathologies. Whenever individuals join together to become a couple, their interactions are liable to trigger unprocessed information from each of their family of origin experiences or previous relationships. Dysfunctional patterns of interaction and defenses are not simply the product of current situations but are rooted in previous experiences. Assessment is needed to identify whether the crisis that brings a couple into therapy is the latest example of a long-standing personal pattern or the result of new traumatization. For instance, in cases of infidelity or abandonment, the wounded partner may be unable to reconcile because she cannot erase the sadness, lack of trust, and mental image of the betrayal. Regardless of what may be happening in the present, even including her partner's great remorse and reassurances, previous experiences will not allow for a sense of safety or reengagement. In this case, EMDR would be used to process the experience to liberate her from the distressing prior events. The EMDR clinician would also want to investigate and process the roots of the earlier betrayal by appropriate history taking from both partners. What previous experiences set the foundation for his actions? What dynamics were inherent in the relationship and/or his previous history to cause this to occur?

No couple relationship starts off completely new; it is always influenced by the experiences that forged each individual's sense of self and others. For instance, as noted by Siegel in the *Foreword* to this book, different kinds of parenting produce children with secure, avoidant, ambivalent, or disorganized attachments. In turn, these children will form relationships that are influenced by these earlier attachment interactions, perhaps inappropriately attacking, dismissing, or withdrawing from their partners. Despite overt intention, the current situations automatically link into the memory networks where the earlier experiences are stored, and the dysfunctional affects and perspectives arise to color the perceptions of the present (see also Shapiro, 1998). A gesture by a partner meant as supportive may be interpreted as overcontrolling or demeaning. What is simple distractedness may be seen as abandonment or disdain.

The AIP model sensitizes clinicians to take appropriate client histories to identify the earlier memories that have set the groundwork for the dysfunction, and then to use EMDR to process these experiential contributors. FST models are indeed salient, as clearly the interpersonal interactions within the family of origin or with other significant people may be the unprocessed distressing events that have been stored in memory. Current interpersonal interactions may trigger the memories, and family dynamics may maintain and exacerbate the symptoms. However, from an AIP perspective, the root cause is internal. For example, a husband's controlling behaviors are viewed as the consequence of earlier experiences that may be feeding current fears of abandonment or inadequacy. Although his overt behaviors may be elicited by the perceptions of his wife's actions and may be exacerbated by her reactions, the essential cause of chronic misperceptions and inappropriate behaviors is understood to be the unprocessed material. That is, even innocent behaviors by the wife, or those that would be deemed appropriate by others, can elicit affective responses in the husband and cause him to be distressed and controlling. Some relationships may need interventions focused only on changing patterns of interaction and communication. However, in the AIP model, chronic and resistant interactional systems are viewed as based on pathological responses within the individual.

In conjunction with appropriate systemic evaluation, the AIP model posits the utility of processing the individual's past experiences that are driving the current dysfunctional behavior. By this means, the family therapist can be more successful in modeling and teaching the relationship and communication skills that are needed. For instance, many perpetrators of violent domestic acts have witnessed these kinds of abusive behaviors between their own parents, with stored affects of fear and anger. EMDR treatment would include processing these experiences along with teaching the necessary self-control and relationship skills. Anecdotal reports have indicated that processing the childhood memories of domestic violence perpetrators frees them from the automatic dysfunctional reactions, just as research involving the processing of sexual abuse perpetrators' childhood experiences has revealed a cessation of automatic reactivity and physiological arousal (see Ricci, 2006; Ricci, Clayton, & Shapiro, in press). Likewise, published reports indicate the utility of EMDR with people who have experienced marital and sexual dysfunction, who are now enabled to move toward much healthier relationships (Kaslow, Nurse, & Thompson, 2002; Keenan & Farrell, 2000; C. Levin, 1993; Protinsky, Sparks, & Flemke, 2001; Wernik, 1993).

A variety of dysfunctional relational behaviors may be rooted in childhood experiences that in some way initially gave the individual a sense of safety or control. As indicated by Siegel ("Foreword,"), children with insecure attachments have an *appropriate* response to their parents' dysfunctional patterns; the pathology resides in the fact that, as an adult, these interactional patterns are no longer functional. The AIP model encourages clinicians to process the remembered interactions that set these patterns and sensitizes them to recognize that the client's parents may be the victims of their own traumatization, which might go back many generations. The inappropriate responses to their children arise from the disturbing experiences that are stored in their own memory networks and that need to be processed. Although evolution has hardwired automatic responses to maintain the survival of the species, trauma can override this programming (Madrid, Skolek, & Shapiro, in press; Schore, 2003; Siegel, 1999). For instance, in contrast to healthy mothers who automatically respond to their children's cries with nurturing and support, the traumatized mother might become anxious and hyperaroused. Consequently, the infant may be avoided or handled roughly when crying, starting a cycle of inappropriate responses by the mother to the baby's basic needs, which can continue throughout childhood.

The AIP model alerts clinicians to the necessity of identifying and processing the parents' disturbing memories in order to change their habitual responses, as well as treating the children by processing their own traumatizing experiences (for detailed case examples, see Shapiro & Forrest, 1997). FST can then be used to teach the appropriate parenting skills and help establish the healthy boundaries and interactions necessary to allow the family to thrive. (Possibly, Structural Family Therapy would be the treatment of choice; see Chapter 2.) If an individual therapist is working with an adult, family reconciliations are not as important because the client has reached an age at which individuation and a variety of choices are possible. For children who are embedded within the dynamics of a dysfunctional family, it is a principle of EMDR that it is important to work with the parents to help change these dynamics, while simultaneously incorporating positive experiences, affects, and resources for the child.

CONCLUSIONS

A child's sense of self is engendered by accumulated interactions with his parents and provides the core filter through which other life experiences are viewed. For instance, Tara's parents consistently treated her in ways that caused her to feel defective, and, due to the affects arising from these unprocessed memories, other events were also experienced with the sense of "I'm worthless/inadequate." This would be the case regardless of whether she entered therapy at age 15 or age 50. Likewise, a client's lifelong depression may be caused by parental responses that instilled the affects and attendant beliefs of "I'm not good enough" and "I'm not in control" during formative years, or his fear and anxiety may be the result of parenting that resulted in an ambivalent attachment.

As an integrative psychotherapy approach, the goal of EMDR is to liberate clients of any age from the experiential contributors that set the foundation for the current pathology. A thorough assessment of the entire clinical picture is used to ascertain limitations of body, mind, emotion, and existential perspective. The AIP model guiding EMDR practice posits that most pathology is influenced or caused by memories of previous experiences that have been inappropriately stored in the brain; a systemic evaluation is needed to explore that foundation and to identify the present situations that are exacerbating any dysfunction.

Whether the client is a child or an adult, it is vital to remember that interpersonal interactions are the product of inner worlds converging. Some relationships can be corrected through education alone, but many clients are in need of profound psychic readjustment to break lifelong patterns of dysfunctional emotional and cognitive responses. The problematic relationship is simply another symptom of a wounded inner world. This book offers clinical guidance to both individual and family therapists by demonstrating AIP-informed EMDR processing in combination with various models of FST. EMDR highlights the inner world of the individual as a primary foundation for interactional behaviors. The myriad forms of FST contribute ways to augment targeting selections as well as procedures for heightening understanding and improving interactions among family members. As no person exists in isolation, the importance of an integrative practice cannot be overstated. It is hoped that this compendium of strategies across the spectrum of EMDR and FST clinical practice will aid in that process.

REFERENCES

American Psychiatric Association. (2000). *Diagnostic and statistical manual of mental disorders* (4th ed., text rev.). Washington, DC: Author.

American Psychiatric Association. (2004). *Practice guideline for the treatment of patients with acute stress disorder and posttraumatic stress disorder.* Arlington, VA: American Psychiatric Association Practice Guidelines.

Andrade, J., Kavanagh, D., & Baddeley, A. (1997). Eye-movements and visual imagery: A working memory approach to the treatment of post-traumatic stress disorder. *British Journal of Clinical Psychology, 36,* 209–223.

Bandura, A. (1977). Self-efficacy: Toward a unifying theory of behavioral change. *Psychological Review, 84,* 191–215.

Bandura, A. (2000). Self-efficacy: The foundation of agency. In W. J. Perrig & A. Grob (Eds.), *Control of human behavior, mental processes, and consciousness: Essays in honor of the 60th birthday of August Flammer* (pp. 17–33). Mahwah, NJ: Erlbaum.

Barlow, D. H., Shapiro, F., & White, M. (2005, December). *Supervision panel.* Evolution of Psychotherapy Conference, Anaheim, CA.

Barrowcliff, A. L., Gray, N. S., Freeman, T. C. A., & MacCulloch, M. J. (2004). Eye-movements reduce the vividness, emotional valence and electrodermal arousal associated with negative autobiographical memories. *Journal of Forensic Psychiatry and Psychology, 15,* 325–345.

Bleich, A., Kotler, M., Kutz, I., & Shalev, A. (2002). *Guidelines for the assessment and professional intervention with terror victims in the hospital and in the community.* Position paper of the (Israeli) National Council for Mental Health, Jerusalem, Israel.

Bradley, R., Greene, J., Russ, E., Dutra, L., & Westen, D. (2005). A multidimensional meta-analysis of psychotherapy for PTSD. *American Journal of Psychiatry, 162,* 214–227.

Brown, S., & Shapiro, F. (2006). EMDR in the treatment of borderline personality disorder. *Clinical Case Studies, 5,* 403–420.

Browning, C. (1999, September). Floatback and float-forward: Techniques for linking past, present, and future. *EMDRIA Newsletter,* pp. 12–13.

Carlson, J., Chemtob, C. M., Rusnak, K., Hedlund, N. L., & Muraoka, M. Y. (1998). Eye movement desensitization and reprocessing (EMDR): Treatment for combat-related post-traumatic stress disorder. *Journal of Traumatic Stress, 11,* 3–24.

Chemtob, C. M., Tolin, D. F., van der Kolk, B. A., & Pitman, R. K. (2000). Eye movement desensitization and reprocessing. In E. B. Foa, T. M. Keane, & M. J. Friedman (Eds.), *Effective treatments for PTSD: Practice guidelines from the International Society for Traumatic Stress Studies* (pp. 139–155, 333–335). New York: Guilford Press.

Christman, S. D., Garvey, K. J., Propper, R. E., & Phaneuf, K. A. (2003). Bilateral eye movements enhance the retrieval of episodic memories. *Neuropsychology, 17,* 221–229.

Davidson, P. R., & Parker, K. C. H. (2001). Eye movement desensitization and reprocessing (EMDR): A meta-analysis. *Journal of Consulting and Clinical Psychology, 69,* 305–316.

De Jongh, A., Ten Broeke, E., & Renssen, M. R. (1999). Treatment of specific phobias with eye movement desensitization and reprocessing (EMDR): Protocol, empirical status, and conceptual issues. *Journal of Anxiety Disorders, 13,* 69–85.

Department of Veterans Affairs & Department of Defense. (2004). *VA/DoD clinical practice guideline for the management of post-traumatic stress.* Washington, DC: Author.

Dutch National Steering Committee Guidelines Mental Health Care. (2003). *Multidisciplinary guideline: Anxiety disorders.* Utrecht, The Netherlands: Quality Institute Heath Care CBO/ Trimbos Institute.

Dworkin, M. (2005). *EMDR and the relational imperative.* New York: Brunner-Routledge.

Edmond, T., Rubin, A., & Wambach, K. (1999). The effectiveness of EMDR with adult female survivors of childhood sexual abuse. *Social Work Research, 23,* 103–116.

Edmond, T., Sloan, L., & McCarty, D. (2004). Sexual abuse survivors' perceptions of the effectiveness of EMDR and eclectic therapy: A mixed-methods study. *Research on Social Work Practice, 14,* 259–272.

Emmelkamp, P. M. G., Bouman, T. K., & Scholing, A. (1992). *Anxiety disorders: A practitioner's guide.* Chichester, England: Wiley.

Fernandez, I., & Faretta, E. (in press). EMDR in the treatment of panic disorder with agoraphobia. *Clinical Case Studies.*

Foa, E. B., & Rothbaum, B. O. (1998). *Treating the trauma of rape: Cognitive-behavioral therapy for PTSD.* New York: Guilford Press.

Grant, M., & Threlfo, C. (2002). EMDR in the treatment of chronic pain. *Journal of Clinical Psychology, 58,* 1505–1520.

Gupta, M., & Gupta, A. (2002). Use of eye movement desensitization and reprocessing (EMDR) in the treatment of dermatologic disorders. *Journal of Cutaneous Medicine and Surgery, 6,* 415–421.

Ironson, G. I., Freund, B., Strauss, J. L., & Williams, J. (2002). Comparison of two treatments for traumatic stress: A community-based study of EMDR and prolonged exposure. *Journal of Clinical Psychology, 58,* 113–128.

Jaberghaderi, N., Greenwald, R., Rubin, A., Dolatabadim, S., & Zand, S. O. (2004). A comparison of CBT and EMDR for sexually abused Iranian girls. *Clinical Psychology and Psychotherapy, 11,* 358–368.

Kaslow, F. W., Nurse, A. R., & Thompson, P. (2002). Utilization of EMDR in conjunction with family systems therapy. In F. Shapiro (Ed.), *EMDR and the paradigm prism: Experts of diverse orientations explore an integrated treatment* (pp. 289–318). Washington, DC: American Psychological Association.

Kavanagh, D. J., Freese, S., Andrade, J., & May, J. (2001). Effects of visuospatial tasks on desensitization to emotive memories. *British Journal of Clinical Psychology, 40,* 267–280.

Keenan, P., & Farrell, D. (2000). Treating morbid jealousy with eye movement desensitization and reprocessing utilizing cognitive inter-weave: A case report. *Counselling Psychology Quarterly, 13,* 175–189.

Kitchur, M. (2005). The strategic developmental model for EMDR. In R. Shapiro (Ed.), *EMDR solutions* (pp. 8–56). New York: Norton.

Korn, D. L., & Leeds, A. M. (2002). Preliminary evidence of efficacy for EMDR resource development and installation in the stabilization phase of treatment of complex posttraumatic stress disorder. *Journal of Clinical Psychology, 58*(12), 1465–1487.

Korn, D. L., van der Kolk, B. A., Weir, J., & Rozelle, D. (2004, September). *Looking beyond the data: Clinical lessons learned from an EMDR treatment outcome study.* Paper presented at the Annual conference of the EMDR International Association, Montreal, Canada.

Kuiken, D., Bears, M., Miall, D., & Smith, L. (2001–2002). Eye movement desensitization reprocessing facilitates attentional orienting. *Imagination, Cognition and Personality, 21*(1), 3–20.

Lamprecht, F., Kohnke, C., Lempa, W., Sack, M., Matzke, M., & Munte, T. (2004). Event-related potentials and EMDR treatment of post-traumatic stress disorder. *Neuroscience Research, 49,* 267–272.

Lansing, K., Amen, D. G., Hanks, C., & Rudy, L. (2005). High resolution brain SPECT imaging and EMDR in police officers with PTSD. *Journal of Neuropsychiatry and Clinical Neurosciences, 17,* 526–532.

Lee, C., Gavriel, H., Drummond, P., Richards, J., & Greenwald, R. (2002). Treatment of post-traumatic stress disorder: A comparison of stress inoculation training with prolonged exposure and eye movement desensitization and reprocessing. *Journal of Clinical Psychology, 58,* 1071–1089.

Lee, C., Taylor, G., & Drummond, P. D. (2006). The active ingredient in EMDR: Is it traditional exposure or dual focus of attention? *Clinical Psychology and Psychotherapy, 13,* 97–107.

Levin, C. (1993, July/August). The enigma of EMDR. *Family Therapy Networker,* 75–83.

Levin, P., Lazrove, S., & van der Kolk, B. A. (1999). What psychological testing and neuroimaging tell us about the treatment of posttraumatic stress disorder (PTSD) by eye movement desensitization and reprocessing (EMDR). *Journal of Anxiety Disorders, 13,* 159–172.

Lovett, J. (1999). *Small wonders: Healing childhood trauma with EMDR.* New York: Free Press.

Madrid, A., Skolek, S., & Shapiro, F. (in press). Repairing failures in bonding through EMDR. *Clinical Case Studies.*

Marcus, S., Marquis, P., & Sakai, C. (1997). Controlled study of treatment of PTSD using EMDR in an HMO setting. *Psychotherapy, 34,* 307–315.

Marcus, S., Marquis, P., & Sakai, C. (2004). Three- and 6-month follow-up of EMDR treatment of PTSD in an HMO setting. *International Journal of Stress Management, 11,* 195–208.

Maxfield, L., & Hyer, L. A. (2002). The relationship between efficacy and methodology in studies investigating EMDR treatment of PTSD. *Journal of Clinical Psychology, 58,* 23–41.

McCullough, L. (2002). Exploring change mechanisms in EMDR applied to "small t trauma" in short term dynamic psychotherapy: Research questions and speculations. *Journal of Clinical Psychology, 58,* 1465–1487.

McGoldrick, M., Gerson, R., & Shellenberger, S. (1999). *Genograms: Assessment and intervention.* New York: Norton.

Mol, S. S. L., Arntz, A., Metsemakers, J. F. M., Dinant, G., Vilters-Van Montfort, P. A. P., & Knottnerus, A. (2005). Symptoms of post-traumatic stress disorder after non-traumatic events: Evidence from an open population study. *British Journal of Psychiatry, 186,* 494–499.

National Institute for Clinical Excellence. (2005). *Post traumatic stress disorder (PTSD): The management of adults and children in primary and secondary care.* London: NICE Guidelines.

Norcross, J. C. (Ed.). (2002). *Psychotherapy relationships that work: Therapist contributions and responsiveness to patient needs.* New York: Oxford University Press.

Perkins, B. R., & Rouanzoin, C. C. (2002). A critical evaluation of current views regarding eye movement desensitization and reprocessing (EMDR): Clarifying points of confusion. *Journal of Clinical Psychology, 58,* 77–97.

Peterson, C., Maier, S. F., & Seligman, M. E. P. (1993). *Learned helplessness: A theory for the age of personal control.* New York: Oxford University Press.

Power, K. G., McGoldrick, T., Brown, K., Buchanan, R., Sharp, D., Swanson, V., et al. (2002). A controlled comparison of eye movement desensitization and reprocessing versus exposure plus cognitive restructuring, versus waiting list in the treatment of post-traumatic stress disorder. *Journal of Clinical Psychology and Psychotherapy, 9,* 299–318.

Protinsky, H., Sparks, J., & Flemke, K. (2001). Using eye movement desensitization and reprocessing to enhance treatment of couples. *Journal of Marital and Family Therapy, 27,* 157–164.

Ray, A. L., & Zbik, A. (2001). Cognitive behavioral therapies and beyond. In C. D. Tollison, J. R. Satterhwaite, & J. W. Tollison (Eds.), *Practical pain management* (3rd ed., pp. 189–208). Philadelphia: Lippincott.

Ricci, R. J. (2006). Trauma resolution using eye movement desensitization and reprocessing with an incestuous sex offender: An instrumental case study. *Clinical Case Studies, 5,* 248–265

Ricci, R. J., Clayton, C. A., & Shapiro, F. (2006). Some effects of EMDR treatment with previously abused child molesters: Theoretical reviews and preliminary findings. *Journal of Forensic Psychiatry and Psychology, 17,* 538–562.

Rogers, S., & Silver, S. M. (2002). Is EMDR an exposure therapy? A review of trauma protocols. *Journal of Clinical Psychology, 58,* 43–59.

Rogers, S., Silver, S., Goss, J., Obenchain, J., Willis, A., & Whitney, R. (1999). A single session, controlled group study of flooding and eye movement desensitization and reprocessing in treating posttraumatic stress disorder among Vietnam War veterans: Preliminary data. *Journal of Anxiety Disorders, 13,* 119–130.

Rothbaum, B. O., Astin, M. C., & Marsteller, F. (2005). Prolonged exposure versus eye movement desensitization (EMDR) for PTSD rape victims. *Journal of Traumatic Stress, 18,* 607–616.

Scheck, M., Schaeffer, J. A., & Gillette, C. (1998). Brief psychological intervention with traumatized young women: The efficacy of eye movement desensitization and reprocessing. *Journal of Traumatic Stress, 11,* 25–44.

Schneider, J., Hofmann, A., Rost, C., & Shapiro, F. (in press). EMDR in the treatment of chronic phantom limb pain. *Pain Medicine.*

Schore, A. N. (2003). *Affect dysregulation and the disorders of the self.* New York: Norton.

Seligman, M. E. (1972). Learned helplessness. *Annual Review of Medicine, 23,* 407–412.

Shapiro, F. (1989). Efficacy of the eye movement desensitization procedure in the treatment of traumatic memories. *Journal of Traumatic Stress Studies, 2,* 199–223.

Shapiro, F. (1991a). Eye movement desensitization and reprocessing procedure: From EMD to EMD/R—A new treatment model for anxiety and related traumata. *Behavior Therapist, 14,* 133–135.

Shapiro, F. (1991b). Stray thoughts. *EMDR Network Newsletter, 1,* 1–3.

Shapiro, F. (1994a). Alternative stimuli in the use of EMDR. *Journal of Behavior Therapy and Experimental Psychiatry, 25,* 89.

Shapiro, F. (1994b). EMDR: In the eye of a paradigm shift. *Behavior Therapist, 17,* 153–158.

Shapiro, F. (1995). *Eye movement desensitization and reprocessing: Basic principles, protocols and procedures.* New York: Guilford Press.

Shapiro, F. (1998). Eye movement desensitization and reprocessing (EMDR): Accelerated information processing and affect-driven constructions. *Crisis Intervention and Time-Limited Treatment, 4,* 145–157.

Shapiro, F. (1999). Eye movement desensitization and reprocessing (EMDR): Clinical and research implications of an integrated psychotherapy treatment. *Journal of Anxiety Disorders, 13,* 35–67.

Shapiro, F. (2001). *Eye movement desensitization and reprocessing: Basic principles, protocols and procedures* (2nd ed.). New York: Guilford Press.

Shapiro, F. (2002). Paradigms, processing, and personality development. In F. Shapiro (Ed.), *EMDR as an integrative psychotherapy approach: Experts of diverse orientations explore the paradigm prism* (pp. 3–26). Washington, DC: American Psychological Association Books.

Shapiro, F. (2005). *Eye movement desensitization and reprocessing (EMDR) training manual.* Watsonville, CA: EMDR Institute.

Shapiro, F., & Forrest, M. S. (1997). *EMDR.* New York: Basic Books.

Siegel, D. J. (1999). *The developing mind: Toward a neurobiology of interpersonal experience.* New York: Guilford Press.

Siegel, D. J. (2002). The developing mind and the resolution of trauma: Some ideas about information processing and an interpersonal neurobiology of psychotherapy. In F. Shapiro (Ed.), *EMDR as an integrative psychotherapy approach: Experts of diverse orientations explore the paradigm prism* (pp. 85–122). Washington, DC: American Psychological Association.

Sjöblom, P. O., Andréewitch, S., Bejerot, S., Mörtberg, E., Brinck, U., Ruck, C., et al. (2003). *Regional treatment recommendation for anxiety disorders.* Stockholm, Sweden: Medical Program Committee/Stockholm City Council.

Smyth, N. J., & Poole, D. (2002). EMDR and cognitive behavior therapy: Exploring convergence and divergence. In F. Shapiro (Ed.), *EMDR and the paradigm prism* (pp. 151–180). Washington, DC: American Psychological Association.

Sprang, G. (2001). The use of eye movement desensitization and reprocessing (EMDR) in the treatment of traumatic stress and complicated mourning: Psychological and behavioral outcomes. *Research on Social Work Practice, 11,* 300–320.

Stickgold, R. (2002). EMDR: A putative neurobiological mechanism of action. *Journal of Clinical Psychology, 58,* 61–75.

Taylor, S., Thordarson, D. S., Maxfield, L., Fedoroff, I. C., Lovell, K., & Ogrodniczuk, J. (2003). Comparative efficacy, speed, and adverse effects of three PTSD treatments: Exposure therapy, EMDR, and relaxation training. *Journal of Consulting and Clinical Psychology, 71,* 330–338.

Van den Hout, M., Muris, P., Salemink, E., & Kindt, M. (2001). Autobiographical memories become less vivid and emotional after eye movements. *British Journal of Clinical Psychology, 40,* 121–130.

van der Kolk, B. A. (1996). Trauma and memory. In B. A. van der Kolk, A. C. McFarlane, & L. Weisaeth (Eds.), *Traumatic stress: The effects of overwhelming experience on mind, body, and society* (pp. 279–302). New York: Guilford Press.

van der Kolk, B. A. (2002). Beyond the talking cure: Somatic experience and subcortical imprints in the treatment of trauma. In F. Shapiro (Ed.), *EMDR as an integrative psychotherapy approach: Experts of diverse orientations explore the paradigm prism* (pp. 57–84). Washington, DC: American Psychological Association.

van der Kolk, B. Spinazzola., Blaustein, J., Hopper, J., Hopper, E., Korn, D., et al. (in press). A randomized clinical trial of EMDR, fluoxetine, and pill placebo in the treatment of PTSD: Treatment effects and long-term maintenance. *Journal of Clinical Psychiatry.*

Van Etten, M., & Taylor, S. (1998). Comparative efficacy of treatments for post-traumatic stress disorder: A meta-analysis. *Clinical Psychology and Psychotherapy, 5,* 126–144.

Vaughan, K., Armstrong, M. F., Gold, R., O'Connor, N., Jenneke, W., & Tarrier, N. (1994). A trial of eye movement desensitization compared to image habituation training and applied muscle relaxation in post-traumatic stress disorder. *Journal of Behavior Therapy and Experimental Psychiatry, 25,* 283–291.

Wachtel, P. L. (2002). EMDR and psychoanalysis. In F. Shapiro (Ed.), *EMDR and the paradigm prism* (pp. 123–150). Washington, DC: American Psychological Association.

Watkins, J., & Watkins, H. (1997). *Ego states, theory and therapy.* New York: Norton.

Wernik, U. (1993). The role of the traumatic component in the etiology of sexual dysfunctions and its treatment with eye movement desensitization procedure. *Journal of Sex Education and Therapy, 19,* 212–222.

Wolpe, J. (1958). *Psychotherapy by reciprocal inhibition.* Stanford: Stanford University Press.

Zabukovec, J., Lazrove, S., & Shapiro, F. (2000). Self-healing aspects of EMDR: The therapeutic change process and perspectives of integrated psychotherapies. *Journal of Psychotherapy Integration, 10,* 189–206.

CHAPTER 2

Family Systems Theories and Therapeutic Applications: A Contextual Overview

Florence W. Kaslow

The purpose of this chapter is to provide a kaleidoscopic overview of the field of family therapy/psychology within which the ensuing chapters can be better understood. To accomplish this massive task within the space limits set, the same format has been followed in the summarization of each of the main theoretical schools. Common key dimensions found in almost all theories are highlighted. The dimensions covered are a synopsis of the theory's basic structure and goals, the techniques and process of each school of therapy, its perceived treatment applicability, and process and/or outcome research on the methodology. When a particular concept or technique is mentioned later in the volume, the reader may wish to use the index to refer back to this chapter for additional elucidation or contextualization. Wherever possible, chapters in the book are alluded to in which the author selectively integrates a particular theoretical perspective and treatment approach with his or her Eye Movement Desensitization and Reprocessing (EMDR) clinical work. (The selection of theories represents the author's choice and is not exhaustive.)

The field has now evolved to the point where the third, fourth, and even fifth generation of family theorists, therapists, psychologists, and researchers are actively engaged in making noteworthy contributions (see Appendix C). Excellent books and articles have been written explicating the various schools of family therapy, and the interested reader can consult these for greater detail (see Goldenberg & Goldenberg, 2004; N. J. Kaslow, Dausch, & Celano, 2003; N. J. Kaslow, Kaslow, & Farber, 1999; Nichols & Schwartz, 2006; see Appendix C on history for recent trends in the field).

SCHEMAS OF HEALTHY, MIDRANGE, AND DYSFUNCTIONAL FAMILIES

It is essential to have a framework in which to view the patients we see as we seek to ascertain their areas of health and strength and to understand their areas of dysfunction and their deficits. Different schemas have been promulgated indicating what constitutes healthy, midrange, and dysfunctional family dynamics and interactional processes (Walsh, 1993) and measuring those characteristics and patterns that help in determining family classification. Such schemas offer a picture of healthy functioning that can serve as the baseline from which clinicians can help distressed families move in the direction of healthier patterns and processes.

Two well-delineated models exist. Olson and colleagues (1983; Olson, Sprenkle, & Russell, 1979) evolved a circumplex model of family functioning predicated on two main variables: adaptability and cohesion. *Adaptability* refers to the system's ability to change its power structure, role relationships, and relationship rules flexibly in response to situational and developmental stress. *Cohesion* refers to the emotional bond family members have with one another. A balance on both variables typifies healthy family functioning, as well as the optimal development of each family member. When families exhibit balance on one dimension and extreme behavior on the other, they are classified as midrange. When their functioning on both variables falls in the extreme range, the family is apt to be dysfunctional; they may either be chaotic or rigid on the adaptability dimension, and disengaged or enmeshed on the cohesion dimension. This model posits four subtypes of dysfunctional families: *chaotically disengaged*—family members feel disconnected from one another, blurred boundaries predominate, leadership and discipline are erratic or almost nonexistent, and roles and rules are poorly defined and shift rapidly; *chaotically enmeshed*— family members are entirely too close with one another, with excessive demands for loyalty and little tolerance for individuality, privacy, or outside friends and activities; this is combined with unpredictability and explosiveness in family leadership and discipline; *rigidly disengaged*—family members experience a sense of isolation and loneliness in a rule-governed, authoritarian milieu where negotiation is rare and stereotypical roles are dictated; and *rigidly enmeshed*— family members feel that extreme family closeness is demanded within a context stressing strict obedience to rules, rigid roles, and subservience to authoritarian leadership. Olson and colleagues (1979, 1983) include *family communication* as the third dimension in this model and posit that communication is a facilitating dimension, which enables families to alter the cohesion and adaptability domains. This classification system provides a framework for change-oriented interventions.

Beavers (1977, 1993) offers a growth-oriented, rather than a change-oriented, model. In his conceptualization, families are labeled healthy, midrange, or dysfunctional based on the following eight variables: systems orientation, boundary issues, contextual issues, power issues, encouragement of autonomy, affective issues, negotiation and task performance, and transcendental values. He purports that healthy families are open systems that interact with the outer world and also have appropriate boundaries between individual members and between generations. Each member is free to express his or her feelings and thoughts. There is respect for individual privacy and permeability of boundaries leading to closeness in relationships. There are clear roles, rules, and expectations, so the confusion caused by mixed messages is avoided. Parental figures share power; thus, there are few battles for control. Age-appropriate autonomy is fostered so that individuals can function relatively independently, while still having a sense of belonging to the family unit. Healthy families encourage the experience and expression of the complete gamut of positive and negative emotions and respond empathically to one another's affective expressions. Such families have good problem-solving skills and are comfortable negotiating when disagreements arise. This enables them to master tasks and cope with life transitions effectively. Finally, these families explicitly and implicitly share a system for meaning and value that helps them to feel part of the larger world context. Dysfunctional families have almost diametrically opposite characteristics on each variable and tend to live in a state of ongoing conflict. They are often quite alienated from one another, the larger community, and/or extended family. Midrange families fall midway between healthy and dysfunctional.

Based on their research, F. W. Kaslow and Hammerschmidt (1992) have added several other dimensions that typify healthy couples in long-term successful marriages. These include having fun together, maintaining a high level of trust in each other, respecting one another's integrity, being good friends and enjoying each other's company, sharing many interests and activities, and being considerate of each other's needs and wants.

To recapitulate, the two most widely accepted classification schemas indicate that the characteristics of healthy family functioning are contingent upon the family's life cycle stage and the sociocultural context in which family members live. Key dimensions along which family functioning is evaluated are cohesion, flexibility, and communication. Optimally functioning families are cohesive, with a clear yet flexible structure, allowing for both closeness and age-appropriate autonomy. Healthy families adapt their power structure, role relationships, and rules in response to situational and developmental imperatives and new information from the environment. A relatively equal power distribution is normative for the spouses, and a clear power hierarchy exists between the parental subsystem and the children; it is modified as the developmental stages of the children change. Standards for behavior regulation are modified using negotiation and problem solving. Family functions are performed so that members are not overburdened with too many tasks and there is role flexibility. Communication about both affective and instrumental concerns is clear and effective, with congruence among the content, intent, and process of communications.

In the cases presented in the chapters in this book one sees most of the clients progress on the continuum from being quite dysfunctional at entry into treatment to falling between the midrange and healthy categories at the time of termination.

INTEGRATIVE PERSPECTIVE

An important and overarching trend, which is particularly germane to many of the cases discussed in this book, is a shift away from a purist family systems approach to a more integrative, comprehensive theoretical and treatment perspective, manifested in numerous spheres of activity (Lebow, 2005). Many family practitioners now integrate a range of theoretical models and the intervention techniques associated with different schools of family therapy into their treatment. Another indicator of this trend is the resurgence of emphasis on the significance of the individual in the family system and the recognition of the mutual and reciprocal impact of the individual on the family and the family on the individual. A corollary of this is concern for understanding the coevolution of the individual and the family such that all of their differing needs are considered and balanced. Given this reemergence of concern for the individual within the family system (Wachtel & Wachtel, 1986), it has become more acceptable to many family therapists to conduct psychological testing, utilize psychopharmacological interventions, do individual or couples therapy concurrently or sequentially with family therapy (Pinsoff, 1995), or to hospitalize a family member with severe symptomatology and impairments that do not respond to outpatient interventions.

OVERVIEW OF CONCEPTUAL MODELS

Theories of family therapy are not monolithic. Rather, this broad categorization subsumes approaches ranging from traditional psychoanalytic and learning theories to systems, communications, and post-modern theories. Family theories are not completely distinct; they share common variables, and there is much overlap. To highlight the main consistent points: The majority of schools view the family as a system whose members are interdependent and see the family as comprised of several subsystems with generational links and boundaries, communication networks, coalitions and alliances, rules, secrets, myths, and rituals. As discussed earlier, three key dimensions of functioning are the focus of multiple approaches: cohesion, adaptability, and communication (Olson et al., 1979).

Most family therapists agree that a major goal of therapy is to change the family systems' interactional patterns, with individual change occurring as a product of systems change (Sander, 1979). Additional goals sought by those of almost all schools include the development of role flexibility and adaptability; a balancing of power, particularly in marital therapy; the establishment of individuality within the family collectivity; and greater clarity and specificity of communication. Main areas around which there is divergence of opinion between adherents of different schools relate to such issues as the definition of family composition (e.g., nuclear, extended), who must be present at therapy sessions, the importance of history versus the centrality of the present, a focus on intrapsychic versus interpersonal dynamics, the nature and meaning of the presenting problems, the role of assessment, the identified ultimate goals of therapy, the idea of problem and solution, and the personality and role of the therapist (Beels & Ferber, 1972; Gurman, 1979; F. W. Kaslow, 1987).

The various approaches, grouped under the major family theories, to be discussed are the following:

- Psychodynamic
  —Object relations
  —Attachment theory
  —Imago relationship therapy

- Bowenian/multigenerational
- Contextual/relational
- Experiential
  —Symbolic experiential
- Structural
- Strategic
  —Narrative
  —Social constructionism and postmodernism
- Systemic
- Psychoeducational
- Behavioral/cognitive-behavioral
  —Brief family therapy
  —Problem- and solution-focused
  —Functional family therapy
- Integrative

Each theory offers its own view of the reality of the family and a perspective on family health and dysfunction. Although some techniques and terminology may be similar, they are not identical because they exist in the context of a different epistemology. This chapter focuses on the theories rather than the therapists most associated with them, although the person of the therapist is at least as important as the techniques that he or she uses (Whitaker, 1976). Each therapist brings his or her own style and personality to the interpretation and application of a theory (F. W. Kaslow, Cooper, & Linsenberg, 1979), as is obvious in the subsequent chapters.

PSYCHODYNAMIC FAMILY THERAPY

This approach is the nearest descendant of individual psychoanalytically oriented psychotherapy and one of the only family models that acknowledges its ties to psychoanalytic thinking, despite the fact that many family therapy pioneers were trained in this tradition. This heritage is also apparent in Bowenian, contextual, experiential, and integrative family therapies. Psychoanalytic family therapy emphasizes the role of the unconscious and past history as determinants of behavior and motivations, posits that insight is a necessary precursor for behavioral change to occur, and highlights the importance of transference and countertransference phenomena. In recent years, a number of clinicians have integrated object relations and family systems theories, referring to their work as *Object Relations Family Therapy* (D. E. Scharff & Scharff, 1987; J. S. Scharff, 1989; Slipp, 1984), which has become the dominant psychoanalytically oriented family therapy approach practiced today.

Basic Structure and Goals

Object Relations Family Therapy, a long-term approach, addresses unresolved intrapsychic conflicts that are reenacted in one's current life, causing interpersonal and intrapsychic difficulties. Session number varies, depending on the presenting problem and the goals of each phase of treatment. Typically, goals include the following (N. J. Kaslow et al., 1999):

- Clarifying and redefining problems in such a way that they become more accessible to resolution
- Delineating boundary issues
- Explicating individual needs and desires and how these can be fulfilled within the marital-family system
- Modifying excessive narcissistic expectations and demands
- Increasing expressive and listening skills
- Decreasing intimidating and blaming statements
- Facilitating problem solving and conflict resolution
- Modifying dysfunctional rules and communication patterns
- Helping family members achieve greater insight
- Strengthening ego functioning
- Recognizing, acknowledging, and reworking defensive projective identifications
- Attaining more mature internal self- and object representations
- Developing more gratifying interpersonal relationships that support one's need for attachment, individuation, and psychological growth
- Reducing interlocking pathologies among family members
- Resolving spousal and therapist-patient transferences
- Encouraging greater trust and closeness
- Supporting heightened appreciation of one's uniqueness
- Fostering greater comfort with and enjoyment of one's sexuality
- Creating a better balance between the cognitive and affective domains of living
- Improving self-image and family esteem for all
- Resolving neurotic conflicts

Many of these goals are consonant with the dimensions that appear in the prior discussion of characteristics of the healthy family (F. W. Kaslow, 1981; Lewis, Beavers, Gossett, & Phillips, 1976; Walsh, 1993).

Techniques and Process of Therapy

In the initial phase, the therapist provides a "holding environment" consisting of a specified time, space, and structure for therapy. This enables family members to feel safe and secure so that they can express their emotions and beliefs openly and feel closer with one another while maintaining a separate sense of self. This is quite compatible with the way an EMDR therapist constructs the therapy milieu. The therapist functions as a "good enough" parent, reparenting the family by providing consistent nurturance and structure to foster the healthy maturation of individual members and the family unit.

During this phase, a comprehensive history of each member is taken, which seeks information about early experiences, presenting problems, and prior treatment. The clinician observes family interaction during open-ended interviews to determine family members' level of object relations, major defense mechanisms, and the relationship between current interactional patterns and family of origin dynamics. Because the spousal pair creates the family unit, it is necessary that the clinician explore their unconscious and conscious reasons for choosing each other, the unfolding of the marital relationship, the experiences, including conflicts, that predated the marriage, and the effects of these on current interactions and affective quality. Because of the impact of the past on shaping the present, the assessment process plays a central role in psychoanalytic family therapy. The underlying significance of the presenting problems and the interactional themes constitute the central foci of the evaluation.

Once a strong therapeutic alliance is established, the therapist empathically interprets conflicts, resistances, negative transferences, defenses, and patterns of interaction indicative of unresolved intrapsychic and interpersonal conflicts. Effective interpretations connect an individual's and family's history with their current feelings, thoughts, behaviors, and transactions, thereby opening the way for more adaptive family interactional patterns and intrapsychic changes to occur.

The clinician encourages and supports affective communication and increased demonstrations of affection, clarifies the nature of the family's communication, challenges assumptions and beliefs and tries to dislodge constricting, rigidly held outdated patterns, and facilitates development of deeper insight into one's self and awareness of other members. Technical errors occur when a safe holding environment has not been created, when interpretations are poorly timed and do not attend to significant intrapsychic or interpersonal dynamics, or when therapist comments reflect unarticulated and unresolved countertransference issues.

Psychodynamic and object relations therapists address transference and countertransference issues to facilitate the therapeutic endeavor (F. W. Kaslow & Magnavita, 2002). They use their own reactions to the family's behavior and interaction patterns to understand the shared, yet unspoken, experiences of each member regarding family interactional patterns. They use their own objective countertransference reactions to interpret interpersonal patterns in which one family member is induced to behave in a circumscribed and maladaptive manner (projective identification) (J. S. Scharff, 1992).

Issues of loss and separation are attended to throughout treatment. During the termination phase, salient conflicts are reviewed and reworked. An opportunity is provided for mourning the anticipated loss of the therapist, who has become an important attachment figure.

Specific techniques are considered secondary to the strength and nature of the therapeutic alliance; therefore, these do not define the practice of Object Relations Family Therapy. Rather, the defining characteristic is the therapist's joining with the family and creating a safe holding environment within which family members can rediscover each other and the lost parts of the self projected onto one another. Although many family therapists emphasize the therapeutic relationship, it is those who are psychoanalytically oriented who focus on the therapeutic alliance as a curative factor, use transference interpretation as the cornerstone of the treatment, and pay attention to countertransference dynamics as these influence the therapeutic work.

Treatment Applicability

Usually clinicians use Object Relations Family Therapy with high-functioning families whose members are psychologically oriented, well educated, and interested in gaining insight and who possess the resources necessary to engage in long-term treatment. Some clinicians also have advocated its use with families with a schizophrenic, borderline, or narcissistic member (J. S. Scharff, 1989); children and adolescents; those who divorce and remarry; and those coping with trauma and loss (D. E. Scharff & Scharff, 1987).

Ideas about the importance of mother-infant bonding, parent-child attachment, and couple bonding are subsumed in Objects Relations Theory under the rubric of object constancy. This concept posits that early attachments should be secure, safe, loving, predictable, and constant and become the prototype for the later relationships one forms (Bowlby, 1969, 1988). Several of the chapters in the current volume draw heavily on attachment theory, the need to create a safe holding environment for good EMDR treatment to occur and lack of bonding to be repaired, and for people to create trusting relationships in the here and now, all of which are also goals of Object Relations Family Therapy. (See, for example, chapters by Moses, Madrid, Wesselmann, and Talan.)

BOWENIAN SYSTEMS THEORY

Bowenian family therapy is also referred to as family of origin therapy. Like the psychoanalysts, Bowen considered mental illness to be a product of disturbed interpersonal relationships. But unlike psychoanalytic approaches that focus primarily on the individual and on intrapsychic change, Bowen asserted that change must occur at the level of the relationship system. Further, whereas in psychoanalytic theory the unconscious is presumed to direct one's conscious thoughts and actions, in Bowenian theory (Kerr & Bowen, 1988) it is the combination of one's degree of unmodulated anxiety and the level of differentiation from one's family of origin that are considered the strongest determinates of one's interpersonal relationships.

A number of core elements of Bowenian theory deserve mention. First, Bowen perceived his theory to be applicable to the human condition in general, not just the family. Second, instead of providing a theoretical framework consisting of dichotomous psychological concepts (nature/nurture, marital problems/child problems, physical illness/emotional illness), he viewed phenomena along a continuum. Third, this school emphasizes the person of the therapist. Specifically, Bowen stressed that it is imperative for the therapist to be well differentiated from his or her own family of origin. He argued that a therapist's capacity to be therapeutic was a function of his or her level of differentiation. Fourth, he posited that chronic anxiety, a pervasive experience characteristic of *all* living systems, is the primary source of psychological dysfunctions and that differentiation is the remedy for chronic anxiety.

Eight interlocking constructs constitute much of Bowenian theory (Friedman, 1991): differentiation of self, emotional cutoff, family emotional system, family projection process, triangulation, sibling position, multigenerational transmission process, and societal regression. Differentiation of self, the cornerstone of this theory, refers to the extent to which individuals differentiate between emotional and intellectual processes and their degree of separation from the family of origin. Highly differentiated individuals are capable of decision making and problem solving without responding to internal emotional stimuli. They are neither overly invested in the emotional climate of their family of origin nor totally withdrawn from or impervious to its importance. Conversely, when a person's intellectual functioning is dominated by emotions and there is a fusion between thinking and feeling, that person is low on the differentiation continuum. For example, some people who superficially appear to function well have trouble differentiating between subjective feelings and objective thoughts. Such fusion and confusion of affective and cognitive processes is most severe in close personal relationships, as in families with a schizophrenic member, which Bowen (1988) characterized as having an "undifferentiated family ego mass."

Differentiation from one's family of origin is an ongoing developmental process. Some individuals who have trouble with the tasks of differentiation try to psychologically or emotionally individuate by withdrawing and denying their family's importance. They may isolate themselves through geographic distancing or severing virtually all contact. Bowen labeled this style of pseudo-differentiation an "emotional cutoff."

The family emotional system is comprised of emotionally interdependent people; it has its own organizational principles, which encompass each member's individual and collective thoughts, feelings, fantasies, associations, and past relationship history. A nuclear family emotional system typically is formed by marital partners with equivalent levels of self-differentiation. When two highly self-differentiated individuals marry, they are likely to create a relatively healthy, stable relationship. Conversely, low levels of differentiation in one or both spouses may be associated with a family of origin system characterized by high levels of emotional fusion, marital conflict, dysfunction in one or both partners, triangulation, lack of self-differentiation of members, or projection of anxiety. Fewer symptoms of distress are noted in multiple generations of a family when there is ongoing emotional contact between individuals in different generations, yet family members still strive toward high levels of self-differentiation.

Bowen identified a "family projection process" through which parents project their difficulties onto the most vulnerable child, regardless of the child's birth order. The child chosen as the recipient of parental projections, and thus triangulated into the marital relationship, ordinarily reveals the lowest level of differentiation and is the most fusion-prone offspring. This child experiences the most difficulty in achieving adaptive age-appropriate emotional separation. The less differentiated the parents are from their respective families of origin, the greater the reliance on the family projection process to stabilize the system and the more probable that more than one child will evidence emotional dysfunction.

Triangles, the basic building blocks of any emotional system, represent the smallest relationship system that is stable (Bowen, 1988). Triangulation is another technique marital pairs utilize to contain the tension in their relationship secondary to high levels of anxiety, stress, and fusion. When the continuity of the dyad is threatened, a vulnerable third party is drawn into their relationship to form a triangle and stave off the crisis. If this triangle fails to dilute the anxiety and stabilize the situation, additional individuals are inveigled in to form interlocking triangles.

Other core concepts include a multigenerational transmission process wherein severe dysfunction is hypothesized to be transmitted through the family emotional systems processes over several generations; sibling position, which reflects Bowen's assertion that interactions between marital partners may be influenced by their own respective birth order; and societal regression, in which societal dynamics (like family dynamics) involve a dialectic between the opposing forces of symbiosis and individuation.

Basic Structure and Goals

Bowenian therapy is a relatively structured and long-term approach, typically conducted by a single therapist with a spousal pair or individual adults. Individual family members, as well as the relational system, are the patient unit. Greater differentiation of self within one's family of origin, rather than emotionally cutting oneself off from one's progenitors, constitutes the main objective of the work. A second, related goal is to detriangulate each person from maladaptive three-party systems by resolving dyadic tensions and emotionally disentangling everyone from the interpersonal conflicts that precipitated the triangulation.

Techniques and Process of Therapy

Family of origin sessions are structured to enable each individual to speak rationally and decrease emotionality. To achieve this, the therapist alternately asks each partner about himself or herself, their responses to each other's comments, the presenting problem, and their nuclear and extended family. The clinician educates the participants about Bowenian theory, encouraging and coaching visits to (each) one's family of origin to work through unresolved emotional attachments from the past and increase differentiation. The focus shifts between the spouses; the therapist purposefully serves as the third point of the triangle. As the couple become cognizant of their triangulation process in vivo in therapy, they gain insight into the repetitive relational maneuvers they utilize to triangulate vulnerable family members. As the therapist works with them toward detriangulation, they will act differently, and the fusion of the family will diminish.

Bowenian therapists emphasize the importance of ascertaining multigenerational historical data about relationships within the family of origin. Presenting problems are interpreted in the context of manifestations of fusion and differentiation. Issues are reframed, needs and wants are clarified, greater reciprocity and cooperation are promoted, and nonfunctional relational system rules are modified. Bowen believed that avoidance of the transference is necessary to raise the likelihood that the intensity of the relationship will be concentrated on the real family members and not redirected into an intense transference relationship with the therapist. These core assumptions heralded a major departure from psychoanalytic theory and practice.

A dramatic technique used to facilitate family of origin work is constructing genograms, visual graphs that depict a family genealogy or family tree (F. W. Kaslow, 1995; McGoldrick, Gerson, & Shellenberger, 1999). Genograms provide information about individual family members and the family's structure and interrelationships over generations. Constructing genograms is a useful modality for engaging with the family. They can offer a rich source of systemic data leading to hypotheses about behavior, beliefs, myths, values, fears, legacies (and illnesses) inherent in a family's functioning. They can enable the therapist to use a systemic perspective in conceptualizing, reframing, and detoxifying current and past family problems to unblock the relational system and encourage increased differentiation. (See chapter by Shellenberger for an in-depth discussion.) As no one theoretical approach undergirds the concept of genogramming, these are used by clinicians with diverse theoretical orientations (Roberto, 1992) throughout much of the world.

Treatment Applicability

Usually family of origin therapy is practiced with individuals and couples who have a good capacity to move toward differentiation and objective processing of emotions. Therapists espousing this orientation tend to work with the most differentiated family members, as these individuals are apt to be the most capable of change. It is valid for those interested in participating in long-term work focusing on core relational issues. It is generally considered inappropriate for individuals and couples in acute crisis.

CONTEXTUAL AND RELATIONAL THERAPY

Boszormenyi-Nagy, the founder of this theoretical school, outlined four separate but intertwined dimensions that serve as the basis for the relational context and dynamics of family functioning (Boszormenyi-Nagy & Krasner, 1986). These are:

- *Facts:* what is provided by one's destiny. Facts may be unavoidable, due to chance and fate (e.g., ethnicity, gender, physical health), or avoidable, reflecting an individual's or family's construction of reality (e.g., family historical context, social context).
- *Psychology:* the individual's emotional experience, behavior patterns, aspirations, and motivations. These processes are indicative of interpersonal patterns and familial dynamics.

- *Transactions:* family organizational patterns regarding roles, communication styles and sequences, power, and intimacy.
- *Relational ethics:* construed as the cornerstone of Contextual Therapy. The concept of relational ethics denotes fair and trustworthy interpersonal interactions in which the welfare and entitlements of oneself and all family members are acknowledged, valued, and respected.

In this theory, legacy connotes "the universal injunction of parental accountability, including the human mandate to reverse the injustices of the past for the benefit of the next generation" (Boszormenyi-Nagy, Greenbaum, & Ulrich, 1991, p. 205). This legacy engenders family loyalties expressed as unconscious (and therefore invisible) repetition of familial expectations, roles, alliances and coalitions, and modes of behavior and communication, and thus the inevitable acquisition of expectations and responsibilities of each individual to the family as a whole.

Ultimately these legacies and loyalties lead each family member to accrue and maintain an invisible ledger of merit and indebtedness, a multigenerational account system of investments and obligations in each relationship. This ledger varies depending on each member's contributions and withdrawals (e.g., exploiting others). When family members mutually credit one another for their contributions to enriching their life, there is an equal distribution of family emotional resources, and adaptive functioning prevails. When individuals or families experience themselves as possessing an imbalance in their ledger of merit and indebtedness, trust is decreased, deprived family members exhibit feelings of destructive entitlement or overindebtedness, and a family scapegoat often emerges. (See chapter by Manon.)

Basic Structure and Goals

Contextual Therapy is a long-term, intensive approach that may be conducted with individuals, family units, or multigenerational systems. It is most valuable when conducted by a cotherapy team, as two therapists provide a balanced, complementary example of give-and-take in human interactions. Including as many family members as possible is considered optimal, *if* family members are willing and able to work together for a mutually beneficial outcome. Whether the therapy includes the individual, marital dyad, nuclear family, or multigenerational family system is contingent on family members' optimal resource potential for enhancing mutual trust and self-validation, a key component of an individual's self-esteem. Although the cotherapists are actively engaged with the family and serve as catalysts for change, family meetings and rituals conducted between sessions are the times when change is consolidated. Homework may be assigned to assist family members in developing more positive and trusting relationships.

The goal of Contextual Therapy is *rejunction,* the rebalancing of one's obligations in family relationships. The rejunction process includes the acknowledgment of equitable multilaterality, resolving problems by making invisible loyalties conscious and explicit, and repairing ruptured or strained relationships, a commitment to a fair balance of give-and-take (relational mutuality), and a process of reengagement (Boszormenyi-Nagy et al., 1991). Therefore, the therapist encourages family members to explore their capacities for correcting imbalances in the ledger of merit and indebtedness through both increased availability toward others and redefined use of others as resources. This process fosters reliance on self-validation or validation derived from fair consideration of others' needs. Although insight into one's family of origin dynamics is considered a necessary component of the change and healing process, and thus a goal of the work, lasting change requires efforts at rejunction and enhancing positive relational resources.

Techniques and Process of Therapy

In this model, effective therapy involves the creation of a trusting milieu within which family members feel safe enough to make conscious their unconscious ledger of merit and indebtedness, make visible their invisible loyalties, and engage in the rejunction process. The therapist assumes the role of advocate for all family members, across generations, whether present, absent, or deceased. This technique, in which the therapist empathically acknowledges each individual's perspective in a nonjudgmental manner, is referred to as exhibiting multidirectional partiality. It allows each family member the opportunity to be heard while conveying his or her position on the issues. Using this technique, the therapist periodically may take sides in order to involve a particularly distant or exploited member, but always with the realization that ultimately a rebalancing must take place. Once people know that they will have the opportunity to speak and be listened to sensitively, they are more apt to begin to hear and acknowledge the other side(s) of an issue. Then the process of give-and-take begins to be enacted within the family, forming the basis for trustworthiness in relationships.

Assessment is an ongoing, rather than distinct, phase; it includes evaluation of the family's competencies and vulnerabilities, current status, and relational patterns. As in Bowenian therapy, it often entails developing a three-generation picture of the family through genogramming. The therapist assesses the relational ethics of the family unit and the individual members' personalities and their transactional patterns. He or she discerns family members' capacity for empathy, reliability, and trustworthiness, the interpersonal conflicts based on competing needs and motives, and the nature and quality of attachments. The inclusion of history taking serves as another vehicle for building trust with the family.

Following the assessment and establishment of a treatment contract and therapeutic alliance, the working-through phase begins. The therapist starts by addressing the presenting problem and encouraging each family member to express his or her view of the problem. Then a quick shift away from the presenting problem takes place, with a redirection of focus to the more basic dynamic issues and associated defenses and resistances. The presenting problem is reframed as reflecting underlying concerns regarding loyalty to one's family of origin and the accompanying imbalance in the family relationships. Exploration of family legacies, invisible loyalties, and the ledger of balances is focal.

The main therapeutic techniques used to enhance the rejunction process include the following:

- Siding with each family member at different times to maintain multilateral partiality, while also holding each member accountable for his or her views and actions vis-à-vis the ledger of merit and indebtedness
- Crediting each family member for his or her efforts and contributions to the family, usually starting with the most vulnerable family member who has been hurt the most
- Eliciting members' spontaneous overtures to address constructively their own difficulties in an attempt to balance fairness between individuals rather than on a systemic level
- Implementing a moratorium during which family members are encouraged to ponder the benefits of making changes and choosing if and when these will be made, without feeling pressured by the therapist to do so
- Utilizing the rejunction process to facilitate family members' making relational changes, reconnecting with members of their immediate and extended family, and rebalancing accounts
- Engaging in loyalty framing in an effort to examine disloyalties and foster appreciation of existing, even if invisible, loyalties
- Helping family members invest in the process of fair exoneration of their parents for their choices and behaviors, with the goal of establishing more adaptive communication with them

Although transference reactions may be manifested between family members or between them and the therapist, transference work is not deemed central. Rather, therapists help family members understand and alter their relationships, highlight the importance of family roles, and provide the essential reparenting to support the rejunction process. Once family members are able to acknowledge invisible loyalties, rebalance unsettled accounts, and exonerate their parents, the termination phase commences. Successful termination embodies addressing and working through issues of loss, separation, and abandonment.

Treatment Applicability

This approach has been criticized as being too intellectual and inappropriate for treating families from lower socioeconomic classes and those who are not highly articulate. Yet, Boszormenyi-Nagy and colleagues (1991) believe that Contextual Therapy is applicable to most human problems, as the theory is built on basic principles relevant to a cross section of families regardless of race, ethnicity, or socioeconomic status. They argue that the concepts of trust, fairness, and reciprocity are basic relational concepts pertinent to the treatment of individuals from all sociocultural backgrounds, manifesting a broad range of symptoms and relational difficulties. This approach is applicable to current problems and also stresses the preventive aspect anchored in the rebalancing of present relationships for the benefit of future offspring (Ducommun-Nagy, 2002). Some clinicians also have addressed the appropriateness of Contextual Therapy for work with children and their families (Goldenthal, 1991).

Although there has been minimal empirical validation for the efficacy of Contextual Therapy, clinical validation abounds. Litt's chapter in this book captures the essence of Contextual Therapy and brings its richness to life in his exposition of how he integrates it with EMDR in his case example.

SYMBOLIC-EXPERIENTIAL THERAPY

Carl Whitaker, another eminent family therapy pioneer, like Bowen, came from a professional background of being an inpatient psychiatrist. His training in child psychiatry had provided him with the opportunity to conduct play therapy. From his personal clinical experiences with children, adolescents, and severely disturbed adults, he gained insight into the nature and utility of primary process ("craziness"), the importance of regression in fostering later growth, the value of entering a patient's world intuitively by permitting one's own unconscious the freedom to spontaneously understand the metacommunication of the patient's unconscious, and the importance of the therapist developing a style consonant with his or her own nature. This approach is rooted primarily in the affective experiences inherent in the process of change. Implicit in Whitaker's writings, teachings, and clinical demonstrations was a clarion call for the experience of therapy to be an *authentic encounter* for all involved, reflecting his kinship with the humanists and existentialists.

Whitaker (1976) asserted that theory actually impedes clinical practice and that the symbolic-experiential approach is largely atheoretical. Nonetheless, some basic tenets and concepts are associated with this approach; these include symbolic experience, growth, psychotherapy of the absurd, battles for structure and initiative, psychotherapeutic impasse, and the importance of playing (Napier & Whitaker, 1978).

Whitaker (Whitaker & Bumberry, 1988, p. 78) considered *symbolic-experiential therapy* "an effort to deal with the representation system underneath what is actually being said." This approach de-emphasizes conscious thinking and reasoning about problems, stressing increased awareness of unconscious and affective experiences to help people expand their range of life experience and live a freer and more creative life. To do so, they must grapple with universal life issues, including sexuality, "craziness," loving and hating, and death.

"Carl" Whitaker also is known for his writing on the healthy family (Whitaker & Bumberry, 1988) and for offering guidelines to keep the therapist alive and to avoid therapist burnout. These guidelines, which convey some of his essence and spirit, include the following:

(1) Relegate every significant other to second place; (2) learn how to love—flirt with any infant available; (3) develop a reverence for your own impulses, and be suspicious of your behavior sequences; (4) enjoy your mate more than your kids, and be childish with your mate; (5) fracture role structures repeatedly; (6) learn to retreat and advance from every

position you take; (7) guard your impotence as one of your most valuable weapons; (8) build long-term relations so you can be free to hate safely; (9) face the fact that you must grow until you die—develop a sense of the benign absurdity of life . . . and thus learn to transcend the world of experience; (10) develop your primary process living; (11) evolve a joint craziness with someone you are safe with; (12) structure a professional cuddle group so you won't abuse your mate with the garbage left over from the day's work. (Whitaker, 1976, p. 164)

Other theorists identified with the experiential school are Satir (1967, 1972), Duhl and Duhl (1981), Kempler (1981), and Kantor and Lehr (1975). Due to space constraints, Whitaker's approach is the only one presented in detail. Several of Satir's Experiential Family Therapy techniques in her family reconstruction approach are also mentioned, given that their significance lies in their great potency in reaching otherwise noncommunicative families with whom strictly verbal approaches are usually ineffective (Satir & Baldwin, 1983).

Basic Structure and Goals

The course of symbolic-experiential therapy typically is of intermediate length, with sessions conducted at variable frequency. Preferably, sessions include the symptomatic family member, nuclear family members residing with the symptomatic person, the extended family, and the index person's social support network. The therapy is built on a "therapeutic suprasystem" (Roberto, 1991) consisting of the family or couple in treatment and a cotherapy team or therapist and consultant. Whitaker recommended a cotherapy team to augment the clinician's power and give each therapist support and a partner to bail him or her out if the therapist becomes embroiled in the family dynamics. This approach enables therapists to alternate functions, consistent with the notion that each member of the family should be able to play all positions on the family team and go beyond stereotypical roles. The team demonstrates a pattern of caring that permits the family to risk becoming more anxious, instead of relying on defensive, self-protective interactional patterns. When a cotherapy team is not feasible, a consultant can provide a systemic view of the family, support the therapist, and enhance the problem-solving potential (Roberto, 1992).

This modality enables individuals to develop an increased tolerance for the absurdity of life and balance interpersonal connectedness with expressions of individuation (Whitaker & Bumberry, 1988). The therapeutic aims are to (a) increase members' sense of family cohesion; (b) help the couple or family support individual members' needs in the process of individuation and negotiation of developmental tasks; and (c) foster creativity, spontaneity, and accessibility of affective experience individually and in the family unit. Operationalization of these objectives is developed jointly by members of the therapeutic suprasystem.

Techniques and Process of Therapy

In symbolic-experiential therapy, a strong therapeutic alliance is crucial; thus, the personality of the therapist should project warmth, flexibility, tenderness, firmness, a sense of absurdity and humor, and genuineness. Although engaged actively in the therapeutic process, therapists do not direct the therapy. Rather, they listen, observe, reflect upon their own emotional responses, and challenge maladaptive interactional patterns without focusing on the etiology of the difficulties. Their role is comparable to that of a coach or surrogate grandparent, requiring a balance of nurturance and caring with structure and discipline. Keith and Whitaker (1981) highlighted the importance of playing with the entire family, actually, symbolically, or metaphorically. In so doing, the therapists give permission to play, freeing the patients to have fun together, thereby making family life less serious and constrained.

Like other family therapy approaches, symbolic-experiential treatment has a beginning, middle, and end phase. In the beginning phase, the therapists focus on joining with the family, with the goal of building enough trust and credibility that the family is willing to invest in treatment. This joining process is enhanced by the clinician's use of self, play, humor, metaphors, and reframes to expand the family's perspective regarding problems. The use of self may include metaphorical allegories and teaching stories, free associations, and memories and fantasies aimed at offering alternative problem-solving strategies and supporting family members' initiatives for change. It should enable families to trust the therapist enough to share their unique inner world (Whitaker, 1976).

The battles for structure and initiative must be waged and won before a sound therapeutic alliance is forged, enabling the family to reorganize to cure the symptomatic (scapegoated) member and increase differentiation (Keith & Whitaker, 1981). The battle for structure, which begins immediately, is a battle over ground rules regarding treatment arrangements, session membership, scheduling, and fees (Napier & Whitaker, 1978). Its aim is to establish the cotherapists as consultants for change. This battle is over when a minimum of a two-generation structure is established, with the therapists in charge and having optimal flexibility in working with the family. When this battle is resolved successfully, family regression occurs, engendering an intense transference relationship and underscoring the seriousness of the therapeutic endeavor.

The battle for initiative then commences, with the cotherapy team encouraging family members to take responsibility for their own growth and life choices. This battle is resolved when the family takes control of the direction of the sessions and institutes changes and when the cotherapy dyad establishes an existential I-thou relationship with each family member, characterized by flexibility, caring, and mutual involvement of all members of the therapeutic suprasystem. During this phase, information is obtained regarding the presenting problem, family of origin, and family interactional patterns.

In the middle phase, clinical interventions create an "interpersonal expansion of the symptom," and the family confronts their life problems. Some of the techniques used to facilitate this process are redefining symptoms as efforts toward growth, explicating covert conflict, separating interpersonal and internal stress and modeling fantasized alternatives, reversing roles, and involving grandparents and other extended family members in the treatment process (Roberto, 1991). Other techniques recommended by Satir (1967, 1972) also may be used during this treatment phase. Specifically, family members may be encouraged to enact scenes in their lives (drama, family reconstruction) and create static (family sculpture) or dynamic (stress ballet) nonverbal presentations that depict their perceptions of family relationships. The use of experiential techniques, in conjunction with the therapists' continued use of self, helps the family develop alternative interactional patterns that are conducive to change and growth.

Many families effectively negotiate the middle phase of therapy, showing improvement and feeling more competent to handle problems. However, for others, the work leads to an "impotence impasse" in which the family does not take responsibility for their own problems, and consequently they do not change (Keith & Whitaker, 1981). This impasse is resolved when the family and cotherapy team mutually agree on treatment decisions.

Whitaker cautioned against engaging in symptom relief, asserting that symptoms have evolved as an adaptation to dysfunctional family or societal situations, implying that symptom relief could precipitate the emergence of symptoms in other family members or disintegration of the family unit. He believed that a symptom cannot be "abandoned" until the symptomatic family member finds it to be too weighty and no longer necessary. Thus, Whitaker suggested paradoxical reframing, or prescribing the symptom until it becomes so exaggerated that it is rejected, and stressed the importance of using this technique with wisdom, warmth, and humor, and not as a gimmick. He practiced "psychotherapy of the absurd" long before others began describing their use of paradox in family therapy.

In the final phase, the cotherapy team disengages from the family system, restricting their interventions to problematic situations that the family is unable to manage alone. This permits the family to reflect on its functioning and assume increasing responsibility for decision making and problem solving. The relationship between the cotherapy team and the family shifts from that of consultant-patient to a partnership. To promote this relational shift, the cotherapists spontaneously self-disclose, express sadness over termination, and ask for feedback about the therapy. When family members demonstrate sufficient self-confidence and competencies in problem solving and managing life events, termination is indicated. It is accomplished by the family members and cotherapy dyad acknowledging mutual interdependence and the loss of a meaningful relationship (Keith & Whitaker, 1981).

Treatment Applicability

Symbolic-Experiential Family Therapy has been used with families presenting with a variety of difficulties, including those in which the index person carries a Schizophrenia Spectrum Disorder diagnosis. Some have argued that this treatment approach has limited efficacy with families in which a member evidences an Antisocial or Narcissistic Personality Disorder. Although empirical studies have not been presented in the literature, the efficacy of the model is suggested in detailed case descriptions (Napier & Whitaker, 1978; Whitaker & Bumberry, 1988).

COMMUNICATION MODEL

Communication theorists hold that because actors in a system are interdependent, the behavior of any one member affects all other members, and the main time and relational dimension is the here and now. Given that the family is the sum of the individual personalities, plus their interactions, it is nonsummative (Olson, 1970). Whether an action makes a temporary impact or is conducive to lasting change depends on the sources from which power is derived: (a) society, or the external system; (b) the specific family's history and tradition of power allocation and dominance; or (c) the family's homeostasis and need for survival and system maintenance at the given time (Stanton, 1981). Thus, rather than conceptualizing the locus of psychological difficulties as within the individual, this model reconceptualized symptoms as reflecting interactional and situational dynamics, underscoring the importance of social context in shaping behavior (N. J. Kaslow et al., 1999).

For illustrative purposes, the following discussion focuses primarily on the Mental Research Institute (MRI) communications school brief therapy approach. (See Appendix C for explication of other approaches subsumed under the communications rubric.)

Basic Structure and Goals

Therapies based in the communications model are typically time limited. Sessions are scheduled weekly or biweekly, with a maximum of 10 meetings. The approach is structured and utilizes active interventions. Sessions are conducted by a single clinician or cotherapy pair, and consultant(s) may be positioned behind a one-way mirror to provide objective input and recommend interventions.

The primary goal is problem resolution aimed at reducing or eliminating suffering. Families are not expected to understand how the change occurred, nor is the development of a strong therapeutic alliance fostered.

Techniques and Process of Therapy

Adherents of this school are pragmatic and problem focused. The approach is behaviorally oriented; insight and awareness are not deemed necessary for change. Because repetitive, dysfunctional behavioral sequences and transactions happen in the here and now and are perpetuated by ongoing behavior, intervention in the present system and not consideration of past events and emotions is essential for alterations to occur (Stanton, 1981). Thus, the therapist must take purposeful steps to change enough aspects of the repetitive problem-maintaining behavior patterns so that the symptom will no longer be needed. Repetitious, maladaptive behavior and communication patterns are replaced with new, healthier ways of communicating and acting.

Communication therapists differentiate between *first-order change,* permissible by families because this entails only superficial tweaking that does not significantly change the system or its members, and *second-order change,* which results from major modifications in the interaction and transaction patterns. It is this second-order change that communication theorists deem critical to a successful therapeutic outcome (Watzlawick, Weakland, & Fisch, 1974).

The MRI brief therapy approach is conducted in the following sequence (Segal, 1991):

- Identification of family members motivated for the intervention
- Data collection about problem behaviors and associated prior problem-solving efforts
- Establishment of a clearly defined and operationalized goal
- Formulation of a plan to promote change
- Implementation of therapeutic techniques aimed at disrupting maladaptive problem-solving efforts and enhancing the use of more effective strategies
- Evaluation of treatment efficacy
- Termination when a small but significant and apparently durable change is noted and the family conveys a capacity to manage problems effectively without the therapist's help

Paradoxical injunctions, often used by MRI brief therapy practitioners, are also utilized by strategic and systemic therapists. Two classes of paradoxical directives may be employed to change the family's attempted solutions. The family may be instructed to change the problem behavior or to increase the frequency and/or intensity of the symptomatic behavior. Such *symptom prescription,* which presents a *therapeutic double bind,* facilitates second-order change by placing the family or its members in an untenable position vis-à-vis the problem, such that any action taken produces change in the problem behavior. Thus, if a symptomatic family member is instructed not to change the problem behavior, that person is caught in a dilemma. If he complies with the therapeutic instruction, it shows that he is capable of controlling the symptom, and he can no longer claim to be behaving symptomatically. Conversely, if he defies the directive, the symptom is alleviated and the desired therapeutic change results.

Solution-focused practitioners (de Shazer, 1985) ask therapeutic questions geared to disrupting problem-maintaining behavioral patterns and altering archaic family beliefs. Three kinds of questions, frequently asked during the first session, are identified with this approach:

1. Miracle questions
2. Exception-finding questions
3. Scaling questions

The miracle question has become the best known and is most frequently asked by therapists of various theoretical persuasions. It asks:

Suppose that one night there is a miracle and while you are sleeping the problem that brought you to therapy is solved. How would you know? What would be different? What would you notice the next morning that will tell you that there has been a miracle? (de Shazer, 1988, p. 113)

It helps the client gradually to construct an image of what a brighter, more fulfilling future will look like when the problem is solved; thus, the appellation "solution-focused therapy." It shares many narrative and restorying features with the postmodern and social constructionist approaches (discussed later under "Strategic Family Therapy").

Treatment Applicability

The validity of the MRI brief therapy approach has been documented in case reports of families in which one member evidences a range of symptomatic behaviors (e.g., depression, sexual dysfunction, child and adolescent behavior problems) that diminish post treatment. However, few systematic treatment outcome studies have been conducted focusing on the effectiveness of this model.

STRUCTURAL FAMILY THERAPY

The structural model, which serves as the basis for much family therapy practice today, was developed mainly by Salvador Minuchin and colleagues (Minuchin, Montalvo, Guerney, Rosman, & Schumer, 1967), as well as by Edgar Auerswald (1985), Harry Aponte (1976), Jay Haley (1963, 1971), Lynn Hoffman (1980, 1981), and H. Charles Fishman (Minuchin & Fishman, 1981).

Its theory and techniques are explicit and lend themselves to being taught systematically and to being imitated. To utilize this approach effectively, the therapist must be comfortable being a conductor (Beels & Ferber, 1972), an active and powerful therapist who conveys expertise and a belief in his or her ability to help the family mobilize its capacity to change.

It is a theory-based approach, conceptualizing adaptive and maladaptive functioning in terms of the organized patterns of interaction between individuals, their families, and the social context (Aponte & Van Deusen, 1981; Minuchin & Fishman, 1981). Structural therapists believe that a family should not be a group of equals; rather, the parents should be in charge as the executives or administrators. A central tenet is the idea of a hierarchical organization based on appropriate boundaries between members and subsystems. The subsystems may include the spouse subsystem (marital dyad), parental subsystem (which may include a grandparent or other adult in a pivotal role and/or a parentified child), parent-child dyads, and the sibling subsystem (the child's first peer group) (Minuchin, Rosman, & Baker, 1978). Awareness of these subsystems and the boundaries separating them is essential to an understanding of the family's health or pathology. Constructing or reinforcing appropriate boundaries is needed for family members to be able to individuate appropriately and grow emotionally.

Alignment refers to the "joining or opposition of one member of a system to another in carrying out an operation" (Aponte, 1976, p. 434). Coalitions, covert alliances between two family members against a third, and the sharing by two individuals of a common interest not held by a third person are two primary forms of alignments in families. Boundaries and alignments depend on power or force and the relative influence each member has on the outcome of any given activity.

Throughout the family life cycle, the family system experiences transitions as its members grow and develop (Haley, 1973). The family structure must adapt to these changes to allow continued growth, while also providing a stable environment. When it cannot adapt, rigid patterns of interaction develop that prevent the family from exploring new alternatives.

Manifestations of dysfunctional family functioning include impairments in boundaries, inappropriate alignments, and power imbalances. Dysfunctional families often present as enmeshed or disengaged, terms referring to the characteristic way family members establish contact with one another. In disengaged families, members do not seem to care about or react to one another; there is a disconnected quality and lack of contact. Enmeshed families, who fall at the opposite end of the range of maladaptive expressions of family involvement, are characterized by much interlocking between members and rapid reactivity to each other's moods and behaviors, so that change begun by one member is met with immediate resistance by the others (Minuchin et al., 1978).

Structural family therapists identify dysfunctional family alignments as needing at least three participants. When two family members repeatedly are in agreement against a third, a stable coalition is formed. When two members agree on identifying a third as the source of the problem, a detouring coalition emerges, lowering stress in the dyad and giving the impression of harmony. Triangulation, the third type of dysfunctional alignment, happens when two family members each insist that a third member side with him or her against the opposing party. The third person, often a child, is apt to feel conflicted about his or her split loyalty, resulting in symptomatic behavior. Dysfunctional family transactions, which manifest the inability of parents to use their authority to implement assigned roles, are indicative of problems in the family's balance of power.

In sum, in this perspective dysfunctional families evidencing maladaptive boundaries, alliances, and power balances, are underorganized, and have a limited capacity to cope effectively due to a rigid but consistently used structure. Conversely, healthy families have well-defined, flexible, and relatively cohesive structures. They accommodate to the changing functions and roles of individual members, family subsystems, the entire family unit, and the sociocultural context.

Basic Structure and Goals

This brief therapy approach is flexible about the number of therapists involved; which family members participate in a given interview; and the location, length, and frequency of sessions. Usually only one therapist is involved; the family members who interact on a daily basis take part in the treatment, which consists of weekly sessions of 5 to 7 months' duration. When the presenting problem is serious, such as severe anorexia, the patient may be hospitalized and the family may be brought in either to live at the hospital temporarily or to undergo intensive outpatient therapy (Minuchin et al., 1978).

The primary goal is resolution of the presenting problem through the restructuring of the family unit so that more adaptive interactional patterns emerge. An additional goal is reformulating the family's construction of reality by encouraging the development of alternative explanatory schemas for conceptualizing the problem. This leads them to develop more adaptive transactions.

Techniques and Process of Therapy

According to structural therapists, families enter treatment when stress has overloaded the system. The family has adapted to changed circumstances in a dysfunctional manner and, when stressed, continues to maintain its equilibrium by repeating the same pathological behavior. The task of therapy is to restructure the family, introducing alternative ways of interacting. The family is presumed to have the capacity to adopt new patterns of behavior; thus, therapists search for competence within the family rather than exploring the roots of dysfunctional behavior.

This includes three cyclical and overlapping stages: joining, assessing, and restructuring. The therapist joins the family rapidly and in a position of leadership to collect data and diagnose the problem. By entering the family system, the therapist learns how they experience reality and gains awareness of family rules, myths, and themes. Maintenance (supporting the existing structure of the family or subsystem), tracking (following the content of the family's communication), and mimesis (adopting the behavior and affective style of the family) are used to ease the joining process. At first, the presenting problem is accepted as the real problem, and interventions are designed to relieve the symptom and improve the system's functioning. Once this occurs, the family has more confidence in the therapist and may decide to work on other problems with greater optimism about the outcome. This is a more symptom-oriented approach than psychodynamic and experiential therapies, yet not as symptom focused as the strategic therapies.

Six domains of family functioning are addressed during the evaluation phase: structural and boundary quality, flexibility and capacity for change, interactional patterns of the subsystems, role of the index person and how the symptomatic behavior maintains family homeostasis, the ecological context in which the presenting problem emerges and is maintained, and the developmental stage of each member and the family unit as a whole. The result of this assessment is the formulation of a family map and diagnosis in which the relationships between structural problems and current symptoms are articulated. Moore discusses some of these domains in her chapter using the structural approach with families with medical problems.

During the restructuring phase, redressing structural difficulties identified during the assessment is the focus of attention. The position taken is that within the hierarchy, the parents should have the power, which the therapist supports if necessary. Process (or how the family interacts), rather than content (or what is said), is the key to therapy. Nonverbal aspects of the communication process are considered important data.

A number of therapeutic techniques are associated with the restructuring process. Spatial interventions may entail changing the seating arrangement in a session or removing members temporarily or having certain members view the session from behind a one-way mirror, thus taking them out of the action temporarily and forcing others to interact. Such spatial interventions, which deal with distance and proximity between family members, seek to change interpersonal boundaries in an attempt to alter the perspectives of the family members. Enactments, fashioned to induce the family to act out dysfunctional and habitual transactional patterns in vivo, offer the therapist opportunities to intervene actively and directly in facilitating structural change. Another tactic for changing embedded family patterns involves the therapist's use of self to disrupt the system's maladaptive homeostasis. The clinician briefly joins or supports particular family members to alter the typical hierarchical configuration and introduce the possibility of new combinations or options. To change members' constructions of reality about the presenting problem, the therapist tries to transform the family's linear view of the problem (i.e., one member is "the problem" or the "identified patient") to one of complementarity (i.e., all family members are involved). Education, including a model of normal family functioning, may be offered in an effort to restructure the family. Paradoxical injunctions can be used to confuse family members, disrupt entrenched thinking, and trigger a search for alternatives.

Additional techniques include escalating stress, marking boundaries, and assigning homework tasks (Colapinto, 1991). The therapist may encourage the family to reenact a dysfunctional transaction and then intervene by escalating stress via prolonging the advent of the enactment, introducing new variables, or indicating alternative transactions. By having the family enact a different pattern of transactions that may include boundary marking, the session serves as a viable new model for interaction outside of the therapy context. Homework tasks serve as a diagnostic probe to ascertain family openness to change and as a mechanism to enable the maladaptive communication patterns and structures to be altered.

To recapitulate, Minuchin (1974) posited that therapy should induce a more optimal family organization that enables family members to realize their own growth potential. This is brought about through a therapeutic process in which the family's perception of reality is challenged, alternative ways of interacting are presented, and new, self-reinforcing transactional patterns are fostered that lead to more gratifying relationships.

Structural family therapists assume an active, authoritative role by asking probing and open-ended questions, giving directions, and assigning homework. As the stage director or producer of the family drama, the therapist expects family members to accommodate to his or her directives, and therefore communicates expertise in facilitating change (N. J. Kaslow et al., 1999).

Treatment Applicability

Empirically based treatment outcome studies show that Structural Family Therapy can be applied successfully to a range of problems and symptoms, such as psychosomatic illnesses, externalizing behavior disorders (see Chapter 11 by

Koedam), and substance abuse, and to families from all economic levels and with various family structures. This approach often is utilized when the identified patient is a child or adolescent and the treatment of choice appears to be family therapy.

STRATEGIC FAMILY THERAPY

The Strategic Therapy of Haley (1976), Madanes (1991), and Hoffman (1981), influenced by Bateson's (Bateson, Jackson, Haley, & Weakland, 1956) communication theory and Ericksonian (Zeig, 1985a, 1985b) hypnosis, perceives problems as metaphors for family dysfunction maintained by faulty and incongruent hierarchies and malfunctioning triangles. Behavior change is their main objective. They believe symptom formation most often occurs at times of transitions in the family life cycle, when a given developmental task is not mastered adequately, thus precipitating a crisis. In such circumstances, an individual's development becomes fixated or "stuck," and symptoms evolve as expressions of the unresolved crisis. The complex, circular behavioral sequences that constitute a family's problem-solving efforts actually perpetuate the presenting problem (Haley, 1976); thus, change within the family system is an absolutely necessary condition for individual change to occur.

The Galveston group, who originally devised multiple impact therapy and then became intrigued by and involved in epistemology, cybernetics, recursiveness, and the work of Humberto Maturana (Dell, 1981), subsequently shifted their focus to a social constructionist perspective (Goolishian & Anderson, 1990), as did other family therapy leaders (e.g., Hoffman, 1992). According to the social constructionist model, meanings and understandings are arrived at through co-construction of events, negotiated through social interactions and achieved through social consensus (Gergen, 1985). Meanings constantly evolve in relation to the social context of a given interaction in which they emerge. To the extent that new explanatory narratives of meaning can be co-constructed, which is the essence of what occurs in many of the cases described in this book when EMDR is utilized or reframing is done, individuals gain a new perspective on their earlier life experiences and then achieve more flexibility in approaching future life events and social interactions. Manon's personal story of the EMDR treatment she received to help her revisit and work through her confusing and abusive childhood experiences illustrates how valuable the co-construction of new explanatory narratives can be. Unlike reframing techniques, in EMDR treatment the shift in narrative structure occurs spontaneously as insights arise during processing.

The following discussion centers mainly on Haley (1976) and Madanes's (1984) problem-solving therapy as illustrative of strategic approaches. In light of the overlap between some of the strategic family therapies and the communications and systemic models, relevant therapeutic structures and techniques addressed earlier are noted only briefly. The shift toward postmodern theories mentioned herein is elaborated later in the chapter.

Basic Structure and Goals

Strategic Therapy, typically a brief intervention, may include the entire family or just one or two of its members for weekly or biweekly sessions. Like the MRI approach, strategic family work is structured: The therapist directs the questioning, gives directives, and intervenes actively. Teaching skills, imparting knowledge, and offering practical advice are not priorities. Sessions are conducted by a single therapist; consultant(s) may be positioned behind a one-way mirror to provide objective input and recommend strategic interventions.

The major goal is to resolve the family's presenting problem within their social context by replacing stereotypical role concepts and behaviors with greater breadth and flexibility, redistributing power for a more equitable balance, and enabling participants to communicate their thoughts, emotions, and wishes more clearly and accurately. To achieve this, small, specific subgoals geared to the resolution of the presenting problems are identified collaboratively. These subgoals are described as increases in positive behaviors, rather than decreases in negative behaviors. This strategy enhances family motivation by igniting a belief that change is possible. The ultimate therapeutic goal is to alter the interactional sequences that maintain problem behaviors, thus facilitating resolution of a family crisis and promoting progress to the next stage of family and individual life cycle development. These changes are congruent with achieving second-order change.

Techniques and Process of Therapy

Adherents of the strategic school are pragmatic and symptom focused. The approach is primarily behaviorally oriented; insight and awareness are not considered essential for change. Because repetitive, dysfunctional behavioral sequences and transactions occur in the present and are perpetuated by continuing behavior, alteration of these require interventions in the present system and not attention to past events and emotions (Stanton, 1981). Thus, the therapist must take definitive, targeted steps to change enough of the repetitive pattern so that the symptom will no longer be needed. The clinician endeavors to replace repetitious, maladaptive behavior and communication patterns with new, better ways of communicating and acting. Strategic therapists are active and authoritative; they exercise their persuasive powers to convince a family to follow their directives.

The first stage of problem-solving therapy consists of an initial interview in which the presenting problem and its context are determined. This interview has five components: social stage, problem stage, interaction stage, goal-setting stage, and task-setting stage. It ends with the administering of the first set of therapeutic directives based on the therapist's understanding of the family diagnosis and presenting problem.

In the middle phase, these tactical interventions are implemented as strategies for addressing each problem (Madanes, 1981). The directives, which may be straight or paradoxical, elicit information about the family (including resistances to change), intensify the therapeutic alliance, and facilitate structural change in interactional sequences maintaining the problem. Straight directives enlist family cooperation with therapist requests and may be valuable in times of family crisis. Frequent use is made of paradoxical directives, therapeutic double binds, and split messages. Whichever half of the contradictory message the family selects to follow will engage them in some facet of improvement. A directive that seems to contradict the desired goals actually serves to generate the family's movement toward change. Thus, once the issue is clearly defined, specific goals have been set, and the paradoxical instructions have been conveyed, the responses are observed and the therapist continues to encourage the usual behavior (symptom prescription), consequently ruling out "rebellious improvement." He or she then expresses confusion over the changes that occur, refusing to take credit for them. Haley (1963) asserted that the basic rule was to encourage the symptom in such a way that it is no longer of any use to the patient.

Main techniques used to challenge the family's homeostasis and foment change in existing behavioral sequences include paradox, reframing, creating ordeals, pretending, and unbalancing. The major paradoxical techniques are utilizing therapeutic double bind communications, positioning (accepting and exaggerating family communications, highlighting the absurdity of the situation, thus causing the family to reevaluate and modify their attitude), restraining (discouraging change by outlining associated dangers), and symptom prescription. With symptom prescription, rather than trying to end the symptomatic behavior, it is recommended that the symptom be increased, ostensibly sanctioning the undesirable behaviors. The therapist's efforts do not stir up resistance from the identified patient, who no longer needs to defend his or her right to maintain the problem behavior. By suggesting exacerbation of the symptom until it no longer serves a useful function in the system, it is alleviated. Once it becomes clear that the person can deliberately make the symptom more severe, the therapist gains leverage to point out that if he or she can control the behavior by increasing it, then control similarly can be exerted to decrease it.

Reframing is a technique in which actions that have been criticized as crazy or disturbed are relabeled positively (positive connotation), thereby introducing a differing view of reality. For example, a rebellious, hostile teenager may be relabeled the family savior; his or her behavior is interpreted as a sacrifice in the service of keeping the parents' shaky marriage together, as the only time they act in unison is when their adolescent gets into trouble. This new view may enable the family to be appreciative rather than critical and may lead to resolution of the marital conflict; this forces the parents to face the reality of the great burden the scapegoat bears, which was the true underlying problem. Thus, reframing redefines the situation in a manner that leads to refocusing on the core, though often denied or ignored, issue or relationship.

Several other techniques used by strategic therapists merit mentioning. Ordeals are generated and utilized as therapeutic maneuvers in which family members are asked to engage in behaviors they dislike but that will improve family relationships (Haley, 1984). Pretending involves a request by the therapist that the symptomatic person feign the symptom. This voluntary exhibiting of the symptom modifies family members' perceptions of the problematic individual and the function of the problem behavior in the family unit. Unbalancing involves the strategic support of one family member, often through the prescription of homework; it disrupts the equilibrium that maintains the problem. Termination is begun when significant diminution in the presenting problem has occurred and the family reveals a capacity to manage problems on its own. In the ending phase, the family is credited for having made the changes, yet cautioned against developing a sense of false optimism about a problem-free life.

Treatment Applicability

Strategic Family Therapy has been utilized in work with couples and families presenting with manifold symptoms, including schizophrenia spectrum disorders, substance abuse, family violence and incest, anxiety disorders, and child and adolescent behavior problems (Madanes, 1990, 1991; Szykula, Morris, & Sudweeks, 1987). There is a paucity of empirical data regarding its treatment efficacy.

SYSTEMIC FAMILY THERAPY

The Milan group (Italy) elucidated systemic family therapy. This approach focuses on process, viewing the family and therapist as an ecosystem in which, over time, each member affects the psychological well-being of all other members. It holds that problem behavior is maintained by rule-governed transactional patterns, with the symptom sustaining the family equilibrium. Congruent with Bateson's (Bateson et al., 1956) view, the family is conceptualized as a nonlinear and complex cybernetic system, with interlocking feedback mechanisms and repetitive behavior sequence patterns. Therapists of this persuasion emphasize the importance of illuminating the meaning of second-order cybernetics.

Basic Structure and Goals

Generally, systemic family therapy sessions are few in number (ranging from 3 to 20), spaced at monthly intervals to permit time for interventions to take root and evoke systemic change. The number of sessions is set at the start of treatment and is adhered to rigorously. Sessions are conducted by a single therapist or cotherapy pair, and consultant(s) may be positioned behind a one-way mirror to recommend systemic interventions. Systemic therapists (Selvini Palazzoli, Boscolo, Cecchin, & Prata, 1978) often use the "Greek chorus," a group of observers behind a one-way mirror, who might call the therapist out and make suggestions, take sides, and/or participate in postsession deliberations.

The overarching goal is to create a milieu in which to explore the family's belief systems, providing new conceptualizations of family problems (cognitive maps) and facilitating change. The treatment team holds a systemic perspective in order to resolve the presenting problem within the family context. Specific goals are stated by each family member, and the therapy team stresses that it is the family's responsibility to make changes. If the therapist disagrees with the family's goals, family wishes are respected, except in instances where their decisions might be harmful to one or more family members (e.g., abuse or incest).

It is not anticipated or necessary that families comprehend how the change occurs, nor is the development of a strong therapeutic bond fostered.

Techniques and Process of Therapy

Incorporating a more evolutionary viewpoint than their strategic colleagues, systemic therapists believe that when the family's rules and conceptual framework for understanding reality (i.e., epistemology) are no longer adaptive, problematic behaviors emerge. Using a framework that brings in new information to sanction and promote the family's development of an alternative epistemology and spontaneous change, sessions are organized according to a relatively standard treatment format. During the presession, data are gathered by the consulting team. Then the therapist(s) meets with family members, provides the information gleaned from the presession, and guides the discussion, allowing for observation of the family's transactional patterns. Next, the therapist/cotherapy dyad and the Greek chorus meet in a separate room to exchange observations, opinions, and suggestions. This meeting results in the formulation of a systemic hypothesis (i.e., diagnosis) and associated intervention plan. The therapist(s) then rejoins the family, provides feedback from the meeting with the consultants, and gives a directive for a task to be completed outside of the session. Usually this directive takes the form of a paradoxical suggestion, symptom prescription, or ritual. It may be given immediately following the consultation in verbal or written form, or sent as a letter or telegram to the family after the session. These prescriptions are designed to increase family connectedness rather than to provoke resistance. Each session concludes with a postsession discussion among team members about family responses to the intervention and the development of a written summary of the session.

In addition to the techniques already described, several other strategies are associated with systemic approaches, including circular questioning (asking one family member to comment on transactions between two other members), positive connotation (reframing all behavior as positive to preserve family homeostasis and cohesion), rituals (prescribing an individualized action or series of actions aimed at altering family roles by addressing the conflict between unspoken and spoken family rules), and counterparadoxical interventions (presenting a therapeutic double bind in which the overt communication is for the family not to change). These techniques elucidate family games (specific repetitive patterns of family interaction; Prata, 1990), introduce a new conceptualization of family problems, and encourage discovery of new solutions to problems through systemic change (N. J. Kaslow et al., 1999).

Termination occurs at the time predetermined at the beginning of therapy. Typically, by then, the problem behavior has been resolved, or at least substantially reduced. The therapist may suggest that the family return for a review session at a later date.

Systemic therapists, unlike their strategic colleagues, historically have adopted a relatively neutral, objective, and *nonreactive stance,* avoiding entanglement in family alliances. They posit that this position affords maximal leverage for creating change, as the therapist may attend to the entire system without being seduced into family games (Selvini Palazzoli, Cirillo, Selvini, & Sorrentino, 1989). Recently, a shift in philosophy has occurred, and systemic therapists are now encouraged to share their systemic hypotheses with the family and curtail the use of paradoxical interventions.

Treatment Applicability

This approach has been used with couples and families experiencing a variety of behavior problems, including psychotic, mood, and personality disorders, alcohol abuse, and psychosomatic illnesses. In a review of 10 empirical investigations of systemic family therapy, Carr (1991) found symptomatic relief in two-thirds to three-quarters of the cases, and systemic change in one-half of them.

BEHAVIORAL AND COGNITIVE-BEHAVIORAL THERAPIES

Behavioral and cognitive-behavioral marital and family therapies encompass a range of techniques and treatment models (see Goldenberg & Goldenberg, 2004; Holtzworth-Munroe & Jacobson, 1991). The behavioral approach to the assessment and treatment of marital and family problems reflects an expansion from the traditional individual approach to behavioral treatment (Bandura, 1969) based on principles from both operant (Skinner, 1974) and classical conditioning (Pavlov, 1941). Behavioral marital and family therapists examine family members' behavior in the context of environmental variables and formulate functional analyses of behavior patterns based on stimulus-response and reinforcement contingencies. Behavior is thought to be influenced by cognitions, stimulus-response patterns, and reinforcement contingencies.

Most behavioral couples and family therapists acknowledge systems concepts, which emphasize the interdependent nature of the behavior patterns between the members (Fay & Lazarus, 1984). According to this perspective, people maintain each others' behavior through reinforcement, and thus behavioral control is a circular or reciprocal process. Behavioral therapists emphasize the importance of family members' learning or relearning more adaptive ways of relating. They assume that people have diverse, idiosyncratic learning histories, and thus a "cookie cutter" application of techniques is not sanctioned.

Behavioral Marital Therapists (BMTs) note and augment potentially reinforcing events and minimize the occurrence of aversive marital interactions to balance the reward-cost ratio for each member of the dyad. BMTs also seek to enhance the couple's capacity to recognize, initiate, and acknowledge positive interactions, decrease hurtful interchanges, develop and employ more adaptive communication skills and problem-solving strategies, and negotiate problem resolution by contingency contracting (Liberman, Wheeler, deVisser, Kuehnel, & Kuehnel, 1980).

Behavioral interventions also have been developed for use with families (Epstein, Bishop, & Levin, 1978). Alexander and colleagues (Alexander & Barton, 1990; Alexander & Parsons, 1982) developed functional family therapy

(FFT), an approach in which all behavior is viewed as adaptive and therefore functional. The therapist determines the interpersonal functions of each family member's behavior before initiating change in the system. Efforts are geared toward modifying members' cognitions and emotional responses to assist the family in conceptualizing difficulties in a systemic manner and sharing responsibility for behavior change. Education is provided and new skills taught that are needed to sustain positive changes.

Finally, methods have been forged for treating couples and families based on an integration of cognitive and behavioral psychology (Epstein, Schlesinger, & Dryden, 1988). Cognitive-Behavioral Family Treatment (CBFT), an outgrowth of individual cognitive therapies (Beck, 1976; Ellis & Grieger, 1977), assumes that cognitive mediation of events affects family relational patterns, as do family members' feelings and actions. Problems arise from family members' distorted beliefs about each other and from dysfunctional transactional patterns. Cognitions and interactions are inextricably intertwined and mutually influential. Assessment focuses on examining such cognitive processes as beliefs, attributions, and behaviors, such as conflict resolution, communication, and negotiation skills. The most frequently used intervention techniques include cognitive restructuring procedures and self-instructional training. The behavioral strategies include communication, assertiveness, and problem-solving training, as well as behavior exchange procedures.

To illustrate these therapies, the FFT model has been selected because it integrates cognitive and behavioral approaches, is based on a well-articulated set of principles, and has received strong empirical support (Goldenberg & Goldenberg, 2004; Nichols & Schwartz, 2006).

Basic Structure and Goals

These therapies are generally brief, time limited, structured, and conducted by a single therapist. The treatment is crafted to engender changes in cognitions and behavior of each individual and in the family unit as a whole. The family is offered alternative explanatory narratives of events, enabling everyone to behave more adaptively and to interact more harmoniously.

Techniques and Process of Therapy

FFT occurs in phases. In the *assessment stage,* three levels of family functioning are evaluated: relationship (interactional patterns and processes), functional (adaptive functions of behavioral sequences of various family members), and individual (identification of behavioral, cognitive, and affective changes required for each family member to change problem behavior).

Family interventions are divided into therapeutic and educational strategies tailored to alter family members' cognitions and affects. Therapy centers around interventions that address family resistances and that mobilize and motivate family members to change and prepare the family to benefit from the educational interventions. Advocates assume that behavior change requires changes in family members' self-perceptions and perceptions regarding other

family members, and thus each one is encouraged to question his or her understanding of family interactional patterns and the presenting problem. This reattribution strategy is reflected in the process, style, and content of therapist-family
communications.

Relabeling is a reattribution technique used frequently by functional family
therapists to bring about change in the family unit. A technique similar to positive reframing, relabeling connotes a message that recasts roles, behaviors, and
emotions perceived negatively by family members into more positive terms
(revalencing) and sensitizes family members to the reciprocal interpersonal effects of each other's behaviors and emotions. Revalencing facilitates alternative
understanding and affective responses that are more in line with family members' expectations. This relabeling implicitly communicates that the dissatisfied
person has much more control over the problematic relational pattern than he or
she realizes. As relabeling revalences behavior, it also implies that there are
ways family members can change to more directly obtain what they want.

In the *educational facet* of the intervention, instruction is given in a manner
consistent with the functional outcomes of family members' behavior and the
therapeutic reattributions that the therapist has fashioned within the family unit.
Therapists choose from a wide assortment of overt behavior change interventions (e.g., contingency contracting and management, modeling, systematic desensitization, time-out procedures, communication skills training, assertiveness
training, problem-solving training) to maximize needed behavior change. Techniques are selected based on goodness of fit with the functions and processes of
the particular family's life.

In behavioral and cognitive-behavioral marital and family therapies, therapists
take a directive stance and function as scientists, role models, and educators.
They acknowledge that a collaborative working alliance is requisite for behavior
change. Functional family therapists are known for their explanations of strategies for developing such a working alliance. They use the following relationship-
building skills to establish the optimal environment and prepare the family for
change: present as warm and empathic, integrate emotions and behavior, adopt a
nonjudgmental stance, use humor to defuse tension, and selectively self-disclose
to provide information to the family. They employ structuring skills to assist the
family in implementing change. During the education phase, these encompass
directiveness, self-confidence, and clarity. Adherents of this approach continually monitor their impact on family members and calibrate their style of interaction to maximize their fit with the family's functional characteristics (Sexton
& Alexander, 2002).

Treatment Applicability

BFT and CBFT have addressed a broad range of behavioral, emotional, and relational problems. Research utilizing FFT has shown that modifying dysfunctional family processes leads to a dramatic reduction in recidivism rates for
juvenile delinquents whose families comply with treatment (Alexander & Parsons, 1982). These interventions are also associated with long-term mainte-

nance of treatment gains and heightened family ability to cope with developmental transitions.

This category of approaches has been the object of more empirical investigation than any other family therapy model. In a review of the literature (Holtzworth-Munroe & Jacobson, 1991), it was asserted that Behavioral Marital Therapy is more efficacious than control conditions in relieving marital discord and promoting marital satisfaction. Variables associated with positive treatment outcome include the development of a collaborative therapist-couple partnership, active client engagement in the intervention process, and compliance with assigned tasks. Child-focused BFT has been shown to be advantageous in ameliorating the presenting problem in a heterogeneous sample of children (Szykula et al., 1987). Treatment outcome research focusing on such sexual dysfunctions as premature ejaculation, female primary orgasmic dysfunction, and paraphilias has yielded high rates of success for behavioral treatments (Heiman, LoPiccolo, & LoPiccolo, 1981). Client variables linked to good prognosis in cognitive-behavioral marital and family therapy include at least average intellectual functioning and capacity for abstraction of all participants, children who are school-age or older, and family members who demonstrate relative acceptance of one another (Epstein et al., 1988).

PSYCHOEDUCATIONAL FAMILY THERAPY

Psychoeducational approaches are designed to correct individual and family difficulties and improve functioning (McFarlane, 1991). These models are intended to train family members to be helpers to their loved one (e.g., parent training for those with disturbed children); teach family members communication, problem-solving, and conflict resolution skills; and prevent the emergence of problems in order to improve the quality of family life. A multitude of theoretical perspectives contribute to the foundational base of psychoeducational approaches, including cognitive-behavioral, psychodynamic, and humanistic; some are atheoretical in orientation. Psychoeducational programs have been developed for parent training (Carkhuff, 1971), marriage enhancement (Jacobson & Margolin, 1979; Stuart, 1969), and family skills training and enrichment (Guerney, 1977; L'Abate & Weinstein, 1987).

Basic Structure and Goals

Family psychoeducation, a structured treatment approach that can be conducted with one family or in a multiple-family group format, usually is provided by two clinicians. Session frequency depends on the patient's psychiatric condition and the stage of the family education process. Treatment is generally long term. Sessions typically are frequent in the early phases, and intervals between sessions are greater during the later phases of treatment.

The two major long-terms goals are relapse prevention and reintegration of the patient into the community. To reach these objectives, short-term and intermediate goals have been delineated, including: stabilization of the patient's symptoms, enlistment of family members in the education process, provision of education regarding psychotic conditions and psychopharmacological interventions, establishment of a treatment team that includes family members and stresses continuity of care, encouragement of the development and use of a social support network, and assistance to the family in managing the stress associated with caring for a family member with a chronic psychiatric condition. Throughout treatment, goals are candidly discussed and negotiated.

Techniques and Process of Therapy

Individual and multiple family psychoeducation approaches include four phases. The first coincides with the family member's first psychotic episode. A collaborative relationship is established with all significant family members available and the patient. While the crisis is being assessed, the family members' responses to the patient's symptoms and the treatment environment are elicited. The family's structure, coping strategies, and social support system are evaluated. At the close of phase 1, a contract is written that specifies the structure of the intervention.

In phase 2, educational information is provided in a day or weekend workshop or a series of brief, ongoing informational sessions interspersed between family meetings. These educational workshops are presented in a lecture and discussion format designed for family members and friends of the patient. In some cases, concurrent education is also presented to the patient in a group format. In addition to offering material on the nature, symptoms, and management of Schizophrenia Spectrum Disorders, the educational component addresses key risk factors associated with relapse and strategies to deal effectively with these stressors.

The third phase, the reentry period, starts when the patient returns to the community and lasts approximately 1 year. Emphasis is placed on stabilization of the patient outside of the hospital. In the fourth and final phase, rehabilitation, therapists and family members collaborate to improve the patient's adaptive functioning. Termination is contingent on both the patient's clinical status and the family's desire for ongoing treatment and/or social support.

Techniques employed in psychoeducation sessions include (a) informal socializing with patient and family at the beginning of the session, (b) reviewing homework assignments, (c) analyzing between-session events, (d) reframing stressors in a manner consistent with the information provided during the educational components, (e) teaching problem-solving and communication skills, and (f) underscoring urgency of medication compliance.

Therapists offer advice, guidance, and information, conveying both their own expertise and their appreciation of the value of the family's experience in assisting their loved one.

Treatment Applicability

Psychoeducational approaches have proven valuable in work with families with a member diagnosed with Schizophrenia or a Mood Disorder (Anderson, Reiss, & Hogarty, 1986). Psychoeducational parent training, marriage enhancement, and family skills training and enrichment programs also have received modest empirical support (Levant, 1986).

INTEGRATIVE FAMILY THERAPY

Integrative models strive to unify previously divergent theories and techniques into a supraordinate structure, with a recognition of the similarities and differences of the perspectives being combined (Gurman, 2005). They reflect a synthesis of general systems theory and at least one additional individual or family therapy approach (Lebow, 1987). These models may differ in terms of their reliance on the amalgamation of intervention strategies from discrete models into a particular approach, integration of two or more approaches into a unitary theoretical and clinical entity, and use of intervention techniques from different schools chosen because of their appropriateness for addressing specific problems (Johnson & Greenberg, 1987; F. W. Kaslow & Lebow, 2002). Theory integration seeks the development of more broadly useful paradigms for understanding and treating marital and family dysfunction, models that flexibly accommodate therapist differences in personality style and skill level and the unique characteristics of each family unit (Aradi & Kaslow, 1987). However, a theory that has good explanatory power with one family may prove inadequate for conceptualizing the dynamics of another, and an intervention strategy that works well with one type of symptomatology or syndrome may lead to an impasse with another.

Aradi and Kaslow (1987) proposed a three-stage process of family therapy theory integration. Stage 1 offers six criteria as the basis for systematic theory examination: the explanatory, diagnostic, therapeutic, prognostic, evaluative, and preventive power of the theory. Theories are considered in terms of their usefulness in conceptualizing and assessing family strengths and dysfunction, generating a treatment approach, predicting the course of dysfunction and treatment outcome, offering an approach for process and outcome research, and addressing prevention. Thus, an integrative approach is contingent upon the therapist's assessment of the appropriateness, applicability, and power of each available theoretical perspective and accompanying intervention model during the course of treatment.

Stage 2 addresses key therapist variables, highlighting the stance that theory integration involves an interaction between the therapist's predilections and personality style and his or her objective assessment of the extant theories. A therapist's views on the nature and definitions of dysfunction, the role and focus of assessment and diagnosis, the structure and process of treatment, the role of the therapist, and intervention goals influence the selection of therapeutic approaches to be integrated. Thus, the goodness of fit between a therapist's belief system and the components of various treatment approaches provide a framework for evaluating a theory's integrative potential for that particular clinician. Similarly, family variables, the focus of Stage 3 in theory integration, represent a key contextual dimension for determining the utility of a model. The therapist must incorporate the family's construction of reality (Reiss, 1981) in developing a conceptual model best suited to the family's interactional patterns and style.

As this model demonstrates, the essence of theory integration is to provide a context for the synthesis of distinct theories and their components into a more holistic approach, specifically adapted to account for unique contextual variables. As such, numerous integrative models of marital and family therapy are possible. (For a fuller discussion on integrative models of marital and family therapy and recent empirical process and outcome research evaluating its efficacy, see F. W. Kaslow & Lebow, 2002; Pinsof, 2002.)

CONCLUDING COMMENTS

This chapter has provided a conceptual road map of the major theories of marital and family therapy, with the hope of increasing the reader's awareness of the existing extant panoply from which the authors of the ensuing chapters integrating EMDR and family systems theory made their selections. In this relatively young field, it is not surprising that no one school of thought contains all of the elements integral to a conceptual schema that merits consideration as a complete theory. Yet, each of the schools has contributed sufficiently to the development of the field to warrant inclusion. It is anticipated that in the next decade the field will continue to exhibit increased intellectual and scientific rigor in the pursuit of a more sophisticated understanding of the processes and outcomes of marital and family therapy that have begun to be expressed since the 1990s, and that this trend will accelerate.

REFERENCES

Alexander, J. F., & Barton, C. (1990). Functional family therapy: A relationship and a process. In F. W. Kaslow (Ed.), *Voices in family psychology* (Vol. 1, pp. 209–226). Newbury Park, CA: Sage.

Alexander, J. F., & Parsons, B. V. (1982). *Functional family therapy.* Monterey, CA: Brooks/Cole.

Anderson, C. M., Reiss, D. J., & Hogarty, G. E. (1986). *Schizophrenia and the family.* New York: Guilford Press.

Aponte, H. J. (1976). Underorganization in the poor family. In P. J. Guerin (Ed.), *Family therapy: Theory and practice* (pp. 432–448). New York: Gardner.

Aponte, H. J., & Van Deusen, J. M. (1981). Structural family therapy. In A. S. Gurman & D. P. Kniskern (Eds.), *Handbook of family therapy* (pp. 310–360). New York: Brunner/Mazel.

Aradi, N. S., & Kaslow, F. W. (1987). Theory integration in family therapy: Definition, rationale, content and process. *Psychotherapy: Theory, Research and Practice, 25,* 598–608.

Auerswald, E. (1985). Thinking about thinking in family therapy. *Family Process, 24,* 1–12.

Bandura, A. (1969). *Principles of behavior modification.* New York: Holt, Rinehart and Winston.

Bateson, G., Jackson, D. D., Haley, J. E., & Weakland, J. (1956). Toward a theory of schizophrenia. *Behavioral Science, 1,* 251–264.

Beavers, W. R. (1977). *Psychotherapy and growth: Family systems perspective.* New York: Brunner/Mazel.

Beavers, W. R. (1993). Measuring family competence: The Beavers systems model. In F. Walsh (Ed.), *Normal family processes* (2nd ed., pp. 73–103). New York: Guilford Press.

Beck, A. T. (1976). *Cognitive therapy and emotional disorders.* New York: International Universities Press.

Beels, C., & Ferber, A. (1972). What family therapists do. In A. Ferber, M. Mendelsohn, & A. Napier (Eds.), *The book of family therapy* (pp. 168–232). New York: Science House.

Boszormenyi-Nagy, I., Greenebaum, J., & Ulrich, D. (1991). Contextual therapy. In A. S. Gurman & D. P. Kniskern (Eds.), *Handbook of family therapy* (Vol. II, pp. 200–238). New York: Brunner/Mazel.

Boszormenyi-Nagy, I., & Krasner, B. R. (1986). *Between give and take: A critical guide to contextual therapy.* New York: Brunner/Mazel.

Bowen, M. (1988). *Family therapy in clinical practice* (2nd ed.). Northvale, NJ: Jason Aronson.

Bowlby, J. (1969). *Attachment and loss: Vol. 1. Attachment.* New York: Basic Books.

Bowlby, J. (1988). *A secure base: Parent-child attachment and healthy human development.* New York: Basic Books.

Carkhuff, R. R. (1971). Training as a preferred mode of treatment. *Journal of Counseling Psychology, 18,* 123–131.

Carr, A. (1991). Milan systemic family therapy: A review of ten empirical investigations. *Journal of Family Therapy, 13,* 237–263.

Colapinto, J. (1991). Structural family therapy. In A. S. Gurman & D. P. Kniskern (Eds.), *Handbook of family therapy* (Vol. 2, pp. 417–443). New York: Brunner/Mazel.

Dell, P. (1981). Paradox redux. *Journal of Marital and Family Therapy, 7,* 127–134.

de Shazer, S. (1985). *Keys to solution in brief therapy.* New York: Norton.

de Shazer, S. (1988). *Clues: Investigation solutions in brief therapy.* New York: Norton.

Duhl, B. S., & Duhl, F. J. (1981). Integrative family therapy. In A. S. Gurman & D. P. Kniskern (Eds.), *Handbook of family therapy* (pp. 483–516). New York: Brunner/Mazel.

Ducommun-Nagy, C. (2002). Contextual therapy. In F. W. Kaslow, R. F. Massey, & S. D. Massey (Eds.), *Comprehensive handbook of psychotherapy: Vol. 3. Interpersonal/humanistic/existential* (pp. 463–488). Hoboken, NJ: Wiley.

Ellis, A., & Grieger, R. (Eds.). (1977). *Handbook of rational emotive therapy.* New York: Springer.

Epstein, N. B., Bishop, D. S., & Levin, S. (1978). The McMaster model of family functioning. *Journal of Marital and Family Counseling, 4,* 19–32.

Epstein, N. B., Schlesinger, S. E., & Dryden, W. (Eds.). (1988). *Cognitive-behavioral therapy with families.* New York: Brunner/Mazel.

Fay, A., & Lazarus, A. A. (1984). The therapist in behavioral and multi-modal therapy. In F. W. Kaslow (Ed.), *Psychotherapy with psychotherapists* (pp. 1–18). New York: Haworth.

Friedman, E. H. (1991). Bowen theory and therapy. In A. S. Gurman & D. P. Kniskern (Eds.), *Handbook of family therapy* (Vol. 2, pp. 134–170). New York: Brunner/Mazel.

Gergen, K. (1985). The social constructionist movement in modern psychology. *American Psychologist, 40,* 266–275.

Goldenberg, I., & Goldenberg, H. (2004). *Family therapy: An overview* (6th ed.). Belmont, CA: Brooks/Cole.

Goldenthal, P. (1991). Contextual therapy with children and families. *Innovations in clinical practice: A sourcebook, 10,* 85–97. (Published annually by Professional Resource Press, Sarasota, FL)

Goolishian, H. A., & Anderson, H. (1990). Understanding the therapeutic process: From individuals and families to systems and language. In F. W. Kaslow (Ed.), *Voices in family psychology* (Vol. 1, pp. 91–113). Newbury Park, CA: Sage.

Guerney, B. G., Jr. (Ed.). (1977). *Relationship enhancement.* San Francisco: Jossey-Bass.

Gurman, A. S. (1979). Dimensions of marital therapy: A comparative analysis. *Journal of Marital and Family Therapy, 5,* 5–18.

Gurman, A. S. (2005). Brief integrative marital therapy: An interpersonal-intrapsychic approach. In J. Lebow (Ed.), *Handbook of clinical family therapy* (pp. 353–383). Hoboken, NJ: Wiley.

Haley, J. (1963). *Strategies of psychotherapy.* New York: Grune & Stratton.

Haley, J. (1971). *Changing families.* New York: Grune & Stratton.

Haley, J. (1973). *Uncommon therapy: The psychiatric techniques of Milton H. Erickson, MD.* New York: Norton.

Haley, J. (1976). *Problem-solving therapy.* San Francisco: Jossey-Bass.

Haley, J. (1984). *Ordeal therapy: Unusual ways to change behavior.* San Francisco: Jossey-Bass.

Heiman, J. R., LoPiccolo, L., & LoPiccolo, J. (1981). The treatment of sexual dysfunction. In A. S. Gurman & D. P. Kniskern (Eds.), *Handbook of family therapy* (Vol. 1, pp. 592–630). New York: Brunner/Mazel.

Hoffman, L. (1980). The family life cycle and discontinuous change. In E. Carter & M. McGoldrick (Eds.), *The family life cycle: A framework for family therapy* (pp. 53–68). New York: Gardner Press.

Hoffman, L. (1981). *Foundations of family therapy.* New York: Basic Books.

Hoffman, L. (1992). A reflective stance for family therapy. In S. McNamee & K. J. Gergen (Eds.), *Therapy as social construction* (pp. 7–24). London: Sage.

Holtzworth-Monroe, A., & Jacobson, N. S. (1991). Behavioral marital therapy. In A. S. Gurman & D. P. Kniskern (Eds.), *Handbook of family therapy* (Vol. 2, pp. 96–133). New York: Brunner/Mazel.

Jacobson, N. S., & Margolin, G. (1979). *Marital therapy: Strategies based on social learning and behavior exchange principles.* New York: Brunner/Mazel.

Johnson, S. M., & Greenberg, L. S. (1987). Integration in marital therapy: Issues and progress. *International Journal of Eclectic Psychotherapy, 6,* 202–215.

Kantor, D., & Lehr, W. (1975). *Inside the family: Toward a theory of family process.* San Francisco: Jossey-Bass.

Kaslow, F. W. (1981). Profile of the healthy family. *Interaction, 4,* 1–15.

Kaslow, F. W. (1987). Marital and family therapy. In M. B. Sussman & S. K. Steinmetz (Eds.), *Handbook of marriage and the family* (pp. 835–859). New York: Plenum Press.

Kaslow, F. W. (Ed.). (1995). *Projective genogramming.* Sarasota, FL: Professional Resource Press.

Kaslow, F. W., Cooper, B., & Linsenberg, M. (1979). Therapist authenticity: A key factor in family therapy effectiveness. *International Journal of Family Therapy, 1,* 184–199.

Kaslow, F. W., & Hammerschmidt, H. (1992). Long term good marriages: The seemingly essential ingredients. In B. J. Brothers (Ed.), *Couples therapy: Multiple perspectives* (pp. 15–38). New York: Haworth.

Kaslow, F. W., & Lebow, J. (Eds.). (2002). *Comprehensive handbook of psychotherapy: Vol. 4. Integrative/eclectic.* Hoboken, NJ: Wiley.

Kaslow, F. W., & Magnavita, J. (Eds.). (2002). *Comprehensive handbook of psychotherapy: Vol. 1. Psychodynamic/object relations.* Hoboken, NJ: Wiley.

Kaslow, N. J., Dausch, B. M., & Celano, M. (2003). The family therapies. In A. S. Gurman & S. B. Messer (Eds.), *Modern psychotherapies: Theory and practice* (2nd ed., 400–462). New York: Guilford Press.

Kaslow, N. J., Kaslow, F. W., & Farber, E. W. (1999). Theories and techniques of marital and family therapy. In M. B. Sussman, S. K. Steinmetz, & G. W. Peterson (Eds.), *Handbook of marriage and the family* (2nd ed., pp. 767–793). New York: Plenum Press.

Keith, D. V., & Whitaker, C. A. (1981). Play therapy: A paradigm for work with families. *Journal of Marriage and Family Therapy, 7*(3), 243–254.

Kempler, W. (1981). *Experiential psychotherapy within families.* New York: Brunner/Mazel.

Kerr, M., & Bowen, M. (1988). *Family evaluation: An approach based on Bowen theory.* New York: Norton.

L'Abate, L., & Weinstein, S. E. (1987). *Structured enrichment programs for couples and families.* New York: Brunner/Mazel.

Lebow, J. L. (1987). Integrative family therapy: An overview of major issues. *Psychotherapy: Theory, Research and Practice, 24,* 584–594.

Lebow, J. L. (2005). *Handbook of clinical family therapy.* Hoboken, NJ: Wiley.

Levant, R. F. (Ed.). (1986). *Psychoeducational approaches to family therapy and counseling.* New York: Springer.

Lewis, J. M., Beavers, W. R., Gossett, J. T., & Phillips, V. A. (1976). *No single thread: Psychological health in family systems.* New York: Brunner/Mazel.

Liberman, R. P., Wheeler, E., deVisser, L. A. J. M., Kuehnel, J., & Kuehnel, T. (1980). *Handbook of marital therapy: A positive approach to helping troubled relationships.* New York: Plenum Press.

Madanes, C. (1981). *Strategic family therapy.* San Francisco: Jossey-Bass.

Madanes, C. (1984). *Behind the one way mirror.* San Francisco: Jossey-Bass.

Madanes, C. (1990). *Sex, love, and violence.* New York: Norton.

Madanes, C. (1991). Strategic family therapy. In A. S. Gurman & D. P. Kniskern (Eds.), *Handbook of family therapy* (Vol. 2, pp. 396–416). New York: Brunner/Mazel.

McFarlane, W. R. (1991). Family psychoeducational treatment. In A. S. Gurman & D. P. Kniskern (Eds.), *Handbook of family therapy* (Vol. 2, p. 363–395). New York: Brunner/Mazel.

McGoldrick, M., Gerson, R., & Shellenberger, S. (1999). *Genograms: Assessment and intervention (2nd ed.).* New York: Norton.

Minuchin, S. (1974). *Families and family therapy.* Cambridge, MA: Harvard University Press.

Minuchin, S., & Fishman, H. C. (1981). *Family therapy techniques.* Cambridge, MA: Harvard University Press.

Minuchin, S., Montalvo, B., Guerney, B. G., Jr., Rosman, B., & Schumer, F. (1967). *Families of the slums.* New York: Basic Books.

Minuchin, S., Rosman, B. L., & Baker, L. (1978). *Psychosomatic families: Anorexia nervosa in context.* Cambridge, MA: Harvard University Press.

Napier, A. Y., & Whitaker, C. A. (1978). *The family crucible.* New York: Harper & Row.

Nichols, M. P., & Schwartz, R. C. (2006). *Family therapy: Concepts and methods* (7th ed.). Boston: Allyn & Bacon.

Olson, D. H. (1970). Marital and family therapy: Integrative review and critique. *Journal of Marriage and the Family, 32,* 501–538.

Olson, D. H., McCubbin, H. I., Barnes, H., Larsen, A., Muxen, M., & Wilson, M. (1983). *Families: What makes them work.* Beverly Hills, CA: Sage.

Olson, D. H., Sprenkle, D., & Russell, C. (1979). Circumplex model of marital and family systems: Cohesion and adaptability dimensions, family types, and clinical applications. *Family Process, 18,* 3–28.

Pavlov, I. P. (1941). *Conditioned reflexes and psychiatry.* New York: International Publications.

Pinsof, W. M. (1995). *Integrative problem centered therapy.* New York: Basic Books.

Pinsof, W. M. (2002). Integrative problem solving therapy. In F. W. Kaslow & J. Lebow (Eds.), *Comprehensive handbook of psychotherapy: Vol. 4. Integrative/eclectic* (pp. 341–366). Hoboken, NJ: Wiley.

Prata, G. (1990). *A systemic harpoon into family games.* New York: Brunner/Mazel.

Reiss, D. (1981). *The family's construction of reality.* Cambridge, MA: Harvard University Press.

Roberto, L. G. (1991). Symbolic-experiential family therapy. In A. S. Gurman & D. P. Kniskern (Eds.), *Handbook of family therapy* (Vol. 2, pp. 444–476). New York: Brunner/Mazel.

Roberto, L. G. (1992). *Transgenerational family therapies.* New York: Guilford Press.

Sander, F. M. (1979). *Individual and family therapy: Toward an integration.* New York: Aronson.

Satir, V. (1967). *Cojoint family therapy.* Palo Alto, CA: Science & Behavior Books.

Satir, V. (1972). *People-making.* Palo Alto, CA: Science & Behavior Books.

Satir, V., & Baldwin, M. (1983). *Satir step by step: A guide to creating change in families.* Palo Alto, CA: Science and Behavior Books.

Scharff, D. E., & Scharff, J. S. (1987). *Object relations family therapy.* Northvale, NJ: Aronson.

Scharff, J. S. (Ed.). (1989). *Foundations of object relations family therapy.* Northvale, NJ: Aronson.

Scharff, J. S. (Ed.). (1992). *Projective and introjective identification and the uses of the therapist's self.* Northvale, NJ: Aronson.

Segal, L. (1991). Brief therapy: The MRI approach. In A. S. Gurman & D. P. Kniskern (Eds.), *Handbook of family therapy* (Vol. 2, pp. 171–199). New York: Brunner/Mazel.

Selvini Palazzoli, M., Boscolo, L., Cecchin, G., & Prata, G. (1978). *Paradox and counterparadox.* Northvale, NJ: Jason Aronson.

Selvini Palazzoli, M., Cirillo, S., Selvini, M., & Sorrentino, A. M. (1989). *Family games: General models of psychotic pressures in the family.* New York: Norton.

Sexton, T. L., & Alexander, J. F. (2002). Functional family therapy for at risk adolescents and their families. In F. W. Kaslow & T. E. Patterson (Eds.), *Comprehensive handbook of psychotherapy: Vol. 2. Cognitive-behavioral approaches* (pp. 117–140). Hoboken, NJ: Wiley.

Skinner, B. F. (1974). *About behaviorism.* New York: Knopf.

Slipp, S. (1984). *Object relations: A dynamic bridge between individual and family treatment.* New York: Aronson.

Stanton, M. D. (1981). Strategic approaches to family therapy. In A. S. Gurman & D. P. Kniskern (Eds.), *Handbook of family therapy* (pp. 361–402). New York: Brunner/Mazel.

Stuart, R. B. (1969). Operant-interpersonal treatment of marital discord. *Journal of Consulting and Clinical Psychology, 33,* 675–682.

Szykula, S. A., Morris, S. B., & Sudweeks, C. (1987). Child-focused behavior and strategic therapies: Outcome comparisons. *Psychotherapy: Theory, Research, and Practice, 24,* 546–551.

Wachtel, E. F., & Wachtel, P. L. (1986). *Family dynamics in individual psychotherapy.* New York: Guilford Press.

Walsh, F. (1993). *Normal family processes* (2nd ed.). New York: Guilford Press.

Watzlawick, P., Weakland, J., & Fisch, R. (1974). *Change: Principles of problem formation and problem resolution.* New York: Norton.

Whitaker, C. A. (1976). The hindrance of theory in clinical work. In P. J. Guerin (Ed.), *Family therapy: Theory and practice* (pp. 154–164). New York: Gardner Press.

Whitaker, C. A., & Bumberry, W. M. (1988). *Dancing with the family: A symbolic-experiential approach.* New York: Brunner/Mazel.

Zeig, J. K. (1985a). *Ericksonian psychotherapy: Structures* (Vol. 1). New York: Brunner/Mazel.

Zeig, J. K. (1985b). *Ericksonian psychotherapy: Clinical applications* (Vol. 2). New York: Brunner/Mazel.

CHAPTER 3

Use of the Genogram with Families for Assessment and Treatment

Sylvia Shellenberger

A picture is worth a thousand words. Likewise, a couple's genogram captures in one graphic depiction much of their history, emotional lives, and current issues. Like a family tree, the genogram represents the biological connections of the family. In addition, it can illustrate the social connections of family members, the quality of relationships between members of the family, dates of major family events, and individual characteristics of key family members. The genogram is utilized by therapists to join with their clients, for clients and therapists to track family patterns, and for therapists to reframe, detoxify, and normalize emotionally laden issues (McGoldrick, Gerson, & Shellenberger, 1999). Genograms also assist the therapist in developing hypotheses about the nature of the relationship between current symptoms and past family events and in determining treatment possibilities. Multiple genograms can be constructed as therapy progresses and thereby serve as a record for family changes over time.

In this chapter, the use of the genogram is highlighted as a tool for couple or family assessment, to determine therapeutic options, and to intervene. Typical symbols used and questions asked for the purpose of building the genogram are described. Several cases are presented, the first of which illustrates the intertwining of assessment and intervention in couple's therapy. The second case presents the challenge of interviewing and drawing a genogram of a family where there are multiple partners, children by different partners, and complex relationship dynamics. The third case shows both the biological and adoptive families of one adult. In the portrayal of the cases, points of referral for Eye Movement Desensitization and Reprocessing (EMDR) therapy are noted. Adaptations of the traditional genogram, including socially constructed genograms, projective genograms, and community genograms, are discussed along with limitations of the genogram technique.

Family systems therapies, based on Bowen Theory (1978; Kerr & Bowen, 1988), often use the genogram as the primary organizing tool for drawing the family constellation across multiple generations to discover clues about family functioning and to resolve struggles in order to promote healthier functioning. Bowen Theory focuses not simply on the client or the client's nuclear family, but on the entire family emotional field, represented pictorially by a genogram drawing of at least three generations. Therapy addresses the clients' relationships in their nuclear family and family of origin and as participants in patterns of interaction across multiple generations. Genograms of clients' families across generations capture the richness and complexity of extended family systems. Bowen Theory purports that there are forces within families pulling people toward togetherness and connection and opposing forces pushing them toward separateness and independence. When individuals have difficulty balancing these two forces, or get caught in emotional struggles related to these forces, dysfunctional relationships may result. Problematic relationships are those that are fused, distant, conflictual, cut off, triangulated, or even abusive. Fused relationships are those in which one person becomes so emotionally attached to another that he or she reacts in response to the actions or emotions of the other; this is the opposite of differentiation (Bowen, 1978). Triangulated relationships occur when a third person is introduced into a dyadic relationship to balance either the excessive intimacy or distance and to provide stability in the system (Bowen, 1978). A common triangle involves two parents and a child, and each parent attempts to have the child side with him or her against the other parent. The genogram graphic portrays these different types of relationships through the use of symbols. These symbols reveal relationships in which struggles may be resolved through differentiation, which, in turn, may lead to less tension or anxiety in the system and healthier family adaptations. Differentiation is characterized by acting with autonomy and without responding to pressure from others in the system.

Historically, professionals in family medicine and family therapy were the first to utilize genograms to record information about families in their practices and to call for the standardization of symbols so other clinicians could read and interpret the family graphic (Jolly, Froom, & Rosen, 1980). The standardized format was decided upon by a committee that included Murray Bowen, Jack Froom, and Jack Medalie and members of the North American Primary Care Research Group (McGoldrick et al., 1999). Using genograms of famous families, McGoldrick and Gerson (1985) and then McGoldrick et al. (1999) further defined the format and interpretive principles, described applications of the genogram, and highlighted the need for research using genograms. The computerized genogram, initiated by Gerson in 1985 and continued by Shellenberger and others, contributed to the standardization and extended the use of the genogram in institutional and educational settings (Genogram-Maker, 1985; Genogram-Maker Millennium, 2005; Relativity, 2003). Numerous fields such as family medicine, pediatrics, nursing, psychology, hospice and palliative care, medical anthropology, health policy, law, social work, and family business have adopted the genogram as a tool for discovery of information relevant to their practice (Carlock & Ward, 2001; Hockley, 2000; Kent-Wilkinson, 1999; Liossi, Hatira, & Mystakidou, 1997; Richards, Burgess, Peterson, McCarthy, 1993; Spoljar-Vrzina, 2000; Visscher & Clore, 1992; Watts & Shrader, 1998).

As a tool in marital and family therapy, the genogram serves many purposes. For the therapist, constructing a genogram assists in the discovery of historic events in the lives of couples that have current significance, aids in the development of goals for therapy, leads to interpretations that may have meaning for the clients, and facilitates decision making about modes of intervention. Through genogram interviewing, points of grief, trauma, and misfortune are discovered, as well as clients' reactions to these events. The following case illustrates a therapist's and couple's use of the genogram.

────────────────── **Case Example** ──────────────────

Case 1: Dilemmas and Disturbances in an Accomplished Couple

Rachel was a high-functioning CEO of her own software company. She and her husband, David, had unresolved issues about whether to have a child. As they began to talk more seriously about this, David's panicky feelings, similar to those he had experienced during his mother's protracted illness, began to resurface. The couple decided to see a therapist and received a referral from their family physician, who explained to the therapist ahead of time why the couple sought therapy.

The therapist introduced herself, inviting the couple to ask questions about therapy with her. Savvy about different modes of therapy Rachel had heard friends talk about, she asked what to expect in their sessions. The therapist commented that her orientation in therapy was a family systems approach, originally conceptualized by Bowen (1978), and then Kerr and Bowen (1988). She explained that the primary tool she used to ground the therapy was the genogram and that she planned to draw the genogram for them to see as they told their story of why they had come. She expected that the genogram would help Rachel and David have a better idea as to why they were unable to move forward with a decision about having a child and why David's panic attacks were reoccurring. Concerned about using their time efficiently, Rachel wondered why it was important to include their past in a discussion that she hoped would focus on their present and future lives. The therapist noted that when decision making becomes difficult, there may be factors related to the family of origin of one or both members of the couple that create anxiety and keep them at a standstill. The genogram could indicate areas of tension related to family messages they had received or family relationships that might be holding them back from making a clear decision about whether to have a child. The genogram could help to distill information related to their family backgrounds in a way that was relevant to their current lives and choices. Rachel nodded her head as if to say she believed this was possible in their case.

Invited to ask more questions, the couple agreed that they felt comfortable with the therapist and were willing to explore the links between their family backgrounds and current difficulties. The therapist encouraged them to ask about the process of their therapy at any time.

In this first encounter, the therapist addressed the couple's concerns by linking the presenting problem to the therapeutic process she envisioned. In the therapist's Bowenian framework, the goal was to help each member of the couple access their intellects as well as their emotions and adapt to change in a flexible manner as they made their decisions. Modeling how to take *differentiated stances,* the therapist remained open to their questions and discussed concerns about their therapy.

CREATING THE INITIAL GENOGRAM

To build a family genogram the therapist ideally needs three things: chart paper or a computer screen (Genogram-Maker Millennium, 2005) on which to draw the graphic; a set of representational tools, including lines, squares, circles, text, and symbols (Genogram-Maker Millennium, 2005; McGoldrick et al., 1999); and a set of interview questions to elicit the presenting problem, family dynamics, and relevant family history. Some therapists create the genogram while face to face with the clients, explaining the theory behind the genogram if couples are curious, as in the case of David and Rachel. Figure 3.1 illustrates the method for drawing family

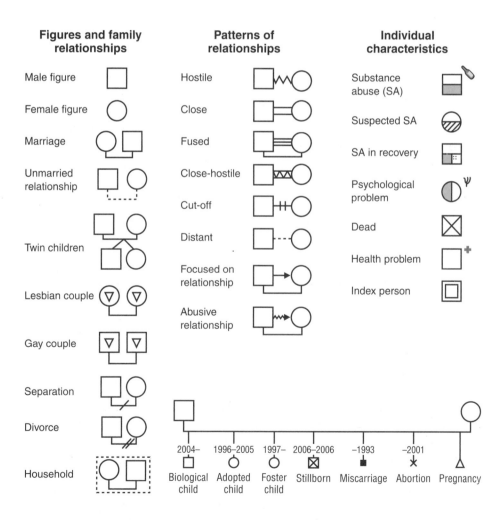

Figure 3.1   Genogram elements, representations, and symbols. © Sylvia Shellenberger, 2006.

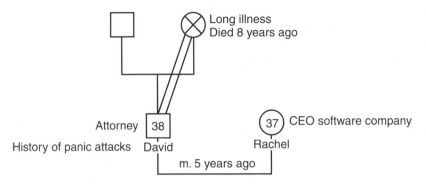

Figure 3.2   Rachel and David's marriage.

connections using the standard tools, the manner of indicating patterns of relationships such as closeness and conflict, and symbols or icons depicting individual characteristics such as substance abuse, psychological problems, and illnesses.

The therapist began the genogram interview by drawing David and Rachel as a
spousal pair and asking what brought them together (see Figure 3.2). Their strong
initial attraction was based on common interests of traveling and professional
ambition. Their 5-year marriage was marked by travels to remote areas of the
globe and accomplishments in their respective jobs. David was a successful attor-
ney who hoped to become a partner in the law firm in a few years. They had married in their 30s, after years of dedication to their respective educations and
careers. David's panic attacks, dating back to the time of his caring for his
mother during her long illness and her death, had subsided during these early
years of their marriage. The attacks began to resurface as Rachel and David
began in earnest to consider attempting to have a child. Rachel, too, described
heightened anxiety as she struggled with the decision to consider becoming a
mother. The couple hoped for help clarifying the decision and addressing David's
panic attacks before they again became debilitating. The initial genogram drawn
by the therapist is seen in Figure 3.2.

In this genogram, David, represented by a square figure, was a 38-year-old at-
torney who had a history of panic attacks. He was close to his mother (indicated
by double lines between David and his mother), who had suffered through a long
illness and died 8 years prior to their beginning therapy. He had married Rachel
5 years before therapy; she was 37 years old and a CEO of her own software
company. The line connecting David and Rachel is a solid line indicating marriage. Usually, the *m* for marriage is followed by the date of the marriage. If
there is a divorce or separation, the letter *d* or *s* and the divorce or separation
date is listed above this line.

EXPANDING THE FAMILY GENOGRAM IN
THE PROCESS OF THERAPY

When conducting a genogram interview, the therapeutic processes of assessment
and intervention are intertwined. For example, questions emerging from the in-

terview (see "Genogram Interview" later in the chapter) lead to assessment of family and individual functioning. Likewise, graphing the information learned about the couple leads to more questions for the couple to contemplate. The gaps in David and Rachel's genogram led to targeted questions from the therapist. For example, David never mentioned his father, and when asked by the therapist about his father's role in their family life, David became tearful and revealed that his mother portrayed her husband as an alcoholic who had beaten her on occasions of his drunkenness. His father abandoned them when David was 2 years old. She never remarried, dedicating herself to her work and to caring for David. When asked about his impressions of his genogram, David remarked that he had not realized how much emotion he felt about his father's abandonment. When asked how this intense emotion might be related to their current lives, David made the connection between the feelings his mother had about her abandonment by her husband, his own sadness about not having a father in his life, and his fear that Rachel might leave him. Rachel commented that she was beginning to understand the reasons David held on tightly to her, something she had found irritating and in the past had believed to be irrational.

When asked about her family, Rachel described an upbringing in which her parents were engaged in their separate professional activities. In response to a question about family members with whom she felt most connected, she named her older sister and her maternal grandmother. Rachel remembered how sad and empty she felt after her grandmother's death from cervical cancer when she was only 10 years old.

The therapist encouraged the couple to reflect on what they saw in their genogram. They were struck by the intensity of the losses they had each experienced at young ages. They held hands as they comforted each other through these difficult memories. The therapist queried how their early experiences might relate to fears about becoming pregnant. They named several fears. David worried that Rachel might abandon him after they had a child, and both were concerned that as parents they might continue to focus on their careers, not their child. Asked what they wanted to do about these fears, both said they wanted to find ways to calm their anxieties, regardless of whether they decided to have a child. David put forth his intention to disclose his preoccupations to Rachel so that they could talk over what was going on between them. Rachel committed to spending time assessing her career path to determine if and how she could make changes that would create time to spend with a child. Together, they pledged to find outlets for relaxation that might be calming as well.

The new genogram included information related to David's father and Rachel's family. Figure 3.3 illustrates several important points about drawing genograms. Siblings are typically drawn using a line from older on the left to younger on the right. There are two sets of relationship lines between David's father and his mother. One line indicates abuse in the direction of David's father toward his mother. The two vertical slashes across the abuse line indicate a cutoff between these two people. There are two ways of depicting a problem with alcohol misuse: One is to show the icon representing a bottle, the other is to shade in the bottom half of the figure.

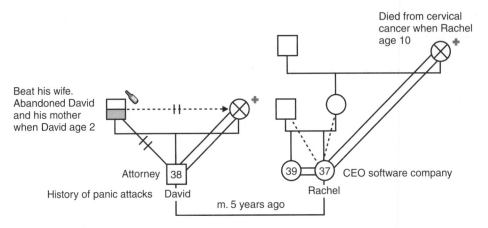

Figure 3.3   David's and Rachel's families of origin.

THE COUPLE'S ANXIETIES ABOUT PREGNANCY

Although they made progress between visits in following through with their commitment to relax more, Rachel's anxiety heightened as she began to explore ways she might change her life to make time for a child. When asked by the therapist to describe more fully her relationship to her parents, she related that her parents not only focused on their professional lives, but they rarely engaged fully with the children. On the genogram, this type of distant relationship is indicated by dotted lines (see Figure 3.4). Perhaps her ambivalence could be attributed in part to her parents' sole focus on their work lives to the exclusion of their children. David was more eager to have children than Rachel was and assured her of his involvement and his commitment to hire the help they would need to care for the child.

Rachel's fears about becoming a parent were not quieted by David's reassurances. She continued to feel great ambivalence about changing the trajectory of

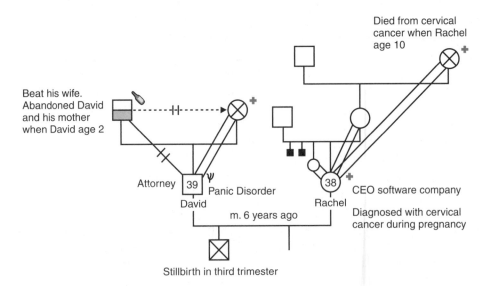

Figure 3.4   Stillbirth and cancer diagnosis.

her life from a focus on her work and David to bringing a child into their lives. During the process of therapy, however, Rachel became pregnant. She felt ill much of the time and resented the pregnancy. She noticed how the lack of energy affected her job performance. David was at first enthusiastic about the pregnancy, but later noted that Rachel seemed distracted and out of touch with him. His panic symptoms increased, and he became fearful of having another attack. Panic Disorder was diagnosed by the therapist. He admitted he was drinking more than usual as a way of self-medicating to avoid panic symptoms. The therapist made a referral to David's family physician for evaluation for medication.

During her third trimester, Rachel realized she felt no movement from the baby. She immediately went to the gynecologist, who determined that the baby was no longer living. Quite disturbing to Rachel and David, she had to deliver the dead baby.

PREGNANCY: A DIFFERENT VIEW

Rachel felt great remorse over her earlier feelings of not wanting to have a child and became determined to become pregnant again. This time, she and David were in synchrony about their desire for parenthood. She described feeling driven to be pregnant again. Genogram interviewing focused on possible family members and friends who could be helpful to them during this time of grief. The therapist asked Rachel what she knew about the pregnancies of her mother, other family members, and friends. Rachel remembered some vague mention by her mother that she had had several miscarriages before giving birth to her two daughters. The decision was made for Rachel to ask her mother more about her pregnancy losses. As Rachel and her mother explored this history, a new bond was formed between mother and daughter.

Soon Rachel became pregnant again. However, 6 weeks into her pregnancy, she was diagnosed with cervical cancer. The news was devastating to both David and Rachel and led to multipronged approaches to rid her of the cancer, including time off from work for both of them, efforts on the part of Rachel and her doctors to save the pregnancy, and more intensive therapy for both of them. The genogram reflects the trauma experienced by them with these major life-changing events. Symbols beside the figures of David and Rachel depict the psychological diagnosis (Ψ) indicating David's Panic Disorder and the cross (✚) representing Rachel's illness. In addition, the ⊠ depicts the death of their unborn child.

The therapist and couple explored possible plans for dealing with this current trauma. The therapist coordinated with David's physician regarding medication for Panic Disorder and with Rachel's physicians about their plans for managing her illness.

A DIFFERENTIATED RESPONSE TO TRAUMA

Even in the midst of crisis, David and Rachel maintained a hopeful attitude and reported success at keeping their fears in check. They attributed much of this forward vision to their therapy, which they believed helped them to be

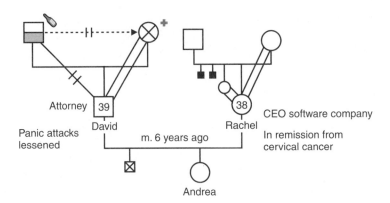

Figure 3.5   The family in recovery.

less reactive to these traumas. At the same time, Rachel believed that the therapy had helped her to forge an alliance with her mother, who became a great source of support during her pregnancy loss and battle with cancer. Within a year, Rachel and David became the proud parents of a baby girl, Rachel's cancer had gone into remission, and David's panic attacks had subsided (see Figure 3.5).

POSSIBLE USES OF EMDR

A therapist, who was trained in EMDR, could have chosen to incorporate it either by conducting the therapy herself or referring to another clinician. In addition to processing the current traumatic situations (the miscarriage and cancer), the genogram indicated the earlier events that were contributing to the present symptoms, including the ambivalence about having a child. Processing these events would be beneficial for the couple. For David, that would include targeting his father's abandonment and his mother's illness. His panic attacks and his fear of Rachel's leaving would be processed as well. For Rachel, useful targets would be her grandmother's death and some of the memories of her parents being distant and unavailable. Her current job-related anxiety would also be addressed. The EMDR three-pronged protocol would address the earlier events, present triggers, and templates for appropriate future action (see Chapter 1). The objectives of EMDR therapy would have been to deal with the painful emotions related to the current and previous crises so that the grief and trauma became integrated, opening the way for the couple to move forward.

GENOGRAM INTERVIEW

The following questions may be used as a guide for what to ask when creating an initial genogram and adding to it as therapy progresses. The therapist may ask these questions in a very different order from those listed here. This list is adapted from McGoldrick et al. (1999) and is meant to stimulate ideas about exploring important family domains.

   I. Ask for a description of the presenting problem from the point of view of each individual.
     A. Develop a time line of the problem from beginning to present.
     B. Ask what attempts have been made to solve the problem. (e.g., Have they looked to other family members for help, or to clergy, medical professionals, or friends? Have they tried therapy, medication, or other modes of treatment?)
     C. Ask what has prevented the problem from being solved.
     D. Ask what would happen if the problem were to be solved.
  II. Ask for a description of the current family.
     A. Members living at home (children, parents, spouses, others).
     B. Members living away from home part or all of the time.
     C. Recent changes in the family.
 III. Ask for a description of the family of origin of each partner.
     A. Parents, important caregivers during childhood, siblings, and siblings' families.
       1. Country of origin of parents and the influence the country of origin currently has on the family.
       2. Cultural or religious issues that are sources of conflict, connection, or strength in the family.
       3. Sibling birth order from oldest to youngest, including miscarriages and stillbirths.
       4. Parents and grandparents, noting other important relationships, such as with uncles or stepsiblings.
       5. Relationships that have resulted in separation, divorce, or remarriage.
       6. Family relationships that have particular meaning for the clients.
       7. Relationships with people close to the family who are considered like family.
       8. If there are adoptions or foster placements, ask who was considered the primary family.
  IV. Ask about previous significant partners of each client.
     A. Beginning and ending dates of relationships.
     B. Reason for ending of the relationships.
     C. Current relationships with previous partners.

     V. Inquire about children from previous relationships.

       A. History of the relationship to each child.

       B. Current relationship to each child.

       C. Current whereabouts of each child.

    VI. Inquire about the nature of significant relationships, such as closeness, conflict, abuse, cutoff (see middle column of Figure 3.1).

   VII. Ask about family rules.

       A. Are there rules about how members should fulfill their gender roles? (e.g., in some families, women are often chosen to be the caregivers of the elders.)

       B. Are there rules about coming into or leaving the family? (e.g., in some cultures and families, children are expected to live with their parents until they are married.)

  VIII. Note individual characteristics of significant persons (see righthand column of Figure 3.1).

       A. Strengths.

          1. Achievements, accomplishments.

          2. Positive relationships.

          3. Family, social, or community connections and contributions.

          4. Efforts to improve family life, such as recovery from substance abuse or participation in therapy.

       B. Other aspects of functioning.

          1. Work history.

          2. Education.

          3. Substance use or abuse.

          4. Psychological problems.

          5. Medical history and problems, including current prescription drugs.

          6. Family role (e.g., caregiver, financial provider).

    IX. Ask about past and current critical events.

       A. Trauma from war, natural disasters, harmful relationships.

       B. Acute or chronic illnesses.

       C. Untimely deaths.

     X. Ask about dynamic changes (positive occurrences that have led to improvements in family life).

       A. End of war, recovery from natural disasters, ending or healing of harmful relationships, acquiring new and more fulfilling job or avocational pursuit.

       B. Wanted pregnancies or births.

       C. Recovery from illnesses, substance abuse.

Case 2: Complex Family Genograms

Complex family configurations can be challenging. The interviewing process may take extra time, and drawing the significant connections may be difficult. But seeing these complexities is often extremely important for understanding the multigenerational dynamics and current struggles of the clients. In this example, an initial therapy session with María is described to show how complex relationships and dynamics can be handled. María presented for therapy on referral by her family physician, who was concerned that María was depressed. In the genogram interview (see Figure 3.5), the therapist asked who was living in the household. María lived at home with her husband, Hugh, and their three children; María's father, who had recently been diagnosed with Parkinson's disease; and her niece, who came to live in the home a year ago, after the death of Hugh's brother and sister-in-law, both by suicide. Asked about her role in her family, María resentfully said she was expected to do everything: cook, clean, wash clothes, supervise the children with their school work, all while she was employed full time. The therapist asked how María was coping with her many responsibilities, and she revealed that she was not sleeping or eating well, and she did not like going home after work. Although she was concerned about her son, José, who was failing in school and beginning to hang out with the wrong crowd, María felt unable to set limits or to discipline him. In her opinion, her husband was too strict with their son, criticizing José at every turn. Moreover, Hugh refused to discuss the situation with María, and he brooded most of the time the two of them were together.

When the therapist asked if María had anyone whom she considered supportive of her situation, she disclosed that she had begun to spend time with a coworker, Samuel, who was consoling about her difficulties. She admitted that they had gone out to have a few drinks after work on several occasions and that she found him attractive. She had not divulged her whereabouts to Hugh when he reached her by cell phone. Further, when asked by the therapist how much she drank, she admitted that she had more to drink on these occasions than she believed was healthy for her. Queries about histories of substance abuse in her family led María to acknowledge that her mother was a heavy drinker most of her life, and her mother's third partner also drank heavily. The drinking led to problems in and dissolution of her mother's significant relationships. When she saw the substance abuse highlighted on her genogram, María vowed to not let alcohol ruin her family life.

The therapist noted on her genogram the many changes experienced in her family in the past year. There were three deaths of close family members, her father's health status changed, she took in a new family member, and her son was failing in school. It was not surprising that María needed some relief from the intense emotional burdens sustained by her family. María expressed relief that the therapist understood her dilemma.

Next, the therapist encouraged María to pinpoint her family's strengths and accomplishments. She related the story of her sister-in-law's and brother-in-law's deaths. The entire extended families on both sides, including María's cousins, aunts, and uncles in Mexico and Hugh's parents in a neighboring U.S. state, rallied to support María and Hugh and the children whose parents had died. María was touched by the outpouring of concern but felt empty when the relatives left to go back to their homes. Together, the therapist and María set the goals for her therapy to include marshalling support on a regular basis from her extended family, improving the way she interacted with her husband and children, and evaluating further her recent drinking habits (see Figure 3.6).

As can be seen in the genogram in Figure 3.6, María was the index client, symbolized by a double circle. The dotted circle around the family members indicate with whom she lived at the current time. She had a conflictual relationship with her husband and a close relationship with her mother, who died in 2005 and who drank heavily. Her mother had three partners, shown by separate lines down and across from her figure. The first and second marriages, reflected by solid lines, ended in divorce. The dotted line to her third partner signified a relationship without marriage. This partnership ended in separation. María's mother had one child by her first marriage and one by her second marriage. María's husband had conflictual relationships with María and their son, José. He had a close relationship to his twin brother, who had died by suicide.

María's therapeutic course was not steady. At first, she hesitated to come to therapy because of her shame about having a relationship outside of her marriage and her drinking, which had become heavier during the past year. Genogram interviewing and family systems therapy were the primary modalities used. Over time, she came to trust the therapist, stopped the heavy drinking, and brought her husband with her to explore their marital difficulties. She began to act in a more differentiated way with her husband, standing up for what she needed from him as her partner and coparent. The children also were included in the

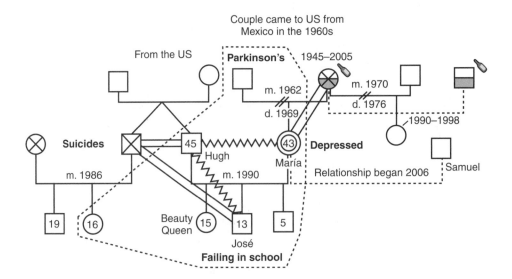

Figure 3.6   Critical events in María's family.

therapy. As his parents' relationship improved, José showed progress in his school performance. Each time a new family member came to therapy, genogram interviewing was undertaken for the purposes of joining with the new member and to incorporate their perspectives on their family history, any abuse, current relationships, and aspects of resilience. EMDR therapy could also have been used to enhance María's treatment. An exploration of her feelings of grief related to her mother's life and death and resentment about her overwhelming family responsibilities would have led to defining targets for EMDR therapy.

──────────────── **Case Example** ────────────────

Case 3: Adoption

Another complex type of family relationship for genogramming exists when there have been adoptions. Two drawings illustrate Marty's biological family (Figure 3.7) and adoptive family (Figure 3.8), both of Arctic cultural backgrounds. Marty was in recovery from alcohol and drug abuse. As can be seen, many members of both his adoptive and biological families abuse alcohol and drugs. A limitation of the genogram is that it is two-dimensional. It would be ideal to be able to picture both of Marty's families in one genogram. It is easy to imagine how cluttered his genogram would look if the two graphics were superimposed. Showing two separate families, as in these diagrams, seems to be the clearest way to represent his families.

In Marty's biological family, Marty and a younger sister were adopted away from the family. All family members but one were known to abuse substances. Marty's father abused his wife and Marty's older brother, Richard, who fought back. Richard finally killed his father, for which he was on probation at the time of Marty's interview. In Marty's adoptive family, neither of his parents abused substances; however, all but two of his siblings did. His adoptive parents were often in conflict, and Marty was abused both by his adoptive father and his oldest brother. Marty's brother went to jail for abusing Marty and committed suicide

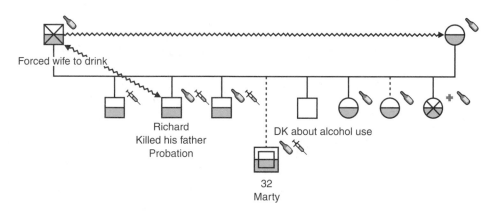

Figure 3.7   Marty's biological family.

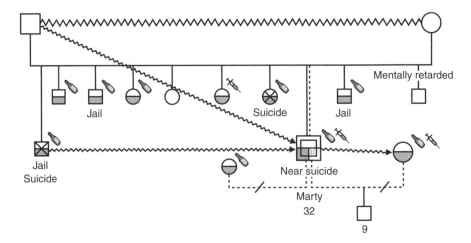

Figure 3.8 Marty's adoptive family.

while in jail. Marty admitted that he nearly committed suicide when he was 17 years old. He has had two significant relationships with women who abuse substances. He had a son with this second partner, but the slash mark across the line connecting them indicates the end of that relationship. In his interview, he identified his areas of strength as his fortitude to have survived in a hostile environment and his tenacity for managing his addiction. Marty was in residential treatment for substance abuse and hoped to soon begin family therapy in order to be allowed legally to parent his son. His intention was also to repair his relationship with his son's mother. EMDR and family systems therapy would be appropriate modalities to assist Marty in improving his family relationships and recovering from past traumas.

There are additional questions that might be particularly relevant for complex families, such as: Who did you consider to be your primary family? What were the connections that people knew about but did not discuss? Which partnership did your mother consider to be her most important? Clients' responses and the accompanying graphic depiction can assist clients and therapists to have a deeper understanding about the real nature of the relational system.

PRACTICAL ASPECTS OF GENOGRAMMING

As in María's and Marty's situations, most people come to therapy ready to tell their stories. In some cases, however, people are reticent to discuss information about their family's past or present lives. Reasons for nondisclosure include shame about some aspect of their current family life or their history, fear of legal problems if behavior is revealed, belief that the past has nothing to do with the current issues, or, as in the case of David and Rachel, wanting therapy to be carried out efficiently. Families often hide or deny traumatic events such as physical, sexual, or emotional abuse or neglect. In these cases, focusing on the present reasons for coming to therapy and drawing the genogram of the people mentioned will build trust with the therapist. The therapist might begin by saying, "For me to get a clear picture of what is happening in the situation you are describing, I'd like to draw a picture of it on this computer screen [or chart paper]. I imagine things will be clearer for you, too, if you see yourselves in this drawing. We will draw how you relate to each other, and we should be able to see what is causing problems for you. Reveal as much as you feel comfortable about the situations." Clients may have questions about whether this will become part of their medical or psychological record or whether the material will be confidential. The therapist will need to explain the limits of confidentiality and how files are handled in the practice. For example, the therapist may explain that if someone is being harmed, the authorities will need to be informed.

Some clients will be curious about the connections and patterns they are discovering in their family. They may want to draw their own genograms, interview other family members to learn more, and bring in new information they have discovered about their family. Therapists may encourage clients to read about family patterns and genograms. Books for the public include *The Dance of Anger* (Lerner, 1994), and *Genograms: Assessment and Intervention* (McGoldrick et al., 1999).

Therapists build trust with clients as the stories of their lives are revealed. Modeling differentiation for clients is the first step in leading them to take differentiated positions within their families. Therapists model differentiation by showing curiosity about why things happened as they have in this family and by communicating interest in their clients' struggles and expressing concern for their clients' lives. The atmosphere becomes one of joint exploration and discovery rather than judgment or shame.

ADAPTATIONS OF THE TRADITIONAL GENOGRAM

Traditional genogram interviewing may be augmented by using adaptations that have been developed for such purposes. For example, Kaslow (1995) developed a projective technique in which clients are just asked to draw their family. This allows clients to start at the most significant and logical place for them in their family history. After the genograms are drawn, the clinician asks a series of questions, such as the following:

- With whom did you begin? Why?
- Whom did you omit or exclude? Why?
- Whom would you like to eliminate? Why?
- Whom would you like to add? Why?

This process is intended to bring unknown or repressed patterns and connections into conscious awareness so that they can be dealt with in therapy.

Another adaptation is socially constructed genograms, where a broader assessment of the social environment is conducted (Milewski-Hertlein, 2001). Based on the idea that the relational system is more encompassing than the

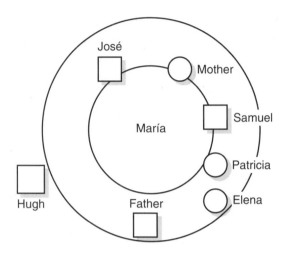

Figure 3.9 María's socially constructed genogram.

nuclear and multigenerational family, and that the idea of a family changes for people over their lifetime, the socially constructed genogram evokes information about the social system and the clients' relationships to this entity. Patterns and experiences relevant to the client are incorporated into the drawing, with clients drawing themselves at the center of a series of concentric circles. Clients are then asked to draw symbols for the people they consider to be family members, though they may not be biological relatives. They are to place the figures on closer or more distant concentric circles, depending on the nature of the relationship with that person. See María's socially constructed genogram in Figure 3.9, where she placed her coworker, Samuel, closer to her than her husband, Hugh.

For EMDR purposes, this social graphic also includes people clients consider important in their lives who are a source of distress. Indicating the source of the difficulties can provide useful targets among peers or authority figures. This construction is intended to be used in conjunction with the standard genogram to bring to the forefront patterns that are evident in social relationships.

Community genograms take an even broader view in order to understand the particular cultural strengths and contextual characteristics impinging on clients' lives. The objective of this process is to build on clients', families', and the community's capacities and resources. Clients are assisted in clinical work to analyze and act on external influences that have affected their lives. Progress in therapy is documented by the changing community genogram (Rigazio-DiGilio, Ivey, Kunkler-Peck, & Grady, 2005).

LIMITATIONS OF THE GENOGRAM

Factors that limit the usefulness of the genogram have to do with the types of information gathered during the interviews. The first type of information collected is factual, such as demographic information, dates of significant occurrences, and the life cycle stages of the family. The second type of data has to do with inferences about family functioning, such as the nature of key relationships, the family triangles, and multigenerational patterns. The reliability and validity of the genogram is limited according to the accuracy with which types of information are generated by the therapist and clients. Inaccurate information may be due to individuals' poor recollections or lack of knowledge of occurrences or their desire to keep secrets from the therapist or other family members (McGoldrick et al., 1999). Therapists may not ask certain important questions because of time constraints or for fear of causing a disruption in their relationship with clients. Although it would be much easier to evaluate the reliability and validity of the genogram if a standard protocol were used, much clinically important information would be lost (McGoldrick et al., 1999). Instead, it is imperative to maintain the integrity of the tool so that the perspectives of a variety of family members can be incorporated into the genogram, the clients and their therapists can consider a variety of explanations for new or repeated patterns, and shifts over time can be recorded. For this to happen, it is essential to maintain flexibility in the genogram interview and openness in generating themes and hypotheses and to use drawing mechanisms that allow for a changing family system.

DISCUSSION

The genogram has been shown to be a powerful therapeutic tool for family systems therapy and as an adjunct to other forms of therapy such as EMDR, Structural Family Therapy, psychodynamic therapy, narrative family therapy, and most of the other forms of family therapy described in Chapter 2. Genogram interviewing can be used to understand and to intervene with family systems of people of different ethnic and racial backgrounds, particular disorders and illnesses (e.g., substance abuse, Huntington's disease, HIV), social challenges (e.g., poverty, marginalization), and life crises (e.g., war, hurricanes). Through the genogram, EMDR targets may be identified and family system dynamics revealed. Using paper or software (Genogram-Maker Millennium, 2005; Relativity, 2003), the genogram may be drawn in the therapy room along with clients or kept by the therapist as an ongoing record of family functioning. A wealth of important family information may be seen at a glance on the genogram, including significant dates of births, deaths, critical family events; healthy and dysfunctional relationship patterns such as closeness, conflict, and abuse; and individual behaviors such as substance abuse, illnesses, and particular roles played in the family. Using genogram interviewing, the therapist and clients discover links between current issues and past family history, multigenerational rules or legacies, and areas of strength and resilience in clients. This information may be used for assessment, interpretation, and intervention.

REFERENCES

Bowen, M. (1978). *Family therapy in clinical practice.* New York: Aronson.

Carlock, R. S., & Ward, J. (2001). *Strategic planning for the family business: Parallel planning to unite the family and business.* New York: Macmillan.

Genogram-Maker (Version 1.0) [Computer Software]. (1985). Atlanta, GA: Humanware.

Genogram-Maker Millennium (Version 1.1.6) [Computer Software]. (2005). Atlanta, GA: GenoWare. Available from http://www.genogram.org.

Hockley, J. (2000). Psychosocial aspects in palliative care: Communicating with the patient and family. *Acta Oncologia, 39*(8), 905–910.

Jolly, W. M., Froom, J., & Rosen, M. G. (1980). The genogram. *Journal of Family Practice, 10*(2), 251–255.

Kaslow, F. (1995). *Projective genogramming.* Sarasota, FL: Professional Resources Press.

Kent-Wilkinson, A. (1999). Forensic family genogram: An assessment and intervention tool. *Journal of Psychosocial Nursing and Mental Health Services, 37*(9), 52–56.

Kerr, M. E., & Bowen, M. (1988). *Family evaluation.* New York: Norton.

Lerner, H. (1994). *The dance of anger.* New York: Harper & Row.

Liossi, C., Hatira, P., & Mystakidou, K. (1997). The use of the genogram in palliative care. *Palliative Medicine, 11*(6), 455–461.

McGoldrick, M., & Gerson, R. (1985). *Genograms in family assessment.* New York: Norton.

McGoldrick, M., Gerson, R., & Shellenberger, S. (1999). *Genograms: Assessment and intervention.* New York: Norton.

Milewski-Hertlein, K. A. (2001). The use of a socially constructed genogram in clinical practice. *American Journal of Family Therapy, 29,* 23–38.

Relativity (Version 3.0) [Computer Software]. (2003). Silver Spring, MD: WonderWare. Available from http://www.interpersonaluniverse.net.

Richards, W. R., Burgess, D. E., Peterson, F. R., & McCarthy, K. L. (1993). A psychosocial assessment tool for hospice. *Hospice Journal, 9*(1), 1–12.

Rigazio-DiGilio, S. A., Ivey, A. E., Kunkler-Peck, K. P., & Grady, L. T. (2005). *Community genograms: Using individual, family, and cultural narratives with clients.* New York: Teachers College Press.

Spoljar-Vrzina, S. M. (2000). Genograms of exile and return families in Croatia: A medical anthropological approach. *Coll Anthropology, 24*(2), 565–578.

Visscher, E. M., & Clore, E. R. (1992). The genogram: A strategy for assessment. *Journal of Pediatric Health Care, 6*(6), 361–367.

Watts, C., & Shrader, E. (1998). The genogram: A new research tool to document patterns of decision-making, conflict and vulnerability within households. *Health Policy and Planning, 13*(4), 459–464.

CHAPTER 4

EMDR Treatment of Family Abuse:
Eye Movement to "I" Movement

Marcelle Manon*

For my first 50 years, I was accustomed to emotional pain coming over me like waves in a turbulent sea, but it always subsided like the ebb and flow of the ocean. Then there came a point when the emotional waves no longer subsided, but became stronger, lasted longer, and became more intense. Finally, they were like a huge undertow followed by a great wall of pounding surf that hit hard and swept away my life, leaving a wake of destruction in its path. I could no longer function, yet went through the routine motions of work and home life and spent more and more time sobbing in an unstoppable way that I had not known before.

My physician had me take an extended leave of absence from work for clinical depression, and I entered a 5-day-a-week intensive outpatient program that included individual therapy, group therapy, anger management, and dealing with relationships and toxic work environments. Because I had already used therapy to deal with obstacles that inhibited my growth and happiness over the years, I welcomed the opportunity.

My individual therapist had been trained to use the Eye Movement Desensitization and Reprocessing (EMDR) approach, and we discussed using the method's

This chapter presents an inside view of EMDR narrated by a client who was requested to tell her story to educate clinicians and clients so that others might be healed. Ms. Manon's vivid account of her emotional history, along with the description of various memories targeted in treatment and the results of her processing sessions, provide an excellent illustration of the therapy. Her emotional upheaval and adult relationships are a reflection of the cauldron of abuse, deceit, and chaos intrinsic to her family of origin. As indicated by the Adaptive Information Processing model (discussed in Chapter 1), her symptoms were largely the result of the earlier negative experiences from childhood that were dysfunctionally stored in her brain. These memories had inherent within them the emotions and perspectives that generated her negative sense of self and inability to function happily in the world. The processing of the memories of these early events resulted in accelerated learning and a concomitant transmutation of her personal identity and self-efficacy. In Chapter 1, Shapiro comprehensively describes the EMDR procedures and protocols employed by the therapist and the AIP model used to guide the treatment. An addendum to the case by Kaslow elucidates the family systems perspective.
*Author's name is a pseudonym to protect identities of all involved.

"self-soothing" techniques. Though I had the ability to nurture others, it seemed as though I had never learned to nurture myself.

FAMILY BACKGROUND

My parents were married for 37 years. I was the middle child, with an older sister and younger brother. There was a large, multigenerational extended family on my father's side that mostly lived within walking distance or in close geographic proximity, and we saw them regularly.

Most of the traumas dealt with in EMDR were rooted in childhood and revolved around or involved my mother and, to some extent, my father and sister. Discussing each family member during therapy was difficult and caused anxiety and tears. I saw my mother as abusive, my father as living in his own self-created utopian world, where he was in denial of any abuse in our home, and I felt that my sister and I had been set up from childhood to be distant from one another and to have an adversarial relationship.

Our mother was the older of two daughters. She always stressed the importance of a firstborn child being a son and disclosed that she felt like a disappointment to her father because she was not male. She stated how unfair it was that her younger sister did not have the same gender burden and therefore felt her parents loved her sister more. My grandparents never expressed such thoughts to me, even though I was close to them until they were in their 80s.

The strength of my mother's feelings carried over to her children, and when her first child, my sister, was born and was not a male, my mother claimed that she was an even greater disappointment to her father (as well as to her husband and his family). She felt that my birth as a second female child made her life worse. It seemed that sometimes her issues with regard to her sister got confused when dealing with my sister and me. Her ranting about our "inferior" gender could last for hours and became both verbally and physically abusive, as exemplified by having our hair combed and brushed so hard that she would pull it out in clumps by the roots while we screamed and sobbed.

Finally, a son (my younger brother) was born, and she had the child she could love openly. She was a different person when he was present and cherished him throughout her life, which was a blessing for them both. He did not get caught up in the cycle of abuse.

She remained fixated on gender throughout the next generation. During my first pregnancy, she told me that if I did not have a son, she, my husband, my father, and my grandfather would never forgive me.

But her definitive statement about gender that stayed with me was the one made by her shrill voice reminding me over the years that she had given birth to "two mistakes and a son" and that she had absolutely no use for the second mistake. EMDR helped me identify and remove the pain from the issues that resulted from thinking of myself as a useless second mistake.

Mother was an intelligent, talented woman who was thin and had the most amazing wardrobe, with matching shoes, hats, and gloves for every outfit. She was heavily involved in our post-WWII community and was always impeccably dressed. She kept a busy social schedule, focused on building neighborhood centers and playgrounds as well as chairing committees for several charities. Publicly, everyone admired her.

But privately, she had a volatile personality. We never knew who we would find when we came in the front door. She could be nice, or she could be raving mad and wielding a leather belt. As a small child, I always hoped we would have company because she behaved well when other people were present. In those moments, I was so proud to be her daughter. The darkest times were when I was alone with her because that is when the abuse happened.

The postscript to our relationship is that in over 20 years since her death, I do not miss her at all—quite a sad reflection on one's relationship with one's mother. The EMDR process helped me understand that though I yearned for the All-American-Mom-and-Apple-Pie—life, it was neither my reality nor my fault that it did not exist in our home.

Dad was the youngest of three sons. He was intelligent, had a great work ethic, made friends easily, and was consistently referred to as a nice man by family, coworkers, and friends. His family was open about how he was always spoiled by his mother, and we saw that she continued to let him have his way as we were growing up. Sometimes when he didn't get his way, he had temper tantrums. A sister-in-law of his told me that, even in his 70s, he was still the self-centered boy she had met more than 50 years earlier. He was known for avoiding people, places, and topics that he disliked. Abuse in our home was probably in that category. If he didn't acknowledge it, it didn't exist.

My sister was 3 years my senior. We were close, and I still remember her wonderful laughter and playing with her at the beach when we were both very young. She was my fearless best friend. Then, when I was 4, seemingly overnight, it all changed—as though a wall went up. Laughter was replaced by an unnatural silence that descended on our house. Some things were not discussed with anyone, not even each other.

Yet it was my sister confirming this silence decades later that was key to my EMDR experience. She had reached a point in her own therapy where she questioned why she had never been angry at our father and remembered that I had expressed anger at him during my teens.

It was only the second time that she called to discuss our childhood during her decades of ongoing therapy. On the first occasion, she had phoned me to validate her memory of a Friday night ritual from our childhood. She then declared the subject closed, never to be spoken of again. I assumed that she wanted to avoid the memory because it brought up a terrible reality, which contrasted with the perfect childhood she had invented and described to others.

In her second phone call, years later, my sister asked about my adolescent anger toward our Dad. To explain this, I had to break the silence that had started decades earlier when, as a 4-year-old, I was sexually molested at nursery school. My sister's reaction was fast, and she shared her recollection. "Mom got a phone call, got mad, and went running out of the house and brought you home." We both remembered my clothing that day, that my dress and shoes were ruined because I had wet myself, that I was sobbing and begging Mother not to hit me anymore. Mother had sworn me to secrecy, but when Dad came home, I reached out to him for comfort. He was not there for me either. That was the first time I got angry with him and stopped believing that either parent would be there to protect me. My sister and I went on to discuss how the anger grew.

Though we shared our memories of that day, she was adamant that I accept that our childhood was wonderful and that Dad had made it that way. I did not agree, and she declared the topic closed. The silence that returned lasted until her death from cancer several years later.

Her fantasy childhood was even clearer to me after her death. I traveled to her memorial service where she lived, and many people who came to pay respects were unaware she even had a sister. There was not even a picture of me in the apartment where she had resided for 27 years. It did seem significant to me, however, that she had discussed my molestation with a cousin, who shared it with another relative, both of whom were in the mental health field.

COUNSELING AND THERAPY BACKGROUND

I began therapy as a teenager, when our parents decided that my sister and I needed it. Both parents refused to go to any sessions as they felt it was not a family issue and they were not the problem. We were just bad children—yet one bad child was class president and a straight-A student and the other bad child was thriving at a school for the academically gifted and in the all-city high school choir.

When this therapy stagnated, I entered a group at a mental hospital where I was the only one who was clean, sober, in school, and had not been to Juvenile Detention. So I learned new things from my group, though not what our parents had in mind, and I sought a path toward quiet rebellion. When things at home got worse, I ran away, straight to my maternal grandparents' or my maternal aunt and uncle's homes, which were always more loving environments. Once that started, therapy ended.

In college, two psychology teachers observed that I was floundering and offered help. I found that if I dealt with specific issues when I reached an impasse, it was possible to find viable alternatives, something I had not known. With the specific issue resolved, I could leave therapy and still return if another issue surfaced. Thus, I started dealing with problems one at a time. So, over the next 30 years, I returned for treatment of specific issues: postpartum depression, the breakup of my first marriage, blending our family during my current marriage, and so on. I viewed therapy as there to help me if I lost my way.

My sister and I differed on our views on therapy. She had sessions several times a week for about 20 years and was seeing two therapists when she died. Strangely, her death was the event that led me to EMDR because it opened a big black abyss to a profound depression like I had never known before. My life would forever change.

EMDR EXPERIENCE

Four years after experiencing EMDR, I evaluate EMDR as a great gift I gave myself to learn that I am an abuse survivor on many issues. With EMDR, I was finally able to do more than cope with the abuse. Now I am no longer a victim of it.

The first few sessions were based on discussing my background, learning what to do to relax and calm myself when I became tense, and laying the groundwork for the actual sessions that would deal with key trauma issues. I also identified a series of positive elements I desired to have in my life, for example, replacing existing negative thoughts (e.g., "I will fail") and related feelings with positive ones (e.g., "I can succeed"). We went over what was true and what was false about my life, taking into account the success of my second marriage rather than feeling like a failure because my first marriage ended in divorce.

I made a list of the specific targets that we would focus on during my EMDR sessions, both specific events and the broader category of distressing feelings. The targets included being a failure, being a disappointment, feeling dishonest, feeling lost all of the time, not feeling lovable, being crippled by fear, being labeled "damaged goods" due to molestation as a young child, coping with various forms of abuse, being inadequate, being told to not show that I am smart or people won't like me, and the conflict caused by having saved my mother's life while wanting her gone. All of these issues caused extreme distress.

Each target was addressed in one or more sessions. We began by identifying an image of the event with its associated negative thoughts and emotions. I rated these on the Subjective Units of Disturbance (SUD) scale from 0 to 10, with 0 being no distress and 10 the highest possible distress. Then we set a goal to replace it with a positive image and thought. This process required that I trust the therapist and myself enough to recall events; feel the sensations that were evoked; and hear, feel, and smell the memories. After identifying and rating the elements of the target event, I focused on these with all the related sensations, while moving my eyes back and forth, following the therapist's moving finger or pencil. This process was repeated as I processed the various aspects of the incident. After each set of eye movements, we talked about what I had experienced and what other images, memories, and feelings I gleaned through the process. This sometimes evoked raw emotion; there was nausea, inability to breath, and not being able to find my voice. We repeated the process of my focusing on the material while engaging in eye movements until there was significantly less stress.

We replaced the negative images and thoughts with positive ones (i.e., screaming voices with soothing words, being sent to my room with being cuddled). What was gained from each session was a more positive feeling about my own worthiness as a person. The session concluded with checking in on the sensations that I now felt about the trauma (i.e., Did I still want to throw up? Did I still feel like I couldn't breathe?). If I still felt these things to any degree, we continued until these sensations were gone. Finally, I evaluated the amount of distress and assigned a SUD rating to the trauma. It was usually 0 to 3, with 0 being the goal of having totally processed the trauma. I understood that the trauma could subside even more as time passed, which was an incredibly comforting thought.

Each subsequent session began with a review of the previous session and my progress. By the fourth session, I not only understood that I was making progress, but I accepted that my soul was healing. It became clear that after each session I felt a little less like my life was spinning out of control. Also, I was being empowered to reclaim the self-esteem and joy lost somewhere in early childhood. It seemed as though age 50 was not too late to begin.

A subsequent session focused on the traumatic events that had initiated my sister's first phone call. These were the ritual Friday night enemas that went back as far as I could remember and stopped around second grade. (I recall ranking this ritual about an 8 on the SUD scale.) Mother would fill an enema container with warm soapy water. First my sister would lie down on the tile floor in the hall bathroom and receive her enema. Then mother would fill the container for me. I would lie down on the tile floor while my sister voided her colon and got into the hot bath. We were told we had to hold the warm soapy fluid until we felt like we were going to burst. If we had an accident on the floor, Mother went ballistic and we were pushed into the feces and then had to clean it up. After I had voided my colon, I would get in the tub with my sister. Then Mother put a big electric space heater in front of the tub so we could not get out, and she left the room. Once, as a toddler, I remember still having to poop after entering the tub; I was too terrified to try getting out, so I pooped in the tub. My sister got upset and cried, and I was beaten. When Mother returned, she took my sister (who was between 5 and 8 years old) with her, leaving me alone in the tub. I remember hearing my sister crying and begging, "Mommy, please, no," but I did not understand why. Because my father kept his store open late on Friday nights, he was not home to witness or stop the ritual from happening.

For 4 decades, my sister and I never mentioned these events, even though we shared a childhood bedroom. On that phone call years later, my sister said Mother took her to the master bath, where she would lie down on the tile floor and make my sister give her an enema. My sister experienced the trauma when she freaked out at her sigmoidoscopy as the doctor put the scope in her rectum. This caused her to call for validation of the memory.

During EMDR, I got to talk about all of the memories related to the Friday night experiences. As well as the narrative of events, I had to experience and work through the sensations of the humidity hanging off the skylight, the coldness of the pink and green floor tiles, the sparks and hot electric smell from the brown heater, the pain and cramping from the fullness of my bowels, the squishy feeling of having my hands rubbed into the feces, and the terror of the huge enema tip going into me, the scalding hot water in the bath, the salty taste of my tears, and the fear of Mother's rage. Though my SUD number was high when we began, it diminished as I went through the sensations and replaced the thoughts with positive images and completed the process. This was extremely helpful when I went for my own sigmoidoscopy, and I did not experience any undue anxiety.

Another negative issue that we dealt with through EMDR was that I always felt dishonest. This stemmed from my parents calling me a liar. Even as a 50-year-old woman, I woke up every morning expecting to have to prove myself to be an honest person. This was particularly hurtful as I had worked hard to maintain my integrity and to live a life based on reality and honesty. Yes, it was true that as a child I had resorted to lies on occasion, but what were the circumstances that drove a little girl to see lying as a necessary part of survival?

EMDR helped me understand that I had started out telling the truth. An example of this is when our father asked, "Who broke the banister?" I replied, "Mommy pushed me down the steps and it broke when I fell down." He didn't believe me, and my answer made Mother angry, so she retaliated the next day with more abuse. So, though I told the truth, I was in worse trouble. I learned to say "I don't know" rather than answer him. In that little girl's mind, I was not lying but choosing not to answer. The way I had processed honesty was that adults would require a child to tell them the truth yet require the child to lie to other adults to protect them. It really confused me as a little girl.

So life became Dad's coming home from work on a day when mother had been abusive and the interrogation would begin: "How did you get that burn?" or "Who took your sister's shirt?" The true answer was Mommy—but the safer answer was "I don't know." That didn't work, and Dad would call me a liar and get really angry. Sometimes he'd lose his temper. Once he took a hammer, destroying all of my dolls and toys, except the ones I had hidden. Those were found and given to a cousin. I was no longer allowed to have toys or children's books. It reinforced my belief that neither of my parents could be trusted and that being truthful or saying "I don't know" didn't work in our house.

Through the EMDR process, I discovered that even as a child I was honest and reached out to other adults with the truth. One aunt said that as a small child I would tell her, "They are mean to me." She approached my parents, who told her I exaggerated a lot and had lied. After the EMDR process on this issue was completed, my integrity was reinforced when I checked with other relatives who recalled talking to my father about Mother and me. They also were rebuffed. Child abuse in the 1950s was not an acceptable topic, certainly not in respectable middle-class families like ours.

Also rating higher than an 8 on my SUD scale was the sense of going through life with the fear of getting lost. This fear had been a part of me since childhood, and though I have a great sense of direction, at the time of my therapy I resorted to relentlessly carrying maps, written directions, and a cell phone. In EMDR we began with the first time I actually remembered being lost.

I was about 3, and the family was at a lake. Dad was playing cards and smoking a cigar. Mother was sunbathing, and my sister (age 6) was watching me. I found something that I just had to show my father and wandered off to find him. I got lost, and the person who found me brought me to the refreshment stand, where I got ice cream and they put me on the loudspeaker saying, "Me, *Marcelle* looking for my Daddy!"

He came running, as did my frightened sister and our mother. I don't remember if Mother was angrier at me for wandering off or at my sister for losing me. She did wait until the next day, when my father was at work, to administer our punishments.

Within a few months, I wandered out the front door and was brought back by a neighbor who found me down the street. The punishment was being put in the coat closet with the camphor odor. Shortly after that, I got sidetracked on the way to the potty at nursery school, and that led to being molested.

During the EMDR session about the incident at the lake, I focused on the images: the smell and sound of the pine trees, the lapping of the water, and chasing the little tadpoles. I had caught one, and the reason I wandered off to find my father was to show him my catch. I can remember the heat, the coolness of the ice cream and the mess it made, hearing the loudness of the sound of my voice coming over the PA, and the smell of the Coppertone tanning oil. In processing the next incident, I remember the darkness inside the coat closet and the overwhelming smell of the camphor and not being able to breath. It was also very hot in the closet, and the coats were itchy because they were wool. This brought forward issues that I struggled with about dark places and claustrophobia.

The process was able to get me to self-soothe the little girl who I used to be and to reparent her the way I wanted. I accepted the reality that adults are responsible for watching over children and not expecting 6-year-old siblings to do so. I also finally understood that neither child had done anything wrong. Through EMDR I got to the point where camphor no longer makes me feel nauseated, I no longer feel I have to move when someone wearing Coppertone sits next to me, and maps are put away except on road trips. The SUD rating is now a 0.

I used EMDR to process a good deal of guilt. Because I grew up watching TV moms like June Cleaver and Harriet Nelson, my expectations made dealing with my mother that much more difficult. On the SUD scale, the fact that I had thoughts of wanting her gone was in the 7 to 10 range. Yet when that chance came, I saved her life, not once but twice, all the while wishing she would die. I used EMDR to help me deal with wishing she had died.

The earliest image of wanting her gone was of my sister and I sitting at the top of the stairs in our pajamas listening to our mother rant and scream at our father and threatening to leave. She packed up her things and got in her car. She left us behind. We were joyous and hugged each other. Within the hour she was back, crying that she had nowhere to go because she couldn't go back to her parents.

The first time I saved her life, I was home alone doing homework and she had been grocery shopping. She came home and was in the kitchen with her shoes off while she unpacked the groceries. I came down to help as she dropped a bottle. It broke and a shard of glass went through a major vein in her foot. Before I could get her to leave the shard in until an ambulance came, she had pulled it out, and blood spurted everywhere. I called for the ambulance and did basic first aid until they arrived. She lost a good deal of blood, and I had a lot of guilt because I had thought about not using first aid. It would have been so easy to leave her, but I found that an immoral choice.

The second time, I was again home alone doing homework. I heard her come back from her night class in our old Fiat and pull up to the back of the house. The engine kept running and the back door did not open, so I went down the stairs and found her in the driveway, slumped over the steering wheel with the engine running. Carbon monoxide was leaking into the cab of the car and could have killed her. I thought about leaving her there just a bit longer, but again I called the ambulance.

In EMDR, I dealt with the guilt I felt for having thoughts of not saving her. During the process, the visuals and other sensations from the incidences were felt, sorted through, and replaced with the feeling that I did make valid choices and I am a good person. It touched on other areas we had also identified. I could see that I had worth and had not been crippled by my fears. I proved that I was far from inadequate. I was anything but a failure. The negative things I had been told about myself and had come to believe were not based on reality.

A very confusing trauma that needed to be resolved was the molestation. I was already at the point where I could mention being molested without discussing the details, but struggled with understanding why, as it was not a violent rape, it was so traumatic—it was, after all, just inappropriate touching. Processing the events with EMDR allowed me to understand that the trauma was more than just that moment.

We worked through the sequence of events prior to, during, and after the molestation. I then understood that the distress levels I felt involved several issues, with the highest level being about how the matter was dealt with once discovered. That issue changed my life and how I defined myself as a woman and a human being.

We started with the image of a happy little girl who loved going to school and having a teacher and classroom, just like my older sister did. We had recently bought pretty new dresses that I could twirl in, and I had a head full of curls. I was wearing one of those dresses that day. Mother walked me to school. Toward the end of class, I had to go to the bathroom. I was sent alone and ran into the janitor. He told me I looked pretty in my new dress and he wanted to show me something in his closet. He wanted to touch my curls and give me a hug. He started to touch my body, and he asked me to touch him "just like a doctor and nurse" examine people. He had his penis out for me to touch and his hand in my underwear. Then the woman who ran the school opened the door.

She grabbed me, took me to her office, and called my mother. She was yelling and told me not to move. She left me there and was yelling at someone in the hall. Mother came in, winded from running, and was angry and screaming at the woman and me. I still had to go to the bathroom, but every time I opened my mouth to ask permission, I was told to be quiet. Eventually I couldn't hold it anymore and peed on the floor. Now Mother was really mad and spanked me, something she rarely did in front of other people. She grabbed me by my arm and marched me home, not even stopping at my classroom for my things. She yelled all the way and periodically grabbed my arm, lifted me off the ground, and spanked me repeatedly for ruining my new dress and shoes. By then I was cold and didn't understand what I had done. I was sobbing so hard I could not catch my breath and wanted to stop. She would not stop but walked faster. My legs hurt, and she started dragging me and bruised my arm. I was warned not to tell anyone about anything that happened. My sister was home from school when we arrived and wanted to know what was wrong. I wanted to tell her but didn't want to get hit again, so I never said a word. I tried cuddling with my father when he came home, but before I could tell him, Mother let him know I was bad and had ruined my clothes and the carpet at school, and he angrily sent me straight to bed.

Then she had my curls cut off. My new pixie haircut had cowlicks sticking up all over—it looked awful! She allowed only pants to be worn to school and made me wear orthopedic shoes. I wondered what I had done that I couldn't be pretty anymore.

She kept me home for days, telling me that I was "damaged goods," a term I did not understand. She instructed me never to tell anyone because if people knew they wouldn't be allowed to play with me or like me. Also, no decent boy would ever marry me. She said my family would not want me around if they knew. So I distanced myself from most of my family because I did not feel worthy of being with them, but mostly because I was afraid that if I talked to them, the secret might slip out. Looking back, although I may not have felt totally worthless, I definitely felt worth less than the rest of my family.

Through the EMDR process, I felt the sensations of the total experience—among them, the depth of feeling unworthy, the joy of the twirling in my dress, and the disbelief of seeing my hair chopped off. I got to shed the tears that had been stopped and break the rest of the silence that had fallen around the whole traumatic episode. Once the SUD level was lowered, I started to understand that the trauma was more than the molestation; it was the devastation from the events that followed. These events were fertile soil in which the negative thoughts and feelings could flourish and become the foundation on which I had built my life.

Working through this trauma and doing the sets with experiencing the images, sensations, feelings, and thoughts was difficult, but the relief was worth the process. The results were amazing. EMDR allowed me to be free for the first time to see the potential for changing many of the things that were rooted in negative thoughts and feelings about myself. I developed a sense of real liberation and am pleased to acknowledge that this early molestation episode and its ramifications now rank a 0 on the SUD scale. That trauma can no longer define who I am, as it had for almost half a century.

Since completing the EMDR process, I have concluded that because I felt unworthy and damaged from the age of 4 until I was past 50, just about every decision I made during that period was based on feeling that I did not deserve happiness. This included two marriages with abuse issues, for I believed that, like my parents, anyone who loved me was entitled to abuse me.

Post-EMDR, I can look back at the reasons I found it acceptable to have a husband who insisted women could not say no to a husband wanting to have intercourse and who would force me to have sex, or a spouse threatening to turn me into a lampshade or bar of soap (like the Nazis did in WWII) if he was mad at me. I could clearly see why I tolerated spousal abuse and considered drug and alcohol abuse acceptable behaviors at home.

Acknowledging any of those abuses prior to going through the EMDR process would have been a 10 on the SUD scale. Now they are a 0 and just a part of how I became the person I am today. The difference is also clear in my ability to set boundaries and make better choices. No other form of therapy was successful in getting me to that point in my development. Other therapists had focused on the gender bias that was part of my mother's issues, and some were even convinced it was sibling rivalry with my brother. EMDR was crucial to understanding how being born female to a woman who wanted a son affected my life. I also learned not to give that idea the power to continue.

One recurrent theme that I see post-EMDR is that I had a multitude of illogical thoughts from a distorted childhood. High among those is the old adage "Children should be seen and not heard." This became the concept that good children stay put and bad children move about. So I learned to sit in silence for hours. The downside was that I was afraid to make noise or move and denied myself normal body functions, like going to a bathroom. I stifled coughs and silenced sneezes. I had a hard time controlling my asthma, which at times was uncontrollable due to allergies or emotions. There were many times that I felt as though an elephant was sitting on my chest and I could not breathe. At those times, I made noise and therefore was told that I was a bad child. Even during the EMDR process, my breathing issue surfaced. My therapist told me repeatedly to remember to breathe because I would forget to do so. Periodically, I find there are times I still have to remind myself that it is all right to make noise breathing and that I will still be a good person.

EMDR helped me to understand that some thoughts are not valid, and I can neutralize them simply by breathing and smiling. So today, I can use the techniques learned in EMDR on an ongoing basis because something from the past may creep into my present. However, these incidents are minor, and I am able to cope easily with them because of the changes that I experienced with EMDR. I am able to refocus on the positive beliefs that I now have about myself and use some of the self-calming and relaxation techniques that I learned in the first few EMDR sessions.

This occurred last weekend, when I was asked why I do not make long-range plans. The EMDR techniques allowed me to remember events 50 years ago in a soothing way. I remembered being taken to a physician over a period of about 4 years. During a visit he told my mother that there was a good chance I would not live to adulthood. I was in the room at the time. As a result, I did not plan on being around long, so made only short-term plans. Using the EMDR techniques, I was not afraid to remember, and the recall was complete with the building location, the smells of the office, the car we arrived in. I even remembered his name and the medical procedures that both my sister and I had, which shocked my dad when I shared that part of the memory with him. The whole experience was liberating. Not only had I lived to adulthood, but I have lived long enough to have my first grandchild this year and make long-range plans to be involved in its life.

Through EMDR I have identified other illogical thoughts that I've carried with me since childhood, such as: (a) If the abuser tells me he is hitting me because he loves me, then I deserve the abuse; (b) I am a bad person because of something another human being did to me; (c) I can do nothing right because it is not done to someone else's expectation; and (d) I deserve less in life than others. These thoughts had organized my life so that each morning when I woke up, I had to start the day from the bottom of the barrel of unworthiness as though no 2 days were connected. Now, almost 5 years since I completed my EMDR sessions, I wake up feeling that each day is a good day and I don't have to start over re-earning my worthiness. Being female is a wonderful part of who I am and not just a gender classification.

As I drew conclusions from EMDR therapy, one thing became clear that I had not experienced in any other therapy: *I am an abuse survivor.* I can hold my head high and know I am no longer vulnerable to an abuser. I will not tolerate it in my family or among my peers or stay in a toxic work environment. Because I no longer doubt myself and my choices are well thought out, people cannot burden me with guilt or negative messages. I heal a little more each day and am learning that my intuitions are good. There is no chance that I will ever feel crippled or incapable of making decisions for fear that I am capable of making only poor decisions.

In the present, I am able to deal with the reality as part of a natural reaction to a situation. A recent example of this is our daughter's diagnosis of and treatment for cancer. Not only is this a severe medical problem, but due to the type of cancer, she will not be able to fulfill her dream of a career of flying Coast Guard helicopters.

This is happening in conjunction with other situations, including potentially life-threatening health concerns, our house being on the market and not selling, my spouse's truck accident, a child in law school, and a child whose wedding will be taking place hundreds of miles away. Five years ago, I would have spiraled into a depression that would have found root in my feelings of failure and inadequacy. Today I can see that although the totality of these events may seem overwhelming, I can allow myself to find the joy in them. My daughter will be a cancer survivor and find another career path, my husband will heal and the truck will be repaired, our child is doing well in law school, and we'll happily celebrate our son's nuptials anywhere.

I still carry my original trauma list in my daily binder to remind me of my good mental and emotional health. On a day when I feel a little down, I turn to the list and see that no matter what the current situation may be, it does not have the power to return me to that dark place in my past. I now have the skills from EMDR to nurture myself and keep things in perspective and the willingness to seek the proper help again if I encounter any of life's true traumas.

To my therapist, who was my guide and companion through EMDR: I will always hold a spot in my heart for you, but all names, including yours, were omitted in this anonymous piece. Your professionalism, kindness, and gentle encouragement remain a part of my healing. You were present in spirit as I was able to retell my life events. Without you, I would still be living with the silence and these words would not have been possible. Many thanks!

ADDENDUM

Analysis of Family Dynamics and Functioning from a Family Systems Perspective

Florence W. Kaslow

(In this commentary, occasionally I allude to the theory on which a specific interpretation is predicated, in parenthesis, and the reader can refer to Chapter 2, where the theories are discussed.)

Clearly, the author grew up in a highly dysfunctional family that presented itself to the outside world as if all within were fine. The mother could be charming and was perceived as such in the community through her numerous involvements. The father was pleasant and superficial, although often physically and emotionally absent. He used avoidance and denial as his major coping mechanisms (psychodynamic theory and ego psychology). He refused to consider this daughter's allegations that his wife was abusing them and colluded with his wife and eldest daughter to keep the family secret hidden from the outside world. Thus, he offered no support or protection to the author. To those of us who use a family relational diagnosis, the mother would be considered to have an Axis II Personality Disorder, probably falling in the borderline area with histrionic features (American Psychiatric Association, 1994; Kaslow, 1996). Within the family constellation she vacillated between expecting the two girls to be close to each other, in that they shared a bedroom and their bath, and yet setting them up against one another so they could not tell each other important bits of information; she also engaged in splitting the girls off from one another and their father, often leaving this daughter feeling alone, scared, and isolated. This family resembles many dysfunctional families that exhibit Axis II symptomatology of abuse, cruelty, secrecy, manipulation, explosive rage, deceit, denial, schisms, and confusion and make one another feel damned if you do and damned if you don't. These were certainly among the characteristics exhibited by the author's family.

In Chapter 6, Madrid writes that it is urgent that maternal-infant bonding occur immediately upon birth and continue thereafter, prior to the attachment phase (psychodynamic, object relations, attachment theory). Rather than experiencing bonding at a basic primitive physical level, the author as an infant was beset by rejection; instead of unconditional love, it appears she felt like a hapless and unwanted mistake—just because she lacked a penis. And so the trauma began almost at birth and was continually replicated and reinforced.

It appears that the author's mother believed that her father and her husband only valued male children and devalued female children—and by extension, girls and women. Her mother had internalized this view to such an extent that she herself lacked self-esteem and was so fixated on this gender issue as the core factor in achieving a positive sense of self-worth that she seemed to loathe herself and her first- and second-born children, just because they were girls.

The weekly enemas seem to have been administered sadistically—not because the girls were ill, but in a ritualistic, repetitive manner that was painful for and odious to these two young children. That the mother also forced the older one to give her an enema each week (making her leave the younger one alone in the bathtub and go with her, screaming, "No, mommy, no") is horrific to contemplate. At once sadistic and masochistic, one wonders what kind of sin she is trying to expiate, to punish herself and the children for. The sin of not bearing sons? If she believed this was so essential for being acceptable, she had a severe cognitive distortion, perhaps an exaggeration of a preference she thought her father had, which she long perpetuated, instead of refusing to assert her own independent thinking that these ideas were just not acceptable and that she and her daughters *were* worthwhile human beings in their own right.

We can deduce that the mother's guilt and shame must have been enormous. She was careful to engage in these abusive acts only on Friday nights, when her husband worked late and there was no one else around to observe her and curtail her intrusive, hurtful behavior. It continued until her son was born; perhaps then she felt fulfilled or vindicated, or both, by being able to give birth to the coveted male baby. It is not possible to determine if the mother's obsession with having a boy was in fact a demand placed upon her by her father, and/or her husband, or one that she put upon herself, as an exaggerated version of the hope of many people of her father's generation that having a son as an offspring was a blessing more desired than having a daughter. Such a belief has remained true in the vast majority of Chinese and many other Asian families into the twenty-first century. That the woman's sister allegedly did not feel stigmatized or devalued because of her gender seems to indicate that the father did not dislike females per se. It is also refuted by the fact that the author went on to become fond of and close to this same maternal grandfather. So there appears to have been a serious cognitive impairment operating in her mother that may or may not have been transmitted intergenerationally (Bowenian and contextual theories). This distortion was later successfully corrected in the EMDR therapy when the patient was helped to see herself anew as valuable and good, not as defaced, besmirched, and worthless.

Despite all of the family pathology, we also realize the author had some very real strengths to draw on and should ponder where these came from. How else would she have managed to return to school after the molestation by the janitor and subsequent humiliation by school officials and her mother, who embellished the trauma and punished her rather than soothing the terrified child, and still gone on to be an excellent student? She had to have been quite bright and very determined to do well, despite her unhappy, conflicted home life. Further proof of her fine intelligence and courage exists here, in this very chapter, which is so well written, so sensitively and thoughtfully retold and analyzed. She appears so appreciative of finally having had the chance to engage in therapy *when she wanted to* with a skilled EMDR therapist who brought her peace of mind, an opportunity to recast her life more positively, to self-soothe, and to rework her second marriage so it could be transformed beyond abuse to become loving and mutually honoring.

Also, she recognizes and pays tribute to her maternal grandparents and her maternal aunt and uncle, her mother's younger sister and her husband—all of whom were there for her with love, affection, and a place to stay when she ran away from home. She could not tell them why, or she would have gotten punished for revealing the unspeakable secret of the abuse, so she told them, "I'm just unhappy and I'd like to stay here for a few days." They called her parents and said she was safe, and she knew she had found herself a much needed day or two of affection and respite.

Obviously, Ms. Manon has gone through at least several losses early in her adult life. She mentions that her mother died about 20 years ago; her first marriage, an abusive one, ended in divorce. Throughout the years her father remained detached, casually peripheral, and emotionally unavailable. Her second marriage, also initially abusive, sounds like it may have been shaky when she was nearly 50 years of age. But it was her sister's death that triggered her decompensation. We know that once her sister entered therapy, she continued to convey very little; probably she still felt too constrained to talk about how they had been mistreated by their mother, as they had not been close since they were very young, and because of an old prohibition. They had had little contact over the prior 4 decades until she started to deal with repressed memories, and this spurred her to call the author only two or three times to see if what she remembered really happened.

In her narrative, the author seems baffled as to why her sister's death became the pivotal event that shattered her ability to continue maintaining her tenuous hold on reality and motivated her to seek therapy. This time she fortunately found someone skilled in EMDR.

My interpretation of the timing, or the answer to the *Why then?* query, is that Ms. Manon was frequently accused of lying or exaggerating to cover the heinous acts of others. The only one who could bear witness to and validate the reality of her sad early life story was her sister. With her sister's demise, there was no one left, or so she feared, to say, "Yes, it really happened. It was not your imagination. You did not make it up. You are not crazy." And because your dad says it did not happen and it did not happen to your brother does not change the fact that it did happen to you.

Postscript

Subsequent to reading the chapter and speaking to the author to offer editorial feedback, I told her that her narrative had evoked several responses and wondered if she might be interested in hearing them. They are included here because they add a little more on how a family systems therapist might have intervened in conjunction with the EMDR therapist if the patient were willing to go further in her treatment. She definitely was, and decided to pursue them.

The main suggestion was that she talk over some of this with her aunt, who is still very much alive and with whom she has always maintained a good relationship. The veil of secrecy is no longer necessary. Her husband is already privy to all of this information. Both she and her husband followed up with lengthy phone conversations with the aunt. The aunt, though startled at the depth and extent of her nightmare, bore witness to the following facts:

• Ms. Manon's beloved maternal great-grandmother brought the custom of giving everyone enemas for almost any ailment from Eastern Europe. The aunt also had been subjected to them, and despised them, but her own mother never used them ritualistically, and the aunt did not pass this on to her children. She found the practice odious.

• When her niece did run away to hide out at their house, she did complain of abuse. They dismissed it as adolescent rebellion, as it was such an unacceptable and unthinkable behavior that they did not believe the abuse really happened. So they offered tea and sympathy but did not try to intervene to protect her. Her aunt expressed regret for being so naive and not being more attuned at that time.

• Her father was portrayed as a superficial Mr. Nice Guy, never deeply emotionally involved with his children, and was not perceived as someone who could be engaged in any relationship of great emotional depth. A suggestion might have been made to invite him in for a two-generation family of origin session. Her brother also could have been included. The author says this was tried, but neither believe in therapy, especially since she and her sister turned to it and it became her aunt's profession.

• The aunt had a warm and mutually loving and respectful relationship with her father. She did not perceive him as macho or as thinking men were preferable to or better than women. Checking this out further validated the author's ability to formulate her own valid impressions.

Obviously, family secrets that camouflage abuse, violence, distortions, shameful behaviors, and parental irresponsibility in the form of silent collusion and shirking the duty to protect one's children from harm are all reprehensible. EMDR offers an opportunity to reinvision oneself being born in a happier way into a caring family in which one is loved and nurtured unconditionally and learns to self-soothe and see oneself in a much more positive light. It is indeed a therapeutic gift. Perhaps as the author continues to find inner peace and self-respect, she can do the same with her children and find a way to heal the one major rift she alludes to, when she engaged in behavior that lacked integrity. Perhaps this will be the next milestone in her healing journey.

REFERENCES

American Psychiatric Association. (1994). *Diagnostic and statistical manual of mental disorders* (4th ed.). Washington, DC: Author.

Kaslow, F. W. (1996). *Handbook of relational diagnosis and dysfunctional family patterns*. New York: Wiley.

PART II

Attachment Problems

CHAPTER 5

Treating Attachment Issues through EMDR and a Family Systems Approach

Debra Wesselmann

John Bowlby, the founder of attachment theory, came to view the attachment between infant and mother as a psychological bond in its own right. In the 1940s and 1950s, as he observed the dramatic effects of long parental separations on children's well-being, he concluded that the nature and stability of a child's attachment relationships had a direct impact on the developing personality. In the decades following, attachment theory was expanded as researchers observed that the quality of attachment in intact families varied with the level of parental sensitivity (Bowlby, 1988).

The difficult behaviors exhibited by children who meet the criteria for a diagnosis of Reactive Attachment Disorder (American Psychiatric Association, 1994) can be challenging to both parents and professionals. The diagnostic criteria include markedly disturbed and developmentally inappropriate interpersonal behaviors combined with a history of pathogenic care. Although not a diagnosable disorder, the term "anxious" or "insecure" attachment describes the quality of attachment of young children who are not readily comforted by the presence of their parents during an experimental situation designed to elevate their anxiety. An anxious attachment status appears to increase the risk for emotional and behavioral problems during childhood and adolescence and to be related to low parental sensitivity and responsiveness during infancy (Ainsworth, 1982; Main, Kaplan, & Cassidy, 1985). In a study by the National Institute of Child Health and Human Development (NICHD) Early Child Care Research Network (2004), affect dysregulation in toddlers was found to be associated with an insecure attachment status and later social, learning, and behavioral problems. Among a group of boys referred to a mental health clinic for behavioral problems, 80% were found to have an insecure attachment status, compared to only 28% in a nonclinical control group (Greenberg, DeKlyen, Speltz, & Endriga, 1997). Another study found that passive withdrawal and aggression in elementary school children, especially boys, were associated with current life stresses and insecure attachments (Renken, Egeland, Marvinney, Mangelsdorf, & Sroufe, 1989).

In a study of mother-teen problem solving, adolescents with insecure attachment showed higher levels of anger and avoidance in comparison to secure teens

(Kobak, Cole, Ferenz-Gillies, Fleming, & Gamble, 1993). Among a group of adolescents faced with risk factors such as low income, insecurely attached teens exhibited less social competence and higher levels of both externalizing and internalizing symptoms compared to the secure group (Allen, Moore, Kuperminc, & Bell, 1998). Another adolescent study found teen suicidal ideation to be strongly associated with a disorganized attachment status (Adam, Sheldon-Keller, & West, 1996). Overall, children and adults with disturbed childhood attachments appear to have difficulty reflecting on or regulating their internal state (Fonagy et al., 1997).

Comparison of Attachment, Adaptive Information Processing, and Family Systems Models

Utilizing the point of view of three models, attachment, Adaptive Information Processing, and family systems, can enhance the clinician's understanding of attachment-related symptoms. Although the models hold shared views, each brings an additional piece of the puzzle to case conceptualization and treatment planning.

Attachment Theory

Bowlby (1944, 1973) first recognized the significance of the mother-child attachment relationship when he discovered high rates of early attachment separations in the histories of juvenile delinquents. In later studies, he observed serious negative effects from lengthy hospital stays without parental contact (due to contamination fears) on young children, including superficiality in the child's relationships and higher rates of delinquency long after reunification with parents (Bowlby, 1973; Robertson & Bowlby, 1952).

Trained as a psychoanalyst, Bowlby developed his theory of attachment in the context of the object relations school of psychoanalysis. Both object relations and attachment theories emphasize the importance of the early mother-infant relationship and view mother-infant interactions as directly influential on interpersonal functioning later in life. However, from the object relations perspective, the mother as love object is tied to the infant's primary need to feed at the mother's breast, whereas attachment theorists view the infant's attachment to mother as primary, not secondary to the need for oral gratification. Bowlby described attachment as vital to the infant's survival as it motivates the infant to seek closeness with the mother (Ainsworth, 1969).

Bowlby's colleague, Mary Ainsworth, studied attachment patterns related to quality of parental sensitivity. She began her research with mother-infant pairs in the 1950s in Uganda (Ainsworth, 1967), where she developed an assessment procedure called the Strange Situation, which involves the mother leaving the year-old infant with a stranger and then returning to the child. Through her studies, she discovered that the infants of sensitive, emotionally attuned mothers developed secure attachments. They confidently explored their environment and returned to the mother for comfort as needed.

Ainsworth (1967) observed that infants whose mother was less sensitive and responsive to the infant's cues developed one of two categories of insecure attachments: ambivalent/resistant or avoidant. Infants classified as ambivalent/resistant in their attachment to their mother appeared excessively clingy and fussy when she returned during the Strange Situation. Their demanding ways were found to be adaptive, however, as their mother was observed to be inconsistent in meeting their emotional needs. Conversely, infants categorized as avoidant in their attachment to their mother appeared unconcerned about her whereabouts, even after she returned. The lack of distress shown by the avoidant infants also appeared to be adaptive, as the mothers of these infants were observed to be uncomfortable with expressed emotions and more able to tolerate closeness when their infant remained emotionally impassive (Ainsworth, 1982; Grossmann, Fremmer-Bombik, Rudolph, & Grossmann, 1988; van IJzendoorn, 1992).

Sroufe (1988) found that by school age, securely attached children were viewed by teachers as cooperative, and ambivalent/resistant children were typically perceived as overly needy, clingy, and sometimes angry. Avoidant children were viewed as aloof, overly independent, and sometimes hostile.

A fourth category, attachment disorganization, was identified when researchers recognized that a small number of observed children exhibited fearful behaviors upon reunion with the parent, including freezing, covering their eyes or mouth, spinning, and flapping their hands. In studies involving maltreated infants, attachment disorganization was found to be strongly associated with abuse (Carlson, Cicchetti, Barnett, & Braunwald, 1989; Main & Hesse, 1990; Main & Solomon, 1986). However, in studies of nonabusive families, attachment disorganization in infants was also found to be linked to unresolved loss or trauma in the parent and associated parental behaviors or symptoms that were in some way frightening to the infants (Lyons-Ruth & Block, 1996; Lyons-Ruth & Jacobvitz, 1999; Main & Hesse, 1990; Main & Solomon, 1990; Schuengel, Bakermans-Kranenburg, van IJzendoorn, & Blom, 1999). By school age, disorganized children appeared to have either caretaking behaviors toward adults or punishing and controlling behaviors (Cassidy, 1988; Lyons-Ruth, Alpern, & Repacholi, 1993).

Attachment style tends to be transmitted intergenerationally. Consistently, researchers have found a 70% to 80% correspondence between attachment status in parents and attachment status in their children (Grossmann et al., 1988; van IJzendoorn, 1992). Benoit and Parker (1994) observed attachment status transmitted in families through three generations with the same consistency.

Adaptive Information Processing Model and Attachment Theory: Shared Views

Bowlby's (1989) Internal Working Model (IWM) of attachment theory and Shapiro's (2001) Adaptive Information Processing (AIP) model share the view that early life experiences are profoundly influential over perceptions and emotions in later life. Bowlby theorized that children's early experiences involving their primary attachment figures have a significant impact on their developing

IWM, that is, their perceptions related to self-worth, the trustworthiness of people, and their view of the world as safe or unsafe (Main et al., 1985). Similarly, Shapiro proposed that when a distressing childhood event is inadequately processed, the memory network containing the related thoughts, images, emotions, and sensations can be triggered by situations in one's current life that are in some way reminiscent of the earlier event.

The AIP model provides a framework for conceptualizing how parents' unresolved, upsetting memories may lead to attachment disorganization in their children. When a parent's experience of closeness with her child taps into the dysfunctionally stored experiences of her own childhood loss or trauma, the related distressing emotions, cognitions, and sensations may be reexperienced by the mother. Therefore, closeness with her child may lead to upsetting thoughts, sensations, and emotions that interfere with her ability to respond sensitively to her child's needs, which in turn may create a felt sense of insecurity in the child. A parent with acute distress related to triggered memories may exhibit facial expressions, voice tones, or other types of emotional and body responses that are frightening and disorganizing for her child.

Family Systems and Attachment Models: Shared Views

Both family systems and attachment models hold the view that styles of attachment and interpersonal behaviors within families, once established, are self-reinforcing and persistent (Bowlby, 1989; Haley, 1963; P. Minuchin, 1985; S. Minuchin, 1974), even across generations (Bowen, 1978; van IJzendoorn, 1992). Marvin (2003), and Stevenson-Hinde (1990) recognized that the categories of attachment—secure, resistant, avoidant, and disorganized—correspond to the four family patterns of closeness and distance observed by family systems theorist Salvador Minuchin (1974): adaptive, enmeshed, disengaged, and chaotic. The adaptive family has appropriate boundaries, allowing members both connection and autonomy, consistent with families who exhibit secure attachments. The enmeshed family is "too close" due to diffuse boundaries between members, consistent with families who exhibit resistant/ambivalent attachments. Disengaged families have rigid boundaries and lack connection, consistent with the signs of avoidant attachments. The chaotic family has erratic boundaries and may share traits with families showing attachment disorganization.

S. Minuchin (1974) observed that healthy families have a hierarchy in which the parents hold most of the power. In a healthy hierarchy, the children respect the power of their parents and also view them as comfort givers. More conflict is experienced in families that lack an appropriate hierarchy. Poor quality attachments interfere with a healthy family hierarchy, as children with a disturbed attachment are unable to fully trust the parent. Consequently, they do not look to the parent for comfort or respect the parent as an authority figure. They lack a sense of "I am the little one, you are the big one, and I can depend on you."

Established family boundaries and hierarchy may become disturbed when new members join. For example, a child bringing an attachment disorder to a blended, adoptive, or foster family may introduce a chaotic pattern of relating to a previously stable and adaptive family, impacting interpersonal behaviors within the family system.

Treatment of Attachment Issues

Researchers studying attachment status in adulthood through the use of the Adult Attachment Interview (AAI) identified a number of adults who held a secure attachment status in adulthood despite acutely disturbing attachment experiences in childhood (Hesse, 1999; Pearson, Cohn, Cowan, & Cowan, 1994). It appeared that these individuals had somehow processed and resolved their early distressing attachment experiences, allowing them to "earn" a secure attachment status. Like children of lifelong secure parents, the children of adults with an "earned secure" attachment status were securely attached, thus breaking any intergenerational transmission process of insecurity that may have existed.

The "earned secure" attachment status may be synonymous with the well-functioning state of an adult who has achieved differentiation, as described by family systems theorist Murray Bowen (1978). Bowen asserted that an individual who lacks differentiation from his or her family of origin naturally projects the original family's patterns onto the spousal relationship and the parent-child relationship; self-differentiation leads to freedom from early pathological dynamics.

Eye Movement Desensitization and Reprocessing (EMDR; Shapiro, 2001) can help clients differentiate from early family of origin patterns by reprocessing distressing early memories. In numerous studies, EMDR has been shown to be an effective method for resolving distressing memories in both adults (Ironson, Freund, Strauss, & Williams, 2002; Lee, Gavriel, Drummond, Richards, & Greenwald, 2002; Power et al., 2002) and children (Chemtob, Nakashima, & Carlson, 2002; Jaberghaderi, Greenwald, Rubin, & Zand, 2004). The EMDR protocol is described as facilitating the natural information processing system, integrating more adaptive thoughts and beliefs related to the event, and relieving affective and somatic distress (Shapiro, 2001). EMDR can help both parents and children process dysfunctionally stored material created in early childhood, including negative affect, somatic responses, and negative beliefs such as "I am unlovable," "Others cannot be trusted," "Closeness is not safe," and "I will be abandoned." The reprocessing of stored negative material related to unresolved loss or trauma may allow parents to have more positive experiences of closeness with their children and remain more responsive to their needs. Similarly, EMDR reprocessing of stored negative material with children may allow them to have more positive experiences of closeness with their parents.

Family systems therapy and EMDR therapy are different but complementary approaches to improving attachment relationships. EMDR can remove the obstacles to affectional bonds within an individual, creating a window of opportunity for closeness. But that window of opportunity may close if the family is not ready to reach out and embrace the family member in return. Instead of supporting and encouraging change, established negative interpersonal patterns within the family system may sabotage it. For example, EMDR may help an adopted child resolve anger and mistrust of caregivers related to earlier experiences, but the child's newfound feelings of trust and desire for closeness will be frustrated if the adoptive parents continue previously established habits of distancing and disciplining with anger. Family therapy can help the entire family establish new patterns of physical affection, emotional closeness, and positive discipline that will reinforce the child's intrapersonal changes. Similarly, EMDR may help a parent let go of feelings of mistrust and anger rooted in the past, but family therapy may be needed to help the family support those changes by developing new family behaviors related to expressing feelings, listening, resolving conflict, and having fun together.

THERAPY PROCESS

The following are some general treatment strategies combining a family systems approach with an EMDR approach, helpful in working with families affected by disturbed parent-child attachments:

- Develop a trusting relationship with each member of the family.
- Identify distressing memories related to attachment that are affecting the child or parent. (These memories may be targeted later with EMDR.)
- Put family therapy strategies into place to increase healthy family behaviors such as care giving, care receiving, communicating, listening, and empathy.
- Engage parents in their own individual EMDR treatment as needed to remove observed blocks in the parents' capacity to develop or repair affectional bonds with their children.
- Coach parents to nurture and hold the child in session, and use bilateral stimulation with the child and parents to strengthen positive affect and sensations associated with care receiving and care giving.
- Reprocess the child's distressing memories using EMDR, and coach the parents to hold the child during the desensitization phase to create a nurturing experience and help with emotion regulation.
- Use EMDR to target and reprocess present triggers for the child and/or parent and build a positive template for patterns of future relating.
- As the child and parent experience successes at home, use bilateral stimulation to strengthen related positive feelings and sensations. Some children have difficulty accepting praise and misbehave following success experiences. In this case, bilateral stimulation may increase tolerance for praise and feelings of success.

Phase 1

The EMDR approach follows eight phases of treatment (Shapiro, 2001). Phase 1, History Taking, typically includes inquiry as to client and family complaints, mental status, and overall readiness for treatment. In addition, the therapist can assess the quality of the attachment relationships within the family system by asking the family member or members completing the interview how they would describe the various relationships in the family and note relationships that appear close, overly close, overprotective, distant, controlling, or abusive. The therapist should look for problems in the hierarchy, that is, problems in care giving or care receiving, setting of limits, and acceptance of authority. A genogram (Kaslow, 1995; Kerr & Bowen, 1988; McGoldrick & Gerson, 1988) can help conceptualize the full generational story as the clinician asks about relationship problems, separations, trauma, and losses in the history of the child, parents, and grandparents.

The therapist should also inquire as to any medical or situational complications experienced prenatally and during birth or postpartum, involving either mother or child, which may have interfered with bonding (Main & Hesse, 1990; Madrid, Chapter 6). In the case of adoption, it is important to gather information about birth parents, reasons for relinquishment, placement prior to adoption, and adjustment following placement. The therapist should also listen for recent situations that may have created family stress and interfered with closeness or trust, such as domestic abuse (Stowasser, Chapter 12), separation or divorce (Klaff, Chapter 14), drug or alcohol abuse, recent trauma or losses, or family stressors such as job loss, working two jobs, or moves.

Phase 2

During Phase 2, the Preparation Phase, the therapist begins establishing the office as a safe place for the family to explore issues and make changes. From the first meeting with the family, the therapist should create a therapeutic alliance by communicating concern for the welfare of each family member (Byng-Hall, 1999).

Sometimes a child strongly desires to connect with his parents but cannot tolerate the feelings of vulnerability associated with the traditional methods of connecting through comfort seeking or approval seeking. He may then misbehave in an attempt to reject, hurt, or irritate his parents. The child's misbehaviors and angry power struggles with the parents help the child feel connected to the parents—a feeling he desperately needs—while he simultaneously avoids feeling vulnerable. The parents' repeated angry responses therefore strongly reinforce the child's provocative behaviors. The therapist can help the parents understand that at a deeper, more primitive level, the child is acting out of a double bind.

The parents' angry reactions to the child's provocations can be decreased through the use of reframing techniques that relabel the child's defiance (Marvin, 2003), and the parents' changed perception serves to reduce power struggles. Parents can also be taught to interrupt the angry power struggle by surprising the child with a paradoxical response. For example, parents can encourage the symptom (Madanes, 1986) by responding with amazement or admiration to the child's artistry, creativity, or skill in tantrum throwing or excuse making (Keck & Kupecky, 2002). The parents can also learn to give the child consequences for his misbehaviors along with expressing sincere sorrow and empathy for the child's poor choices and the unfortunate outcome (Cline & Fay, 1992; Levy & Orlans, 2000).

Care giving and care receiving between parents and child can be encouraged by coaching the parents to hold or snuggle close to the child while in the office (Hughes, 1997; Keck & Kupecky, 2002). The child may be asked to listen to the parents as they give the child loving affirmations. The therapist can then ask the child and parents to notice the related positive affect and sensations, while the clinician employs bilateral stimulation with both child and parents (tapping, eye movements, or auditory tones) to strengthen positive feelings, internalize the positive messages, and develop tolerance for the feelings related to closeness.

Because secure attachment is associated with emotional attunement, emotional communication work is an important component of Phase 2. For example, one family member can be instructed to talk about feelings uninterrupted for 1 or 2 minutes, while the listener is instructed to then paraphrase what was said. The speaker can then be asked to rate the accuracy of the paraphrasing from 0% to 100% and repeat anything that was left out of the paraphrase. The speaker and the listener should then switch places. This kind of communication work can increase empathy and understanding between parents and children or between partners.

Prior to Phase 3, the therapist should also guide the child or adult preparing to begin EMDR by visualizing a "safe place" and reinforcing the safe image with bilateral stimulation. Later, the safe place can be used whenever it becomes necessary to close an incomplete EMDR session. An imaginary container can be similarly installed to hold the upsetting emotions and images between sessions.

Phases 3 through 8

After a sense of safety has been established both in the office and within the family system, specific events in the child's or parent's history that may have led to affects or cognitions blocking a sense of trust, self-worth, and security in relationships can be targeted and reprocessed with EMDR. Specific targets are sometimes difficult to identify when children or adults have suffered more covert or chronic trauma. In such situations, the therapist should look for representational memories: those memories that seem to be most triggering in the present and representative of the overall situation.

During Phase 3, the Assessment Phase, the use of cards or posters illustrating facial expressions associated with various emotions can help the child who has difficulty describing how she feels. The parent can be coached to gently help the child identify feelings and beliefs, thus increasing the parent's sensitivity to the child's feelings. Prior to beginning Phase 4, the Desensitization Phase, the therapist can prepare the parent to hold or cuddle the child in a nurturing manner during the EMDR reprocessing. This provides an excellent opportunity for the parent to provide comfort while the child is in a vulnerable, more receptive state, increases the parent's emotional attunement, and also helps the child remain regulated.

Although EMDR typically facilitates the child or adult client in his or her own processing, blocks to processing occasionally require the therapist to unobtrusively introduce new material or a new perspective through *Cognitive Interweaves* (Shapiro, 2001, pp. 249–276). This situation is not uncommon during

EMDR work with children, as children often lack the information they need to make the cognitive shifts. If a parent is providing supportive holding of the child during EMDR, the parent can be utilized to help provide Cognitive Interweaves when necessary. For example, if the child is unable to move beyond self-blame, the therapist may turn to the parent and ask, "Mom, can you think of any situations in which it is okay for an adult to harm a child?" This provides the parent an opening to respond emphatically, "Of course not! It is never all right for an adult to harm a child!" thus supplying the child with information he needs to successfully shift perspective. Simultaneously, the parent is reinforced as caregiver and authority figure in the child's eyes.

Phases 5 through 8—Installation, Body Scan, Closure, and Reevaluation—are followed according to the standard protocol (Shapiro, 2001).

The Three-Pronged Approach

EMDR is a three-pronged approach addressing past, present, and future. After past experiences are reprocessed, current experiences to which negative associations have been developed for children or their parents should be targeted and reprocessed. Current situations that trigger negative reactions on the part of children with disturbed attachment status may seem surprisingly benign. For example, receiving comfort, receiving a compliment, achieving a success, or participating in a traditional family celebration may trigger a negative reaction in a child who has learned that closeness is not safe or that positive experiences do not last. After reprocessing memories and current triggers, the child or parent can be guided in imaging future successes, while bilateral stimulation is utilized to strengthen the positive associated affect, sensations, and cognitions. Similarly, each time the parent or child reports a success experience, such as a calm response to a tough situation or a positive experience of closeness, the clinician can strengthen the associated positive affect, sensations, and cognitions with bilateral stimulation.

CASE EXAMPLES

Case 1: Jack and Foster Mother

Jack, age 7, was brought to therapy by his foster mother because of his severe behavioral problems. Jack and his 3-year-old biological brother had been placed with the foster mother 4 months earlier after two prior foster placements had failed. The foster mother was divorced and had two grown daughters. The boys had been out of their birth home for close to a year because of abuse and neglect by their birth mother. Their birth mother had since been incarcerated for illegal drug activities, and the state was taking steps to terminate her parental rights.

Jack's symptoms met the *Diagnostic and Statistical Manual of Mental Disorders* (*DSM-IV;* American Psychiatric Association, 1994) criteria for Reactive Attachment Disorder, Posttraumatic Stress Disorder, Oppositional Defiant Disorder, and Attention-Deficit/Hyperactivity Disorder; he was being treated for the last with a stimulant medication. His foster mother reported that Jack was having frequent out-of-control rages. On some occasions, the rages were triggered when his demands were refused; at other times, Jack awoke in an agitated, irritable state and exploded without reason. He was destroying property; he had broken objects in the home, torn chunks of wallpaper off the walls, and urinated down a heating vent. He did not comply with instruction or redirection and did not respond to rewards and consequences. Jack clearly did not respect his foster mother as an authority figure, nor did he accept her comforting or nurturing. The foster mother appeared capable of nurturing and providing comfort, as evidenced by her good caregiving with the 3-year-old.

During the Preparation Phase of EMDR, the therapeutic relationship with the foster mother was central. She needed to know that the therapist clearly understood what she was going through, and it was also important that she trust the therapist's expertise. Jack, on the other hand, needed to know he could not provoke the therapist or control the therapy, and he also needed to feel understood. This was accomplished through empathy, humor, and the setting of clear boundaries.

Jack's misbehaviors were reframed by explaining to the foster mother that Jack engaged her in angry control battles to connect with her, without triggering intolerable feelings of vulnerability. Jack's misbehaviors were also reframed for him. Knowing that he had a need to feel powerful and in control in order to feel safe, the therapist let Jack know how sad it was that his "emotion brain" was in control of him and hurting him. Sympathetically, the therapist reminded Jack how much time he spent serving disciplinary consequences when he could be having fun. The therapist also told Jack, again with great sympathy, that she hoped he would get stronger soon, so that he could overcome his emotion brain and make the choices that would give him a happier life.

The foster mother was taught how to use a paradoxical approach to Jack's misbehaviors to break the power struggles. She learned to thank Jack for misbehaving; because he received chores as consequences for his misbehavior, she was getting much more housework done. At the same time, she showered him with sympathy for missing out on so much playtime and reassured him lovingly that he was a smart boy and would learn to make better choices soon. This allowed the foster mother to provide comfort when Jack was attempting to provoke anger, and it gave ownership of Jack's problem behaviors to Jack. The foster mother also learned to make light-hearted comments in response to Jack's attempts to manipulate, such as "Nice try!" (with a genuine smile). When he raged, she responded by complimenting him in a sincere voice on his excellent "technique" and "artistry."

After putting these strategies into place, bilateral stimulation was utilized for resource strengthening. The foster mother was asked to hold Jack in an infant position, and Jack was instructed to notice the feelings of physical comfort in his body while he listened to bilateral tones through headphones until he was completely relaxed. In addition, the therapist provided bilateral stimulation to the foster mother with alternating taps, while she observed her own positive feelings and sensations associated with holding Jack. Next, Jack was asked to listen to nurturing messages from his foster mother while she continued to hold him in her lap and he continued listening to the bilateral tones. Jack and his foster mother were instructed to continue cuddling together at a regular time each day at home.

At the following session, while he was held by his foster mother, the therapist guided Jack in creating a safe place, which, in his case, was an imaginary tree house. Jack also created an image of a giant metal trunk to hold all of his upsetting memories and feelings between sessions. Both images were strengthened with auditory bilateral stimulation.

Following the Preparation Phase, two of Jack's most traumatic representative memories were targeted and reprocessed with EMDR. The therapist asked Jack's foster mother to hold him during the reprocessing to aid in emotion regulation and to provide comfort while he was feeling vulnerable. The first memory that Jack processed involved waking up in the middle of the night to discover that he was completely alone in his birth mother's apartment. The second involved a severe beating with a belt. *Negative Cognitions* related to both memories included "I am bad," "I am unlovable," "I am not safe," and "I cannot trust." During the Installation Phase, Jack was able to install "It wasn't my fault," "I am lovable," and "I can trust my new mom to take care of me, I am safe now." Jack accepted nurturing from his foster mother at the end of each session. Immediately following the completion of the EMDR trauma processing, the foster mother noticed that Jack's pattern of waking up first thing in the morning in an irritable and explosive mood had stopped.

Six months into the therapy, Jack's birth mother's rights were terminated, and the foster mother started the adoption process. Jack's feelings of grief and loss surfaced, along with feelings of guilt and disloyalty toward his birth mother. His foster mother told him that one of the reasons she loved him was because he was a loving boy who loved his birth mother, which gave Jack permission to love them both. EMDR was used to help him process his feelings of loss and grief.

After completing the work with past events, current and recent triggers were reprocessed. For example, the arrival of a new foster brother triggered jealous outbursts, and being told "No" often triggered an oppositional response. Therefore, these situations were targeted with EMDR. EMDR was also used to install and strengthen positive images of future holidays and other family celebrations. As his foster mother and Jack began reporting success experiences, auditory bilateral stimulation was used to strengthen access to the associated positive affect and sensations.

One session was devoted to the reading of a story (see Lovett, 1999) about Jack, written by the foster mother with the guidance of the therapist. The story described how Jack was overcoming his past beliefs and behaviors and discovering love and safety in his life today. Bilateral stimulation was provided to strengthen the feelings of empowerment created by the story. To increase positive experiences of closeness at home, Jack and his foster mother continued to read the story together at bedtime.

Many sessions were devoted to the important work of helping Jack verbalize his feelings with his foster mother and helping her attune to Jack and provide

Table 5.1   Pre and Posttreatment Incidents Documented over One Month

	Physical Aggression	Arguing	Whining	Ignoring a Direction	Leaving a Task Incomplete
Pretreatment	6	47	62	28	98
Posttreatment	0	9	10	2	8

nurturing and comfort. The foster mother reported Jack to be increasingly cooperative and affectionate, and he sought her regularly for comfort. After 14 months of therapy, the adoption was finalized. Regular weekly therapy was concluded, and Jack and his foster mother were switched to maintenance therapy as needed.

Table 5.1 shows the frequency of behaviors as documented by the foster mother for 1 month prior to therapy and for 1 month after completing the regular weekly therapy. Reported numbers for the month prior to therapy are probably lower than actual numbers, as Jack spent weekends at respite care that first month where he was not under observation by the foster mother.

The synthesis of EMDR and family therapy provided effective intervention for Jack and his new mother. EMDR removed the blocks to the development of affectional bonds, and the family therapy helped Jack and his mother become emotionally attuned, break negative, entrenched relational patterns, and establish adaptive behaviors.

Case 2: Julie and Her Mother

Julie, age 13, was brought to therapy by her biological mother because Julie had been defiant at home, skipping school, and spending all her time with friends. Julie's mother was involved in individual EMDR therapy, working to resolve her experiences of childhood neglect and emotional abuse. Julie's mother and father had divorced when Julie was 3 years old, after it was discovered that Julie had been molested by her father. She had had no further contact with him. Julie had one older sister. During Julie's first therapy session, both alone and with her mother, she was stubbornly silent.

Julie's symptoms were consistent with the *DSM-IV* criteria for Oppositional Defiant Disorder (American Psychiatric Association, 1994). It was hypothesized that she had developed a disorganized attachment related to Mother's unresolved trauma as well as Julie's early trauma.

The therapy process was similar to that of Jack and his foster mother, except that Julie's mother had attachment issues of her own. Probably because of the work Mother had completed thus far in her own individual therapy, she was able to admit readily that she had never been very affectionate with Julie, and she was willing to try to do whatever was asked of her. Mother's own EMDR work had helped remove negative affect, sensations, beliefs, and reactions, which may have interfered with her ability to be sensitive and affectionate with Julie in the past, but she now needed very directive coaching in family therapy to repair intentionally the damaged bonds in her relationship with her daughter. The therapist worked with Mother on developing a list of nurturing messages to give her daughter prior to the session with the two of them. In session, the therapist coached Mother to hold her daughter and then to share the nurturing messages with her, while the therapist strengthened Julie's associated positive sensations and affect with bilateral stimulation. Julie was quiet but tearful throughout the session, but then was eager to repeat the session the following week. The first holding and nurturing session was videotaped, after which Mother and the therapist watched the videotape together. Mother was able to critique herself, and she noticed that Julie had curled up on her lap "and looked like she was 3 years old." The therapist acknowledged Mother's observations and stated that Julie's regression would give Mother a chance to make up for the bonding that was missed when Julie was small.

The nurturing session was repeated several times as part of the Preparation Phase. Finally, Mother held Julie, providing comfort and emotion regulation, while the sexual abuse was reprocessed using EMDR.

Following the reprocessing, Julie became much more verbal. She stated that she felt closer to her mother in the sessions, but she asked if they could try to get closer at home. Julie, her mother, and the therapist brainstormed ideas. Finally, both agreed to eat dinner together each evening without the company of television and to use the time to discuss the day. They also agreed to snuggle at bedtime, looking at old family photo albums and sharing family stories. When therapy was terminated, Julie was having no problems with school attendance, was cooperative at home, and continued to seek time with her mother.

Case 3: Ben, a Stepfather

Ben came to therapy for the first time shortly after his marriage to Gail. The therapist had worked with Gail in the past. She had two adolescent boys from her first marriage. She had called for an appointment because Ben was becoming increasingly angry with her two sons.

Ben had grown up in foster care in South America. He had been physically and sexually abused by an older brother, who had also lived in the foster home. As an adult, Ben had developed an alcohol addiction, but he had been sober for the prior 2 years. He had never been married before. It was hypothesized that Ben held unresolved memories in relation to his past attachment loss and trauma and that his past traumas were interfering with his ability to develop a positive relationship with Gail's sons.

As part of the Preparation Phase, the therapist guided Ben in the "affect bridge," a method utilizing present affect to bridge to an earlier experience associated with present-day reactions (Shapiro, 1995; Watkins, 1971). First, Ben was asked to bring up a situation with the boys that had caused him to become angry and to allow the recent situation to become vivid in his mind. Ben was then asked to notice the anger he was feeling, pay attention to the associated sensations in his body, and let his mind "float back" to childhood. Ben immediately thought of a situation in which his older brother had been abusive to him.

The brother had been around the age of Ben's two stepsons, and the exercise helped Ben understand how his past was affecting his responses with the boys.

Following EMDR resource development work, Ben's early experiences were targeted and reprocessed with EMDR. This was followed by family therapy. For example, when the boys complained that Ben never played with them, he explained that he had started working in the fields when he was 5 and had never learned to play. The boys agreed to teach Ben how to play some games. In the weeks following, they taught him to play card games and pool, increasing positive experiences of connection and fun between them. Ben described new-found feelings of closeness to the boys, and he reported that his anger outbursts had ceased.

DISCUSSION

Children diagnosed with Reactive Attachment Disorder and children with an insecure or disorganized attachment status may exhibit internalizing and externalizing symptoms that are extremely challenging to both parents and professionals. There are many roads to disturbed parent-child attachment relationships. For example, children may have an insecure attachment due to the insecure attachment status of their parents, or they may have attachment disorganization due to a parent's unresolved trauma or loss. An adopted child may suffer from attachment disorganization caused by early maltreatment, and members of the adoptive family may exhibit negative interpersonal patterns in response to the child's symptoms. A foster child may suffer from Reactive Attachment Disorder caused by parental abuse and multiple foster home placements, and children living with their parents may exhibit attachment related symptoms due to early painful medical interventions and lengthy hospital stays.

Bowlby's (1988) Internal Working Model (IWM) is consistent with the EMDR Adaptive Information Processing (AIP) model in that both recognize the influence of an individual's earliest relationship experiences on patterns of interpersonal relating in later childhood, adolescence, and adulthood. Bowlby observed that early distressing experiences with caregivers can lead to a negative IWM, that is, negative perceptions related to others, self, and the world. The negative perceptions can then become a self-fulfilling prophecy. For example, a child's mistrust of others and feelings of unlovability can lead to sullen withdrawal and angry acting out, inviting negative reactions from the people around him or her—and further reinforcing the child's negative perceptions.

EMDR (Shapiro, 2001) can resolve early trauma and loss and allow a child or adult to break free from old patterns of responding to experience current relationships in a new way. To prevent established negative patterns in the system from sabotaging positive changes made by individual members, family therapy can be utilized to interrupt negative patterns, change unhealthy boundaries, and increase communication, empathy, care giving, and care receiving. Whether poor quality attachments are inherent in the family system or are the result of events outside the current family, the integration of family therapy with EMDR can help the system adapt to and support positive changes in family members.

As shown in the three case studies, with appropriate interventions, a family affected by poor quality attachment relationships can be helped to break free from negative entrenched patterns related to mistrust and insecurity and to develop more secure family bonds. Once established, the new patterns can become a healthy legacy for the family's future.

REFERENCES

Adam, K. S., Sheldon-Keller, A. E., & West, M. (1996). Attachment organization and history of suicidal behavior in adolescents. *Journal of Clinical and Consulting Psychology, 64,* 264–272.

Ainsworth, M. D. S. (1967). *Infancy in Uganda: Infant care and the growth of love.* Baltimore: Johns Hopkins University Press.

Ainsworth, M. D. S. (1969). Object relations, dependency, and attachment: A theoretical review of the infant-mother relationship. *Child Development, 40,* 969–1025.

Ainsworth, M. D. S. (1982). Attachment: Retrospect and prospect. In C. M. Parkes & J. Stevenson-Hinde (Eds.), *The place of attachment in human behavior* (pp. 3–29). New York: Tavistock.

Allen, J. P., Moore, C., Kuperminc, G., & Bell, K. (1998). Attachment and adolescent psychosocial functioning. *Child Development, 69,* 1406–1419.

American Psychiatric Association. (1994). *Diagnostic and statistical manual of mental disorders* (4th ed.). Washington, DC: Author.

Benoit, D., & Parker, K. (1994). Stability and transmission of attachment across three generations. *Child Development, 65,* 1444–1456.

Bowen, M. (1978). *Family therapy in clinical practice.* New York: Aronson.

Bowlby, J. (1944). Forty-four juvenile thieves: Their characteristics and home life. *International Journal of Psycho-Analysis, 25,* 19–52, 107–127.

Bowlby, J. (1973). *Attachment and loss: Vol. II. Separation—Anxiety and anger.* New York: Basic Books.

Bowlby, J. (1988). Developmental psychiatry comes of age. *American Journal of Psychiatry, 145,* 1–10.

Bowlby, J. (1989). The role of attachment in personality development and psychopathology. In S. I. Greenspan & G. H. Pollack (Eds.), *The course of life: Vol. 1. Infancy* (pp. 119–136). Madison, CT: International Universities Press.

Byng-Hall, J. (1999). Family and couple therapy: Toward greater security. In J. Cassidy & P. R. Shaver (Eds.), *Handbook of attachment: Theory, research, and clinical applications* (pp. 625–645). New York: Guilford Press.

Carlson, V., Cicchetti, D., Barnett, D., & Braunwald, K. (1989). Disorganized/disoriented attachment relationships in maltreated infants. *Developmental Psychology, 25*(4), 525–531.

Cassidy, J. (1988). Child-mother attachment and the self in 6-year-olds. *Child Development, 59,* 121–135.

Chemtob, C. M., Nakashima, J., & Carlson, J. G. (2002). Brief-treatment for elementary school children with disaster-related PTSD: A field study. *Journal of Clinical Psychology, 58,* 99–112.

Cline, F. W., & Fay, J. (1992). *Parenting teens with love and logic.* Colorado Springs, CO: Pinon.

Fonagy, P., Target, M., Steele, M., Steele, H., Leigh, T., Levinson, A., et al. (1997). Morality, disruptive behavior, borderline personality disorder, crime, and their relationship to security of attachment. In L. Atkinson & K. J. Zucker (Eds.), *Attachment and psychopathology* (pp. 223–274). New York: Guilford Press.

Greenberg, M. T., DeKlyen, M., Speltz, M. L., & Endriga, M. C. (1997). The role of attachment processes in externalizing psychopathology in young children. In L. Atkinson & K. J. Zucker (Eds.), *Attachment and psychopathology* (pp. 196–222). New York: Guilford Press.

Grossmann, K., Fremmer-Bombik, E., Rudolph, J., & Grossmann, K. E. (1988). Maternal attachment representations as related to patterns of infant-mother attachment and maternal care during the first year. In R. A. Hinde & J. Stevenson-Hinde (Eds.), *Relationships within families: Mutual influences* (pp. 241–260). Oxford: Clarendon Press.

Haley, J. (1963). *Strategies of psychotherapy.* New York: Grune and Stratton.

Hesse, E. (1999). The Adult Attachment Interview: Historical and current perspectives. In J. Cassidy & P. R. Shaver (Eds.), *Handbook of attachment: Theory, research, and clinical applications* (pp. 395–433). New York: Guilford Press.

Hughes, D. (1997). *Facilitating developmental attachment: The road to emotional recovery and behavioral change in foster and adopted children.* Northvale, NJ: Aronson.

Ironson, G., Freund, B., Strauss, J. L., & Williams, J. (2002). Comparison of two treatments for traumatic stress: A community-based study of EMDR and prolonged exposure. *Journal of Clinical Psychology, 58,* 113–128.

Jaberghaderi, N., Greenwald, R., Rubin, A. S. D., & Zand, S. O. (2004). A comparison of CBT and EMDR for sexually abused Iranian girls. *Clinical Psychology and Psychotherapy, 11,* 358–368.

Kaslow, F. W. (1995). *Projective genogramming.* Sarasota, FL: Professional Resource Press.

Keck, G. C., & Kupecky, R. M. (2002). *Parenting the hurt child: Helping adoptive families heal and grow.* Colorado Springs, CO: Pinon.

Kerr, M. E., & Bowen, M. (1988). *Family evaluation.* New York: Norton.

Kobak, R. R., Cole, H. E., Ferenz-Gillies, R., Fleming, W. S., & Gamble, W. (1993). Attachment and emotion regulation during mother-teen problem solving: A control theory analysis. *Child Development, 64,* 231–245.

Lee, C., Gavriel, H., Drummond, P., Richards, J., & Greenwald, R. (2002). Treatment of PTSD: Stress inoculation training with prolonged exposure compared to EMDR. *Journal of Clinical Psychology, 58,* 1071–1089.

Levy, T. M., & Orlans, M. (2000). Attachment disorder as an antecedent to violence and antisocial patterns in children. In T. M. Levy (Ed.), *Handbook of attachment interventions* (pp. 244–258). San Diego, CA: Academic Press.

Lovett, J. (1999). *Small wonders: Healing childhood trauma with EMDR.* New York: Free Press.

Lyons-Ruth, K., Alpern, L., & Repacholi, L. (1993). Disorganized infant attachment classification and maternal psychosocial problems as predictors of hostile-aggressive behavior in the preschool classroom. *Child Development, 64,* 572–585.

Lyons-Ruth, K., & Block, D. (1996). The disturbed caregiving system: Relations among childhood trauma, maternal caregiving, and infant affect and attachment. *Infant Mental Health Journal, 17*(3), 257–275.

Lyons-Ruth, K., & Jacobvitz, D. (1999). Attachment disorganization: Unresolved loss, relational violence, and lapses in behavioral and attentional strategies. In J. Cassidy & P. R. Shaver (Eds.), *Handbook of attachment: Theory, research and clinical applications* (pp. 520–554). New York: Guilford Press.

Madanes, C. (1986). Integrating ideas in family therapy with children. In H. C. Fishman & B. L. Rosman (Eds.), *Evolving models for family change: A volume in honor of Salvador Minuchin* (pp. 183–203). New York: Guilford Press.

Main, M., & Hesse, E. (1990). Parents' unresolved traumatic experiences are related to infant disorganized attachment status: Is frightened and/or frightening parental behavior the linking mechanism? In M. Greenberg, D. Cicchetti, & E. M. Cummings (Eds.), *Attachment in the pre-school years: Theory, research, and intervention* (pp. 161–182). Chicago: University of Chicago Press.

Main, M., Kaplan, N., & Cassidy, J. (1985). Security in infancy, childhood, and adulthood: A move to the level of representation. *Monographs of the Society for Research in Child Development, 50*(1/2, Serial No. 209), 66–104.

Main, M., & Solomon, J. (1986). Discovery of an insecure-disorganized/disoriented attachment pattern. In T. B. Brazelton & M. Yogman (Eds.), *Affective development in infancy* (pp. 95–124). Norwood, NJ: Ablex.

Main, M., & Solomon, J. (1990). Procedures for identifying infants as disorganized/disoriented during the Ainsworth Strange Situation. In M. Greenberg, D. Cicchetti, & M. Cummings (Eds.), *Attachment in the pre-school years* (pp. 121–159). Chicago: University of Chicago Press.

Marvin, R. S. (2003). Implications of attachment research for the field of family therapy. In P. Erdman & T. Caffery (Eds.), *Attachment and family systems: Conceptual, empirical, and therapeutic relatedness* (pp. 3–27). New York: Brunner-Routledge.

McGoldrick, M., & Gerson, R. (1988). Genograms and the family life cycle. In B. Carter & M. McGoldrick (Eds.), *The changing family life cycle* (2nd ed., pp. 164–186). New York: Gardner Press.

Minuchin, P. (1985). Families and individual development: Provocations from the field of family therapy. *Child Development, 56,* 289–302.

Minuchin, S. (1974). *Families and family therapy.* Cambridge, MA: Harvard University Press.

NICHD Early Child Care Research Network. (2004). Affect dysregulation in the mother-child relationship in the toddler years: Antecedents and consequences. *Development and Psychopathology, 16,* 43–68.

Pearson, J. L., Cohn, D. A., Cowan, P. A., & Cowan, C. P. (1994). Earned- and continuous-security in adult attachment: Relation to depressive symptomatology and parenting style. *Development and Psychopathology, 6,* 359–373.

Power, K., McGoldrick, T., Brown, K., Buchanan, R., Sharp, D., Swanson, V., et al. (2002). A controlled comparison of eye movement desensitization and reprocessing versus exposure plus cognitive restructuring versus waiting list in the treatment of post-traumatic stress disorder. *Clinical Psychology and Psychotherapy, 9,* 299–318.

Renken, B., Egeland, B., Marvinney, D., Mangelsdorf, S., & Sroufe, A. L. (1989). Early childhood antecedents of aggression and passive-withdrawal in early elementary school. *Journal of Personality, 57*(2), 257–281.

Robertson, J., & Bowlby, J. (1952). Responses of young children to separation from their mothers. *Courrier Centere Internationale Enfance, 2,* 131–142.

Schuengel, C., Bakermans-Kranenburg, M. J., van IJzendoorn, M. H., & Blom, M. (1999). Unresolved loss and infant disorganization: Links to frightening maternal behavior. In J. Solomon & C. George (Eds.), *Attachment disorganization* (pp. 71–94). New York: Guilford Press.

Shapiro, F. (1995). *Eye movement desensitization and reprocessing: Basic principles, protocols, and procedures.* New York: Guilford Press.

Shapiro, F. (2001). *Eye movement desensitization and reprocessing: Basic principles, protocols, and procedures* (2nd ed.). New York: Guilford Press.

Sroufe, L. A. (1988). The role of infant-caregiver attachment in development. In J. Belsky & T. Nezworski (Eds.), *Clinical implications of attachment* (pp. 18–38). Hillsdale, NJ: Erlbaum.

Stevenson-Hinde, J. (1990). Attachment within family systems: An overview. *Infant Mental Health Journal, 11,* 218–227.

van IJzendoorn, M. H. (1992). Intergenerational transmission of parenting: A review of studies in nonclinical populations. *Developmental Review, 12,* 76–99.

Watkins, J. G. (1971). The affect bridge: A hypnoanalytic technique. *International Journal of Clinical and Experimental Hypnosis, 19,* 21–27.

CHAPTER 6

Repairing Maternal-Infant Bonding Failures

Antonio Madrid

Maternal-infant bonding (MIB) is the powerful, instinctual connection that exists between a mother and child—the strong emotional glue that attaches her to her child, enabling her to undertake and enjoy the exhaustive and selfless tasks of motherhood (Klaus & Kennell, 1976). It is palpable and enduring; it is the glow radiating from her as she looks at her child. A complex, intricate dance between mother and child, it encompasses biological, emotional, behavioral, and spiritual domains. It is considered the foundation of all relationships in the child's life (Klaus, Kennell, & Klaus, 1995).

When MIB is absent, the mother most often knows it. She might say, "Something is missing here" or "I feel differently about him than my other children" or "I don't have any maternal feelings for this child."

MIB problems are often flagrant and fairly easy to detect. One mother may say that she loves her child but does not like him or her. Another may openly confess that she does not love the child. Many mothers remember that they felt something was wrong with their child from birth. Some mothers say that when they first held their baby, they wondered if they were given the wrong child. A mother might comment that her baby was always unaffectionate, hard to soothe, fussy, colicky, demanding, or even rejecting of her. Counselors may have noticed that parenting problems have existed for the entire life of the child.

Surprisingly, MIB problems are usually accidental, the fault of neither mother nor child. With appropriate and focused clinical inquiry, their causes are obvious, and their resolution is straightforward.

Maternal-Infant Bonding

The concept of human maternal-infant bonding was first proposed by pediatricians Marshall Klaus and John Kennell, from Case Western Reserve, in 1976. They reviewed studies demonstrating that animal mothers separated from their offspring at birth will reject their babies (Klaus & Kennell, 1976, 1982). For example, if lambs are separated at birth and the separation continues for 4 hours, 50% of ewes will reject their lambs. If the separation lasts for 12 to 24 hours, the rejection rate climbs to 75%. By contrast, if the 24-hour separation does not commence until 2 to 4 days after birth, all ewes will reaccept their lambs (Poindron & Le Neindre, 1979).

Studies with monkeys are equally telling. Mothers who are separated from their infants for 1 hour after birth will still show a preference for them in a choice situation. If the initial separation lasts for 24 hours, the mother's preference for her neonates seems to disappear. The sooner after birth the separation occurs, the stronger the effects.

Klaus and Kennell (1976) proposed that a maternal-infant bond also occurs in humans and that this bond is biological, psychological, and emotional. They perceived it as a complex interaction in which a strong emotional response pattern is mutually appreciated, anticipated, and reinforced. Klaus and Kennell posited that maternal-infant bonding is hardwired into humans and will occur spontaneously unless something serious impedes it, and that the two most common impediments to bonding are physical separation at birth and emotional separation during pregnancy, birth, or soon afterward. Emotional separation is usually caused by something traumatic in the mother's life, evoking in her emotions that are incompatible with bonding.

If either of these impediments to bonding (physical or emotional separation) is present, the chances of bonding are greatly reduced. M. H. Klaus (personal communication, Summer 2004) noted that a mother will make great efforts to bond, even in the face of separation or trauma, and there is ample proof that these obstacles are frequently overcome. There are many routes to bonding, said Klaus, because humans are highly adaptable; however, when these impediments are not surmounted, a bonding problem usually results.

Mother-Infant Bonding Problems

Mothers who do not bond often act differently from bonded mothers. Several studies compared mothers who had early or extra contact with their child immediately after birth (i.e., 2 or 3 hours of uninterrupted contact) with mothers whose child was taken into the nursery immediately after birth. Klaus et al. (1972) found that mothers with extra contact were more affectionate and soothing, even 1 year later. Sousa et al. (1974) noted that 77% of mothers with extra contact were still breast-feeding at 2 months, compared to 27% of the mothers with a normal routine. Johnson (1976) likewise noted that 83% of mothers with early contact were still breast-feeding, compared to 16% of mothers with late contact. De Chateau (1976) found that mothers with early contact were more affectionate: They kissed and looked lovingly at their baby more often, cleaned their baby less, and breast-fed more. At 3 months, their baby smiled, laughed more, and cried less.

More serious consequences have been noted by other authors. During a 17-month study, O'Connor and associates (O'Connor, Vietze, Sherrod, Sandler, & Altemeier, 1980) found that babies who had limited early contact with their mother experienced more abuse, neglect, abandonment, and nonorganic failure to thrive. In a hospital in Thailand, the introduction of rooming-in and early contact with suckling reduced the frequency of abandonment from 33 in 10,000 births a year to 1 in 10,000 (Kennell & Klaus, 1998). Similar results were found in Russia, the Philippines, and Costa Rica when early contact and rooming-in were introduced.

Children who have not bonded develop a wide range of difficulties, including medical problems. Cassibba, van IJzendoorn, Bruno, and Coppola (2004) found that children with recurrent asthmatic bronchitis appeared to be less secure with their mother than were healthy children. Mead (2004) theorized that disruptions in early bonding are capable of causing long-term imbalances in autonomic regulatory function and may be at the root of Type 1 diabetes. Mantymaa et al. (2003) documented that mother-infant interaction problems are a significant predictor of chronic and recurrent health problems in the child and that interactional issues are related to the child's subsequent physical health.

Bonding problems seem to introduce chronic stress into the child's life. Klinnert et al. (2001) documented that parenting problems noted at 3 weeks may cause stress that is so severe that it impacts the immune system of the young child.

When a mother is not bonded to her child, stress is introduced into the entire family. Families often come into therapy because of the problem between the mother and the nonbonded child. Nothing that the child does seems to please his or her mother, and this often causes conflict between the mother and father. Although there can be much help through behavioral strategies or family therapy, the underlying pain of the family may not get touched until the bond itself is addressed and repaired.

When an MIB problem is clearly identified, MIB Therapy can be introduced as an important part of a wider treatment package. It is not an alternative to family therapy, but it can make family therapy more effective by eliminating the seemingly impenetrable obstacle between mother and child. When the mother begins to feel her love for the child, the child feels it and responds accordingly; this can change the dynamics of the entire family. We have heard mothers say, "When I finally got connected to my child the whole family got well."

Mother-Infant Bonding and Attachment

The importance of the mother-infant relationship was recognized by psychodynamic and object relations theorists. In his emphasis on psychosocial development throughout the life span, Erickson (1963) postulated that the infant's ability to trust and feel secure was critical for healthy development. Mahler (1971) and Klein (1975) hypothesized that the quality of children's early relationship with their mother determined the quality of their relationships in adulthood, and Kernberg (1975) and Kohut (1977) posited that adult mental health problems can be understood as resulting from deficits in the early mother-child relationship.

Although the terms "bonding" and "attachment" often are used interchangeably, for the purpose of this chapter "maternal-infant bonding" is considered to be a set of primitive and instinctual emotions and behaviors that exist in the mother, and "attachment" is understood to be the feelings and behaviors that exist in the child (Kennell & Klaus, 1998). Attachment is the result of maternal actions, conscious and especially unconscious, that probably start from this initial bond and that continue over the course of the child's infancy. Schore (2003) wrote that attachment is the product of a mother's being attuned to her baby and resonating to his needs. Through a network of communications between mother and baby, the child expects that his needs will be satisfied, his internal states mirrored, and his heightened negative emotions modulated by her.

In secure attachments, normal breaks in this synchronistic pattern are regularly mended. This leads to the expectation in the child that soothing is not far off, which is an important ingredient in forming an internal structure to handle stress (Kohut, 1977). The attunement and resonance that are the essential components of attachment spring, in part, from the mother's instinctual bond to her baby. Without this maternal-infant bond forming the foundation for their interwoven pattern of relating, it is hard to imagine that attachment can occur. In fact, MIB can be considered a necessary, though not sufficient, condition of attachment.

Attachment problems are not the same as MIB problems. Attachment deficits are often the result of prolonged separation at a later age or of continuous misattunement between mother and child. Maladaptive attachment may result in pathological behaviors in the child (Bowlby, 1973; Schore, 2003). Disruptions in the maternal-infant bond do not necessarily result in a *Diagnostic and Statistical Manual of Mental Disorders* diagnosable disorder.

THERAPY PROCESS

Repairing MIB problems is generally straightforward and quick. Because infants are phylogenetically engineered to bond with their mother (Klaus & Kennell, 1982), they will usually do so automatically when their mother bonds to them. Even older children will often respond positively to the change in their mother. The focus of MIB Therapy is to remove the impediments to bonding so that the mother-child relationship is repaired.

MIB Therapy (Madrid, Skolek, & Shapiro, 2006) is a four-step process: (1) identifying the original impediment to bonding, (2) processing the event, (3) installing an alternative birth, and (4) following up. MIB Therapy incorporates and parallels the eight phases of Eye Movement Desensitization and Reprocessing (EMDR; Shapiro, 2001). The first step parallels the first three phases of EMDR treatment: History Taking, Preparation, and Assessment. The second step of MIB Therapy implements EMDR Phases 4 through 6; the third step is an additional expansion and modification of EMDR's Phases 5 through 7. Finally, the fourth step of MIB Therapy is comparable to EMDR's eighth phase (Shapiro, 2001).

MIB treatment, although not developed from family systems therapy, has many elements in common with the postmodern constructionist approach and the Narrative Therapy of Michael White and David Epston (1990). White and Epston asserted that language shapes events by providing meaning and interpretation; they hypothesized that an individual's sense of reality is organized through the stories she tells about herself and her life. White developed the technique of "externalizing" problems, in which difficulties are redefined as existing outside of the person, rather than being perceived as characterological and residing within the individual. Clients are assisted in "restorying" problems;

they reconstruct their life stories to create new narratives that provide more adaptive views of themselves and their situations. The changed narrative is thought to result in more effective interpersonal interactions.

These two main elements of Narrative Therapy, deconstructing historical stories and reconstructing alternate narratives (Goldenberg & Goldenberg, 2000), have parallels with the approach taken in MIB Therapy. MIB treatment reconceptualizes bonding failures as resulting from a lack of opportunities, not deficient parenting. In MIB Therapy, the patient develops and adopts a new birthing story. However, unlike Narrative Therapy, which also focuses on exceptions and changing current behavior, the MIB focus is primarily on revising the historical experience. Also, unlike most family therapies, MIB treatment primarily provides individual sessions to the mother (or nonbonded caregiver).

Identifying the Original Impediment to Bonding

When a mother hears that her feelings of estrangement from her child are the result of some event that was accidental or out of her control, she often feels a great sense of relief and hope. She has been carrying a huge burden around with her for the life of the child, and finding out that she is not the cause will be the first step in making a difference. This reformulation will fuel the motivation needed for therapy and engage her as an active participant in the process.

It is imperative to identify the impediment to bonding. As mentioned earlier, two impediments are most often at the root of MIB problems: physical separation at birth and emotional separation (usually trauma based) around the time of birth:

1. *Physical separation* can occur because of things that happen in the hospital that keep a child away from his or her mother, including the mother's need for general anesthesia, cesarean delivery, a stay in an intensive care nursery, placement in an incubator, mother getting sick, mother or baby being overmedicated, and mother being sent home without her baby. The birth of twins and triplets often results in the mother being able to bond with only one baby (Klaus & Kennell, 1976). Adopted children also frequently suffer from bonding problems (Madrid & McPhee, 1980).

2. *Emotional separation* occurs when the mother is experiencing another emotion so intense that it is incompatible with, and blocks, bonding. As most of these emotions are brought about by traumatic events, EMDR surfaces as the treatment of choice in remedying these emotional impediments* to bonding. Elicited from the mother through a careful history, these events may include a death in the family, marital problems, illness during pregnancy, homelessness, extreme poverty, or other severe trauma.

The Maternal-Infant Bonding Survey (MIBS; see Madrid, Ames, Horner, Brown, & Navarette, 2004; Madrid, Ames, Skolek, & Brown, 2000) was developed to assist in identifying these events. A shortened version (Madrid et al., 2006) in checklist form is presented in Table 6.1.

---

*From the Latin *impedimenta,* baggage.

Table 6.1   Quick Reference Maternal Infant Bonding Survey

Physical Separation

    Mother was separated from child at or after birth.

    Mother had a very difficult delivery.

    Child was sick at birth.

    Child was twin or triplet.

    Child was in intensive care nursery or incubator.

    Mother was anesthetized at birth.

    Mother was heavily medicated.

    Mother was very sick after the birth.

    Mother was separated from child in first month.

    Child was adopted.

    Other separation _____

Emotional Separation

    Mother had emotional problems during pregnancy.

    Mother had emotional problems after birth.

    Mother had a death in the family within 2 years of birth.

    Mother had a miscarriage within 2 years of birth.

    Mother and father were separated before birth or soon after.

    Mother was addicted to drugs or alcohol at birth.

    Mother moved before or soon after birth.

    Severe financial problems.

    Unwanted pregnancy.

    New romance in mother's life.

    Other emotion _____

Source: "Repairing Failures in Bonding through EMDR," by A. Madrid, S. Skolek, and F. Shapiro, 2006, *Clinical Case Studies, 5,* 271–286.

These events were termed by Pennington (1991) nonbonding events (NBE). There is often more than one NBE in a mother's history. Occasionally, during the course of therapy, the identified NBE is a red herring and the core NBE is some other event. For example, one mother processed a red herring NBE, identified as losing her mate before the child was born. Following the treatment, there was no improvement in the relationship with her child. Subsequently, another NBE was uncovered: her soul-shattering guilt about having a child out of wedlock. Once identified and processed, there was an immediate resolution in her bonding with her child.

Processing the Nonbonding Event

This step of MIB Therapy implements EMDR's Phases 4 through 6 (Desensitization, Installation, and Body Scan) subsequent to the standard Preparation and Assessment Phases. The purpose of this step is to process and metabolize the event or events that blocked bonding. The target is the NBE, identified by the mother and the therapist, keeping in mind that there may be more than one NBE. For example, the mother's brother may have died 2 months before she conceived; her husband may have lost his job; and she may have been very ill during the pregnancy. Each NBE must be processed until the score on the Subjective Unit of Disturbance (SUD) scale reaches 0 or 1 (if ecologically valid).

It is not uncommon for a mother to be surprised by the intensity of her reactions to the NBE. She may have sequestered the emotions and the memories of the event to the back corners of her consciousness to reconstruct her life. Without a strong emotional reaction, it is unlikely that the core NBE has been unearthed. As an example, a mother was processing an assumed NBE: being homeless and single when she delivered her child. There was only a moderate SUD of 4, and there was no emotional expression as she lowered the SUD to 0. However, when she remembered that she had to move in with her very critical parents, her SUD for this event rocketed to 9 and she worked through this trauma with intense feelings. The result of metabolizing this NBE brought about a closer bond with her daughter.

When a mother is separated from her child after birth, the separation itself may constitute a trauma. Many stories have been reported in which the mother was forcibly detained from going to the nursery to see her baby; the separation may have occurred for hours or days, causing traumatic emotional pain. When there are no more feelings around an NBE associated with the birth of the child, then the mother is ready to work on an alternative birth.

Installing an Alternative Birth

The fifth phase of EMDR's standard protocol is to strengthen and enhance a cognition related to the original incident that reflects a positive self-perception. In MIB Therapy, this *Positive Cognition* is further enhanced by installing an image of an alternative birth that is positive and satisfying to the mother. This also functions as a positive template.

At times, the beginnings of the alternative birth will be apparent in the second step. When that occurs, one can encourage the client to explore what that might feel like. For example, a mother may be processing the death of a brother that occurred before she conceived her child; she may reflect that it would have been so nice to have a pregnancy without grief. She could be encouraged to find out how that would be.

Certain events are important to imagine in the new birth. One must make sure that the mother can joyfully imagine the following:

- Each of the trimesters
- An easy delivery and birth
- The baby's first breath
- The baby lying on the mother's chest
- The first couple of hours
- The first couple of days
- Returning home

The alternative birth must also include the resolved NBEs. The impediments to bonding now gone, she can imagine *and experience* a birth without the NBEs. For example, she can feel what it is like to be pregnant without the grief from the death of someone dear to her. She can find out what a healthy pregnancy feels like, without being nauseated throughout the day. She can know what it is like to hold her child right after he or she is born. She can experience what it is like to go home with her baby. She can be awake and alert and healthy while she holds her baby for as long as she wants. She can have a warm home where she can live with her baby. She can have her husband stay with her throughout labor and delivery.

When checking for the strength of these images, our team uses a grading scale from A to F. Anything not approaching a grade of A should be suspect; it usually means that more work needs to be done on processing the NBE. When a new birth is successfully installed, tears and intense emotion often accompany the image.

Following Up

The following-up step of MIB Therapy incorporates the present and future prongs of the standard EMDR protocol (Shapiro, 2001). In subsequent sessions, the mother is encouraged to identify any current triggers that are inhibiting her new bonding experience. These triggers are targeted according to the standard EMDR protocol. For example, one mother felt distant from her teenage daughter when she expressed a lack of appreciation for her mother's care.

Occasionally, the bond will be ripped asunder. Being new, it may be tender, fragile, and susceptible to tearing, but it can usually be repaired. The mother needs to identify what happened around the time of the new disruption. Usually it is some kind of emotional assault to the mother or child. For example, a mother of a child with asthma told her son in an argument that he would be sorry when she died. The asthma immediately returned. When she realized how terrible this angry outburst was, she returned home and apologized. The wheezing stopped within an hour. Returning to the standard EMDR protocol and processing the trigger that caused her overreaction and incorporating a template for alternative positive behavior (e.g., other ways to verbalize her feelings) would assist in preventing another breakdown.

In another case, a mother was visited by her own parents and was so hurt by their verbal abuse and disrespect that she "lost" her daughter that weekend. She processed her parents' insults through EMDR and "found" her daughter again. Once again, comprehensive processing to assist in strengthening interactions that will support an ongoing bond includes the event underlying her reaction, the trigger, and an alternative positive future template.

The mother is also encouraged to identify future situations where she might feel uncertain about her new perspective. For example, a mother wondered how she would feel holding her friend's newborn baby. This was successfully processed with EMDR. It is also very helpful to reeducate the mother about MIB and the events that can assault it. She can be taught how to fix things herself. She is encouraged to make contact with the therapist if she needs help doing this.

Following a successful course of MIB Therapy, mothers commonly report that there has been a substantial change in their relationship with their child. They say that they now love their child, that he is more affectionate, that he is not as much trouble. The child will respond immediately to being loved by his mother. Little children often calm down, are more affectionate, and are less demanding. Mothers have reported that their teenagers will crawl into their lap and that their grown-up children will phone for no reason and say that they love them.

The individual maternal bonding therapy described has the greatest family impact with young children, under 8 years of age. However, as children get older, they may have issues of their own that have developed over time, which may need to be included in the process. If a teenage girl has a long-held resentment about not feeling loved and being treated distantly by her mother, she may benefit from first targeting those feelings with EMDR and then creating a new, close childhood, which can be installed with EMDR. Fathers who feel estranged from a child for reasons that fit into the MIB paradigm can also be treated. For example, the father of a 4-year-old whose own father died when his son was born can process the death of his father with EMDR and create a new birth of his son with the experience of being unencumbered with grief.

CASE EXAMPLE

Lucile was the mother of a 5-year-old girl. She was referred by her friend, who was a counseling graduate student who knew about MIB Therapy. The student stated that Lucile was a textbook case of nonbonding.

Lucile said that she liked nothing about being a mother. Her daughter drained her; she was a pest. Lucile did not even like being around her. She was very disappointed about this because she had wanted to be a mother, yet the actuality was a terrible experience. Her daughter, she said, was not a very happy little girl.

She blamed herself for these feelings. She had tried to get closer to her daughter through individual therapy, but it did not work. Her friend told her about maternal-infant bonding, and for the first time she had some glimmer of hope and self-respect.

Her history was a classic case of an MIB disruption; it was filled with several serious NBEs. In the beginning of her pregnancy, she moved from a nice town where she had many friends to an ugly town where she knew no one. She was so severely nauseated throughout the entire pregnancy that she had to spend most of the time lying down. The labor was very long and excruciatingly painful, ending as a cesarean section delivery. Totally exhausted, she was not alert enough to know the condition of the baby or even its sex. She fell asleep for 3 hours, and when she awoke and asked for her baby, the staff would not accommodate her. Several long hours later, she held her baby and remembered thinking, "Something is wrong here. I don't have any feelings for this baby."

During the hospitalization she was told that she had a serious adult-onset medical condition that would need to be treated for the rest of her life. She returned home feeling battered and defeated. She went into individual therapy after 5 months and was placed on antidepressants. She said that the entire first year was a nightmare.

The first session was spent gathering this information and explaining to her that anyone would be devoid of feelings with this history. The theories regarding MIB were discussed, and she wept with relief. The targets for EMDR were identified: moving, being ill during pregnancy, the long labor and C-section, not seeing her baby, getting ill in the hospital, and returning home in a battered state. EMDR was practiced with a *Safe Place* exercise.

In the second meeting, Lucile worked on the move and the nausea during pregnancy. She was able to process completely the sadness about moving and the loneliness in her new town. She could not fully process the nausea of her pregnancy. She was stabilized using a safe place and was asked to store the rest of the feelings about her pregnancy at the office. She was encouraged to keep notes between sessions about feelings and images that occurred to her.

The third session was devoted to processing the nausea during pregnancy. She remembered with great emotion how horrible she felt, that no one knew how terrible it was, and how impossible it was to love someone who made her feel so sick. She thought about lying on the couch, writhing with nausea, and twice she brought the SUD down to 1. She spontaneously began to think about how it might have been if she had been healthy during the pregnancy. She was encouraged to play with those thoughts for a while. She graded those thoughts a B for reality. This indicated that there was probably more to do about the pregnancy.

The fourth session began with Lucile's report that she and her daughter "were getting along much better, for no apparent reason." We checked out the SUDs for the move (0) and the pregnancy (4); she spent the remainder of the session processing the feelings and images of the pregnancy, the torturous delivery, and the poor medical care she received afterward. All of these targets were brought to SUDs of 0 or 1.

The fifth session started with her reporting that she and her daughter continued to get along better. The SUDs were checked for moving (0), pregnancy (5), and the delivery (4). Each target was processed, during which she remembered different painful events and thoughts, and she was filled with intense emotion during most of the session. Each target was again checked, and she registered SUDs of 0 or 1 for each of them, indicating that she was ready for installing an alternative birth.

She had begun to imagine a new birth in the previous two sessions; she was already straining at the bit. She was asked to imagine the first trimester, this time healthy and joyful. She did so, and graded its reality A for feeling real. Two sets of seven eye movements cemented it. She imagined the second trimester and gave it a grade of C; more work needed to be done. She was asked what still bothered her about the second trimester. She spoke of how sick she was, how little medical help she received, and how difficult it was to love someone who made her so violently ill. These targets were processed with EMDR until her SUDs were 0. Returning to imagine a healthy second trimester recorded an A, and it was solidified with two sets of seven eye movements. The third trimester went in a similar fashion: initially low grade, more EMDR processing, and then a good image. She could imagine the entire pregnancy as joyful and healthy, and she then could imagine the baby being born and placed on top of her. She beamed with joy with this image.

Lucile began the seventh session stating that her daughter had changed from being a chore to "the love of her life." She also stated that this was the first time since her daughter's birth that she was not seriously depressed at this time of year. These were two clear indications that bonding had worked. That session was spent checking to see if anything needed more work. The SUD level for all targets was still at 0, and the new pregnancy and birth felt real (A). Lucile claimed that when she thought about her daughter's birth, she happily imagined that "she popped right out; I breast-fed; she slept with me."

The follow-up session was 3 weeks later. She reported that she and her daughter continued to enjoy each other. She felt wonderful when she thought about her daughter's birth.

She spoke about how she and her daughter had recently met with the graduate student friend. Lucile told her friend about the therapy. Her daughter was very attentive throughout the story, and when she was done, her daughter came over to her and held her head and looked deeply into her eyes. They were both stunned and moved by this ecstatic experience.

We checked in on the targeted areas (pregnancy, delivery, postnatal times), which were still at a SUD of 0. She mentioned that she still felt bad about the time after the birth, when she went home and was depressed, was lonely, still had not been validated, and was with a child she did not love. All of these targets were processed and reduced to 0. She now could imagine the first year as a healthy, joyful mother. She stated, "Now I know what it's like to love my daughter." She felt that treatment was completed.

Six months later, she was contacted and reported that she was still doing fine. Her life had changed and her daughter's as well. One year later, she wrote a note, saying, "We are doing really well. I still feel like we really, finally bonded. The other day she said: 'Mom, I wish I had three of you, then if I lost one, I'd still have two more.' She is always saying things like that. And often, when she plays by herself, she is singing or humming. I feel like she's really a happy kid."

The focus of the treatment was solely on the traumas surrounding the pregnancy and birth, and she was able to work through those traumas and imagine an alternative birth. Occasionally, a mother might balk at a new birth, feeling that it is not real and should not be imagined. It often helps to explain that this new history is an "emotional history" and will not interfere with the physical history. It is like a parallel highway, with each history on either side of the center divider. She can ride on either side whenever she wants or whenever it is appropriate.

MOTHER-INFANT BONDING: ASTHMA AND BONDING

Childhood asthma is epidemic in the United States, having affected an estimated 5 million children in 1994. It is the most common chronic childhood illness, accounting for more missed school than any other disease (Lara et al., 2002).

The connection between childhood asthma and mother-child problems has been documented by 6 decades of study. Authors have labeled the mothers distant (Turnbull, 1962), rejecting (Gerard, 1953; Miller & Baruch, 1950; Purcell, Bernstein, & Bukantz, 1961), resentful (Bentley, 1975), engulfing (Abramson, 1954; Garner & Wenar, 1959), narcissistic and cold (Sandler, 1964), overprotective (Bentley, 1975; Rogerson, Hardcastle, & Dugiud, 1935), conflicted about dependency (Mohr & Richmond, 1954), and depressed (Mrazek, Klinnert, Mrazek, & Macey, 1991). Some authors noted that these mothers had parenting difficulties (Bentley, 1975; Klinnert et al., 2001; Lilljeqvist, Smorvik, & Faleide, 2002).

Parting from these studies, which seem to blame mothers for their child's asthma, three researchers found that children with asthma had birth histories compatible with bonding problems (Feinberg, 1988; Pennington, 1991; Schwartz, 1988). Between 70% and 80% of the mothers of asthmatics were judged nonbonded, compared to 25% of the mothers of healthy children, and asthmatic children frequently had two or more NBEs in their history. The results were so compelling that Schwartz wrote, "If a child has asthma, he most likely is not bonded" (p. 92). One of the conclusions of these studies was that the personality of the mother had little to do with causing their children's asthma; rather, the mothers were the victims of a disruption in bonding.

With the suggestion that disruptions in MIB may be linked to the development of childhood asthma, it seemed logical that asthma symptoms might be helped if the bonding were improved. Two pilot studies demonstrated this to be true. In the first study (Madrid et al., 2000), six mothers of asthmatic children were treated with a therapy aimed at repairing the bond. Five children experienced complete or nearly complete improvement; this occurred concurrent with reduction in medications. Two infants had total remission of all symptoms. In the second study (Madrid et al., 2004), 15 mothers of asthmatics were treated with the same type of therapy. Twelve children's symptoms improved, including seven Mexican Americans whose mothers were treated in Spanish. Eight of 10 children regularly taking medications no longer needed them.

These studies used the four-step treatment described earlier. Although the particular vehicle for processing the traumas in these studies was hypnosis, explorations using EMDR are showing that the results are equally helpful and in some cases better.

DISCUSSION

Animals who do not bond abandon their offspring. Humans, though they may sometimes feel inclined in that direction, tend to stay the course and do the best they can, despite having few of the feelings that make parenting enjoyable. Without these rewarding feelings, mothers carry out the duties of parenting often in a heroic, selfless fashion, compensating as best they can for a lack of "instinctual" feelings of love (Madrid & McPhee, 1980).

Devoid of their mother's feelings of love, children act as if they are always looking for something unattainable; they are nervous, cranky, pestering, despondent. Mothers report that there was always something different about, or missing from, this child. Lack of bonding can lead to more serious problems: increased stress, abuse, failure to thrive, and medical problems. Coupled with chronic issues of misattunement, attachment problems may follow, along with personality disorders and other forms of severe psychopathology.

Maternal-infant bonding problems are the fault neither of the mother nor of the child. They most often occur accidentally. They arise from easily identified causes: physical separation at birth or emotional separation (usually trauma based) around pregnancy or birth.

If caught early enough, bonding problems can be remedied quickly and efficaciously. The therapy involves identifying the NBE, metabolizing it through EMDR (or other trauma-focused process), re-creating a new birth, and following up to deal with the effects.

When it seems that bonding is an issue, when the events that interfered with bonding are identifiable, and when the child is young enough, then MIB Therapy can be a valuable part of a family therapy plan. This tool is easy to learn and most often is effective the first time a therapist tries it. The maternal-infant bond is driven by such a powerful primitive instinct, that mother and child are waiting with their minds, bodies, and souls to be connected. Herein is the primary force behind the effectiveness of MIB Therapy.

REFERENCES

Abramson, H. (1954). Evaluation of maternal rejection theory in allergy. *Annals of Allergy, 12,* 129–140.

Bentley, J. (1975). Asthmatic children away from home: A comparative psychological study. *Journal of Asthma Research, 13,* 17–25.

Bowlby, J. (1973). *Attachment and loss: Vol. 2. Separation, anxiety, and anger.* New York: Basic Books.

Cassibba, R., van IJzendoorn, M., Bruno, S., & Coppola, G. (2004). Attachment of mothers and children with recurrent asthmatic bronchitis. *Journal of Asthma, 41,* 419–462.

de Chateau, P. (1976). *Neonatal care routine: Influences on maternal and infant behavior and on breast feeding.* Umea, Sweden: Umea University Medical Dissertations.

Erickson, E. H. (1963). *Childhood and society* (2nd ed.). New York: Norton.

Feinberg, S. (1988). *Degree of maternal infant bonding and its relationship to pediatric asthma and family environments.* Unpublished doctoral dissertation, San Francisco School of Professional Psychology.

Garner, A., & Wenar, D. (1959). *The mother-child interaction in psychosomatic disorders.* Chicago: University of Illinois Press.

Gerard, M. (1953). Genesis of psychosomatic symptoms in infancy: The influence of infantile trauma upon symptom choice. In F. Deutzch (Ed.), *The psychosomatic concept in psychoanalysis* (pp. 124–130). New York: International Universities Press.

Goldenberg, H., & Goldenberg, I. (2000). *Family therapy: An overview* (5th ed.). Pacific Grove, CA: Brooks/Cole.

Johnson, N. W. (1976). Breast feeding at one hour of age. *American Journal of Maternal Child Nursing, 1,* 12.

Kennell, J. H., & Klaus, M. H. (1998). Bonding: Recent observations that alter perinatal care. *Pediatric Review, 19,* 4–12.

Kernberg, O. F. (1975). *Borderline conditions and pathological narcissism.* New York: Aronson.

Klaus, M. H., Jerauld, R., Kreger, N., McAlpine, W., Steffa, M., & Kennell, J. (1972). Maternal attachment: Importance of the first post-partum days. *New England Journal of Medicine, 286,* 460–463.

Klaus, M. H., & Kennell, J. H. (1976). *Maternal-infant bonding.* St. Louis, MO: Mosby.

Klaus, M. H., & Kennell, J. H. (1982). *Parent-infant bonding.* St. Louis, MO: Mosby.

Klaus, M. H., Kennell, J. H., & Klaus, P. H. (1995). *Bonding.* Reading, MA: Addison-Wesley.

Klein, M. (1975). *The psychoanalysis of children.* New York: Dell.

Klinnert, M., Nelson, H., Price, M., Adinoff, L., Leung, D., & Mrazek, D. (2001, October). Onset and persistence of childhood asthma: Predictors from infancy. *Pediatrics, 108,* 4 [Online]. Available from http://www.pediatrics.org/cgi/content/full/108/4/e69.

Kohut, H. (1977). *The restoration of the self.* New York: International Universities Press.

Lara, M., Rosenbaum, S., Rachelefsky, G., Nicholar, W., Morton, S., Emont, S., et al. (2002). Improving childhood asthma outcomes in the United States: A blueprint for policy action. *Pediatrics, 109*(5), 919–930.

Lilljeqvist, A., Smorvik, D., & Faleide, A. (2002). Temperamental differences between healthy, asthmatic, and allergic children before onset of illness: A longitudinal prospective study of asthma development. *Journal of Genetic Psychology, 163*(2), 219–227.

Madrid, A., Ames, R., Horner, D., Brown, G., & Navarrette, L. (2004). Improving asthma symptoms in children by repairing the maternal-infant bond. *Journal of Prenatal and Perinatal Psychology and Health, 18*(3), 221–231.

Madrid, A., Ames, R., Skolek, S., & Brown, G. (2000). Does maternal-infant bonding therapy improve breathing in asthmatic children? *Journal of Prenatal and Perinatal Psychology and Health, 15*(2), 90–112.

Madrid, A., & McPhee, X. (1980). The treatment of pediatric asthma through maternal-infant bonding in hypnosis. *Journal of Pre and Perinatal Psychology Association of North America, 1*(1), 24–28.

Madrid, A., Skolek, S., & Shapiro, F. (2006). Repairing failures in bonding though EMDR. *Clinical Case Studies, 5,* 271–286.

Mahler, M. S. (1971). A study of the separation and individuation process. *Psychoanalytic Study of the Child, 26,* 403–422.

Mantymaa, M., Puura, K., Luoma, I., Salmelim, R., Davis, H., Tsiantis, J., et al. (2003). Infant-mother interaction as a predictor of child's chronic health problems. *Child Care, Health, and Development, 29,* 181–191.

Mead, V. P. (2004). A new model for understanding the role of environmental factors in the origins of chronic illness: A case study of Type 1 diabetes mellitus. *Medical Hypotheses, 63,* 1035–1046.

Miller, H., & Baruch, D. (1950). The emotional problems of childhood and their relation to asthma. *AMA Journal of the Diseases of Children, 93,* 242–245.

Mohr, G., & Richmond, J. (1954). A program for the study of children with psychosomatic disorders. In G. Caplan (Ed.), *Emotional problems of early childhood* (pp. 78–104). New York: Basic Books.

Mrazek, D. A., Klinnert, M. D., Mrazek, P., & Macey, T. (1991). Early asthma onset: Consideration of parenting issues. *Journal of the American Academy of Child and Adolescent Psychiatry, 30,* 277–282.

O'Connor, S., Vietze, P. M., Sherrod, K. B., Sandler, H. M., & Altemeier, W. A. (1980). Reduced incidence of parenting inadequacy following rooming-in. *Pediatrics, 66*(2), 176–182.

Pennington, D. (1991). *Events associated with maternal-infant bonding deficits and severity of pediatric asthma.* Unpublished doctoral dissertation, San Francisco School of Professional Psychology.

Poindron, P., & Le Neindre, P. (1979). Hormonal and behavioral basis for establishing maternal behavior in sheep. In L. Inichella & R. Panchari (Eds.), *Psychoneuroendocrinology in reproduction* (pp. 147–178). Amsterdam: Elsevier/North-Holland Biomedical Press.

Purcell, K., Bernstein, L., & Bukantz, S. (1961). A preliminary comparison of rapidly remitting and persistently "steroid-dependent" asthmatic children. *Psychosomatic Medicine, 23,* 305–310.]

Rogerson, C. H., Hardcastle, D., & Dugiud, K. (1935). A psychological approach to the problem of asthma and asthma-eczema-prurigo syndrome. *Guy's Hospital Report, 85,* 289–308.

Sandler, L. (1964). Child-rearing practices of mothers of asthmatic children, Pt. II. *Journal of Asthma Research, 2,* 215–255.

Schore, A. N. (2003). *Affect regulation and repair of the self.* New York: Norton.

Schwartz, M. P. (1988). *Incidence of events associated with maternal-infant bonding disturbance in a pediatric population.* Unpublished doctoral dissertation, Rosebridge Graduate School, Walnut Creek, CA.

Shapiro, F. (2001). *Eye movement desensitization and reprocessing: Basic principles, protocols, and procedures* (2nd ed.). New York: Guilford Press.

Sousa, P. L. R., Barros, F. C., Gazalle, R. V., Begeres, R. M., Pinheiro, G. N., Menezes, S. T., et al. (1974, October). *Attachment and lactation.* Paper presented at the 15th International Congress of Pediatrics, Buenos Aires.

Turnbull, J. (1962). Asthma conceived as a learned response. *Journal of Psychosomatic Research, 6,* 59.

White, M., & Epston, D. (1990). *Narrative means to therapeutic ends.* New York: Norton.

CHAPTER 7

Enhancing Attachments: Conjoint Couple Therapy

Mark D. Moses

Marriage is the triumph of hope over experience.
—Oscar Wilde

Couples and Attachment

An individual's drive to attach is at the core of all relationships. This need is both normal and healthy (Zimberoff & Hartman, 2002). On the most basic level, two individuals who desire, seek, and join in attachment form a couple. The sexual nature and complex socioemotional factors distinguish adult romantic unions from other relationships (Feeney, 1999).

The choice of a partner commonly constitutes a search for qualities missing from one's family of origin, and/or a desire to sustain what was satisfying and familiar, or a need to heal emotional wounds (Shaver & Hazan, 1993). The individual implicitly, perhaps unconsciously, chooses a partner in the hope and promise of a sense of completeness (Donovan, 2003; Scharff & Scharff, 1987). When common values, aspirations, and mutual support are present in the match, harmony and satisfaction prevail (Gottman, 1999). To illustrate: Dave sees in Sarah a quality that reminds him of his mother's calm and quiet manner. Sarah is attracted to Dave's passion for life, which she experiences as an exciting contrast to the members of her disengaged family.

For most, the initial fascinations and attractions sustain themselves for months and perhaps years before challenges ensue. When events in the relationship are experienced as breaches of the attachment bond, the resulting wounds, if unresolved, compromise the relationship. How can attachment problems be understood and resolved in therapy? This chapter addresses the nature of attachments, attachment issues, related difficulties encountered in couples, and a couple therapy treatment approach that integrates Eye Movement Desensitization and Reprocessing (EMDR; Shapiro, 2001).

Attachment Theory

Attachment theory is viewed as one of the most cogent and researched explanations of adult love relationships (Johnson, Millikin, & Makinen, 2001; Shaver & Hazan, 1993). Bowlby (1988) conceptualized that *proximity* (contact), *a secure base* (security), and *a safe haven* (comfort and protection) are fundamental to healthy human attachments. Bowlby built attachment theory on the mother-infant (or caregiver-child) bond and later noted "conspicuous similarities" established in adult relationship bonds (Hazan & Zeifman, 1999). He proposed that these are lifelong, cradle-to-grave needs.

Attachment Styles

Based on the research of Bartholomew and Horowitz (1991), four adult attachment style prototypes have been identified: *secure* plus three insecure styles, *preoccupied, dismissing,* and *fearful.* Secure people are characterized by seeking intimacy with little concern about abandonment. They readily self-disclose, are inclined to turn to their partner in times of need, but also have the resiliency to manage emotional stress in themselves and the emotions expressed by their partner. Preoccupied people also seek intimacy, yet they tend to exhibit high levels of anxiety about abandonment. Dismissing people are characterized by significant levels of avoidance of intimacy and low levels of anxiety about abandonment, and fearful people are characterized by high levels of both avoidance of intimacy and anxiety about abandonment (Davila, 2003).

What are the implications and predictions in the matching of attachment styles in couples? Banse (2004) corroborated the strong correlation between relationship satisfaction and the style of attachment. There was a negative correlation between relationship satisfaction and fearful attachment in both women and men. Banse found that the negative effects of fearful and dismissing styles could be compensated by the partner's style or the combination of the couple's styles. However, a preoccupied attachment style in husbands is related to low satisfaction in both partners, with no compensation to balance the relationship (e.g., an attending wife).

Does attachment security naturally change over time in a marriage? Treboux, Crowell, and Waters (2004) explored the degree of perceived attachment security, comparing couples in new relationships to couples married for 6 years. They found that attachment security generally increased over time. Treboux et al. also corroborated the value of secure style as offering safe haven in stressful situations, as the secure relationship did affect marital satisfaction. As predicted from attachment theory, the same was not true in the insecure relationships.

A key question is: Can attachment styles change? Mounting research indicates that it is possible to enhance *attachment security* (Gottman, 1994; Mikulincer, 1999). Attachments styles can fluctuate through the life cycle due to contextual, environmental, and situational stressors, including partner match (Love & Murdock, 2004). The possibility of changing attachment styles by repairing attachment injuries and modifying relational patterns has been validated (Bartholomew & Horowitz, 1991; Johnson, 2004; Johnson & Whiffen,

2003). The therapeutic relationship itself may cultivate relationship security if it includes the elements of healthy attachment (e.g., safety, validation, understanding, and reliability) paired with therapist attunement.

Unresolved Attachment Experiences: Inherent Problems

Attachment injuries are wounds that occur when a significant figure, parent or partner, fails to respond during a critical time of need. In a couple's life together, these painful incidents left unresolved from an invalidating past are susceptible to being triggered by similar events having a recurring theme. When this occurs, barriers are created in the relationship (Johnson, 2004).

To illustrate a common issue, consider Bill and Carla, who after several years of marriage are plagued by a pattern of disconnection. Bill suffers from a fear of abandonment rooted in the childhood loss of his father. Carla survived a chaotic and emotionally abusive family environment, in which raised voices represented hostility. Carla has a fearful attachment style, and Bill has a preoccupied attachment style. When stress presents itself, Bill erupts by raising his voice in a harsh tone and Carla typically withdraws by storming out, resulting in severe misunderstandings and limitations in their intimacy. Their respective activated attachment issues have marooned them in perceptions of abandonment and betrayal, respectively. The marriage is at an impasse, stuck in negative interactions that perpetuate the continuation of injuries and disconnection.

Karpel (2001) characterized the manifestations of impasses as intense reactivity (triggering), significant affective arousal or flattening, perceptual distortions, inflexibility of responses, predictability (repetition) of interaction, decreased ability for empathy with partner, and a lack of learning in therapy. According to attachment theory, impasses are direct results of blocks or erosions in the connection between the couple. From a systemic view, the over- or under-reactions of partners feed dysfunctional *interactional sequences.*

These impasses color the experience of the relationship and obscure the *softer emotion.* For Bill and Carla, the deeper, primary, softer feelings of sadness and fear lie beneath the secondary surface expressions of anger and rejection. *Softening events,* characterized by a shift from hostility to warmth in energy, are also blocked by defensive barriers. Both softer emotions and softening events are necessary for intimacy and healthy attachments (Gottman, 1994).

Targeting Couples' Attachment Injuries

Viewed from an EMDR Adaptive Informational Processing perspective (AIP; Shapiro, 2001), a couple's overreactions and overregulation (e.g., shutting down) in repetitive interactions are fueled by traumatic material encapsulated in the brain and triggered by one's partner. When incompletely processed and stored, small "t" (small traumas) attachment experiences become triggered, and distortions and other blocks can occur (Shapiro, 1995). A study by Protinsky, Sparks, and Flemke (2001) applying EMDR to couples with attachment issues found that painful incidents from an invalidating past environment must first be accessed and processed before the couple can move forward. Kaslow, Nurse, and Thompson (2002, p. 303) suggested that, through EMDR, "[couples] move toward the same goal of vital attachment with increased closeness, a major principle of family systems therapy." Shapiro (2001, p. 288) lent further support when she stated, "By using EMDR to defuse earlier memories, the couple can achieve a healthier dynamic and give appropriate weight to present problems and disagreements."

A Couple Therapy Approach to Attachment Issues: The Synthesis

A hypothetical couple enters therapy, and some improvement is made in stabilizing their current crisis. However, their progress stalls in a negative pattern and they remain disconnected. They cannot move beyond certain impasses. The therapist suspects that underlying residuals from attachment injuries are impeding their progress. The therapist implements an EMDR–Family Systems Integrative approach conjointly (both present) to address these obstacles, ultimately freeing the relationship to move forward.

The EMDR and Conjoint Couple Therapy protocol (Moses, 2002, 2003) is a hybrid of three family therapy frameworks: experiential (Emotionally Focused Therapy: EFT), psychodynamic (Object Relations), and Social Construction (Narrative Therapy). All approaches interface in several ways and are compatible with EMDR, an *integrative therapy*. As Maxfield (2002, p. 403) pointed out, "EMDR has elements of many traditional psychological orientations . . . [including] interactional therapies." The union of these approaches is outlined next.

During the assessment phase of treatment, the therapist employs aspects of EFT, Object Relations, and Narrative Therapy when interviewing for personal history. Family of origin genograms (Kaslow, 1995; McGoldrick, Gerson, & Shellenberger, 1999) are constructed, and attachment styles, traumatic events, and patterns are identified.

Then the therapist implements the EMDR protocol to process these attachment injury residuals so new pathways can open. Conjoint EMDR addresses these obstacles, ultimately freeing the relationship to move forward. In the final phase, EFT and Narrative Therapy provide a structure for the couple to retell their stories, practice new skills, and imagine a more positive future.

In the following, a brief discussion of these family therapy approaches, their various interfaces, and the ways they accommodate the EMDR protocol, is presented.

Object Relations

The core concept of Bowlby's (1988) original theory of attachment is based on the innate human need for attachment and is grounded in Object Relations Theory. When relationship development is impeded, Psychodynamic/Object Relations Theory proposes, "The effects of past traumas interfere with current functioning, the related developmental trajectory, or both" (Kaslow et al., 2002, p. 311). EMDR is compatible with psychodynamic information processing (Shapiro, 2001; Wachtel, 2002). Two main features of Psychodynamic/Object Relations Therapy are *free association* and *transference* (Scharff & Scharff, 1987). Free association is congruous with the free flow of thoughts, feelings, and images encouraged in EMDR processing. In couple therapy, the transferences are addressed between the partners, rather than a working-through between the patient and therapist, as in individual Psychodynamic Therapy (Donovan, 2003).

Emotionally Focused Therapy

As an experiential therapy, EFT holds emotions as key in organizing attachment beliefs and behaviors. The goal in EFT is to "reprocess experiences and reorganize interactions to create a secure bond between partners" (Johnson, 2004, p. 12). Emotional "shifts" are seen as important signals of attachment distress. Congruent with the principles of experiential therapies, EMDR facilitates a natural processing with minimal input or direction from the therapist. EMDR also focuses on bodily felt experience, carefully tracked, while connecting cognitive information with emotional material. Divergence exists, as EMDR places less emphasis on verbalization (i.e., articulating symbolic experiences and reflective listening) during processing than do most experiential therapies (Bohart & Greenberg, 2002).

Narrative Therapy

The goal of Narrative Therapy is the *deconstruction* of old and problematic stories and the *reconstruction* of new and hopeful narratives about the self and the relationship through constellations of questions and extensive dialogue (Freedman & Combs, 2000; White & Epsom, 1990). Narrative Therapy is derived from social constructivism, which postulates that the discourses from individuals' various social contexts (e.g., family, friends, and partners) shape their reality. In Narrative Couple Therapy, each partner witnesses the retelling of his or her respective stories, with the goals of understanding, modification, and integration (Freedman & Combs, 2000). Similarly, EMDR strives to change the *Negative Cognitions* to *Positive Cognitions* by using the raw material of *preferred cognitions* and *Cognitive Interweaves* to construct a *positive future template* (Shapiro, 1995). Both approaches encourage a reframe of subjective realities about the self in relational contexts. However, Narrative Therapy and EMDR differ in focus and procedure. Narrative Therapy is primarily concerned with cognitive shifts through extensive questioning and discussion, whereas EMDR is focused on a shift in the experience as well as cognition, with a minimum of questioning or dialogue.

Applying EMDR to Couple Therapy

EMDR has been applied to couple therapy, both as parallel individual treatments and conjointly, with both partners present (Karpel, 2001; Kaslow et al., 2002; Litt, 2000; Moses, 2002, 2003; Protinsky et al., 2001; Shapiro, 1995; Zangwill, 2000).

Advantages of Integrating EMDR and Couple Therapy

In a task analysis study, Protinsky et al. (2001, p. 163) indicated that couples in conjoint EMDR treatment, compared to a control group who received EFT without EMDR, benefited from a "heightened emotional experience," and as a result, partners were "more interested in emotional engagement." Protinsky et al. found that EMDR as an intervention in Conjoint Couple Therapy appeared to increase therapeutic effectiveness. EMDR was intended, in the Protinsky et al. application, as a brief intervention of rapid processing in the context of the couple therapy. Systemically, the relationship is always viewed as the "patient," and the couple system is thus worked with conjointly. The intent of applying EMDR in this model is to help the relationship and the couple progress through impasses; it is not intended as two comprehensive parallel individual therapies. Building on these findings and anecdotal reports from EMDR therapists, an EMDR couple therapy protocol was developed (Moses, 2002, 2003).

THERAPY PROCESS

> *All experience is knowledge: everything else is just information.*
>
> —Albert Einstein

Goal of Therapy

Conjoint Couple Therapy applying EMDR increases empathy in the *witnessing partner,* as the *working partner* breaks through the reactivity of attachment triggers (Moses, 2003). Johnson and Whiffen (2003) proposed that couple therapy can offer alternative patterns of response and renewed ways to connect. The strengthening of the pair bond provides a relational resiliency and mutual emotional protection.

Guidelines

Therapists working conjointly with EMDR should ensure that they establish the following elements:

- *Safety:* by establishing stability, sufficient resources, and commitment.
- *Balance:* by establishing equanimity; for example, both partners must participate.
- *Containment:* by establishing sufficient contextual support systems.

The Process of EMDR with Couples

The aim of integrating EMDR into couple therapy is to repair attachment wounds while providing a tangible experience of availability, empathy, and the promise of reliability. This experience allows the couple to build trust by melting their defenses (protective attachment styles) and rekindling an intimate attachment. When partners first meet and fall in love they share more personal narratives of positive as well as painful experiences and fears. Revelations of this type and with a depth of feeling, according to Hazan and Zeifman (1999), may constitute a test of commitment and future reliability, as well as a bid for caring and mutual acceptance. "As the members of couples start to serve as mutual sources of emotional support, their relationship takes on an additional component of attachment—namely *safe haven*" (p. 350).

The schematic (Figure 7.1) illuminates a couple's natural proclivity to attach. This typically begins with sharing and often the promise of mutual healing. Over time, injuries (i.e., betrayal, abandonment, rejection, nonvalidation, and nonresponsiveness) occur in the relationship and can result in chronic distancing or conflict. The couple may seek therapy. In therapy, stability and surface behavior (first-order change) improve. Deeper, more sustaining change (second order) is sought. If an impasse is reached and the couple remains stuck, EMDR is considered to process the individual attachment issues and bridge the reattach-

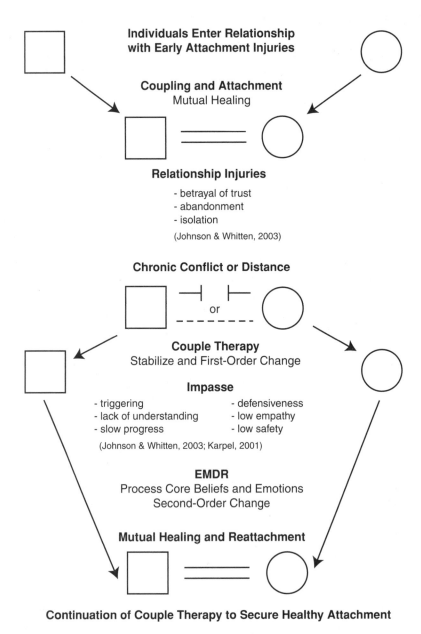

**Individuals Enter Relationship
with Early Attachment Injuries**

Coupling and Attachment
Mutual Healing

Relationship Injuries

- betrayal of trust
- abandonment
- isolation

(Johnson & Whitten, 2003)

Chronic Conflict or Distance

or

Couple Therapy
Stabilize and First-Order Change

Impasse

- triggering   - defensiveness
- lack of understanding   - low empathy
- slow progress   - low safety

(Johnson & Whitten, 2003; Karpel, 2001)

EMDR
Process Core Beliefs and Emotions
Second-Order Change

Mutual Healing and Reattachment

Continuation of Couple Therapy to Secure Healthy Attachment

Figure 7.1   A model for EMDR and attachment issues in couple therapy.

ment between partners. Then the relationship therapy can continue with the couple more securely attached.

Treatment Processes and Procedures

The protocol for couples (Moses, 2003) offers safety through structure, as does the eight-phase, three-pronged EMDR protocol (Shapiro, 2001) integrated in the approach presented here.

Phase 1: History

The therapist gathers information, which includes a thorough *trauma history,* particularly related to attachment injuries. According to Byng-Hall (1999), a major measurement of attachment security in a marriage is the degree of coherence in partners' narratives about family relationships. The therapist tracks the affect and coherence of narratives about family of origin as well as current relationships, using the following tools.

A *genogram* is useful in identifying transgenerational and relational patterns (McGoldrick et al., 1999). Genograms may be developed with a thematic structure (e.g., health issues, addiction, gender roles). Another approach developed by Kaslow (1995) is the projective genogram, which emphasizes a series of open-ended questions, encouraging free association, and clients drawing their own genograms. An attachment genogram is an interview focused on the attachment bonds with the family of origin focused on associations for projective and thematic value. Adapted from the Adult Attachment Interview (see Bartholomew & Horowitz, 1991), the following may be queried and explored: (a) relationship with father and mother, and the parent to whom you were closer; (b) relationship with siblings; (c) relationship with significant extended family members and any parentlike figures; (d) general sense of proximity, secure base, and safe haven in one's family of origin; (e) any trauma history experienced or witnessed; (f) any beliefs about self in relationships; (g) any rejections, separations, threats, or losses; and (h) therapist attentiveness to any attachment style themes and beliefs. (See Chapter 3 by Shellenberger.)

It is as vital to identify the *positive resources* within the relationship as it is to note the areas of difficulty. Examples of these are working cooperatively as parents, sharing a common humor, and "positive deviations" around the problems presented.

The couple's appropriateness for conjoint EMDR intervention needs to be assessed. The following circumstances would signal concern: (a) if the commitment to the relationship is unclear; (b) if the trauma issues require individual therapy before readiness for couple therapy; and (c) if safety within the couple system has not been established.

Phase 2: Preparation

The therapist explains the EMDR procedure to the couple, mutual consent is obtained, and the procedure instructions and processing order are presented. The instructions for the witnessing partner are carefully explained. The therapist positions the witnessing partner according to the working partner's preferences (e.g., next to or behind working partner), then instructs him or her about the parameters for *compassionate witnessing:* "Stay focused, be still and silent, look away during passes, do not track light [or fingers]. Closure instructions will be offered at the end of the processing session" (see later discussion). The therapist assists the working partner to identify and visualize a safe place, and then leads the client in a set of eye movements or other bilateral stimulation. Relaxation techniques are introduced, if needed, to provide the client with self-soothing methods to deal with disturbance that might emerge in or between sessions.

Phase 3: Assessment

This phase targets attachment injury events and patterns. The therapist always begins with the relationship issues, then tracks whatever direction the client's pathways take. The therapist generally uses one of three methods to identify targets: (1) clear target identification by the couple or individual during the assessment phase, (2) *float-back* instructions focused on bodily sensations, or (3) the use of the float-back technique through guided imagery (Moses, 2003; Zangwill, 2000) to induce a memory. Once a target is identified, the following associated components are verbalized: Negative Cognition, Positive Cognition, physical sensations and locations, Subjective Units of Disturbance, and Validity of Cognition. This establishes a baseline for processing (see Shapiro, 2001; Chapter 1).

Phases 4 through 7: Processing

Phases 4 through 7 are the core of desensitizing and reprocessing. The therapist focuses on the current attachment injury first, and then explores any related *feeder memories.* It is beyond the scope of this chapter to describe the details of EMDR processing (see Shapiro, 2001), but Phase 7, session Closure, is explicated in the following five components:

1. *Debrief the working partner* by identifying any unfinished work and explaining that internal processing may continue during the week (memories, dreams, etc.). The working partner is asked to note any pertinent material that may arise and share at the next session check-in.

2. *Closure instructions and reflections for the witnessing partner* consist of the therapist's statement, "Without labeling, pathologizing, interpreting, or problem-solving, limit the focus of your comments to how you were emotionally impacted."

3. *Bridging material* may help connect content from the session in a meaningful manner. Following the witnessing partner's "emotional impact statement," the therapist sensitizes the witnessing partner to see how he or she might have inadvertently triggered the partner. In addition, issues may have been triggered in the witnessing partner, which can be identified at this time. Possibilities for new interactions and future templates can also be harvested and developed with the therapist.

4. *Mutual appreciation* is shared with the following instructions: "Share with one another one quality about the other that you deeply or profoundly appreci-

ated in our time together today. Make contact with one another, at least eye contact, and I will simply listen."

5. *Instructions for the time between sessions* involve the therapist's advising the couple to avoid discussing the EMDR session to ensure that any continuing individual processing is not interrupted. In the event that the working partner does share material, his or her mate should be coached to respond as a compassionate listener.

Phase 8: Reevaluation

In the next session, both partners check in. The therapist then determines whether further EMDR sessions are required for the first partner before shifting to the other partner. To maintain balance, each turn in EMDR processing is limited to 2 or 3 sessions for each partner, if possible. The alternation of turns may occur several times throughout a couple's treatment. When partners are ready for the shift, the protocol described earlier is repeated.

Reflections on the Therapy Process

A three-pronged EMDR protocol is applied by initially identifying the triggers in the *current* relationship, processing the *earlier* feeder memories, and installing templates for a more connected *future* relationship. The therapy becomes systemic by bridging respective individual issues to the relationship interactions. This process is a working within and between (Johnson, 2004). The therapist functions as an interpreter of issues and a peacemaker for mutual disarmament of triggers. It is vital to recognize competition and comparison in the couple relationship. The therapist should be especially cautious in planning the treatment, including deciding the order of processing when: (a) one partner has more traumas or is more severely traumatized than the other; (b) one partner is more familiar or experienced with EMDR; (c) one partner has a more dramatic or "impressive" response; (d) one partner does not have much or any response; or (e) there is a rivalry as to who is the "better client."

CASE EXAMPLES

Case 1: Meg and Greg: A Case of Abandonment and Betrayal

The Presenting Problem

Meg and Greg, married 9 years, now in their early 30s, entered marital therapy in crisis following Greg's outbursts, which were related to Meg's extramarital encounters (see Figure 7.2).

Background

Meg perceived her father as distant and her mother as "critical and controlling." Meg individuated through rebellion and developed a *dismissing attachment style*. People with this style tend to have a relatively low need for relationships, are content to be self-sufficient, and are not emotionally open or affectionate

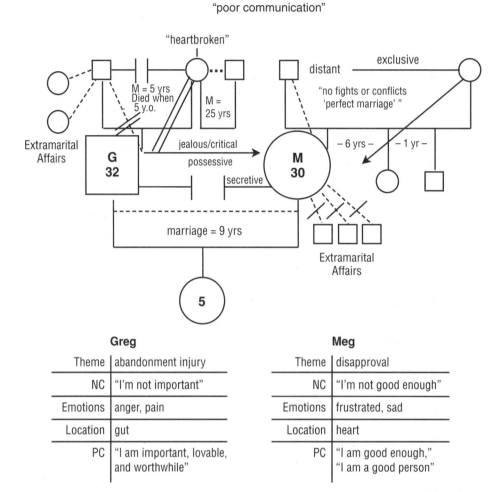

Figure 7.2   Genogram Greg and Meg.

(Davila, 2003). Greg was an only child of a conflicted marriage. His parents divorced when he was 5, following his father's extramarital affairs. Greg felt that he and his mother never healed from the father's abandonment, leaving Greg with a *preoccupied attachment style*. People with this style tend to question whether they are worthy of love, obsessively worry about rejection, and are dependant in relationships. They seek reassurance about their partner's love and commitment. They idealize partners, yet are hypercritical of them when needs are not met (Davila, 2003).

Course of Treatment

The initial sessions focused on joining, history taking, and identifying interactional systems in the marriage (e.g., distancer and pursuer). The emotional tenor included anger and desperation on Greg's part, and guilt and suffocation on

Meg's. Over the next four sessions a frame for understanding, responsibility, and forgiveness developed. A mutual decision was made to introduce EMDR into the conjoint therapy. Greg chose to work first.

Greg's Processing

Greg's Negative Cognition was "I am not important," and his Positive Cognition was "I am good enough!" His score on the Validity of Cognition (VOC) scale was 2 (on a scale 1 to 7, where 7 is completely true), and his identified emotions were "anger and pain." His score on the Subjective Units of Disturbance (SUD) scale was 8 (on a scale 0 to 10, where 10 is the most disturbance imaginable), and the location of feeling was his gut.

Greg chose to position Meg next to him and held her hand. Meg became a *compassionate witness*. Next, a safe place was established. The target was Greg's interaction with his abandoning father, and the picture was a baseball game as a boy, one attended by his father. As Greg began processing the painful scene, his agony was palpable. Related channels involved his anger toward his father and identification with his mother's compromise. His SUD neutralized, and the belief "I'm important, lovable, and worthwhile" became valid (VOC = 7).

Meg wept at Greg's boyhood pain. She offered, "I feel so badly for him. I never want to hurt him like that" (a softening event). The session ended with expressions of appreciation and a silent, poignant gaze that had not been present for some time (*proximity*). At the next session, during check-in reevaluation, Greg reported, "I am not angry anymore, and I can sleep now." The decision was made for a shift to allow Meg to process.

Meg's Processing

Meg's target memory was interaction with her critical mother, and her target was a scene of her mother inquiring about something when Meg was 10 years old. The perceived implication was that she had fallen short of her mother's expectations. Meg's Negative Cognition was "I am not good enough." The emotions "frustration and sadness" were located in her heart with a SUD of 8. Her Positive Cognition was "I am good enough and I am a good person," with a VOC of 2.

Meg held Greg's hand, as if he provided some important grounding to her. After establishing a safe place, she pictured a typical mealtime scene, distressed by her mother's judgments. She described her "heart beating fast" and an urge to "escape and have a secret life." Meg's processing was emotionally intense with sobs, resulting in a neutralizing of her SUD at 0 (release and relief). We installed a Cognitive Interweave of "My mother is not the authority of my worth," which led to a confidence that "I am good enough! I am a good person," with a VOC of 7.

Greg reflected, "I felt her hurt. . . . I felt good for Meg when she finally said, 'I am a good person'" (softening event). Realizing a link to the marriage and what he might offer, Greg vowed to be "less critical and more thoughtful in how I bring things up. . . . I don't want to sound like her mother." The session closed with expressions of deep mutual appreciation.

At the next session, Meg disclosed that she was thrilled to feel affection for Greg and reported a renewed physical relationship. She realized that her guilty feelings and unworthiness had blocked her emotional progress. Concurrently, Greg reported none of his previous suspicion and was "more confident" (secure base) in the marriage.

After a 2-month break from treatment, they returned to, in their words, "work on a few sexual issues." Four sessions of focused work helped them in negotiating mutual initiation. Their intimate reattachment, emotionally and sexually, was maintained at a 6-month follow-up.

In Retrospect

The impasses in the treatment dissolved as a result of the EMDR processing, which allowed a shared emotional experience leading to increased attunement, that is, deeper understanding, empathy, and connection. After two EMDR sessions each, the couple therapy progressed more rapidly and successfully.

Case 2: Tim and Sarah: A Case of Nonresponsiveness and Nonvalidation

Married for 20 years, now in their 40s, the glue for Tim and Sarah was their three children, who were all doing well and launching into their own lives (see Figure 7.3).

Presenting Problem

The concern was mutual disconnection. Tim had had a major depressive episode 5 years earlier and periodically fell into a "sad and disconnected state." Sarah complained of "lack of passion" in the marriage. Both expressed commitment and desire to stay together, although Sarah admitted to having fantasies of leaving to seek passion and connection with someone else. She had had urges over the years, but had never acted on those impulses. Sarah was in individual therapy, where she was finding her voice and was encouraged by her therapist to enter marital therapy to face her long-standing issues with Tim.

Background

Tim grew up, the youngest of three boys, in a "successful family" where the emphasis was on performance. His father and one brother were physicians, and his other brother was a lawyer. There was a wall of privacy around emotions as expression of feelings was seen as weak in this male-dominant, competitive family. Tim owned a clothing store and worked long hours. He enjoyed moderate success until an economic recession resulted in bankruptcy, unemployment, and depletion of his sense of self-worth. This situation precipitated a 9-month depressive episode. Tim's Negative Cognitions, "I'm deficient" and "I'm not good enough," emerged in his processing work. The trigger in the relationship was regularly sensing Sarah's disappointment in him. Even though he desperately wanted to please his wife, he was confused about how to accomplish this daunting goal. Tim demonstrated a *fearful attachment style*. According to Davila (2003), people with this style tend to question if they are worthy of

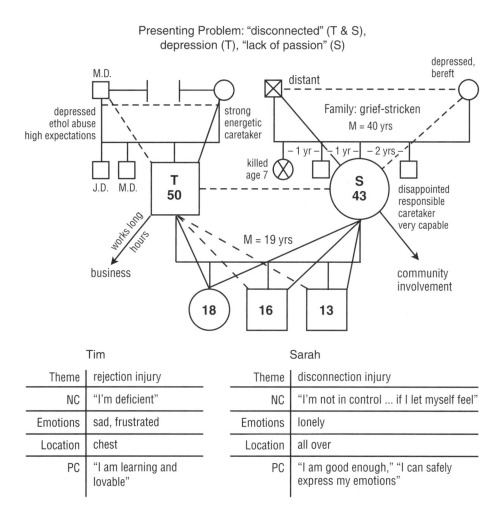

Figure 7.3   Genogram Tim and Sarah.

love; they fear rejection yet yearn to be in a relationship. Once in a relation-ship, they fear intimacy and are inclined to be inhibited (emotionally) and pas-sive (physically).

Sarah came from a supportive and loving middle-class family. The second daughter, third of four children, she benefited from a secure start in life. When Sarah was age 5, her family was marked by the tragic death of her older sister in an automobile accident. Sarah, her mother, and her two brothers survived the ac-cident. Her mother was the driver and felt deeply responsible; she fell into a chronic depression from which she never truly recovered. As the surviving daugh-ter, Sarah learned to avoid burdening her now unavailable mother with any of her needs, especially emotional ones, and to provide nurturing to her father and broth-ers. Sarah grew up to be a capable, dependable caregiver as a wife, mother, friend, and community member. Her Negative Cognition emerged as "I am not in control if I let myself feel." She had developed a predominantly *preoccupied attachment style.* Typical of this style, people who provide much caregiving, often to the point of excess, have a potential to be demanding, feeling as though their needs are never fully met (Davila, 2003).

Course of Treatment

The initial sessions focused on joining and history taking. The therapist learned that Sarah lived in quiet desperation, reluctant to express her needs. Tim felt profoundly inadequate, baffled at how to be an acceptable husband to Sarah. The degree of mutual triggering and impasse was Sarah feeling "fed up" and Tim feeling "hopeless," which led to a decision to introduce EMDR into the treatment. Sarah worked first. This order tipped the balance, as Tim had been viewed as the patient, beginning with his depression, and Sarah felt that others' needs always went before hers. The following excerpts are from the next two sessions.

Sarah's Processing

Sarah positioned Tim next to her without any contact. After establishing a safe place, she targeted her deep emptiness and pain when she was alone with Tim. She recalled feeling hopelessly alone during Tim's depressive episode 5 years earlier.

Therapist: Can you bring up a picture that represents that experience?

Sarah: Yes, I see Tim staring out of the window, sitting motionless and expressionless.

Therapist: And what words go best with that picture which express your distressing belief about yourself now?

Sarah: I am not in control. . . . I am alone. . . . I will disappear.

Therapist: Bring up that picture. . . . What would you like to believe about yourself now?

Sarah: I am in control enough that I will be okay expressing my feelings. (VOC = 3)

Therapist: What do you feel now when bringing up that picture?

Sarah: I feel hopeless and panicked.

Therapist: On a scale of 0 to 10, with 10 most distressing, what level of disturbance (SUD) do you have?

Sarah: It is very strong, maybe an 8.

Therapist: Where do you feel it in your body?

Sarah: Here (gestures to her heart) . . . and all over. . . . I can't get him to respond.

Therapist: (Instructs Sarah to track fingers: eye movements [EMs]) Can you let your mind float back to an earlier time when you had that same feeling? . . .

Sarah: Wow! My mother just popped up . . . kind of superimposed on the scene. She is standing at the sink, staring out . . . she's not there . . . like in a trance . . . not really there . . . and I am a little girl, feeling alone.

Therapist: (EMs) Let it go . . . (EMs) What comes up?

Sarah: I needed to be a good little girl, or I would be alone and disintegrate. . . .

Sarah: I can express my feelings and be okay.

Therapist: (EMs) What comes up?

Sarah: I feel a little calmer. I have a bit more distance from the picture. . . . I see my mother as a sad woman and feel compassion about her loss.

Therapist: (Back to target memory) Can you bring up the original incident?

Sarah: I don't feel so frustrated. . . . I feel compassion for Tim. He was grieving a loss, too . . . like my mother . . . and had sad feelings about it. . . .

Sarah: It is okay for me to have feelings and needs, too.

Therapist: Go with that. . . . (EMs)

Sarah: (SUD = 0; VOC = 6) I can let Tim know what I need.

Witnessing Partner Reflection

Therapist: Tim, without labeling, pathologizing, interpreting . . . how were you affected?

Tim: (To Sarah) I can see, for the first time, the similarities of your mother not being available, and when I was depressed. I'm terribly sorry and don't want to keep affecting you that way. (softening effect)

Mutual Appreciation Sharing

Therapist: Share with one another one quality . . . that you deeply . . . appreciated. . . .

Sarah: I appreciate how you were really here. . . . I mean emotionally, I felt you here.

Tim: I appreciate that you shared what you need. Now I can help you. (safe haven)

Tim's Processing

After two EMDR processing sessions with Sarah, Tim chose to focus on his feeling of inadequacy in the marriage. The scene with Sarah rapidly linked to a scene as a 10-year-old at a school play, Tim feeling "not good enough" in his father's eyes, compared to his older brothers. His preferred cognition of "I am learning and I am loveable" was installed, with a renewed confidence in his ability to stay more emotionally engaged with Sarah. During the mutual appreciation sharing, Sarah welled up (a softening event), expressing her pride in Tim's efforts to understand and be available to her. (safe haven)

In Retrospect

Although this couple worked on many more issues and negotiations in the next 4 months of treatment, 6 EMDR sessions moved them beyond the impasses that had plagued them for years. The focused processing also gave Sarah and Tim hope and the resultant motivation to experiment with different ways that they could be engaged as a couple. At termination they had begun daily check-ins, were going out dancing, and had resumed their physical intimacy. Because both Sarah and Tim were in individual treatment, a few phone contacts with their respective therapists bridged a successful coordination of treatment that avoided triangulation.

DISCUSSION

Each partner brings strengths and issues to the relationship. The etiologies of many attachment issues are found in small "t" trauma experiences, resulting in attachment limitations, such as bonds that are blocked by impasses. In contrast, large "T" traumas, that is, those related to life-threatening events, such as assault, abuse, and other serious trauma, require special assessment and cautions to determine if conjoint EMDR is indicated or contraindicated. Attachment injuries are at the foundation of the couple's impasses. When wounds are triggered by specific events and current situations in the couple's life, encapsulated emotional residuals can fuel reactions, leading to dysfunctional patterns, symptoms, and constraints in the relationship. Repairing attachment injuries can result in reconnecting the couple and has been shown empirically to be corrective (Hazan & Zeifman, 1999).

The therapist can conceptualize the qualities of a secure attachment style as a template for a healthier, more supportive and stable relationship (Davila, 2003). Insecure attachment styles (i.e., fearful, preoccupied, and dismissive) are characterized and often tainted by themes of abandonment, nonvalidation, or betrayal. The therapist can be guided by determining each partner's respective attachment style, holding the various attachment styles in mind as "channel markers" in the treatment process. Discussion of the styles, their origins, and their interrelationships can sensitize the partners to each other's struggles. In addition, an understanding of the dynamics of the couple's attachment styles may help the therapist chart a shorter course for therapy by identifying cognitions and emotions in preparation for EMDR processing.

The limitation of categorizing attachment styles lies in the mixed and variable aspects of styles that occur for individuals in reality. Thus, as valuable as these schemas are, fixed labels, assumed or imposed, are best avoided. A respectful curiosity about clients' unique narratives, beliefs, and styles will prove more workable.

Certainly the goal in all therapies is to help the partners develop more adaptive interactions, more positive skills, and healthier connections. *So why apply EMDR?* EMDR's promise lies in its uniquely rapid processing of attachment injuries that are often at the core of relational issues. Through EMDR processing, each partner has an opportunity to recount and desensitize residuals from past attachment injuries in a safe environment and, consequently, to sensitize each other to painful triggers. By breaking through these impasses, the couple is free to grow cognitively, affectivity, and spiritually.

Why Work Conjointly?

The efficacy of EMDR with individuals is well established, but its adaptation to couple therapy is less fully documented. However, from a systems approach, the couple is viewed as the patient. Working conjointly balances the system, as neither partner is identified as the "problem," and both have an opportunity to experience insights into each other's past that might not be shared on a conscious level. Working conjointly, each individual has an opportunity to access past injuries as the respective partner compassionately witnesses, vicariously experiences the pain, and activates mutual attunement. This increased empathy and understanding can precipitate a fundamental shift as old, hard, distressing narratives are replaced by new, softer, and more loving stories. The reduced emotional charge of past experience allows the couple to respond without reactivity, with less emphasis on the past, and with more energy on present interaction. In this way, the treatment is corrective to the system.

Outcome studies of couple therapy indicate that cognitive techniques alone do not produce sustained change unless accompanied by an emotional, behavioral, and experiential shift (Atkinson, 1999; Johnson, 2004). Still, understanding is important in the therapy process. Holmes (1998, p. 69) pointed out that developing an awareness of the other's *unmet early attachment needs* encourages acceptance that he or she is not acting in a "deliberately contrary way, but rather following unconscious working models."

Three therapy approaches and their respective processes—EFT, Narrative Therapy, and EMDR—are integrated into various stages of the treatment. The integrative couple therapy approach presented in this chapter includes EFT in the exploration of attachment patterns and styles. Techniques associated with Narrative Therapy are used to gather history, identify attachment issues, and develop softer and more hopeful future possibilities, as can be seen in the case studies. EMDR's reprocessing of attachment issues provides a powerful emotional experience that breaks through impasses in the relationship that have blocked progress.

Regarding the challenge of integration, none of the family therapy approaches are applied in a completely orthodox manner. That is, the integration of these approaches requires selection of components and modification of each model in the synthesis, the combination leading to a new assimilation. However, the intent is to preserve the fundamental integrity of each family therapy approach as well as the fidelity of the EMDR protocol.

When Is EMDR Appropriate in Couple Therapy?

The therapist is cautioned to apply EMDR conjointly only after ascertaining commitment, safety, and mutual consent by the partners. Conjoint EMDR is contraindicated in cases of severe trauma or reluctance, hostility, or intolerance by either partner because of the emotional intensity involved. EMDR with couples is also an approach to be used only by experienced, well-trained, and secure therapists with the resources to handle the strong feelings the therapy can generate.

Indications and Contraindications

In ascertaining the appropriate use of conjoint EMDR, the following have emerged from both the literature and therapist anecdotal reports regarding indications and contraindications.

EMDR is indicated in couple therapy (a) for couples seeking mutual understanding, empathy, and sensitivity to triggering events; (b) for couples with difficulty being vulnerable with one another; (c) for couples who are at an impasse in treatment and need the safety of a structure to process underlying issues; and (d) for couples who cannot get beyond personalizing or projecting.

Contraindications to working conjointly with EMDR include (a) a history of complex or severe trauma (large "T"); if an exception is made, the therapist should be very cautious, assuring sufficient resources and close coordination with a required primary individual therapist; (b) significant dissociation in either partner; (c) when either partner is reluctant to try EMDR with the partner witnessing; (d) a lack of commitment to the relationship; (e) the therapist's inability to control the conjoint sessions sufficiently to provide safety; (f) intense hostility or conflict, in which case, one must first reduce the intensity of the hostility; (g) the propensity for the witnessing partner to use the working partner's revelations against him or her (Litt, 2000); (h) if the witnessing partner is likely to be unable or unwilling to let the working partner have all the therapist's attention, or interrupts the process by talking or moving around (Litt, 2000); (i) a lack of tolerance by either one of the partners or the therapist for the emotional intensity; and (j) insufficient time to do the work.

When Conjoint Treatment Is Not Recommended or Possible

If conjoint EMDR is not indicated or possible, individual treatment remains an option (for one or both) and may be the treatment of choice. Each therapist should have a policy regarding mixing individual with couple therapy.

The following cautions are to be considered. First, the risks involved in unbalancing the system could do more harm than good to the relationship or to either of the partners. Despite therapists' best efforts to be even in our respective individual sessions, a very sensitive or competitive partner could feel rejected or less favored. Second, there is a potential for enhanced client emotional attachment to the therapist when meeting individually, and therefore one-on-one sessions are usually best avoided. Unless extenuating circumstances exist, there is no need to add more complexity for couples that come with substantial challenges. With these cautions in mind, the therapist can refer out if individual treatment is indicated, remain available for the couple, and coordinate treatments.

Third, triangulation is a risk when the other therapist involved is unfamiliar with or misinformed about EMDR. It is imperative to educate the individual therapist and to view him or her as a resource. To avoid triangulation, it is important to coordinate the conjoint EMDR treatment with any other individual therapists involved.

Finally, the development of treatments for couples who are challenged by attachment issues relies on continuing research. More rigorous study is needed to determine the most effective factors in the synthesis of various couple therapy models and the specific applications of EMDR. Three areas of empirical research that would benefit the development of EMDR in couple therapy are the establishment of the most efficient assessment tools for readiness, the refinement of indicators and contraindicators, and outcome efficacy studies with longitudinal follow-up.

REFERENCES

Atkinson, B. (1999, July/August). The emotional imperative: Psychotherapists cannot afford to ignore the primacy of the limbic brain. *Family Therapy Networker, 22–23.*

Banse, R. (2004). Adult attachment and marital satisfaction: Evidence for dyadic configuration effects. *Journal of Social and Personal Relationships, 21*(2), 273–282.

Bartholomew, K., & Horowitz, L. (1991). Attachment styles among young adults. *Journal of Personality and Social Psychology, 61,* 226–244.

Bohart, A., & Greenberg, L. (2002). EMDR and experiential psychotherapy. In F. Shapiro (Ed.), *EMDR as an integrative psychotherapy approach* (pp. 239–261). Washington, DC: American Psychological Association.

Bowlby, J. (1988). *A secure base.* New York: Basic Books.

Byng-Hall, J. (1999). Family and couple therapy. In J. Cassidy & P. R. Shaver (Eds.), *Handbook of attachment: Theory, research, and clinical applications* (p. 628). New York: Guilford Press.

Davila, J. (2003). Attachment processes in couple therapy. In S. Johnson & V. Whiffen (Eds.), *Attachment processes in couples and family therapy* (pp. 124–143). New York: Guilford Press.

Donovan, J. M. (2003). *Short-term object relations couples therapy.* London: Routledge.

Feeney, J. (1999). Adult romantic attachment and couple relationships. In J. Cassidy & P. R. Shaver (Eds.), *Handbook of attachment: Theory, research, and clinical applications* (pp. 355–377). New York: Guilford Press.

Freedman, J. H., & Combs, G. (2000). Narrative therapy with couples. In L. J. Bevilaqua (Ed.), *Comparative treatments for relationship dysfunction* (pp. 342–361). New York: Springer.

Gottman, J. M. (1994). *What predicts divorce?* Hillsdale, NJ: Erlbaum.

Gottman, J. M. (1999). *The marriage clinic: A scientifically based marital therapy.* New York: Norton.

Hazan, C., & Zeifman, D. (1999). Pair bonds as attachments. In J. Cassidy & P. R. Shaver (Eds.), *Handbook of attachment: Theory, research, and clinical applications* (pp. 336–354). New York: Guilford Press.

Holmes, J. (1998). Defensive and creative uses of narrative in psychotherapy: An attachment perspective. In G. Roberts & J. Holmes (Eds.), *Narrative in psychotherapy and psychiatry* (pp. 49–68). Oxford: Oxford University Press.

Johnson, S. M. (2004). *The practice of emotionally focused couple therapy.* New York: Brunner-Routledge.

Johnson, S. M., Millikin, J., & Makinen, J. (2001). Attachment injuries in couples relationships: A new perspective on impasses in couples therapy. *Journal of Marital and Family Therapy, 27,* 145–155.

Johnson, S., & Whiffen, V. (2003). *Attachment processes in couples and family therapy*. New York: Guilford Press.

Karpel, M. (2001). *EMDR in couples therapy: Targeting the repetition compulsion in chronic conflict*. Handout from presentation at Smith College, School of Social Work, Northampton, MA.

Kaslow, F. (1995). *Projective genogramming*. Sarasota, FL: Professional Resource Press.

Kaslow, F., Nurse, A., & Thompson, P. (2002). EMDR in conjunction with family systems therapy. In F. Shapiro (Ed.), *EMDR as an integrative psychotherapy approach* (pp. 289–318). Washington, DC: American Psychological Association.

Litt, B. (2000). *EMDR in couples therapy: An ego state approach*. Paper presented at the EMDR International Association Convention, Toronto, Ontario, Canada.

Love, K., & Murdock, T. (2004). Attachment to parents and psychological well-being: An examination of young adult college students in intact families and stepfamilies. *Journal of Family Psychology, 18*(4), 600–608.

Maxfield, L. (2002). Commonly asked questions about EMDR and suggestions for research parameters. In F. Shapiro (Ed.), *EMDR as an integrative psychotherapy approach* (p. 403). Washington, DC: American Psychological Association.

McGoldrick, M., Gerson, R., & Shellenberger, S. (1999). *Genograms: Assessment and intervention* (2nd ed.). New York: Norton.

Mikulincer, M. (1999). Adult attachment style and affect regulation: Strategic variation in self-appraisals. *Journal of Personality and Social Psychology, 75,* 420–435.

Moses, M. (2002, June). *EMDR and conjoint couples therapy*. Paper presented at the EMDR International Association conference, San Diego, CA.

Moses, M. (2003). Protocol for EMDR and conjoint couples therapy. *EMDRIA Newsletter, 8*(1), 4–13.

Protinsky, S., Sparks, J., & Flemke, K. (2001). Using eye movement desensitization and reprocessing to enhance treatment of couple. *Journal of Marital and Family Therapy, 27,* 157–164.

Scharff, D., & Scharff, J. (1987). *Object relations family therapy*. New York: Aronson.

Shapiro, F. (1995). *Eye movement desensitization and reprocessing: Basic principles, protocols and procedures*. New York: Guilford Press.

Shapiro, F. (2001). *Eye movement desensitization and reprocessing: Basic principles, protocols and procedures* (2nd ed.). New York: Guilford Press.

Shaver, P., & Hazan, C. (1993). Adult romantic attachment: Theory and evidence. In D. Perlman & W. Jones (Eds.), *Advances in personal relationships* (Vol. 4, pp. 29–70). London: Jessica Kingsley.

Treboux, D., Crowell, J., & Waters, E. (2004). When "new" meets "old": Configurations of adult attachment representatives and their implications for marital functioning. *Developmental Psychology, 40*(2), 295–314.

Wachtel, P. L. (2002). EMDR and psychoanalysis. In F. Shapiro (Ed.), *EMDR as an integrative psychotherapy approach* (p. 124). Washington, DC: American Psychological Association.

White, M., & Epsom, D. (1990). *Narrative means to therapeutic ends*. New York: Norton.

Zangwill, W. (2000, June). *Integrating EMDR into sex and relationship therapy*. Poster presented at the EMDR International Association conference, Toronto, Canada.

Zimberoff, D., & Hartman, D. (2002). Attachment, detachment, nonattachment: Achieving synthesis. *Journal of Heart-Centered Therapies, 5* (1), 3–94.

PART III

Marital Problems and Conflicts

CHAPTER 8

Integrating EMDR and Bowen Theory in Treating Chronic Relationship Dysfunction

Nancy Knudsen

Finding and maintaining a healthy relationship with a mate is a life goal for the vast majority of people. For some, this process occurs naturally; for others, the pursuit of a lasting and healthy relationship is a source of chronic disappointment. Some individuals are so preoccupied by their inability to find satisfaction in this area of their life that they become symptomatic. Reports of low self-esteem, isolation from others, hopelessness, despair, and social anxiety are some of the more common complaints. These individuals are often estranged from their family or have conflictual relationships with them.

The concept of *Chronic Relationship Dysfunction* was developed by the author to describe the experience of those who are unable to find and maintain a healthy relationship with a mate *and* who feel considerable related emotional distress. The types of experiences that people with this problem typically present in a clinical setting include the inability to make any meaningful contact with an appropriate partner and making a series of poor choices so that no relationship lasts.

Clients seeking treatment for relationship problems can be effectively treated using a Bowen family systems perspective (Bowen, 1978; Kerr & Bowen, 1988) as the theoretical backdrop for understanding the bigger relational context. In addition, the Adaptive Information Processing (AIP) model (Shapiro, 2001) can be used to understand the physiological link between critical early life experiences and current dysfunction. Together these theories provide a cohesive theoretical base and integrative treatment approach for use with clients with chronic relationship dysfunction.

Bowen Theory views the family as an emotional unit and uses systems thinking to describe the complex interactions within it (Bowen, 1978). The family system is seen as the appropriate unit of study because of the highly social nature of humans and the intense sensitivity that members of families have toward one another. Change in the functioning of any individual family member is predictably followed by a change in the emotional functioning of others.

From a Bowen perspective, the problem of Chronic Relationship Dysfunction is seen as applying to a certain segment of the population who operate at a lower level of differentiation. Instead of individual diagnoses, Bowen Theory focuses on the entire family emotional field (Kerr & Bowen, 1988), which includes the family of origin and the extended families of each of the parents. The atmosphere of this family emotional field determines the skill with which an individual balances the basic emotional force for interpersonal connection with the compelling drive for individuality. The unresolved struggle between these two opposing forces can absorb an enormous amount of emotional energy and result in constant disappointment (Kerr & Bowen, 1988). Individuals caught in this struggle can be viewed as having chronic relationship dysfunction.

From the perspective of the AIP model (Shapiro, 2001), chronic relationship dysfunction is seen in the manifestation in adulthood of a series of difficult interpersonal experiences that have occurred over time and that were never fully processed through the brain's natural information processing system. The AIP model proposes that within each individual there is a physiological information processing system in which new information is adaptively incorporated into existing memory networks by means of forging associations with previously stored material. A difficult experience in childhood, such as perceived rejection from a parental figure, may remain frozen in time in an unprocessed state, along with strong emotions and physical sensations that continue to become activated when current events trigger the earlier memory (see also van der Kolk, 2002). Irrational beliefs that were forged at the time of the original event are generalized to other situations that resemble it. By facilitating the activation of a natural physiological system, the AIP model and the Eye Movement Desensitization and Reprocessing (EMDR) approach address current symptoms such as chronic relationship dysfunction by allowing the individual to reprocess the old material, thus integrating it with current information.

Bowen Theory Major Concepts

Bowen Theory uses a family systems perspective that serves as a road map for understanding human relationship patterns. Murray Bowen (1978; Kerr & Bowen, 1988) used the natural sciences as a point of reference in his family systems conceptualization. Three of the eight concepts that compose his theory are discussed in this section: *differentiation of self, triangles,* and the *nuclear family emotional system.*

Differentiation of Self

The concept of *differentiation of self* (Bowen, 1978; Kerr & Bowen, 1988) is the cornerstone of Bowen Theory. Taken from the field of biology, the concept of differentiation refers to that critical time in the development of a cell when it loses the flexibility to develop into any of a number of different kinds of cells and is instead inwardly directed to fulfill a certain destiny, one that serves the whole and yet simultaneously sets its own course. Borrowing this idea from biology and then applying it to humans in families, Bowen used the term *differentiation of self* to describe the capacity of any individual to successfully balance two opposing natural forces: the force toward separateness that pushes each person toward being independent and unique, and the force that propels humans toward togetherness, that inherent desire for belonging to the group, for connecting with others who offer love and acceptance.

This capacity for balancing these two forces differs from family to family and, to some extent, within individuals in the same family. When things are calm in a family system, there may be more room for individuals to express their differences and unique qualities, but when there is more emotional intensity, the family exerts more emotional pressure to fall into line and be "one of us." The extent to which any individual can stand up to this pressure while continuing to stay involved with members of the family in a calm and thoughtful manner is an indicator of the level of differentiation.

Differentiation also refers to the ability to distinguish thoughts from feelings and to choose between being guided by one's intellect or one's emotions (Bowen, 1978). Individuals with higher levels of differentiation are better able to cope with stress because they are able to feel strong emotions, yet base their actions on logical, rational thinking. In contrast, more poorly differentiated individuals are highly reactive to others and base their actions on emotionally charged, often irrational thoughts.

A third indicator of the level of differentiation of self is the relationships that an individual has within the family of origin. When emotional pressure to conform becomes very intense, some people succumb to that pressure and lose themselves in the process (*fusion*); others cut themselves off emotionally, either internally or physically, in an effort to assert their right to be a separate person (*cutoff*). Those with higher levels of differentiation are more successful in being able to resolve relationship issues with their parents without sacrificing either themselves or their connections to family members.

Triangles

Thinking in terms of *triangles* is instrumental to a practical application of Bowen Theory. Borrowing again from the field of biology, the human family system can be viewed as a single cell, with the basic molecular unit of that cell being the triangle (Bowen, 1978). Bowen posited that a two-person emotional system is inherently unstable, and that under stress, a third person will be "triangled in" to create stability. Systems of more than three persons become a series of interlocking triangles.

There are several common triangle configurations. The most basic triangle occurs with the first child's birth. Triangles occur naturally in all human families and extend from the family of origin into the nuclear family. Families with higher levels of differentiation can adapt to change with flexibility, but families with lower levels tend to form rigid triangles. For example, a child may fuse identity with one parent while distancing from the other. Triangles can bond two people against a third. Yet, if conflict emerges between the two closer people, closeness with the third one can be solicited by either party, and the alliances may shift.

Nuclear Family Emotional System

A third important Bowen Theory concept is the *Nuclear Family Emotional System* (Bowen, 1978). As a new family unit is formed, each partner brings into it a certain number of unresolved issues from the past, proportionate to the level of differentiation from their family of origin. These unresolved issues tend to carry over in their nuclear family in the following ways: (a) marital conflict, (b) projection onto a child, and (c) dysfunction in a spouse. A particular family might exhibit one of these symptoms predominantly or all three simultaneously.

Families that pass on their anxiety via *marital conflict* tend to be headed by spouses who lock horns as a way of managing their anxiety. Each partner seeks a sense of togetherness that is based on the other giving up his or her autonomy. Differences are poorly tolerated and are interpreted as a lack of love.

Projection onto a child refers to the way families transfer anxiety out of the marital relationship. Children who are labeled "special" in some way that draws greater focus, be it positive or negative, can unwittingly take on the unresolved issues of the family system and actually fare more poorly than their siblings. The *dysfunction of a spouse* might be physical, emotional, or social; regardless, an interdependence between the two partners at their differing levels of functioning emerges and is maintained by the system. Rather than deal with their issues directly, these families unwittingly sacrifice the autonomy of one individual for the sake of togetherness. Although the spouse who functions at the higher level might be perceived as more differentiated, this is not necessarily the case. There is a trade-off for overfunctioning as much as there is for underfunctioning. Each position makes an individual more vulnerable to emotional or physical distress and accompanying symptoms (Kerr & Bowen, 1988).

The description of these three concepts provides the reader with an introduction to Bowen Theory. The remaining five concepts, *family projection process, multigenerational transmission process, sibling position, emotional cutoff,* and *societal emotional process,* all contribute to a fuller understanding of the theory (Kerr & Bowen, 1988).

Review of the Literature

Both Bowen (1978; Kerr & Bowen, 1988), with his theory of family systems, and Shapiro (1995, 2001), with her AIP model and the EMDR approach, have made significant contributions to the field of human behavior. Each has challenged contemporaries to rethink the extant prevailing theories and clinical tools and consider new ways of thinking about change. Each has utilized the natural sciences and what is known about the brain to inform their theories (Kerr & Bowen, 1988; Shapiro, 2001).

Bowen's (1978, pp. 3–16) original National Institute of Mental Health study of hospitalized schizophrenics and their families in the 1950s laid the groundwork for his theory. He proposed a scale for describing the basic level of differentiation of self that went from 0 to 100, but he provided only broad profiles of how people function emotionally and intellectually at each of four scale ranges (Bowen, 1976). However, several attempts have been made to create effective assessment tools for measuring levels of differentiation (Skowron & Friedlander, 1998; Skowron & Schmidt, 2003). There have also been assessment tools developed that measure aspects of differentiation of self, such as the impact on adult children of parental expectations (Bray, Williamson, & Malone, 1984) and the level of behavioral and emotional reactivity (Bartle & Sabatelli, 1995). These assessment tools have allowed marriage and family researchers to conduct a number of significant studies that positively correlate level of self-differentiation and marital success (Benson, Larson, Wilson, & Demo, 1993; Miller, Anderson, & Keala, 2004; Rosen, Bartle-Haring, & Stith, 2001; Skowron, Holmes, & Sabatelli, 2003).

Several researchers have investigated treatment effects using these assessment tools (Bartle-Haring, Glade, & Vira, 2005; Bray, Williamson, & Malone, 1986). Murdock and Gore (2004) assessed the interaction between levels of differentiation and levels of stress and demonstrated that coping with stress is more difficult for individuals with lower levels of differentiation. Their conclusion is that, although in the short term the acquiring of coping strategies is a useful way for individuals to reduce the impact of stress on their life, focusing treatment on increasing differentiation of self will over time elevate functioning.

Relevant to the treatment of chronic relationship dysfunction is the clinical application of EMDR for clients with family-based trauma or distressful memories. Several researchers have specifically focused on this population and found rapid resolution of profoundly disturbing family-related memories, such as incest and chronic abuse (Edmond, Rubin, & Wambach, 1999; Lazrove, Triffleman, Kite, McGlasshan, & Rounsaville, 1998). Even more relevant is the work of a growing group of family therapists who have documented the use of EMDR in their treatment as a way to introduce change throughout the system (Bardin, 2004; Kaslow, Nurse, & Thompson, 2002; Keenan & Farrell, 2000; Protinsky, Sparks, & Flemke, 2001; Snyder, 1996).

Advantages of Integrating EMDR and Bowen Theory

There are a number of compelling reasons to consider the integration of EMDR and Bowen Theory. Much of human pain and trauma is directly related to the intense sensitivity family members have to one another. Bowen Theory offers an objective view that can explain why family members behave as they do. Yet for many people, insight alone does not undo the strong emotional responses that have gotten locked in the neural network system. The AIP model offers a way to understand the gap that can keep newly acquired information from being enough to mitigate the high arousal levels of strong emotional responses, and EMDR provides the therapeutic structure to fully integrate the two. Together, these approaches emphasize the development of a healthy balance between self and other in the present and encourage strengthening family relationships as a preparation for adult relationship readiness.

THERAPY PROCESS

Chronic relationship dysfunction can be viewed as a result of a series of disturbing experiences that occurred within the family system. Some of these experiences fall in the category of single incidents; many of them blend together as repetitive events. The treatment model described here utilizes the basic structure of the EMDR protocol with the clinical application of Bowen Theory at certain key times. The therapy is structured in three basic stages. In the first stage, during the History Taking, Preparation, and Assessment Phases of EMDR, the therapist assists the client in developing a conceptualization and understanding of relationship patterns in his or her family of origin and current situation. In the second stage, the client processes EMDR targets while changing the pattern of his or her relationships with family members and prospective partners. In the third stage, the client begins working on relationships with future partners, consolidating and improving one-on-one relationships with key family members, and employing new skills while using EMDR to process any related anxiety.

Stage 1: Client History and Case Conceptualization

The first session begins with the client describing the presenting symptoms. For clients with chronic relationship dysfunction, there is a notable struggle between longing for closeness and despair about not finding love. It is important to take note of the interactive pattern of the most recent failed attempts. For example, does the client have a history of falling in love at first sight with partners who seem indifferent to him or her? Or does the client reject each potential partner so quickly that no relationship gets started? Whatever the interactive pattern, it is likely that it has occurred more than once and has roots in the family of origin.

A thorough history includes an extensive review of the family emotional system as well as the client's adult relationships. The creation of a family diagram or genogram that tracks at least three generations is an excellent method for gathering this information (Bowen, 1980; McGoldrick, Gerson, & Shellenberger, 1999). Questions are asked as the genogram is being drawn, such as "What do you know about your maternal grandparents' marriage?" "How was it affected by the birth of each child?" "Did either of your parents have a child whom they favored?" and "How did this affect that child's relationship with the other parent?" Cutoff relationships as well as intensely involved relationships are identified. Special relationships with grandparents, aunts, uncles, cousins, siblings, and relatives through marriage, such as stepparents, are noted as well. Acquiring this information allows the clinician to assess the family system by understanding the key triangles, the basic level of differentiation, and the ways that the nuclear family emotional system operates.

As therapist and client take a look at the family system with this broad lens, the client's view of himself is challenged as he begins to understand how the system has operated over time. By identifying triangles that have a certain predictability, the client perceives family behavior in a more objective way. Connections are made between earlier and current interactive patterns.

For example, Sara found herself in a series of short-term relationships with men who were married or otherwise unavailable. Just as her father was married to a wife who disappointed him, the men in Sara's life tended to be involved with other women whom they were unable to truly love or leave. Sara was in the same interactive pattern with these men as she was with her father. In each case, she was functioning within a triangle in which her presence took the focus off the couple's ability to resolve their differences directly. Helping Sara see the way the past was reverberating in the present allowed her to have a more objective view of her own role in the system.

As the history-taking process reveals the multigenerational patterns that relate to the client's presenting problem, it is important to formulate a comprehensive treatment plan that includes two essential elements: the development of a strategy for enhancing the client's current capacity for coping and functioning in the current extended family system, and the organizing of EMDR targets that served as precursors for current dysfunctional interactive patterns.

To maximize client stability in the present, the therapist assesses the client's strengths and resources and explores the quality of the client's current family relationships. Strategies are developed for managing these relationships during the first stage of treatment. Interventions are planned so that the client can use his or her new knowledge to shift the configurations of the key triangles.

Some clients will have cut themselves off from certain family members due to actual or perceived threat, and it is important to respect this choice as good self-care while continuing to maintain objectivity about the larger system. Other clients, whose family members are still overly involved in their life, require assistance in altering their responses to these family members. This will help them to develop some essential new interpersonal skills along with better self-care. For example, encouraging clients to be more proactive about introducing change in the system might begin with simple limit setting about the length or nature of a visit.

Sara might be coached to refrain from speaking negatively about her mother with her father. She might also consider spending time alone with her mother to forge a new, more adult relationship. It would be predicted that there will be resistance to her effort to introduce a change in the system, and various scenarios would be reviewed, emphasizing Sara's effort to stay calm and nonreactive.

To complete the client history and case conceptualization phase, a time line is created that details key events over the course of the client's life. This time line includes memories of discrete incidents that occurred as well as composite memories of typical encounters that are associated with a certain time period. In the process of composing the time line, nodal events that represent significant change, such as the birth of a sibling, the death of a grandparent, a divorce or remarriage, or a move to a new location, are listed as well as disturbing events.

Once the time line is complete, the therapist and client determine which incidents are relevant targets for EMDR processing. Because there may be a number of difficult memories related to each of the client's childhood parental figures, it is important to keep the triangles in mind. Is there a disturbing childhood memory that includes both parents (or the two other members of the triangle involved)? If the memory is only about Dad, is there a corresponding one about Mom? A target list is compiled that includes all variations of the dysfunctional interactive pattern, beginning with the primary triangle, usually of mother, father, and client, and ending with the most recent relationship. For instance, the first memory processed by Sara was of herself as a 6-year-old witnessing her father criticize her mother; then, after her mother ran crying from the room, Sara curled up on her father's lap as he praised her for being his "perfect little girl."

EMDR is explained to the client as the heart of the treatment in that by reprocessing each of these disturbing memories, the strong emotions stored in the body since childhood will become integrated with more recently acquired knowledge. Only then can the level of reactivity toward key family members become lowered enough to learn to relate to them in a new way. Once this task is accomplished, current relationship patterns are able to shift.

Stage 2: Processing and Changing Relationship Patterns

The setting up and processing of the relevant memories listed in the time line using the standard EMDR protocol follows the preparation work. After the first target is fully processed, the level of disturbance on the other items on the list may have altered. Each item that is still active in the present is processed until the list is exhausted. As this may take a number of months to complete, the therapist continues to coach the client in managing his or her family contacts in calm and thoughtful ways, applying acquired knowledge and insights enhanced by the EMDR processing.

Again utilizing the case of Sara, this coaching involved a series of discussions about how to plan for more successful visits with her parents in the present time, including spending more time with her mother and not succumbing to her father's reflexive criticism. Once the client's EMDR work reaches the present, the most recent manifestations of the dysfunctional relationship patterns are targeted. At the same time, healthy screening devices for partner selection and other building blocks of healthy relationship skills are taught and practiced. The therapist acts as a coach to the client, who is now trying to apply her new gains to her day-to-day life. The future template, the rehearsal of new skills and attitudes regarding anticipated relationship encounters, is the last stage of the EMDR's three-pronged protocol. Any anticipated fears that arise are then processed and a positive outcome is installed.

For example, Sara was no longer drawn to men who used her as an alternative to their primary partner, and she was able to understand her own role in choosing a familiar interactional pattern that reverberated back to her own family emotional system. Because she was able to forge new relationships with each of her parents that showed promise of dismantling the old order, Sara was now prepared to seek an adult relationship with an appropriate and available partner. The processing of the recent relationship targets was able to go very quickly. Criteria for potential partners were discussed, and a future template of successfully screening out inappropriate choices was implemented.

Stage 3: Establishing Healthy Asdult Relationships

As these last stages of the EMDR protocol are completed, relationships within the family systems have altered notably. For instance, in Sara's case, as she stuck to her goals to relate one-on-one to each of her parents, the entire family reconfigured. Her mother began functioning on a more differentiated level, and her father became overall less critical. Throughout the treatment, there has been an ongoing repairing and reworking of the relationships within the family of origin. Individual relationships have begun to be built outside of the entrenched triangles in which they have operated. Clients are beginning to shift their position in the system and to anticipate the emotional pull to revert to old patterns. As EMDR targets are resolved, there is a marked lowering of reactivity to family members, thus paving the way to positive, healthy connections.

If there is a family member previously thought to be too dangerous to have contact with, it is now time to rethink this position and possibly test the waters with the client's newfound strength. The goal of the proposed meeting is not to expect that the other has changed, but simply for the client to experience himself as an adult, looking eye to eye with a parental figure he used to see as larger than life but can now see as just another human being. Obviously, there are those individuals who are truly dangerous. Yet, even in these most extreme cases, a scaled-down version of an actual meeting can take place, for example, in the form of a letter, phone call, or facilitated meeting in a secure location.

The act of making peace with the family one grew up in is a giant step toward differentiation of self and the opening of the doorway to successful relationships. Can the client express who she is as an individual even in the face of the pressure of the family emotional system? Can she stay connected to them even if she does not conform? Can she hold her own in a calm and centered manner? These are the challenges she faces, not only with her family of origin, but with whomever she may partner. Using her own family as the vehicle to develop these capacities will give her the strength not only to make an appropriate choice, but also to manage herself at a higher level of differentiation.

In the final stage of treatment, the therapist acts as coach in the ongoing maintenance and strengthening of new skills as a new significant relationship unfolds. This generally occurs with sessions spaced farther apart. When termination takes place, it is always with the option of returning when or if the need arises for fine-tuning of any aspect of the therapy experience.

CASE EXAMPLE

Stanley, 48, came to treatment lonely and depressed. He wanted to be able to have a successful relationship with a woman but felt quite hopeless about this due to his dismal relationship history. Stanley had once been married for 7 years to a woman whom he said never loved him. One day he left her for another woman and never looked back. In the 15 years since, he had had a series of relationships that lasted approximately 2 to 3 months, at which point he would become disillusioned and abruptly walk away. At the time he entered therapy he had not been in a relationship for over 2 years, and his efforts at dating had practically ground to a halt because he "no longer saw the point." Stanley had been taking antidepressants on and off for years. He felt that they helped him to some extent, but he wished for a more fulfilling life.

Stanley was born in Poland, the youngest of three children born to Jewish parents, each of whom had lived through the Holocaust. Both of his parents' families of origin had been severely impacted by the war. His father lost his entire family at the age of 15, and his mother lost her father when he left Poland abruptly and never returned. Given this harsh backdrop of cutoff relationships as a result of war, Stanley's parents brought into their marriage the legacy of unresolved losses and their reluctance to ever really trust anyone again.

As the family genogram was created (see Figure 8.1), the nature of the triangles in Stanley's family was revealed. His parents' marriage was characterized by high levels of conflict, and each of the three children was drawn into their drama in a particular way. Both the older siblings were treated harshly by their father, who beat them and humiliated them with name-calling and threats. Stanley, on the other hand, was his father's favorite. He reported being treated like a little pet who was expected to deliver hugs and kisses in exchange for a constant stream of gifts and special status. Stanley's mother treated all of her children harshly but was especially hard on him. She was the one who beat Stanley while his father passively stood by. Occasionally, she would crawl into bed with Stanley at night and hold him, asking him whom he loved more, his father or her. Both parents berated each other to the children as they attempted to pull them onto their side of their ongoing conflict.

When Stanley was 13 years old, the family left Poland with their life savings sewn into their clothing and emigrated to the United States. Fitting into their

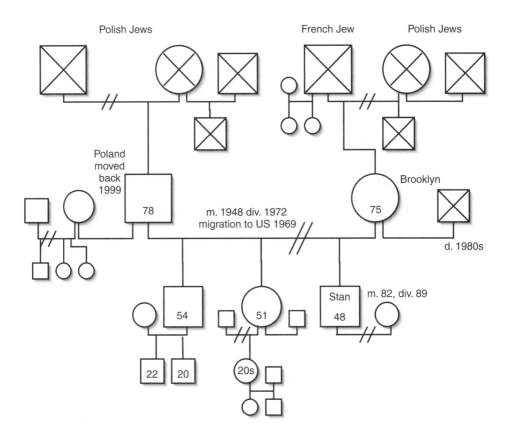

Figure 8.1   Stanley's family diagram.

new environment in New York City was stressful on each family member in different ways, and the conflicts between the parents reemerged with new ferocity. Stanley remembered coming home one day when he was 14 to find that his mother and brother had moved out. Three days later, they were back, without a word spoken about it. During the next year, both siblings moved out, and then one day without warning, Stanley's mother was gone. Stanley was left alone with his devastated, broken-down father. Around this time, Stanley became involved in alcohol and drug use. He found himself full of contempt for his father, who seemed pathetic to him in his grief.

Stanley's relationship history with women began in this family context and under the chronic use of substances as a way to deal with his emotional pain. Bright and good looking, he apparently had no trouble attracting girls. In fact, he had a steady girlfriend whom he adored for 2 years. However, at the age of 17, he abruptly broke up with her and walked the other way, never to look back, wondering even then what was wrong with him. Several short-term relationships later, at the age of 20, he met Amy, who was to become his wife. This was a tumultuous relationship with high levels of conflict. Then one day, after 13 years, Stanley walked out on Amy for a woman he ended up being with for 2 months.

At the age of 35, Stanley finally addressed his 20-year substance abuse problem and became sober. A few years later, he went back to school and got a degree in a new field of interest. He entered therapy and was treated for depression with medication. During his adulthood, Stanley had gone 10 years without any contact with his family members, whom he had written off as "pathetic people not worth his time." Each of his parents had remarried, and his two siblings had married and had children. His father had eventually moved back to Poland with his second wife. At the age of 48, Stanley had little to do with any of them except for occasional superficial contact. He had made no connection between his level of cutoff from his family and his own difficulties in finding a sustained meaningful relationship.

Case Therapy Process

Given Stanley's presenting problem, it made sense to approach this case using both Bowen Theory and EMDR. The initial assessment included gathering the history, creating the family genogram, and compiling a time line. Concepts of family theory were explained, as Stanley was encouraged to look at his family over several generations. His curiosity was stimulated by looking at his family system more objectively, and he was able to gain a broader perspective about why people, including himself, behaved the way they did. Systems concepts were used to illustrate how his current symptoms were the result of the unresolved issues in his family of origin. However, this did not impact his visceral emotional responses to past events or current contact with family members. EMDR and the AIP model were presented as the vehicle for getting at this highly charged emotional material in a way that would truly allow him to put it behind him. Thus, he could absorb his new knowledge and fully integrate it with a more adaptive range of emotions.

In preparation for doing EMDR processing of the targets listed on the time line, a session was spent enhancing coping strategies and installing a safe place using eye movements. The time line was then reviewed for target selection. It was decided to start with the first beating Stanley recalled receiving from his mother, after he had tracked mud into the house when he was 6 years old. This target was chosen because it was the pivotal experience in which Stanley felt "the bond of love had been severed, and my heart closed." Although this memory involved his mother and not his father, previous discussion and analysis of the family triangle informed the context in which this scene occurred. A friend of Stanley's mother was present during the beating, and like his father during many of the beatings that came later, she sat there passively and watched.

This first target was set up using the standard EMDR protocol. The *picture* was Stanley sitting on a chair in the kitchen wearing his muddied galoshes while his mother stood over him pounding his head against the wall. The *Negative Cognition* (NC) was "I don't matter," and the *Positive Cognition* (PC) was "I matter." His score on the Validity of Cognition (VOC) scale was 2, and the identified *emotions* were sadness, hopelessness, and loneliness. His score on the Subjective Units of Disturbance (SUD) scale was 7, and he identified no *body sensations.* (Note that the VOC rates the validity of the Positive Cognition on a scale where 1 = Not true and 7 = Completely true; the SUD rates disturbance, where 0 = No disturbance and 10 = Severe disturbance.)

It took two sessions for this memory to process to the level of no disturbance. In the second session, the NC was "I'm going to die," and the PC was "I am safe." Upon installing the PC at the end of the session, Stanley added, "I am safe and I can love." The EMDR processing of this target involved a lot of intense emotions as he gradually brought into the scene his adult thinking and capacity to embrace the pain of others, including that of himself as a child and, to a degree, that of his mother.

The second target chosen involved another incident of his being beaten by his mother, this time with his father watching. Once again, the NC was "I'm not safe," and the PC was "I am safe." Interestingly, the processing primarily involved Stanley's feelings of hurt and humiliation at having his father, whom he had experienced as an ally against his mother, side with her against him. Stanley was now processing the way he felt betrayed by the switching of alliances that can go on in a family triangle. The parents' low levels of differentiation caused them to draw their child into their struggle by one of them favoring him while the other rejected, then occasionally joining together by turning against him.

Each memory with current disturbance was processed chronologically. The relationship of the parents and the way the triangle functioned was a theme that came through in each of Stanley's EMDR sessions. His emotions were raw and visceral. As the memories were slowly processed, the insights allowed him to view his family more objectively, gradually adding to a new sense of integration.

A target that was particularly difficult to process was his father's face, with wet lips puckered up to kiss Stanley; this was a memory of the countless times when he experienced his father's needy affection as repulsive. Over the course of four EMDR sessions, Stanley expelled the sense of his father's invasive physical affection as a constant threat to his own personhood. He was able to gain emotional distance from this aspect of his relationship with his father for the first time. This allowed him to take in a wider perspective of what was going on throughout the system. For example, he could see his mother's jealousy and resentment of his father's affection for him and his siblings' longing to attain any positive attention from their father.

Stanley went on to process the target of his mother walking out on him and his father when he was a teenager, and then the series of women on whom he had walked out. As he gradually made his way to the present, he was able to resolve his struggle between yearning for closeness and being terrified of being possessed as an object for someone else's gratification, and to recognize how this had reverberated within the family system. A newfound strength emerged along with a desire to love.

At this point in the therapy, 4 months had passed. Stanley had begun searching on Internet dating sites for women he might like to meet, an activity he had done on and off for years. In addition to the EMDR processing work described, a topic of discussion had been ways he could develop his social life. Stanley casually mentioned that he had had a date. Several weeks later, he announced that he had a really good feeling about the woman he was dating, and that she had told him he was "warm." He found himself feeling very excited about the possibility of this relationship developing into something. That day, his EMDR processing took him from the Negative Cognition "I'm heartless" to the Positive Cognition "I'm likeable," which, when installed, developed into "I'm a decent person." Within several weeks, he reported that things were going very well with Eve, who lived a few hours away, and that they were planning a 5-day trip together. In the therapy, he was now up to processing his marriage, a very loaded period of not feeling worthy of love. Stanley was very excited by the rapid progress and the impact the work was having on his newly unfolding relationship.

Around this time, the therapist reminded Stanley of his reoccurring experience of getting into relationships that would seem to go fine for 2 months or so before he would find the woman flawed in some way and walk away. She suggested to him that this might still be ahead for him, but could be dealt with differently. A discussion was initiated of the value of his making contact with the members of his family of origin. This effort would allow him to test his greater capacity to hold on to his sense of self while in the presence of those most likely to throw him off. Stanley was intrigued and saw this challenge as part of a process that could ultimately free him to be more fully himself without having to cut off from others. He began the process of planning two trips, one to New York City and one to Poland.

Planning for contact with a family such as Stanley's requires thought and realistic goal setting. A number of sessions were devoted to this topic, as well as the unfolding of the new relationship with Eve and the subsequent plans for him to relocate to her city. As was predicted, 10 weeks into the relationship, the moment arrived when Stanley's old pattern reared up full force. On a camping trip they took together, they had a conversation in which Stanley felt that Eve was not listening to what he was really saying. Something inside him snapped, and he found himself jumping to the conclusion that she was not a person who could ever understand him. He became silent and turned away from her for the rest of the evening.

In the therapy office several days later, Stanley was in a great deal of pain about the downward turn the relationship had taken. The rest of the trip had been awkward between them, and they had not spoken since. He felt hopeless because he now saw Eve as flawed and "not good enough." He felt judgmental about her in all kinds of ways he had not felt before. Suddenly, she did not seem pretty enough or smart enough either. He was raising questions to himself about whether he wanted to go on in the relationship. He did not see his own role in the interaction at all.

Fortunately, he was able to identify what had happened as the interactive pattern that had been predicted: the turning away from love he had been doing all his life, as had his parents before him. EMDR was used to target the recent event, using the following setup. The picture was Stanley lying next to Eve in the tent, giving her the silent treatment. His NC was "I'm not worthy of having needs," and his PC was "I can have needs." His VOC score was 2, and the identified emotion was sadness. His SUD score was 9, and his body sensation was numbness. Here is a segment of the processing he did (Note: BLS refers to bilateral stimulation.):

> I felt a wave of sadness, then I thought about her, how kind and good a person she really is. (BLS) There's a sensation in my stomach like nausea. I feel like I don't want to go there. It's a feeling of fear that I have. (BLS) The thought is "If you love me, then there is something screwed up about you." (BLS) I want to be loved, yet at the same time I don't. I'm really afraid of it. (BLS) I'm afraid to be loved because something will be demanded of me that I won't be able to give. Then images of my parents come in with the idea that they made demands on me that I couldn't give. (BLS) Eve. If I could be open and soft, I could be really happy with her. I pictured a moment of happiness. (BLS) More images of my parents (tears). I felt their attempts to love me, yet their love felt so awkward and weird that I don't want it at all. I have suspicions of this love. (BLS) So I see that I defend against this love by finding fault with the other person.

When Stanley was brought back to the initial target, he tuned into an entirely different part of the day together that was quite lovely and tender. He felt ready and eager to reconnect with Eve now that he had dislodged the huge boulder that had been in his way. By the next week, Stanley reported that the relationship was now stronger than ever. A reevaluation of the last target, however, revealed that there was still more work to do. This time the processing included the following:

> This time I feel my judgments dissipating without my going in my mind to breaking up. (BLS) Just now I saw the face of my father and remembered how many times I disengaged from him. It was like disengaging from myself. (BLS) I used to hate it when he'd take credit for the things I did well. I distanced to pull away from his being able to own any part of me. Now I would like to reengage with those disowned parts of me. (BLS) Rejecting people was also his M.O. I want to reengage with the disowned parts that were him. I'm not whole and

I want to be. (BLS) I just got this great desire to be a whole person. To have healthy boundaries, to know where I am and what is another person. (BLS) I'm getting pictures of cubes of me that are bleeding and wounded being reintegrated into me. (BLS) I can do this. I'm making friends with these wounded parts. Then my mother was there because some of them were hers too. (BLS) I'm thinking about how much time and energy went into rejecting these parts that belonged to them. (BLS) I'm feeling hopeful. It's not only do-able, but I'm really close.

This session ended with an installation of "I can be whole," along with an enthusiasm and excitement about getting there. Stanley was now looking forward to his family visits. He was not expecting that his parents had changed, but he wanted to experience himself as a healthier adult about to handle himself well in their presence.

There were three more sessions over a 7-week stretch. Stanley was able to visit his mother and two siblings in New York City, the first time in 34 years the four of them had been together. This visit was quite challenging in many ways as he felt such strong judgments about each of them that made it hard for him to think clearly about the goals he had set. Nonetheless, he was able to relate with each of them more authentically without walking away. This visit was discussed in detail, and suggestions were made as to what he could do in future interactions to further "hold on to himself."

The trip to Poland occurred a month later. Stanley came back reporting that he still did not find his father a likeable man. He said, "He still favors me and that made me very uncomfortable. I would not let him kiss me on the lips. I had the insight that if someone really likes me, I shrink away from that and run in the other direction." However, the visit was very productive in that Stanley was able to stay relatively calm in the presence of his father, was able to set good boundaries, and was able to relate to his father from an adult vantage point. The trip seemed to him an important piece of his healing that now had him even more excited about moving in with Eve.

Because Stanley moved out of the geographic area, treatment was terminated at this point. Ideally, there would have been occasional meetings to continue the work on Stanley's ongoing relationships, both with his family of origin and with Eve, as he ran into snags or found himself triggered into old patterns of withdrawal. A future template using EMDR would also have been employed had there been more time. A 6-month follow-up contact with Stanley revealed that he and Eve had gotten married, and he was pleased with the quality of their relationship.

DISCUSSION

This case offers a clear illustration of the benefits of integrating EMDR with Bowen Theory. The presenting problem of "walking away from love" could be viewed as the result of an intergenerational legacy with recognizable component parts. Raising Stanley's level of differentiation allowed him to become less reactive and more capable of staying in relationships even in the face of conflict.

EMDR provided the means to efficiently dismantle the intense reactivity that Stanley grew up with in his family emotional system. By systematically revisiting and processing the still disturbing events of the past, Stanley was able to integrate what he had learned about family functioning with the emotions that had been driving his behavior. The fundamental struggle between the forces of togetherness and separateness, connecting with others yet having an independent self, which is at the heart of the effort of differentiation of self, moved from impossibly difficult to, in Stanley's own words, "actually do-able." The EMDR processing integrated with Bowen Theory allowed Stanley to come more fully into his adult self, a more highly differentiated self, capable of managing himself and his emotions rather than being managed by them.

The integration of Bowen Theory and EMDR provides a powerful and effective treatment approach for individuals suffering from chronic relationship dysfunction. Disturbing memories of things that occurred in the context of family life are often at the root of current relationship difficulties. Insufficient understanding about how families operate, unresolved relationships with key family members, and irrational, feeling-based conclusions about past events all contribute to the replication of dysfunctional patterns in adult life. The EMDR protocol, when properly implemented, allows the strong emotions and residual body sensations that feed the irrational thinking to subside as more adaptive information takes hold in a wider web of associations.

Bowen Theory holds a key for making sense of what can often feel like an incomprehensible series of traumatic events within a family. The perpetual questions of why these things happen in families, or how it is that parents treat their children badly, can be understood in a wider context, so that blame can be lifted and responsibility for change can be seen as starting with the self. Having this information prior to EMDR processing allows for a more complete integration of an adult perspective. The elegance of the three-pronged EMDR protocol allows for a thorough internal reworking of earlier obstacles to change.

As EMDR processing proceeds through the time line of targets related to the dysfunctional relational pattern, clients will find themselves less reactive to others in general. This lowered reactivity is accompanied by clearer and more objective thinking, a hallmark characteristic of differentiation of self. To then test these newfound attributes where they will be most difficult to retain, clients are directed back to their family of origin. This begins the actual reworking of the stuck relationships within the family, thus paving the way for optimal present-day functioning.

REFERENCES

Bardin, A. (2004). EMDR within a family system. *Journal of Family Psychology, 15,* 47–61.

Bartle, S., & Sabatelli, R. M. (1995). The Behavioral and Emotional Reactivity Index: Preliminary evidence for construct validity from three studies. *Family Relations, 44,* 267–277.

Bartle-Haring, S., Glade, A. C., & Vira, R. (2005). Initial levels of differentiation and reduction in psychological symptoms for clients in marriage and family therapy. *Journal of Marital and Family Therapy, 31,* 121–131.

Benson, M. J., Larson, J. H., Wilson, S. M., & Demo, D. H. (1993). Family of origin influences on late adolescent romantic relationships. *Journal of Marriage and the Family, 55,* 663–672.

Bowen, M. (1976). Theory in the practice of psychotherapy. In P. L. Guerin Jr. (Ed.), *Family therapy: Theory and practice* (pp. 42–90). New York: Gardner Press.

Bowen, M. (1978). *Family therapy in clinical practice.* New York: Aronson.

Bowen, M. (1980). Key to the use of the genogram. In E. A. Carter & M. McGoldrick (Eds.), *The family life cycle: A framework for family therapy* (p. xxiii). New York: Gardner.

Bray, J. H., Williamson, D. S., & Malone, P. E. (1984). Personal authority in the family system: Development of a questionnaire to measure personal authority in intergenerational family processes. *Journal of Marital and Family Therapy, 10,* 167–178.

Bray, J. H., Williamson, D. S., & Malone, P. E. (1986). An evaluation of an intergenerational consultation process to increase personal authority in the family system. *Family Process, 25,* 423–436.

Edmond, T., Rubin, A., & Wambach, K. G. (1999). The effectiveness of EMDR with adult female survivors of childhood sexual abuse. *Social Work Research, 23,* 103–116.

Kaslow, F. W., Nurse, A. R., & Thompson, P. (2002). EMDR in conjunction with family systems therapy. In F. Shapiro (Ed.), *EMDR as an integrative psychotherapy approach: Experts of diverse orientations explore the paradigm prism* (pp. 289–318). Washington, DC: American Psychological Association.

Keenan, P., & Farrell, D. (2000). Treating morbid jealousy with eye movement desensitization and reprocessing utilizing cognitive interweave: A case report. *Counseling Psychology Quarterly, 13,* 175–189.

Kerr, M., & Bowen, M. (1988). *Family evaluation: An approach based on Bowen theory.* New York: Norton.

Lazrove, S., Triffleman, E., Kite, L., McGlasshan, T., & Rounsaville, B. (1998). An open trial of EMDR as treatment for chronic PTSD. *American Journal of Orthopsychiatry, 69,* 601–608.

McGoldrick, M., Gerson, R., & Shellenberger, S. (1999). *Genograms: Assessment and intervention* (2nd ed.). New York: Norton.

Miller, R. B., Anderson, S. A., & Keala, D. K. (2004). Is Bowen theory valid? *Journal of Marital and Family Therapy, 30,* 453–466.

Murdock, N., & Gore, P. (2004). Stress, coping, and differentiation of self: A test of Bowen theory. *Contemporary Family Therapy, 26,* 319–335.

Protinsky, H., Sparks, J., & Flemke, K. (2001). Using eye movement desensitization and reprocessing to enhance treatment of couples. *Journal of Marital and Family Therapy, 27,* 157–164.

Rosen, K. H., Bartle-Haring, S., & Stith, S. M. (2001). Using Bowen theory to enhance understanding of the intergenerational transmission of dating violence. *Journal of Family Issues, 22,* 124–142.

Shapiro, F. (1995). *Eye movement desensitization and reprocessing: Basic principles, protocols and procedures.* New York: Guilford Press.

Shapiro, F. (2001). *Eye movement desensitization and reprocessing: Basic principles, protocols, and procedures* (2nd ed.). New York: Guilford Press.

Skowron, E. A., & Friedlander, M. L. (1998). The Differentiation of Self Inventory: Development and initial validation. *Journal of Counseling Psychology, 45,* 235–246.

Skowron, E. A., Holmes, S. E., & Sabatelli, R. M. (2003). Deconstructing differentiation: Self regulation, interdependent relating, and well-being in adulthood. *Contemporary Family Therapy, 25,* 111–129.

Skowron, E. A., & Schmidt, T. A. (2003). Assessing interpersonal fusion: Reliability and validity of a new DSI fusion with others subscale. *Journal of Marital and Family Therapy, 29,* 209–222.

Snyder, M. (1996). Intimate partners: A context for the intensification and healing of emotional pain. *Women and Therapy, 19,* 79–92.

van der Kolk, B. A. (2002). Beyond the talking cure: Somatic experience and subcortical imprints in the treatment of trauma. In F. Shapiro (Ed.), *EMDR as an integrative psychotherapy approach: Experts of diverse orientations explore the paradigm prism* (pp. 57–83). Washington, DC: American Psychological Association.

CHAPTER 9

Integrating EMDR and Imago Relationship Therapy in Couple Treatment

Beverly S. Talan

Relationship conflict is inevitable. Studies reveal that marriages and relationships lose intimacy and satisfaction because of the couple's inability to resolve conflict and thus to heal their ruptured connection. Relationship conflict may develop from many sources: infidelity, sexual dysfunction, posttraumatic stress, past trauma, and domestic violence. One partner often feels misunderstood by the other. Couples in difficult relationships frequently do not have the knowledge they need to resolve conflicts and lack the understanding, skills, and tools that are necessary to mend the break in their connection (Gottman, 2000; Protinsky, Sparks, & Flemke, 2001).

The structure of marriage has changed in recent decades. Expectations of the marital relationship have broadened to include friendship, support, fun, intimacy, and good sex (Love, 2001). Power struggles resulting from misunderstandings or boredom, partners working, the women's movement, free love, open marriage, cohabitation, and the possibility of divorce have all affected traditional marriage. Research on marital conflict has found that many of the issues faced by partners have their roots in childhood experiences. In particular, poor attachment in childhood is often related to attachment struggles in adult relationships (Hendrix, 1992, 2001; Solomon, 2002).

History of Origins of Marital Conflict:
From Freud to Mahler

The first person to describe the impact of childhood relationships and experiences on adult relationships was Sigmund Freud, the father of psychoanalysis (Morris, 2003). His theories about the progressive stages of maturation focused on the inner life and conflicted drives of the individual. In particular, he maintained that adult neurosis has its roots in the Oedipal stage of maturation, which occurs during ages 3 to 5. Freud's concepts were developed further by Hyman Spotnitz, a proponent of modern psychoanalysis (Morris, 2003). He believed that the roots of neurosis began much earlier than the Oedipal phase and treated pre-Oedipal patients by using various techniques, including mirroring. Margaret Mahler later renamed this phase of maturation the identity stage.

Mahler (Mahler, Pine, & Berman, 1975) hypothesized that humans move through developmental stages of growth and wounding. In the early weeks, the newborn does not experience any differentiation between the self and mother and is in a symbiotic relationship. Mahler's early stages of child development are related to the reaction of the mother to the child's needs. Mahler (1968) posited that when the child's individuation process is disturbed, the child may regress and attempt to use the mechanism of symbiosis. She also hypothesized that the process of symbiosis may be internalized and used throughout the individual's life in an attempt to attach to others, relieve stress, and find love.

Other theorists also have remarked on the importance of the mother's response. For example, John Bowlby (1973) asserted that behaviors such as crying, making eye contact, and smiling, which invite warm and reliable attachment responses, result in the child's developing a better ability to cope with the world. If the parent does not encourage and validate the child and provide comfort, security, and warmth, wounding usually occurs. Bowlby postulated that the child develops a cognitive representation of early attachment relationships, which he referred to as an "internal working model." In this way, the child's initial interpersonal experiences become a working model for future relationships.

Attachment Theory

Mary Ainsworth's research emanated from Bowlby's work on attachment theory. She studied young children in relation to their mother (Gabler, 2002) and observed that after a mother's brief separation from her child, he or she showed one of three reactions. Some were angry, difficult to soothe, inconsistent, and chaotic. Ainsworth referred to these children as "anxious-ambivalent." A second group of children, who appeared to suppress feelings of anxiety and who did not appear to make contact with their mother, were referenced as "avoidant." A third group of children made contact with their mother, were easily soothed, and quickly returned to their play. Ainsworth classified these children as having a "secure" attachment style. Shaver and Clark (1994) noted that the mother's relational style influenced the child's behavior during the first few years of life. It was as though the child was thinking, "Can I count on my mother to be available when needed?" Children will perceive their mother as (a) consistently responsive, leading to the development of a secure child; (b) consistently unresponsive, resulting in a child who is avoidant; or (c) inconsistent, linked to a child who is anxious-ambivalent (Gabler, 2002).

Verzulli (1999) contended that attachment problems in children include such symptoms as poor impulse control, destructive tendencies, cruelty, aggression, irresponsibility, depression, hopelessness, blaming, and defensiveness. Sensitive responses toward an infant by parents will result in secure attachment, but disrupted attachment may lead to deficits in behavioral and emotional regulation because the child does not trust or feel safe. These issues can generalize to adulthood relationships, so that the marriage will be a struggle when one or both do not trust the other or feel safe. Attachment styles, created in response to childhood experiences, often account for conflict in relationships. A disrupted attachment cycle in childhood, due to abuse, neglect, multiple caregivers, separation from parents, or other negative causes, can result in unmet needs affecting the individual's development. Although adults with attachment disturbances may function well at their jobs and in friendships, their defenses may begin to break down in intimate relationships, and they may have difficulty accepting affection or love, resulting in relationship conflict.

Childhood attachment deficits can impact marital relationships in many ways (Hendrix, 2001). Attachment may affect choice of partner (e.g., an individual seeks the safety and security that he missed in childhood) or contribute to themes of marital conflict (e.g., the partner of the symbiotic attachment-disordered adult feels as though she has little or no value; Verzulli, 1999). Often disagreements occur when a partner triggers and evokes a response reminiscent of childhood behaviors, and the attachment-wounded person feels manipulated or controlled. Change may be difficult depending on the depth of the old wound and the severity of the defense. In addition to studies regarding the influence of attachments on couple's conflict, neurobiological studies of early childhood have increased knowledge about social and emotional development and have influenced our understanding of relationship discord and its developmental roots (Siegel, 1999, 2002).

Imago Theory

Imago theory was developed by Harville Hendrix (1992, 1996, 2001), who incorporated and synthesized concepts from several theories, including those related to early childhood development, attachment, and object relations (Slipp, 1984). Imago theory describes the unconscious course of most adult relationships from the initial attraction to romantic love and into the power struggle. Hendrix postulated that when people are attracted to someone, their unconscious mind chooses an ideal "Imago match," someone who will give them what they did not get in childhood. Although similar to Bowlby's (1973) Internal Working Model concept, the Imago represents the unconscious messages that enable one to pursue an ideal relationship. Imago refers to the mental image or picture that is developed from the accumulation of positive and negative messages received in interpersonal experiences. Hendrix (1996) proposed that these messages from parents, grandparents, siblings, aunts and uncles, peers, teachers, and partners are stored in the person's unconscious mind.

Hendrix (1996) posited that relationship intimacy is related to the level of the partners' self-esteem. When ignored, criticized, or judged, individuals tend to repress, deny, or disown some negative and positive parts of self. This results in feelings of disillusionment, frustration, fear, anger, disappointment, and even the inability to give or receive love (Hendrix & Hunt, 2004). Occasionally some individuals are thought to project their unwanted traits onto their partner. There may be a reactive power struggle in which one partner insists that the other accept his or her perspective (e.g., to acknowledge that his or her truth is the only truth). Hendrix (2001) proposed that an individual's insistence that the partner change represents a symbiotic need from childhood, which can be resolved only when each person is willing to change by acknowledging and incorporating his or her own missing traits (Hendrix & Hunt, 2004).

Hendrix (1992, 2001) proposed that the power struggle is a normal stage for relationships, in that it provides an opportunity for a couple to recommit, go through transformation, and ultimately emerge into real love and a healthy conscious relationship. He used the term "complementarity" to refer to the balance of power in marital relationships; one partner is referred to as the "minimizer" and the other as the "maximizer." The character traits of the minimizer, who constricts or diminishes affect, include withholding and being pseudo-independent, closed, excluding, self-centered, compulsive, implosive, and dominant; in contrast, the maximizer expands or exaggerates affect and is overly dependent, grasping, diffuse, other-centered, impulsive, explosive, and submissive. Gabler (2002) posited that these roles direct the course of power struggles, which are thought to eventually result in a healing process.

Hendrix's theory has some commonalities with other family system approaches (Gerson, 1996). In particular, Imago theory recognizes the intergenerational transmission of levels of maturity and emotional functioning proposed by Bowen (1978). Gerson posited that, although individual psychoanalytic or behavioral concepts dominated the mental health field, systemic thinking appears to have revolutionized psychotherapeutic practice. Family issues are understood to span the generations, with systemic anxiety impacting couples and families. For example, evidence presented by Fauchier and Margolin (2004) showed that interactions in one family subsystem influence other family subsystems. They examined the connection between marital and parent-child relationships, focusing on how conflict in the marriage can disrupt parenting.

Research studies that investigated the relationship between attachment status and partner selection have produced inconsistent findings. For example, Brennan and Shaver (1995) found nonsignificant correlations between partners' attachment-style ratings. Hazan and Shaver (1994) suggested that there is evidence that partners are selected for their ability to confirm attachment-related positive or negative expectations. There is some research that indicates that people marry their defensive style complement (Marrone, Hannah, Bause, Long, & Luquet, 1998). For example, a passive-aggressive person might be unconsciously attracted to an aggressive personality. Gabler (2002) explored theoretical and empirical relationships between attachment theory and Imago theory. She used attachment theory constructs to examine a largely unsupported element of Imago theory: the complementary nature of partners' defensive styles. The study provided empirical support for the notion that partners show different attachment styles.

The therapeutic value of emotional processing has been emphasized by various theorists. Van der Kolk, McFarlane, and Van der Hart (1996) asserted that accessing disowned painful emotions may be essential for adequate processing. Similarly, Greenberg and Pavio (1997) stated that experiencing this pain in emotionally oriented therapy is more likely to result in a successful outcome. Johnson and

Williams-Keeler (1998) found that trauma recovery was better predicted by receiving comfort from a significant other than by the severity of the trauma history.

Imago Relationship Therapy

Imago Relationship Therapy (IRT; Hendrix, 1996, 2001) is designed to process negative experiences to heal early wounds of childhood, resolve marital conflict and criticism, and increase connection and intimacy. The goal of treatment is for the partners to become individually whole and conscious and an "intentional couple"; this concept emphasizes the importance of making conscious and deliberate choices rather than being reactive. The couple is encouraged to identify their defenses and reveal their wounded vulnerable selves to each other, thus moving out of reactivity into the conscious stage of their relationship. IRT draws from attachment theory and Object Relations Theory as it attempts to re-create the connection that was lost in childhood and to increase couple intimacy (Slipp, 1984). Memories of one's core self, as well as cognitive, affective, sensory, and behavioral memories, are shared safely with the partner so that the wounded person may be held literally and figuratively and validated in order to recover underdeveloped parts of the self (Hendrix & Hunt, 2004). Experientially, "lost selves" are identified, and one's hidden potential may be discovered.

EMDR

Eye Movement Desensitization and Reprocessing (EMDR; Shapiro, 1995, 2001) is a psychotherapy created to access and process the disturbing memories and deep wounds of childhood and bring them to adaptive resolution (Shapiro, 2001; Shapiro & Maxfield, 2002). The Adaptive Information Processing (AIP) model that

> governs EMDR practice invites clinicians to view the overall client picture to identify the past events that contribute to the dysfunction, the present events that trigger disturbance, and the skills and internal resources that need to be incorporated for healthy and adaptive living in the future. (Shapiro, 2002, p. 27)

"EMDR is a positive, self-actualizing approach, not just a trauma desensitization model where we just address the obvious issue and then let them continue to limp along with other inhibiting issues" (Shapiro, 2003).

The Integration of EMDR and Imago Relationship Therapy

EMDR and IRT are both comprehensive integrative therapies based on several approaches, including psychodynamic, behavioral, cognitive, experiential, body-mind-oriented, family of origin systems, transpersonal, interpersonal, attachment theory, and Object Relations Theory (Hendrix, 1992; Shapiro, 2001). Each therapy has a standardized protocol, and Shapiro (2001) and Hendrix (2001) both proposed that, to get the most efficient and effective results, therapists need to follow these protocols.

Gabler (2002) noted that EMDR, when combined with an emotionally and experientially oriented couple therapy, was found useful when reprocessing emotions that typically fuel dysfunctional couple interactions. Her research indicated that this combination might amplify intimacy, increase connection, and promote change. Protinsky et al. (2001) investigated the treatment of couples with EMDR combined with an emotionally and experientially based approach. The outcome of their study indicated that the combined treatment seemed to enhance the emotional experience that Johnson and Talitman (1997) have identified as important to the successful outcome of therapy.

In a second study, Flemke and Protinsky (2003) found intimacy to be greatly enhanced with couples when integrating EMDR and an Imago technique, *Parent-Child Dialogue*. This study suggested that combining a family therapy, such as IRT, with EMDR might promote change and resolution and increase compassion and intimacy in marital and relationship conflict. The protocol used by Flemke and Protinsky used Imago dialogues to create emotional arousal, self-disclosure, and partner empathic response. If the couple appeared to be at an impasse, and an unprocessed trigger could be identified, EMDR was introduced for greater healing of childhood wounds. The authors concluded that processing childhood wounds and traumas by integrating EMDR and IRT might help couples establish a more intimate connection.

THERAPY PROCESS

In the integrative therapy approach described in this chapter, IRT is used to organize the approach to therapy, identify unprocessed targets for EMDR processing, facilitate communication between the partners, and help couples become less reactive and more intentional, separate and ultimately more connected. The couple is asked to commit to 12 sessions of therapy. EMDR is implemented, with both partners present, by having one partner process an issue while the other partner listens, observes, focuses on the partner's experiences and his or her own internal experiences, and takes notes to be shared later (Protinsky et al., 2001). The listening partner may hold the other, literally or figuratively, while the processing partner expresses pain in a safe environment. The couple experiences bonding and connection.

The role of the therapist is to create a safe environment for the expression of emotion and to facilitate dialogue, thus increasing the partners' knowledge of themselves and each other. The therapist maintains a focus on the marital relationship and works with the couple, rather than with the individuals separately.

The basic steps of IRT are (a) understanding childhood wounds and frustrations, (b) creating profiles of parents and partners, (c) learning the Couples Dialogue, (d) resolving anger, (e) experiencing containment and self-soothing, (f) expressing caring and appreciation, and (g) developing a relationship vision of the future (Hendrix, 2001). The couple moves through the steps sequentially.

The Couples Dialogue

The Couples Dialogue becomes a tool of transformation, helping the partners to become more separate as individuals and to reach toward each other in connection. The Dialogue is a strategic communication technique and includes variations designed to assist couples in expressing frustration, anger, and fear, as well as needs and desires, in a calm and safe manner. The Couples Dialogue consists of three parts:

1. The first is mirroring, where one partner (sender) expresses feelings about a frustrating feeling or event, and the listening partner (receiver) mirrors or reflects back what is heard, enabling the sender to know he or she has been heard. The listener invites the sender to express more about the message and continues to mirror until the message is complete.

2. The second component of the Dialogue is the receiver's validation that what the sender expressed makes sense and is true for the sender. The listener may not agree with the sender but only needs to accept and validate that what the listener heard is true for the sender. The receiver may explore what hurts or frightens his or her partner and what childhood memories are related. This process assists the listening partner to place reactivity aside and to become more conscious and compassionate.

3. The third step of the Dialogue is empathy expressed by the receiver, who needs to step outside of his or her feelings and become attuned with the sender, imagining what the sender might feel. When the sender feels understood and experiences validation and empathy, the process reverses and the receiver asks to become the sender and vice versa (Hendrix, 2001).

Parent-Child Dialogue

Another form of the Couples Dialogue is the Parent-Child Dialogue; it addresses childhood wounds and is used as a vehicle for healing. One of the partners (the sender) is encouraged to retreat to a painful time in childhood and requests the other partner (the receiver) to assume the role of the sender's parent. The receiver asks the sender to express the deepest hurt and the worst frustration from childhood, and the role-playing partner mirrors the message, validates, and empathizes. The parent/listener asks the child/sender what he or she needs from the parent to heal the pain. The couple then assumes its original role as two partners. The listener asks, "As your partner, what do you need from me to help you heal that?" Frequently the partner who plays the parent is more compassionate and understands what the partner missed in childhood, which often reflects what he or she misses in their adult relationship. This Parent-Child Dialogue is often powerful enough to unleash and process deep-seated wounds and allows the partners to grow and heal in the relationship (Hendrix, 2001, 2005).

Phases of Treatment

The sequencing of treatment phases used in this integrative model combines aspects of both EMDR and IRT, and follows the protocols of both approaches.

Client History, Treatment Planning, and Preparation

During the early phases of treatment, the therapist establishes rapport with the clients. Development of attunement by the therapist is often crucial in both IRT and EMDR, because the therapist's expertise can function as a resource in therapy (Hendrix, 2001; Shapiro, 2001, 2002). During this phase, the couple is educated about the effects of early childhood experiences on development and later relationships. The basic concepts of IRT and EMDR are explained. The first EMDR phase involves taking a clinical history to determine the clients' readiness for EMDR, and a treatment plan is conceptualized by identifying past, present, and future template targets. New targets continue to be identified as processing commences. Likewise, the Imago therapist also may take a history of the couple in the first and second sessions; this process continues throughout treatment, as historical information is elicited during the use of the Couples Dialogue.

In both EMDR and IRT, the clients' positive resources are explored to strengthen the ego, enhance the therapy, and establish sufficient stabilization. Examples of resources utilized in EMDR are visualization of a safe place (Korn & Leeds, 2002; Shapiro, 2001), relaxation exercises, meditation, and positive memories to remind clients of times when they felt in control and could handle emotional distress. Correspondingly, IRT uses guided visualization exercises to help clients establish a safe place so that when they are confronted with painful experiences or negative cognitions they can be reminded that they have a place of safety. Other IRT resources are positive memories, appreciations, affirmations, and flooding a partner with affirmative messages to remind the couple of the potential healing of these ideas (Hendrix, 2001).

The client and therapist also identify possible large "T" and small "t" traumas as targets to be processed in EMDR, including past and current disturbing events that evoke stress. IRT is used to explore early developmental wounding of each client, for example, during early attachment, exploration, and identity stages. In EMDR, the float-back technique assists a client in recalling an earlier event and helps identify and reprocess the implicit memories that are frozen due to early trauma. The float-forward technique aids the couple in the creation of a mutual vision by addressing any anxieties they may have about their future. Reprocessing their fears may result in the identification of resources, such as solutions and coping strategies (Shapiro, 2002, 2003; Young, Zangwill, & Behary, 2002).

Processing

It is the purpose of both EMDR and IRT to identify, reprocess, and transform dysfunctional stored memories and to move the individual toward increased mental health. Both approaches stress the importance of processing early events and moving out of reactivity and into consciousness. Processing means working to break the legacy of old memories and to create new associations and more effective adaptations. EMDR uses dual stimulation, such as eye movements or bilateral taps and tones (Shapiro, 2001); Imago therapy uses various forms of the Couples Dialogue to expedite the process. IRT also uses anecdotes, poetry, and movies to deepen emotions and the process. For example, showing a movie clip from Disney's *The Kid* visually illustrates the parent-child power struggle. In both approaches, the therapist facilitates and stays out of the way of the clients, allowing them to follow the process, which naturally moves them in the direction of healing and change (Hendrix, 2001; Shapiro, 2001).

The therapist assists the partners with the Couples Dialogue, using mirroring, validating, and empathizing, to continue processing incomplete issues. To be certain that the couple is in a state of emotional balance, self-control techniques learned in the Preparation Phase may be used. If it is evident that some painful experience has not been accessed and processed during IRT, or the couple has difficulty moving forward, introducing EMDR to deal with the impasse and to process unprocessed material appears to allow transformation to occur more readily (Shapiro, 2001, 2002). EMDR is used according to the standard protocol, but with the partner present to provide support and validation.

As processing continues and early traumas and issues become less painful, the past and present appear to be increasingly more tolerable. Furthermore, processing childhood wounds with IRT and EMDR works to increase the partners' compassion and intimacy, establishing a healing connection and creating change in difficult relationships (Protinsky et al., 2001).

Future-Oriented Exercises

When the EMDR desensitization is complete and past and present disturbances have been targeted and reprocessed, the therapy focus shifts to enhance the client's ability to make future choices (Shapiro, 2001). Similarly, IRT introduces experiential flooding of positive characteristics and appreciation exercises to the couple, such as reromanticizing, re-visioning, restructuring anger, and other future-oriented exercises (Hendrix, 2001). Reimaging each other, from a cruel and abusive person to someone who is emotionally wounded, is effective during the Imago Holding Dialogue. One partner holds the wounded partner and asks, "What was it like as a child living in your family?" and "What was the worst part?" Another way to reimage the other is through guided imageries, when each partner invites the wounded partner to join him or her in a safe place, to return to the childhood home, and to hold each other in their new positive thoughts. The Imago process continues with reromanticizing (appreciations, flooding, caring, and fun exercises), restructuring the relationship by asking for what each needs, learning how to deal with anger more effectively, and writing a mutual relationship vision of the future to promote healing, connection, and healthier mature love.

Transformation

EMDR and IRT appear to work together to enhance transformation through deeper processing and resolution of early childhood wounds and trauma. Through curiosity and the use of the Couples Dialogue, the couple learns about themselves, each other, and the relationship. The couple moves from the unconscious love relationship and the power struggle into the stages of a conscious love relationship, which includes commitment, understanding resistance, resolving anger and fear, taking risks, and embracing real love. Information is gathered, painful experiences are processed, options are discovered, and new decisions are made.

CASE EXAMPLE

Ellen and Marty came into therapy in the midst of a severe power struggle. Married almost 30 years and with two married children, they reported that they had been trying to survive the marriage since its inception. Recently, Marty had had an affair and wanted to leave the marriage. Ellen was stunned. Marty agreed to go to marital therapy, and they arrived in crisis.

Imago Relationship Therapy initially was chosen as the treatment modality. By means of the Couples Dialogue, history was disclosed and Ellen and Marty's developmental stages were explored. Through the course of treatment, they learned the Couples Dialogue in several forms, creating a seamless flow of therapy. To complete the protocol, even when they may have felt uncomfortable, the couple made a commitment to stay in therapy and in the process for at least 12 sessions. They also agreed to include the resolution approach of EMDR. The goal was to desensitize their trauma and to reprocess information gathered in the course of therapy. The therapy sessions continued well beyond the original contract of 12 sessions.

Ellen and Marty's histories were similar. Abandonment and rejection began at the attachment stage, which set the platform for the rest of childhood and was reawakened in their marital relationship. Ellen adapted to her past by becoming a maximizer; Marty's early adaptation was to be a minimizer. The more Ellen displayed anger and fought for what she did not get as a child and what she wanted and needed in the marriage, the further Marty pulled away out of terror of becoming too close and experiencing his childhood abandonment and rejection wounds again.

Ellen and Marty may have unconsciously chosen each other so that each could become more like the other. Although they were defended against owning their negative, denied parts and their positive, disowned parts, their hidden desire may have been to be more like their partner. It appears that the maximizer and minimizer connected unconsciously to become an Imago match, so that they could heal early childhood wounds.

Ellen

Ellen was 9 years old when her mother died. It was Ellen's responsibility to do household chores and to care for her siblings and her father, who was an alcoholic. Although her father remarried, Ellen's stepmother had a stroke and lived with her and Marty throughout their married life. Responsibilities increased, and Ellen's role as caretaker became a heavier burden.

The loss of her biological mother was a significant past target for Ellen, and the picture that represented the worst part of that incident was her father telling her that her mother had died. She was "stunned." She had not been allowed to visit her mother, and Ellen expected that her mother would come home from the hospital. Because she was expected to care for younger siblings and her alcoholic father, she never was allowed to grieve or cry. Ellen did not have an opportunity to say good-bye to her mother. For the first time in her life, during EMDR processing she began to grieve over the loss of her mother, which became the target.

Ellen expressed anger and frustration with Marty because of his affair. It triggered Ellen's early childhood feelings of abandonment by her mother. Marty listened and mirrored back everything Ellen told him. Marty was encouraged to put aside his reactions to Ellen's communiqué and to see "her world," knowing he would have a later opportunity to respond. He checked with Ellen to see if he "got it right" and continued to mirror until he "got it all." When Ellen was finished, Marty validated and empathized, given all that he had learned about Ellen, experienced her pain, and grew more compassionate.

Given her pain and anger with her father around her mother's death, Ellen agreed to do a Parent-Child Dialogue and asked Marty to be her as-if father. As instructed, she closed her eyes and allowed herself to go back to the morning her father told her that her mother died. Marty put aside being Ellen's husband to be her as-if father and asked Ellen, "What is it like for you this morning, learning that your mother died?" He mirrored, validated, and empathized as she described her pain to her "father." Following two sessions of the Parent-Child Dialogue, EMDR became the therapy of choice to clear out unresolved trauma over this issue for Ellen, and eventually to install Positive Cognitions. The Parent-Child Dialogue of IRT helped her get through the pain and angry feelings toward her father and helped her feel more comfortable with other issues around her mother's dying, such as her difficulty returning to school after her mother died.

EMDR allowed deeper processing and resolution. Although IRT was extremely helpful to Ellen and Marty in identifying and processing their early childhood wounds, EMDR was added to supplement and deepen the therapy process. Ellen chose buzzers in her hands coordinated with auditory tones through a headset for the dual stimulation to be used in EMDR, and watching the picture on a video in her mind with her eyes closed. The Parent-Child Dialogue of IRT helped her get through the pain and angry feelings about her father. Using the EMDR float-back technique, Ellen was able to get in touch with her Negative Cognitions, which included "I am not okay," "I lack confidence," and "I am powerless." When IRT was insufficient to reach and completely reprocess these negative issues, EMDR often was able to desensitize and reprocess Ellen's negative thoughts and feelings. Often EMDR and IRT were used in the same session. If time did not allow for both therapies, EMDR was provided in subsequent sessions. Ellen's Positive Cognitions were "I am in control and secure" and "I am okay as I am"; these were installed when the desensitization phase was complete.

A present-day target for Ellen was her inability to trust Marty, given his affair and his frequent lies. Ellen's familiar childhood adaptation of her role as a caretaker continued with her husband, her two children, and, eventually, her grandchildren. Hurt and anger were deep-seated for many years. She and Marty were committed to the process and to using the Imago Couples Dialogue, but Ellen was not able to cry or to express anger over her abandonment as a child, which was retriggered when Marty had his affair. With the additional help of EMDR and the loss of her mother as a target, she was able to process and clear out the blockages that interfered with healing the old wounds. Marty was able to hold her in her pain and supported her in her new desire to take care of herself without shame and guilt. Once the past and present targets were cleared, Ellen was able to create a future template and rewrite the relationship vision for her future. The AIP model of EMDR and Imago dialoguing were helpful in creating a healthy future vision for Ellen.

Marty

When they first came for therapy, Marty had little recollection of his childhood. He had difficulty remembering events with his parents or siblings or about himself. With the use of the Parent-Child Dialogue and the introduction of EMDR to process deep childhood wounds, Marty began to remember more about his early dysfunctional childhood. Triggered by Ellen's need to take care of him, which made him feel uncomfortable, he recalled himself at age 5, wearing overalls, sitting on the steps looking for someone with whom to talk. No one was there. He had no playmates. He had no toys and could not have fun. He was hungry and his mother was calling him, but he was afraid to go home. Marty's mother was overwhelmed, sacrificing to raise seven children with no money. Ellen's need to coddle Marty was unsafe for him, given his mother's lack of attention. This scene from his past became Marty's past target.

The Couples Dialogue enabled Marty to express in a safe way the terror he felt growing up, how "I do not deserve love, am a bad person, am not lovable, do not trust myself." He had difficulty expressing all this, and that "I do not deserve good things" and felt he was a "disappointment." Ellen was able to mirror, validate, and empathize throughout while crying and being compassionate. She held Marty literally and figuratively by staying in his world and putting her issues aside. He was able to reprocess his negative childhood coupled with his Positive Cognitions: "I deserve love, I am a good person, I am lovable, I can trust myself, I am okay."

Another factor exacerbating the marital conflict was Marty's anxiety, anger, depression, and flashbacks of his combat time in the Vietnam War. He was the only survivor in his group, and he suffered undue guilt and feelings of responsibility for the incident. To compound his negative feelings around his war issues, the current incompetence of his fellow workers resulted in Marty's assuming more tasks himself. His increased focus on work impacted his time and attention on his relationship with Ellen and increased her feelings of rejection and abandonment. His posttraumatic stress diminished when survivor guilt became the target, and EMDR was used to decrease the impact of Marty's negative feelings. Although IRT was powerful in the healing of the relationship, incorporating EMDR around his Vietnam War issues resulted in a more significant improvement in Marty's self-esteem and his ability to connect with Ellen.

Change in the relationship became evident when Marty's feelings of terror and inadequacy were desensitized and reprocessed by using the Imago Dialogue and by healing his unresolved past pain with EMDR. In this case, the integration of IRT and EMDR seemed very successful. Using both methods appeared to speed up the process and to increase the healing of his early childhood wounds. Both Ellen and Marty had nurturing deficits and deprivation as children. Their adult relationship mirrored their pasts and replicated the attachment wounding of their childhoods. Safety was established in the therapy using the Couples Dialogue and guided imageries, and they were able to replay early incidents with their partner present to hold them in their pain. When this was clear, other channels were successfully targeted and processed. Four sessions of EMDR were conducted, with Ellen holding Marty with eye contact, validation, and empathy. Often she reached for Marty and held him in her arms. Her attunement and empathy were very healing and were accepted by Marty. There was a breakthrough of many of the blocked early childhood traumas.

Exercises such as flooding each other with positive phrases, re-visioning each other as wounded rather than mean or abusive, and learning to ask for what each wanted or needed helped transform Ellen and Marty and their relationship. Other positive activities they learned were having fun, gifting, and showing care. They became able to give and receive love. Ellen and Marty eventually attended therapy less often, felt more secure in their relationship, and had the tools and techniques they needed to continue their journey toward healthier separateness and connection.

DISCUSSION

As illustrated in the example of Marty and Ellen, the integration of EMDR and IRT can result in thorough and comprehensive processing and transformation of the marital relationship. Both practices assist clients in processing unconscious or implicit memories that hold unfulfilled needs of childhood, defenses related to early childhood wounds and trauma, and past experiences that appear to have an effect on current and future relationships.

IRT is designed to create marital transformation by processing negative experiences with the Couples Dialogue to heal early wounds of childhood, resolve marital conflict and criticism, and increase connection, communication, and intimacy. Reprocessing with EMDR changes the individual by resolving traumatic memories, desensitizing triggers, eliminating emotional distress, and reformulating associated beliefs; it changes the couple through the systemic effects of each partner's personal growth and the shared experience within the session.

Despite the unique methods of EMDR and IRT, they tend to be similar in their goals and philosophies. Advantages of integrating EMDR and IRT may include faster and deeper resolution of early childhood wounds and trauma and increased compassion and intimacy, enabling the couple to establish a healing connection, which breaks the symbiosis created in early childhood. Separation due to personal growth allows the couple to honor each other's differences and often results in greater connection. The integration of EMDR with IRT appears to provide more comprehensive desensitization, reprocessing, and healing than either of these therapies might provide individually.

REFERENCES

Bowen, M. (1978). *Family therapy in clinical practice.* New York: Aronson.

Bowlby, J. (1973). *Attachment and loss: Vol. 2. Separation: Anxiety and anger.* New York: Basic Books.

Brennan, K., & Shaver, P. (1995). Dimensions of adult attachment, affect regulation, and romantic relationship functioning. *Personality and Social Psychology Bulletin, 21,* 267–283.

Fauchier, A., & Margolin, G. (2004). Affection and conflict in marital and parent-child relationships. *Journal of Marital and Family Therapy, 30*(2), 197–211.

Flemke, K. R., & Protinsky, H. (2003). Imago dialogues: Treatment enhancement with EMDR. *Journal of Family Psychotherapy, 14*(2), 31–45.

Gabler, G. J. (2002). Complementarity of defensive style in intimate relationships. *Journal of Imago Relationship Therapy, 5*(2), 29–43.

Gerson, R. (1996). Family systems theory and imago therapy: A theoretical interpretation. *Journal of Imago Relationship Therapy, 1*(1), 19–41.

Gottman, J. (2000). The timing of divorce: Predicting when a couple will divorce over a 14 year period. *Journal of Marriage and Family, 62*(3), 737–745.

Greenberg, L., & Pavio, S. (1997). *Working with emotion in psychotherapy.* New York: Guilford Press.

Hazan, C., & Shaver, P. (1994). Attachment as an organizational framework for research on close relationships. *Psychological Inquiry, 5,* 1–22.

Hendrix, H. (1992). *Keeping the love you find: A guide for singles.* New York: Pocket Books.

Hendrix, H. (1996). The evolution of imago relationship therapy: A personal and professional journey. *Journal of Imago Relationship Therapy, 1*(1), 1–17.

Hendrix, H. (2001). *Getting the love you want: A guide for couples.* New York: First Owl Books. (Original work published 1988)

Hendrix, H. (2005). *Getting the love you want: Couples workshop manual.* New York: Imago Relationships International. (Original work published 1979)

Hendrix, H., & Hunt, H. (2004). *Receiving love: Transform your relationship by letting yourself be loved.* New York: Atria Books.

Johnson, S. M., & Talitman, E. (1997). Predictors of success in emotionally focused marital therapy. *Journal of Marital and Family Therapy, 23,* 135–151.

Johnson, S. M., & Williams-Keeler, L. (1998). Creating healing relationships for couples dealing with trauma: The use of emotionally focused marital therapy. *Journal of Marital and Family Therapy, 24,* 25–40.

Korn, D. L., & Leeds, A. M. (2002). Preliminary evidence of efficacy for EMDR resource development and installation in the stabilization phase of treatment of complex posttraumatic stress disorder. *Journal of Clinical Psychology, 58,* 1465–1487.

Love, P. (2001). *The truth about love.* New York: Simon & Schuster.

Mahler, M. (1968). *On human symbiosis and the vicissitudes of individuation.* New York: International Universities Press.

Mahler, M., Pine, F., & Berman, A. (1975). *The psychological birth of the human infant: Symbiosis and individuation.* New York: Basic Books.

Marrone, J., Hannah, M., Bause, M., Long, J., & Luquet, W. (1998). The Imago Developmental Adaptation Profile (IDAP): Preliminary scale development. *Journal of Imago Relationship Therapy, 3,* 49–62.

Morris, J. (2003). Maturation: Imago theory versus psychoanalytic theory. *Journal of Imago Relationship Therapy, 5*(2), 1–13.

Protinsky, H., Sparks, J., & Flemke, K. (2001). Using eye movement desensitization and reprocessing to enhance treatment of couples. *Journal of Marital and Family Therapy, 27*(2), 157–164.

Shapiro, F. (1995). *Eye movement desensitization and reprocessing: Basic principles, protocols, and procedures.* New York: Guilford Press.

Shapiro, F. (2001). *Eye movement desensitization and reprocessing: Basic principles, protocols, and procedures* (2nd ed.). New York: Guilford Press.

Shapiro, F. (2002). EMDR treatment: Overview and integration. In F. Shapiro (Ed.), *EMDR as an integrative psychotherapy approach* (pp. 27–56). Washington, DC: American Psychological Association.

Shapiro, F. (2003, September). *Adaptive information processing and case conceptualization.* Paper presented at EMDRIA Conference, Denver, CO.

Shapiro, F., & Maxfield, L. (2002). Eye movement desensitization and reprocessing (EMDR). In M. Hersen & W. Sledge (Eds.), *Encyclopedia of psychotherapy* (Vol. 1, pp. 777–785). New York: Elsevier Science.

Shaver, P., & Clark, C. (1994). The psychodynamics of adult romantic attachment. In J. M. Masling & R. F. Bornstein (Eds.), *Empirical perspectives on object relations theory* (pp. 105–156). Washington, DC: American Psychological Association.

Siegel, D. (1999). *The developing mind: Toward a neurobiology of interpersonal experience.* New York: Guilford Press.

Siegel, D. (2002). The developing mind and the resolution of trauma: Some ideas about information processing and an interpersonal neurobiology of psychotherapy. In F. Shapiro (Ed.), *EMDR as an integrative psychotherapy approach* (pp. 85–122). Washington, DC: American Psychological Association.

Slipp, S. (1984). *Object relations: A dynamic bridge between individual and family therapy.* New York: Aronson.

Solomon, M. F. (2002). Connection, disruption, repair: Treating the effects of attachment trauma on intimate relationships. In M. F. Solomon & D. J. Siegel (Eds.), *Healing trauma: Attachment, mind, body and brain* (pp. 372–345). New York: Norton.

van der Kolk, B. A., McFarlane, A. C., & Van der Hart, O. (1996). The black hole of trauma. In B. van der Kolk, A. McFarlane, & L. Weisaeth (Eds.), *Traumatic stress* (pp. 3–19). New York: Guilford Press.

Verzulli, S. (1999). Disturbed attachment, abuse, and imago therapy. *Journal of Imago Relationship Therapy, 4*(1), 1–16.

Young, J., Zangwill, W., & Behary, W. (2002). Combining EMDR and schema-focused therapy. In F. Shapiro (Ed.), *EMDR in conjunction with family systems therapy* (pp. 181–208). Washington, DC: American Psychological Association.

CHAPTER 10

EMDR and Emotionally Focused Couple Therapy for War Veteran Couples

Nancy Errebo and Rita Sommers-Flanagan

A veteran of the global war on terror, married just 18 days before deployment to Iraq, came home to his wife a different man. The couple came to the Vet Center for help. "His eyes look hollow," said the young woman, her own eyes reflecting confusion and concern. "He is no fun anymore, so I go out dancing by myself—just to relax or maybe to make him jealous. It seems like the only way to get his attention is to make him mad. I'm just about to give up."

To help veteran couples such as this one, therapists need to understand the effect of war on the warrior, the impact of the warrior's experience on intimate relationships, and effective individual and couple treatments. These considerations are discussed in this chapter.

War Trauma and Complex Posttraumatic Stress Disorder

Silver and Rogers (2002) delineated several unique elements of war trauma that help explain why veterans often develop complex Posttraumatic Stress Disorder (PTSD):

- Prolonged exposure sets the autonomic nervous system at higher levels of arousal and solidifies negative views of self, other, and world.

- Multiple traumas are highly likely.

- War trauma is deliberately inflicted by and on one's fellow human beings.

- Veterans are likely to be both victim and perpetrator; many young people who enlist in the military for the noble reason of protecting their country discover the grim reality that surviving combat requires one to experience and inflict brutality.

- Veterans are both powerful and powerless; they are authorized to use deadly force to dominate the enemy, yet there is every possibility that same lethality will be used against them. This dichotomy causes enormous inner confusion.

- Having repeatedly witnessed the worst that can happen, veterans feel the need to constantly anticipate and prepare for the worst.

- Because veterans have put their lives on the line for their country and fellow citizens, they have unique relationships with society, the government, and the flag for which they fought. Therefore, social upheavals, natural disasters, terrorist threats, and war are more personal and problematic to veterans than to other citizens.

Effects of Posttraumatic Stress Disorder Symptoms on Veterans and Their Intimate Relationships

The National Vietnam Veterans Readjustment Study (Kulka et al., 1990) found that families of combat veterans with PTSD exhibit more violence, marital problems, parenting problems, and children's behavioral problems than families of veterans without PTSD. The symptoms of PTSD impair the veteran's attempts to reenter society and reestablish the closeness and intimacy that he* experienced in his family prior to deployment.

Reexperiencing Symptoms

Intrusive memories preoccupy some veterans in the daytime and invade dreams at night. To his horror, a veteran may wake up from a nightmare of mortal combat to find his hands closing around his wife's throat. Thus, fear may replace security in the marital bed.

Hyperarousal Symptoms

Hyperarousal of the autonomic nervous system may make a veteran an insomniac, irritable, intense, and unpredictable (Foa, 2000). In response, the tension in the household can regularly build to an unbearable level until sometimes only a violent eruption of words or actions can bring relief (Errebo, 1995).

Emotional Numbing Symptoms

The intrusive and arousal symptoms of PTSD are devastating, yet emotional numbing can produce an even sadder and more pernicious casualty of war: the disruption of attachment bonds (Ainsworth, 1989; Mitchell, 1999). Emotional numbing is grouped with the avoidance cluster of PTSD symptoms and is characterized by diminished interest in significant activities, feelings of detachment from others, and restricted range of affect. Litz and colleagues (1997) found a significant correlation between symptoms of emotional numbing and those of hyperarousal; they hypothesized that numbing is a response to intolerable levels of arousal. Veterans know only too well how fragile life is and how

---

*Although increasing numbers of women are serving in the military and now constitute a large veteran group, in this chapter, we refer to the veteran as "he." Much of the research cited has been conducted on male veterans, and males still make up the large majority of combat soldiers.

much it hurts to lose someone you depend on and love. Therefore, they frequently resist attachment. As one Vietnam veteran explained to his therapist, "The worst thing about this PTSD is that it changes you so that you can't love anyone. If you love someone, you can lose her. And then you're afraid again." Another veteran said, "I have big problems with my wife going out without me. Our neighbor cheated on her husband while he was in Iraq. And a lot of my buddies got Dear John letters over there. I just can't trust my wife like I used to, and it isn't even based on anything *she* did."

Avoidance Symptoms

In avoiding the pain of fear, guilt, and sadness, veterans may withdraw from society, their family, and even from their own dreams and desires (Errebo, 1995; Haley, 1978). Therefore, their families are forced to make decisions for them. For instance, making plans, be it for a weekend outing or long-range financial investment, is very often aversive or overwhelming to veterans because war taught them that plans go awry, things always turn out for the worst, they probably will not live long enough for the plans to materialize, and they do not deserve a future because they survived when so many others died. This impacts the marital relationship because anticipating the events and joys of a shared life together is one of the most intimate things a couple can do.

As the late Sarah Haley wrote in 1978:

> We have been particularly concerned with the pervasiveness of a seeming trade-off to passivity in order to counter fears of the past. . . . Although Vietnam veterans have been characterized in the public and clinical media as having explosive aggressive reactions, these episodes are often punctuation marks in a more stultifying passivity. (p. 262)

A passive coping style, coupled with the ongoing anticipation of danger, makes it more difficult to cope with ordinary, expectable life challenges.

Problems in Veterans' Marital Relationships

Unresolved traumatic experiences can have long-lasting negative effects in intimate relationships. Several studies have examined the impact of veterans' PTSD on their female partners and have found subsequent difficulties in communication and intimacy in these relationships (Coughlan & Parkin, 1987; Maloney, 1988; Verbosky & Ryan, 1988). In a study of the quality of intimate relationships of male Vietnam veterans, Riggs and colleagues (Riggs, Byrne, Weathers, & Litz, 1998) found that over 70% of PTSD veterans and their female partners reported clinically significant levels of relationship distress compared to 30% of non-PTSD couples. They reported a wide range of distress and had taken more steps toward separation and divorce than non-PTSD veterans and their partners. The degree of relationship distress was correlated with the severity of PTSD, especially emotional numbing. Veterans with PTSD reported greater anxiety around intimacy with their partner than veterans without PTSD. Also, partners of veterans with PTSD expressed more anxiety around intimacy than partners of veterans without PTSD.

Certainly, not every veteran develops PTSD, but many experience difficulties in readjustment to civilian life due to traumatic exposure and prolonged separation from family and culture (Burham, 2004). Intimate relationships reverberate in response. War experiences often create ongoing and profound suffering for veterans and their families (Coughlan & Parkin, 1987). From a family systems perspective, the alternating numbing and hyperarousal symptoms that may exist even without a diagnosis of full PTSD disrupt attachment and intimacy and cast the veteran into the identified patient role (S. M. Johnson, 2002). The couple gets caught in a cycle of withdrawing and criticism. Due to her husband's withdrawal, the wife may resort to shouldering all responsibility, managing her husband's moods, and buffering him from the environment. The result is increasing exhaustion, anger, and resentment (D. R. Johnson, Feldman, & Lubin, 1995). Eventually, she, too, may withdraw.

Attachment bonds to the partner may also suffer because of competition from the veteran's relationship to war memories that are more vivid and dramatic than everyday family life. The veteran sometimes thinks that nothing is important that does not have life-or-death consequences (Hayman, Sommers-Flanagan, & Parsons, 1987). Therefore, he withdraws from his wife into an inner landscape he does not invite her to share. As one veteran said, "My wife and I were strangers when I came back from Vietnam. There are no words to describe a war zone, and I wouldn't want to inflict it on her anyway."

If the veteran does try to open up about his experiences, he risks rejection if his wife is horrified by what she hears. For example, a soldier phoned and e-mailed his wife as often as he could, telling her everything that was going on in Fallujah and Mosul, Iraq, the deaths he had witnessed, and the killing he had done. His wife asked him to stop, confessing that she could not stand to hear about the war. Later, as he related this in therapy, he sobbed:

> She thinks I am a monster. I am a trained killer and I did what I had to do. She said I was like a ghost to her. We were madly in love at one time. She can't deal with the fact that I killed so many people. I went on strafing runs all alone with my Bradley. They depended on me to lead—so many bullet holes in that Bradley. In my dreams, I'm in a small clay hut all alone. The insurgents are coming at me, and then they turn into demons. I need my wife to comfort me, but now I can't tell her what I'm going through.

Treatment Considerations

Comprehensive treatment for couples affected by war trauma will include individual sessions for both partners as well as conjoint couples sessions.

Individual Therapy

The treatment of war veterans has been widely studied, and the U.S. Department of Defense and Veteran Affairs (VA/DoD, 2003) developed a comprehensive *Practice Guideline* for individual treatment. One of the recommended therapies is Eye Movement Desensitization and Reprocessing (EMDR; Shapiro, 2001). Various studies (e.g., Carlson, Chemtob, Rusnak, Hedlund, & Muraoka, 1998) have demonstrated the efficacy of EMDR for the treatment of PTSD with war veterans.

EMDR was empirically derived by the observation of the effect of saccadic eye movements on the felt sense of old memories. It is guided by the Adaptive Information Processing (AIP) model, which posits that everyone has an inherent information processing system that normally heals emotional distress, but that can be overwhelmed by severely disturbing and traumatic experiences. The veteran with PTSD is trapped in negative cognitive, emotional, behavioral, and relational patterns because his war trauma has remained unprocessed (Shapiro, 1995, 2001). The trauma memory is considered to be stored in a state-dependent somatosensory form; when it is stimulated, the veteran is often helpless to choose his reaction. EMDR treatment facilitates the processing of these memories and proceeds in eight phases. For instance, in treating the couple reported at the end of the previous section, EMDR would be used with both the veteran and his wife to process the memories of the war experiences and intimacy difficulties. Whereas the veteran had the direct experience of the war memories, the wife's reaction to her husband's letters would also be categorized as a trauma for her and in need of processing (see Shapiro, 2001). The essence of the three-pronged protocol is to help a distressed individual to process painful memories, and in so doing become more responsive to the present and better able to shape the future (Shapiro, 1995, 2001).

Marital Therapy

The research on family and couple therapy for combat veteran couples is sparse. Glynn and colleagues (1999) assessed the effects of adding behavioral family therapy to exposure treatment for combat-related PTSD. Although exposure therapy helped with some of the PTSD symptoms, these researchers did not find an additive effect for the behavioral family therapy. In a small pilot study, Monson, Schnurr, Stevens, and Guthrie (2004) provided Cognitive-Behavioral Couple's Treatment (CBCT) to seven couples in which the husband was diagnosed with PTSD due to combat-related experiences. Husbands endorsed only modest improvement in PTSD symptoms but did not report relationship improvement; wives reported both relationship improvement and perceived improvement in their partner's PTSD symptoms.

There are several clinical models for working with trauma in couples and families. Some of these include Emotionally Focused Therapy (S. M. Johnson, 2002), Critical Interaction Therapy (D. R. Johnson et al., 1995), and Figley's (1988) Five Step model. Other couple therapy approaches, including psychoanalytic, narrative, cognitive-behavioral, structural, and strategic models, have also been utilized with veterans.

Emotionally Focused Couple Therapy (EFT; S. M. Johnson, 2002) has been found to be very helpful with veteran couples. It draws on several theories, including the systemic-structural theory of Salvador Minuchin (Minuchin & Fishman, 1981); the nonpathologizing humanism of Carl Rogers (1961); the here-and-now, experiential stance of Fritz Perls (1973); and John Bowlby's (1978) theory of attachment. The EFT method was empirically derived by observation of how couples repaired their relationship in therapy, and it has been validated by controlled studies (e.g., S. M. Johnson & Greenberg, 1998).

The essence of EFT is to help a distressed couple construct a more secure attachment by focusing, in the present moment of the therapy session, on the emotional experience of each partner and the interpersonal dynamics between them. Specifically, the EFT therapist helps clients develop and differentiate their emotions by noticing, reflecting, and validating the affect of each partner and actively restructuring their interpersonal enactment (S. M. Johnson, 2004).

THERAPY PROCESS

The therapy process described here is an integration of EFT and EMDR. In case conceptualization and treatment planning, EMDR and EFT can be woven together harmoniously; many of their theoretical concepts and procedural steps are compatible with or parallel to one another.

EFT and EMDR are first described separately. Next, the parallels between the two treatments are discussed. Then a plan is presented for combining EMDR and EFT in comprehensive treatment for couples affected by war trauma.

Emotionally Focused Couple Therapy

The first goal of EFT is to facilitate shifts in rigid, negative interactional patterns by accessing and reprocessing each partner's emotional responses. The second goal is to help the couple interact in the session in new ways that create a relationship of safety, security, protection, and comfort. The partners then are able to help each other regulate negative affect and strengthen each other's sense of self. These changes occur first in session with the support of the therapist. In time, the couple spontaneously behave in the new ways outside the session.

Stages of Emotionally Focused Couple Therapy

EFT is accomplished in three stages and nine steps (S. M. Johnson, 2004):

Stage 1: De-Escalation of Negative Cycles of Interaction

Step 1. Together, the therapist and the couple create an alliance and define core conflicts in the couple's enactment of insecure attachment issues. When an attachment figure is unresponsive, humans respond with anxiety or avoidance. When attachment is threatened but not severed, intense attachment efforts such as clinging, begging, pursuit, and even aggressive cornering may ensue. Avoidant strategies such as obsessive focus on tasks and limiting or avoiding emotional engagement occur when hope for a response is tenuous. A third insecure attachment style, called fearful avoidant, is a combination of seeking closeness and then pushing it away when it is offered. Specifically, how do the partners employ strategies of anxious clinging and detached avoidance that are the hallmarks of insecure attachment?

Step 2. The negative interactional cycle wherein these conflict issues are expressed is identified by the couple's descriptions and the therapist's observations of their interactions. Is the couple caught in a cycle of pursue/withdraw, withdraw/withdraw, attack/attack, or some combination of the three? The pursue/withdraw pattern might be typified by a wife who angrily criticizes and demands attention from an emotionally inexpressive husband. The more she pursues, the more he withdraws. The withdraw/withdraw pattern is seen in partners who both fear emotional engagement. It can also happen when a pursuer gives up.

In some couples, tension and hostility escalate to the point that both angrily criticize and blame each other or even engage in physical violence. This can happen when a withdrawer feels driven to fight back when cornered by a pursuer.

Step 3. Unacknowledged emotions underlying interactional positions are accessed. For instance, the pursuer acknowledges fear and longing that drive her demands, and the withdrawer expresses the shame that underlies his stonewalling.

Step 4. The problem is reframed in terms of the negative cycle, underlying emotions, and attachment needs. The couple unites in viewing the cycle as the common enemy and the source of emotional deprivation and distress.

Stage 2: Changing Interactional Positions

Step 5. Disowned attachment emotions, needs, and aspects of self are integrated into couple interactions. For example, a withdrawn husband acknowledges and expresses how much he fears his wife's criticism and how he longs to be accepted.

Step 6. Each partner's experience and new interactional responses are accepted by the other partner. The therapist helps each partner assimilate the new responses into his or her view of the other.

Step 7. Expression of needs and wants, emotional engagement, and bonding events redefine the attachment between partners.

Stage 3: Consolidation and Integration

Step 8. New solutions to old relationship problems emerge. The partners find themselves behaving in new ways outside of the therapy session.

Step 9. New positions and new cycles of attachment behaviors consolidate and become the couple's new dance.

Emotionally Focused Therapy Adapted for Trauma Survivors

In *Emotionally Focused Couple Therapy with Trauma Survivors,* S. M. Johnson (2002) embedded and consolidated the nine EFT steps into the following three-stage structure that conforms to McCann and Pearlman's (1990) stages of therapy for individual trauma survivors. This adapted protocol addresses complex PTSD in which systems of meaning, perceptions of self and other, and the capacity for affect regulation have been deeply affected by trauma.

Stage 1: Stabilization

Task 1. Creating a safe context. Establishing safety and trust with trauma survivors takes longer and must be explicitly collaborative. The therapeutic alliance is vital and is monitored throughout the therapy process.

Task 2. Clarifying interactional patterns and the emotions that shape them. Negative interactional cycles of attack and alienation are tracked. Emotional responses that reflect the impact of the trauma and of attachment insecurity are identified. Partners are helped to view each other as allies in a common fight against the negative cycle.

Stage 2: Restructuring Bonds: The Building of Self and Relational Capacities

Task 1. Expanding and restructuring emotional experience. Partners feel safe enough to acknowledge and express their fears and insecurities and the ways they protect themselves.

Task 2. Expanding self with other. Expressing vulnerabilities creates a new sense of self, which enriches the relationship with the other.

Task 3. Restructuring interactions toward accessibility and responsiveness. The focus turns from blaming the partner to examining how each individual habitually engages the other.

Stage 3: Integration

In each stage, the influence of the "dragon" (S. M. Johnson, 2002, p. 33) of trauma on the couple's interactions is explicitly addressed and the couple is enabled to face the dragon together. In this way, the individual partners stop blaming each other and realize that the negative emotional cycle is the enemy.

EMDR for Couples Affected by War Trauma

The standard eight-phase, three-pronged EMDR protocol needs little, if any, modification for reprocessing war-related traumatic memories. Targets are selected from a thorough military and civilian trauma history and can be sequenced chronologically or in clusters. Clusters can be grouped by type of incident (e.g., firefights, deaths of friends, or being powerless or abandoned) or around themes of responsibility, safety, and choice.

In preparing the veteran for EMDR processing, it is essential to understand that veterans often have trouble identifying a safe place. Therefore, it is wiser to use the idea of a place of calm or well-being where it is possible to relax to some degree (Silver & Rogers, 2002). *Resource Development and Installation* (Korn & Leeds, 2002) can be valuable, particularly for helping individuals use the marital relationship as a resource. For example, a veteran realized that he had lost touch with the tenderness and intimacy he had once felt toward his wife. As he pictured himself sitting close to her on their wedding night, he was amazed to feel the physical sensations of his arm around her and her head on his shoulder. The sensations strengthened with bilateral stimulation and were installed as a positive resource. That night he brought her flowers and cooked a special dinner. The renewed feeling of connection provided comfort during his reprocessing of a memory of street fighting in Baghdad.

The Role of Small "t" Trauma in War Trauma and Veteran Couples

Small "t" trauma is Shapiro's (1995, 2002) term for disturbing experiences that do not meet *Diagnostic and Statistical Manual of Mental Disorders (DSM)* criteria for PTSD. Though less dramatic and more commonplace than large "T" traumas such as war and rape, these events may be equally distressing and should not be underestimated in working with veterans. They should be formally assessed in the History Phase and reprocessed with EMDR. A common small "t" trauma for veterans is the way they were treated after the war. Many Vietnam veterans remember being spit on or called "Baby Killer."

It is also helpful to use EMDR for the emotional wounds one spouse may have deliberately or inadvertently perpetrated against the other. The partners of veterans commonly report that veterans, in their preoccupation with intrusive memories or in their preferred state of emotional numbness, ignore or attempt to prohibit their partner's emotional needs. In turn, veterans claim to have no emotions of their own except anger. Gentle inquiry about the reasons for withholding feelings often yields "I told her how I felt one time, and she used it against me." When asked to clarify that statement, they reply that their wife laughed, changed the subject, told someone else their confidence, or brought up the disclosure as a sign of weakness in an argument at a later time. These responses would have negative effects in their own right, but they are compounded in that these interactions also remind some veterans of feeling rejected by society on returning from war.

Parallels between EMDR and Emotionally Focused Therapy: Assumptions, Concepts, and Interventions

Understanding parallel concepts and interventions of EMDR and EFT facilitates a smooth integration of the two therapies. These parallels are considered next.

Similar Assumptions

EMDR and EFT are both information processing therapies and assume that negative emotions and beliefs block people's access to their inner resources. AIP, which underlies EMDR, assumes that distress is caused by information dysfunctionally stored in the memory network. When this information is stimulated by present-day triggers, it produces a cascade of associated memories, painful emotions, body sensations, and negative self-beliefs. Reprocessing the traumatic memory with EMDR results in an adaptive resolution (Shapiro, 1995, 2001, 2002). EFT, rooted in attachment theory, assumes that faulty information processing causes negative cycles. Insecurely attached people are understood to selectively attend to and distort perceptions of their partner's behavior. Their "intense, chronic fear reduces working memory, increases superficial processing of information, generates extensive cognitive bias, and preempts all other processing" (S. M. Johnson, 2002, p. 51). When the emotions associated with the core attachment issues are accessed and reprocessed, the partners feel safer with one another and can use the communication skills they already possess (S. M. Johnson, 2002).

Similar Therapist Stances

The first and most important EMDR lesson is "Stay out of the way of spontaneous processing." The stance of the EFT therapist is very similar. Rather than acting as strategist, creator of insight, or expert, the EFT therapist is a consultant who collaborates with the couple in restructuring their relationship. Individuals are not seen as deficient or unskilled, nor are their desires for connection, needs for validation, and emotional responses to their partner viewed as pathological. Rather, clients are seen as stuck in rigid, negative patterns of processing, emotional expression, and interaction (S. M. Johnson, 2002).

Small "t" Traumas and Attachment Injuries

A small "t" trauma is a distressing incident that does not meet *DSM* criteria for a traumatic event but may be key to a client's pathology. These small "t" traumas may become EMDR targets in future phases of treatment. The EFT parallel to the small "t" trauma is the attachment injury, defined as abandonment and violation of trust within the couple's relationship itself. Attachment injuries occur when one partner, in utmost vulnerability, reaches out to the other partner and is ignored or rejected, whereupon the injured partner's trust disintegrates.

Cognitive Interweave and Empathic Inference

Although the therapist stays out of the way of spontaneous reprocessing as much as possible, specialized interventions are applied when processing seems blocked or when individuals lack the positive experiences, learning, and concepts necessary for integrating the trauma into adaptive memory networks. In EMDR, a *Cognitive Interweave* is used to help the client access the needed resource. For example, when a veteran has trouble letting go of survivor guilt, the therapist might say, "What if it happened to your child?" A parallel EFT concept is the empathic inference. S. M. Johnson (2002) offers a simple statement that helps clients extend and unfold their understanding of their experience. For example, the therapist might say, "I think I hear you saying that you are not only ambivalent about trusting here, but one part of you rebels at the very idea" (p. 91).

Assessment Phase and Evocative Inquiry

To be reprocessed, negative emotions must be accessed, experienced, and tolerated long enough for resolution to occur. In the Assessment Phase of EMDR, the patient identifies the traumatic image, *Negative Cognition,* emotion, and body sensation. Assessment is immediately followed by Desensitization, during which the therapist makes soothing statements to encourage the client to stay with the emotional processing until it naturally shifts. The EFT intervention for accessing, experiencing, and tolerating emotions is "evocative inquiry," in which the partners are asked to focus on different body sensations and associated desires and meanings. The therapist makes soothing statements to maintain connection to them and to encourage them to stay with their emotional experience.

Positive Cognition and Expanding Self

The EMDR therapist asks the client to identify a *Positive Cognition* that is the opposite of the "Negative Cognition" associated with the trauma. The Positive Cognition provides a direction for reprocessing. A visualization of future behavior, based on the Positive Cognition, may spontaneously evolve during reprocessing, or the visualization of future behavior may be selected as a target in a subsequent session. In the parallel EFT intervention of "expanding self," the client visualizes a preferred identity. As that identity is enacted in the therapy session, the sense of self begins to shift.

Integrated EMDR and Emotionally Focused Therapy Treatment for Couples Affected by War Trauma

The treatment, which includes both individual and couple sessions, is designed to be utilized by one therapist working alone, although a team approach could be used. It is implemented in 25 to 45 sessions spanning 12 to 24 months. The length of the treatment reflects the reality that the treatment of war trauma is complex. Whereas the standard EFT protocol is designed for 8 to 20 sessions, S. M. Johnson (2002) found that about 30 sessions are needed for war veteran couples. Twelve EMDR sessions were needed to reprocess the memories of war veterans, eliminating the diagnosis of PTSD in 78% of participants (Carlson et al., 1998). The challenge for the therapist is to focus equally on individual trauma processing and the restructuring of couple interaction. It should be noted that this treatment is not appropriate when active life-threatening substance abuse, suicide attempts, or domestic violence are present.

Therapeutic Goals

There are four main goals in this integrated therapy: (1) to bridge the gap between the way each partner structures the individual inner emotional experience and the dynamic system of their intimate relationship (S. M. Johnson, 2002); (2) to reprocess war memories so they will not affect daily life; (3) to reprocess attachment injuries; and (4) to recreate the relationship as a safe haven for both partners.

Stabilization, History, and Preparation: Sessions 1–10

In the first few sessions with the couple, the therapist fosters a positive attachment with both partners by being accessible, transparent, and responsive to their concerns and questions. The connection to the therapist will provide structure and comfort as the partners explore the intimidating world of unacknowledged emotions and unprocessed traumatic memories.

Establishing trust with a veteran may take some special attention. Veterans often ask, "You weren't there, so how can you understand what I have been through?" The therapist validates the concern and confidently states, "I haven't experienced what you have, but I can see how you are suffering, and I am proficient in treatments that have helped other veterans."

Also, in these initial sessions, the negative emotional cycle and the core insecure attachment struggle are assessed and a focused treatment plan and objectives are worked out, thereby creating hope and confidence that a closer, safer relationship and relief from PTSD symptoms can be achieved. Because veterans with war trauma frequently alternate between hyperarousal and emotional numbing, they may seek closeness but push it away once it is offered. The veteran often distrusts the spouse and views the self as unlovable (S. M. Johnson, 2002). This avoidant attachment style is developed in war; one learns not to get close because a friend may be lost in an instant. Many veterans with long-term marriages are well aware of this pattern although unable to change through awareness alone. The therapist often hears, "I don't know how she put up with me all these years." A Vietnam veteran, recalling how he stayed out drinking every night and turned away from his wife's pleas for attention, said remorsefully, "What right did I have to crush all her dreams for our marriage?"

Individual Sessions for Each Partner

After the initial conjoint sessions, one or two individual sessions for each partner are scheduled. The goals for the individual sessions are to strengthen the therapeutic alliance with each partner, to observe and interact with each independently of the other, and to obtain information that might be censored in the presence of the other partner. A thorough trauma history is taken in the individual sessions, including large "T" and small "t" traumas from family of origin, military, and postmilitary events. Special attention is paid to attachment injuries that have occurred within the couple's relationship, because resolution of these injuries is vital to the partners' feelings of emotional safety.

The individual partners are helped to identify traumatic negative self-beliefs, present triggers, and desired future beliefs and behaviors that will become EMDR targets in the next phase of treatment. Positive resources are identified. Partners are encouraged and helped to share this information with the other partner in the next conjoint session; this process is the beginning of increased emotional opening to each other.

Partners are helped to develop emotion regulation, a necessary prerequisite for both EMDR Phases 4 through 7 and for the couple's EFT work. In the therapy session, with the therapist's support, each partner learns to access emotion without becoming overwhelmed by it. The *Safe Place* exercise and EMDR for Resource Installation may be useful here. It is not expected that couples will be able to change negative emotional patterns outside of the sessions during this phase.

The second task of the first stage is clarifying interactional patterns and the emotional responses that shape them (S. M. Johnson, 2002). The therapist and the couple see how cycles of attack and alienation are the dragon to be conquered. Now it is clear how emotional responses of each partner reflect traumatic states and attachment insecurity. The therapist tracks how the pair communicates and reflects those observations in a coherent narrative, thereby enabling them to observe the dance, step back, and ally against the dragon. For example, the therapist might say, "You folded your arms when she reached for your hand. Is that what happens when she pushes for closeness? You can't quite accept that touch?" When the couple resonates to the therapist's narrative of their negative interactions, the therapist tentatively inquires about and infers their underlying emotional responses and frames these in terms of trauma and insecure attachment.

The therapist helps each partner stay with emotions rather than pushing them away. The therapist might say, "Your voice sounds angry when you say he ignores your pain, yet I see tears in your eyes, so perhaps you feel sadness and longing as well. Is that true? Can you tell him in a simple way how abandoned you feel and how much you long for him to be there for you?"

Restructuring Bonds and Reprocessing Disturbing Memories: Sessions 11–39

In this stage, EMDR and EFT support and deepen each other. EMDR helps process traumatic memories so that the past is released and present interactions no longer constitute triggers. EFT enables the couple to re-create their relationship as a safe haven in which they can calmly and confidently face the trauma dragon together.

In EFT terms, a couple is ready to start the second stage when they are aware of their negative cycle, less overwhelmed, more hopeful, and more engaged with each other. This stage has three tasks:

Task 1. Expanding and restructuring emotional experience. The individual partners express avoided emotions and integrate them into the self-concept and the conversations with the other partner. Attachment needs for being held, listened to, understood, and treasured, as well as insecurities and fears, are clarified and conveyed to the partner. The therapist actively helps the partners move between emotional expression and emotional containment so they can feel comfortably in control of themselves. Here it is important to note that expressions of caring can be as disconcerting as criticism. "What happens as she tells you how dear you are to her? Can you look at her? What do you see in her face?" The therapist heightens the core emotions and attachment responses to emphasize their significance. "It's hard to grasp that she could value you so much, isn't it? It's hard to keep looking at her. Shame and the belief 'I am worthless' make you freeze and look down." EMDR would be used to identify and process the memories that are causing this affect and belief.

Task 2. Expanding self with other. Partners integrate now acknowledged primary emotions and attachment needs into a new sense of self. It is a chance for a veteran who has been damaged by war to claim a coherent, organized sense of self. The therapist notices when one of the partners is able to reach out to the other in the midst of trauma or attachment issues and use the relationship as a safe haven. The therapist heightens the responsiveness of the partners by asking them to turn and look at each other and ask for what they need.

Task 3. Accessibility and responsiveness. The therapist helps each partner own his or her habitual interactional style and even more actively structures the couple's interactions to build secure bonding. Emotional risk taking and sharing of vulnerabilities are encouraged and validated. The therapist might note, "John, you are openly telling Mary how hard it is for you to ask to be held. Do you see her leaning forward and reaching out to you? Can you look at her and tell her what this means to you?" EMDR sessions are scheduled for reprocessing of war memories and attachment injuries. The individuals' responses, affects, and beliefs are used to identify the specific memories that are the foundation of the pathology. The couple and therapist decide whether to cluster the EMDR sessions or intersperse them with couple sessions.

Couple Work and EMDR Sessions

EMDR is an individual treatment. There are advantages and disadvantages to having one partner present for the other's EMDR session. The witnessing partner may gain insight and empathy that could bring the couple closer. However, the traumatized partner may not be ready to disclose some of the material, especially if it involves negative feelings about the witnessing partner. Also, the witnessing partner may find it difficult to manage his or her own feelings throughout the session. The therapist and couple can discuss these considerations and together decide what would be best.

Consolidation and Integration: Sessions 40–45

In the Integration Phase of EFT, improvements in self-definition, relationship definition, and each partner's resilience to traumatic stress are noted in positive statements about the self, the relationship, and resilience. In EMDR terms, the trauma has reached an adaptive resolution marked by the absence of triggering, a valid Positive Cognition, and improved functioning.

CASE EXAMPLE

Bart and Cindy

The couple was seen at a Vet Center, one of 206 community-based outpatient treatment centers that compose the Readjustment Counseling Service of the Department of Veterans Affairs. A similar approach might be followed by a private practitioner, either independently or in conjunction with a Veterans Affairs program.

Bart and Cindy, each 38 years old, fell in love and married when both were serving in the Army. Cindy's eyes sparkled as she described her handsome capable soldier husband. "Everyone respected him. Even the colonel asked his advice." Bart was drawn to Cindy's warmth, playfulness, intelligence, and integrity. "She has the finest values of anyone I've ever known, and she's sexy, smart, and fun at the same time." During courtship and early marriage, they had great fun as they developed a close emotional and sexual bond.

In 1991, Bart was deployed to Saudi Arabia for Operation Desert Storm while Cindy stayed in the United States. Because he was in a medical unit, Bart never expected to be in a firefight. However, while on assignment to another unit, there was an ambush, and he shot and killed an Iraqi soldier. Shaken and ashamed, he never told anyone about it—even his wife.

In 1992, both were discharged from the army and started civilian careers, Bart as an emergency medical technician and Cindy as a home health care nurse. A daughter was born in 1993 and a son in 1995. Despite career and parenting successes, their relationship was empty and disappointing. They never had any fun, and their sexual relationship dwindled to nothing. The following exchange illustrates how their attachment to each other had deteriorated:

Bart: Cindy used to be warm and open. Now she dresses in another room. I feel rejected and unloved.

Cindy: I never stopped loving you. Your low self-confidence is the problem.

Bart: I have a stressful job. I want to go to Cindy for a hug to make it all better.

Cindy: And that's all our sex life is about. I don't want to participate in it anymore.

Case Therapy Process

In 1992, Bart and Cindy were briefly seen shortly after discharge from the army. They learned about trauma responses and made a trusting connection with the Vet Center team. Nine years went by before they returned. It is common for young veterans to seek brief assistance with readjustment to civilian life and then return to therapy when life problems build up.

In 2001, they began 2 years of intensive therapy. The case description clearly shows that veterans, even bright, successful individuals like Bart and Cindy, often need a lot of support. EFT/EMDR treatment can be highly beneficial to veteran couples such as this one.

Stabilization, History, and Preparation

Bart and Cindy described an intricate dance of anxious clinging and detached avoidance in which each played the roles of pursuer and withdrawer:

Cindy: (Shrilly and tearfully) He works 11-hour days. When he comes home, he yells at the children. I have to step in to protect them because they're afraid of him. He eats on the run—doesn't even sit down with the rest of us. Then he goes out for another three hours to help one of his friends fix his truck or sheetrock his basement. I'm sick of it.

Bart: (Defensively) Look, I'm the major breadwinner here. My job is stressful, to say the least. I'm tired when I come home, and I expect some appreciation from my family—or at least some peace and quiet. The kids are out of control, so, yeah, I get a little irritated. Oh, and Cindy didn't mention that instead of meeting me at the door with a kiss like she used to, she is sitting at the computer playing some online fantasy game with her virtual buddies.

Cindy: (Still crying) I have tried everything to get some emotional response from Bart. Now I have officially given up. He tries to make me feel guilty for playing this game, which is my only creative outlet and my only contact with intelligent adults. And even though he shows no affection at any other time, when he gets home from his friend's house about 10:30, he is for sure going to try to wheedle me into having sex. I'm through with that, too.

Bart: We haven't had sex for a year. I sleep on the couch almost every night. I don't understand what is going on. Everything I do is for Cindy, yet nothing I do is right in her eyes.

Therapist: (Reflecting on the negative cycle and its underlying emotions) So, Cindy, I think I understand that you feel neglected. You have searched for ways to reach Bart and nothing has worked. You sound angry. Yet I can't help wondering if you are also sad and afraid. Bart, you work so hard, and it sounds like you are longing for Cindy's affection and admiration. Tell me, are you frightened that you may have lost her for good?

The therapist's description of the negative cycle and the underlying emotions resonated with Cindy and Bart and gave them hope. In individual sessions, they each revealed traumatic memories that were targeted with EMDR in the second stage of therapy.

Alone with the therapist, Bart told about killing the Iraqi soldier, and also revealed that when he was 12, he realized his mother was having an extramarital affair. Both events were playing themselves out in his relationship with Cindy. He believed he was a bad person and was in danger of losing her. Therefore, when she criticized him, he tried to make her happy by being a "better person," which meant doing anything she wanted and working overtime so he could buy her things. He resented that his efforts did not produce sex, approval, and affection, but instead of confronting her, he was obsequious, reserving his irritability and criticism for the children.

In her individual session, Cindy remembered that at age 6 she stepped between her parents to stop a fight. From that moment on, she "took control of the family" because she believed "I can depend only on myself." She was playing the same role as an adult: stepping between her husband and children whenever there was conflict between them. Cindy also recalled an attachment injury that occurred right after Bart returned from Saudi Arabia. Distraught over the sudden death of her beloved father, she was stunned when Bart gruffly ordered her to stop crying, saying, "One day of crying is enough." His behavior was a vivid contrast to his loving support when she had a miscarriage the year before the war.

In subsequent couple sessions, they gained increased awareness of how these events were being reenacted in their negative cycle. They were ready to begin the second stage of therapy.

Restructuring Bonds and Reprocessing Disturbing Memories

Task 1. Expression and integration of avoided emotions. Reprocessing of traumatic memories. The following transcript shows progress in working with avoided emotions:

Bart: When Cindy and I aren't touching I feel fear, sorrow, and pain in my stomach.

Therapist: What's that like for you, Bart, to express this fear, sorrow, and pain? I sense that you desperately need Cindy's touch but are not able to reach out for her.

Bart: I shut down. If I keep busy and don't let Cindy cook for me or wait on me, then I'm not vulnerable to being abandoned. I don't need her because I'm self-sufficient. I feel like I have to work harder and make more money and give her whatever she wants so she will give me what I want in bed. But it doesn't work, and I'm scared and frustrated.

Therapist: Such tremendous fear and longing. Bart, can you turn to Cindy and tell her how desperately you need her touch and how afraid you are to reach out to her?

Bart: I can try. Cindy, I need you. You're the reason I come home at night. I love my children, but I come home to my wife. I feel so lost and scared when you won't touch me.

Therapist: Cindy, what is it like for you to hear Bart express his need for your touch and how scared he feels when you push him away?

Cindy: Sex is a drug that he uses to make himself feel better. I hate it that he's afraid of me. Why can't I help him be the confident, strong man he used to be?

The couple became skilled at both expressing and containing their emotions as they focused on their negative cycle in session. They started taking walks together and meditating. At this point, they each began their private EMDR sessions, interspersed with couple sessions.

The first EMDR target was Cindy's memory of breaking up her parents' fight. At the end of that session, her Positive Cognition was "I can trust my husband." She then gave up stepping in between Bart and the children whenever there was conflict between them. It was a welcome change for Bart and lessened his sense that he had to walk on eggshells to avoid Cindy's disapproval.

Cindy also had an EMDR session targeting the memory of Bart demanding that she stop crying about her father's death. In the course of reprocessing, she realized that she had lost her trust in and attachment to her husband that night and that her whole perspective on her marriage changed. As the pain drained out of the image of Bart's coldness in the face of her grief, she saw his response through the lens of his war experience and was able to forgive him.

Impressed with Cindy's EMDR experiences, Bart was ready to focus on the worst day of his life. The session began with the following image: sand flying in the wind; people running; chaos; overwhelming fear and tension. His Negative Cognition was "I am a bad person." His preferred Positive Cognition was "I am a good person; I deserve to be happy." His score on the Validity of Cognition (VOC) scale was 2 on a Likert scale (1 = Not true at all and 7 = Completely true). He felt guilt and shame in his gut and chest, rated as 8 on the Subjective Units of Disturbance (SUD) scale (0 = No distress and 10 = Extreme distress).

At the end of the session, he said, "I feel warmer and calmer. Anyone would make the same choice. It doesn't make me a bad person." At that time his SUD rating was 5.

At his next session, 2 weeks later, it was obvious that processing had continued (see Shapiro, 2001, for discussion of between-session processing):

Bart: (Describing a meditation session) I was looking at the face of the Iraqi soldier and feeling somber. Out of nowhere the image shifted to seeing myself standing there and I felt joy . . . the joy of being alive.

(See Zangwill & Kosminsky, 2002, for a discussion of meditation and EMDR.)

Therapist: When you think of the incident, what do you get now?

Bart: I remember the chaos, but now it looks more serene. I still see his eyes and the blood. I still feel sorrow, but not so critical of myself. At that point it wasn't a choice. Any other action would have been suicide.

Bart reported that his SUD was 3. EMDR processing commenced with the previous dialogue as the starting point:

Bart: (After several sets of eye movements) Cindy said that sex was a drug for me. Maybe it's true. When I felt bad, I'd go to Cindy. Was that about feeling shame for taking another man's life? (After the next set of eye movements) I deserve better than just being a roommate to my wife.

The session ended with a SUD of 0 and a VOC of 7 for the positive statement "I am a good person. I deserve to be happy."

The following transcript is from his third EMDR session 2 weeks later:

Therapist: When you bring up the war memory, what do you get?

Bart: I see a guy lying in the sand. (SUD = 0) I killed him in the line of duty. I would do the same thing again. (Changing the subject) I told Cindy I am not happy just being a roommate, and I am not going to live like this. I said, "You can take half my paycheck and I'll go find my own happiness somewhere." I didn't apologize. That night when I got home she was cooking dinner . . . including my favorite dessert. She hasn't cooked in months.

Task 2. Expanding self with other. After the initial EMDR sessions, it was easier for the couple to acknowledge their emotions and needs and to incorporate them into a new sense of self:

Therapist: So we learned from the EMDR sessions that neither of you has felt safe in the other's arms since the war. How has it been for you to realize that?

Cindy: I lost my caring husband. In his place was a cold, insensitive stranger.

Bart: It makes me think less of myself. I want to be the shoulder you can cry on again.

Bart's and Cindy's statements were developed into EMDR targets according to the three-pronged protocol. Cindy developed a future template of being sexually responsive to a strong, sensitive Bart. Bart developed a future template of comforting Cindy as she cried in his arms.

Task 3. Accessibility and responsiveness. Positive responses toward each other were encouraged and validated by the therapist:

Bart: Why mourn what I can't change instead of rejoicing in what I have, who I am, and the good I'm doing? I was trying to eliminate my guilt by becoming a draft horse.

Cindy: Trying to externally fix what was internally wrong—his injured sense of self.

Therapist: Cindy, as you speak, I see you leaning toward Bart with tenderness in your eyes. Do you see it, too, Bart? Can you tell Cindy what it is like for you to see this?

Bart: Cindy, it's like the sun is out, and the ice in my heart is melting.

Consolidation and Integration

The following vignette shows the couple's new dance:

Bart: It's safe to disagree with Cindy now. I tell her what I want from her.

Cindy: He's not aggressive, so I'm not afraid of him. He's not backing down, so I respect him. Bart is back in our bed now. I can be sexually uninhibited because he has the courage to be someone new. I've changed, too. I don't always have to control everything.

DISCUSSION

In this chapter, therapists are offered a method to integrate EFT with EMDR for war veterans and their intimate partners. In 25 to 45 sessions spanning 12 to 24 months, by focusing on both the individual war and childhood traumatic memories and the attachment injuries within the relationship itself, a therapist can help a veteran couple work through traumatic memories and re-create the relationship as a safe haven for both partners.

The goal of therapy is to achieve the most comprehensive treatment effects in the shortest time, while maintaining a stable client in a stable system (Shapiro, 1995, 2001). The integration of EMDR and EFT in psychotherapy with veterans helps accomplish this goal in several ways. First, blending the two treatments increases the comprehensiveness of therapy by reducing the reactivity of both partners to current triggers of past traumas while simultaneously increasing the emotional safety and stability of the relationship itself. Second, EFT and EMDR are both trauma-focused and emotion-focused treatments, and they get to the heart of the problem very quickly, thus motivating couples to stay longer and work harder. Finally, including the wife in the treatment enlists her support as more than a caretaker and shifts the veteran out of the identified patient role.

The case example of Bart and Cindy illustrates the efficiency and synchronicity of combining the two methods. The couple was excited to discover how their negative emotional cycle of criticism, blame, and withdrawal had been created and maintained by traumatic experiences. This motivated them to systematically work through the large "T" trauma of war, the small "t" traumas of childhood, and the attachment injuries in their own marriage. Within 2 years, they had emerged from despair into renewed trust, respect, and connection to one another.

Bart and Cindy are obviously a unique couple with problems particular to their own lives, yet their struggles are quite representative of the traumas, issues, and concerns faced by veteran couples. The benefits of combining EMDR with EFT are likely to be relevant for a wide range of veterans and their partners.

REFERENCES

Ainsworth, M. (1989). Attachments beyond infancy. *American Psychologist, 44*(4), 709–716.

Bowlby, J. (1978). Attachment theory and its therapeutic implications. *Adolescent Psychiatry, 6*, 5–33.

Burham, G. (2004). One teammate's journey with PTSD. *Blast,* 36–38.

Carlson, J. G., Chemtob, C., Rusnak, K., Hedlund, N., & Muraoka, M. (1998). Eye movement desensitization and reprocessing (EMDR) treatment for combat-related posttraumatic stress disorder. *Journal of Traumatic Stress, 11*, 3–24.

Coughlan, K., & Parkin, C. (1987). Women partners of Vietnam vets. *Journal of Psychosocial Nursing and Mental Health Services, 25*(10), 25–27.

Errebo, N. E. (1995). Object relations family therapy and PTSD: Family therapy with four generations of a Vietnam veteran's family. In D. K. Rhoades, M. R. Leaveck, & J. C. Hudson (Eds.), *The legacy of Vietnam veterans and their families: Survivors of war—Catalysts for changes: Papers from the 1994 National Symposium* (pp. 420–427). Washington, DC: Agent Orange Class Assistance Program.

Figley, C. R. (1988). Post-traumatic family therapy. In F. M. Ochberg (Ed.), *Post-traumatic therapy and victims of violence* (pp. 278–294). New York: Brunner/Mazel.

Foa, E. B. (2000). Psychosocial treatment of posttraumatic stress disorder [Special issue]. *Journal of Clinical Psychiatry, 61*(Suppl. 5), 43–51.

Glynn, S. M., Eth, S., Randolph, E. T., Foy, D. W., Urbatis, M., Boxer, L., et al. (1999). A test of behavioral family therapy to augment exposure for combat-related posttraumatic stress disorder. *Journal of Consulting and Clinical Psychology, 67*, 243–251.

Haley, S. A. (1978). Treatment implications of post-combat stress response syndromes for mental health professionals. In C. R. Figley (Ed.), *Stress disorders among Vietnam veterans* (pp. 254–267). New York: Brunner/Mazel.

Hayman, P. M., Sommers-Flanagan, R., & Parsons, J. P. (1987). Aftermath of violence: Posttraumatic stress disorder among Vietnam veterans [Special issue]. *Journal of Counseling and Development: Counseling and Violence, 65*(7), 363–366.

Johnson, D. R., Feldman, S., & Lubin, H. (1995). Critical interaction therapy: Couples therapy in combat-related posttraumatic stress disorder. *Family Process, 34*, 401–412.

Johnson, S. M. (2002). *Emotionally focused couple therapy with trauma survivors: Strengthening attachment bonds.* New York: Guilford Press.

Johnson, S. M. (2004). *The practice of emotionally focused couple therapy: Creating connection* (2nd ed.). New York: Brunner-Routledge.

Johnson, S. M., & Greenberg, L. (1998). Relating process to outcome in marital therapy. *Journal of Marital and Family Therapy, 14,* 175–183.

Korn, D. L., & Leeds, A. M. (2002). Preliminary evidence of efficacy for EMDR resource development and installation in the stabilization phase of treatment of complex posttraumatic stress disorder. *Journal of Clinical Psychology, 58*(12), 1465–1487.

Kulka, R. A., Schlenger, W. E., Fairbank, J. A., Hough, R. L., Jordan, B. K., Marmar, C. R., et al. (1990). *Trauma and the Vietnam war generation: Report of findings from the National Vietnam Veterans Readjustment Study.* New York: Brunner/Mazel.

Litz, B. T., Schlenger, W., Weathers, F., Caddell, J., Fairbank, J., & Lavange, L. (1997). Predictors of emotional numbing in posttraumatic stress disorder. *Journal of Traumatic Stress, 10,* 607–618.

Maloney, L. J. (1988). Post-traumatic stresses on women partners of Vietnam veterans. *Smith College Studies in Social Work, 58*(2), 122–143.

McCann, I. L., & Pearlman, L. A. (1990). *Psychological trauma and the adult survivor.* New York Brunner/Mazel.

Minuchin, S., & Fishman, H. C. (1981). *Family therapy techniques.* Cambridge, MA: Harvard University Press.

Mitchell, S. A. (1999). Attachment theory and the psychoanalytic tradition: Reflections on human rationality. *Psychoanalytic Dialogues, 9*(1), 85–107.

Monson, C. M., Schnurr, P. P., Stevens, S. P., & Guthrie, K. A. (2004). Cognitive-behavioral couple's treatment for posttraumatic stress disorder. *Journal of Traumatic Stress, 17,* 341–344.

Perls, F. (1973). *The Gestalt approach and eye witness to therapy.* New York: Bantam.

Riggs, D. S., Byrne, C., Weathers, F., & Litz, B. (1998). The quality of intimate relationships of male Vietnam veterans: Problems associated with posttraumatic stress disorder. *Journal of Traumatic Stress, 11,* 87–101.

Rogers, C. R. (1961). *On becoming a person.* Boston: Houghton Mifflin.

Shapiro, F. (1995). *Eye movement desensitization and reprocessing: Basic principles, protocols, and procedures.* New York: Guilford Press.

Shapiro, F. (2001). *Eye movement desensitization and reprocessing: Basic principles, protocols, and procedures* (2nd ed.). New York: Guilford Press.

Shapiro, F. (2002). EMDR treatment: Overview and integration. In F. Shapiro (Ed.), *EMDR as an integrative psychotherapy approach: Experts of diverse orientations explore the paradigm prism* (pp. 27–55). Washington, DC: American Psychological Association.

Silver, S. M., & Rogers, S. (2002). *Light in the heart of darkness: EMDR and the treatment of war and terrorism survivors.* New York: Norton.

Verbosky, S. J., & Ryan, D. A. (1988). Female partners of Vietnam veterans: Stress by proximity. *Issues in Mental Health Nursing, 9*(1), 95–104.

Veteran Affairs and Department of Defense Clinical Practice Guideline Working Group. (2003, December). *Management of post-traumatic stress.* Washington, DC: Veterans Health Administration, Department of Veterans Affairs and Health Affairs, and Department of Defense Office of Quality and Performance (10Q-CPG/PTSD-04).

Zangwill, W. M., & Kosminsky, P. (2002, December). The need to strengthen the mindfulness component of EMDR. *EMDRIA Newsletter,* 4–5.

CHAPTER 11

Sexual Trauma in Dysfunctional Marriages: Integrating Structural Therapy and EMDR

Wilhelmina S. Koedam

Sexual trauma is a debilitating event. When it occurs during childhood, the abuse can have a lifelong impact. Clearly, suffering abuse as a child represents a significant risk factor for multiple physical and mental health problems in adulthood (McCauley et al., 1997: Sachs-Ericsson, Blazer, Plant, & Arrow, 2005). These studies have also shown that abuse in childhood is a significant risk factor for later depression, alcoholism, substance abuse, and suicide attempts.

Incidence of childhood sexual abuse in the United States is estimated to have been perpetrated against 16% to 20% of men and 33% of women. In clinical populations these estimates increase significantly to 30% for men and 50% for women (Briere, Evans, Runtz, & Wall, 1988). Numerous studies have established that childhood abuse contributes to difficulties in adult relationships (e.g., Rumstein-McKean & Hunsley, 2001) and incidence of violent behavior against spouses and children (e.g., Davis & Petrectic-Jackson, 2000). More specific references to the long-term effects of childhood sexual abuse on romantic and intimate relationships are found in Jacquet (1999), who concludes that survivors experience problems with sexual intimacy, trust, conflict, negativity, and commitment volatility. Finkelhor, Hotaling, Lewis, and Smith (1989) suggested that sexual abuse survivors report more marital disruption and less sexual satisfaction than individuals with no history of abuse.

Based on their study, Jacob and Veach (2005) suggested that male sexual abuse trauma survivors suffer significant chronic stress, with symptoms of irritability, anger, depression, and anxiety. Additionally, couples reported engaging in reenactments of the abuse in terms of "colluder and enabler roles" as well as emotional disconnection, power, and control struggles (p. 294). Other studies looking at male sexual abuse survivors demonstrate growing evidence that rather than men not being affected by sexual abuse, the abuse appears to have significant effects on masculine gender identity and domestic violence (Kia-Keating, Grossman, Sorsoli, & Epstein, 2005; Lisak, 1994, 1995; Mejia, 2005). The relationships of survivors of sexual or emotional trauma are often fraught with conflict and problems related to the original abuse around power, trust, and boundary issues. Sexual abuse survivors may struggle desperately in their marital relationships, especially in the arenas of intimacy, sexuality, and attachment (Jacquet, 1999; Rutter, 1993), and often have difficulty with the expression of sexuality (Najman, Dunne, Purdie, Boyle, & Coxeter, 2005). Nonetheless, trauma survivors can be amazingly resilient and adaptive. They are often so cognizant of children's pain and suffering that they become very sensitive and aware parents.

Abuse also impacts the survivor's interpersonal functioning in terms of contributing to poor communication skills (Champion De Crespigny, 1996) and minimal family cohesion (Nelson & Wampler, 2000). Furthermore, survivors may manifest symptoms related to distortions of sexual identity and Dissociative Identity Disorder (Basham & Miehls, 2002; Koedam, 1996).

Herman (1992) outlined the effects of interpersonal trauma on survivors and proposed a new diagnostic category, Complex Posttraumatic Stress Disorder. She argued that intentional violence in interpersonal relationships results in a distinct clinical pattern that includes three broad areas of disturbance: multiplicity of symptoms, characterological changes with identity disturbance, and vulnerability to repeated harm. In empirical evaluations (Pelcovitz, van der Kolk, Roth, Mandel, & Resick, 1997; van der Kolk et al., 1996), this construct was found to be intrinsically related to Posttraumatic Stress Disorder (PTSD). The symptoms currently listed among the associated features of PTSD in the *Diagnostic and Statistical Manual of Mental Disorders IV* (American Psychiatric Association, 1994, p. 425) include the following:

> More commonly seen in association with an interpersonal stressor . . .; impaired affect modulation; self destructive and impulsive behavior; dissociative symptoms, somatic complaints; feelings of ineffectiveness, shame, despair, or hopelessness; feeling permanently damaged; a loss of previously sustained beliefs, hostility; social withdrawal; feeling constantly threatened; impaired relationships with others; or a change from the individual's previous personality characteristics.

Sexual abuse survivor couples who choose to engage in marital therapy often present with problems around attachment, intimacy, infidelity, rage, a sense of entrapment, feelings of betrayal, low self-esteem, powerlessness, codependency, and a need to control or have power. Their individual histories become critical to understanding what type of interventions to implement as these individuals continue to respond to one another in an almost stylized and predictable manner.

Structural Family Therapy

Structural Family Therapy (SFT) (Kaslow, 1981) is one of many systems approaches to family intervention. The family systems theory articulated in the work of Murray Bowen (1966), known as Bowen systems theory, seems to have been one of its antecedents. Bowen's work centers on the emotional forces that influence the way nuclear and extended families function. His work evolved at the Menninger Clinic in the 1940s to 1950s, where he sought to involve the family while treating a young psychotic patient, and developed into a hypothesis regarding the mother-patient relationship. His continued clinical work and research led to the development of the Bowen family systems theory, which initially posited six interlocking concepts: triangles, nuclear family, emotional process, family projection process, multigenerational transmission, and sibling position (Bowen, 1966; Toman, 1961). Later, two more concepts were added: emotional cutoff and societal regression (Bowen, 1976). A key underpinning of system theory is the concept that there are automatic, predictable behavioral patterns among family members (Papero, 1983). The fundamental theoretical premise is homeostasis and the idea that forces that oppose one another create a dynamic balance. Disruptions of this homeostatic state cause symptoms of dysfunction to emerge (Papero, 1983). Additionally, Bowen (1972) introduced concepts of togetherness and individuation as major forces operating in the family system.

Salvador Minuchin and his colleagues (Minuchin, Montalvo, Guerney, Rosman, & Schumer, 1967), who were working with boys in residential treatment at the Wiltwyck School for boys in New York, found that the children's individual therapeutic changes were not maintained when they returned to their home. These findings were found again later in Minuchin and Montalvo's work with Dr. Lester Baker (Minuchin, Rosman, & Baker, 1978) a pediatric endocrinologist, in the Children's Hospital in Philadelphia, who found his diabetic patients did poorly when sent back to their home. Their findings in psychosomatic research suggested that family characteristics such as enmeshment, overprotectiveness, rigidity, and lack of conflict resolution contributed to the reoccurrence of the children's acute medical episodes (Rosenberg, 1983).

The theoretical underpinnings of structural therapy assume that a family is more than the sum of its individual dynamics; it is an array of relationships among family members that are structured around specified arrangements that form the structure of the family (Minuchin, 1974). According to SFT, the dysfunctional family unit is characterized by enmeshment (family members tend to be overinvolved and intrusive to other members), disengagement (little cohesiveness between family members), boundaries (members of the family have too rigid or too loose boundaries), and a lack of healthy homeostasis (Aponte, 1992; Huycke, 2000; Minuchin, 1974; Rosenberg, 1983). These concepts have much in common with the Bowen Theory of homeostasis, triangles, individuation, emotional cutoff, togetherness, and anxiety contributing to the disruption of the family process.

Minuchin (1974) posited that the structural approach to families is based on the concept that a family is more than the sum of the individual biopsychodynamics of its members. Family members relate according to certain arrangements, which govern their transactions. These arrangements, though often not explicitly stated or even recognized, form a whole; this is the structure of the family. The reality of the structure is of a different order from the reality of the individual members. In this model of couple therapy, context is a central concept in that "it is the breaking or expanding of the interpersonal contexts in which the person is embedded that allows new possibilities of behavior to emerge for that individual" (Melito, 1988, p. 32). Minuchin also postulated the importance of boundaries in functional families, stating that the boundaries should neither be too diffuse nor too rigid and that the goal is to create an ideal structure in which the essential functions of the family are support, nurturance, and socialization of its individual members.

When the sexual or emotional trauma suffered by one or both marital partners is unresolved, it tends to exacerbate interpersonal conflicts and disrupt interactions. Trauma survivor couples exhibit many of the classic interactive patterns targeted in SFT; these include enmeshment and disengagement, rigid and diffuse boundaries, and lack of conflict resolution skills.

Basham and Miehls (2002) present an overview of *synthetic couple counseling* for couples with a history of trauma. The aim of synthetic counseling is the synthesis created by building "a unified plan with disparate constructs" (p. 254). Metaphor is helpful in describing this synthetic stance. If you visualize staring at a crystal, the texture and color look different depending on what part of the multifaceted glass you are observing. Similarly, the fabric of this theoretical synthesis shifts color and shape during the course of different phases of couple therapy. Synthetic couple counseling is a fluid dynamic model in which different therapy models emerge and retreat as the phases of counseling develop (phase-oriented couple therapy) and the presenting issues evolve over time. It encompasses many SFT treatment components, such as the use of enactments, distancing, boundary ruptures, and communication skill training. Basham and Miehls also include in their model PTSD issues such as sexual and identity disorders, affectively laden associations, and "victim-victimizer-bystander" role fluidity. These clinicians posit that trauma survivors often reenact the patterns of the victim, victimizer, and bystander in their adult relationships. These individuals may shift in all of these roles with their partner or children. These reenactments can trigger tremendous stress and dysfunction in the family dynamic and homeostasis.

SFT has been utilized with cases of mild to moderate conjugal violence (Bagarozzi & Giddings, 1983; Goldenberg & Goldenberg, 2004; Straus & Gelles, 1986; Taylor, 1984). Another model for treating couples whose members suffered trauma is cognitive-behavioral therapy, which incorporates psychoeducational approaches (Compton & Folette, 1998; Riggs, 2000).

Eye Movement Desensitization and Reprocessing

Shapiro's (2001) Adaptive Information Processing (AIP) model (2001) posits "a neurological balance in a distinct physiological system that allows information to be processed to an 'adaptive resolution'" (1995, p. 29). Accordingly, what is useful in the experience will be learned and stored for the future. She postulates that when a severe trauma is experienced by an individual, an imbalance occurs in the nervous system, which then causes the system to cease functioning, and the images, sounds, feelings, and physical sensations are maintained in a disturbed state. The components of the trauma continue to be triggered by internal and external stimuli and can be exhibited in common symptoms of PTSD, such as nightmares, flashbacks, body memories, and intrusive thoughts. Shapiro further posits that most pathologies are "derived from earlier life experiences that set in motion a continued pattern of affect, behavior, cognitions and consequent identity structures" (1995, p. 29).

Shapiro (1995, p. 30) hypothesized that bilateral stimulation (i.e., eye movements, knee tapping, a flashing light bar, auditory bilateral stimulation) triggers a physiological mechanism that activates the information processing system. She developed a treatment approach, Eye Movement Desensitization and Reprocessing (EMDR), in which the client engages in eye movements in structured procedures while focusing on the disturbing material of the trauma. With EMDR, the individual is able to reprocess the material in a more adaptive way and create an adaptive resolution.

In her book on EMDR, Shapiro (1995, p. 14) states:

> The model regards most pathologies as derived from earlier life experiences that set in motion a continued pattern of affect, behavior, cognitions, and consequent identity structures. . . . The ongoing repetitive negative responses to present day stimuli is similar to the initial response to the early traumas. Often individuals have no cognitive connection to their present day reactions and early memories of trauma. EMDR is an information processing system that accesses the initial traumas, defines the cognitive distortions or belief systems associated with the traumatic memory, the emotions still held that are connected to the trauma and where in the body those emotions reside. As these components of early trauma memory are identified the EMDR information processing technique functions to desensitize and decrease the disturbing impact of the trauma and allows the individual to reprocess the event and its cognitive and emotional sequelae to a healthier more adaptive response to the memory and present day stimuli.

Descriptions of the use of EMDR in marital therapy are fairly new in the literature. Protinsky, Sparks, and Flemke (2001, p. 161) describe a case in which EMDR was used in conjoint sessions in an attempt to enhance intimacy and vulnerability with a "successful compassionate witnessing," which these clinicians state is "crucial for therapeutic success."

THERAPY PROCESS

Treatment Overview

This chapter describes a treatment approach that combines SFT and EMDR in marital therapy when one or both partners have a history of childhood sexual abuse. In this approach, the therapist begins with SFT and then shifts to EMDR treatment of the traumatized partner. This shift is to process the survivor's abuse experience so that he or she can come to an adaptive resolution. This sets the stage for the survivor to respond differently to the possible triggers in his or her life as well as in the relationship. Once the EMDR process is complete and the couple participates in joint debriefing of the EMDR intervention, they reengage in the SFT marital sessions while integrating insights and adaptations the trauma survivor has gained from the EMDR work. This approach involves the applications of the EMDR standard protocol. It also uses the core elements of SFT, such as joining, restructuring diffuse and rigid boundaries, relabeling, and enactments.

Joining involves the therapist connecting with each partner from the inception of treatment and creating a sense of safety. Joining is essential in the treatment of traumatized individuals because it reduces their fear of being unsafe in emotionally charged situations; this fear is central to survivors' responses and reactions in social and emotional settings. For example, if the traumatized partner suffers from a sense of worthlessness and shame due to the childhood experiences, it is imperative that the clinician verbally recognize a positive attribute or accomplishment of the individual during the marital sessions. Additionally, the therapist assures the partners that it is safe to explore the difficulties they face in the relationship and that these issues will not be dealt with in a shame-based fashion.

Boundaries are restructured by redefining these in the family. When a couple is enmeshed and lack individuation or there is a significant degree of emotional disconnection, the therapist plays a role in helping them redefine and create new structures to bring the members into a more functional and emotionally healthy equilibrium. This may entail more time apart and less scrutiny of each other or helping the individual who is disconnected to try approaching his or her partner in a more intimate and trusting manner.

Relabeling changes the definition of an event to make it seem more reasonable and understandable. It revises the couple's perspective on a problem so that they can consider different solutions. In some couples, for example, the wife may see her husband as overcontrolling, when actually the husband is attempting to allay fears of abandonment by always knowing where and what his partner is doing. By relabeling the behavior as based on fear of abandonment, the wife may be able to engage in some reassurance behaviors rather than withdrawing from the perceived sense of being controlled.

Enactments are therapist-facilitated interactions that bring the marital conflict and presenting problem into the couple session. The therapist can then help the couple experience their dysfunctional communications and behavioral patterns in a safe environment. Often, couples will repetitively engage in the same scripts, so that the context and underlying message of the interaction is the same, although the content may vary depending on actual interaction, such as one partner always shaming and intimidating the other to maintain control of the relationship. Highlighting the script in sessions and helping the couple establish different, more spontaneous responses can be invaluable tools.

Often, one partner's abuse history interferes with marital therapy; he or she is blocked from working on the relationship because of the traumatic sequelae. For example, Seth was unable to resolve conflicts with his wife and wanted to terminate treatment because he felt so frustrated and distressed. Although this inability looked like unwillingness and resistance, his responses were determined by trauma-based reactivity. Further, a traumatized partner may experience an emotional abreaction during reenactments, experiencing a reliving of the trauma. At such points, it is prudent for the therapist to digress from the traditional model of SFT and shift to EMDR to work through the trauma that is being triggered by the partner or current situations. There are two approaches that can be utilized. Shapiro (1995) suggested that EMDR be implemented on an individual basis because it can be threatening for the survivor to be so vulnerable in the presence of the partner who is triggering the reactions. Conversely, Protinsky et al. (2001) recommended allowing the partner to participate during the EMDR process as a "compassionate witness," because this tends to enhance the couple's intimacy and compassion. In the integrated model discussed herein, the survivor is given the choice of conjoint or individual EMDR sessions. Following the EMDR session, the therapist uses SFT strategies to assist the couple in incorporating the insights and adaptations generated from the EMDR work with the restructuring of the relationship and shaping of competence in improving the family dynamics.

Initial Session

The initial session with a couple in crisis entails gathering not only the reasons the couple has chosen to enter marital therapy but also a comprehensive history taking of families of origin, prior marriages, relationships, medical concerns, sexual histories, therapeutic experiences, and an assessment of abuse history. The personal history becomes critical in understanding what type of interventions to initiate, as these individuals continue to respond to one another in a stylized and predictable manner. It is vital that the therapist present information about PTSD and its impact on the individuals and their relationships. The therapist uses this information to *relabel* the abused partner's triggered behaviors as resulting from his or her reactivity to internal and external stimuli; the relabeling changes the couple's perspective on the problem. The therapist further explains that although they are in the office to engage in marital therapy, the sessions might revolve around individual history, behaviors, and reactions to triggering stimuli. The therapist also introduces the possibility of using EMDR in the context of couple counseling. Due to the issue of the survivor's fears of vulnerability, the option of individual EMDR sessions is presented. The survivor is then asked if he or she is willing to share with and debrief the partner regarding the EMDR process to increase the partner's compassion, understanding, and intimacy. This is done at the end of the EMDR session or at a later couple session, depending on the EMDR participant's level of emotionality at the end of the EMDR sessions.

Structural Family Therapy

The initial session with a couple in crisis entails gathering not only the intake information, including the reasons the couple has chosen to enter marital therapy, but also a comprehensive history of the families of origin, prior marriages, relationships, medical concerns, therapeutic experiences, and an assessment of abuse history. When it is clear that either partner has a history of abuse or neglect, presenting the theory of PTSD is vital. This will enable the members of the couple to better understand their partner's behaviors and reactivity to internal and external stimuli that are triggering the individual in the context of the relationship.

This is especially true when the enactments, bringing the conflict and presenting problem into the couple session, occur in SFT; one may actually see abreaction occurring during the session. As the marital therapy begins, the therapist must be able to join fluidly with each member of the couple to create a sense of connection and safety with each. This joining with patients in SFT is essential and should be ongoing for traumatized individuals as their fear of being unsafe in emotionally charged situations is central to their responses and reactions in social and emotional settings. As traumatized individuals struggle with trust and often go to great lengths to avoid additional pain, *resistance* manifested in early termination of therapy is a common dilemma a structural therapist may encounter. Joining with the couple, especially the survivor, is essential, so that he or she will gain trust and confidence that the therapeutic interventions will help and that the therapist understands, can relate to the marital concerns, and is compassionate regarding the trauma history and its effect on the relationship.

The concept of relabeling, which enables the couple to change their perspective on a problem and therefore perceive different solutions, is also central in this model. The therapist will often reframe or relabel so the family can develop alternative ways to view a problem and be open to additional solutions and alternative behaviors to deal with said problems. Trauma survivors also have many boundary issues, as their personal boundaries were violated when they were subjected to abuse. Thus, couples in which one or both are abuse survivors struggle with creating healthy boundaries in the context of their intimate relationships. Structural theory considers diffuse and rigid boundaries as a component of the dysfunctional homeostasis in families. Couples with trauma survivor issues often cross personal boundaries or create impenetrable walls and need to learn new ways of interacting and communicating based on trust, safety, and compassion. Enactments involve bringing the problem behaviors into the session so they can be observed by the therapist. However, the structural interventions can be frightening and perceived as shaming by trauma survivors. Structural therapists may exacerbate or highlight the conflict in the session to help the couple create new interactions and solutions in a safe, controlled environment. The structural therapist works toward symptom reduction in an effort to restructure the family transaction patterns so the changes will last.

EMDR Intervention Process

Phase 1: Client History and Treatment Planning

Although the therapist has already gathered the general history during the initial marital therapy intake session, the client's trauma history is explored in more detail prior to EMDR processing. Treatment planning includes identifying specific targets: past memories that trigger the pathological response set, current situations that trigger the individual, and the goal for future responses in the individual's life situations. It is recommended that the survivor's partner be present during this phase to provide support and increase his or her compassion and understanding. The partner can also help identify treatment targets. This creates a new kind of alliance within the couple that can be very curative. Not only can they identify the painful and difficult transactions in the relationship, but they can also clarify misunderstood and misinterpreted behaviors and communications.

Phase 2: Preparation Phase

This phase sets the therapeutic framework and defines the client's expectations. Having the partner share in this phase strengthens the alliance, increases determination, and fosters different expectations, which may help shape a sense of competence in the couple.

The therapist evaluates client safety because the individual work of the trauma survivor may be very emotionally charged and abreactive. The positive rapport with the therapist, already established through joining in the SFT sessions, is essential as the client may experience feelings of vulnerability and loss of control. The inclusion of the partner in the post-EMDR debriefing stage increases the survivor's sense of support. It is often therapeutically appropriate to have the partner available to drive the client home after an EMDR session, whether or not a joint debriefing and sharing has occurred.

Phases 3 through 7: Processing

Phases 3 through 7 are generally done solely with the client, unless one is using the conjoint therapy model (Protinsky et al., 2001). These phases follow the standard EMDR protocol (Shapiro, 2001). After completing Phase 7, the EMDR session and process is reviewed with the individual and the partner. This allows the partner to anticipate, highlight, and aid in logging the images, memories, and behavioral manifestations between EMDR sessions.

Phase 8: Reevaluation

Phase 8 opens the follow-up session with assessing how well the target material has been resolved and if new processing is needed. During this time, new material may have surfaced, which will need to be processed with EMDR. The input of the partner can create a strong couple alliance and positively influence the restructuring of the relationship as the couple can now unite with empathy, understanding, and new views about each other. Changes in the survivor's belief system and increased safety in the relationship create changes in marital behavior. Often the partner will gain an understanding of the survivor and no longer react and misinterpret his or her behaviors, thus reducing their conflicts.

The Three-Pronged Protocol

The three-pronged protocol overview is necessary for success with EMDR. The first stage processes the past events that are the foundation of the current dysfunction. The second stage targets the present and addresses current stimuli that trigger problematic responses. The third stage focuses on the client's future behavior and choices (Shapiro, 1995). This meshes well with the overall family therapy focus in that the purpose of SFT is to change dysfunctional behaviors and communications, identify the triggers in the context of the relationship, and restructure the marriage with new perspectives, communication skills, and behaviors.

Reimplementation of Structural Family Therapy

Upon completion of the EMDR, the more traditional implementation of SFT is indicated. If new traumatic material emerges in the ongoing marital sessions EMDR may again be implemented to deal with these newly surfaced issues. Attention will be refocused on the presenting issues in the relationship and how to relabel and create more appropriate communications, boundaries, and structure in the relationship. The compassion for and sensitivity to the survivor's issues that have evolved are helpful in creating a far safer emotional climate, which helps enable the couple to try new behaviors and interactions. A review of the original couple issues that brought them into therapy is now indicated, with a new understanding of the possible triggers and dynamics that led to the problematic behaviors. As the survivor has processed his or her reactivity to triggers, recognizes them as such, and has processed more adaptive ways as a result of the EMDR work, new solutions to marital issues and the dismantling of the impasse should pave the way for the couple to engage in positive restructuring of the marriage using the SFT model.

CASE EXAMPLE

Family Composition

The husband, Seth, was age 37, the wife, Emily, was age 36, and their children were 9-year-old Amanda, 3-year-old Leslie, and 1-year-old Danny. Seth was a successful business entrepreneur, and Emily was a stay-at-home mom. Seth and Emily had been married and divorced and then remarried approximately 5 years after their initial divorce. The eldest daughter was born during the first marriage and the two younger siblings were born after the couple remarried. The middle child was born with a birth defect, which required her to undergo serious medical interventions. This put tremendous stress on the couple's relationship as she needed 24-hour monitoring during the first year of her life and there were constant concerns regarding her health. Leslie suffered through numerous surgeries to correct her disfigurement. In addition, the birth of Danny while Leslie was still undergoing significant medical care and interventions put even more stress on Seth and Emily.

Referral

Emily was referred by a friend who had been in counseling in the past and recommended they try marital counseling because of the volatile and chaotic relationship she witnessed. Emily scheduled a session because she believed Seth was "having a midlife crisis and the marriage was falling apart."

Presenting Problem

Emily called for an appointment as she was distraught when she heard rumors that Seth was having an affair. He continued to lie to her about the allegations and became enraged in response to her confrontations. When she persisted in confronting him about his extracurricular activities he became violent, pushing and shoving her, punching walls, and breaking car windshields. He then stormed out and finally moved out of the marital home. The couple came into the initial session in crisis. The issues of his violent temper and acting-out were addressed in the first session, and a safety contract was established. Emily was counseled to resist confronting Seth with her suspicions and allegations when she began to see him become agitated and wait until she came to therapy, where there was a safer, controlled environment in which to present her suspicions. Seth was requested to ask her to stop pressing him and, if she would not, to let her know he was leaving the house for a short period so as not to escalate the situation, but also not to abandon her or discount her fears and suspicions.

Marital History and Assessment

The therapist's analysis suggested that the issues of enmeshment and disengagement were critical factors in this couple's interactions. They were continually conflicted around Seth's frustration over what he viewed as Emily's desperately needing to be overinvolved in every aspect of his life and her suspiciousness to the point of monitoring all of his activities. Seth also complained that he felt Emily was sexually rigid. Emily reported that given her belief that Seth was engaging in extramarital sexual activities and blatantly lying to her, her behaviors were justified. Seth, on the other hand, was determined to use his rage, his financial and interpersonal power, and his sense of entitlement to disengage from his spouse and children. Neither seemed capable of resolving conflict effectively.

There was a history of years of dysfunction and strife. In addition to multiple alleged affairs on the part of Seth, Emily confessed to one extramarital affair. Although Seth had a history of sexual infidelity, he was unable to emotionally tolerate Emily's one affair.

As the marital sessions continued, the therapist hypothesized that the couple's progress was blocked due to Seth's continued tendency to rage, womanize, and abandon Emily and their children. Because each member of the couple remained entrenched in their stylized dyadic interactions, the therapist conducted a deeper exploration of their individual histories.

Each partner suffered from trauma-related sequelae. Emily had suffered severe psychological and sexual trauma and incest. She had engaged in previous individual therapy and appeared to have somewhat better coping mechanisms and exhibited fewer PTSD symptoms than Seth, who had never participated in any therapeutic interventions. However, Emily exhibited many of the characteristics of an incest survivor and an adult child of an alcoholic in her codependency (Beatty, 1992), alternating between becoming angry, then crushed, and finally accepting Seth's behaviors (both violent and sexual) by allowing him to repeatedly come home, starting the cycle again (Courtois, 1988; Loring & Cowan, 1997). Emily reported that her self-esteem was eroding as a result of his verbal abuse, constant criticism, and overt extramarital affairs.

Seth's assessment revealed that he was struggling with untreated symptoms of PTSD. These were related to a series of untreated and severe psychological and sexual traumas at the hands of several men and one woman. Seth also had undiagnosed dyslexia and suffered tremendous shame because he could not succeed in school. One of his most painful secrets continued to be his current inability to read beyond a primary level. He became dependent on Emily to review all written material, such as business and legal documents, prior to his completing any business transaction. This increased Seth's resentment toward Emily as he felt shamed and disempowered by his disability. He began a course of treatment for his dyslexia, but soon abandoned the reading program. When Emily broached this in session, Seth stated that he was unwilling to commit the time to the remedial reading program as it would take away from his lucrative business; he acknowledged that his financial success was vital for his self-esteem. Seth exhibited classic signs of dysfunctionally stored memories that were expressed in distorted belief systems and behaviors. His labile affect, womanizing, and desertions appeared to be an escape from the overwhelming feelings triggered by the conflict in the marriage.

Seth evidenced many of the symptoms that Herman (1992) described as the sequelae of childhood trauma. These included flashbacks and intrusive thoughts, identity distortions (although no evidence of dissociation), labile affect, sexual addictions, compulsive behavior, steroid use, and antisocial behavior with rages, reenactments, and hypersexuality. Seth began to take on the role of the abuser during his rages, using both verbal and physical abuse. This response to trauma by a male may be partially accounted for by the social beliefs and expectations of masculinity and is underscored in research findings:

> Male survivors of trauma are more likely than women to externalize their pain and, in the process, to perpetuate interpersonal violence and continue the tragic cycle of pain. . . . [Often] male gender role socialization is linked to shame and the shutdown of emotional and communicative coping capacities in males. (Mejia, 2005, pp. 32–33)

Family violence was another component of this couple's interaction. When Seth was confronted with his lies and infidelity, he would resort to pushing, shoving, and punching. He stated, "She will not leave me alone and this is the only way I know how to get away from Emily when she harasses me."

Case Therapy Process

Initially Seth and Emily came to the office for help in dealing with their ongoing dramatic conflicts that would escalate into violent episodes of screaming, pushing, punching, and Seth moving out. Because they exhibited many of the classic issues that are targets in SFT, such as enmeshment, disengagement, lack of conflict resolution skills, poor communication skills, rigidity, and lack of boundaries, SFT was the treatment approach used with them. Their boundaries were quite diffuse; Emily was extremely enmeshed and codependent, and Seth continually disconnected.

During the initial sessions, maladaptive repetitive patterns of communication were evident. These patterns were pointed out to Seth and Emily to emphasize that the therapeutic focus would be on the repetitive behavioral and verbal patterns rather than the details of specific incidents.

Treatment goals of honoring fidelity; establishing healthy boundaries; communicating with kindness, respect, and consideration; being aware of each other's struggles; and supporting each other were set in the initial sessions. The safety contract was discussed, and as a containment procedure Seth and Emily agreed to try to implement de-escalation tactics such as time-out and waiting until therapy before discussing volatile topics.

The process of joining with both husband and wife was begun early in the interactions. This is often accomplished by finding common areas of interest or tapping into the expertise of each partner, thereby building a sense of mutual respect and connection.

One of the primary premises of SFT is that attempting to reconstruct disputes and family problems that occur outside the therapy session is less effective than enactment, a technique that brings the conflict or problem into the session. This process helps the family experience their dysfunctional behavioral interactions in a controlled situation. The presence of the therapist gives them a heightened awareness, and by examining their roles, behaviors, and communications they can consider alternative, more functional ways, of behaving. Once the couple has experienced a new way of interacting as a result of the enactment they are is encouraged to implement these adaptive changes at home.

Although Seth and Emily were actively engaged in the marital therapy, Seth would revert back to his rages, lies, and infidelity. When "caught again" he would cope by moving out, physically lashing out, or disappearing to punish his wife for the confrontation. Despite the therapist's efforts to use such SFT techniques as joining, enactment, and relabeling, Seth continued to respond in an extremely volatile manner. He would attempt to intimidate Emily verbally during the session; if that was unsuccessful, he would storm out of the therapist's office, just as he did at home. These actions stirred Emily's feelings of abandonment and her abuse issues as she, too, was a trauma survivor as well as an adult child of an alcoholic. It became evident that their individual and intertwined pathologies were so deep-rooted and intense that using SFT alone was insufficient to bring about the lasting changes they needed and wanted.

It was apparent that Seth's trauma history and individual belief system had to be addressed first, as his life was driven by his damaged self-concept. This was manifested in his ongoing behaviors of womanizing to prove his manhood, making a great deal of money to hide his illiteracy (his biggest and most shameful secret), and bullying anyone who "crossed him" to assert his personal power.

It became eminently clear that the implementation of EMDR for treating Seth's early trauma was indicated prior to continuing the marital therapy. Emily and Seth agreed that Seth needed to access, process, and adaptively resolve the effects of his traumatic history, and he consented to EMDR treatment.

Next they explored their individual trauma histories in conjoint sessions, in the application of Phases 1 and 2 of the EMDR protocol. This process was liberating to both as they gained some insight into their long-standing patterns. Seth and Emily expressed that sharing their traumatic histories in session fostered new feelings of closeness and trust which had been absent in their relationship. Both noted that after sharing these painful histories, they believed they could be more supportive and kind to one another.

Through the discussion of EMDR theory and gaining an understanding of the impact of their prior trauma, Seth and Emily were able to relabel their enduring dysfunctional beliefs and behaviors. This was not only freeing for both of them but also immensely helpful as they began to shift toward restructuring their interactions. After this theory session, Seth began individual EMDR.

Seth's First EMDR Session

Seth began his EMDR session with a description of the trigger incident, when he was approximately 9 years old an apartment superintendent lured him into the apartment basement filled with pellet guns, minibikes, motorcycles, and scuba gear and then sexually molested him. His *Negative Cognition* was "I'm stupid and gay." He reported feelings of confusion, anger, shame, and sadness, with tightness and heaviness in his chest. His *Positive Cognition* was "I'm a normal heterosexual who made a poor childhood choice." As he began the EMDR he was able to describe the perpetrator and the initial incident and then stated, "After it happened I didn't care: So he was abusing me a little bit? I went back there, then I went one time a week and he took me to his apartment. This went on for more than a year. I figured he already did it and I liked all the stuff in the basement that I did not get to have at home."

He then became very tearful about his parents' lack of interest in him and the shaming he received from them regarding his inability to do well in school. He also discussed his mother's need for him to be super clean, to the point of rubbing him raw in the bathtub and not permitting him to play and get dirty. "They never told me they loved me, even to this day!"

At this point, the rejections and family abuse were processed.

After each set of eye movements, Seth recounted additional memories of attempted or actual molestations. For example, during his next set of eye movements he stated:

> About 1 or 2 years later I was in a private school, one of the teachers, older man. He was a speech therapist. Two or three of the kids would mess around together. I was one of the group on a field trip to Manhattan in his house. Kids were 12 or 13 years old playing, fondling each other, we left. One of the kids told me he wanted me to be his boyfriend, he was older. Scared of him. Answered No! Boy ran after me. Why? Why? Still see kid's face; wanted to hit him. NO WAY!!!!

In between eye movement sets he admitted how upset he was that this boy thought he was gay.

The next set of eye movements began and he stated: "The police came and asked my mom if I stayed overnight at his [the speech therapist's] house. I told them I don't know nothing and leave me alone. . . . Stopped going to the basement."

After another set of eye movements he stated:

Female tutor 22 years old, had sex with her. Wanted to prove I was a man and not gay. Lonely misguided unloved little boy. I did everything for attention. I do not think I'm gay. I've been beating myself up—stupid! I'm 40 years old. I cannot read or write!!!!

At this point in the EMDR he became very tearful and stated, "This is my biggest shameful secret. My friend said to me. 'What, are you stupid?' It hurts." He was crying.

Seth stated that his deepest underlying negative belief is not that he is gay but that he is stupid; he declared that he spent his life trying to disprove both negative beliefs. He described some new insights and explained that he attempts to prove to himself he is not gay by womanizing and exhibiting aggressive behaviors to be manly. He also reported realizing that he worked out and took steroids to look big, strong, and manly and that he is driven to prove he is not stupid by becoming a very successful business entrepreneur while hiding the fact that he can barely read.

Seth chose to do the EMDR work in a 2-hour session as he felt he would be able to tolerate this better.

During the following sessions, the EMDR work was reprocessed and the second prong of the protocol was instituted by focusing on and discussing current triggers in his life, such as his reading disability, which he encountered on a daily basis in conducting his business and various law suits; his business, which put him in daily contact with women; and his choice to work out with steroids to look strong and big. Future issues (prong 3) were discussed in terms of ongoing individual therapy, reading therapy, and weaning from the steroids.

Couple Debriefing of the EMDR Session

Seth invited Emily to attend the debriefing of the EMDR sessions with him so she would have a deeper understanding of his underlying beliefs and the kinds of stimuli that trigger him. During the debriefing, the theories of EMDR were reviewed. One of the primary concepts covered was that past traumatic events are the underpinnings to current dysfunctional responses to life and that Seth was responding to stimuli that triggered him on a daily basis. Additionally, the therapist highlighted the concept that the individual connects these traumatic events to other events in life, similar to hyperlinking on the Internet, so that current events and interactions can trigger the person's dysfunctional responses. This relabeling validated and reframed his cognitive distortions and beliefs.

The debriefing was helpful for both. Emily was able to see Seth as a vulnerable human being who had been terribly hurt rather than the raging, shaming womanizer he had become to her. Seth was able to gain tremendous insight as well as resolve some of the dysfunctional beliefs he held about himself.

Resumption of Couple Therapy

The integration of EMDR in this couple's marital therapy enabled them to dismantle the stylized, repetitive patterns of communication and interaction that they engaged in almost daily. In SFT the dismantling of these dysfunctional patterns is essential for improvement in the marriage.

A positive expectation in a marital subsystem is that the husband and wife will communicate with intimacy, support each other, and exhibit loving and sexual connections. Seth and Emily showed none of these attributes when they began therapy. After the EMDR intervention they were able to connect and communicate on a more intimate and honest level. Seth expressed that Emily felt "like a best friend for the first time in [their] marriage," realizing how much she loved him unconditionally. This was such an amazing awareness for him that he had difficulty integrating the concept that he was worthy of any kind of unconditional love given the history of his family of origin.

As they reengaged in marital counseling, a positive alliance between Emily and Seth was evident. They began to communicate without constantly arguing and shouting. Rather than continually crossing each other's boundaries and getting into physical confrontations, they learned to find ways to physically distance themselves and allow time to cool down with a specified and agreed-upon waiting period before continuing their discussions. They also began to define and form boundaries between them so there was less enmeshment, yet a loving connection. Both started to be more cognizant of each other's triggers and attempted to be compassionate and considerate in not exacerbating responses that ignited these triggers. They practiced reframing, which helped them modify their reactions and attitudes toward each other in a more productive and honoring manner.

Instituting SFT techniques created a sense of competence in both Emily and Seth. This integrated approach was very productive as it overcame the impasse in the marital process. By diverting to the individual therapy issues in the context of the marital therapy, the husband had a unique opportunity to divulge painful memories and to be vulnerable in a controlled, safe environment. In addition, the wife was able to participate in the debriefing and offer him comfort and understanding.

One of the challenges in this approach is to present the implementation of a very powerful individual treatment approach, EMDR, to a couple and have them both understand and ally with the concept of diverting the focus on the crises in the family to individual concerns. Another challenge is engaging the individual who is a candidate for EMDR to trust both the therapist and the spouse to do this kind of intense therapy work and share it with the spouse. The advantage of integrating EMDR and couple therapy in this case was that it allowed the husband to overcome his overwhelming emotional responses to minor events, which would then lead to escalating the drama between the couple. In addition, the recognition of his personal history and his identity crisis as a result of his childhood traumas allowed him to reprocess his dysfunctional beliefs and become emotionally accessible for further couple work.

DISCUSSION

Sexual trauma survivors often exhibit significant interpersonal difficulties, especially when engaging in intimate, long-term relationships. Their relationships may be marred by intense conflict, distrust, and control and sexual issues. Destructive behaviors, to self and others, are hallmarks of their relationships.

SFT (Minuchin, 1974) is the family system model chosen for the treatment of these couples. However, if the individual dysfunction of the trauma survivor overpowers the couple therapy, a departure from the marital treatment is critical to ensure a successful outcome. Then the application of EMDR for the processing of past traumas is indicated.

As shown in the case study, marital therapy became stalled when the couple was unable to resolve conflict and restructure boundaries. It was clear that Seth and Emily were plagued by a continual reenactment of their past traumas with related distorted interpretations of intimacy, trust, and conflict. As this couple had become lost in the rigid confines of their dynamics, it was apparent that the individual trauma sequelae needed to be addressed before marital therapy could be continued.

The integrative approach described in this chapter involves departing from marital therapy to deal with one partner's individual trauma history through an essentially individual treatment, EMDR. The EMDR sessions were shared with the partner either in a debriefing session or through her participation as a witness. After this, the couple therapy was continued. Although the use of this protocol apparently is still unusual, as it has been rarely reported in the marital literature, it can be very effective.

This intervention requires the therapist to establish a good trust level and to bond or join effectively with members of the couple. The vulnerability that trauma survivors experience while engaging in EMDR is significantly multiplied by knowing they will be expressing painful, shaming events with their partner, whom they love but with whom they are embedded in conflict. The emotional risk is great and it takes great courage to engage in this process. Yet the positive outcome for the couple's mutual understanding is dramatic. Furthermore, the resolution of past issues frees the couple so that they can progress in creating change and moving toward growth and intimacy.

The combination of SFT and EMDR may have tremendous therapeutic benefit for couples where one or both partners have suffered sexual trauma or physical, emotional, or verbal abuse. Ongoing clinical research in the integration of EMDR with various family system approaches is a rich and promising area of study that can expand a treating therapist's clinical repertoire.

REFERENCES

American Psychiatric Association. (1994). *Diagnostic and statistical manual of mental disorders* (4th ed.). Washington, DC: Author.

Aponte, H. (1992). Training the person of the therapist in structural family therapy. *Journal of Marital and Family Therapy, 18*(3), 269–281.

Bagarozzi, G. A., & Giddings, C. W. (1983). Conjugal violence: A critical review of current research and clinical practices. *American Journal of Family Therapy, 11*(1), 3–12.

Basham, K., & Miehls, D. (2002, March). Transforming the legacies of childhood trauma in couple therapy: The biopsychosocial assessment as compass and anchor. *Smith College Studies in Social Work, Northampton, 72*(2), 253–278.

Beatty, M. (1992). *Codependent no more.* Center City, MN: Hazeldon.

Bowen, M. (1966). The use of family theory in clinical practice. *Comprehensive Psychiatry, 7,* 345–374.

Bowen, M. (1972). Toward the differentiation of a self in one's own family. In J. Framo (Ed.), *Family interaction: A dialogue between family researchers and family therapists* (pp. 111–173). New York: Springer-Verlag.

Bowen, M. (1976). Theory in the practice of psychotherapy. In P. Guerin (Ed.), *Family therapy* (pp. 42–90). New York: Gardener.

Briere, J., Evans, D., Runtz, M., & Wall, T. (1988). Symptomology in men who were molested as children: A comparison study. *American Journal of Orthopsychiatry, 58,* 457–461.

Champion De Crespigny, J. (1996). The experience of couples in intimate study. *Dissertation Abstracts International, 58*(9), 5109B.

Compton, J., & Folette, V. (1998), Couples surviving trauma: Issues and interventions. In V. Folette, J. Ruzek, & F. Abueg (Eds.), *Cognitive-behavioral therapies for trauma* (pp. 321–352). New York: Guilford Press.

Courtois, C. (1988). *Healing the incest wound: Adult survivors in therapy.* New York: Norton.

Davis, J. L., & Petrectic-Jackson, P. A. (2000). The impact of child sexual abuse on adult interpersonal functioning: A review and synthesis of the empirical literature. *Aggression and Violent Behavior, 5,* 291–328.

Finkelhor, D., Hotaling, G., Lewis, I., & Smith, C. (1989). Sexual abuse and its relationship to later sexual satisfaction, marital status, religion, and attitudes. *Journal of Interpersonal Violence, 4,* 379–399.

Goldenberg, I., & Goldenberg, H. (2004). *Family therapy: An overview* (6th ed.). Pacific Grove, CA: Brooks/Cole-Thomson Learning.

Herman, J. (1992). *Trauma and recovery.* New York: Basic Books.

Huycke, J. D. (2000, Spring). Unpublished manuscript, University of Wisconsin, Milwaukee, School of Social Welfare, Course in Social Work Practice.

Jacob, C., & Veach, P. (2005). Intrapersonal and familial effects of child sexual abuse on female partners of male survivors. *Journal of Counseling Psychology, 3,* 284–297.

Jacquet, S. (1999). Sexual abuse experiences and family environment in childhood as predictors of sexual dysfunction and premarital relationships in adulthood. *Dissertation Abstracts International, 60*(9), 4501B.

Kaslow, F. (1981). A diaclectic approach to family therapy and practice: Selectivity and synthesis. *Journal of Marital and Family Therapy, 7,* 345–351.

Kia-Keating, M., Grossman, F., Sorsoli, L., & Epstein, M. (2005). Containing and resisting masculinity: Narratives of renegotiation among resilient male survivors of childhood sexual abuse. *Psychology of Men and Masculinity, 6*(3), 169–185.

Koedam, W. (1996). Dissociative identity disorder in relational contexts. In F. W. Kaslow (Ed.), *Handbook of relational diagnosis and dysfunctional family patterns* (pp. 420–433). New York: Wiley.

Lisak, D. (1994). The psychological impact of sexual abuse: Content analysis of interviews with male survivors. *Journal of Traumatic Stress, 7,* 525–548.

Lisak, D. (1995). Integrating a critique of gender in the treatment of male survivors of childhood abuse. *Psychotherapy, 32,* 258–269.

Loring, S., & Cowan, G. (1997). Codependency: An interpersonal phenomenon. *Sex Roles: A Journal of Research, 36,*115–123.

McCauley, J., Kern, D. E., Kolander, K., Dill, L., Schroeder, A. F., DeChant, H. K., et al. (1997). Clinical characteristics of women with a history of childhood abuse: Unhealed wounds. *Journal of the American Medical Association, 277*(17), 1362–1368.

Mejia, X. (2005, Winter). Gender matters: Working with adult male survivors of trauma. *Journal of Counseling and Development, 83,* 30–37.

Melito, R. (1988). Combining individual dynamics with structural family dynamics. *Journal of Marital and Family Therapy, 14*(1).

Minuchin, S. (1974). *Families and family therapy.* Cambridge, MA: Harvard University Press.

Minuchin, S., Montalvo, B., Guerney, B. G., Jr., Rosman, B. L., & Schumer, F. (1967). *Families of the slums.* New York: Basic Books.

Minuchin, S., Rosman, B. L., & Baker, L. (1978). *Psychosomatic families: Anorexia nervosa in context.* Cambridge, MA: Harvard University Press.

Najman, J. M., Dunne, M. P., Purdie, D. M., Boyle, F. M., & Coxeter, P. D. (2005). Sexual abuse in childhood and sexual dysfunction in adulthood: An Australian population-based study. *Archives of Sexual Behavior, 34,* 517–526.

Nelson, B., & Wampler, K. (2000). Systemic effects of trauma in clinic couples: An exploratory study of secondary trauma resulting from childhood abuse. *Journal of Marital and Family Therapy, 36,* 171–184.

Papero, D. (1983). Family systems theory and therapy. In B. Wolman & G. Stricker (Eds.), *Handbook of family and marital therapy* (pp. 137–158). New York: Plenum Press.

Pelcovitz, D., van der Kolk, B. A., Roth, S., Mandel, F. S., & Resick, P. (1997). Development of a criteria set and a structured interview for disorder of extreme stress (SIDES). *Journal of Traumatic Stress, 10,* 3–16.

Protinsky, H., Sparks, J., & Flemke, K. (2001, April). Using eye movement desensitization and reprocessing to enhance treatment in couples. *Journal of Marital and Family Therapy, 27*(2), 157–164.

Riggs, D. S. (2000). Marital and family therapy. In E. B. Foa, T. M. Keane, & M. J. Friedman (Eds.), *Effective treatment for PTSD* (pp. 280–301). New York: Guilford Press.

Rosenberg, J. B. (1983). Structural family therapy. In B. Wolm & G. Stricker (Eds.), *Handbook of family and marital therapy* (pp. 159–185). New York, Plenum Press.

Rumstein-McKean, O., & Hunsley, J. (2001). Interpersonal and family functioning of female survivors of childhood sexual abuse. *Clinical Psychology Review, 21,* 471–490.

Rutter, M. (1993). Resilience: Some conceptual considerations. *Journal of Adolescent Health, 14,* 626–631.

Sachs-Ericsson, N., Blazer, D., Plant, E. A., & Arrow, B. (2005). Childhood sexual and physical abuse and the 1-year prevalence of medical problems in the National Comorbidity Survey. *Health Psychology, 24,* 32–40.

Shapiro, F. (1995). *Eye movement desensitization and reprocessing: Basic principles, protocols, and procedures.* New York: Guilford Press.

Shapiro, F. (2001). *Eye movement desensitization and reprocessing: Basic principles, protocols, and procedures* (2nd ed.). New York: Guilford Press.

Straus, M. A., & Gelles, R. J. (1986). Societal change in family violence from 1975–1985 as revealed by two national surveys. *Journal of Marriage and the Family, 48,* 465–479.

Taylor, J. W. (1984). Structured conjoint therapy for spouse abuse cases. *Social Work, 63,* 259–265.

Toman, W. (1961). *Family constellation: Its effects on personality and social behavior.* New York: Springer.

van der Kolk, B. A., Pelcovitz, D., Roth, S., Mandel, F., McFarlane, A., & Herman, J. (1996). Dissociation, somatization, and affect dysregulation; The complexity of adaptation to trauma. *American Journal of Psychiatry, 153,* 83–93.

CHAPTER 12

EMDR and Family Therapy in the Treatment of Domestic Violence

Julie E. Stowasser

Domestic violence (DV) has been defined as a pattern of verbal and physical behavior intended to control another person in an existing, former, or desired intimate relationship (Walker, 1979). DV is distinguished from "simply dysfunctional" behavior by one person's repetitive use of power and control tactics to coerce another to behave or perceive in a manner that he or she would not otherwise choose. This conduct can take numerous forms and can be difficult for victims, perpetrators, and even therapists to recognize, particularly when the abuse is subsequently minimized or denied (Harway & Hansen, 1993).

When treating individuals with DV issues, it is important to promote the cessation of all behaviors in the categories of control and abuse, and not simply limit intervention to dealing with threats of violence or actual physical abuse. Without effective intervention, the cycle of violence can progress from verbal and psychological abuse to physical assault, resulting in bodily injury and, in some cases, the death of the victim, the perpetrator, or both (Dutton, 1998; Herman, 1997; LaViolette & Barnett, 2000; Walker, 1979, 1989, 1994). Children can also be harmed psychologically and physically, either by being abused or by witnessing DV directed against someone else (American Psychological Association [APA], 1996; Jacobson, 2000; Jaffe, Wolfe, & Wilson, 1990; LaViolette & Barnett, 2000). Further damage occurs if the abuser's behavior interferes with the parent-child relationship or disrupts the child's attachment to caregivers. Abuse can also affect neighbors, business associates, and others if the impact extends into those relationships.

A carefully worded initial intake (Harway & Hansen, 1993) with victims is needed to illuminate all forms of abuse, including the subtler and secretive forms. Similarly, direct questioning of the abuser may result in getting a more complete disclosure (Peterman & Dixon, 2001). A thorough history of adults involved in abusive relationships will often reveal that they experienced direct or indirect exposure to DV in childhood (APA, 1996; Cooley & Severson, 1993; Dutton, 1998; Jacobson, 2000; Kwong, Bartholomew, Henderson, & Trinke, 2003; Walker, 1994). Some authors (Kwong et al., 2003; Walker, 1994) refer to this as the "intergenerational transmission of violence."

Although DV is not confined to heterosexual unions or to males as abusers, this chapter focuses on heterosexual males as offenders because 85% of DV is directed by men toward women (Rennison & Welchans, 2000). Victims can experience psychological symptoms including but not limited to depression, anxiety, Posttraumatic Stress Disorder (PTSD), dissociation, eating disorders, somatic complaints, and poor self-esteem (Dutton, 1998; Herman, 1997; LaViolette & Barnett, 2000; Walker, 1979, 1989, 1994). Efforts have been made to categorize batterers into types; however, there is no precise profile for a DV perpetrator (APA, 1996; Dutton, 1995, 1998; Sonkin & Dutton, 2003; Wallace & Nosko, 2003) and no profile for a victim (APA, 1996; LaViolette & Barnett, 2000; Walker, 1994).

First proposed by Lenore Walker (1979) as a model with which to understand and treat domestic violence, the Cycle of Violence Theory hypothesized that although each abusive relationship is unique, most abusive incidents can be mapped to follow a violent cycle that consists of three phases: (1) the escalation of tension, (2) the abusive release, and (3) the loving, contrite, "honeymoon" phase. She posited that only the abuser can interrupt the escalation phase, which otherwise will continue until violently released (Walker, 1994). The victim can act to shorten, but not prevent, the escalation phase and may not have the choice to leave. Once the abuser expels his tension, his thoughts and feelings normalize, allowing awareness and remorse to follow in the honeymoon phase, where promises and attempts to repair and reconnect with the victim are made (Walker, 1979, 1994). Over time, some couples may no longer experience the honeymoon stage of the cycle. The abuser often denies the abuse or reorganizes the event to minimize or justify his behaviors or to place blame on the victim (Dutton, 1998). If confronted with his behavior, he may even threaten more violence against the victim, choose a new victim (e.g., the therapist), or threaten to abandon the family (Madanes, 1995).

Eye Movement Desensitization and Reprocessing

Eye Movement Desensitization and Reprocessing (EMDR; Shapiro, 1995, 2001) is an integrated method of psychotherapy that incorporates aspects of cognitive-behavioral, gestalt, psychodynamic, systems, and other established therapies. EMDR has been demonstrated to be efficacious in the treatment of PTSD (American Psychiatric Association, 2004), and preliminary evidence suggests that it may be helpful for children and adults affected by interpersonal violence (Edmond, Rubin, & Wambach, 1999; Maxwell, 2002; Pollock, 2000). Although some EMDR studies on PTSD included victims of domestic violence, the victims were a subset and not the specific population focused on. To date, there are no published studies on EMDR that address the specific treatment of victims or perpetrators of domestic violence. However, McMulin (1998) has combined EMDR and relapse prevention with sex offender treatment, and Pollock (2000) reported success in treating a perpetrator's PTSD that developed subsequent to his homicidal offense. EMDR was also shown to be effective in reducing sensitivity to physical pain, a benefit to victim survivors who experience chronic or intermittently triggered somatic symptoms (Grant & Threlfo, 2002).

EMDR is an eight-phase psychotherapy that addresses original injurious memories rather than the traumatic sequelae alone. EMDR treatment includes a three-pronged approach that targets the past events related to the trauma and its present triggers and facilitates an understanding of the client's appropriate options for the future in the context of that original memory; it thus provides a comprehensive approach to treatment (Shapiro, 2001; Shapiro & Maxfield, 2002). EMDR can relieve the negative symptoms and disorders caused by child abuse and neglect and childhood and adulthood exposure to domestic violence by targeting those memories that contribute to and maintain the current dysfunction. Though aware of the past, it does not seek to explore and understand it. Like some family therapy approaches (e.g., Minuchin, 1974), EMDR is prospective in its orientation to the client's present symptomatology and future accommodations.

Therapy of Social Action

Minuchin (1974; see also Becvar & Becvar, 1988; Kaslow, 1982) was an early innovator in the systems school of family therapy and the developer of Structural Family Therapy, one of the most widely used family systems orientations today (Green & Framo, 1981). Joined by Jay Haley in 1962, he designed and led Structural Family Therapy training and treatment programs (Kaslow, 1982). Cloe Madanes followed later, and in 1976 she and Haley forged Strategic Family Therapy. Madanes and Haley subsequently separated, and Madanes went on to develop the Therapy of Social Action (TSA), a blended application of strategic (Madanes, 1981, 1990, 1995) and structural (Becvar & Becvar, 1988) family therapy. TSA is distinguished by its view of the family structure as one wherein some family members have more causative power, choice, and therefore personal responsibility than others; for example, a parent has more choice and responsibility than a child. TSA declares that the adult abuser has more power and responsibility for the family structure and is authentically the first-order change agent for the family. TSA is also prospective and is designed to assist the perpetrator in taking full responsibility for his actions and relieving the burden of hurt he has caused his family members. It can also be used to assist some batterers with their own suffering, which resulted from having committed offensive interpersonal behaviors (Madanes, 1981, 1990, 1995; Pollock, 2000; Waldo, 1987).

TSA is a 12-step method of treating perpetrators, victims, and their families. The 12 steps are (1) account for the offense, (2) demonstrate why it was wrong, (3) communicate the spiritual pain it caused, (4) understand the pain it also caused the victimizer, (5) acknowledge other offenders and victims in the family, (6) understand the pain it caused all those who care for the victim, (7) apologize from the heart, (8) allow other family members to apologize to the victim, (9) delineate consequences for future offenses, (10) organize the family to protect against further victimization, (11) establish and make reparation for the offense, and (12) reorient the family to a "normal" life (Madanes, 1995). Steps 1 through 7 and 11 are parts of the perpetrator's "apology," a critical and required component of TSA treatment.

The victim's only role in TSA treatment is to determine that the perpetrator's apology is sincere and demonstrates accountability and responsibility. McNamara and Dhami (2003) examined the function an apology plays in increasing offender empathy, reducing antisocial behavior, and increasing victim safety. Their research has shown valuable but inconsistent relief for victims and perpetrators regardless of the accountability in or perceived sincerity of the apology. There has been only one outcome study assessing TSA. Madanes (1995) contacted 72 of the first 75 families treated with TSA 2 years after treatment completion. She reported a 96% success rate, with 69 families remaining offense-free.

THERAPY PROCESS

The DV therapist joins the family as a strong and directive person who provides leadership and strengthens or changes the family structure as needed. Abiding by ethical and legal mandates (Cervantes, 1993) to inquire about past and current abuses, he or she asks specific questions to illuminate all forms of DV. The therapist assesses for lethality and prohibits conjoint therapy when any single item is present on any lethality checklist (e.g., Bograd & Mederos, 1999; Hart, 1990), when there is a restraining order, or if the batterer is receiving legally mandated treatment. The therapist also rules out conjoint sessions when the perpetrator denies responsibility, the victim expresses fear, or there is active physical violence (within 12 months), threats of violence, substance abuse, or personality disorder (Berry, 1995; Bograd & Mederos, 1999; deBecker, 1997; Hart, 1990). Should any of these concerns arise during treatment, the clinician makes appropriate referrals and conducts only individual sessions, as safety is the first goal in DV treatment. In such instances, neither will be present for their partner's Phases 2 through 8 of EMDR and the apology will not be attempted. If partners are seen together, sessions focus solely on psychoeducation, safety planning, and monitoring of interpersonal behavior until the couple is ready to resume conjoint sessions.

When integrating EMDR and TSA in the treatment of couples with domestic violence issues, current DV History Taking is intensive and is initially conducted separately to enhance the safety of the victim and increase the potential for her full disclosure. In TSA Step 1, in addition to accounts of violence in previous generations, the perpetrator's History Taking also includes an accounting of his offenses toward the victim. As perpetrators can deny, minimize, or avoid full accountability (Dutton, 1995, 1998; Madanes, 1995; Walker, 1979, 1989, 1994), the victim's and other family members' accounts of the couple's violence can be cross-referenced against his.

Material collected in Phase 1 of EMDR is complementary with Step 1 of TSA, where the perpetrator and victim are asked about the worst thing that ever happened to them. The EMDR therapist also asks the client about his or her small "t" traumas (e.g., rejections and disappointments) and large "T" Traumas (e.g., abuse and assaults). As the history is narrated, the therapist monitors the client to assess for necessary EMDR preparatory work (EMDR Phase 2) and identifies target memories for reprocessing (EMDR Phase 3).

Concurrent with Phases 1 through 3 of EMDR and Steps 1 through 6 of TSA, EMDR and TSA education is provided, as well as information about other issues such as parenting and PTSD. Further goals include in-depth education on (a) DV, including its effects on the victim, children, and perpetrator (APA, 1996; Jaffe, Wolfe, & Wilson, 1990); (b) the cycle of violence (Walker, 1979); and (c) strategies that the couple can use to resolve conflict and change the cycle (Stowasser, 2001). Essential behavioral goals are established and the couple work toward these using TSA and EMDR. These include the following goals:

- Eliminate physical violence and threats.
- Reduce denial and victim blaming.
- Use nonviolent conflict resolution skills.
- Increase each individual's personal power and responsibility.
- Enforce boundaries appropriately.
- Develop empathy for self and others.
- Repair relationships where appropriate.

The therapist may creatively utilize any number of interventions designed to stabilize the family and limit escalations. For example, written time-out instructions (Stowasser, 2001), negotiated in advance, stress open communication and the cooperation of each partner; they provide guidelines for the calling of a time-out and suggest specific behaviors to consider if the other partner is uncooperative. When initiated by one partner without the awareness or cooperation of the other, the time-out can potentially be unsafe (Rosen, Matheson, Stith, McCollum, & Locke, 2003). EMDR can be used to imaginally rehearse the use of such tools prior to reprocessing traumas (and also while in the third prong). TSA can strengthen the sense of responsibility to do so. Such interventions are warranted prior to EMDR reprocessing of DV in the family.

As the TSA therapist readies all parties for the apology, he or she seeks to motivate them to stop DV now and into the next generation. The therapist attempts to make meaning of the violence and change their metaphor from something that glorifies violence and distorts strength and power to something that signifies impotence, weakness, powerlessness, and defeat. Victims and their children will often try to protect the father from the consequences of his behavior. The TSA therapist is always on guard to prevent the family from minimizing the seriousness of the violence and will clearly state that the abuse is wrong and point out the spiritually painful consequences of abuse to the family. The therapist makes clear that each family member, not just the perpetrator, is responsible for his or her actions, regardless of provocations. Keeping abuse a secret is psychologically harmful and can be interpreted by the victim as proof that the abuse was somehow her fault. Secrecy is also a subtle form of denial that the abuse happened and can result in the victim's adopting a faulty self-assessment, such as "I am crazy" for believing it happened or for feeling distress.

EMDR reprocessing in Phases 4 through 8 can increase client safety when it is strategically employed to resolve the perpetrator's distressing memories related to current maladaptive behaviors. Reprocessing the perpetrator's earlier experiences as a victim may facilitate an increase in empathy for himself and for others. For example, his inability or unwillingness to tolerate the negative affect and faulty cognitions associated with his own victimization can inhibit his acceptance of the distress experienced by others. In turn, reprocessing his memories of the abuse he committed toward another may increase his sense of accountability and responsibility to that victim, for those actions, and, when the third prong is employed, may assist him in easing toward behavioral options that are psychologically and physically healthier for him, his victim, and his family.

Reprocessing of past abuse is also beneficial in assisting the victim in clearing out shameful recall of her past abuse, relieving her of the burdens of and blame for the abuse (first and second prongs), and strategically imagining preemptive options (safety plans) and alternatives to static responses such as freezing or escalating in times of verbal or physical assault (third prong). EMDR lends speed to TSA by enhancing the client's ability to tolerate painful affect. Resolving these core DV issues will help reduce and eliminate strife at home; consequently, EMDR can be considered an ethical choice to offer the family members affected by DV.

CASE EXAMPLE

EMDR and TSA were integrated in the treatment of a couple, Rick and Jennie Roth. Both of their families of origin were historically steeped over several generations in verbal, emotional, and physical violence. As children and teenagers, each witnessed and were subject to these abuses. Jennie also experienced emotional, physical, and medical neglect. The Roths met as children, became high school sweethearts, and after a college-age separation of 3 years, reunited and married; they then had two children. Rick first physically assaulted Jennie 4 years into their marriage, after the birth of their second son. His physical DV continued intermittently over the next 12 years as he regularly employed control and other forms of abuse. After 16 years of marriage, Jennie left Rick because of his perpetration of another physically violent incident, and he entered therapy at a DV agency. Rick was a typical batterer, minimizing some of his abusive behaviors and outright denying others (Dutton, 1998; Madanes, 1995). At the same time, however, he admitted his behavior was hurtful and that no one, including his wife, knew how much he loved her. His stated therapeutic goals were to be able to show his love and respect for her and "to be a human being." Rick received 4 months of DV education, and in preparation for the TSA apology, began an accounting of the abuse he perpetrated against his wife and children. His concurrent EMDR sessions, in which he reprocessed traumatic childhood experiences, included physical and emotional child abuse he received from his older sister, and which his father often instigated as a form of family entertainment. He also addressed his childhood attempt to kill this sister. He stated that he was feeling calmer and that his wife was noticing that this "weird" therapy was working.

Rick's treatment was interrupted due to his therapist's relocation, and the TSA component was not completed. He stayed on with another therapist for 15 months of intermittent traditional DV talk therapy treatment. He was stable and, though still anxious and angry at times, was not experiencing rage. His home life had improved considerably and he had returned to live with his family.

Three and a half years after Rick's EMDR therapy, he referred his wife for EMDR treatment. She had previously participated in talk therapy, intermittently, for about 5 years, focusing on DV, difficult people at work, a life-threatening brain tumor, and other, similarly themed victim situations. However, despite the lengthy work, she still suffered from chronic PTSD.

Jennie's family was intergenerationally abusive, alcoholic, and frequently bloody and violent, in contrast to the controlled violence of Rick's family. She reported that on her mother's side, the women were severely physically abused but would eventually fight back violently. Jennie grew up being brutally verbally abused and was called stupid, ugly, and a whore on a regular basis. On some occasions, she was physically, emotionally, and medically neglected. She had had chronic bronchitis, pneumonia, and vertigo early in life and made sense of it all by adopting the *Negative Cognitions* "There is something wrong with me" "I don't deserve" "I am unworthy" and "It's my fault."

She arrived for her third session in physical and emotional distress and described a recent dinner at their home with Rick's father as guest. Jennie stated that the dinner was stressful and caused her body to ache. She targeted the dinner with EMDR and during the reprocessing phase connected back to the last physical assault from her husband, which had occurred 4 years previously and which took place *in preparation* for a visit and dinner with Rick's father. In hindsight, she saw that most of the past physically abusive episodes had occurred in anticipation of, or soon after, contact with Rick's father. She left the session pain free, emotionally intact, and startled by the awareness that her body could "hold" pain and that old pain could be triggered by current events. It gave Jennie a new context in which to think about herself rather than thinking she was physically defective and mentally crazy. Due to her work obligations, Jennie's first EMDR treatment ended after four sessions, although incomplete.

Five years after Rick concluded his initial therapy and 2 years after Jennie ended hers, they returned to treatment as a couple. They were doing well in their individual careers; Rick owned one company and supervised at another. Jennie was successfully employed as a government scientist. However, the verbal abuse of some male colleagues was triggering Jennie's symptoms, and she did not always feel safe at home because Rick and her now adult sons still had controlling behaviors and the boys were sometimes verbally abusive.

Although prediction is not science, Rick's potential for homicide and violence was assessed as being very low to zero using Hart's Lethality Assessment

(1990) and clinical information (Bograd & Mederos, 1999; Cattaneo & Goodman, 2003; Peterman & Dixon, 2001), and the couple met the very narrow criteria for couples therapy with abusive families (Bograd & Mederos, 1999). Rick was taking responsibility and did not blame or justify his behavior. He did not assault outside his family and had not threatened anyone or been violent in his family for 5 years, well beyond the recommended violence-free period of 12 months. He had no criminal history and had had no substance abuse issues for more than 20 years. Rick had narcissistic and PTSD traits but he was not diagnosable under *Diagnostic and Statistical Manual of Mental Disorders* (*DSM-IV;* American Psychiatric Association, 1994) criteria.

Jennie suffered from chronic PTSD (American Psychiatric Association, 1994) and was verbally abused at work and at home by her sons. She was clearly willing to heal, but unresolved traumas made it difficult to address current stressful interactions. She was not taking medication and had no substance abuse or criminal histories. Jennie had a safety plan and also knew its limits in protecting her (de Becker, 1997) if Rick was intent on violence. Meanwhile, she had assaulted Rick physically while waiting for couples therapy to begin. This behavior was assessed as an aggressive outburst and a test of Rick's commitment to nonviolence but not part of an escalating pattern of domestic abuse. Regardless, the therapist, per TSA, set clear limits about such behaviors and clarified the potential legal consequences.

They were seen as a couple, individually, and conjointly with the other observing. Avoidance and anxiety about their remaining DV issues were quickly evident as they initially focused on their children and the effects that Rick's violence and control had had on their sons and their relationships with women. The avoidance was respected as their stated needs were addressed with education provided to reorient them to the treatment goals previously set forth. Targets for reprocessing were selected, and *Safe Place* (Shapiro, 2001) and other relaxation exercises were executed, including one designed to help strengthen a sense of a secure self (Steele, 2004). Previous sessions were reassessed and deemed sufficient to reduce the need for further resource work beyond the standard options in EMDR Phase 2. Jennie's prior experiences with medical and psychotherapy professionals left her with issues that required, from time to time, crisislike interventions that extended therapy and diverted the process from stated treatment goals but remained within the flexible guidelines of both EMDR and TSA.

Reprocessing of crisis-oriented targets with EMDR Phases 3 through 8 and education and support allowed the couple to settle into the treatment. Rick slowly prepared his apology to his wife and children. As shame is a feature of many batterers (Dutton, 1995; Wallace & Nosko, 2003), and as Rick was increasingly aware of and simultaneously hurt by (Pollock, 2000) the pain he inflicted on his family, it was crucial to structure the apology so that it could be a healing experience for Rick as well.

Rick's EMDR Sessions

Rick's EMDR sessions addressed family issues related to physical abuse in childhood and ongoing emotional abuse by a parent and sibling. Other targets included his anger, his fear of not being perfect, and his own abusive behavior as a child and as an adult. The resolution of these issues seemed to provide an easier transition that allowed him to address his abuse of his wife and reduce his demeaning stance toward, and isolation from, others.

Rick's First EMDR Session

Rick reported frustration that Jennie still had PTSD symptoms saying, "It's getting kind of tiresome . . . is it really worth all this? . . . I'm kind of in a damned if I do, damned if I don't position [just as he had been while growing up]. . . . She definitely knows what she doesn't want, and I'm pretty much everything she doesn't want." He added, "She's very angry and I don't know why," while at the same time expressing conflicting awareness that "I'm not good enough and it's all my fault." Rick was presenting as a victim. Checking in, he reported a score on the Subjective Units of Disturbance (SUD) scale of 7, where 0 = No disturbance and 10 = Worst disturbance possible.

Accessing an earlier memory through the sensation (Shapiro, 2001) of frustration at "not getting it" led to an earlier experience with his father and the formulation of an earlier target, "Dad's demeanor." The imagery was of watching his father's cocky "know it all" walk: "He walks like he's better than anyone else, like he's someone special." Rick's feelings were "funny," "really funny [laughing]," "really good," "embarrassed," and "fantastic." "Having a dad like that, it really was [fantastic]. . . . Being a Roth, we were on a whole different plane in the universe. The Roth family was so superior to anyone else." (In setting up the EMDR target, the therapist refrains from providing corrective information, as he or she might when working from the TSA model.) When exploring the sensations associated with those feelings, Rick described an awareness of its being funny in his head, nausea in his stomach, and an overall tenseness in his body. His *Negative Cognitions* (NCs) were "I'm not good enough, I have to be perfect and in control" and "I am in danger." The *Positive Cognition* (PC) he chose first was "I'm far superior to what I was"; he explained this by saying, "If I met myself back then, I'd shoot him." Upon further reflection he stated, "I am an excellent person. I am learning and getting better all the time. I don't have to be perfect, it's okay to make mistakes." His score on the Validity of Cognition (VOC) scale was 6.5, where 1 = Completely invalid and 7 = Completely valid. He rated his emotional distress as 1 on the SUD.

The target, Rick's first foray into his narcissistic traits, was allowed to remain without deeper inquiry despite the higher SUD that the NC of "I am in danger" might suggest. Rick denied feeling any strong sensations when reprocessing, despite his rigid posture, clenching jaw, and tight fists. The target was reprocessed to a SUD of 0 and VOC of 7, with his PC adjusting to the awareness that he could be special in the presence of others without behaving like his father or being abusive and could feel the concurrent specialness of others. His processing also involved experiencing some insight into, and empathy for, how his and his father's behaviors were intergenerationally transmitted and learned, which then allowed forgiveness for his father and himself to follow.

Rick's Second EMDR Session

Rick chose as his next target "I need to be ahead of people"—to be first in line on the sidewalk, on the freeway, and in the grocery store. He recalled his father's speedy driving and how his father thrust his way to the front of the line, stating, "I always had to be the one everybody was following. I always had to be in front." His conflict was apparent. He knew his behavior was rude and potentially dangerous, yet it felt intensely pleasurable to be "special." His image was seeing open space in front of him on the freeway, on the sidewalk, and in the grocery store and was accompanied with the urge to simply get in front of others. His NC was "No one knows how special I am if I'm not in front." Emotions and sensations were frustration, impatience, intolerance, anger, and anxiety, and they were felt as tenseness of all his muscles and an indefinable sensation in his stomach. His SUD score now was more appropriately reported as 10. PC was "I'm good enough—right where I am." His VOC score was 4.

Therapist: (Tapping bilaterally on the client's knees).

Rick: (With some surprise) It's a nauseous feeling in my stomach.

Therapist: (Tapping bilaterally on the client's knees) Okay, go with that.

Rick: That feels better. Weird. A weird image popped into my head. It's morning and I'm sitting on my deck having my coffee. I see somebody coming down the mountain, and I think, "Ya know, if I leave right now, I'll be ahead" (laughs).

Therapist: (Tapping bilaterally on the client's knees) Notice the sensations in your body as you go with that.

Rick: That was calming. I [imagined I] just fixed myself another cup of coffee and then went off to work. I can remember times I'd get two-thirds of the way down the mountain and remember I forgot my sunglasses. (Rick is noticing that the need to be first is not always beneficial.)

Therapist: (Tapping bilaterally on the client's knees) Just go with that.

Rick: (Softly) Much more relaxing. There's a lot less tension (reflecting). I really am good enough. (Rick stopped to discuss how his father's behavior had seemed normal, and how his own behaviors now seemed "ignorant." He stated that he had flashed on several images of the past and wondered how strange it must have been for others to interact with him when he was trying to be first. The therapist guided him back to his target and solicited his SUD, which was now reported to be a 2 to 3.)

Rick: There is still something . . . that says I really am more special than anyone else.

Therapist: (Tapping bilaterally on the client's knees) Okay, go with that.

Rick: I'm still toying with that specialness.

The therapist offered a paradoxical interweave regarding Rick's conflict and the hurtful burden of being special and alone rather than common and connected to others. Rick corrected the therapist, stating, "It's a matter of not being more special than anyone else, but that we are all uniquely special." At this, the therapist offered, "Go with that."

Therapist: (Tapping bilaterally on the client's knees).

Rick: That's more realistic . . . it feels pretty good . . . in my stomach and head. I was just going over my sensations in situations like that, and now I am noticing a melting, it feels good.

He reported a SUD of 1 or "a half" and made spontaneous connections to several pleasant memories of his abusive older sister taking him to cultural activities as a younger child. Those positive memories were strengthened with more bilateral tapping. The VOC moved to 6.75. He believed he would go to 7 after some time driving or going to the grocery store. A future template application was offered, and he stated he would look forward to the potentially enjoyable experiences while grocery shopping. Subsequent assessments of this target revealed that though Rick still sometimes drove fast, it was without the compulsion to be in front and was now enjoyable. At 1-year follow-up, he laughed stating, "I even let people get in front of me."

With the additional reprocessing of his helplessness about Jennie's health and work issues, guilt at the control he had exerted on his boys, his father's specialness, and his own need to be first, Rick's defenses against sitting with the painful affect regarding his abuse of his family declined. His overall affect tolerance and empathy also increased and he became more comfortable talking directly about the harm he had done to his wife and children, how it affected them then and now, and how it interfered with their relationships with each other. He also expressed more gratitude for Jennie's mothering of their sons, because without her attentiveness, he thought, his boys would have been "even more damaged" by his behavior.

Rick's Eighth EMDR Session

Rick's first recollection of rage was of himself as a young child chasing after his dog, wanting to kill it. (The second incident, of attempting to kill his sister, had been reprocessed 5 years earlier.) The dog had entered his bedroom, where he hid from his family and soothed himself by making toy models. The dog was excited to see him and ran amok, breaking several of his models.

Therapist: (Tapping bilaterally on the client's knees and noticing his clenched jaw and pulsing neck and temple veins) How was that?

Rick: It was intense . . . kind of an out-of-body experience . . . it looked pretty scary. (He appeared scared, and Jennie, who had been observing, interjected that his jaw had been clenching and unclenching, his face turned red, and veins throbbed. Rick stated that he was not aware of this.)

Additional sets of knee taps were administered with no change in affect or picture, and though appearing present in the room, Rick seemed to be dissociated from his feelings. Based on clinical judgment and intuition, and feedback that Rick was stuck observing the boy as he chased his dog and was then punished, a *Cognitive Interweave* was offered: Rick was asked if he would go back into that memory and be with his little boy self and see what the boy felt.

Therapist: (Tapping bilaterally on the client's knees) And what do you get now?

Rick: It was comforting to know he [the boy] had someone there who understood.

Therapist: And where do you feel that comforting sensation?

Rick: (Indicating his heart) In here.

Processing continued until his affect lessened, awareness that the event was oversolidified, VOC went to 7, body scan was clear, and a future template was successfully installed.

Rick's Last EMDR Session

Rick targeted his worst and last incident of rage, "the monster in the shed." This event occurred as he and Jennie readied their home for dinner with Rick's father; this was the incident that had brought the family to therapy more than 5 years earlier. Jennie, his victim, was again present for his session. Observing the image, he said even he would be in danger from his rageful self, "the monster." Of note, Rick was now reporting feeling his feelings and was not suggesting a disconnect with or dissociation away from his feelings, which included a sense of uneasiness and shock, with tension in his jaw and facial muscles. NC was "I have no choice." In exploring his PC, Rick stated about himself as a monster, "He serves no purpose anymore, there is no reason for his existence. Before I felt I had no choices, it was the only way I could feel whole. I was heard. I was feared. I was able to express myself. Whereas I felt I couldn't otherwise. That was the only way people were going to 'get' it. But I have so many choices now." His PC was "I have massive amounts of choices."

Therapist: (Tapping bilaterally on the client's knees).

Rick: Feels safe. In my head. (Note that although Rick denied lacking safety at the target setup, he now says that he feels safe, suggesting that safety may have been an important issue. However, during EMDR reprocessing, the therapist does not confront the client about the apparent contradiction, as he or she might during TSA, but instead, simply trusts the process.)

Therapist: (Tapping bilaterally on the client's knees). Just notice that.

Rick is again clenching his jaw, his veins throb, and his body is rigid as his knees are tapped. Jennie has been watching silently, with some concern on her face, but this time does not interrupt. After a few sets, his physical symptoms subside, and he is directed back to his target paired with his emerging PC that he states is at a VOC of 6, "I have choices not to be that person anymore," and begins the body scan. He reports feeling relaxed and confident. He is asked what he would do in a similar situation in the future and reports confidence in staying calm and not escalating in anticipation of being judged by his father as "not being perfect."

Jennie's EMDR Sessions

Jennie had more incidents to reprocess than Rick had, and she scored higher overall on her respective SUD. She addressed early childhood abuse and neglect as well as the first physically abusive incident, and several others, by her husband. Like Rick, all of her processed incidents addressed current triggers and involved a future template to install new behavioral responses should any similar event occur in the future.

Small crises (off the treatment plan) were attended to from time to time, but Jennie withheld from the therapist her suicidal ideation and realistic fears of being labeled "crazy" and of being hospitalized. She had been hospitalized previously when disclosing the same to an inexperienced bachelor-level counselor. Her concerns increased as the affect associated with both working on the material and living with her ex-abuser roused her self-hate for having stayed with him. The conflict was tremendous, as she did not see her husband now as the man he was then. One-third of the way into her treatment, she disclosed that she had considered leaving treatment several times. The hospitalization incident was targeted and successfully reprocessed. The following week, after observing an accident where several male police officers stood by appearing to neglect a frail female victim, Jennie noted a shift in her response; rather than the extreme outrage she would have felt, she now experienced a calm concern and attributed this shift to her EMDR work, saying to herself, "This . . . works!" With that, she clarified her intent to continue therapy to completion.

Jennie's Eighth EMDR Session

After reprocessing Rick's first event of physical abuse that occurred after the birth of her second son, and a representational event of verbal abuse at work, Jennie chose to work on her life-threatening brain tumor and its treatment. This target appeared to have several active connections to the past and the present. Her targeted image was of being her adult self in a fetal position in bed. Her NCs were "I'm a bad person. I must have done something bad. I deserve this." Emotions were "helplessness, anger, hopelessness, sadness, and complete devastation" that was felt all over her body. She was visibly shaking. Her SUD score was at 10. Her PC was "It's over. I am a survivor. I deserve the best," with a VOC of 2.

> **Therapist:** (Tapping bilaterally on the client's knees).
>
> **Jennie:** That brought up feeling anger all over, and I'm numb in my legs.
>
> **Therapist:** (Tapping bilaterally on the client's knees) Just notice.
>
> **Jennie:** (Sobbing and rocking) Everyone thought they took care of me back then, but they didn't.

Several sets later, this target appeared to be at SUD of 0 and VOC of 7. Yet during the body scan, Jennie reported again feeling suicidal. When asked to "just notice that," she spontaneously connected with a memory of being age 7, neglected physically and emotionally, until later cared for by a female neighbor. She stated, "That's when I first thought of suicide. I thought if I kill myself, maybe they will notice me!" She reported that since that time her suicidal ideation occurred daily, sometimes with significant intensity. With several more sets of processing, she addressed questions of her own judgment of her health and messages from others that she was crazy. "They said it's all in my head." Jennie then got stuck on survivor guilt, as she is the only remaining member of her cancer support group. She felt guilty and angry that she, who was labeled "bad," was alive, but the "good" Christians were dead. It didn't make sense to her. A Cognitive Interweave was offered:

Therapist: What would you tell a little child who says, "The priest told me this happened because I was bad?"

Jennie: That's bullshit! Get another priest! (laughs).

Therapist: (Tapping bilaterally on the client's knees) Go with that.

Jennie: (Pulling out the learning benefits) It [the brain tumor] changed my life. I gave up a lucrative career where I was always gone 60 to 80 hours a week, and I never saw my boys. It led me into knowing I was in a battering relationship, I didn't even know it. It actually opened up a lot of doors.

Therapist: (Tapping bilaterally on the client's knees) Just notice that.

Jennie: (Feeling stuck and referring to her anger) It just won't go away. Why am I still dealing with this?

Therapist: Is there anything you would like to say to it?

Jennie: Yea, I want to say, f_____ you, and give it the bird.

Therapist: (Tapping bilaterally on the client's knees) Go with that.

Jennie: Okay . . . hmm . . . cool! I told it to f_____ off and go away, but I thanked it for changing my life.

Processing then swiftly proceeded to a SUD score of 0 and VOC of 7 related to being a strong survivor, able to trust her judgment, knowing her brain tumor treatment and her childhood were over, and that she is a good person and deserving of life. When asked at the following session what she got when she brought up "brain tumor," she expressed surprise at not having experienced any of the suicidal ideation that had previously been evident on a daily basis.

Therapy of Social Action Family Therapy Focus Resumes

Once their targets and current triggers were addressed and new behavioral responses were installed, the TSA focus was resumed. Rick was ready to apologize to his family. Their now adult sons who had long ago opted out of their own individual treatment were asked to attend an extended session and came willingly. Each shared their recall of Rick's emotional and physical abuse of their mother and some of the emotional and physical abuse they had experienced at that time.

The family was then strategically posed such that Jennie sat across from Rick, with her sons, Aaron and Rick Jr., flanking her. Rick first apologized to Jennie for abusing her from the day they began to go steady in high school. He apologized for interfering with the right Jennie had to a close and loving relationship with her sons, for making her feel she was crazy, stupid, or unlovable, and for making her feel afraid of him. He culminated in promising to spend the rest of his life being the husband she always deserved, celebrating each day together, doing everything in his power to ensure she knew she was treasured and loved. Jennie, from whom nothing was asked per TSA instructions, accepted his apology and kissed him. Rick continued with separate apologies to each of his sons.

Debriefing with the family after the apology, Rick shared his fears that they could have rejected his efforts and his belief that they would have had that right. During the process, the boys had maintained physical contact with their mother and unbroken and vigilant visual contact with their father. Rick Jr. thoughtfully expressed that he could not recall ever having felt so light in his body, and was amazed by the process. He noted that he was rapidly making "so many connections" between the ways he was raised and how he conducted himself in relationships with women. The therapist again joined the family and strengthened Rick Jr.'s emerging perceptions that he could change his dating behaviors and also resume the close relationship he had once enjoyed with his mother. He agreed; he had still not removed his hand from his mother since the apology had begun. The family was encouraged that they could now reorient to a safe and abuse-free dynamic. Aaron stated he felt loved and connected, and he rose, gathering his family for a hug.

In the couple's follow-up session, each reported that the family was doing well. Jennie thought her sons were closer and that the elder was initiating more contact with the younger. It was as she had always hoped. She felt secure in her choice of staying with her husband and softened considerably when asked how things were going with them. Rick was grateful for his family and revealed that he was opening up more to men he had previously considered to be only acquaintances. Although the benefits of therapy offered to each of the adult children were not acted on, it appeared that the family was in a good place to stop treatment.

As a courtesy, Rick's and Jennie's comments are included. Although their 4 months of therapy were spread over a 6-month period, they stated that due to the strong affect they each experienced, they would likely have dropped out if sessions were not structured, led, and contained by the therapist, or if sessions had been limited to 50 minutes. Sessions were $1\frac{1}{2}$ to 2 hours, and up to 4 hours long when conducted back to back, allowing time for more complete processing and debriefing as their issues warranted. They reported that the therapist's qualities of warmth, genuineness, congruence, sense of humor, and confidence in the efficacy of EMDR and the therapeutic process inspired trust and a willingness to stay when therapy became difficult. The couple also stressed that they were able to reduce avoidance when reprocessing, as the EMDR target work-up was written on a white board for their easy view.

DISCUSSION

TSA and EMDR appear to be a powerful combination for the treatment of DV. When used with carefully selected couples, EMDR and TSA can repair the damage caused to the victims, strengthen relationships, inhibit abuser and victim tendencies in children, eliminate PTSD, increase personal responsibility, develop nonviolent conflict resolution skills, and increase empathy for self and others.

EMDR effectively reprocesses individual traumas, simplifies resolution of current issues, and provides alternative behavioral options for the future. It strengthens the likelihood that an abuser will voluntarily continue in TSA treatment. TSA provides a context for EMDR treatment by facilitating the abuser's sense of responsibility, thereby increasing the victim's safety. EMDR and TSA clear the way for the perpetrator's progression from a shameful to a more responsible recall of his past behaviors and can increase his self-esteem more rapidly for the same reason. Reducing shame will make it more likely that the abuser can tolerate negative affect in the presence of the victim, fulfill the TSA apologizing steps, and participate in an appropriate reorganization of the family. Utilizing EMDR and TSA together is an ethical choice to reduce the intergenerational transmission of domestic violence and its associated behaviors.

In working with those affected by domestic violence, there are numerous cautions and safeguards to consider. Most important, the primary goal of working with domestically violent families is to promote safety. In a perfect world, treatment would be administered under an umbrella of a "coordinated community response" (Murphy, Musser, & Maton, 1998) with specialists in domestic violence treating Rick, Jennie, and their children quickly and effectively.

Domestic violence as a label has no corresponding diagnosis in the *DSM-IV* (American Psychiatric Association, 1994). However it results in mental and physical harm and can culminate in homicide or suicide, warranting adequate training and supervision of treating therapists so that they are competently operating within their scope of practice and standards of care. A variety of issues that the therapist should attend to include safety planning, the handling of the client's transferential issues, the therapist's countertransference, and the hairpin turns that treatment can take as life outside the sessions impacts the therapeutic process. Consultation and supervision are recommended for inexperienced therapists. An introductory course in domestic violence does not provide the necessary levels of skill in assessment and treatment that these potentially lethal couples deserve.

Harway and Hansen's (1993) study underscores the need for adequate therapist DV education. Two vignettes were reviewed and assessed by members of the American Association for Marriage and Family Therapy. The results for one vignette concluded that 40% of therapists failed to address the issue of a couple's violence; 91% of the therapists who did identify the violence minimized it. Further, 55% of those therapists *would not intervene,* and only 11% said they would seek immediate help for the victim. Sadly, 14% incorrectly diagnosed the issue of violence as one of communication. The other vignette was based on a true-life couple where homicide of the female occurred. In this vignette, only eight (2%) of the 362 respondents correctly anticipated the husband's lethality.

DV is largely transmitted intergenerationally, and this chapter presents one option for effective and comprehensive treatment not only for the victim and the perpetrator, but for their children as well. These methods are also likely to produce results when the women are perpetrators and the men are victims, when there is "mutual" violence, and within same-sex couples. Although the treatment suggested can facilitate healing, early intervention with batterers, their victims, and their victim children will prevent much suffering and may interrupt the intergenerational transmission of violence.

As families with intergenerational histories of violence have complex issues that permeate much of their lives, it is recommended that parties maintain some connection to their EMDR and TSA work posttreatment. That may involve checking in with their treatment provider, attendance at 12-step programs, or other growth-oriented activities where accountability is a key feature.

REFERENCES

American Psychiatric Association. (1994). *Diagnostic and statistical manual of mental disorders* (4th ed.). Washington, DC: Author.

American Psychiatric Association. (2004). *Practice guideline for the treatment of patients with acute stress disorder and posttraumatic stress disorder.* Arlington, VA: American Psychiatric Association Practice Guidelines.

American Psychological Association. (1996). *Violence and the family.* Washington, DC: Author.

Becvar, D. S., & Becvar, R. J. (1988). *Family therapy: A systemic integration.* Boston: Allyn & Bacon.

Berry, D. B. (1995). *The domestic violence sourcebook.* Los Angeles: Lowell House.

Bograd, M., & Mederos, F. (1999). Battering and couples therapy: Universal screening and selection of treatment modality. *Journal of Marital and Family Therapy, 25,* 291–312.

Cattaneo, L. B., & Goodman, L. A. (2003). Victim-reported risk factors for continued abusive behavior: Assessing the dangerousness of arrested batterers. *Journal of Community Psychology, 31,* 349–369.

Cervantes, N. N. (1993). Therapist duty in domestic violence cases: Ethical considerations. In M. Hansen & M. Harway (Eds.), *Battering and family therapy* (pp. 147–155). Newbury Park, CA: Sage.

Cooley, C. S., & Severson, K. (1993). Establishing feminist systemic criteria for viewing violence and alcoholism. In M. Hansen & M. Harway (Eds.), *Battering and family therapy* (pp. 42–53). Newbury Park, CA: Sage.

de Becker, G. (1997). *The gift of fear.* New York: Little, Brown.

Dutton, D. G. (1995). *The batterer: A psychological profile.* New York: Basic Books.

Dutton, D. G. (1998). *The abusive personality: Violence and control in intimate relationships.* New York: Guilford Press.

Edmond, T., Rubin, A., & Wambach, K. G. (1999). The effectiveness of EMDR with adult survivors of child sexual abuse. *Social Work Research, 23,* 103–117.

Grant, M., & Threlfo, C. (2002). EMDR in the treatment of chronic pain. *Journal of Clinical Psychology, 58,* 1501–1520.

Green, R. J., & Framo, J. L. (1981). Introduction to structural family therapy. In R. Green & J. Framo (Eds.), *Family therapy* (pp. 443–444). New York: International Universities Press.

Hart, B. (1990). *Assessing whether batterers will kill.* St. Paul: Minnesota Center Against Violence and Abuse. Retrieved November 6, 2005, from http://www.mincava.umn.edu/documents /hart/hart.html.

Harway, M., & Hansen, M. (1993). Therapist perceptions of family violence. In M. Hansen & M. Harway (Eds.), *Battering and family therapy* (pp. 42–53). Newbury Park, CA: Sage.

Herman, J. (1997). *Trauma and recovery.* New York: Basic Books.

Jacobson, W. B. (2000). *Safe from the start: Taking action on children exposed to violence.* Washington, DC: U.S. Department of Justice, Office of Juvenile Justice and Delinquency Prevention. Retrieved July 2, 2004, from http://www.ncjrs.org/pdffiles1/ojjdp/182789.pdf.

Jaffe, P. G., Wolfe, D. A., & Wilson, S. K. (1990). *Children of battered women.* Newbury Park, CA: Sage.

Kaslow, F. W. (1982). History of family therapy in the United States: A kaleidoscopic overview. In F. Kaslow (Ed.), *The international book of family therapy* (pp. 5–37). New York: Brunner/Mazel.

Kwong, M. J., Bartholomew, K., Henderson, A. J., & Trinke, S. J. (2003). The intergenerational transmission of relationship violence. *Journal of Family Violence, 17*(3), 288–301.

LaViolette, A. D., & Barnett, O. W. (2000). *It can happen to anyone: Why battered women stay.* Thousand Oaks, CA: Sage.

Madanes, C. (1981). *Strategic family therapy.* San Francisco: Jossey-Bass.

Madanes, C. (1990). *Sex, love, and violence.* New York: Norton.

Madanes, C. (1995). *The violence of men.* San Francisco: Jossey-Bass.

Maxwell, J. P. (2002). The imprint of child physical and emotional abuse: A case study on the use of EMDR to address anxiety and a lack of self-esteem. *Journal of Family Violence, 18,* 281–293.

McMulin, T. (1998). Combining EMDR with relapse prevention programs to enhance treatment outcomes with sex offenders. *EMDRIA Newsletter, 3*(2), 20–24.

McNamara, M. R., & Dhami, M. K. (2003, June). *The role of apology in restorative justice.* Paper presented at the 6th International Conference on Restorative Justice, Vancouver, British Columbia, Canada.

Minuchin, S. (1974). *Families and family therapy.* Cambridge, MA: Harvard University Press.

Murphy, C. M., Musser, P. H., & Maton, K. I. (1998). Coordinated community intervention for domestic abusers: Intervention system involvement and criminal recidivism. *Journal of Family Violence, 13,* 263–284.

Peterman, L. M., & Dixon, C. G. (2001). Assessment and evaluation of men who batter women. *Journal of Rehabilitation, 67*(4), 38–42.

Pollock, P. H. (2000). Eye movement desensitization and reprocessing (EMDR) for post-traumatic stress disorder (PTSD) following homicide. *Journal of Forensic Psychiatry, 11,* 176–184.

Rennison, C. M., & Welchans, S. (2000). *Bureau of Justice special report: Intimate partner violence.* Washington, DC: U.S. Department of Justice, Office of Justice Programs. Retrieved July 2, 2004, from http://www.ojp.usdoj.gov/bjs/pub/pdf/ipv.pdf.

Rosen, K. H., Matheson, J. L., Stith, S. M., McCollum, E. E., & Locke, L. D. (2003). Negotiated time-out: A de-escalation tool for couples. *Journal of Marital and Family Therapy, 29,* 291–298.

Shapiro, F. (1995). *Eye movement desensitization and reprocessing: Basic principles, protocols and procedures.* New York: Guilford Press.

Shapiro, F. (2001). *Eye movement desensitization and reprocessing: Basic principles, protocols and procedures* (2nd ed.). New York: Guilford Press.

Shapiro, F., & Maxfield, L. (2002). Eye movement desensitization and reprocessing (EMDR): Information processing in the treatment of trauma. *Journal of Clinical Psychology, 58,* 933–946.

Sonkin, D. J., & Dutton, D. G. (2003). Treating assaultive men from an attachment perspective. In D. Dutton & D. Sonkin (Eds.), *Intimate violence: Contemporary treatment innovations* (pp. 105–134). New York: Haworth Maltreatment and Trauma Press.

Steele, A. (2004). *Developing a secure self: An approach to working with attachment in adults.* Gabriola Island, British Columbia, Canada: Author.

Stowasser, J. E. (2001). *The packet: An integrated handbook for perpetrators and victims of domestic violence.* San Luis Obispo, California: Author.

Waldo, M. (1987). Also victims: Understanding and treating men arrested for spouse abuse. *Journal of Counseling and Development, 65,* 385–388.

Walker, L. (1979). *The battered woman.* New York: Harper & Row.

Walker, L. (1989). *Terrifying love.* New York: Harper & Row.

Walker, L. (1994). *Abused women and survivor therapy.* Washington, DC: American Psychological Association.

Wallace, R., & Nosko, A. (2003). Shame in male spouse abusers and its treatment in group therapy. In D. Dutton & D. Sonkin (Eds.), *Intimate violence: Contemporary treatment innovations* (pp. 47–74). New York: Haworth Maltreatment and Trauma Press.

PART IV

Child and Family Problems

CHAPTER 13

Complex Separation, Individuation Processes, and Anxiety Disorders in Young Adulthood

Laura Rocchietta Tofani

In family systems theory, an individual's passage through young adulthood is a crucial phase in the family life cycle (McGoldrick, Gerson, & Shellenberger, 1999). This development phase can be isolating, and many forms of psychopathology are considered to have their onset during this period of life. In young adulthood, the individual goes through a process of separation and individuation, which involve tasks for himself or herself and the multigenerational family system. These include developing an autonomous boundary system and mature patterns of interaction that allow the youth to become more responsible and self-directed, with a more stable sense of self. The young adult can then pursue intimacy versus isolation in relationships outside the family of origin, create emotional bonds without fear of rejection or fusion, and develop new self-regulatory schemas of action for a wholly independent life. In addition, as the young adult separates and individuates, the family system must change. Older generations (i.e., parents and relatives with a parenting role) must renegotiate their interpersonal relationships.

In many cultures, people continue the process of differentiation throughout their entire life span. However, the leaving-home phase is the most delicate one because a good outcome makes a significant difference on an individual's subsequent psychological development (Cancrini & La Rosa, 1991). Any therapeutic intervention in the leaving-home phase must have the purpose of helping a young person develop the tools for this important leap. At the family level, some complex family emotional forces can interfere with this leap, such as family projection processes, sense of loyalty toward family myths, and family patterns passed down through generations (Neill & Kniskern, 1982). The family projection process was conceptualized by Bowen (1978) as occurring when parents project part of their immaturity onto one or more of their children. The child who is the object of the projection is thought to develop a lower level of differentiation of self.

In families with moderately dysfunctional patterns (Beavers & Voeller, 1981), young family members in the leaving-home phase may develop neurotic symptoms, including anxiety disorders with phobic and obsessive symptoms. Research has shown that anxiety in children is highly influenced by parenting style, perception of family support (Rapee & Melville, 1997), and family relational patterns.

Social Anxiety Disorder (American Psychiatric Association, 1994) is considered to be a common disorder in young adults. Its onset typically occurs during adolescence, and it is the third most prevalent psychiatric disorder, following substance abuse and depression (Kessler et al., 1994); it increases a patient's lifetime risk of depression approximately fourfold (Schneier, Johnson, Hornig, Liebowitz, & Weisman, 1992). Symptoms can be triggered by the requirements of this developmental phase, which necessitates movement toward autonomy in many aspects. Social Anxiety Disorder is characterized by a marked or persistent fear of one or more social or performance situations and preoccupation with possible embarrassment and humiliation. Exposure to the feared social situation provokes anxiety, which may take the form of a situationally predisposed panic attack. The avoidance, anxious anticipation, or distress in the feared social or performance situation interferes significantly with the person's occupational or relational functioning, or there is marked distress about having the phobia. It is severely debilitating and demoralizing over time.

According to Shapiro's (1995, 2001) Adaptive Information Processing model, a neurotic symptomatic situation in a young adult with an unfinished separation process may be connected to unresolved separations and other past traumas. Moreover, many patients report that their phobia began in response to a specific embarrassing and traumatic experience (Schneier et al., 1992), resulting in a more or less severe impact on mental states and a related inability to face the new developmental stage.

Research and Clinical Evidence

In family systems research, many studies have reached the same conclusion: The development and transmission of anxiety within a family derive from a lack of individuation in family members (Namyslowska & Siewierska, 1994). Families with an identified patient in the anxiety spectrum of disorders present with enmeshment and tend to distribute psychological tension in one or more "emotional triangles" (Oppenheimer & Frey, 1993). The concept of triangles was introduced by Bowen (1978), who proposed that when anxiety increases between two family members, a vulnerable third person is predictably recruited into the system to reduce anxiety levels.

Authors have reported parental metacommunications instructing the anxious young adult to avoid explorative behavior that the parents consider dangerous; consequently the young adult learns to act independently only in those areas that his or her parents consider safe (Rapee & Melville, 1997). In these families, interactions among family members focus on controlling emotions to avoid both interpersonal and intrapersonal conflict (Laurent, 2000). Attachment theories support similar findings: Children with anxious attachment are thought to have anxious mothers, who are characterized as intrusive and highly controlling and available to the child only at certain times (Crittenden, 1997).

Ugazio (1998) described a specific family relational pattern in which the mother encourages independence and personal autonomy in other family members, while developing a fused relationship with the phobic-anxious child that is based on the mother's emotional needs. So the child is in a double bind: A strong protective relationship with the mother makes him feel safe and loved but not self-confident, whereas being more independent satisfies his self-esteem but increases his anxiety, as he feels unprotected when he is outside the important bond.

Treatment

At both an individual and a family level, it is important for the therapist to work on these two polarities: the child's need for protection (with risk of low self-esteem) versus the need for independence (accompanied by fear of new situations). These are the two mental schemas that permeate the child and his or her extended family's mental world.

The clinical effectiveness of Eye Movement Desensitization and Reprocessing (EMDR; Shapiro, 2001) with Anxiety Disorders and Panic Disorder is supported by multiple observations and research (Feske, 1998; Goldstein & Feske, 1994; Shapiro & Forrest, 1997). EMDR therapy is appropriate for treating anxiety syndromes because it addresses traumas in the attachment relational patterns and the unprocessed anxiety-promoting memories that underlie anxious thoughts, feelings, and behaviors in the young adult (to better understand how "states become traits," see Perry, Pollard, Blakely, Baker, & Vigilante, 1995). Reports and clinical experience have also supported the use of a specific EMDR protocol for anxious-phobic individuals (Shapiro, 1999). The related 11-step phobia protocol includes the standard eight steps (Shapiro, 1995) plus phases developed to address anticipatory anxiety and avoidance behavior. More specifically, EMDR has shown effective results in clinical practice with performance anxiety (Foster & Lendl, 1996), test anxiety (Maxfield & Melnyk, 2000), social phobias (Smith & Poole, 2002), and Generalized Anxiety Disorder (Lazarus & Lazarus, 2002).

The Power of Integration

The integration of family systems therapy and EMDR can maximize outcome, with each approach providing a specific contribution (Shapiro, 2002) according to its potential. Family therapy identifies and treats the dysfunctional family patterns that impact self-image and identity development (Shotter & Gergen, 1989). EMDR reprocesses the elements of overwhelming events, creating change in the individual. EMDR can help in defining and treating the intrapersonal cognitive and emotional conflicts and personal affect dysregulation in the identified patient *that cannot be addressed as well at a family level.*

THERAPY PROCESS

Recursive Help in a Double-Level Intervention

Family systems therapy and EMDR are integrated in the treatment of young adults with complex separation problems to modify structural aspects, defenses, and responses of the individual and the family. These two approaches induce individual and family change *in a recursive way* (Siegel, 1999), so that each influences the other in a circular fashion. In fact, the aim of integrating family therapy and EMDR is to accelerate change by creating an *impact wave* between the dynamics and outcomes of the two forms of therapy. To obtain such an *impact wave* effect, the therapist interweaves sessions considering the specific contributions and resources of each therapeutic approach. These concepts are discussed next.

Family systems therapy and EMDR share two important purposes. First, both approaches promote self-awareness and self-responsibility and allow the individual and the family to move in a *self-regulatory way* in directions chosen by the system. Second, both work on integrating emotions and cognition. In fact, in Experiential Family Therapy, cognitive and emotional "self-awareness often brings about an integration of fragmented or unfinished aspects of the Self that have been outside awareness" (Piercy & Sprenkle, 1986, p. 56). Therefore, family systems therapy and EMDR have different potentials and can complement each other, realizing both interpersonal and intrapsychic goals with a real integration of both approaches and not only a conjoint use (Malagoli Togliatti & Rocchietta Tofani, 2002).

In this integrated treatment procedure, family therapy follows the experiential family systems therapy approach (Giat Roberto, 1992; Napier & Whitaker, 1978), with elements of multigenerational and Structural Family Therapy styles (Bowen, 1978; Minuchin & Fishman, 1992). Therefore, it includes such techniques as working on the genogram and emotional triangles, exploring family myths, and restructuring boundaries and roles. Experiential Family Therapy has been shown to be particularly helpful in families with a young adult who is transitioning out of the home, because it emphasizes the importance of personal choices and awareness of the ongoing process of individuation and the young person's responsibility and competence (Neill & Kniskern, 1982). Therapy focuses on unlocking direct emotional expression, stimulating expanded experience within the family, and promoting self-disclosure among family members to break rigid cycles of automatic behaviors and to change the family myth about family unity.

The family systems treatment techniques are designed to promote individuation, reestablish proper emotional and organizational boundaries between generations, and treat family reactions to separation and unresolved emotional issues between the young adult and his or her family of origin. Family therapy techniques based on psychological detriangulation (Bowen, 1978) are also used.

The EMDR standard protocol is followed. The eight phases are utilized together with the three-pronged principles (processing past experiences contributing to dysfunction, processing present triggers, and developing imaginal templates of skills and behaviors for more adaptive future action). Targets are chosen that connect with anxiety-promoting materials or aspects of unsatisfactory relational patterns. EMDR contains various elements of cognitive and emotional processing that are thought to be clinically effective. These include identification of the sensory effects of the trauma and separating them from the affective interpretations of these sensations, free associations, elicitation of information and insight, guided imagery creation, and dismissal of imagery. One of the phases of the phobia protocol (Shapiro, 1999), the proactive future template, is often used.

Minor modifications were introduced in administering EMDR inside the integrated procedure. Establishing an appropriate therapeutic relationship, assessment of the entire clinical picture, and reevaluation of behavioral changes are often carried out during family therapy sessions or are enriched by elements derived from family observations. Emotional and cognitive resources are also identified in the exchanges between family members.

Alternating different types of therapy sessions is already common in family therapy, mainly with adolescents and young adults. This is done to promote individuation and separation, with a shift from individual modalities to family modalities, which can be offered concurrently (maintaining a systemic frame of reference or combining individual and family approaches). In the integrated approach, there are frequent switches from family sessions to individual EMDR sessions. This technique can be particularly effective, with the therapeutic effect being amplified if the therapist manages to transfer key contents from the family context to the individual one and vice versa in such a way that an impact wave is caused on the two clinical situations. Moreover, the therapist pays careful attention to time the switch according to emerging therapeutically relevant needs.

CASE EXAMPLE

The following case example illustrates this process (see also Figure 13.1). The treatment consisted of family sessions and individual EMDR sessions. The time interval between individual sessions was 7 to 10 days and between family sessions was 15 to 20 days over a total time period of almost 10 months.

A Family in Transition

This case concerns a young adult in the leaving-home developmental phase who presented with panic reactions and an anxious depressive mood as part of a generalized social phobia. The 20-year-old young woman, Joanne, was diagnosed with Generalized Social Phobia (*International Statistical Classification of Diseases,* 10th revision, World Health Organization, 2005) also called Social Anxiety Disorder (*Diagnostic and Statistical Manual of Mental Disorders,* fourth edition, American Psychiatric Association, 1994). It appeared that her severe loss of autonomy was secondary to her fear of sensory responses, such as trembling, dizziness, palpitations, and panic, and to her anxious anticipation of

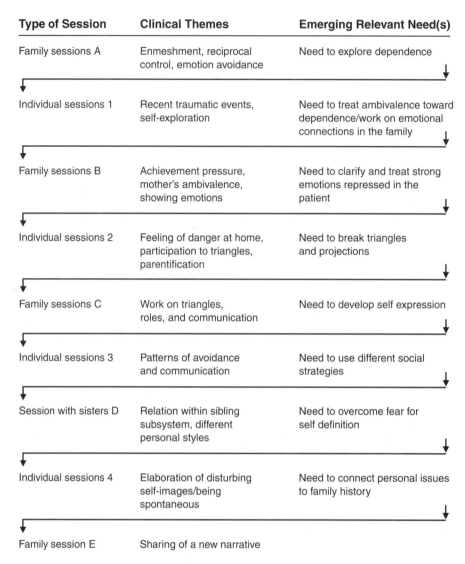

Type of Session	Clinical Themes	Emerging Relevant Need(s)
Family sessions A	Enmeshment, reciprocal control, emotion avoidance	Need to explore dependence
Individual sessions 1	Recent traumatic events, self-exploration	Need to treat ambivalence toward dependence/work on emotional connections in the family
Family sessions B	Achievement pressure, mother's ambivalence, showing emotions	Need to clarify and treat strong emotions repressed in the patient
Individual sessions 2	Feeling of danger at home, participation to triangles, parentification	Need to break triangles and projections
Family sessions C	Work on triangles, roles, and communication	Need to develop self expression
Individual sessions 3	Patterns of avoidance and communication	Need to use different social strategies
Session with sisters D	Relation within sibling subsystem, different personal styles	Need to overcome fear for self definition
Individual sessions 4	Elaboration of disturbing self-images/being spontaneous	Need to connect personal issues to family history
Family session E	Sharing of a new narrative	

Figure 13.1   Schema summarizing the interconnection of type of sessions, clinical themes and therapeutic relevant need(s). The arrow shows how the appropriate type of session is determined by the emerging relevant therapeutic need(s).

distress, helplessness, and embarrassment. Her personality appeared to be organized around her social phobias.

Family Therapy

The family genogram (Figure 13.2) summarizes the family structure and the quality of family relationships. Joanne's father died when she was 6. Joanne lived with her mother and two sisters and was very close to her maternal grandmother, great-grandmother, and aunt. The seven women lived in two apartments on the same level of a large country house. Often the three girls stayed with their relatives, moving back and forth between their mother's

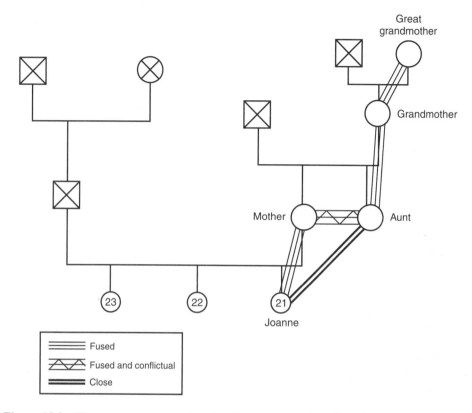

Figure 13.2   The genogram summarizes family structure and quality of relationships.

apartment and their grandmother's apartment. Individuation was not easy in this four-generation female family, because the older generations had the habit of monitoring every matter. All four generations went on summer vacations together, and everybody knew everything about the others. Joanne's sisters attended university and came home on weekends, as Joanne was beginning to do in her first year away from home.

The three girls were each in the leaving-home phase of the family life cycle, but when her family came to therapy, Joanne had developed in a short time such rapid regression in autonomy and self-reliance that she seemed completely stuck. In fact, at the onset of therapy she was sleeping again in her mother's bed and sought her mother's assistance with her schoolwork, just as she had done at the age of 16, when she had suffered from depression. Joanne had experienced anxiety or panic reactions for the 2 months prior to therapy. After she failed a university exam, she began avoiding public places and social situations and refused to leave the house for fear of panic reactions. Other symptoms included generalized anxiety, difficulty falling asleep, withdrawal, and depressive thoughts such as "I'm worth nothing." Joanne's family had such an epistemology, or philosophy of life, that they could not accept and understand how a relatively small failure (the exam) could be followed by symptoms they characterized as "weakness."

The following headings describe the interconnection of types of sessions described in Figure 13.1.

Family Sessions A

All seven family members attended the first three sessions. Family therapy techniques were used to develop an understanding of major dysfunctional patterns of interpersonal relations. These included family mapping, home assignments, and circular questioning, in which each individual was asked the same question. The family pattern, dynamic, and multigenerational history were assessed in the first three family sessions conducted with the extended family. The main foci included:

- *Structural problems:* The boundaries among family members were enmeshed and blurred, with fused boundaries between Joanne and her mother and a diffused parenting role among mother, aunt, and grandmother.

- *Problems connected to interpersonal images:* Joanne's self-image was that of a weak and sick person. During adolescence, she had received treatment for an anxious depressive mood. The family thought of itself as composed of very strong and independent women except for Joanne, who was regarded as too sensitive, as her deceased father was also regarded. In addition, in the initial assessment of symptoms, it was reported that Joanne's mother also suffered from anxiety attacks, with peaks at specific moments. Consequently, the adults in the family, fearful that this would also be Joanne's destiny, reinforced Joanne's self-image.

- *Communication:* Communication was based on avoidance of any conflict and open confrontation. Joanne particularly avoided expressing feelings and ideas, covertly controlling reactions of the other members during family therapy sessions. The family sent a double message, primarily to Joanne: on one hand, to stay focused on self-expression and realization; on the other hand, to suppress all individual needs that were inconsistent with the "family identity." Joanne showed more spontaneity in individual sessions than she did in family sessions, which was a sign of her difficulty in individuation within the family context, but also a sign of her positive attitude toward therapy.

- *Family life cycle and multigenerational patterns:* The family was in the leaving-home developmental phase of the family life cycle. The difficulty with separation of the youngest and weakest member seemed to cause significant anxiety for Joanne's mother and an anxious-depressive mood in Joanne. The genogram revealed a pattern of strong alliance between the mother of every generation and her youngest daughter. Joanne's mother expressed the danger she attached to the situation when she said that there was an urgent need to solve Joanne's difficulties in studying and being independent because otherwise the problem itself would become like a "gangrene" that destroys an organism.

In accordance with family systems concepts, at the end of the first three family sessions, problems were reframed with reference to family life developmental change. The following positive restructuring definition was given to the family:

> It is not Joanne's personal problem, but a family challenge. It is difficult for her to differentiate, find her own way, and leave home in a family with such close connections and with an important loss in her past. It is also not easy because the family has difficulties in blessing a daughter who is so different from the others. Plus there is such a strong feeling of danger, both in Joanne and the mother. . . . This is really a family challenge.

According to experiential family systems concepts, this reframing was conceived to set a family goal connected to the emotional field and to underline the sense of unity while introducing the idea of autonomy and pointing out the importance of family choices and responsibility.

Individual Sessions 1

Joanne was offered a separate space to explore family realities; this allowed for a better definition of personal boundaries, which was considered important both for the development of individuation and the treatment of her anxiety. The goals of Joanne's individual therapy were to determine the root of the diffused interpersonal boundaries in the family and to address her emerging need to explore her independence.

In the first of three individual sessions, Joanne spoke about the importance, for her and her family, of being intelligent and always proper; her feelings of inadequacy in comparison with her sisters; her anxiety related to future exams; and her fears of leaving the house and attending university because of panic reactions. The problems of impotence, low self-esteem, and guilt about not meeting expectations coexisted. Joanne colluded with family projections of herself as the weak member, and her everyday function was highly impaired. However, her family expected a quick resolution, so individual treatment with EMDR was proposed.

In her first EMDR session, Joanne worked on her exam failure, the target being the scene "Professors laughing at me." She recalled the moment when professors kept teasing her, saying that she "should have known." This target was accompanied by a *Negative Cognition* (NC) of "being always unable" and a preferred *Positive Cognition* (PC) of "being more able to react." Her score on the Validity of Cognition (VOC) scale was 2, where 1 represents untrue and 7 represents completely true. On the Subjective Units of Disturbance (SUD) scale she rated her distress at 8, where 0 represents no distress and 10 severe distress. Joanne identified physical sensations of pressure in her chest and sweating hands.

During processing, Joanne worked on the image of herself as speechless and almost fainting in front of her teachers. Ambivalent feelings emerged: a mixture of anger and shame. These gradually began fading as Joanne recalled other events characterized by the same mixed feelings, where she had not been considered or protected and where her image of herself had been threatened. She disclosed that avoidance or giving up was the strategy she typically used to cope with such distressing situations.

In reprocessing the main target, Joanne "discovered" her dependency on the "opinion of important adults," revealed by thoughts like the following: "I was angry at the teachers. . . . They did not help me. . . . I feel attacked by adult people not helping me." Her images went back to situations in which she made comparisons between herself and her sisters. In a flash, she developed a "mental link." She had the perception that her mother protected and controlled her too much, but also that she, Joanne, wanted to be protected, an unending loop.

During the EMDR desensitization phase, with its free association and elicitation of insight, a reconfiguration of internal connections began to take shape: "I did my best. . . . I can make a mess but I can try to handle things. . . . I can learn to do better." At the end of the session, Joanne ran a mental videotape of possible future actions in situations similar to the one reprocessed in the target. She expressed relief and reported a SUD score of 0 to 1.

During reprocessing, other issues had emerged. For example, Joanne caught a glimpse of a specific feeling of danger for herself: "In my family I cannot show how I feel. . . . Both if I am well and if I feel bad, I feel uneasy." It was decided to work on this issue in a subsequent EMDR session. Joanne processed this and other related targets in later individual sessions.

Other elements were identified as more appropriate to be addressed in subsequent family sessions. These included the sense of duty and high expectations on everybody in the family, Joanne's need to become independent and follow personal paths, and roles played by Joanne in the family network.

Nuclear Family Sessions B

The choice to switch to a family setting was due to two particular factors. First, exchanging personal feedback, being "blessed" to evolve in your own way, and emotional connections with family members are typical family issues. Second, Joanne had worked on herself and it was important to share some of her changes with family members to support her emotional change by stimulating a "circular exchange." In experiential family systems therapy, this is accomplished by coaching family members to experience each other more directly and enhancing self-disclosure among participants, which also favors directness. Three family sessions were conducted with only Joanne, her mother, aunt, and sisters to articulate a clear boundary around the nuclear family, which was understood as including the aunt.

During these family sessions, they discussed the mother's belief "My daughters can realize themselves as they want, but they *must realize* themselves and always be very active." This revealed a dimension of subtle control in the family and undefined boundaries. Moreover, this family philosophy expressed a very dichotomous way of thinking (all black or white, well-defined values) that was evidently connected to anxiety around self-realization.

The therapist kept the focus on emotional issues and coached Joanne's mother to talk about her perception of herself in the family of origin. She explained that although she was very connected to and supported by her family, she also felt controlled by them. This was recognized by Joanne as the same ambivalent emotions about her mother's control that she had discovered during EMDR. She recognized herself in this mixture of feelings and connected her emotional states to family ones. The therapist assisted the members in perceiving emotions about personal constraint in the family network. For instance, Joanne's two sisters spoke about how each had felt pressured and compared to the other, with the family promoting a spirit of competition.

Everybody was encouraged to collaborate in thinking of new ways to exert less reciprocal judgment, as well as less interference around Joanne. Joanne's sisters had the task of going out on Saturday nights and leaving Joanne at home alone, as she wanted, without making comments about her choice. This could make a big difference to Joanne because in her family, not to be willing to go out was considered a sign of psychological retreat and looked at with anxiety.

Individual Sessions 2

At this point, the family sessions had highlighted and developed issues that could be best treated at an individual level. In fact, it was important to help Joanne explore and clarify for herself which strong emotions she was controlling, or at least not expressing, and which ones caused her anxiety. At the beginning of the next two individual sessions, Joanne indicated that she was now able to sleep by herself and to concentrate more on studying. She said that she was willing to go out of the house but still preferred to stay with her sisters. She was uncomfortable about going to university classes and felt uneasy about meeting new people and participating in a group, which were long-standing problems. Joanne explained that she had never had a boyfriend, even though boys had approached her.

The therapist proposed EMDR to reprocess the theme about feeling uneasy and in danger in the house. The chosen target was the emotional and cognitive perception of danger. During EMDR stimulation, Joanne brought up a specific thought, "If I speak, I take sides and I am lost," which initially seemed to be disconnected from other aspects. As the processing continued, this thought connected to feelings of anxiety and powerlessness, as in the following: "I feel overcome by people, I don't know why. . . . I cannot have people suffering because of me." She recalled the time of her father's death and how she had thought, "I have to work it out and not to make a mess in the house."

At that point, a vivid image came up. Joanne recalled a traumatic scene that occurred many years before, when her aunt and grandmother tried to prevent her mother from going to a party with colleagues from work by accusing her of abandoning her daughters. All the adults began to throw things at each other, including glasses, in front of Joanne and her sisters. Joanne recalled trying to calm down all of the adults or, at least, feeling this was her responsibility.

Processing this episode as a target, focusing mainly on the moment of the fight and the screaming and shouting, Joanne went through the following thoughts: "I have more responsibility than my sisters. . . . I could not accept my mother being attacked . . . she was powerless. I remember my aunt Clara did not talk to my sisters and me for many days, which was a big threat to me. . . . I have felt psychologically unsafe and unsure about people since that time." With changes in trauma-related sensory experience and cognitive judgment and with cognitive information being integrated emotionally, Joanne could say to herself, "Perhaps we daughters were really left too much to ourselves, as my relatives were saying, but I worried because nobody took care of my mother. . . . I don't know the past relationship between my mother and her relatives. . . . I cannot take part in their struggles." She explored her connection to her aunt, recalling images of herself at different ages, which indicated that she was closer to her aunt Clara than to her mother. Joanne commented that this was the reason she could not tolerate her aunt's lengthy silence and distance after the family fight and why she had felt abandoned by both her aunt and her mother.

During EMDR processing, Joanne moved through different emotions: from alertness to anxiety, from sadness to relief. She also moved from the Negative Cognition "I am powerless and alone" to the Positive Cognition "I can react for my good," and she worked on mentally testing different ways to respond in anxious family situations.

Family Sessions C

At this point, two issues of great interest for family sessions arose from the individual work with Joanne. The first issue concerned the roots of dependency between Joanne and her mother. While Joanne behaved like a parental child, with excessive mature worries for her mother and family, she was also enmeshed with her mother. She had ambivalent feelings about this: a mixture of satisfaction about closeness and guilt about needing protection. The second issue concerned the triangle between Joanne, her mother, and her aunt. It was decided that a family session would provide the most useful context at this time to facilitate Joanne's individuation and to break family triangles (and projections).

The next family session began with Joanne's progress report. She said that she was not experiencing any panic reactions and had experimented with a more balanced emotional distance from her relatives during their 2-week family vacation. She was less uneasy with strangers and was attending less to others' judgments.

The family was confronted about their indirect communication style, which was very evident between Joanne's mother and aunt. This prompted some highly emotional responses. Joanne's mother expressed her dissatisfaction and was encouraged to limit the help she received from her relatives in her parenting role. In addition, Joanne's mother focused on the fact she had been closer but "less in agreement" with Joanne than she was with her other daughters, to the point where she thought she had "damaged" Joanne too much and could not "let her go."

The therapist invited direct communication and self-disclosure during sessions by providing a caring but firm relationship with each person. Everyone worked on checking her own automatic emotional participation in family triangles, with the aim of unblocking rigid cycles of automatic behavior.

Individual Sessions 3

Because it seemed to be very difficult for Joanne to unblock more authentic and spontaneous emotional expressions and articulate her thoughts, individual sessions were chosen to address her avoidance patterns. In the next two individual sessions, Joanne talked about her task of observing communication at home. She had noticed that when a family member refused another's offer to do something together, that person took the risk of being considered untrustworthy and losing the other's affection. Joanne often felt trapped in having to choose between being considered "strange" or participating in unwanted activities to please others. Now that she was beginning to make more personal choices instead of feeling coerced in the usual pattern of a passive or self-damaging responder, the feedback she received had been less anxiety-provoking than expected. The family therapist concluded that Joanne's family members were learning to differentiate between the anticipation of a behavior and the actual new behavior of other family members, which is a fundamental step in differentiation.

Joanne was now more conscious of her difficulty in saying no to young men who asked her to go out and in expressing disagreement with others in general conversation. In the past, she had usually avoided any conflict by lying, sometimes to the point where the lie would become apparent and she would feel ashamed and unable to react. With EMDR Joanne targeted the following scene, which was chosen because it was a past episode with strong impact: She was on the telephone with a boy she had tried to keep away from her with absurd lies. She got confused about which of the different versions of her other engagements she had given, to the point that her lying was discovered. She had felt very ashamed and, as usual for her, had been close to fainting.

Reprocessing this scene, Joanne faced her inability to take responsibility for her choices and to directly confront others; she recognized that these were the same patterns she had followed at home with her relatives. At first, Joanne recalled other images of her indirect way of communicating, and then she slowly moved toward a different perception of the specific episode with the boy: "I feel relieved. . . . I don't see myself pale and weak at the telephone any more. . . . I am only acting like an adolescent . . . this is my childish side. . . . This scene makes me laugh now." The image faded and similar episodes and strategies were looked at with less anxiety and less self-denigration. Joanne told herself that lying could be a defense but could not be the only one. She stated that she needed to develop better social competence; this was an emerging relevant need, which seemed to be highly significant at this point. Apart from working with imaginal templates for future contact with her peers, an important resource could come from her family system; therefore, a family session was planned with only Joanne and her two sisters.

Family Session with Sisters D

This grouping of the three sisters was chosen to encourage sharing social habits and to work on communication within the sibling subsystem, which could offer Joanne peer support in her process of differentiation. During the session with Joanne and her sisters, Joanne talked about her fear of confronting them because it involved facing unpleasant feelings of conflict and the emotional consequences of breaking the "law of fused female unity." Joanne received more positive personal feedback than she expected. The three sisters talked together about common memories and different personal strategies in their relationships. Joanne expressed relief and pleasure in belonging to the sibling subsystem in a more satisfactory position, but again said that she had both a strong desire for self-expression and also a fear of expressing disagreement with others or conflicting with others.

Individual Sessions 4

Joanne returned to individual sessions to work on her deeply rooted social anxiety. She tended to believe that she was "evil" to others if she contradicted them. The situation seemed stuck, and the therapist suggested using EMDR to find a symbolic image that would represent what she feared. During this EMDR session, Joanne said that she occasionally thought of herself as a wolf: "I can hurt with the voice even if I stand completely still. . . . I can bite without wanting to bite. . . . I am so scared of acting like a wolf to the point that I prefer always to say yes to others." Continuing the EMDR processing, Joanne began thinking about aggressiveness without connecting it to danger, at which point she further integrated her wolf image, stating, "Now the image of the wolf becomes a picture, it isn't alive any longer. It's like a memory. . . . I am not so dangerous. . . . I can be angry and not so dangerous."

When the VOC remained a 4 with respect to the Positive Cognition "I can be myself," the therapist asked Joanne what prevented it from becoming a 7. Joanne replied, "I feel that if I control everything, I destroy myself because I do not express myself. If I behave spontaneously, I feel unsure about myself . . . and then I stay at home not to be anxious . . . and my relatives make me enraged because they think I am antisocial. I can see myself in a giant spider web, trying to roll away from all these sticky points!" Through EMDR Joanne identified her inability to overcome this conflict as an important part of her difficulty in separation. She connected all these points to elements of family history. Cognitive integrative interventions were proposed to Joanne as she recalled the very strict teaching in her family not to be violent and not to be too self-conscious. Her impasse could be connected to inhibited aggressiveness.

At the therapist's question "What are you taking home today?," Joanne answered, "That I am not antisocial. . . . I can behave spontaneously. I am not obliged to roll away from something." At the end of three individual sessions, Joanne was willing to go out to attend social events, and a short time later she joined a local music group.

Considering information and clinical themes both from family therapy and EMDR, it was possible to assess that anguish and anxiety were the usual family answer, the one that crossed the four generations and that was used by the "undifferentiated mass of the family ego-state" (Bowen, 1978, p. 545). These emotions and their associated behaviors were used to maintain self-control and to avoid overwhelming feelings, especially those connected to separations. Anxiety was expressed in the family whenever there was a high level of stress for internal or external factors and when the other defenses of rationalizing and constant activity were not enough. The family myth was "Staying close to each other and helping each other is the only remedy."

Whole-Family Session E

The last therapy session with the whole family included sharing the following narrative according to new story lines that emerged in both family sessions and EMDR sessions. The loss of the father had caused a greater closeness in an already rigidly organized family. Joanne had assumed behaviors consistent with her father's attributes, such as being calm and shy. The basic orientation of the family to "always be active and avoid conflict" had increased after the loss of the father. As time passed, Joanne's behavior had been labeled as contrasting with the style of the other family members, who were at least outwardly tough and doing their best to be actively helpful to each other. So Joanne grew up receiving images of herself as an introverted girl, sensitive and intelligent but neither strong nor autonomous. The attention that she received had the function of diverting family tension among the adults.

Joanne had actually expressed the "sad" side of the family mood, the consciousness of the "open wound" of the father's loss and, simultaneously, an "unconscious protest" against the pressure to be similar to others. Her family could not access normal feelings of sadness, vulnerability, or conflict and could not reject the family myth about family unity. The phase of family life in which the adult daughters were leaving home caused a movement of differentiation within the family. The system, unprepared to face these changes, had gone through an important crisis. The therapy promoted the utilization of already existing resources in the family and stimulated goals of self-expression and differentiation.

At a follow-up session 8 months later, Joanne was asymptomatic and enjoying university life. In her family, there was much more role flexibility, reflecting better boundaries and communication, and there was an openly expressed sense of well-being from all family members.

DISCUSSION

The integrative model of family systems therapy and EMDR appears to be connected to a quicker problem resolution. Special competence is required by the therapist, who must be able to shift roles from that of a family-oriented therapist to an individually oriented therapist, choosing the appropriate intervention for the modality activated at that moment (see Figure13.1). These shifts require specific skills and caution about switching between the two therapeutic contexts and modalities and about respecting personal boundaries of all family members.

A Clinical Model of Integration

The case of Joanne and her family demonstrates that it is possible to enhance the potentialities of EMDR and family therapy by appropriate *choice of issues,* transposed from one setting to the other, and by the relevant *timing of the switches* from the individual to the family setting.

Choice of Issues

The therapist must attend to *focal issues* and *clusters of conflict.* In Joanne's therapy, examples of focal issues were the danger connected to being independent in and outside the family and the family myth about always being together and in agreement. Clusters of conflicts are well exemplified by how Joanne and her mother both wanted to be helped by and connected to family members but at the same time felt limited and judged. The opposite and conflicting emotions of wanting and fearing to be independent had to be treated to allow the development of more adaptive behavior. *Clusters of emotional and cognitive conflicts specific to an individual and a family must be processed both at family and individual levels to optimize treatment.*

Switching between the Different Types of Sessions

When making decisions about switching and interweaving the two different types of sessions, therapists can base their choices on two basic principles: the better method for the relevant clinical need of the moment and the better setting to find cognitive and emotional resources for that relevant clinical need. Examples taken from Joanne's therapy are summarized here.

During the individual sessions, the theme of Joanne's dependence on her mother emerged. Issues surfaced about Joanne's behavior as a responsible parental child and about her enmeshment with her mother to the point that she needed her help for everything. After individual processing, the better method for this central issue was a family session in which Joanne's perceptions could be compared with her mother's memories and a corrective experience in real life could be elicited among all the family members.

Later in therapy, at the end of one individual session, it was clear to Joanne that she needed more social competence. She had to consider and acquire new social skills and find the courage to openly interact with peers. The best setting to find cognitive and emotional resources seemed to be the sisters' subsystem, this time used as a place for open dialogue and sharing of social ways to behave, facilitated by the therapist.

At different times in therapy, relevant clinical goals were set. Joanne needed to better define her strong but vague feeling of personal danger and to explore disturbing images of self. Considering the importance of finding personal answers and resources, individual EMDR sessions provided the best place to focus and elaborate.

As can be seen in Figure 13.1, it is basically the emergence of relevant clinical needs from family sessions or individual sessions that determines the switching between the two types of sessions. The interconnection of clinical themes and emerging relevant needs in therapy sessions and types of sessions is summarized in Figure 13.1. Switching appropriately optimizes the use of personal or family inner energies and creates a unique output.

Summary

Family systems therapy and EMDR can be integrated because it is possible to utilize them concurrently, while maintaining a conceptual and therapeutic coherence with both reference models. Their objectives are compatible. The Experiential Family Therapy approach allows the family in treatment to move toward goals *chosen by the system.* Likewise, specifically in cases in which the patient is an adolescent or young adult, EMDR administered in individual sessions encourages exploration of *truly personal directions and promotes a thorough self- differentiation,* from the psychological point of view, *through the creation of a personal mental safe place.*

The aim of integrating family therapy and EMDR is to accelerate change by creating an impact wave between the dynamics and the outcomes of the two forms of therapy. The integration of the two therapeutic methods stimulates deep change processes in both the individual patient and the family. Both approaches contribute to restoring better functional integration in the self of the young adult member. In the treatment of separation and individuation, the integrated approach helps the therapy process move from overcoming enmeshment and anxiety to addressing self-definition and enhancement of personal resources.

In the integrative model, EMDR offers good insight into family dynamics through the individual eye. For example, EMDR was a powerful lens for focusing on the emotional triangle between Joanne, her mother, and her aunt, as well as identifying alliances and other relational patterns. Moreover, EMDR can be particularly useful in exploring the root of dependency, which keeps the young family member bound to his or her family. It can also help the young person to identify and process what is important and vital in the family mental space. EMDR is useful in defining clusters of cognitive and emotional conflicts that prevent the development of more adaptive behaviors. Finally, it is an important resource when family transactions get stuck in therapy.

Family therapy is particularly helpful in the elaboration of emotions in family group sessions. An example is the family reelaboration about how Joanne's mother was differently connected to each of her three daughters and how she felt guilty about this difference. Moreover, the emergence of issues from family sessions eased and enriched processing during EMDR sessions.

The same elements are a source of material for appropriate integrative interventions. In fact, therapists can use their knowledge of family rules and communication patterns observed in family sessions to formulate proper integrative interventions. For example, in one of the first EMDR sessions Joanne was in a loop with repetitive negative thoughts. She was stuck on her responsibility for being unable to communicate in a direct way both at the university and at home. Considering family avoidance of conflict and open confrontation, it was possible to propose the following integrative intervention: "Are your relatives always direct to each other? Could you learn from them? Do you think you can learn to do that as an adult?" This was helpful in stimulating Joanne's adaptive network.

A special aspect allowed by the integration of the two types of therapy is the better evaluation and treatment of developmental problems. For instance, in the case example, it was possible to examine the experience of psychological dependence along the four generations and to consider and treat it at the individual and family levels.

Research in the integration of the two approaches is recommended to identify core treatment issues and to study the parallel process between self-image modification in EMDR and changes after positive relabeling and/or reframing in family systems therapy.

The integrative model of family systems therapy with EMDR presented in this chapter has shown good clinical results in the treatment of many presenting problems in young adults, including social and cognitive inhibition, fears and phobic reactions, alimentary disorders in otherwise well-functioning clients, and stuttering. The integration allows for shortened recovery times and improved therapy outcomes. Coupling the two therapeutic approaches expands the results of family therapy in the delicate intervention with young adults as a result of more rapid improvement in separation and individuation processes.

In conclusion, EMDR and family therapy treatment are complementary, their objectives are congruent, and their synergistic effect improves and accelerates outcome.

REFERENCES

American Psychiatric Association. (1994). *Diagnostic and statistical manual of mental disorders* (4th ed.). Arlington, VA: Author.

Beavers, W. R., & Voeller, M. N. (1981). Family models: Comparing and contrasting the Olson circumplex model with the Beavers systems model. *Family Process, 22,* 250–260.

Bowen, M. (1978). *Family therapy in clinical practice.* New York: Aronson.

Cancrini, L., & La Rosa, C. (1991). *Il vaso di Pandora: Manuale di psichiatria e psicopatologia* [Pandora's vase: Psychiatry and psychopathology manual]. Rome: Nuova Italia Scientifica.

Crittenden, P. M. (1997). A dynamic-maturational perspective on anxiety disorders. *Italian Journal of Psychiatry, 3,* 28–37.

Feske, U. (1998). Eye movement desensitization and reprocessing treatment for posttraumatic stress disorder. *Clinical Psychology: Science and Practice, 5,* 171–181.

Foster, S., & Lendl, J. (1996). Eye movement desensitization and reprocessing: Four case studies of a new tool for executive coaching and restoring employee performance after setbacks. *Consulting Psychology Journal: Practice and Research, 48,* 155–161.

Giat Roberto, L. (1992). *Transgenerational family therapies.* New York: Guilford Press.

Goldstein, A., & Feske, U. (1994). Eye movement desensitization and reprocessing for panic disorder: A case series. *Journal of Anxiety Disorders, 8,* 351–362.

Kessler, R. C., McGonagle, D. K., Zhao, S., Nelson, C. B., Hughes, M., & Eshleman, S. (1994). Lifetime and 12 months prevalence of *DSM-III-R* psychiatric disorders in the United States (Results from the National Comorbidity Survey). *Archives of General Psychiatry, 51,* 8–19.

Laurent, M. (2000). I disturbi ansioso-fobici in una prospettiva sistemica [Anxious-phobic disorders in a systems theory perspective]. *Psicobiettivo, 20*(2), 21–45.

Lazarus, C. N., & Lazarus, A. A. (2002). EMDR: An elegantly concentrated multimodal procedure. In F. Shapiro (Ed.), *EMDR as an integrative psychotherapy approach* (pp. 209–223). Washington, DC: American Psychological Association.

Malagoli Togliatti, M., & Rocchietta Tofani, L. (2002). *Famiglie multiproblematiche: Dall'analisi all'intervento su un sistema complesso* [Multiproblem families: From analysis to intervention in a complex system]. Rome: Carocci Editore.

Maxfield, L., & Melnyk, W. T. (2000). Single session treatment of test anxiety with eye movement desensitization and reprocessing. *International Journal of Stress Management, 7,* 87–101.

McGoldrick, M., Gerson, R., & Shellenberger, S. (1999). *Genograms: In family assessment.* New York: Norton.

Minuchin, S., & Fishman, H. C. (1992). *Techniques of family therapy.* Cambridge, MA: Harvard University Press.

Namyslowska, I., & Siewierska, A. (1994). Anxiety in the family. *Psychiatry in Poland, 28,* 547–555.

Napier, A. Y., & Whitaker, C. (1978). *The family crucible.* New York: Harper & Row.

Neill, J., & Kniskern, D. (Eds.). (1982). *From psyche to system: The evolving therapy of Carl Whitaker.* New York: Guilford Press.

Oppenheimer, K., & Frey, J. (1993). Family transitions and developmental processes in panic-disordered patients. *Family Process, 32*(3), 341–352.

Perry, B., Pollard, R. A., Blakely, T. L., Baker, W. L., & Vigilante, D. (1995). Childhood trauma, the neurobiology of adaptation and use-dependent development of the brain: How states become traits. *Infant Mental Health Journal, 16,* 271–291.

Piercy, F., & Sprenkle, D. (1986). *Family therapy source book.* New York: Guilford Press.

Rapee, R., & Melville, L. F. (1997). Recall of family factors in social phobia and panic disorder: Comparison of mother and offspring reports. *Journal of Depression and Anxiety, 5,* 7–11.

Schneier, F., Johnson, J., Hornig, C., Liebowitz, M., & Weisman, M. (1992). Social phobia: Comorbidity and morbidity in an epidemiological sample. *Archives of General Psychiatry, 49,* 282–288.

Shapiro, F. (1995). *Eye movement desensitization and reprocessing: Basic principles, protocols and procedures.* New York: Guilford Press.

Shapiro, F. (1999). Eye movement desensitization and reprocessing (EMDR) and the anxiety disorders: Clinical and research implications of an integrated psychotherapy treatment. *Journal of Anxiety Disorders, 13*(1), 35–67.

Shapiro, F. (2001). *Eye movement desensitization and reprocessing: Basic principles, protocols and procedures* (2nd ed.). New York: Guilford Press.

Shapiro, F. (Ed.). (2002). *EMDR as an integrative psychotherapy approach.* Washington, DC: American Psychological Association.

Shapiro, F., & Forrest, M. (1997). *EMDR.* New York: Basic Books.

Shotter, J., & Gergen, K. J. (Eds.). (1989). *Texts of identity.* London: Sage.

Siegel, D. J. (1999). *The developing mind: Toward a neurobiology of interpersonal experience.* New York: Guilford Press.

Smith, N., & Poole, A. (2002). EMDR and cognitive behavior therapy: Exploring convergence and divergence. In F. Shapiro (Ed.), *EMDR as an integrative psychotherapy approach* (pp. 151–180). Washington, DC: American Psychological Association.

Ugazio, V. (1998). *Storie permesse, storie proibite* [Life experiences permitted, life experiences prohibited]. Torino, Italy: Bollati Boringhieri.

World Health Organization (2005). *International statistical classification of diseases and related health problems* (10th rev.). Geneva, Switzerland: Author.

CHAPTER 14

Children of Divorce

Frances (Frankie) R. Klaff

Adults choose to divorce, but it is their children who bear the consequences of this decision. In the United States, with 50% of marriages ending in divorce, more than a million children are implicated, representing about 30% of the child population below the age of 18 (U.S. National Center for Health Statistics cited in U.S. Divorce Statistics, 2006). In Western societies, the nuclear family, comprising mother, father, and children, is traditionally considered to be the basic unit for socializing children (Parsons, 1951). Because many families no longer conform to this traditional model, the question is raised as to whether children can thrive emotionally in a nonstandard nuclear family. Further, what criteria relating to changed family structure might foster or impede healthy child development? Much attention has been devoted to examining whether divorce negatively impacts children's psychological adjustment, or whether divorce is now so prevalent that it can be considered a normative transitional event (Kaslow, 1981). Divorce brings many structural and functional changes. These include the logistic and emotional complications of a nonresidential parent, financial disequilibrium, and two systems with differing rules and expectations. Additionally, there are new subsystem components, such as parental figures, step- and half-siblings, and extended families with a potentially motley cast of new characters and different environments impacting the system. What constitutes "family" for children of divorce is often quite different from what is traditionally viewed as the nuclear family.

Divorce Effects on Childhood Adjustment

Standard views of childhood adjustment stress the importance of the parent-child relationship. The quality of this relationship usually changes with divorce. Feelings of guilt, sadness, anger, and confusion, plus issues regarding loyalty and alliances often color the child's perceptions of parents and life. It is not only the postdivorce situation that affects adjustment, but the nature of the predivorce experience (Forehand & Long, 2002). In fact, reviews of the divorce research literature clearly indicate that the emotional climate pre- and postdivorce, as measured by interparental conflict, has been the most consistent predictor of child adjustment (Amato & Keith, 1991; Emery, 1982). Wallerstein (1983) described maximal adjustment as the accomplishment of certain psychological tasks based on Erikson's (1950) conceptualization of life cycle stages. These are acknowledging the reality of the marital disruption, disengaging from parental conflict and distress, and resuming customary pursuits. Necessary steps involve resolution of loss, anger, and self-blame; acceptance of the permanence of the divorce; and development of realistic hope regarding relationships. This formulation implies that the child must accept the *external systemic structural changes,* as well as reach *internal reconciliation within the self.* Three themes prevail: resolving issues from the *past,* accepting and adjusting to the *present* situation, and transitioning to normalcy for the *future.*

Family Systems-Based Treatment of Divorce

Family therapy has long been recognized as an effective treatment modality for children's problems in general (Nichols & Schwartz, 1998) and for problems relating to divorce in particular (Isaacs & Abelsohn, 1986). Pioneers like Minuchin (1974) based treatment methods on family systems theory, in which the requisite elements of effective family functioning require a hierarchical structure, with parents in authority and clear boundary distinctions between individuals as well as between generations. When this format is disrupted, symptomatic behaviors ensue. A well-aligned hierarchical structure involves appropriate alliances between family subsystems with clear roles, rules, and boundaries, which are neither too permeable (resulting in enmeshment) nor too rigid (resulting in disengagement). Research and clinical literature confirm that in the divorced family, a structural breakdown in hierarchy, authority, roles, and rules of family relationships occurs. Power shifts, hierarchical and boundary changes redefine familial interrelationships, and these disruptions in alignment can in turn result in children's adjustment difficulties (Schulman, 1982; Weltner, 1982). A commonly reported example of boundary violation occurs when a child becomes triangulated in the conflict between feuding parents and is expected to take sides in alliance with one parent against the other. Ideally, despite changes in structural composition, the family system should still embrace the organizing principles of hierarchy, with parents in charge, clear roles and rules, and appropriately permeable boundaries between subsystems.

From the perspective of this systemic model, the whole family was viewed as the treatment unit (Haley, 1980). Treatment interventions were aimed at shifting the structural patterns of interactions between various family subsystems. Interestingly, with the shift in emphasis to treatment of the family as a whole unit, the individual as a subsystem of importance became neglected. Attention to past behavior shifted to present interactions, and focus on *intrapsychic* dynamics was replaced by emphasis on *interpersonal* relationships, exemplified in statements such as "For the purpose of inducing structural change, the therapist must focus not on the family members' private experience, but on their *behavior*" (Gurman & Kniskern, 1981, p. 316). Then, during the 1980s and 1990s, there was a gradual but marked recognition that although systems theory appeared to be sound, the restructuring of families was neither simple nor the sole formula for solving family problems. It became evident that the individual's experience (perceptions, beliefs, and feelings) was also valid and an important target of treatment (Nichols & Schwartz, 1998).

When evaluating children of divorce it is important to consider both systemic and intrapersonal perspectives. Consideration of the whole family system is clearly crucial as the operation of this structural dynamic affects the child's experience and functioning. Consideration of the impact of children's personal experiences of *past* and *current* events is also of critical importance. At best, they have witnessed the eroding parental relationship; at worst, they have become active participants in the conflict, often long before the actual divorce process was enacted and long after it has ended.

Adaptive Information Processing Model Applied to Divorce Issues

The Adaptive Information Processing model (Shapiro, 2001) is particularly applicable to children's experiences of divorce, with its emphasis on past, present, and future elements of experience. Children typically report distressing memories of parents being physically combative or arguing. Other commonly experienced past incidents, such as departure of a parent, diminished finances, changed residence, and even change of entire social systems, including school and friends, can be experienced as traumatic. The impact may remain even after the family has apparently stabilized. Past memories may be stimulated in the present, such as when a parent complains about the ex-spouse regarding child support. Such events, unprocessed, may link to emotional, somatic, and behavioral symptoms, as well as to distorted cognitions. Emotions for this population typically include sadness, anger, guilt, hurt, and feelings of loss and abandonment. Physical sensations often persist in the form of stomachaches and headaches (Greenwald, 1999).

Cognitive distortions, such as "It's my fault," "I am not important," and "I must take care of my mother," may become core beliefs. For instance, 40-year-old Tony was inconsolable after discovering that his girlfriend had been unfaithful. During therapy, he realized that he had always felt guilty for not preventing his own mother's infidelity when he was 6, which led to his parents' divorce. Now, years later, the impact of that experience intensified his reaction to his girlfriend. EMDR treatment helped Tony adaptively process the painful elements of his childhood memory. Treated earlier, he might have become less enmeshed in his parents' problems and more able to cope with the divorce.

EMDR can help the child release irrational feelings of having to assume personal responsibility for problems and care of family members. In addition to the *internal* resolution of past experience, current *external* changes must be fostered to support the child's intrapsychic and behavioral progress. Typically, these involve changes in parental behavior and in that of other involved family subsystems. Thus, the combination of family therapy and EMDR facilitates the overall treatment goal of the child's healthy adaptation to the changes wrought by divorce.

THERAPY PROCESS

Family systems therapy is integral to all eight stages of EMDR treatment of child and divorce issues, utilizing the three-pronged principle of targeting past, present, and future problems. Specifically, the child's past upsetting memories pertaining to the divorce are sought and addressed, as well as present distressing stimuli. While these distressing issues are processed individually, family therapy helps restructure the dysfunctional family interactions. Future challenges are identified and possible solutions sought. EMDR is used to visualize coping skills and behavioral alternatives, which are developed in conjunction with the child, sometimes with parental input.

During the history collection phase, perspectives from parent(s), child, and other subsystems contribute to an understanding of family structure and functioning and provide information for treatment planning. In the preparation phase, family systems work addresses interrelationship mechanics, which may be currently dysfunctional. Insight is gained regarding predivorce issues that may have disturbing associations for the child. Addressing systemic dysfunction at this stage aims at strengthening the family as a base of safety and may aid in stabilizing the child's specific emotional reactions before disturbing material can be processed with EMDR. A parent may need to inform, reassure, or make actual environmental changes to increase safety before past upsetting incidents can be processed. Structural issues regarding boundaries and hierarchy may need attention so that a child does not overfunction by assuming too much responsibility in the new family system or underfunction by regressing to elicit nurturance. These examples highlight some of the structural problems in divorce that may disrupt normative adjustment.

The assessment phase, which involves target selection, may also include family therapy components. A parent may identify disturbing incidents, but the child, aided by the therapist, selects the actual targets. Structural Family Therapy at this stage might involve boundary setting to decrease enmeshment, such as requesting that the parent allow the child to talk independently or encouraging the child to remain alone with the therapist, thereby sometimes facilitating freedom of expression. This is particularly important in cases where a child might be afraid to upset a parent or fear recrimination, or during adolescence, when privacy and individuation are prime considerations. Targets often involve systemic factors, such as triangulation (enmeshment) in past or current parental arguments, and boundary violations, such as a parent berating the ex-spouse to the child or expecting the child to be a message bearer. Emotional components often include missing the absent parent, distress over an unreliable parent, unrealistic hopes for reconciliation, loss of social status, or jealousy over a parent's new relationship. If information does not emerge spontaneously, the therapist can elicit possible targets with general questions, such as "What's the worst part about your parents' divorce?" or specific ones, such as "Whose fault is it that your parents didn't get along?" "What did you do when they were mad at each other?" "Does Dad phone you?" and "Does Mom ask you questions about Dad's girlfriend?"

During the desensitization stage, developmentally guided *Cognitive Interweaves* may be necessary to aid in shifting of stuck material or emotion. Categories include:

- *Responsibility:* "Is it your fault your parents are fighting?" "Whose job is it to get you back to Mom's on time?" These questions address systemic issues of role definition, hierarchy, alliances, boundaries, and enmeshment.

- *Choice:* "What can you do if you feel sad at Dad's new house?" "Can you tell Mom how you feel when she says that?" These questions aim to increase boundary permeability, within realistic limits.

- *Safety:* "What can you do if you are scared?" "Where do you feel safe?" Developing concrete elements of safety is essential before addressing perceived internal insecurity with resource-building elements such as "What can you tell yourself if you feel scared?"

- *New information:* "Is it a child's fault if parents don't get along?" Distortions and misinformation about causality, relationships, appropriate roles, or other systemic matters are addressed.

During the processing phase, restructuring of family relationships may continue, such as setting boundaries for an overly engaged parent or activating a more disengaged parent by prompting for Cognitive Interweave: "Mom, will you pick Patty up on time?" (safety).

- *Future templates* include visualizing successful handling of a problematic systemic issue, such as "Imagine telling your aunt you don't want to talk about Mom," or anticipate glitches and how the child may handle them more confidently.

The reassessment phase should include evaluation of family dynamics as well as the child's individual emotional progress. Further therapy may be needed to address continued dysfunction. Other family members who may benefit from EMDR themselves are usually best referred to a colleague, as complications with alliances become a professional hazard.

CASE EXAMPLES

Case 1: The Dunn Family

Pam (34) sought treatment for her sons, Kendall (7) and Scott (4). Their father, Jay (36), had recently moved from the family home after living in their basement for a year, during which time the couple vacillated between conflict and attempted reconciliation. Pam, attractive and articulate, had a college degree in music education and worked as a chiropractor's assistant. Although poorly paid, she enjoyed both the job and its flexible hours. Jay was a computer technician in an automobile manufacturing plant. Pam described the volatile atmosphere and ongoing conflict over parenting issues during the disintegration of the marriage. She was concerned that Kendall was inattentive in school and had stomach distress. He was not verbal and denied problems. Pam noted that in the last year of marriage, Jay had been physically abusive to her on a few occasions. During that period, Pam described Kendall as a "watchdog," sometimes readying his fists to intervene on her behalf. Once, during a good period, Kendall saw the couple embracing and tried to separate them, misinterpreting the situation as conflictual.

Pam was also worried about Scott's sadness. Although he was more outgoing and expressive than Kendall, he was clingy. When Pam read him the title on a Christian calendar, "A Happy Family Is Heaven on Earth," he had mournfully responded, "That's not our family."

Pam still harbored anger at Jay whom she described as currently sabotaging her parenting efforts, bad-mouthing her to the boys, and not getting them to do their homework while they were with him. Jay's sole complaint was that Pam interfered with his ability to have fun with the kids because she was overfocused on schoolwork. She had enrolled them in a private Christian school, but Jay refused to help with transportation or tuition fees as he felt public school was good enough. Consequently, Pam bore the financial burden as well as driving and other school-related responsibilities. She had initiated legal action to collect increased child support funds from Jay, although the boys were unaware of this.

Treatment: Family Therapy Component

Pam agreed to attend a couple's session with Jay "for the sake of the boys," although she despised him. Jay reluctantly attended and agreed to return if requested, but never initiated contact. The stated therapeutic agenda was the adjustment of the children. Using Minuchin's (1974) structural constructs, the goal for the Dunns was to realign the family system, shifting dysfunctional relationships by clarifying parental roles. This involved establishing a two-family system, with discretely separate hierarchies and permeable but clear boundaries, thereby detriangulating the children and enabling them to have healthy relationships with each parent separately. The task was accomplished by psychoeducation aimed at normalizing the divorce process and offering information about steps to healthy adjustment to facilitate parental recognition of the impact of their own behavior on the boys.

Restructuring the system necessitated challenging the parents to separate their marital issues from the children, neither expecting them to be messengers nor vying for their allegiance. Pam needed to acknowledge the limits of her control over Jay and to modify her expectations regarding homework in his home. It was anticipated that as Pam backed off in her criticism of Jay, he in turn might feel more autonomous and respond more favorably to shifting his parenting style. The therapist also treated the boys apart from mother to support their individuation, encourage freer expression of their thoughts without their fearing consequences, normalize their feelings, strengthen developmentally appropriate boundaries, and reinforce appropriate autonomy of the sibling subsystem.

In summary, the global aim was to facilitate the developmental process of transition to an adaptively functional, postdivorce two-family system. Proper alignment entailed mediating the parental relationship from "fiery foes" to "cooperative colleagues" (Ahrons & Rodgers, 1987) and helping the children disengage from their conflict. Family sessions were provided to various subsystems, such as father and children, mother and children, and each separately, to normalize their new structural reality. These goals align with the body of divorce research, which consistently concludes that continued relationships with both parents in an atmosphere of support and cooperation minimizes psychological injury (Kaslow, 1981; Klaff, 1983; Kressel, 1985).

Treatment: EMDR Component

Preparation with positive "front loading" was included to ensure adequate resources and a sense of safety to lay the groundwork for the later focus on distressing events. Positive resources were elicited with questions such as "What do you like to do?" and "What's best about being with Mom/Dad?" The resultant positive affects were increased through bilateral stimulation (see Shapiro, 2001). Building a comfortable and trusting therapeutic relationship with the boys was an important component of treatment (Dworkin, 2005). In addition, providing or maximizing a sense of safety was an essential element for these children due to the physical altercations they had witnessed.

EMDR treatment attended to the individual intrapersonal elements by focusing on the often neglected perceptual components of the children's experience of the divorce (Klaff, 1983). Individual sessions with the boys targeted their own upsetting memories and distressing feelings and events: past, present, and anticipated future. Painful experiences prior to the dissolution of their parents' marriage as well as upsetting matters and anticipated concerns were addressed. Both positive and negative memories were elicited by the therapist with general inquiry, such as "How are things now in your life?" and specific questions, such as "What's the worst thing you remember about Dad leaving?" Information from parents was addressed with the children separately as appropriate. Pam was initially present in sessions with Scott because he was so young and connected to her; also, her attunement to the therapist served to reinforce Scott's trust in the therapist. Pam was included supportively in administering bilateral stimulation such as tapping during processing and as an informational resource for Cognitive Interweave. As Scott's trust increased, individual sessions facilitated the exploration of previously unexpressed material.

Treatment Summary

Kendall chose to do EMDR without his mother present. This comprised three sessions. Scott attended six sessions combining EMDR and play therapy, with

Pam present for some of the EMDR sessions. Family therapy was incorporated at the beginning and conclusion of each session. The purpose of these interventions was to process emergent concerns (with permission) such as Kendall's desire to spend more time with Dad. Follow-up sessions tracked progress and identified new issues.

During EMDR, Kendall and Scott addressed concerns, memories, and emotions, some of which they had previously acknowledged and some of which had been unexpressed. Targets included unhappiness about their parents' splitting up, desire for reconciliation, feelings of loss, missing Dad's presence, and wishing for more time with him. In their individual treatment, the boys resolved sadness and fear from the past, accepted their parents' separation, and recognized that they were not to blame and were loved by each parent. In family sessions, they learned to negotiate for some changes and recognized that the rules at each house differed, similar to school classes with different teachers. The treatment focus then shifted to Pam's personal issues as a single mother, including future worries, such as the impact of dating. A more in-depth analysis of the work with Scott follows.

EMDR with Scott

During the preparation phase, Scott identified positive resources such as visiting grandparents and playing with cousins. As he thought of past positive experiences, painful feelings of loss were also elicited. Discussion about structural family changes helped him consider more realistic expectations, normalize the divorce process, and isolate areas of discomfort to process with EMDR, such as not seeing his dad enough, missing his mom while he was visiting his dad, and sadness over the fighting between his parents. The safe place established before targeting past memories was in fact a safe base, composed of accessing positive resources: people and experiences. These also served systemically to validate his separate relationships and bonds to each parent. The following moment demonstrates this stage, when Scott excitedly shared that it was photo day at school:

> **Therapist:** Who will you give photos to?
>
> **Scott:** Mom and Dad.
>
> **Therapist:** Oh, you can give a photo to each of the people who are important to you and who love you? (Mhm) Does your Mommy love you?
>
> **Scott:** Yes (installed with a few passes of bilateral stimulation [BLS]).
>
> **Therapist:** Does your Daddy love you?
>
> **Scott:** Yes (BLS).
>
> **Therapist:** So they both love you?
>
> **Scott:** Yes (BLS).

Following this establishment of a secure base and resource, a distressing divorce-related memory target from the past was sought:

Therapist: What was the worst part of the divorce?

Scott: Them fighting.

Therapist: Can you remember a really bad time? (Scott identified a time when his parents were in the basement fighting over a postcard. This was actually a wedding invitation addressed to Pam, which Jay had opened. Interestingly, Kendall selected the same memory for his first target, although Pam had no idea that the boys had even been aware of the incident, and neither had ever divulged their memory to her or each other. This highlights the importance of exploring children's own perceptions of events and of identifying and reprocessing them.)

Bilateral stimulation for Scott was varied to maintain interest and accommodate a child's shorter attention span and included tracking hand movement, knee taps, hand taps. Sets for children are briefer than for adults, approximately equaling the age of the child, although there is no hard and fast rule. Scott's excellent focus and attention allowed for sets of about 10 to 12 passes. Pam, when present, sometimes administered BLS while Scott cuddled up to her. He sometimes sat on the therapist's lap during processing. This demonstrates the practice of making processing as comfortable and natural as possible while adhering to the protocol:

- *Safe place:* Playing with Kendall. (*Interesting to note that he chose his brother as his safe place while remembering his family war zone.*)
- *Target memory:* Mom and Dad in the basement fighting over a postcard.
- *Image:* Parents fighting in the basement. Scott is standing at the top of the basement stairs. (He drew a picture of the fight and looked at it while processing. He also drew himself with large tears pouring down his face; see Figure 14.1).
- *Cognition:* Cognitions sometimes need to be suggested by the therapist as children have more difficulty abstracting. At the time of this session, the therapist had previously aided Scott in developing a cognition "It's their stuff."
- *Subjective Units of Disturbance scale:* 10.
- *Body sensation:* Head.
- *Emotion:* Bad, sad.

The following sequence indicates Scott's responses after each set of BLS:

1. Don't remember.
2. I'm in the mudroom.
3. I ran up to my room and jumped under the covers so I couldn't hear them.
4. Same.
5. Nothing.

6. Same.

7. Sad.

8. We were in Florida. I can go on the moon walk with Kendall. He was kicking me on the moon walk (laughs). (How do you feel now?) Happy (*accessed positive memory*).

9. Nothing. (*"Nothing" is always something. It could mean nothing new to report or no change in feeling or no further distress, or not thinking about the incident.*)

10. Same. (Was Florida before or after the divorce?) Before. (Okay. Keep going.)

11. Same thing, but another ride (*recalling another family memory*).

12. Nothing. (What do you feel?) Sad (*memory now evokes the loss*).

    I want to feel that they like each other (*typifies children's reconciliation fantasy*). (Maybe it's best to think of how they each like you.) (*The overall therapeutic goal is acceptance of the fact of the divorce. This Interweave is aimed systemically at acceptance of the new family structure and*

Figure 14.1 The fight.

boundaries, detriangulating him from parental conflict and validating his relationships with each parent separately.)

13. Same thing. (What?) What you just said.

14. A little mad.

15. Same. (Where do you feel it?) (*question aimed to shift possible looping*). My legs.

16. Nothing. (What about the mad feeling?) It's gone. I feel sad. Still there in my face, in my eyes. (*Note that "nothing" was "something," and his body sensation is suggestive of blocked tears.*)

17. Same.

18. Mad again. (*Perhaps he is struggling with his sadness and previously unexpressed anger at his parents.*) (It's their stuff.) (*This Interweave addressed detriangulation. Therapeutic guesses sometimes miss the mark. In retrospect, Scott may still be processing anger at his parents for causing this. Technically, the Interweave did not address that aspect.*)

19. Same. (Where do you feel it?) In my brain. (What would you like to say?) (*Interweave goal to empower verbalization of feeling and release somatic tension.*) I hope they would get back together. (*Interweave goal is acceptance of reality.*) (Do you think it would happen?) No. (Think of that.) (*It was very tempting to comfort Scott, but the therapist held back, recognizing that Scott was processing toward internal acceptance of the facts, ultimately a longer lasting outcome than solace.*)

20. Same. It's in my brain. (What can we tell your brain?) (*Access to self-soothing. Scott does have reserves of positive resources from which to draw.*) It's okay to be sad. (Yes. Think of that.)

21. Nothing. (What do you feel?) (*checking for current meaning of "nothing"*). A little mad and a little sad.

22. Nothing. But the sad feeling went away. (*Return to target to assess current disturbance.*) (Look at the picture you made.)

23. Nothing. It went away. (When you look at the picture, what do you get?) A little bit sad. (It's okay to be sad. It's their stuff.) (*This Interweave supported and normalized both the emotional and the systemic elements.*)

24. Same, what you said.

25. Same thing. (What do you feel?) A little bit happy.

(*Achieving a SUD score of 0 would not be ecologically appropriate to the situation. He is, after all, dealing with a current problem and continued parental conflict.*) (Do you want to work some more, or have you had enough?) (*This was geared toward giving Scott some control, particularly important because children have so little choice and control in their lives. Giving control in the EMDR process fosters autonomy and self-esteem.*) I've had enough.

(*To close down the session, a future template is introduced to help actualize emotional and cognitive shifts that have occurred in processing and to imaginally rehearse new behavior.*) (So when you go home, what will you think?) It's their stuff. (Okay, think of it.)

26. Okay. (*Seems to happen in many cases, where the processing appears to continue between sessions.*) (smiles). (And how does it feel right here?) (between the eyes). Better.

   SUD = 3. (*It is interesting how clearly even small children assess their SUD level.*)

In the next session, Scott reported that the memory no longer disturbed him. Continued processing often occurs without conscious effort. In another session, Scott again drew a picture of the fight (see Figure 14.2). He reported feeling sad

Figure 14.2   Target: Picture of parents arguing over postcard.

about the divorce. When the therapist asked, "What is the worst part of it now?" Scott answered, "Not enough time with Dad." The previous processing had targeted a past event, but he now identifies a present *trigger,* which is another channel to address. Resolution of a complex event such as divorce involves coming to terms with several channels and triggers for children. Once representative examples are processed, generalization often follows. Scott's image depicted the Sunday night return from Dad. His SUD was 8 and the body sensation was in his legs. During the processing, his SUD dropped to 2 as he recalled pleasure being with his father.

The next step involved a family systems intervention integrated into EMDR processing. Pam was invited into the session to offer a Cognitive Interweave (new information) by reminding Scott that he would soon spend an extended summer vacation with his dad. Processing continued with Pam in the room. Scott's SUD dropped to 0. The systemic maneuver was also to help Pam support the importance of both families for Scott. This was further reinforced in a separate session with Pam in which she was encouraged to "lighten up" on the Sunday return time, restructure homework schedules, recognize her boundaries, and detriangulate the boys from the conflict with Jay. She was educated that her angry attitude toward him was filtering through to the kids with adverse effects. Having a "fun" relationship with their father was reframed as healthy for their male bonding needs. Systemically, an attempt was made to restructure Pam's belief that all the negative consequences on the boys stemmed from their father. This idea is particularly difficult for feuding parents to accept, and it is doubtful that she ever fully assimilated this possibility without personal therapy directed at her divorce experience. Pam might have benefited from EMDR sessions, but realistic time and financial constraints prevailed.

Further sessions with Scott addressed other current upsetting aspects of the divorce arrangement. He identified a typical confusing problem experienced subsequent to divorce. During visits with his father, he missed his mother. This was addressed with EMDR, bolstered by Cognitive Interweaves to increase felt safety and empower choice: "What can you do to feel better? Can you phone Mom?" Family therapy then further processed generated options. It would be futile or even damaging to propose solutions during EMDR that the child cannot implement for developmental, psychological, or practical reasons.

The overall goal was to work on acceptance of the fact of the two separate family systems and to manage the affective components. Cognitive Interweaves acknowledged Scott's feelings and the immutability of the situation, but also validated his power to activate some changes, strengthen the attachments with both parents, and disengage from their personal discord. *Future* templates for coping were included in the processing, and future anticipated fears and problems were addressed. Family therapy with the parents reinforced the importance of separating their stuff from the children (boundaries and control) and not expecting the boys to be messengers (enmeshment and alliances). Care is essential if the therapist chooses to convey information gained in the EMDR session to a parent. Protecting the children is important. Children sometimes report that their parents "act nice" in session but berate them later for bringing up certain issues. This problem constitutes an issue of boundaries in and of itself; consequently, it is preferable whenever possible to check with the child about talking to the parent regarding the problem and to address issues with the child present, acting as the child's advocate.

Longitudinal Follow-up

Kendall and Scott both remembered the EMDR sessions and their content, years later, when they were 14 and 11, respectively. A year earlier, Pam had married a man whom they both liked. Alas, he was unfaithful and this union, too, ended in divorce. The boys denied feeling as wounded as previously as this was not their biological father, with whom they still maintained a strong bond. Jay and Pam were no longer embroiled in heated conflict. The boys were quite clear in their directive to their mother that they did not want her to marry again. This desire certainly reflects the hierarchical shift typical of divorced families, where children become more equal partners in decision making (Wallerstein & Kelly, 1980).

During the 9/11 disaster, Scott experienced nightmares and fears of being alone in the house and requested an EMDR session, which alleviated his anxiety. At the time of current writing, the boys are personable, talented young men of 18 and 15. Kendall composes, sings, and plays guitar, and Scott plays guitar in his own band. They have a good relationship with each other and are still involved in athletics. Kendall has just graduated from high school and will be majoring in music in college. They are involved with both parents, but they tell Pam that they know they cannot count on Dad. These parents did manage to set proper boundaries and mostly detriangulate the boys from their issues and create separate meaningful relationships with their sons.

The systemic issues of divorce are similar for younger children and adolescents. Boundary violations, with one parent seeking alliance against the other, are quite common, and the tasks of adaptation to the divorce are the same. Although an adolescent may be cognitively more developed than a younger child, similar emotional distress may occur. Cognitive confusion may also arise because there is still an emotional allegiance and longing for a parent even in the event that the adolescent recognizes improper behavior of that parent as a spouse. This allegiance in turn can infuriate and confuse the more responsible parent. Conflict can then ensue in the household as the adolescent is asked to judge and confirm that parent's "cause." This is well demonstrated by the following case.

Case 2: The Pline Family

Tess, an intelligent, engaging 14-year-old, requested therapy for conflict with her mother, Galen, an anthropologist, with whom she lived along with her 18-year-old brother, Bradley. The parents had separated and divorced 2 years earlier, when Galen discovered that Dick had been having an affair with her friend, Jill. Following parental separation and divorce, Dick moved to New Mexico, where he now lived with Jill. When Tess was 10, her family had visited Jill's family in New Mexico. Tess and Jill's 9-year-old son, Jason, were asleep on the porch and were awakened by strange sounds. Tess's father and Jill were lying in a sleeping bag next to the children, sexually involved. Tess to this day denies that she knows quite what they were doing. She and Jason talked about the "weird thing that happened," and she finally told her mother after Dick had moved in with the now divorced Jill and her two sons. Tess had infrequent phone contact with her father and dreaded the annual visit to his new home.

Treatment: Family Therapy Component

The first few sessions of therapy were directed at resolving some of the conflictual issues between mother and daughter. Conflict was mild and interspersed with periods of pleasant communication. At first, this appeared to be Tess's individuation, normal at best. Each was seen alone and together to honor subsystem differentiation, but Tess requested more individual therapy time. She then expressed her anger with Mom for telling her that her father was not sending child support and that they were consequently financially strapped. The systemic goal was again to create boundaries and appropriate hierarchy so that Mom kept her stuff from Tess and respected that Tess still loved her father. Tess also did not want to be Galen's buddy, and she resented her brother, who did not want to participate in therapy. His mother reported that he was bright but unmotivated and failing 12th grade. These sessions soon resulted in reduction of conflict. Galen was also in individual treatment including EMDR with another therapist.

Treatment: EMDR Component

Tess denied that she had any distressing memories from the past. She was very cooperative and friendly, said she was fine with the divorce, and focused on normative non-divorce-related issues. However, immediately prior to an impending visit to her father, she reported anxiety and sleeplessness and expressed great reluctance about the visit. She agreed to do EMDR on the issue. When asked if she could identify a past disturbing memory, she identified as a target an incident that had occurred during the most recent visit to her father. Interestingly, although she had not chosen the earlier porch incident involving her father and his lover, the theme of the selected target is resonant of that event.

- *Image:* Last summer, Jill's sons Pete, 17, and Jason, 13, were there. Jason is my age but very immature and ADHD. Pete knocked on Dad and Jill's bedroom door and they wouldn't answer. It was awkward. Pete got angry and Jason was disgusted. (And you?) I screamed at my Dad afterward when I found a condom in their trashcan while I was cleaning their bathroom for them. Dad's shirt was unbuttoned and I confronted him. He said, "I'm hot." But it was not hot in the house. (What time of day was it?) This was at lunchtime.
- *Feeling:* (When you think of that scene, what feeling do you have?) Embarrassed. Grossed out. I think of my dad and mom and then him with Jill. It makes me angry.
- *SUD:* (How bad is that distress now?) 10.
- *Cognition:* (How would you like to cope with it?) I would like to make less of it. They do live together and have needs. They are real people. (*The order was*

reversed here because the EMDR session was not actually preplanned and seemed to flow out of the natural conversation. She had done EMDR previously and was familiar with the routine. The Negative Cognition was not elicited, but her statement was treated as a Positive Cognition and a Validity of Cognition [VOC] scale score was elicited.) (That's what your head says, but how true is that?) Four. It's hard to think about it, but I guess I understand.

• *Body sensation:* (Where do you feel it in your body now?) Stomach is queasy. (Go with it.)

1. I was angry at Dad, then mad at Jill. I felt she took Dad from me. I'm still mad but not as mad. (Number?) Four. In my stomach and chest.

2. I was confused. I didn't know why.

3. I understand it more. I have less harsh of a feeling.

4. It's not as strong. Not as mad.

   (*Still processing. Long silence. Her face is somber and looks as if tears are welling.*) (Are you sad? I thought I saw tears.) Kind of, because I'm losing my Dad. (Go with that.)

5. Not really anything.

   (What's your number now?) A low number. I don't really feel the anger.

   (Your stomach?) It's not churning now. (So what can you say to yourself to help yourself?) (*This Cognitive Interweave elicits elements of responsibility and choice.*) He's a real person, too, and even though he's my dad, I have to let him live.

   (Would you be able to say to your dad "I accept you with Jill but can you be appropriate; it's embarrassing for a kid?") (*Interweave selected to help set appropriate boundaries because she is older and able to articulate, and she does have some power.*) I could say that.

   (How might he respond?) (*This interweave tests the safety of her choice.*) Since he works away from home during the week now, he might say he sees me less often and so he'd like to do what he wants. (And do you accept that [choice]?) (*also checking for emotional distress*).

6. It's hard because it's the only time I see him, too. (*sad face again*). (It's painful.)

7. I think he's choosing her over me.

   (Can you ask him for something for you?) I don't know.

8. I guess I could go on hikes with him, even though I don't like them, to get some time with him (Lunch?) (*Cognitive Interweave to help expand options.*)

9. Yeah, that would be good. I have fun when it's just me and him.

   (And you see him differently from your mom. He's your father.) (Mhm.) (*Interweave sets boundaries in system and shifts alliance expectations.*) (What comes to you now?)

10. Happiness. I know I can probably find some way to be with him. (How's that stomach?) Good. I'm getting, I don't know, no real emotion. I haven't seen him for a year, except I saw him one day this June at graduation.

11. I feel calmer. I'm looking forward to it because it might be nice to see him. (And Jill?) (*Search for possible unresolved triggers.*) Okay.

At this point, Tess's SUD score was 0. Her body sensations were absent, and her cognition was congruent (VOC 7). A future template imagining handling the visit well was introduced.

Treatment Summary

Following this session, Tess comfortably visited her father in New Mexico. An unexpected outcome ensued. Frantic phone calls were received from Galen, Tess, and Dick, each with different motivational agendas. Tess was so happy in New Mexico she decided she wanted to stay there and attend school, which was beginning within a week! Dick thought this was a splendid plan, even though he would be out of town for his job from Sunday evening through Friday night. He was relocating to Vermont within 6 months, and Tess would essentially be in the care of Jill.

Tess's longing for her father and desire to be with him is typical of the conflicts wrought by divorce. That her reconnection with Dick had not occurred on a prior visit presented the therapist with a troubling thought: Had the EMDR worked too well? Individual and family concerns brewed. Both parents contacted their lawyers, and telephone therapy with each family member became essential. Tess's feelings about wanting to have time with her father were validated by both the therapist and, amazingly, her mother. Galen was able to do this because her lawyer, personal therapist, and family therapist had informed her that a court intervention would likely take months as there was no identifiable emergency to support Tess's move and many good reasons in terms of her stability, peer group, and parental availability to predict that her father would not gain residential custody. However, despite therapeutic intervention, Dick remained narcissistically focused on his agenda rather than recognizing what was best for his daughter.

Tess agreed to return home to resolve the matter through the courts. She was under the impression that her wishes would be immediately granted, and neither the therapist nor her mother disabused her of that opinion—an example of a therapeutic alliance and collusion with a chosen parental subsystem because of the therapist's belief that this was in Tess's best interest. She wrote a letter to the judge under her father's tutelage, and indeed with her mother's support. This systemic maneuver was designed by the therapist to defuse conflict, which could result in Tess resisting returning home and ultimately strengthened the mother-daughter subsystem.

Upon her return, Tess processed a dilemma posed by the therapist: What if the judge did not support the move? She targeted the possible scenario with EMDR. During processing, she reported feeling sorry for her father not being able to see her. This, too, typifies divorced children's reactions. A Cognitive Interweave challenged her belief that she was responsible for her father's feelings and behaviors: "Whose choice was it that your father moved so far away?" This helped her to gain a different perspective and shift emotionally. In systemic terms, it helped her to redefine her alignment with her father, which also relieved her of having to protect him. She reported that she could come to terms with the situation and recognized the dilemma of not wanting to be separated from either parent. She recognized, too, that it was normal to experience sadness about what the divorce had brought her.

Tess returned to school and immediately reconnected with friends and became excited about her school program. Resolving her systemic conflicts and the attendant affect allowed her to refocus on normatively appropriate matters, and peer relationships became her major focus. The family therapy facilitated the healing process so that Galen was able to realign her behavior yet provide emotional support. Even though Dick appeared immutable at that time, once Tess was settled at her mother's home, the pattern of contact reverted to what it had been (in systemic terms, the system returned to homeostasis), and he did not pursue the matter further. Tess enjoyed visits to her father about twice a year and had no regrets about returning home. The integrated EMDR and family interventions appear to have helped her resolve the developmental tasks in acceptance of the divorce reality.

To complete the tale, Bradley, then 20, had just returned to his mother's home after having spent 8 months living with his father and working on a farm. He enrolled in an adjunctive university program to prepare for admittance to college and requested therapy to deal with "anxiety" and "low motivation." He was receiving EMDR treatment. Galen remained in treatment with another EMDR therapist throughout the entire divorce process.

Longitudinal Follow-Up

A year later, Tess, age 15, returned to therapy. Her father had recently moved to Massachusetts and filed for custody without consulting Tess.

Tess did not display much emotion but reported to her therapist that she did not want to move to her father, although she liked him and his family. In the session, unaided, she wrote an eloquent letter to the judge expressing her opinion, but it was disallowed in court, as was a letter written by the therapist stating that it was in the best interest of Tess's emotional health to remain in the environment in which she had long-term positive relationships and a sense of community.

Tess desired only 3 weeks of visitation with her father in the summer, as she had already established other plans and was excited about participating in a 10-day humanitarian mission in Mississippi and a 3-week camp, both under the auspices of her church. Her father again responded out of his narcissistic needs and refused to consider the teenager's developmental needs or wishes and to recognize the importance of maintaining her stability within her comfort zone.

The meeting with the judge was stressful for Tess. The court ruling supported Tess remaining in her domain but increased summer visitation to 5 weeks, with 1 weekend midway with her mother. Her father appeared to accept this decision without malice. Nevertheless, Tess immediately began sleeping excessively and stopped all peer activity. Half of the next therapy session was devoted to a debriefing of the court experience with mother and daughter, followed by EMDR with Tess alone.

- *Picture:* I am sitting in the chair and the judge is saying "I am not telling you where I am going to let you stay, but how long would you like to visit the *other* parent?"

  I said, "If it's with my mother then . . ." (longer). She said, "No" and would not let me continue. She just wanted me to respond generically.
- *Negative Cognition:* I betrayed my father.
- *Positive Cognition:* I know the right decision in my heart. (VOC = 6.)
- *Emotion:* Guilt. Worry.
- *Location:* Stomach.
- *SUD:* 8.

The following sequence indicates Tess's responses after each set of BLS:

1. Lesser feeling of guilty, but I still feel guilt.
2. Less, since I know what's right in my heart. Still feel guilty, but it's not as strong.
3. Kind of a black void. But it's a positive void.
4. I feel positive about it. How I felt in there was nervous and overstimulated. I was worried that I would hurt a parent.
5. I think that the decision I made was right for me. My parents' influence wasn't part of my decision.
6. I feel at peace with it. (How's your stomach?) Fine. (So let it roll again.)
7. I told myself I know what's right for me. (Do you anticipate in the future what will come up?) Dad will bring it up. (*Cognitive Interweave: The goal is to release her from her enmeshment and being a pawn in the marital conflict as well as to reframe the problem to be developmentally congruent for an adolescent.*) (It's not about choosing between your parents. It's about your life, school, friends.) Mhm. (Picture yourself in the future.)
8. A good feeling. I'm in control of the situation.
9. What number is it [SUD] now? One. (What would drop it to zero?) If it hadn't happened or if we could've foreseen he was going to do this and done this [EMDR] before it happened. (Do the words "I know what's right in my heart" still fit, or are there some other words that fit better?) I know what I said was right for me and for this time in my life.
10. I'm a zero now, and the guilty feeling has gone away. My stomach feels calm.

Tess returned to therapy 5 days later. Her positive feelings remained despite the fact that her father had begun instant-messaging her about summer arrangements. She reported that she told him that this was a matter between him and her mother and that she felt uncomfortable. He agreed and then persisted with two more messages, which prompted her to divert by saying that she had to sign off to do her homework. She said she was able to do this because of "the amazing EMDR." Her excessive sleeping ceased after this EMDR session and she resumed peer relations. Alas her father at this writing has again filed for custody(!) which has resulted in further stress for both mother and daughter. Further sessions will continue to support Tess through this process.

Tess's challenges are typical for children of divorce where repeated themes of unresolved conflict permeate their lives and create conflict (often around family celebrations) and foster stress, guilt, and other complex emotions. Family therapy is useful in processing systemic issues, even when all members of the family, as in this case, are not accessible for therapy. The EMDR session outcome demonstrates the speedy efficacy of processing current conflictual divorce issues that may recur in the hope that their impact will be lessened and the child's coping strategies increased, thereby alleviating children's emotional burdens in situations not of their making.

DISCUSSION

Ultimately, from a structural system's perspective of the divorced family, the child's adjustment is dependent on family realignment with a new bimodal hierarchical structure, clear boundaries, with parental roles uncontaminated by personal agendas—a difficult task to achieve in reality! The family component of treatment is clearly important, as the changing structure of the family itself becomes an activating source of disturbance for the child. Both the Dunn and Pline families illustrate family systems elements of structural disintegration, breakdown in hierarchy, alliance conflicts, triangulation of children as go-betweens, and the accompanying consequences. As can be seen in these examples, the restructuring of the family system was a necessary element in healing. Also apparent was the importance of attending to the children's internal distress through individual EMDR processing. Integration of both models offered a more complete treatment approach.

As is evident in the examples presented, for toddlers, children, and adolescents, merely attending to structural factors is not sufficient to resolve the child's problems, as the internally stored experience must also be addressed. The internal experience is composed of memories, thoughts, feelings, and viscerally stored reactions accumulated during the sometimes protracted process of predivorce conflict, transitional instability, and recomposition of the new family structure. EMDR accesses the child's perspective, which is often difficult to elicit through talk therapy, play therapy, or family therapy alone. EMDR activates material related to the systemic and affective complications of the divorce, stemming from the past, occurring in the present, and anticipated for the future. These elements are often infused with indelible imagery, emotional intensity, cognitive distortions, and factual realities. EMDR provides an opportunity to unravel and process this internal unresolved material, and there follows a more comfortable settling within the context of the re-structured family system. However, if changes within the family system do not support the well-being of the child, the task of therapy becomes more difficult and the goal becomes helping the child to cope with instability and continued distress.

To help the child cope with and adjust to the sequelae of the divorce experience, it follows that if both external realities (e.g., changed external structure of the family) and internal perceptions of the current system and past hurts are attended to in therapy, more satisfactory outcomes may ensue. Bearing this in mind, the elegance of including the information processing model of EMDR in the treatment plan offers a more complete treatment option. The systemic and affective complications of divorce stemming from the past, activated in the present, and anticipated for the future are all addressed. The child is able to process the perceived information with its elements of emotional intensity, cognitive distortions, and factual realities toward resolution and acceptance and, hopefully, become more adjusted in the context of the restructured family system.

Thus, a feasible treatment protocol for children of divorce needs to address both elements of the family structural process as well as the internal experience of the child. In the integrated treatment process described in this chapter, structural family systems therapy addresses the *external* structural elements contributing to the child's experience, and EMDR addresses the *internal* cognitive, perceptual, affective, and somatic elements of the child's stored experience, which in fact *includes* the experience of the whole family system. To help the child cope with and adjust to the sequelae of the divorce experience, it follows that if factual *realities* such as the changed external structure of the family and the *perceptions* of both realities and their meaning from past, present, and future are attended to in therapy, more satisfactory therapeutic outcomes may be facilitated. The integration of family systems therapy and Adaptive Information Processing as represented by EMDR offers a comprehensive contextual model for the treatment of children of divorce. The equation *The whole system plus the whole child equals the whole treatment* sums up the breadth and depth of the integrative family therapy and EMDR approach.

REFERENCES

Ahrons, C., & Rodgers, R. (1987). *Divorced families: A multidisciplinary developmental view.* New York: Norton.

Amato, P. R., & Keith, B. (1991). Parental divorce and the well being of children: A meta-analysis. *Psychological Bulletin, 110,* 26–46.

Dworkin, M. (2005). *EMDR and the relational imperative: The therapeutic relationship in EMDR.* New York: Routledge.

Emery, R. E. (1982). Interparental conflict and the children of discord and divorce. *Psychological Bulletin, 92,* 310–330.

Erickson, E. (1950). *Childhood and society.* New York: Norton.

Forehand, R., & Long, N. (2002). *Parenting the strong-willed child.* New York: McGraw-Hill.

Greenwald, R. (1999). *Eye movement desensitization and reprocessing (EMDR) in child and adolescent psychotherapy.* Northvale, NJ: Aronson.

Gurman, A. S., & Kniskern, D. P. (Eds.). (1981). *Handbook of family therapy.* New York: Brunner/Mazel.

Haley, J. (1980). *Leaving home: The therapy of disturbed young people.* New York: McGraw-Hill.

Isaacs, M. B., & Abelsohn, D. (1986). *The difficult divorce.* New York: Basic Books.

Kaslow, F. W. (1981). Divorce and divorce therapy. In A. S. Gurman & D. P. Kniskern (Eds.), *Handbook of family therapy* (pp. 662–696). New York: Brunner/Mazel.

Klaff, F. (1983). *Children of divorce: Adjustment with relationship with parents.* Unpublished dissertation thesis, The Fielding Institute

Kressel, K. (1985). *The process of divorce.* New York: Basic Books.

Minuchin, S. (1974). *Families and family therapy.* Cambridge, MA: Harvard University Press.

Nichols, M. P., & Schwartz, R. C. (1998). *Family therapy, concepts, and methods* (4th ed.). Boston: Allyn & Bacon.

Parsons, T. (1951). *The social system.* New York: Free Press.

Schulman, G. L. (1982, Summer). Divorce, single parenthood and stepfamilies: Structural implications of these transactions. *International Journal of Family Therapy, 3,* 88–112.

Shapiro, F. (2001). *Eye movement desensitization and reprocessing: Basic principles, protocols and procedures* (2nd ed.). New York: Guilford Press.

U.S. divorce statistics. (2006). *Divorce Magazine.* Retrieved July 27, 2006, from http://divorcemag.com/statistics/statsUS.shtml.

Wallerstein, J. S. (1983). Children of divorce: The psychological tasks of the child. *American Journal of Orthopsychiatry, 53,* 230–243.

Wallerstein, J. S., & Kelly, J. B. (1980). *Surviving the breakup: How children and parents cope with divorce.* New York: Basic Books.

Weltner, J. A. (1982). Structural approach to the single parent family. *Family Process, 21*(20), 203–210.

CHAPTER 15

The Child as Identified Patient: Integrating Contextual Therapy and EMDR

Barry Litt

It is estimated that as many as 2% of children under age 12 and from 5% to 18% of adolescents suffer from a depressive disorder (Birmaher et al., 1996; Northey, Wells, Silverman, & Bailey, 2003) that will likely persist into adulthood (Northey et al., 2003; Wagner & Ambrosini, 2001). Depressed children who seek outpatient treatment have higher rates of comorbidity and poorer academic and social functioning (Hammen, Rudolph, Weisz, Rao, & Burge, 1999) than their nondepressed counterparts. Moreover, depressive symptoms are strongly related to suicidal behavior in adolescents (Spirito, Valeri, Boergers, & Donaldson, 2003)—the third leading cause of death in children between ages 10 and 19 years (Centers for Disease Control, 1999). Despite the severity of the disorder, research into childhood depression is in its early stages, and little is known about its etiology or effective treatments (Messer & Gross, 1995; Northey et al., 2003).

Research into the development of depressive disorder has focused on the contribution of genes (Eley & Stevenson, 1999; Whiffen, Kerr, & Kallos-Lilly, 2005), psychological variables (Gladstone & Kaslow, 1995; Joiner & Wagner, 1995), psychosocial environment (DiFilippo & Overholser, 2000; Messer & Gross, 1995), or the interaction between two or more of these domains (Eley, 2003; Reinherz, Paradis, Giaconia, Stashwick, & Fitzmaurice, 2003; Schwartz, Kaslow, Seeley, & Lewisohn, 2000). Therapies that have received the most attention in the form of randomly controlled trials include psychopharmacological intervention (Wagner & Ambrosini, 2001; Wagner, Robb, Findling, Gutierrez, & Heydorn, 2004), psychological intervention (Brent et al., 1997; Mufson et al., 2004; Reinecke, Ryan, & DuBois, 1998), and a combination of cognitive-behavioral therapy plus medication (March et al., 2004). Although family-based interventions hold promise for treating childhood depression, the research literature available as of 2003 shows systemic family therapy being subjected to the rigors of empirical validation only in the Brent et al. study (Cottrell, 2003; Northey et al., 2003). This is surprising considering that parental criticism, parental conflict, poor parent-child communication, and excessive aversive interactions are associated with the onset and course of childhood depression (Cottrell, 2003; Hammen et al., 1999; Messer & Gross, 1995).

Moreover, there is some limited research that suggests that children's distorted sense of responsibility for their parents' marital conflict is positively related to increased levels of psychosocial maladjustment (Buchanan, Maccoby, & Dornbusch, 1991; O'Brien, Margolin, & John, 1995).

Childhood Depression from a Family Systems Perspective

The systems approach on which family therapy is based assumes that mental illness is an irreducible phenomenon that results from the complex, recursive interaction of biology, psychology, family, and culture (Nichols & Schwartz, 1998). Historically, family therapy has proceeded on the complementarity, systemic axioms of *equipotentiality* and *equifinality* (from a single event, many outcomes, and vice versa; Simon, Stierlin, & Wynne, 1985). The assumption is that maladaptive family processes exacerbate, maintain, or simply miss opportunities to ameliorate symptoms in the identified patient (Framo, 1982; Prince & Jacobson, 1995). Systemic therapy is not diagnosis-specific, and the goal is to improve family functioning with the expectation that the symptoms—whatever they may be—will remit (Northey et al., 2003).

This is not as unreasonable as it may sound, considering the wealth of data relating family factors to childhood mental illness (Cummings, Davies, & Campbell, 2000), the fact that parents, symptomatic children, and therapists do not always agree on treatment goals when therapy is targeted to the diagnosis (e.g., Garland, Lewczyk-Boxmeyer, Gabayan, & Hawley, 2004), and the general finding that family therapy is more efficacious than no treatment for a wide variety of adult and childhood mental disorders (Northey et al., 2003; Pinsof & Wynne, 2000; Shadish & Baldwin, 2003). Moreover, as Northey and colleagues point out:

> Children and families rarely present for treatment with "pure" disorders and no contextual stressors. It is the rule rather than the exception that children and families who present to clinics often have multiple comorbidities, functional impairments, and contextual stressors that impact on their presenting clinical picture. (p. 538)

Therapy models must take these factors into consideration in a way that research designs aimed at a particular diagnosis do not. The holistic nature of family therapy is well suited to this, as it directs the clinician to examine contextual stressors and to offer treatment options that go beyond the presenting problem. Theoretically, then, family therapy may be an effective intervention for correcting pathogenic processes before they lead to functional impairments and ameliorating disorders that are already manifest.

Childhood Depression from an Adaptive Information Processing Perspective

Shapiro's (2001, p. 16) Adaptive Information Processing (AIP) model proposed that most psychopathological conditions are "derived from earlier life experiences that set in motion a continued pattern of affect, behavior, cognitions, and consequent identity structures." Disturbing experiences that are insufficiently processed become locked into the nervous system in state-specific form. Present-day exposure to the salient excitatory stimulus triggers the affects, beliefs, and behaviors of the original, dysfunctionally stored material. Shapiro asserted that a wide variety of pathologies, including some types of depression, might be configured by early life experiences.

This hypothesis is as yet untested with respect to the matter at hand; there are no randomly controlled trials of EMDR in the treatment of adults or children with a mood disorder. However, existing research on EMDR shows promise with regard to the reduction of symptoms associated with depressive disorder. For example, numerous studies of adults with Posttraumatic Stress Disorder (PTSD; see Maxfield & Hyer, 2002) and at least one study of children with PTSD (Chemtob, Nakashima, & Carlson, 2002) showed EMDR to be effective in reducing participants' comorbid depressive symptoms.

EMDR also has been shown to transform negative self-beliefs and maladaptive attribution style (Shapiro, 2001), two features of cognition that are associated with depression in adults (Beck, Rush, Shaw, & Emery, 1979) as well as in youth (Garber & Robinson, 1997; Muris, Schmidt, Lambrichs, & Meesters, 2001; Schwartz et al., 2000). Finally, EMDR has been shown to correct the undifferentiated attributions of responsibility that adult survivors of childhood abuse have for the behavior of the perpetrator (Edmond, Ruben, & Wambach, 1999; Edmond, Sloan, & McCarty, 2004; Shapiro, 2001).

The Contextualization of EMDR

Contextual Therapy can be considered a metatheory, in that it bridges Object Relations Theories with family systems theories; historical and developmental (vertical) elements with here-and-now (horizontal) elements of family functioning; and individual meaning making with transactional patterning (Fowers & Wenger, 1997; Hibbs, 1989). Contextual Therapy is a differentiation-based (e.g., Kerr & Bowen, 1988; Schnarch, 1991) approach in that it promotes self-determination in the face of family pressure for compliance, reliance on internal resources for self-validation rather than dependence on others for approval, and the overcoming of emotional discomfort in the interests of responsible action (Boszormenyi-Nagy & Krasner, 1986). In fact, from a contextual perspective, responsible relating is inextricable from psychological well-being.

Principles of Contextual Theory

Central to contextual theory is the dialectical principle of relatedness, that is, that the experience of self exists as figure to the ground of a relating not-self, or other. Without relating partners to act on as other, the phenomenological experience of self cannot exist. Insofar as the other is an inextricable feature of one's identity (i.e., attachment figures), self and other are said to be *ontically* dependent (Boszormenyi-Nagy, 1965).

Because the developing child is forming a self in relation to the family as a not-self referent, the introjected family system—its rules, obligations, and entitlements—forms an internalized *relational need template* which determines the criteria, or "fit," for future attachment relationships (Boszormenyi-Nagy, 1965; Framo, 1965, 1982). A woman who grew up in a violent household may find her experience of self validated by marrying an abusive husband. Rigid adherenceto complementary roles of victim and abuser bind each partner reciprocally in a familiar but stagnant self-validating context that inhibits self-delineation and growth.

Self and other manifest their ontic dependence through a dialogue of subject and object roles. The subject role is characterized by receiving attention, the object role by giving it. The mature, or differentiated, personality is capable of alternating subject and object roles on mutually acceptable terms with a relating partner (Boszormenyi-Nagy, 1965; Friedman, 1960). The resulting equitable balancing of self needs with other needs characterizes the dialogic mode of relating, which is the vehicle for trust building (Boszormenyi-Nagy & Krasner, 1986).

A pathological condition exists when there is a chronic imbalance of subject and object positions in a committed relationship. Familiar expressions such as "It's always about him" and "She takes up a lot of space" are testament to the widespread dissatisfaction with those who dominate the subject role. Similarly, a pathological condition arises when being the object of the other's needs eclipses one's own autonomy. Many women have been socialized to believe that their role is to "renounce their own personal ambitions and become merely a ground or context for the strivings of their husbands and children" (Boszormenyi-Nagy, 1987, p. 93).

The balancing of giving and receiving attention and concern implies an ethical dimension to relationship. The dimension of relational ethics—an original and signal contribution by Boszormenyi-Nagy (Fowers & Wenger, 1997)—is the centerpiece of Contextual Therapy. It is also an easily misunderstood concept (e.g., Boszormenyi-Nagy, 1997) because fairness refers to the balancing of ontic needs primarily—the sharing of subject and object positions in a relationship—and functional (i.e., instrumental) needs only secondarily. An equitable division of labor can be a vital resource for a committed couple, but such functional fairness may belie a deeper, ontic reality. A doting husband may perform caretaking tasks for his functionally dependent wife, yet in his need to be needed, he dominates the subject role.

Because parents and children have asymmetrical options for giving and receiving attention and concern, the relationship is ethically unbalanced: Parents give more to their children than the children can return. This fact of children's *indebtedness* stimulates in them a motivational configuration called *filial loyalty* (Boszormenyi-Nagy, 1987; Boszormenyi-Nagy & Krasner, 1986). Filial loyalty may be experienced subjectively as gratitude, guilt, a sense of duty or obligation toward one's parents, need for approval, or not consciously at all.

But in this context, loyalty is about commitment, not feelings. A child's ability to offer age-appropriate concern for the parent, and the parent's ability to receive and acknowledge it, allows that child to progressively discharge the debt and thereby earn *entitlement,* that is, the freedom to make legitimate claims for attention and concern from others. More specifically, the child earns the right to individuate: separate, leave home, and form extrafamilial loyalties. Parents who frustrate their offspring's age-appropriate loyalty efforts, or fail to acknowledge them, entrap their children in a position of chronic indebtedness (Boszormenyi-Nagy & Krasner, 1986).

A Contextual Approach to Pathogenesis

Like other systemic therapies, contextual theory assumes that many mental illnesses, including depression, are developed or maintained through pathogenic family processes (Boszormenyi-Nagy & Krasner, 1986). The principal pathogenic relational configuration affecting children is *parentification.* Unlike the parentified child described by Minuchin (1974), parentification in an ethical context occurs when a child is maneuvered into an object role in the service of the parent's (ontic) ego needs, whether or not that child takes on parentlike (functional) tasks. In addition to obvious forms of exploitation such as physical and sexual abuse, parentification can take the form of scapegoating, infantilizing, or manipulating a child such that loyalty to one parent is disloyalty to the other—a relational configuration called *split loyalties* (Boszormenyi-Nagy & Krasner, 1986).

A needy parent's unconscious need to extract validation from a dependent child shapes the child's personality in a complementary fashion, such that the child learns to accept the ethical imbalance as "normal." The chronically parentified child may develop a *counterautonomous superego* (Boszormenyi-Nagy, 1965) that inhibits individuation with excessive guilt and anxiety. The child is thereby groomed to feel responsible for the parent's well-being and will likely transfer this maladaptive attributional set to other significant relationships (Boszormenyi-Nagy, 1987).

Contextual Theory and the Adaptive Information Processing Model: A Synthesis

Both the contextual approach and the AIP model predict that formative childhood experiences affect both psychological health and relational functioning. The AIP model attributes pathology to the accumulation of discrete traumatic events, and the contextual approach embeds these traumas, large and small, in their relational context. Discrete traumas from a client's family of origin experience, both past and present, are markers of continuously operating, rule-bound patterns of ethically unbalanced relating.

Watching his mother beat his sister while their father passively looked on was a traumatic event for Hal, but the fact that it happened at all reflected the ethical reality of everyday family life: that his mother's needs—even her need to discharge her sadistic impulses—were more important than the children's safety or welfare. The trauma of the event itself is compounded by the lasting effect that ongoing parentification has on personality structure. With its systemic paradigm and its ethical dimension of relationship, the contextual approach is complementary and additive to Shapiro's (2001) AIP model. The contextual approach shows the clinician where to look for the targets, and Eye Movement Desensitization and Reprocessing (EMDR) provides the potency to transform the experience.

THERAPY PROCESS

A general structure of phase-oriented therapy can be described that accounts for most, if not all, referrals for treatment. An assessment phase, a contracting phase, and an intervention phase characterize the main tasks of the therapist. In practice, these phases may overlap, coincide, or repeat themselves over the course of minutes, weeks, or months. This chapter describes only those practices that are unique to the integrated approach.

The Assessment Phase

Consistent with the objectives of EMDR's Phase 1 (Shapiro, 2001), the objectives of this phase are to assess pathology from the biomedical, sociocultural, psychological, transactional (systemic), and ethical domains and develop a working hypothesis of the problem. Methods for assessment specific to this discussion include evaluating transactions and eliciting *Negative Cognitions,* history gathering, and identifying family of origin issues. The formal assessment phase concludes with exploring therapeutic options for each client.

Conjoint sessions are invaluable for observing transactions that reflect deeper, ethical imbalances in the family. These meetings also provide the clinician with a unique opportunity to observe maladaptive cognitive schemas in action. When a conflict or impasse arises in session, a client becomes defensive, or a pathological transaction is observed, the clinician can stop the unfolding interaction and ask involved parties the questions "When this happens, what does it make you believe about yourself?" and "What feelings and sensations do you notice right now?" Negative Cognitions elicited in situ need very little priming on the part of the therapist, and clients have immediate access to the gestalt of corresponding emotions and somatic sensations. The follow-up question "When have you felt this way before?" invites tracing of the present trigger to its family of origin context. These experiences lay the groundwork for Phases 2 and 3 of the EMDR approach (Shapiro, 2001).

History gathering in the initial phase of treatment is accomplished in conjoint family sessions and also in private sessions with the parents. These private sessions are useful for gathering information about the couple relationship and identifying family of origin issues of each adult. A three-generation genogram (e.g., McGoldrick, Gerson, & Shellenberger, 1999) aids in revealing legacies of entitlements and indebtedness and exploring possibilities for earning entitlement through rejunctive action. The genogram also provides an economical blueprint for cataloguing targets for later EMDR sessions. This phase culminates in the development of a working hypothesis regarding the salient pathogenic beliefs, transactions, and ethical imbalances in the family.

The Contracting Phase

Incorporating EMDR's Phase 2 (Shapiro, 2001), the objective of this phase is to present the assessment and treatment options to the responsible parties in a succinct, comprehensible manner and to establish informed consent for therapy. When the child is the identified patient, common options for therapy stemming from this approach are biomedical intervention (i.e., referral for psychiatric or physical evaluation), EMDR, Conjoint Family Therapy, and consultation with teachers and school officials. Parents may be offered the same options, with the addition of couples therapy and family of origin work.

A practical task in this phase, and one likely to be renegotiated periodically, is to determine the who, what, and when of therapy. As the contextual approach stresses autonomy and personal responsibility, the menu of treatment options is presented; the adults and, depending on their maturity, the children are then invited to contract for an individualized treatment plan. For example, one parent may choose to pursue individual therapy (e.g., EMDR and family of origin work), whereas the other parent may wish to participate only in conjoint work with the child, and all parties agree that the child could benefit from a psychiatric evaluation and EMDR.

Working both conjointly and individually with various family members is clinically synergistic and cohesive and affords the therapist an unparalleled opportunity to observe the interlocking relationship between psychic structure and transactional patterning. The logic of this approach is intuitive to many clients who appreciate having a single therapist who is accountable to the whole family, and vice versa. Nevertheless, it is likely that most therapists are not trained to work this way, and some may find it useful to seek consultation on managing boundary and confidentiality issues peculiar to this approach.

The Intervention Phase

As mentioned earlier, the parentification of children is of paramount concern in Contextual Therapy because it is considered a pathogenic relational configuration that can affect generations to come. Various behavioral and systemic interventions may be used to stop exploitation at the transactional level, but changing the more subtle (but more profound) balance of give-and-take is predicated on increasing the parents' own affect tolerance, self-soothing capacity, access to adaptive internal resources (e.g., mindfulness, impulse control, positive self-talk; Schnarch, 1991), and reliance on dialogue as a relational resource (Boszormenyi-Nagy & Krasner, 1986). Consider the parent who asks his son, "Am I a good father?" The father's plea for reassurance undermines his parental role: The child is being asked to parent his father. This, and the countless other double binds that no doubt prevail, are symptoms of the father's inability to soothe and validate himself. To help the son, the therapist must help the father.

Parentification begets parentification. As family of origin experiences from childhood are the main contributors to arrested development, and present-day family of origin relating maintains the arrested personality structure, it follows that these relational configurations themselves are natural targets for EMDR. Kitchur (2005) offers guidelines for targeting family relationships in her strategic developmental model. In most cases, the first target for the desensitization phase is a memory of conflict between the parents. The second and third targets are the relationship with each parent. Ensuing targets include traumas small and large, nodal family events (e.g., birth, moves, serious illness, death), and transactional traumas (e.g., favored sibling, parent-sibling conflict). Consistent with Shapiro's (2001) recommendation, Kitchur favors desensitizing targets in chronological order.

The first three targets (parents' relationship, each parent) are especially rich in the material they generate, and often great progress can be made by their resolution. Reprocessing memories of the parents' conflictual relationship can relieve the bind of split loyalties and a distorted sense of responsibility for the parents' marriage. Reprocessing memories of a parent is therapeutic whether it is event-specific or generic (e.g., the client's most vivid image of Father) because issues of self-worth are personalizations of unearned merit (i.e., lack of worth) in the eyes of the parent. Children confound their own existential self-worth with their experience of their value in the family, what Boszormenyi-Nagy and Spark (1973) called *merit-based accounting of the family*. As a result, maladaptive cognitions such as "I'm not good enough," "I don't measure up," and "I'm worthless" become internalized. EMDR can be effective in reprocessing these Negative Cognitions and their accompanying gestalt and pave the way for transforming the relational paradigms they engender.

Looping, or blocked processing in which distress remains high for numerous consecutive sets (Shapiro, 2001), is common in this type of work. Two original interweaves specific to this aspect of the therapy have been indispensable. The first, the *differentiation interweave,* is essentially a *Cognitive Interweave* (Shapiro, 2001) with a slant on issues of differentiation of self. Central to this strategy is the transformation of the client's paradigm of comparative self-worth to one of existential self-worth. The former, all too common paradigm is based on the family's ledger of merit and implies a hierarchy of human value in which the client is trying to be good enough for the parent or bask in the parent's approval. The latter is an acceptance that all human beings have intrinsic merit that is not subject to quantitative judgment. *Positive Cognitions* indicative of existential self-worth include "I'm worthy" or simply "I am."

Specifically, the differentiation interweave includes techniques such as having the client think about the parent by name and not by title and challenging tacit assumptions during the desensitization phase. The following are some examples for a client who is desensitizing a target of his mother, Martha:

- Why is Martha's opinion of you more important than your own?
- What if nobody could make Martha happy? What if you won the Nobel Prize and she still was disappointed in you, what would that mean?
- Did Martha disappoint her mother? Perhaps your grandmother should be the final judge?
- Do you suppose Martha is looking to you for approval? What would that mean?

- Do you suppose that Martha has impeccable parenting skills gleaned from her own nurturing background, but chose not to use those skills with you because you are different somehow?
- If Martha suddenly thought that you were perfect and showered you with praise, would you be a better person than you were yesterday?
- Notice Martha's unhappiness. Whose problem is it?

Socratic questioning, irony, and perspective taking punctuate the desensitization phase to shatter the illusions and magical thinking of the child perspective and install executive, adult reasoning.

As a companion technique, the *somatic interweave* works synergistically with the cognitive intervention. During the dual attention stimulation (DAS), the client is asked to push both arms out straight "like you are pushing against a great weight." With baffling reliability, and to the astonishment of many a client, this action alone drops the intensity of the affect noticeably—even without the dual attention stimulation. More significantly, this action simulates (or stimulates) the effect of having a more healthy ego boundary. Clients report greater detachment from the parent figure, more compassion for the parent as an individual, and a visceral sense that the "problem" resides with the parent, not with the self. When the score on the Subjective Units of Disturbance scale reaches zero, the client repeats the procedure with a relaxed posture.

With successful resolution of past and present relational experiences, resentment and fear give way to compassion and curiosity, and adult clients are more open to improving their family of origin relationships. The future template aspect of EMDR's three-pronged protocol (Shapiro, 2001) is an important tool for preparing clients for this difficult work. The therapist and client discuss possibilities for rejunctive action with specific family members; this can occur during family visits or in conjoint therapy (e.g., Framo, 1976). Much of the future template work centers on inoculating the client against defensive reactions and mistrust from family members. The criterion for success lies with the integrity of the client's action, not with the response from others.

These interventions are aimed at the adults with the goal of establishing responsible parenting practices, but EMDR also can be used for healing the psychic wounds the child has suffered from parentification. However, the younger the child is, the more vulnerable that child will be to pathogenic family processes. EMDR is no substitute for responsible parenting. Provided that the parentification process is remitting and the ethical imbalances are being discussed openly in the family, EMDR can help to correct the child's maladaptive attributions associated with a history of parentification and, within limits, can be aimed at inoculating the child from further instances of the injustice.

CASE EXAMPLES

Case 1: A Family Approach

This section illustrates the principles of contextually informed EMDR with a clinical vignette. For the purposes of this chapter, only those aspects of the treatment germane to this approach are discussed, including family assessment, contracting, and the intertwining of EMDR and Contextual Therapy interventions.

The Assessment Phase

The Blue family is a White, middle-class, intact family of four who presented for therapy with concerns about 13-year-old Judy's mood swings, self-deprecation, and declining academic performance. Matters reached a crisis point when parents Carol and Hank caught Judy lying about her developing relationship with an older boy. In the ensuing confrontation, Judy stated that she wished she were dead, and Carol and Hank decided she needed therapy. Because both parents shared concerns for their daughter, and the older brother was away at college, Carol, Hank, and Judy were invited to the initial session. This discussion focuses on the mother-father-daughter triad.

As is usual for an initial family interview, the parents were asked to share their concerns about Judy in turn, then follow with their observations of her contributions to the family generally and to each of them in particular. Having the parents speak first, and inviting them to credit their daughter, is an elemental method in Contextual Therapy (Boszormenyi-Nagy & Krasner, 1986). The following questions are helpful in eliciting the child's earned entitlement and assessing the capacity of each parent to credit the child. Each question is followed by its implicit goal in parentheses:

- *Who is Judy to you?* (Reveals existential merit plus merit in the eyes of the parent)
- *How is she helpful to you personally?* (Explores parent's knowledge of Judy's loyalty contributions)
- *Does she seem sensitive to your moods? How can you tell?* (Elicits unexplored areas of Judy's earned merit through caretaking)
- *What kind of challenges has Judy had to face that may make things hard for her?* (Invites consideration of earned merit through hardship)

Carol and Hank were very forthcoming in acknowledging their daughter's contributions but unaware of the cost to Judy. Both parents credited Judy for being a great comfort to them emotionally, being a good sport at tolerating their bad moods, and, alongside her brother, being the most important thing in their lives.

It came as little surprise, then, when Judy admitted worrying about her parents' happiness, feeling the need to be perfect, and trying to put on a "happy face" because she knew how sensitive they were. Judy also described her despair that she could not live up to her brother David's academic success and that she felt that she was "stupid" and a disappointment to her father in particular, who prized academic achievement. Finally, Judy confided that she needed to keep her relationship with her boyfriend secret because she wanted something that belonged just to her—something that was not shared with her parents.

Subsequent meetings with Carol and Hank, both as a couple and individually, rounded out the assessment phase of treatment. The couple revealed that the marital relationship had been stagnant, with each parent receiving more comfort from their daughter than from each other. Carol and Hank were stunned but open to hearing how this fact alone, apart from any corresponding transactional behavior, placed enormous parentlike responsibility on their daughter. Judy's perfectionism, self-deprecation, and privileging of her parent's well-being over her own self-expression were all evidence of a counterautonomous superego. Judy had to go behind her parents' backs to assert her self-delineation needs (to be a subject), because growing up was disloyal to parents who depended so heavily on her availability as an object. Her choice of an older boy is suggestive of a search for substitutive parenting.

Both parents began to appreciate the dynamics of parentification better as their own family histories were explored. In an individual session, Hank revealed that, like his daughter, he had always felt like a disappointment to his parents. He could never please his seemingly infallible father, nor could he comfort his mother, whose need for reassurance was insatiable. Also like his daughter, Hank pursued his self-delineation in secret, in his case, by using illicit drugs and skipping school.

Hank's subjective (dependency) needs were eclipsed by an emotionally needy mother toward whom his offers of care could never be enough and a seemingly flawless father to whom he could never measure up. Psychologically, Hank's parentification experience was personalized in the form of two dominant Negative Cognitions: "I'm a disappointment" (existential failure) and "I don't measure up" (functional failure). Hank coped with these schemas by reenacting them in his current family, yielding transactional behavior in which he alternately played the "poor me" role (after his mother) and the "infallible" role (after his father).

Carol's family history was significant for the fact of her father's death when she was a young child. The bond between daughter and mother intensified as the latter drew comfort from Carol's devotion and availability. Carol's mother soon remarried a man that "would take care of the family," and Carol was compelled to call him Daddy and treat him with affection. This, and her mother's abrogation of the earlier intimacy of the mother-child dyad, constituted injustices that filled Carol with rage. Carol found the adults unable or unwilling to hear her. Except for a brief period of acting-out in her adolescent years, she appeared ever the loyal daughter to her mother and stepfather but maintained a superficial and distant relationship with them.

Carol's loss of her father and subsequent parentification earned her the *destructive entitlement,* or justification, to seek compensatory parenting from a safer figure, her daughter. *Invisibly loyal* (Boszormenyi-Nagy & Spark, 1973) to her mother and stepfather, she displaced and acted out her betrayed trust onto Hank, with whom she remained distant and distrustful. Psychologically, Carol's experience of going from Mother's confidante to being an outsider to the new marriage left two seemingly conflicting Negative Cognitions: "I'm responsible" (for mother's well-being) and "I don't matter." Contextual theory resolves the paradox by recognizing that Carol mattered as an object who gives, but did not matter as a subject who receives. This paradox gave rise to double-binding transactions with Judy. Appearing to give to her daughter by being permissive and acting more like a sister, Carol was actually taking unilaterally from Judy by withholding appropriate discipline and tacitly leaving Judy to mature without parental urging (e.g., Boszormenyi-Nagy & Spark, 1973, p. 82).

With unresolved issues vis-à-vis their families of origin, unfaced issues in the marriage, and a son who had left home, Carol and Hank were living vicariously through their daughter, who found herself in multiple double binds and split loyalties:

- On one level, Judy knew that her parents expected her to mature and act responsibly; on another level, she intuited her parents' need to possess her as a captive object.

- Though Hank expressed his disappointment in Judy, she provided for him the much needed service of being the scapegoat: a self-delineating object against whom Hank was relieved of the burden of himself being "the disappointment."

- As her father set limits and expressed disappointment in her noncompliance with chores, her mother was indulgent and colluded with Judy against Hank. If Judy joined in her mother's cold war against Hank by neglecting chores that he promulgated, she was disloyal to her father. If she performed her age-appropriate tasks, she abandoned her mother.

- Though Judy experienced considerable angst, she was unable to express these issues with her parents both because it would be disloyal and because until now her parents were not conscious of her predicament. They would respond to her by stating that she was the most important thing in the world to them, not realizing that that was the problem. The resulting guilt in Judy would reinforce her self-deprecation and helplessness.

The net effect on Judy's psychological functioning of these facts, transactions, and ethical binds was that she suffered from depressed mood, lacked age-appropriate affective regulation, and had internalized multiple Negative Cognitions and maladaptive attributions. These included "I'm a disappointment, I'm responsible" (for her parents' well-being) and "I'm not good enough." The resemblance to her parents' Negative Cognitions—right down to some of the word choices—was uncanny considering that her parents had not shared their Negative Cognitions with her.

The Contracting Phase

After five sessions of assessment (the first with all three, the second with the parents, the third, fourth, and fifth with each member alone) and two more to contract for therapy, the following treatment plan was agreed to:

- Family sessions for Carol, Hank, and Judy (and later, David, when he returned home for school breaks) to set better boundaries and begin to deparentify Judy. Carol and Hank would be jointly responsible for setting the number, frequency, and timing of these sessions.

- Individual therapy, including EMDR, for Carol to address her family of origin issues. Carol would take responsibility for scheduling her own sessions.
- Individual therapy for Hank, including EMDR, to address his family of origin issues and to accept Judy as she is. Hank would take responsibility for scheduling these sessions.
- Couples therapy, to be delayed until sufficient individual therapy had been accomplished, to be negotiated by Carol and Hank.
- Individual therapy for Judy, including EMDR, to address her Negative Cognitions.
- Psychiatric evaluation for Judy for antidepressant therapy.

The Intervention Phase

This section focuses on the intersection of EMDR and Contextual Therapy in the Blue family's treatment. By this point, Phase 1 (history and treatment planning) and most of Phase 3 (assessment) had been completed. For Phase 2, Carol and Hank were each advised of the risks and benefits of therapy and assessed for tolerance of desensitization (see Shapiro, 2001). For the most part, the model described previously (i.e., targeting family of origin relationships and experiences) guided the therapy.

Carol

Carol's EMDR sessions were punctuated by Conjoint Family Therapy and individual meetings in which she developed new options for relating with her parents and siblings. The talk therapy, the family of origin work, and the EMDR, with judicious use of the somatic and differentiation interweaves and future template work, combined synergistically to foster her development. In one pivotal EMDR session, arms outstretched and focusing on her stepfather, Carol's bitterness melted away as she realized how she had rejected him out of loyalty to her deceased father. Chronically filled with resentment toward her parents, Carol now looked with compassion on the young family of which she was a part. She realized that her parents, through no fault of their own, lacked the wisdom and maturity to navigate the predicament in which they found themselves. Only recently aware of her own blind spots, she wondered aloud if she herself could have done any better.

The benefits generalized to many other areas of her life as well. Carol not only tolerated her own affect better; she was no longer manipulated by her mother's martyrlike stance or intimidated by her stepfather's gruff demeanor. She also better tolerated Judy's frustration and found it easier to set limits and hold Judy to them. She found herself becoming closer to Hank as her chronic resentment faded away.

Hank

Hank also spent many months working gradually through the first three family-based targets. In a dramatic moment during EMDR, augmented with the differentiation interweave, he felt visceral relief when he realized that his mother was an ordinary person and it was not his duty to make her happy. His relationship with her became easier at once, and he found that she was more relaxed around him in response to his new attitude.

Neutralizing his inferiority schema vis-à-vis his father took longer, and the shift was more gradual. Individual and family meetings interspersed with Hank's EMDR sessions provided ongoing feedback about his lapses into the introjected roles of his parents and helped to fine-tune the EMDR targets. Carol's and Judy's increasing courage and insight sparked them to hold Hank accountable for regressing, and his familiar roles had less of a negative impact on the family.

Judy

EMDR sessions with Judy were less successful and possibly ineffective initially. Judy's mood was improved with antidepressant therapy, but her Negative Cognitions did not begin to transform until her family dynamics were significantly improved. Talk therapy, both individually and conjointly, gave her insight into the dynamics of her family and helped her to externalize the binds to which she had been subjected. As the parentification process diminished, she was able to make use of the somatic interweave in EMDR to gain perspective and build courage to confront her father when he regressed. Gradually, her depression lifted and she gained more self-acceptance.

The Family

With Carol and Hank each reducing their emotional reactivity through EMDR, they could participate more constructively in couples therapy. As the parentification process abated, Judy became empowered to hold her parents accountable. Carol's collusion with her daughter gave way to a healthier boundary: Carol and Hank teamed together as parents and began to set effective limits with Judy, who responded with increasing responsibility and self-regulation. In sum, the *tribunal function of the family* (Boszormenyi-Nagy & Krasner, 1986), that is, the family's ability to fairly consider the needs of each member, was enabled.

Case Discussion

Contextual family therapy facilitated by EMDR was used to improve the overall functioning of the Blue family and increase the differentiation of each member. Judy received targeted intervention for depression in the form of antidepressant therapy and EMDR aimed at depressogenic attributions, and systemic intervention in the form of family therapy. The net effect of the integrated approach included improvements in mood, attributional style, self-worth, adaptive self-referencing beliefs, and overall psychosocial functioning, plus improved communication and boundary maintenance in the family.

Case 2: An Individual Approach

Conjoint therapy may not be indicated or feasible for some youth, particularly adolescents. Ruth, a 19-year-old college student from an intact family, was seen for depression and PTSD on a short-term, individual basis. The young woman had experienced an exceptional number of losses of relatives and peers at an early age and had became convinced that her life would probably be cut short, too. Ruth began living only for immediate gratification. She started abusing substances in her teens, was date-raped, and subsequently became depressed and hopeless. As EMDR was used to resolve the losses, it soon became apparent through chaining associations and affect bridging (Shapiro, 2001; Watkins & Watkins, 1997) that a germinal stressor for Ruth was her relationship with her mother, who, from Ruth's descriptions, evidenced borderline personality traits.

Like Judy and some other depressed youth (Campbell et al., 2003), Ruth was a parentified child who had internalized an overresponsible value orientation and a profound sense of helplessness as she could never please or soothe her mother. Ruth's parentification may have laid the foundation for her to personalize the losses in her life and identify with the helplessness and futility of her deceased peers. EMDR, augmented with the differentiation and somatic interweaves, was used to target Ruth's relationship with her mother. Incipient resolution of her overresponsibility schema springboarded her into a renewed sense of hope, and she resumed her college career with unprecedented vigor.

DISCUSSION

Although little is known about the causes of depression in children, systemic treatment that intervenes in the biomedical, psychological, and family process domains is a rational approach that offers great promise. Contextual Therapy is a metatheoretical paradigm that incorporates multiple dimensions of concern to the psychotherapist. It is an inclusive theory that offers insight into the motivation and meaning making of individuals, sources of pathology in families, and goals for differentiation and growth. The concept of filial loyalty explains a child's willingness to become the captive object of a parent's dependency needs, and the ensuing parentification is a putative mechanism contributing to depression and other forms of pathology.

EMDR is a powerful therapeutic intervention that can accommodate to, and be assimilated within, many theoretical models (Shapiro, 2001). The marriage of Contextual Therapy and EMDR offers the clinician a comprehensive framework through which pathogenic family processes can be identified and both systemic and intrapsychic interventions can be implemented. Healing the psychic wounds of the adults enhances their ability to parent their children responsibly, and thereby create a healthy context for their children's self-delineation.

Judy and her family improved with integrated therapy. Although it is impossible to know which interventions affected which changes, or how they combined, it is noteworthy that the EMDR had little apparent effect on 13-year-old Judy's depression while pathogenic family processes persisted. In contextual terms, Judy's filial loyalty, manifested in her overresponsibility and counterautonomous guilt, was proportional to her parents' unmet dependency needs. As her parents progressed, their need to possess her in a captive object role diminished, and Judy was free to experience a more adaptive, differentiated sense of self. In AIP terms, until this occurred, Judy lacked sufficient experiences of her earned entitlement (i.e., merit) for her to form the adaptive networks necessary for EMDR processing to take place.

By contrast, 19-year-old Ruth improved without the benefit of family intervention. It is likely that, up to a point, the influence of family dynamics on cognitions and behavior are inversely correlated with age. Accordingly, EMDR alone is not sufficient to improve childhood depression—in the face of pathogenic family dynamics—until a child reaches late adolescence and can rely more on autonomous internal resources and extrafamilial relational resources.

REFERENCES

Beck, A. T., Rush, J. A., Shaw, B. F., & Emery, G. (1979). *Cognitive therapy of depression.* New York: Guilford Press.

Birmaher, B., Ryan, N. D., Williamson, D., Brent, D. A., Kaufman, J., Dahl, R. E., et al. (1996). Childhood and adolescent depression: Pt. I. A review of the past 10 years. *Journal of the American Academy of Child and Adolescent Psychiatry, 35,* 1427–1439.

Boszormenyi-Nagy, I. (1965). A theory of relationships: Experience and transaction. In I. Boszormenyi-Nagy & J. Framo (Eds.), *Intensive family therapy: Theoretical and practical aspects* (pp. 33–86). New York: Harper & Row.

Boszormenyi-Nagy, I. (1987). *Foundations of contextual therapy: Collected papers of Ivan Boszormenyi-Nagy, M.D.* New York: Brunner/Mazel.

Boszormenyi-Nagy, I. (1997). Response to "Are trustworthiness and fairness enough? Contextual family therapy and the good family." *Journal of Marital and Family Therapy, 23,* 171–173.

Boszormenyi-Nagy, I., & Krasner, B. (1986). *Between give and take: A clinical guide to contextual therapy.* New York: Brunner/Mazel.

Boszormenyi-Nagy, I., & Spark, G. (1973). *Invisible loyalties.* New York: Brunner/Mazel.

Brent, D. A., Holder, D., Kolko, D., Birmaher, B., Baugher, M., Roth, C., et al. (1997). A clinical psychotherapy trial for adolescent depression comparing cognitive, family, and supportive therapy. *Archives of General Psychiatry, 54,* 877–885.

Buchanan, C. M., Maccoby, E. E., & Dornbusch, S. M. (1991). Caught between parents: Adolescents' experiences in divorced homes. *Child Development, 62,* 1008–1029.

Campbell, D., Bianco, V., Dowling, E., Goldberg, H., McNab, S., & Pentecost, D. (2003). Family therapy for childhood depression: Researching significant moments. *Journal of Family Therapy, 25,* 417–435.

Centers for Disease Control. (1999). Deaths: Final data for 1997. *National Vital Statistics Reports, 47,* 1–108.

Chemtob, C., Nakashima, J., & Carlson, J. (2002). Brief treatment for elementary school children with disaster-related posttraumatic stress disorder: A field study. *Journal of Clinical Psychology, 58,* 99–112.

Cottrell, D. (2003). Outcome studies of family therapy in child and adolescent depression. *Journal of Family Therapy, 25,* 406–417.

Cummings, E. M., Davies, P. T., & Campbell, S. B. (2000). *Developmental psychopathology and family process: Theory, research, and clinical implications.* New York: Guilford Press.

DiFilippo, J. M., & Overholser, J. C. (2000). Suicidal ideation in adolescent psychiatric inpatients as associated with depression and attachment relationships. *Journal of Clinical Child Psychology, 29,* 155–177.

Edmond, T., Rubin, A., & Wambach, K. (1999). The effectiveness of EMDR with adult female survivors of childhood sexual abuse. *Social Work Research, 23*(2), 103–116.

Edmond, T., Sloan, L., & McCarty, D. (2004). Sexual abuse survivors' perceptions of the effectiveness of EMDR and eclectic therapy: A mixed-methods study. *Research on Social Work Practice, 14,* 259–272.

Eley, T. C. (2003). Something borrowed, something blue. *Psychologist, 16,* 626–629.

Eley, T. C., & Stevenson, J. (1999). Using genetic analyses to clarify the distinction between depressive and anxious symptoms in children and adolescents. *Journal of Abnormal Child Psychology, 27,* 105–114.

Fowers, B. J., & Wenger, A. (1997). Are trustworthiness and fairness enough? Contextual family therapy and the good family. *Journal of Marital and Family Therapy, 23,* 153–169.

Framo, J. L. (1965). Rationale and techniques of intensive family therapy. In I. Boszormenyi-Nagy & J. Framo (Eds.), *Intensive family therapy: Theoretical aspects* (pp. 143–212). New York: Harper & Row.

Framo, J. L. (1976). Family of origin as a therapeutic resource for adults in marital and family therapy: You can and should go home again. *Family Process, 15,* 193–210.

Framo, J. L. (1982). Symptoms from a family transactional viewpoint. In J. L. Framo (Ed.), *Explorations in marital and family therapy: Selected papers of James L. Framo* (pp. 11–57). New York: Springer.

Friedman, M. S. (1960). *Martin Buber: The life of dialogue.* New York: Harper Torchbooks.

Garber, J., & Robinson, N. S. (1997). Cognitive vulnerability in children at risk for depression. *Cognition and Emotion, 11,* 619–635.

Garland, A. F., Lewczyk-Boxmeyer, C. J., Gabayan, E. N., & Hawley, K. M. (2004). Multiple stakeholder agreement on desired outcomes for adolescents' mental health services. *Psychiatric Services, 55,* 671–676.

Gladstone, T. R., & Kaslow, N. J. (1995). Depression and attributions in children and adolescents: A meta-analytic review. *Journal of Abnormal Child Psychology, 23*(5), 597–606.

Hammen, C., Rudolph, K., Weisz, J., Rao, U., & Burge, D. (1999). The context of depression in clinic-referred youth: Neglected areas in treatment. *Journal of the American Academy of Child and Adolescent Psychiatry, 38,* 64–71.

Hibbs, B. (1989). The context of growth: Relational ethics between parents and children. In L. Combrinck-Graham (Ed.), *Children in family contexts: Perspectives on treatment* (pp. 26–45). New York: Guilford Press.

Joiner, T. E., Jr., & Wagner, K. D. (1995). Attribution style and depression in children and adolescents: A meta-analytic review. *Clinical Psychology Review, 15*(8), 777–798.

Kerr, M. E., & Bowen, M. (1988). *Family evaluation.* New York: Norton.

Kitchur, M. (2005). The strategic developmental model for EMDR. In F. Shapiro (Ed.), *EMDR solutions: Pathways to healing* (pp. 8–56). New York: Norton.

March, J., Silva, S., Petrycki, S., Curry, J., Wells, K., Fairbank, J., et al. (2004). Fluoxetine, cognitive-behavioral therapy, and their combination for adolescents with depression: Treatment for Adolescents with Depression Study (TADS) randomized controlled trial. *Journal of the American Medical Association, 292,* 807–820.

Maxfield, L., & Hyer, L. (2002). The relationship between efficacy and methodology in studies investigating EMDR treatment of PTSD. *Journal of Clinical Psychology, 58,* 23–41.

McGoldrick, M., Gerson, R., & Shellenberger, S. (1999). *Genograms: Assessment and intervention* (2nd ed.). New York: Norton.

Messer, S. C., & Gross, A. M. (1995). Childhood depression and family interaction: A naturalistic observation study. *Journal of Clinical Child Psychology, 24,* 77–88.

Minuchin, S. (1974). *Families and family therapy.* Cambridge, MA: Harvard University Press.

Mufson, L., Dorta, K. P., Wickramaratne, P., Nomura, Y., Olfson, M., & Weissman, M. M. (2004). A randomized effectiveness trial of interpersonal psychotherapy for depressed adolescents. *Archives of General Psychiatry, 61,* 577–584.

Muris, P., Schmidt, H., Lambrichs, R., & Meesters, C. (2001). Protective and vulnerability factors of depression in normal adolescents. *Behavior Research and Therapy, 39,* 555–565.

Nichols, M. P., & Schwartz, R. C. (1998). *Family therapy: Concepts and methods* (4th ed.). Needham Heights, MA: Allyn & Bacon.

Northey, W. F., Wells, K. C., Silverman, W. K., & Bailey, C. E. (2003). Childhood behavioral and emotional disorders. *Journal of Marital and Family Therapy, 29,* 523–545.

O'Brien, M., & Margolin, G., & John, R. S. (1995). Relation among marital conflict, child coping, and child adjustment. *Journal of Clinical Child Psychology, 24,* 346–361.

Pinsof, W. M., & Wynne, L. C. (2000). Toward progress research: Closing the gap between family therapy practice and research. *Journal of Marital and Family Therapy, 26,* 1–8.

Prince, S. E., & Jacobson, N. S. (1995). A review and evaluation of marital and family therapies for affective disorders. *Journal of Marital and Family Therapy, 21,* 377–401.

Reinecke, M. A., Ryan, N. E., & DuBois, D. L. (1998). Cognitive-behavioral therapy of depression and depressive symptoms during adolescence: A review and meta-analysis. *Journal of the American Academy of Child and Adolescent Psychiatry, 37,* 26–34.

Reinherz, H. Z., Paradis, A. D., Giaconia, R. M., Stashwick, C. K., & Fitzmaurice, G. (2003). Childhood and adolescent predictors of major depression in the transition to adulthood. *American Journal of Psychiatry, 160,* 2141–2147.

Schnarch, D. M. (1991). *Constructing the sexual crucible: An integration of sexual and marital therapy.* New York: Norton.

Schwartz, J. A. J., Kaslow, N. J., Seeley, J., & Lewinsohn, P. (2000). Psychological, cognitive, and interpersonal correlates of attributional change in adolescents. *Journal of Clinical Child Psychology, 29,* 188–199.

Shadish, W. R., & Baldwin, S. A. (2003). Meta-analysis of MFT interventions. *Journal of Marital and Family Therapy, 29,* 547–570.

Shapiro, F. (2001). *Eye movement desensitization and reprocessing: Basic principles, protocols, and procedures* (2nd ed.). New York: Guilford Press.

Simon, F. G., Stierlin, H., & Wynne, L. C. (1985). *The language of family therapy: A systemic vocabulary and sourcebook*. New York: Family Process Press.

Spirito, A., Valeri, S., Boergers, J., & Donaldson, D. (2003). Predictors of continued suicidal behavior in adolescents following a suicide attempt. *Journal of Clinical Child and Adolescent Psychology, 32,* 284–289.

Wagner, K. D., & Ambrosini, P. J. (2001). Childhood depression: Pharmacological therapy/treatment. *Journal of Clinical Child Psychology, 30,* 88–98.

Wagner, K. D., Robb, A. S., Findling, R. L., Gutierrez, M. M., & Heydorn, W. E. (2004). A randomized, placebo-controlled trial of citalopram for the treatment of major depression in children and adolescents. *American Journal of Psychiatry, 161,* 1079–1083.

Watkins, J. G., & Watkins, H. H. (1997). *Ego states: Theory and therapy.* New York: Norton.

Whiffen, V. E., Kerr, J. A., & Kallos-Lilly, V. (2005). Maternal depression, adult attachment, and children's emotional distress. *Family Process, 44,* 93–104.

CHAPTER 16

Integrating EMDR and Family Therapy: Treating the Traumatized Child

Anita Bardin, Joel Comet, and Deborah Porten

When children experience a traumatic event, the effect on them can be profound. Studies have documented that children, and even infants, can experience the full range of posttraumatic stress symptoms (Zero to Three, 2005). Other problems include depressive and anxiety reactions, withdrawal, somatic complaints, aggression, and delinquent behavior. The negative impact of these reactions is evident in the children's family and peer relationships and school performance (Cohen, Berliner, & March, 2000; Pynoos, Steinberg, & Goenjian, 1996; Scheeringa & Zeanah, 2001).

The child's reactions to and understanding of the trauma are strongly influenced by the attitudes and responses of his or her parents (Tinker & Wilson, 1999). After the trauma, children need to feel secure and to perceive their parents as strong and protective, as capably coping with the aftereffects. However, parents often experience a profound sense of helplessness, as well as anxiety for their child, and may feel overwhelmed, anxious, depressed, and unable to meet their child's needs (Chansky, 2004; Figley, 1989). Consequently, it is imperative to engage the parents in the treatment of their traumatized child because they are the child's greatest support in the healing process.

At the Shiluv Institute in Jerusalem, the family therapy approach used is systemic/structural and developmental. Family systems theory provides a lens through which to understand the flow of interactions among family members. This perspective examines the impact of an individual's traumatic experience on the interactional patterns within the system that reverberate back on the individual (Kaslow, Nurse, & Thompson, 2002). These patterns range on a continuum from facilitating healing to causing retraumatization or regression.

The Structural Family Therapy (SFT) approach developed by Salvador Minuchin (1974) views the family as a unit of subsystems determined by generation, gender, and function. The term *structural* "refers to the interactional patterns that arrange or organize a family's component subsystems into constant relationships" (Umbarger, 1983, p. 198). Minuchin's theory uses several other key concepts. These are (1) *Circularity,* which denotes the interrelationship of these parts that influence and are influenced by each other; (2) that changes in each member will affect all; (3) *Hierarchy,* which describes the power balance within the family; and (4) *Boundaries,* which refer to the rules regulating the amount of contact between individuals and subsystems (Minuchin & Fishman, 1981).

The family structure must adapt to predictable developmental life cycle changes as well as to unforeseen circumstances such as trauma. After a child's traumatic experience, his subsequent behavioral and emotional reactions will impact his family. They, too, will respond emotionally, behave reactively, and search for some explanations of the event. If, for example, parents find their spiritual beliefs questioned, inducing self-guilt (e.g., "I have sinned"), they will find it difficult to provide security for their children. If there were previous dysfunctional patterns, these may become activated (Figley, 1988, 1989). Families who experience secondary traumatization, or for whom earlier traumatic experiences are reawakened, or whose family history is generally traumatic and dysfunctional will have difficulty providing the needed supportive context (Nichols, 1989).

Family therapy has developed from an almost totally systemic perspective into an integrated approach incorporating individual needs within its focus. The field of traumatology evolved from a focus on healing the individual victim to examining the family context in which recovery takes place. The examination of marriages of Vietnam veterans (Nelson & Wright, 1996) and sexual abuse victims (Johnson, 2002) are examples of this approach.

This wider focus is reflected in research investigating factors that predict the development of trauma reactions in children. These studies identified significant family variables, such as marital conflict, upsetting family talk about the disaster (La Greca, Silverman, Vernberg, & Prinstein, 1996), paternal symptoms of Posttraumatic Stress Disorder (PTSD; Kilic, 2003), and the child's perception of parental upset and anxiety (Laor et al., 1997; Riggs, 2000). When McFarlane (1987, p. 766) found that the adjustment of parents was "an important determinant in the adjustment of children and the adjustment of the children in turn contributed to the . . . adjustment of the family," he discussed this in circular terms; however, most other studies have examined the data only in a linear fashion.

Although there is much descriptive data, no empirical research has examined the effectiveness of family interventions as a therapeutic approach for children with PTSD (Riggs, 2000). In fact, an Internet site, Clinical Evidence from the BMJ Publishing Group, rating treatment efficacy for PTSD evaluated 20 treatment approaches but did not even list family therapy (Bisson, 2004). Given the impact of family and parental functioning on traumatized children, family therapy is clearly an appropriate component of any trauma treatment (Chansky, 2004).

Integrative Treatment Model: EMDR and Structural Family Therapy

The integration of Eye Movement Desensitization and Reprocessing (EMDR; Shapiro, 2001) and SFT in a treatment process allows for healing on both the intrapersonal and the interpersonal levels (Siegel, 2002). EMDR targets the individual's dysfunctionally stored perceptions of a traumatic event. These are assessed and treated in accordance with the three-pronged protocol: identifying past and present areas of dysfunction and positive alternatives for the future. The overwhelming nature of traumatic events can block the brain's natural capacity to process material to a healthy, adaptive resolution. Through EMDR, this unprocessed material is targeted, activated, and processed using dual attention stimulation (see Shapiro, Chapter 1).

SFT addresses the dysfunctional family behavior that exacerbates children's reactions, increases their sense of vulnerability, and inhibits their healing. These issues are addressed directly through such interventions as psychoeducation about trauma, development of parenting skills, treatment of conflictual issues, and restabilization of the family's functioning. SFT posits that to provide the necessary support, families need to have clearly delineated functions, age-appropriate hierarchy, clear boundaries, and functional communication patterns (Minuchin, 1974). A weak parental system, a conflicted spousal system, cross-generational coalitions, and rigid boundaries are dysfunctions that interfere with the system's ability to focus on the needs of a traumatized child.

THERAPY PROCESS

Work with the after effects of a traumatic event is more focused and efficient when following clear therapeutic stages. Next is a brief summary of these stages that include both trauma and family systems perspective.

History and Assessment

Treatment is based on an assessment of the family structure as well as the child's individual developmental history and present functioning. Family involvement facilitates the assessment of the child by clarifying changes in the child's behavior from pre- to posttrauma functioning, including information about the existence of any previous traumas the child may not remember. Evaluation of any posttrauma reorganization of the family structure into dysfunctional patterns is necessary. Examples include a family that avoids facing their own emotional responses by focusing exclusively on the child (detouring; Umbarger, 1983) or issues of secondary gain such as extra attention for the child or intensified closeness of the parents. The family's culture and beliefs are explored. Additionally, current reality-based fears may be present and need to be addressed through education and skill development of both parents and child. Whether there is parental provision of basic safety in and outside the house is also ascertained. Goals are then identified, discussed, and mutually agreed on.

Preparation Phase

In the Preparation Phase of EMDR therapy, the "clinician strengthens the therapeutic alliance so that it is firmly rooted in trust and a sense of security" (Shapiro, 2002, p. 35). When working with children it is critical that the family alliance is similarly rooted. Anchoring the family as a safe place is a basic requirement. Enactment in the therapy room (Minuchin & Fishman, 1981) is used to create scenarios of desired family patterns and communication. This includes asking parents about their child's strengths and best memories. Their responses often reveal inner resources that can be enhanced through *Resource Installation* or used during processing as *Cognitive Interweaves*. This also generates a supportive bond between parents and child that strengthens the child's sense of safety. Homework assignments of challenging family activities can be used to highlight the child's courage and provide successful experiences (e.g., horseback riding, martial arts). The ability of family members to manage their distressing emotions and sensations is also addressed. Self-control techniques (e.g., creating an imaginal safe place) can be taught both to the child and other family members.

Trauma, Desensitization, and Reprocessing

In processing the trauma, the EMDR protocol may need to be adapted to the developmental age of the child (Greenwald, 1994, 1998; Tinker & Wilson, 1999). In the cases described in this chapter, the children preferred mechanical hand tappers or tapping by family members as the method of dual attention stimulation. When the direct targeting of the traumatic material is too frightening, flexibility is used in choosing the initial focus for treatment. For example, a child can tell her story rather than focus on her worst memory (Lovett, 1999). Additional modifications included more frequent use of directed questioning to prompt the child to continue with the processing.

When evaluation reveals that the family is providing safety and the individual child is ready, direct work on the traumatic experience begins. Parental participation through their presence in the room, or by actually holding or tapping the child, provides a supportive holding environment as the child processes his trauma. As the treatment proceeds toward closure, changes in the child's behavior occur. Because these will impact the family system, it is critical to track not only the child's positive or negative emotional experiences and behaviors, but also those of the family members and their mutual impact on one another. Shapiro's (2001, p. 198) directive to attend to whether "an adequate assimilation [has] been made within a healthy social system" is expanded as both the social system and the individual are in treatment. Lack of movement in the child's recovery or stalled processing indicates a need for a closer look at the family's functioning: Are the parents working together and encouraging growth? Is the child's symptomatic behavior being reinforced? An analysis of circular patterns of interactions will determine whether additional therapeutic systemic interventions are necessary. At times, additional family members request EMDR for themselves after seeing the positive changes in the child. A constant evaluation utilizing individual and systemic lenses facilitates the healing and integration of the family unit by identifying and processing current distress and future apprehensions.

CASE EXAMPLES

The following three cases illustrate the integration of the family systemic approach with EMDR.

Case 1: Yoav and His Family

Yoav, a 9-year-old boy, and his 17-year-old brother, Zack, had been stabbed. Yoav exhibited symptoms of Acute Stress Disorder (ASD) and was the initial focus of the treatment. The inclusion of all the family members allowed for the recognition of the specific needs of each person, such as signs of ASD or secondary traumatization (Bardin, 2004). The parents' intense feelings of helplessness inhibited their sons' attempts to overcome their own fears. For the parents to help their sons recover, they needed to recoup their own strength, already depleted by their having immigrated to Israel 5 months before the referral.

During the adjustment to a new society, the immigrant family is vulnerable and its members feel dependent on the authorities. This state of vulnerability was the background on which the violent attack occurred. The family came from a patriarchal, traditional culture, where relationships between children and parents were formal and hierarchical. In Israel, the father's inability to provide for the family and his need to rely on his sons to be his translators and buffer with the authorities challenged his role and self-image, changing the traditional hierarchy. After the violent stabbing attack, the father felt he had failed by not protecting his children. The older sons were confused and embarrassed, seeing their father in a weak position. They compensated by trying to feel strong.

On the day of the attack, Zack was in charge of Yoav, his youngest brother, while their parents were at work. They were attacked and stabbed in the family apartment after school. The attacker was unknown and was not apprehended. The middle son, Mann, 14, arrived home from school to find police and ambulances. He spent that first traumatic day with relatives while his parents each sat in the hospital with a wounded son. Yoav and Zack required emergency hospitalization; each had been stabbed severely and was lucky to be alive.

Two weeks after the attack, Yoav exhibited symptoms that worried both his family and school. He was afraid to go by himself to any room (including the toilet) in the family's small apartment. He screamed uncontrollably in the middle of the night and was afraid to sleep without his mother. He refused to leave the apartment by himself. Zack presented himself as fine and denied any problems. Like everyone in the family, he was concerned about his youngest brother. The father expressed concern that Zack was "at the age where he wouldn't admit to being afraid."

Although not typical of the team's work, home visits were made because Yoav was not well enough to travel. This turned out to provide wonderful opportunities. The entire family was present for the first session. The therapist talked with the family, feeling their warmth and learning about their concern for Yoav. The history of the traumatic event was taken, Yoav's symptoms were described, and Yoav chose a safe place. To begin processing, Yoav chose to use the hand tappers (tactile stimulation). Later, eye movements were used as well. Yoav and the therapist sat near each other, with the rest of the family in a semicircle around them. The therapist identified two difficulties in following the standard protocol. First, Yoav was unable to recall any of his nightmares. He was unaware of his own screaming in the night. Second, his affect of smiling and joking was unconnected to the intensity of the event. This demonstrated how overwhelmed he was and how he was protecting himself emotionally. Focusing on a specific scene was too threatening. The therapist thus decided to start with the retelling of the traumatic event in sequential order. Yoav held the hand tappers and told his story to the therapist. He talked quickly, quietly, with inappropriate smiles.

He described how a strange man entered the unlocked door. The older brother asked what the man wanted, then:

Yoav: Suddenly he came and stabbed me and pushed my brother. I was in shock and saw his knife doing things. Zack said, "Mommy, Mommy." The man left. I got up.

After each set of associations, Yoav stopped as if finished. The processing was rapid and sketchy with flat affect. The therapist focused him back on the event by asking questions:

Therapist: He stabbed you?

Yoav: Yes. Both of us. He stabbed Zack and then me.

Therapist: Where?

Yoav: In the arm, near the heart. He stabbed Zack three times. The police came.

He held the tappers as he continued to describe the ambulance, the hospital, the doctors, and the pain of the treatments. The therapist's interventions connected Yoav to the feelings of fear and sadness that began to appear on his face. It was hard for him to express those feelings. For instance, after describing the stabbing of his brother and his brother's bloody back, he said he was feeling "nothing."

The family sat in silence, listening to Yoav's story. Their faces showed pain and distress. The therapist thought that in addition to the child's defenses against his own intense emotions, he had been concerned about increasing his family's distress. This concern to protect his parents is an example of an inappropriate inverted parent-child hierarchy.

In SFT, the hierarchical position of parents incorporates teaching children through modeling. In this case, the necessary modeling was of resilience: the expression of both vulnerability and coping. Such modeling by the parents would give permission to the boys to express their own feelings without fear of being thought of as weak or of endangering their parents. They would see that their parents can acknowledge pain and continue to function. The therapist therefore created an enactment by having each family member tell his or her own story. Parental ability to express vulnerability reduced Yoav's anxieties and need to protect them. A more functional hierarchy was strengthened. The sharing of these personal experiences enabled each member to connect with his or her own secondary traumatization and needs for healing.

Each family member spoke with feeling, and in spite of the tension and sadness, all experienced mutual caring. Although each one told his or her own story, they all expressed great concern for their youngest member, Yoav. The difference in the parents' reactions was apparent. Father felt that God had punished his children because of something that he must have done, and Mother, although bewildered, was able to express relief that her sons were alive.

In response to the traumatic event, the family had organized around Yoav's fears and regressed behaviors in an overprotective manner that insulated them from facing their own stress. This could morph into a structure of a symptom-bearing child whose regressed behavior functions to deflect and detour family issues. Parental overprotectiveness could reinforce the child's behavior (Minuchin, 1974). Although this organization was an attempt by the system to nurture and protect its members, it could interfere with everyone's recovery and block Yoav's growth toward independence. Helping Yoav work through his anxieties would not only be empowering for him, but would also free the other family members for their own therapeutic work and enable the whole system to reorganize into a more functional unit.

Interrelationships are circular, and a change in any one part will create change in the others. A small change in Yoav's behavior could provide reassurance to his family and thereby help them relate to him in a more growth-producing manner. With this in mind, the therapist decided to shift to the present focus of the EMDR three-pronged protocol and assess his current level of fear. Yoav was asked to attempt to walk to the bathroom by himself. Initially he took only two steps and said he was afraid. At this point, the therapist created an enactment by giving clear directions to the family on how to encourage him. Yoav continued to walk until stopped by his fear. The therapist returned to EMDR to process the fear. Yoav focused on the bathroom:

Yoav: Someone is coming.

Therapist: Think about that.

Yoav was silent for a while. He repeated the same thing. The therapist jump-started the blocked processing through a series of focused questions and a change to the use of eye movements (EM):

Therapist: Who are you afraid of?

Yoav: Thieves! But I am afraid! Someone is coming (continued looping).

Therapist: Think about the fear.

Yoav: I am afraid.

Therapist: Where do you feel the fear in your body? Does it hurt anywhere?

Yoav: Doesn't hurt anywhere.

Therapist: Right now, think about what you are afraid of, what you feel.

Yoav: Yes, that someone will come.

The processing began to flow again, and during successive sets of EM, he talked of his fears of strangers and of attack. Spontaneously, he had positive associations: "In the hospital the doctor will take care of me." After more processing: "One more day, I will be home. One more week, I go to school. That's it. No more." However, after a bit more processing:

Yoav: Wait (Closes his eyes tightly). I go to school. I have friends. That's it.

The EMDR processing, together with the family's support, enabled Yoav's inherent strengths to reemerge. An unexpected visit by a friend caused him to become restless. He wanted to play. He and his friend soon left. Both parents were surprised. This was the first time Yoav had left the apartment without a parent since his return from the hospital. The father was so fearful that he started to follow the boys. Mother had to hold him back. It was clear that the father's anxiety, if unchecked, would sabotage Yoav's gains. The difference between the mother and the father was noted as a dysfunction that the therapist would have to address directly.

Following this initial session, Yoav was no longer screaming in his sleep, although he reported experiencing frightening dreams in the mornings. He was still fearful but had returned to school. Although needing an escort on the way to school, he was cheerful while there. These impressive gains allowed the family, especially the mother, to sleep and feel more hopeful.

The second home visit found Mother and Yoav waiting. As soon as Yoav saw the therapist, he cried out proudly, "I went to the bathroom alone!" Although he was still afraid to fall asleep alone, he slept through the night. Behavioral and emotional changes indicated Yoav's move toward healing. The family's continued support and their change from pained silence to a mutual sharing of the posttrauma feelings supported this healing. It was now time to work directly with the worst memory. Yoav asked to continue with the tappers. He described the knife going into his brother's back. He became restless. He could not picture the attacker's face. His discomfort increased, and he said he wanted to stop. The therapist accessed positive resources. Yoav was asked to concentrate on what he would like to do to the attacker. As he continued holding the tappers he said, "Hit him! Hit him hard." He was asked to concentrate on that. His body and facial expression changed. He felt good and asked to end the work.

While his mother listened, the pain on her face deepened. She was asked if she would like to work. She readily accepted. She, too, was suffering from nightmares. The therapist followed the standard EMDR protocol. The mother rated her distress at 10 on the Subjective Units of Disturbance (SUD) scale where, 0 = No distress and 10 = Extreme distress. Her *Negative Cognition* (NC) was "I am a bad mother" who failed her children. She believed they had been punished because of her. Her *Positive Cognition* (PC) was "I did the best I could" and "It's over." While processing, she continued crying and blaming herself. She repeatedly returned to her confusion and feelings of guilt, saying, "Perhaps God is punishing me." Cognitive Interweaves were helpful in unblocking her processing: "Can we always protect our children?"; "Can we always understand why things happen?" The session ended with a final Cognitive Interweave:

Therapist: What are your kids like?

Mother: They are all good.

Therapist: Then are you a good enough mother?

Mother: (Smiling) Okay.

Her SUD had reached a bearable and ecologically valid 2. She felt relieved and stronger and did not desire more EMDR. Her inner resources brought her to the acceptance that she is a good mother and that things may happen for which there are no satisfactory explanations.

On the third visit, Yoav related dreams he now remembered that showed attempts at self-defense. His natural strengths were reappearing. In one of the dreams, he fought back and ran after a "bad man." Another dream showed his continued (and understandable) anxiety about being protected. In that dream, his mother, who was the main source of emotional support for Yoav, "got sick." Although bad dreams returned occasionally, Yoav's general mood and functioning remained improved. He continued to sleep through the night.

The parents and Yoav came to the Institute for the fourth session. Parental roles and functioning were strained by the traumatic event. The difference in Mother's and Father's reactions was causing conflict between them. The process of moving from overprotecting to empowering Yoav remained more difficult for the father. To decrease this tension, the therapist decided to do individual EMDR with the father with the goal of addressing his depression, anxiety, and overprotectiveness. The father's NC concerned his feelings of guilt. He felt he had sinned, quoting Exodus 20:5, "The sins of the fathers are visited on their sons." Although associating and verbalizing spontaneously with appropriate affect, he found it difficult to follow the protocol. The father needed to vent his self-reproach and express his confusion and pain as he searched for understanding. He spoke about his responsibility for bringing his family to the new country, where his sons were hurt. He spoke of his change in status in Israel from a small businessman to a dishwasher. His sense of self was diminished. Although the session was diffuse, it was cathartic. He was able to reaffirm that he was a loving father, doing his best. These inner resources were installed through eye movements. He left feeling calmer.

During the following week, one individual session was held with Zack at Shiluv. Zack had seen the improvement in his family, and, despite his early proclamations to the contrary, he now wanted to work on his traumatic experience. He completed a full protocol. His NC was "I am weak and small." His SUD was 8 to 9. His PC was "It's over. I'm okay," and his score on the Validity of Cognition scale was 4. Using the hand tappers, he focused on his feelings of guilt: "I did wrong. It was because of me." His pained affect accompanied a detailed description of being stabbed in the back, falling to the floor, and seeing the man's feet "go to Yoav, who didn't make a sound." He described the hospital experience where, for the first time, he saw his father cry. At the end of processing, he said, "It was not really my fault. We always left the door unlocked." EMDR enabled him to move from inappropriate guilt to a more realistic assessment. His eyes were closed for most of the processing. When he opened them, he said, "I feel better. It is over."

Deciding to use EMDR with a client in the presence of his family is based on the family's ability to tolerate stress, its attitude to the client (supportive or blaming), and the needs and developmental stage of the client. Whereas Yoav, age 9, felt comfortable and secure to work in front of his family, Zack, at 17, needed privacy to express weakness and vulnerability.

In his second session, Zack reported that he continued to feel better and felt no need for additional EMDR. He was less afraid, and he accepted that he could not have fought off a man armed with a knife. He was involved with school and making appropriate plans for his future.

The last family session was divided between the parents and Yoav. The parents described improvement in Yoav yet disagreed on how to proceed. The mother was able to express her fears and recognized that she could control them so that her sons would feel safer. She was angry with her husband for still acting fearful around the boys (e.g., calling home six times a day). The father now acknowledged his difficulty and could accept his need to change for his sons' sake. The therapist worked with the parents to improve their ability to make mutual decisions. The enactment of their arguments in the room was an opportunity for them to learn to listen to each other. They both could acknowledge their differences: that father remained more anxious and mother more able to give their sons age-appropriate independence. They were able to agree on actions to support Yoav's recovery. For example, they decided to allow him to walk to school without an adult. They also agreed on reducing the number of telephone calls the father made to the boys each day. The parents could now encourage Yoav to let go of the residual dependent behaviors that had developed as a result of the trauma. Yoav's satisfaction as he regained his independence was a clear message for the parents. They could see his growth. The therapist then addressed Yoav to check if more processing was needed:

Therapist: What is the most frightening memory from that day?

Yoav: Nothing.

Therapist: You told me that the worst part was seeing him stab your brother.

Yoav: Yes.

Therapist: Think about that now. (Yoav is now holding the hand tappers.)

Yoav: I can't.

Therapist: If you think about this frightening thing now, what happens?

Yoav: Don't want to. . . .

Therapist: Okay. . . . But we want you to think about the difficult things so that we can get rid of the bad feelings.

Yoav: So I won't be afraid? I want to be someone who is not a coward.

Here Yoav's NC, "I am a coward," was stated clearly for the first time:

Therapist: You want not to be afraid. Not to be a coward? Do you feel like a coward?

Yoav: A little.

Therapist: Just think about that. (Yoav is still holding the tappers.)

Yoav: (After a moment) It's sad . . . (He continued to repeat this.)

As the processing stalled, the therapist focused Yoav on his body:

Therapist: When you are sad, where do you feel the sadness . . . in your body?

Yoav: Don't know. (silence)

Therapist: In the place where you were stabbed?

Yoav: No. I won't be stabbed and that's all.

Therapist: Are you afraid in your body?

Yoav: Don't know. I'm afraid—the whole body.

Therapist: Just think about that. I know it is hard. But we are doing this to help. We want to throw away the fear. (silence for a few moments, while Yoav still holds the tappers). What are you noticing?

Yoav: Nothing . . . a little . . . my body is afraid now.

The therapist asked where he felt it in his body. He said, "All over." He explained that his body is not afraid in school, only in the home. He became quiet:

Therapist: What are you thinking? (silence) Hard to talk?

Yoav: Yes. (in a sad voice)

Therapist: It's difficult to feel a coward.

Yoav concentrated, then said, "It's finished . . . really. There is just a little fear in my body." He smiled and his body relaxed. He spontaneously handed the therapist the tappers and asked if they were finished. He smiled and asked to go out. He had been very cooperative for his age. His markedly changed mood indicated that he felt positive. Yoav's final statement seemed a good summary. At the end of treatment he exhibited marked improvement in his behavior and expressed appropriate feelings. Changes in the family system had enabled not only Yoav but all the family members to become enablers for each other.

Yoav finished the school year successfully. Two months after termination, a phone call found Yoav proudly saying that he had walked alone in the neighborhood. His mother believed the whole family was fine. Zack made every effort to ensure that he would be drafted into the Israeli Army. He, too, had successfully recovered.

Yoav's symptoms after an acute traumatic experience became the natural focus for this caring immigrant family. The treatment integrated individual information processing through EMDR, with the restructuring of the dysfunctional family system through SFT. The therapist focused on helping the most distressed member of the system find his natural strengths, while helping the family support each other's growth.

Systemic theory postulates that change is part of both action and reaction. Yoav's positive behavioral changes allowed the family to release some of their anxieties about him. The parents' increasing skill as enablers lessened their feelings of helplessness and provided Yoav with the safety and support he needed. A mutually reinforcing cycle created hope and supported competence for both Yoav and his entire family.

Case 2: Ruti and Her Mother Revisiting an Old Trauma

Ruti, a 10-year-old girl, had been sexually molested by an adult male neighbor. Her mother's traumatic history combined with Ruti's previously "forgotten" molestation at age 6 interfered with the treatment of her current second trauma. Ruti was the third of eight children in an ultraorthodox family. Her father worked until late at night. Mother took pride in her role of homemaker but felt disappointed by the emptiness of her marriage.

Ruti served as her mother's companion in an unhappy marriage. Caught in this cross-generational coalition, Ruti was alienated from her father. Addressing the dysfunctional family structure was a requisite for effective use of EMDR. Ruti's current molestation reawakened the mother's memories of her own molestations during adolescence. Mother's unprocessed traumatic experiences led to her overprotection, which impeded Ruti's healing process.

When Ruti went to borrow something from their neighbor, she was confronted by a naked adult male who attempted to touch her. She screamed and ran back to her apartment. Despite the shame that such an incident might bring on their family in its close-knit, religious community, the mother immediately reported the molestation to the police, confronted the attacker, and sought a treatment center for her daughter.

Several weeks after the incident, Ruti reluctantly entered the therapy room, clinging to her mother, a heavy, disheveled woman. Ruti haltingly disclosed what had happened and described her new fears of leaving the house and riding the school bus. She feared the intrusive image of the attacker's face, which was especially distressing at sleep time. Her mother noted a marked regressive quality in Ruti's postincident behavior. Ruti was clingy and showed little independence. Although this burdened Mother, she accompanied Ruti to the school bus and tucked her in each night. Ruti enjoyed her special status with her mother, but the secondary gains did not compensate for her loss of freedom and sense of safety.

The therapist's original plan was to follow the standard protocol of targeting the most terrifying events, but Ruti chose to begin with the picture of leaving her house by herself. "The face is too scary to think about," she said. She readily provided an NC (equivalent to "I am in danger"), "It is scary because he can hurt me." Her SUD was 8. She could not relate to a Positive Cognition other than saying, "I don't want to think about it." Even though neither was formulated as a self-belief, the therapist accepted Ruti's NC and PC because they were appropriate for her developmental level (Lovett, 1999). As processing progresses, it is then easier to elicit a self-statement. When asked to think of a safe place, Ruti smiled and wriggled into her mother. Eye movements seemed strange to her, but she readily held the tappers. As she concentrated on the image of walking alone, she was visibly upset and complained of stomach pain. This remained unchanged through several sets. Processing was stuck, so a Cognitive Interweave was introduced. Ruti was asked if she could imagine a friend she might walk with. Her face lit up as she talked about her girlfriend. This was targeted for several sets. The SUD dropped to 2. Ruti then spontaneously proceeded to talk about her big family. Mother had been watching attentively throughout and responded eagerly when asked to help Ruti think of things to do on the bus so she would not feel frightened if the face appeared. Mother suggested some puzzles and favorite stories. As processing was incomplete, no formal PC was attempted. The session ended with teaching Mother how to do relaxation exercises with Ruti. Both wanted to return to target bedtime.

Ruti and Mother began the second session by reporting that Ruti had walked to and from the school bus by herself. They had prepared puzzles for Ruti for the long ride. Ruti was still frightened by the attacker's face when she was in bed. Her NC, expressed descriptively and in an age-appropriate fashion, was "I am scared. He can get me." Her SUD was 9 to 10. This statement is typical of a child's way of articulating the Negative Cognition of helplessness. She felt the fear in her stomach. She articulated a clear desire: "I want to be able to go to sleep at night like I used to." Her clear wish was for safety.

It was too frightening for Ruti to stay focused on her chosen target. She dropped the tappers. Only then did Mother mention an earlier molestation, when Ruti, age 6, had been pulled into an alley near their house. Ruti remembered the incident and nodded, showing no anxiety, as her mother described what had happened. The therapist, seeing no signs of traumatization, asked Ruti what she thought about being able to protect herself. "I am getting much bigger," she said. This new strength was reinforced with sets of EMs and through a discussion with her mother about how Ruti was bigger now and had protected herself from the neighbor by running away. At the end of the session, the SUD level had dropped to 2 to 3. Ruti's positive self-belief was now a resource for her. Highlighting her increased competence reduced her anxiety.

Between sessions, Ruti continued to go to and from school on her own. However, she was refusing all contact with her father. Mother was puzzled and asked to see the therapist alone. At this session, Mother recounted that after the incident, she had told Ruti that men could be dangerous and she should protect herself from *all* men. Mother felt this phrase had caused Ruti's refusal to let her father approach her. Bitterly disappointed in her marriage, Mother had built her life around her children. She then mentioned two incidents in which men in the community had attempted to fondle her when she was an adolescent. She explored the implications of her exclusive connection with her children and her anger toward her husband and men in general.

Realizing the impact of her feelings on Ruti, she was eager to offer Ruti an alternative message. When Ruti rejoined the session, Mother spoke about Father and how much he missed Ruti. She explained that she had said harsh things about him because she had been upset after the molestation. They talked about different men in the family. Mother conveyed the message that men can be friendly and not dangerous. She asked if she could come by herself to process her memories of molestation, her anger at men, and her feelings about herself as a woman. As Mother's anger toward men diminished, she no longer needed Ruti in an overly close relationship. She could allow Ruti to reconnect with Father and continue toward independence.

Case 3: David and His Family within a Larger Health Network

In this case, the parenting in a multiproblem dysfunctional family inhibited the natural healing process of a child's trauma and produced continuing retraumatization. The inverted hierarchy and the unprocessed early trauma both needed to be addressed. EMDR was used as one element in a wider, overall systemic approach. Family therapy, parent guidance, and interventions by social service support agencies preceded the EMDR referral and continued after treatment.

The G. family was referred by their family therapist, who was working with the parents and their 17-year-old son, a delinquent youth. The referral concerned David, age 12, who had suffered from sleep disturbances for 6 weeks. David's behavior involved getting up hourly at night, awaking at 5:30 A.M., going to school, where he was unable to function, returning home at 6:30 P.M., and crashing on the living room couch at 8. His parents reported that he was fearful and anxious. The referral to the Trauma Unit was based on the family's supposition that David's behavior was linked to a trauma.

David was the fourth of six children. David's two older siblings lived primarily outside the home and returned for school vacations. Both had histories of severe acting-out. The family's structure was characterized by an inverted power hierarchy, with ineffective parents and out-of-control, anxious children. Although the parents had learned new parenting skills over the past 2 years, they continued to be challenged by their older sons, including David. David often became argumentative and threatening when he did not get his way. He took out his frustrations physically on his younger siblings. He would not accept feedback or help from his parents concerning his sleep disturbance. The circularity of parental ineffectiveness and children's problematic behaviors is seen clearly in this family.

An assessment of the family's trauma history revealed the following: death of a baby brother when David was 2.5 years old; David's being hit by teachers; David's transfer to four different schools over 8 years; the parents' past physical disciplining style; the father's major illnesses; and a history of David's being bullied and humiliated by his older brothers because of his weight, babyish behavior, and laziness.

From this trauma assessment, two dominant themes emerged: David perceived the world as a dangerous and unpredictable place, and he felt powerless and unprotected. In response, he had developed mechanisms, at a young age, to protect himself. His mother described how, when his baby brother died, David repeated to her, "I am a hero. I don't cry." His current bullying behavior, when contrasted with his immaturity and fearfulness, was seen as an attempt to feel tough and invincible. David's parents reported that from the time the baby died until David was 7, he would not stay in any room with the door closed. When David was 8, he developed a fear that robbers would kidnap one of his younger siblings. At the time of the therapy, he could not stay in the house at night if he was the oldest child there.

Due to the intrusiveness of David's sleep problem, it was decided to make that the first treatment goal. Neither David nor his parents were able to identify any specific stressor that may have caused the onset of the current symptoms. They interpreted it as an extension and exacerbation of old fears. The therapist decided to target the earliest trauma, the crib death of his baby brother. David had no conscious recollections of the event. Based on Lovett's (1999) methodology, the parents were asked to write out the story of the event as it would have been experienced by a 2.5-year-old child. David and his parents were taught a relaxation technique.

In the following session, EMDR commenced. The mother read the story while the father alternately tapped David's arms as he embraced him in a holding position. Following the reading, the mood was one of grief and pain. Because this was not a conscious memory for David, the therapist probed indirectly for a Positive Cognition. David was asked what he would tell a younger, scared brother who might suffer from similar fears. He replied, "It's over. You are safe now." Thus, David created an internal image (resource) of himself as a wiser, older brother who could reassure himself of his current safety. The family hugged and said a prayer together for the deceased baby.

The EMDR work was combined with parental guidance aimed at strengthening the parents in their position as caregivers and protectors. Strengthening their hierarchical position would provide David with a sense of security. This involved the parents keeping David up until normal bedtime, encouraging him to use his relaxation technique, and giving him positive support. By the next session, David's sleep patterns had adjusted to a normal pattern. Two aspects of change were noticeable. First was David's cooperation, thus demonstrating his newly developed absence of fear about going to sleep. The second aspect was a clear shift in the parent-child relationship. From antagonistic, angry interactions in which David rejected any intervention from his parents, he was now able to accept their support.

David's history of fears, along with its latest manifestation, was understood as reverberations from an early, unprocessed trauma. These fears were reinforced by the additional traumas. Given that most of these issues continued to be actively problematic in the family (e.g., his relationship with his brothers), or potentially so (recurrence of illnesses), the team did not expect resolution of all of David's fears from this one intervention.

There were two elements in the EMDR processing that enabled the changes that did occur. The first involved providing David the opportunity to process his unresolved grief, enabling him to reach his Positive Cognition "It is over. I am safe now." This led to a reduction in his anxiety about going to sleep. The second element was the correction in the hierarchy between David and his parents. In processing the earliest trauma, with his mother reading the script and his father embracing him, David was able to incorporate the additional "new" and reassuring knowledge that his parents were available to care for and protect him. He was freed from protecting them. These changes, behavioral and emotional, changed the rigid circularity of the parent-child relationship. The parents experienced themselves as empowered; they shifted from blaming to a supportive stance.

Though the sleep issue remained corrected, the positive shift in parent-child dynamics could not withstand the ongoing challenges presented by the continuing dysfunctional family patterns. The parents remained insufficiently effective in protecting David from the harsh teasing of his brothers and in confronting David's own aggression, leaving him feeling vulnerable. It was decided to target David's fear of thieves and being home alone in order to provide him with an empowering experience and strengthen his sense of self. During the EMDR processing, David's anxiety was high, and threatening images of thieves arose. These were followed by images of helpless responses (e.g., his running away, being tied up). During continued associations, his responses became more adaptive and effective (calling someone to untie him, calling the police). Following three sessions of EMDR, David felt confident that he could stay home as the babysitter.

David's problematic behavior had also kept him in a central position and brought him attention and a sense of power. Although the new changes created a sense of relief and greater protection by his parents, they also threatened this position. David responded by trying to reassert the centrality that he had become accustomed to. He began blackmailing his parents through unreasonable demands (such as insisting that they buy him expensive toys) as a condition for babysitting. The parents reverted back to ineffective, aggressive responses.

The therapeutic work that had freed David from his debilitating fears and strengthened the parents in their appropriate hierarchical position needed consolidation. Despite a stronger, warmer bond that had developed between David and his parents, problematic interactions within the entire family continued. The parents required continued intensive structural work to firmly establish their authority: to set limits, provide structure, and set consequences for both the older children and David. Without such change, it would be difficult for David to sustain his personal gains. The family was therefore referred back to their primary family therapist to continue work on dysfunctional family patterns.

DISCUSSION

Successful treatment of the traumatized child is dependent on assessment of the child's family system and its role as a potential source of strength or interference in the healing process. Often, the parents' active participation in the treatment is crucial. The traumatized child retreats into the relative safety of his home as he attempts to cope with his overwhelming loss of safety and trust. The ability of the parents to respond to this need is foremost in their child's healing process. When family members are secondarily traumatized or when parenting is deficient, treatment must directly address these issues. Only then can EMDR be maximally effective. Thus, SFT understandings and interventions with the child's family pave the way for successful processing of the child's trauma.

In the case of Yoav and his family, the presence of the family during the EMDR processing of its youngest member gave him the support and safety that allowed him to process his traumatic memories. EMDR for the other members enabled them to move forward and gain strength, which in turn strengthened the positive moves of the young child. SFT interventions strengthened the parental unit by helping them release Yoav from a detouring position that infantilized him. They gave the nurturing and support so crucial to his healing. In the case of Ruti, the natural healing process was blocked by a disappointing, distant spouse relationship. An overly close mother-daughter relationship kept Ruti hostage to her mother's antagonism to men. Only as Mother uncovered and confronted her own resentment toward men and her own previous molestation could her daughter be free to process her own trauma. In David's case, enlisting the parents in EMDR gave him an experience of closeness and support rarely felt in his chaotic family. Their direct involvement in therapy sessions revealed a history of traumatic family events that also needed to be processed. Because of the chronic weakness of the family system, the case was sent back to the referring agency for continuing family work.

Parental presence in the therapy room provides much needed information that young children cannot be expected to provide: trauma history, critical events, family members' reactions to the trauma and in general to their child. Observing family interactions offers another dimension of knowledge of the family. Creating new interactions through enactments provides the family with the ability to develop new growth-inducing patterns and skills. The opportunity to witness their child coping with her trauma as she proceeds through the EMDR processing gives parents the hope that their child can recover and that they can dare to support the child's move back to her former functioning.

When working with children it is often necessary to modify the EMDR protocol to meet the cognitive and emotional level of the child. In general, it is preferable initially to accept the child's formulation of NC and PC even when these are not formulated according to standard protocol. Often, children will start with an external, descriptive statement for the NC and PC, but after a set (or two) of EMs, they can generally give a self-statement, especially if the therapist asks again, "What thoughts about yourself come up or go with that picture?" It is helpful to follow the child's lead so as to encourage his involvement; for example, some children need questions to help them articulate what they are experiencing, others may be able to concentrate for only short periods of time. In the cases reviewed in this chapter, strengthening the parental function was important to free the child for positive individual changes. These changes were either enhanced or curtailed by the system's reactions. This wide perspective on the individual embedded within the family context allows for incorporation of treatment approaches that relate to both the individual and the context. EMDR and family systems/structural therapy, complementing each other, do just that.

REFERENCES

Bardin, A. (2004). EMDR within a family system perspective. *Journal of Family Psychotherapy, 15,* 47–61.

Bisson, J. (2004). *Mental health: Post-traumatic stress disorder.* Retrieved August 16, 2005, from British Medical Association, Clinical Evidence web site: http://www.clinicalevidence.com /ceweb/conditions/meh/1005/1005.jsp.

Chansky, T. E. (2004). *Freeing your child from anxiety.* New York: Norton.

Cohen, J., Berliner, L., & March, J. (2000). Treatment of children and adolescents. In E. Foa, T. Keane, & M. Friedman (Eds.), *Effective treatments for PTSD* (pp. 106–138). New York: Guilford Press.

Figley, C. R. (1988). Helping traumatized families. *Journal of Traumatic Stress, 1,* 127–141.

Figley, C. R. (1989). *Treating stress in families.* New York: Brunner/Mazel.

Greenwald, R. (1994). Applying eye movement desensitization and reprocessing to the treatment of traumatized children: Five case studies. *Anxiety Disorders Practice Journal, 1,* 83–97.

Greenwald, R. (1998). EMDR: New hope for children suffering from trauma and loss. *Clinical Child Psychology and Psychiatry, 3,* 279–287.

Johnson, S. M. (2002). *Emotionally focused couple therapy with trauma survivors.* New York: Guilford Press.

Kaslow, F. W., Nurse, A. R., & Thompson, P. (2002). EMDR and family systems. In F. Shapiro (Ed.), *EMDR as an integrative psychotherapy approach: Experts of diverse orientations explore the paradigm prism* (pp. 289–318). Washington, DC: American Psychological Association Books.

Kilic, E. Z. (2003). The psychological effects of parental mental health on children experiencing disaster: The experience of Bolu earthquake in Turkey. *Family Process, 4,* 485–495.

La Greca, A. M., Silverman, W. K., Vernberg, E. M., & Prinstein, M. J. (1996). Symptoms of posttraumatic stress in children following Hurricane Andrew: A prospective study. *Journal of Consulting and Clinical Psychology, 64,* 712–723.

Laor, N., Wolmer, L., Mayes, L., Gershon, A., Weizman, R., & Cohen, D. (1997). Israel preschool children under Scuds: A 30-month follow-up. *Journal of the American Academy of Child and Adolescent Psychiatry, 36,* 349–356.

Lovett, J. (1999). *Small wonders: Healing childhood trauma with EMDR.* New York: Free Press.

McFarlane, A. (1987). Posttraumatic phenomena in a longitudinal study of children following a natural disaster. *Journal of the American Academy of Child and Adolescent Psychiatry, 26,* 764–769.

Minuchin, S. (1974). *Families and family therapy.* London: Tavistock.

Minuchin, S., & Fishman, C. (1981). *Family therapy techniques.* Cambridge, MA: Harvard University Press.

Nelson, B. S., & Wright, D. W. (1996). Understanding and treating post-traumatic stress disorder symptoms in female partners of veterans with PTSD. *Journal of Marital and Family Therapy, 22,* 455–467

Nichols, W. C. (1989). A family systems approach. In C. R. Figley (Ed.), *Treating stress in families* (pp. 67–96). New York: Brunner/Mazel.

Pynoos, R., Steinberg, A., & Goenjian, A. (1996). Traumatic stress in childhood and adolescence. In B. van der Kolk, A. McFarlane, & L. Weisaeth (Eds.), *Traumatic stress* (pp. 331–358). New York: Guilford Press.

Riggs, D. S. (2000). Marital and family therapy. In E. Foa (Ed.), *Effective treatments for PTSD* (pp. 354–355). New York: Guilford Press.

Scheeringa, M., & Zeanah, C. (2001). A relational perspective on PTSD in early childhood. *Journal of Traumatic Stress, 14*(4), 799–815.

Shapiro, F. (2001). *Eye movement desensitization and reprocessing: Basic principles, protocols and procedures* (2nd ed.). New York: Guilford Press.

Shapiro, F. (2002). *EMDR as an integrative psychotherapy approach: Experts of diverse orientations explore the paradigm prism.* Washington, DC: American Psychological Association Books.

Siegel, D. J. (2002). The developing mind and the resolution of trauma: Some ideas about information processing and an interpersonal neurobiology of psychotherapy. In F. Shapiro (Ed.), *EMDR as an integrative psychotherapy approach: Experts of diverse orientations explore the paradigm prism* (pp. 85–121). Washington, DC: American Psychological Association Books.

Tinker, R. H., & Wilson, S. A. (1999). *Through the eyes of a child: EMDR with children.* New York: Norton.

Umbarger, C. (1983). *Structural family therapy.* New York: Grune and Stratton.

Zero to Three. (2005). *Diagnostic classification of mental health and developmental disorders of infancy and early childhood* (Rev. ed.). Washington, DC: Author.

CHAPTER 17

Integrative Treatment of Intrafamilial Child Sexual Abuse

Louise Maxfield

A child's disclosure of sexual abuse perpetrated by a family member usually precipitates an immediate crisis for the entire family. At the same time as family members deal with the often devastating personal impact and overwhelming emotions of shock, grief, betrayal, anger, fear, guilt, shame, and confusion, police officers and child protection workers demand interviews and scrutinize the family's function and safety. Following their investigation, child protective services typically refuse to allow the child to live at home unless the offender has been removed from the household. The family finds itself struggling with the reconfiguration of the family structure. The children's behavior usually deteriorates, challenging the stretched resources of the nonoffending parent(s). Unfortunately, in many cases, members of the extended family often take the side of the accused offender, isolating and reviling the children and their parent(s), and, as a consequence, the family loses these loved ones and an important part of their support system. Sometimes the child is required to testify in criminal court against a loved one, of whom he or she may also be very afraid.

As time goes by and the parents work to reestablish the structure and stability of the home, they often discover many problems that need to be addressed. Commonly there are long-standing problems with poor communication and inadequate boundaries. These issues have become further compounded by relational and individual distress. Later, there may be familial controversies and challenges regarding future contact with the offender. Individual symptoms related to posttraumatic stress, depression, substance abuse, and conduct problems must also be addressed.

Childhood Sexual Abuse

Child sexual abuse (CSA) is a relatively common occurrence, constituting 10% of all child protective investigations in Canada, with 38% of these investigations substantiated (Trocme & Wolfe, 2001). Only 2% of children were sexually abused by strangers, 27% were sexually abused by known nonrelatives (e.g., babysitters), and 69% were sexually abused by family members (25% by primary caregivers and 44% by other family members). Similar rates of sexual abuse are reported in the United States (National Clearinghouse on Child Abuse and Neglect, 2005). It should be noted that it is widely acknowledged that the number of reported cases represents only a small portion of actual cases because many children and youth do not disclose to anyone (e.g., Alaggia & Kirshenbaum, 2005; London, Bruck, Ceci, & Shuman, 2005).

The prevalence of CSA has been investigated in a number of studies with community samples of more than 1,000 participants. For example, in the National Comorbidity Study, CSA was reported by 13.5% of women and 2.5% of men (Molnar, Buka, & Kessler, 2001). Other researchers have reported prevalence rates varying from 6% to 34% for girls and from 2% to 11% for boys (Walker, Carey, Mohr, Stein, & Seedat, 2004). This range in variance may be attributed to methodological differences in operational definitions or to true differences in the actual populations surveyed.

CSA frequently has a deleterious impact on the victims. A review of 45 studies by Kendall-Tackett, Williams, and Finkelhor (1993) determined that sexually abused children have more symptoms than nonabused children, although one-third of abused children are asymptomatic. Symptoms commonly reported include fears, posttraumatic stress, behavior problems, sexualized behaviors, and poor self-esteem. Kendall-Tacket et al. reported that most recovery occurs within the first 12 to 28 months postdisclosure.

The impact of CSA often continues into adulthood, with CSA related to an increased risk for multiple physical and mental health problems (e.g., McCauley et al., 1997; Sachs-Ericsson, Blazer, Plant, & Arnow, 2005). CSA often occurs as part of a larger pattern of childhood adversity, associated with maladaptive family behaviors. The Adverse Childhood Experiences studies (e.g., Dube et al., 2005; Edwards, Holden, Felitti, & Anda, 2003; Felitti et al., 1998) have determined that childhood abuse and household dysfunction are associated with the development, decades later, of the chronic diseases that are the most common causes of death and disability in North America, including heart disease, cancer, chronic lung and liver disease, and injuries. These studies have also determined that abuse in childhood is a significant risk factor for depression, alcoholism, substance abuse, and suicide attempts.

In a population sample of adult female twins, Kendler et al. (2000) found that CSA was a nonspecific risk factor for the development of subsequent psychiatric and substance abuse disorders and that the risk increased with the severity of the abuse. In an examination of the data from this abused adult twin study, Bulik, Prescott, and Kendler (2001) found no evidence that certain patterns of abuse were uniquely associated with specific psychiatric syndromes, thus confirming prior findings that CSA acts as a nonspecific risk factor for psychiatric disorders. The risk of psychopathology was greater if the perpetrator was a family member, if intercourse was attempted or completed, if force or threats were used, and if "someone the victim told about the abuse either did not believe her, did not support her, or punished her for the abuse" (p. 447).

The Role of the Family after Disclosure

Bulik et al. (2001) identified an important protective factor: The child had a better outcome if he or she told someone about the abuse and that person acted to stop it. This finding is consistent with that of other studies that have identified family support as predictive of resilience (Romans, Martin, Anderson, O'Shea, & Mullen, 1995; Spaccarelli & Kim, 1995). Additionally, research in the field of child development has found that the best predictor of adolescent well-being is the adolescent's relationship with his or her mother (Demo & Acock, 1996).

Parents are often traumatized by their child's disclosure and may have difficulty mobilizing the resources needed to support their child (Elliott & Carnes, 2001). Manion et al. (1996) and Hiebert-Murphy (1998) found that support from friends and family was critical to the function of these parents, illustrating the importance of the psychosocial network response to the family system.

An association between the symptoms of abused children and their nonoffending mother was reported by Deblinger, Steer, and Lipmann (1999). Mothers who were depressed were more likely to describe their children with posttraumatic symptoms and internalizing behaviors. Children who reported depression were more likely to perceive their mother as rejecting, and children with higher posttraumatic stress scores were more likely to perceive their mother as intrusive and controlling. These relationships are correlational in nature, not causative; they are descriptive of the systemic effects of abuse.

Theoretical Conceptualizations

Shapiro's (2001) Adaptive Information Processing model views behavioral disorders and psychological symptoms as having linear causality. Specifically, Shapiro hypothesized that an unresolved or unprocessed traumatic experience, such as CSA, results in a range of emotional, cognitive, somatic, and behavioral symptoms, which then may be exacerbated by family interactions. On the other hand, family systems theory conceptualizes symptoms as being created and maintained in a circular fashion (Nichols & Schwartz, 1995; see also Chapter 20). From this perspective, a child's anxiety is viewed as increased by the parents' attention, and the parents' overprotectiveness as strengthened by the child's symptoms. With regard to CSA, whereas many family systems therapists (especially feminist family theorists) hold that the offender is responsible for his abusive behavior, family dynamics are usually understood as maintaining the system, inhibiting disclosure and/or preventing protection. Family systems theorists also recognize the influence of other external systems (e.g., child protective services, schools) on the family system. There are two family systems therapies that are especially relevant in the treatment of CSA: Strategic Therapy (Madanes, 1990) and Structural Therapy (Minuchin, 1974). Strategic Family Systems Therapy (FST) focuses chiefly on patterns of communication; Structural FST attends to family structure and roles and related power and authority.

Family Systems Therapy

Structural Family Therapy was developed by Salvador Minuchin and colleagues (Minuchin, 1974; Minuchin, Montalvo, Guerney, Rosman, & Schumer, 1967) during his years at the Wiltwyck School for Boys in New York. It focuses on reestablishing parental hierarchical authority, creating appropriate boundaries, and altering alliances. In families with intrafamilial sexual abuse, family structure is often skewed. When the child becomes a sexual partner of the father, he or she is covertly triangulated within the marital subsystem, and the boundary between the parents becomes more rigid. Some abused children attain inordinate power within the family system, whereas others are devalued and dismissed; in both instances, other disturbances often reverberate within the sibling subsystem. In addition, there are problems in the parent-child subsystem because the mother has abrogated her role as protector.

Jay Haley and Cloe Madanes were colleagues of Minuchin's at the Philadelphia Child Guidance Center; they later founded the Family Therapy Institute of Washington, DC, where they developed and taught Strategic Family Therapy (Goldenberg & Goldenberg, 2000). Strategic Family Therapy addresses maladaptive communication patterns. Because of the intense secrecy surrounding abuse in the family, communication is typically distorted and there are deficits in the family's ability to problem-solve. Madanes (1990) developed a 16-step model for treating the offender, victim, and family as a unit. Her approach involves the family's revealing all the secrets, apologizing to the victim, and the victim, hopefully, extending forgiveness.

Neither Strategic nor Structural Family Therapy has been empirically investigated in the treatment of CSA. However, abuse-focused cognitive-behavioral therapy for the child and family has been evaluated and found to be helpful in a number of studies (e.g., Cohen, Deblinger, Mannarino, & Steer, 2004). On the other hand, a similar study by King et al. (2000) found no advantage for including parents in their cognitive-behavioral program.

One of the expected benefits of family therapy is its focus on issues that are known to create later pathology. For example, Whiffen and MacIntosh (2005) concluded that the effects of CSA on adult pathology were mediated by several variables, including shame or self-blame, interpersonal difficulties, and avoidant coping strategies. Family therapy addresses these variables in an interpersonal framework. Further, the strengthening of self-regulation and communication skills and healthy boundaries in family therapy sessions often can contribute to the child's development of psychological strengths and resources.

Eye Movement Desensitization and Reprocessing

Eye Movement Desensitization and Reprocessing (EMDR) is a treatment approach developed by Shapiro (1995, 2001) to assist patients in effectively processing past traumatic and distressing events. It is based on Shapiro's Adaptive Information Processing model and employs an eight-phase approach to therapy, which addresses past memories, current triggers, and future plans. EMDR has been determined to be efficacious in the treatment of adults with Posttraumatic Stress Disorder (PTSD; American Psychiatric Association, 2004; Maxfield & Hyer, 2002). There has been only one randomized study that investigated EMDR treatment of sexually abused children. Jaberghaderi, Greenwald, Rubin, Zand, and Dolatabadi (2004) compared the outcomes of cognitive-behavioral therapy and EMDR for teenage Iranian girls who had been sexually abused. They found that both treatments produced similar significant effects with improvement of posttraumatic symptoms and behavior. Because EMDR did not require the child to spend time on therapy-related homework, the investigators concluded that it was a more efficient treatment. Other studies using EMDR with traumatized children have confirmed its effectiveness with this population (e.g., Chemtob, Nakashima, Hamada, & Carlson, 2002; Fernandez, Gallinari, & Lorenzetti, 2004; Greenwald, 1999; Lovett, 1999; Soberman, Greenwald, & Rule, 2002; Tinker & Wilson, 1999).

THERAPY PROCESS

A combination of family therapy and EMDR can provide thorough comprehensive treatment for the child and nonoffending family members. Generally, EMDR is used to process the distressing memories and emotions, and family therapy is used to address relational problems of family structure (e.g., boundaries, roles, rules); transactional patterns; family issues around safety, blame and guilt; communication; and parenting difficulties. Consequently, the integration of these two approaches can address and resolve the key issues and problems faced by the family and its members.

The integrated treatment process developed by this author has four stages: Stage 1: Stabilization/Advocacy; Stage 2: Family Assessment; Stage 3: Processing; Stage 4: Reevaluation and Termination. These stages may overlap. In family therapy, sessions are conducted with various configurations of the family (i.e., parent-child dyad, children together) as well as the entire intact nuclear family. Sometimes a session is conducted with extended family members. If appropriate and safe, a session may be conducted with the offender and family members.

The treatment of intrafamilial sexual abuse is complicated because of variations in family dynamics and histories. As mentioned earlier, 44% of CSA was found to be perpetrated by family members, such as siblings, cousins, uncles, aunts, and grandparents, and 25% by primary caregivers, such as parents and stepparents (Trocme & Wolfe, 2001). When the offender resides in the same home as the child, child protective services usually insist that either the victim or the offender leave the home. Treatment is more complicated in such cases because the family must adjust to the mandated change in its configuration and the loss of one of its members. The following section summarizes the stages of therapy and highlights important treatment issues and targets.

To simplify this section, the family situation is configured as a nonoffending protective mother with a child abused by the mother's husband or live-in boyfriend.

Stage 1: Stabilization

After disclosure, the family often struggles with the loss of the father and husband, and many related emotions, such as grief, anger, and fear, are elicited. The reorganization of the family may be complicated and painful. In addition, the loss of the offender's income may necessitate the family's leaving their home and applying for financial assistance. The child and his or her family often experience other related losses, and the child is sometimes blamed for causing these losses.

The family is usually involved with multiple community agencies. Typically, child protective services and the police department conduct parallel investigations, interviewing most family members; criminal and family court processes may follow. Counseling services may be provided to the abuse victim and his or her family. There may also be involvement with the forensic systems assessing and treating the offender, as well as related probation or parole agencies. Although families may present for treatment some months after the original disclosure, they usually continue to have contact with various community systems for an extended period.

It is essential that the therapist provide all members of the family with clear information about the legal limitations to confidentiality so that they are aware of the therapist's obligation to report child abuse. The therapist needs to get informed consent forms signed by all family members involved in treatment in order to communicate with other involved agencies.

The therapist also ensures that the family is aware of confidentiality related to personal privacy. For example, the child may tell the therapist personal information (e.g., about social activities or substance use) with the request that the parent not be informed. In many states and provinces, the child's privacy is legally protected and the therapist cannot inform the parent without the child's permission. This issue should be discussed prior to beginning treatment, and all members should understand the therapist's position.

Although the goals of this stage are similar to creating a therapeutic alliance (Shapiro, 2001) and joining with the family (Minuchin, 1974), the therapist also takes an active role as an advocate, providing support and information and guiding the family through the various community systems. During this process, the therapist begins a preliminary evaluation of family dynamics.

It is essential that the therapist monitor issues related to safety, urging the child's protection from the offender and compliance with any court orders that prohibit or restrict contact with the offender. Sometimes children have supervised visits with the offender, and the therapist should review the nature and quality of these visits to identify any emotional abuse.

Stage 2: Family Assessment

The family assessment stage incorporates EMDR's Phases 1 and 2. The first treatment session is typically with the mother alone, to permit the sharing of complicated family histories and secrets, the status of the legal processes, the type of contact that the offender currently has with the family, and the challenges confronting the family (e.g., financial, legal, interpersonal). The exclusion of the children in this session allows for appropriate boundaries around information and reinforces the mother in her role as the parental authority. In many families, the mother's position in the parental hierarchy has previously been eroded. One of the goals of family treatment is to support the mother as she reclaims and asserts her authority so that the recognition of her position is established from the onset of therapy. The therapist also assesses the mother's ability to adjust to the massive transformation in her life situation and her willingness to comply with court orders regarding contact with the offender. In addition, the therapist determines if and where advocacy may be required.

The next few treatment sessions are usually family ones, attended by the mother and her children. The purpose is to develop a treatment plan, facilitate communication, work on role allocations, strengthen boundaries, and ensure safety. The therapist and family develop guidelines to ensure the emotional safety of all members during the family sessions. For example, there may be rules prohibiting name-calling and interrupting. This process models the establishment of appropriate structures, boundaries, and mutual respect.

Although history taking is an integral part of most treatment protocols, in this setting, history taking can be better conceptualized as history rewriting, as each member realizes that his or her version of family history was incomplete or inaccurate. In families where there are many secrets, most members have different experiences about which the others know nothing. This sharing of information is usually done in one or more family sessions with all members of the intact family. The family members discuss what happened, who knew what was happening, and related feelings. Often, one family member will have questions for another. For example, the child may ask his mother why she was unaware of the abuse; a mother may ask a child if abuse occurred on a certain occasion. The history-taking session is often very emotional for all members, and it allows for expression of validation and nurturing. The therapist may need to be directive to assist the members in appropriate responses to others' disclosures. After the session, family members typically feel relieved, as they understand more about each other and what has happened. The session also identifies issues that need to be addressed in future family or EMDR sessions.

Stage 3: Processing

CSA is not simply an individual trauma, it is a trauma to the entire family; furthermore, the disclosure of CSA involves a cascade of responses and changes for the individual members and the family as a unit. Although these problems (and their treatment) are described separately in this chapter, many of them occur simultaneously, exacerbating the level of distress within the family. The treatment of these complex issues requires flexibility and recognition of each family's unique presentation and needs. Most families are confronted with similar core issues, and these issues respond well to a combination of EMDR and family therapy. The process of integrating these two treatment approaches varies, depending on how each specific family addresses the various concerns.

EMDR may be administered either in a conjoint fashion (e.g., with the mother present to support her child) or to an individual alone. When the child receives

EMDR individually, it is usually best if the mother joins the child for the last part of the session, when she can be provided with an overview of the material that the child has processed. This reinforces her role as the parental authority and allows for appropriate nurturance and validation, with the therapist prompting such responses, if necessary.

The Traumatic Event

Trauma processing is usually done with EMDR, followed by family debriefing, if appropriate. Shapiro's (2001) Adaptive Information Processing model guides the choice of targets for EMDR treatment; these include past abuse incidents, current symptoms and triggers, and fears about future situations. For example, after a client has processed her experience of being sexually abused, she will then target current events that trigger discomfort, such as being kissed by her boyfriend. After this, she will process anticipated future events that create apprehension, such as her fear of seeing her molester-father at a family gathering.

Initially, EMDR treatment typically involves processing traumatic events. For each target memory, the client identifies a compelling visual image, the current *Negative Cognition* (NC) related to the memory (e.g., "I'm powerless"), a desired *Positive Cognition* (PC; e.g., "I'm competent"), the current associated emotions, and the location of the related body sensations. The client is asked to rate the validity of the PC when it is paired with the image on the Validity of Cognition (VOC) scale (1 = Not true, 7 = Completely true) and the level of emotional distress on the Subjective Units of Disturbance (SUD) scale (0 = No distress, 10 = Severe distress).

In addition to the experience of CSA, the child may identify other distressing events, such as the police coming to arrest Dad, Mom crying all day, and the anger expressed by other family members. A child may feel guilty about the abuse of his younger sibling or cousin, thinking that the other child would have been protected if he had only disclosed at an earlier time. Some children are shamed by their peers (e.g., called "gay"); others become immobilized by fears. Children often prefer to process the sexual trauma without their mother present because of discomfort at discussing the details of sexual behavior. Rather than shaming the child, this need can be reframed as the creation of appropriate boundaries around sexual privacy. With EMDR, children are usually able to rapidly resolve the distressing emotions, cognitions, and somatic sensations related to the event. As mentioned earlier, it is usually best if the mother can join the child in the debriefing of the EMDR sessions. During that process, the therapist can prompt the mother, if needed, in nurturing and validating responses.

The mother will probably also need to process her child's abuse. Although mothers rarely witness the actual abuse, they often create their own visual images of what happened, and these visual images can be used as a treatment target. Sometimes the images involve distress about their child being hurt and damaged; at other times, they elicit jealousy and anger. For example, one mother said, "I know that it wasn't her fault, but when I visualize her in my bed with my husband, I feel angry, as though she is the other woman. What am I supposed to do about that?" EMDR is helpful to her in resolving these feelings; during processing, the memory is linked to and integrated with other adaptive and contextual information, which transforms the meaning and the stored affective content of the memory.

When a mother was also sexually abused as a child, her reactions to her own abuse often interfere with her ability to respond appropriately to her child. This is especially true if the mother was also abused by the same person who abused her child (e.g., mother's father). Treatment in such cases is often complex and lengthy. EMDR is invaluable and family therapy is essential.

Responsibility

The issue of responsibility for the abuse is often a contentious topic, eliciting shame, blame, guilt, and anger. Family systems theorists (e.g., Faust, 2001; Madanes, 1990) have typically recommended that the child not be asked why she did not disclose, as it is thought that such a question unfairly implies blame and indicates that the child is perceived as responsible. This author disagrees with this position, and argues that there may be important reasons why the child did not disclose, and similarly why the nonoffending parent did not perceive and/or protect. For the family to freely discuss such issues, it is imperative that the concept of responsibility be clarified.

The Responsibility Triangle (Maxfield, 1988; Wakefield & Maxfield, 1991) provides a simple illustration of this construct (see Figure 17.1); it is explained in a family session. In this model, the offender, the nonoffending parent, and the child are each depicted as having unique responsibilities. The offender is seen as being 100% responsible for his own behavior and for the abuse; no one else is responsible for his actions. The nonoffending parent is responsible to protect (as

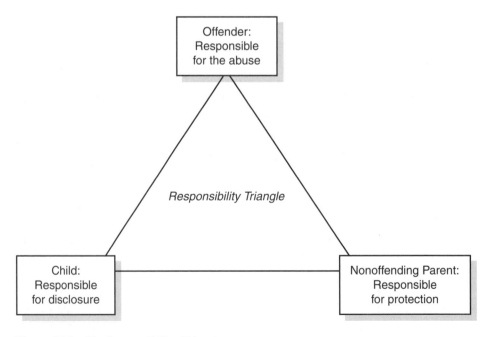

Figure 17.1   The Responsibility Triangle.

are extended family members and community figures). There may be a number of reasons why the mother did not recognize the abuse (e.g., it was well hidden) or did not protect (e.g., fear of injury, fear of losing custody; Jensen, 2005). Whatever the reasons, protection is still the mother's responsibility. The responsibility of the child is to disclose. There may be many reasons why the child did not tell (e.g., threats of harm, love for the offender). Whatever the reasons, it is often difficult or impossible for others to protect the child if he or she refuses to disclose.

This model places the responsibility for the abuse completely on the offender. It also allows the mother and child to identify and address issues related to their own role in the continuation of the abuse. Clarifying these concepts in a family session can help the family to resolve related emotions. For example, the mother takes responsibility for her failure to protect and apologizes to the child for her failure. Note that she does not apologize for the actual abuse, as this is not her responsibility. The child explains why he or she was unable to tell ("He said he'd kill my pet!"), and the mother validates her child's fears and reinforces the concept that the child was not responsible for the abuse. The family can then problem-solve about how future difficulties can be avoided through better protection and communication. These concrete and practical plans about family safety strengthen boundaries and roles.

Sometimes, concerns about responsibility continue to distress the mother or child. In such instances, individual EMDR treatment is used to process these emotions and bring them to a resolution. With EMDR, the child realizes that she could not control the offender nor force him to stop and that he is the one responsible. She asserts, "I was only a little girl!" The mother recognizes that although she originally failed to detect the abuse, she has now taken action to protect her child. Nevertheless, it is quite likely that the mother will continue to feel some guilt and that this will never be completely eradicated. This is what Shapiro (1991) referred as an "ecologically valid" emotion, or as one mother explained, "I did not protect my child, and I will always feel some grief and guilt about that."

Child Conduct Problems and Parenting Difficulties

One might expect that after disclosure, life would become simpler and safer for the child; instead, one usually sees an escalation of distress, conduct problems, and fears. These may be related to the multitude of unexpected and unpredictable changes in the child's life, as well as the flood of overwhelming, confusing emotions and thoughts. The child's behavior can become unmanageable. Simultaneously, the mother may feel guilty and worried about her child's adjustment to all the changes, and she may become overindulgent to compensate, thus exacerbating the child's conduct difficulties. Furthermore, if the mother was previously passive, relinquishing authority to the father, the family may now find itself without any authority figure.

In this instance, the goal of family therapy is to assist the mother in establishing a parental hierarchy, creating appropriate roles, rules, and boundaries. This can be taught in some individual sessions with the mother and in family sessions addressing roles and relationships. EMDR may also be used to help the mother target her feelings of incompetence or guilt and to assist the child in adjusting to the lifestyle changes.

Sometimes children develop more severe behavioral problems, such as aggression, sexualized behaviors, substance abuse, and Conduct Disorder. Specialized programs have been developed to assist with these populations (e.g., see Soberman et al., 2002). A detailed description is beyond the range of this chapter.

Relationship with the Offender

Decisions about the current relationship with the offender almost always result in familial conflict. In some jurisdictions, offenders may be incarcerated for lengthy periods. In other places, offenders receive very short sentences or are placed on probation, thus requiring the family to make decisions about ongoing contact. Prior to the disclosure, the offender was often a loved and valued family member, and individuals' affections did not necessarily change with the revelation of CSA. This can create much personal confusion and familial conflict. Personal confusion responds well to EMDR treatment, but familial conflict requires communication, negotiation, and, often, compromise. Sometimes individual treatment is needed to provide a member with privacy to discuss and accept his or her feelings about the offender.

For example, 10-year-old Bobby loved his father and, even though he had abused him, wanted to maintain contact with him. His mother, on the other hand, was so furious with her husband that she prohibited all contact and flew into a rage whenever his name was mentioned. Bobby experienced severe grief about the loss of his father, worried continually about his well-being, but could not share any of these emotions with his angry mother. Such situations are not easily resolvable because of the intense emotions involved. Bobby's mother refused individual treatment for herself and was incensed by her belief that she had been betrayed. Consequently, treatment focused on helping Bobby adjust to the loss of his father.

Stage 4: Reevaluation and Termination

Reevaluation is conducted as per Shapiro (2001) at the beginning of each session. This review evaluates processing of all identified targets. In particular for EMDR targets, past, present, and future elements are reassessed. For family therapy, planned changes are evaluated in terms of specified goals and behavioral changes. As treatment goals are achieved, termination is planned in appropriate ways. Occasionally, long-term follow-up is organized to ensure that treatment goals are maintained.

CASE EXAMPLE

The Smith family—mother Irene (age 40), daughter Mary (13), and son Sam (9)—were in treatment for about 1 year. They received family, individual, and dyadic sessions, as well as a session with father John (40), who had sexually abused Mary.

Family History

A family physician called to refer 13-year-old Mary for treatment. She had made a minor suicide attempt, and he had diagnosed her with Major Depressive Disorder and PTSD. Mary lived with her mother and her brother. Mary's father had sexually abused her on a single occasion 15 months previously, and he had been living apart from the family since that time. John had pled guilty in court and had received a sentence of 18 months probation. He was allowed supervised access to the children, but few visits had been held. Irene had divorced John and was now dating. She had been forced to find employment to support the family, and her new hospital job involved evening shifts. John had started a new relationship and was now living with his girlfriend, a waitress with a daughter (age 7) and two sons (3 and 5).

Four years previously, Mary had disclosed sexual abuse by her paternal grandfather, George. George had three adult children (John, another son, and a daughter) and eight grandchildren. It was discovered that George had sexually abused all the grandchildren including Mary and Sam. He pled guilty and received a 3-year prison sentence, which was now completed.

After the disclosures about George, Mary, Sam, Irene, and John had been involved in a full course of family therapy. Currently, the family had no contact with the grandparents, although the children said that they missed their grandmother. They also had no contact with their uncle; he was angry about the children's disclosures and his father's incarceration, even though his own sons indicated that they had also been abused.

Stage 1: Stabilization

Because Mary's disclosure of her father's abuse and related investigations had occurred 15 months previously, the family had little current contact with authorities and community systems. John was completing his sex offender treatment and his probationary period. Currently, the children had supervised visits with John, and he was pushing for more contact.

Mary's symptoms were quite severe and met diagnostic criteria for Major Depressive Disorder and PTSD. She was socially withdrawn, did not even answer friends' phone calls, and isolated herself in her room; in school, her marks had dropped from 75% to 50%. Both children were having difficulty adjusting to their mother's absence in the evenings. Mary said, "Before [the abuse] we had both our parents at home, and now it's just Sam and me." Both children expressed feelings of loneliness and fear. Although John had never come to the house, Mary and Sam were afraid he might appear when they were unprotected. Consequently, to provide stabilization for the first few months of treatment, it was recommended that Irene reduce her work schedule so that she could be home in the evenings. This allowed her to establish herself as the parental authority who protects, nurtures, and ensures safety. Irene made these adjustments, even though it caused financial hardship. At Irene's request, the therapist, as an advocate, wrote letters to Irene's employer explaining this need.

Stage 2: Assessment

The therapist assessed both the family and its individual members.

Assessment: The Family

Problems within the family system existed prior to John's abuse of Mary. Irene described John as self-centered, narcissistic, and demanding. Everyone agreed that he had a bad temper and that his rages were frightening and intimidating. Mary depicted him as having an alcohol problem and described fights between him and Irene when he would rage, throw things, and punch holes in walls and Irene would cry.

Mary stated that she was not close to her mother, whom she saw as "different" and "annoying," and claimed not to remember any experiences of safety with her mother. Instead, Mary reported that she felt closer to her father and explained that he used to participate in many activities with her and that he was often proud of her. She said, "He was either happy or angry." Sam was not close to his father, and both he and Irene described John as being very critical of Sam, dismissive, and cruel. Nevertheless, Sam clarified that John could be "fun" at times.

Prior to John's abuse of Mary, it appears that the family structure was dysfunctional. There were problems in the marital and parental subsystems; John was dominant and Irene was disengaged, passive, and depressed. There seems to have been an alignment between Mary and John long before the abuse occurred. Sam was often scapegoated and left out.

After the abuse and John's removal from the family, it was difficult for the family to establish a new and functional structure. Irene had difficulty establishing herself as the authoritative parent, and she was still emotionally removed. Her frequent absences were experienced by the children as an abrogation of her parental responsibility for their protection and safety. Mary disengaged from her mother, isolating herself in her room, and Sam acted out his distress and fears.

Assessment: Irene

Irene described herself as very depressed for about 2 years after her children's disclosures of sexual abuse by her father-in-law. She had responded appropriately to her children's disclosures of abuse, reporting these immediately to the authorities. She did not blame her children and was very supportive of their needs. Currently, she felt very positive and was enjoying her new job, although it required her to be absent from home in the evenings. She was dating and establishing a new life for herself. She did not think she needed individual therapy but was eager to participate in family sessions and was committed to doing all she could to help her children.

Assessment: Mary

For the first year after her father's abuse, it appeared that Mary was coping adequately. However, she had recently attempted suicide because she felt overwhelmed by several events. These included finding out that her father was going to marry his girlfriend ("I feel like he's replaced us!"); her worry about the safety of his 7-year-old stepdaughter ("I keep thinking that he's going to abuse her and wonder if I need to protect her"); and her mother's new job, which necessitated evening shifts ("I'm so scared at home alone. What if my dad came over?"). Further, her classmates had found out about her father's abuse and teased her, calling her "Dad's toy." She felt humiliated and vulnerable and said, "A lot of people know about my reputation." Mary described her grandfather's abuse as severe and frightening and explained that she had coped by dissociating: "I just wasn't there."

Assessment: Sam

Sam had many posttraumatic symptoms and was often sad. He identified multiple fears and worries (grandfather, father, bears, aliens, big wind). He was somewhat oppositional, argued a lot with his sister, and did not like being left alone at home with her. He was very anxious about visits with his father. Sam had intrusive memories regarding John's anger. Although he saw his father as having no control over his anger and behavior, Sam said, "I thought it was my fault he was mad." Sam also expressed distress about his grandfather's abuse and described his fear of his grandfather as "100 times" worse than his fear of his dad. When asked what he wanted to change, Sam said, "I don't stand up for myself."

Stage 3: Processing

Processing included both family sessions and individual EMDR sessions.

Processing: Family Sessions

The overall goal for the family therapy was to alter the family's structure so that they could function more effectively and each member could develop appropriately. This involved changing communication patterns, responsibilities, and roles; shifting alignments; and improving boundaries. Specific goals were strengthening Irene's parental authority, decreasing the disengagement between Mary and Irene, and resolving conflict and distress about visitation with John. A number of strategies were used to achieve these goals.

Irene was coached to be clear in her directives and consistent with consequences. Strategies were developed in sessions alone with Irene and with the children. Irene also made an effort to be home in the evenings, thus providing the children with an essential sense of safety and stability.

The Structural Family Therapy technique of enactment was used with Mary and Irene, who reenacted their conflict about Mary's isolating behaviors, with the therapist then providing suggestions for modifications. Communication skills were taught and modeled. It was agreed that there needed to be clearer boundaries around Mary's time alone, with more respect provided by Irene and more family time attempted by Mary. This resulted in a significant reduction in their conflict, and the boundary between Mary and Irene became less rigid.

Mary confronted Irene about John's abuse, asking, "Did you notice anything prior to that day?" Irene explained that she had not noticed any signs of his sexual interest in Mary. The two then discussed possible prevention of the molestation and came to the conclusion that the abusive incident probably had been inevitable. This discussion was validating for both and strengthened their connection and warmth.

The Structural Family Therapy technique of reframing was used on a variety of occasions to relabel behavior in a less pathological manner. For example, Mary felt very "different" from her peers, and providing some psychoeducational material was helpful in normalizing her experience. She spoke to others about this, including a teacher and a fellow student, and reported feeling empowered and assertive.

One of the most difficult issues confronting this family was contact with John. Irene was very angry with him and would have preferred her children to have no contact with him whatsoever. She recognized, however, that this was not necessarily what her children needed and wanted, and she agreed to do what would be best for them. Mary and Sam worked on their feelings about John in individual sessions (see later discussions), and their feelings changed over the course of treatment, with the resolution of past traumas and an increase in the sense of personal mastery.

After John completed his sex offender treatment and near the end of family treatment, a session was held with John and the children. They both confronted him about the abuse and he apologized to them. They also discussed their wishes and the various options for visitation. Mary decided that she wanted the freedom to pop in and out of John's house for a few minutes at a time (John lived in the same neighborhood). Sam requested continued supervision of visitation, as he still did not feel safe with his father. John was very affirming with the children and allowed them to express their feelings and respected their wishes.

Following this there was a session with Sam, Irene, and Irene's boyfriend to ensure that Sam's wishes and needs were adequately expressed, so that plans could be put in place to ensure his safety and comfort when visiting his father. Sam felt realistically vulnerable around his father; he worried that John might sexually abuse him at a future time and also could not trust his father to always treat him with respect and kindness. Supervised visitation was continued and safety plans were established; for example, Sam was allowed to cut a visit short if he wished.

Processing: Mary

In the Preparation Phase of EMDR, Mary identified a number of strategies that she used when having a "bad day." These included journaling, calling a friend, listening to music, instant-messaging friends, and going away in her imagination. The EMDR *Safe Place* protocol was employed and Mary identified an imaginary beach; during processing, she expressed enjoyment and started laughing in response to some positive thoughts about the beach.

Mary worked on a number of different issues in treatment. EMDR was provided to target the most upsetting incidents, which were the abuse by her grandfather and the humiliation at school. Interestingly, the abuse by her father was not very upsetting to Mary; she had much greater distress related to losing her father to his new family. As changes were made in the family sessions to accommodate her need to have a relationship with him, the distress dissipated.

Mary targeted her grandfather's abuse; her NC was "I'm not strong enough"; her PC was "I'm becoming independent," with a VOC rating of 3; emotions were anger, sadness, and shame, with a SUD rating of 7; and her body felt "closed up." Processing moved through various emotions, with memories of different incidents surfacing. She finished by remembering that she had confronted both her offenders and that as a result of her disclosures, both had been arrested and found guilty. Her PC changed to "I'm powerful" and she gave that a VOC rating of 7, with a SUD of 0. It should be noted that the therapist was not convinced that Mary had processed all elements of her grandfather's abuse and was concerned that she had not completed the present and future prongs of the protocol. Nevertheless, Mary asserted that she was unwilling to do more EMDR on the abuse and claimed that she was no longer troubled by it and that there were no current triggers and no future apprehensions.

Mary also used EMDR to process the teasing at school, the shame related to everyone knowing about her father's molesting her, and his related arrest and brief incarceration. She chose an incident when she walked into her classroom to discover all the students laughing at her. Her NC was "I'm not acceptable"; her PC was "I'm okay," with a VOC of 4. Her emotions were humiliation and anger, with a SUD of 8. During processing, Mary recalled events when she had felt embarrassed about her victimization ("They called me Dad's toy") and other times when she was angry ("I was out of control"). She then spontaneously began accessing adaptive and positive information; for example, she recalled other friends and family who had been supportive and recalled information about CSA previously provided in treatment. As her distress quickly abated, she mentioned that there were no current triggers, but that she was worried about attending high school in September. (Note that Mary's processing naturally shifted to the second and third prongs of EMDR.) She said, "I'm afraid I'll do something, and everyone will laugh." However, as she processed a future template about attending the new, much larger school, she rapidly concluded, "I'm not that worried, my friends will be with me," which shifted to "I'll be fine" and other statements about looking forward to this new developmental phase. The session finished with a SUD of 0 for the original teasing and a VOC of 7 for the PC "I'm okay."

Mary continued to progress well, and there was no evidence that more EMDR was required. When treatment finished, she was reminded that she could return to therapy if memories started to trouble her in the future. Family therapy resulted in many positive changes in Mary's behavior; she became less disengaged and less angry; she expressed feeling safer and more connected to her mother. Her behavior also changed at school: Her marks improved, she became more socially involved, and she began dating. She expressed comfort with her sexuality and her emerging identity as a competent and confident young woman.

Processing: Sam

Sam also worked through many different issues with EMDR. His first targeted image was his grandfather drawing on a picture Sam had made and not listening to Sam's request that he stop. This was an interesting metaphor, and a safer target for Sam to choose than the actual abuse. His NC was "I can't stand up for myself," and his PC was "I can stand up for myself," with a VOC rating of 2. His emotion was described as "bad," with a SUD rating of 9 and pain in his heart.

On the second set of eye movements, the memory shifted to the day his father had been forced to leave the home. "I see him taking his boxes out of the house." As processing continued, Sam expressed feelings of anger and sadness. He then spontaneously visualized himself "in a boxing ring, battling with the bad feelings." At the end of the session, he said, "I don't feel so sad, but I am more angry."

At the beginning of the next session, he reported that he had been remembering some nice memories of his father. Processing of the target (Dad moving out) continued. When he considered the incident, he stated, "It's not as upsetting as last time. . . . But it's still a bit upsetting. I'm all alone." He identified feelings of sadness and anger, which he located at the base of his throat. The SUD rating was 10. During the processing he brought up different experiences with his father, and at the end of the session he felt much relieved. The SUD rating was 1; he explained that it could not be 0 "because I can't just go over to his house—*yet.*"

In another session, Sam targeted the abuse by his grandfather. This time, rather than using a metaphor, he provided vivid details of the event. The image was his grandfather tickling him, then stroking his penis; the NC was "It's my fault," the PC was "I'm okay," the VOC was 2, the affect was "bad," the SUD rating was 10, and the body location was the top of his chest. During processing, Sam thought about issues of responsibility and power. He stated, "It was his choice, he had a choice. It's not my fault!" This was a very positive affirmation for Sam. He finished the session by imagining himself saying to his grandfather, "*No.* Leave me alone!" The SUD rating was 0.

When this memory was reviewed in a later session, the SUD rating remained at 0. Sam explained, "I know it was Grandpa's fault." The memory of Dad leaving the house was also checked, and Sam stated, "I don't feel inferior now. I'm not sad. I'm not unsafe. I'm glad he left. It's more safe. Dad can't hurt anyone." The present and future prongs of the protocol were also completed. For example, Sam had expressed some discomfort about being hugged by his father and handling this in future interactions. Later he reported, "That doesn't bother me anymore." Further, he asserted about his grandfather, "There are a lot of things I could do if he ever tried to touch me again!" In addition, he described himself acting in an assertive manner at school, with successful results. "I used to feel like anyone could do anything to me, but I don't feel like that anymore."

Stage 4: Reevaluation and Termination

All the goals of the Smith family were met in treatment. The altered family structure was more functional, with closer relationships, clearer boundaries, and better communication. Mary was doing well in school and had an active social life. Her depression and PTSD were in full remission. Sam was no longer troubled by intrusive memories, and he felt assertive and competent. The issues with visitation were resolved to everyone's satisfaction. Treatment was terminated with the understanding that the family could return if any problems resurfaced.

DISCUSSION

This chapter has addressed the issues commonly faced by families where the CSA was perpetrated by the mother's husband or boyfriend. This situation is very difficult because of the multiple levels of betrayal, combined with the disruption caused when the father is forced to leave the family home. Because of space limitations, it was not possible to describe the reactions of families when the offender is a grandparent, aunt, uncle, mother, cousin, or sibling. Coping with such disclosures and adjusting to changes within the larger extended family can be exceptionally painful and very challenging. The relationship of other family members with the victim and the offender are impacted by the disclosure and undergo an unexpected transformation.

As is apparent in the proceeding case example, successful treatment of CSA requires working with the child and his or her family and focusing on both individual and family problems. EMDR is invaluable for the individual members in addressing and processing trauma and distress. After EMDR, clients usually are no longer reactive, but instead are able to respond with more freedom and flexibility toward various life and family stressors. It is also anticipated that resolving issues related to CSA will decrease or eliminate its long-term deleterious effects.

Because intrafamilial CSA occurs within the family context and impacts most of the members, there are multiple family aspects that must be addressed. Typically, the family structure is dysfunctional prior to disclosure, and the family often lacks the resources to reconfigure the family into a healthier unit postdisclosure. Furthermore, the family is often reeling with the challenges created by the rupture. Family therapy assists the family in working through these aspects, improving communication, establishing clear and healthy boundaries, realigning the subsystems, establishing parental authority, and forging positive connections between individuals. The therapist also helps the family sort through the often contentious issue of contact with the offender and related safety concerns. The integration of EMDR and family systems therapy provides a powerful combination, addressing both intra- and interpersonal factors, looking at content and context. Therapy sessions can move from one modality to another, with each informing the other, thus maximizing effects.

REFERENCES

Alaggia, R., & Kirshenbaum, S. (2005). Speaking the unspeakable: Exploring the impact of family dynamics on child sexual abuse disclosures. *Families in Society, 86,* 227–234.

American Psychiatric Association. (2004). *Practice guideline for the treatment of patients with acute stress disorder and posttraumatic stress disorder.* Arlington, VA: American Psychiatric Association Practice Guidelines.

Bulik, C. M., Prescott, C. A., & Kendler, K. S. (2001). Features of childhood sexual abuse and the development of psychiatric and substance use disorders. *British Journal of Psychiatry, 179,* 444–449.

Chemtob, C. M., Nakashima, J. J., Hamada, R. S., & Carlson, J. G. (2002). Brief-treatment for elementary school children with disaster-related posttraumatic stress disorder: A field study. *Journal of Clinical Psychology, 58,* 99–112.

Cohen, J. A., Deblinger, E., Mannarino, A. P., & Steer, R. A. (2004). A multisite, randomized controlled trial for children with sexual abuse-related PTSD symptoms. *Journal of the American Academy of Child and Adolescent Psychiatry, 43,* 393–402.

Deblinger, E., Steer, R., & Lipmann, J. (1999). Maternal factors associated with sexually abused children's psychosocial adjustment. *Child Maltreatment, 4,* 13–20.

Demo, D. H., & Acock, A. C. (1996). Family structure, family process, and adolescent well-being. *Journal of Research on Adolescence, 6,* 457–488.

Dube, S. R., Anda, R. F., Whitfield, C. L., Brown, D. W., Felitti, V. J., Dong, M., et al. (2005). Long-term consequences of childhood sexual abuse by gender of victim. *American Journal of Preventive Medicine, 28,* 430–438.

Edwards, V. J., Holden, G. W., Felitti, V. J., & Anda, R. F. (2003). Relationship between multiple forms of childhood maltreatment and adult mental health in community respondents: Results from the Adverse Childhood Experiences study. *American Journal of Psychiatry, 160,* 1453–1460.

Elliott, A. N., & Carnes, C. N. (2001). Reactions of nonoffending parents to the sexual abuse of their child: A review of the literature. *Child Maltreatment, 6,* 314–331.

Faust, J. (2001). Post traumatic stress disorder in children and adolescents: Conceptualization and treatment. In H. Orvaschel, J. Faust, & M. Herson (Eds.), *Handbook of conceptualization and treatment of child psychopathology* (pp. 239–265). Amsterdam: Elsevier Science.

Felitti, V. J., Anda, R. F., Nordenberg, D., Williamson, D. F., Spitz, A. M., Edwards, V., et al. (1998). Relationship of childhood abuse and household dysfunction to many of the leading causes of death in adults: The Adverse Childhood Experiences (ACE) study. *American Journal of Preventive Medicine, 14,* 245–258.

Fernandez, I., Gallinari, E., & Lorenzetti, A. (2004). A school-based EMDR intervention for children who witnessed the Pirelli Building airplane crash in Milan, Italy. *Journal of Brief Therapy, 2,* 129–136.

Goldenberg, I., & Goldenberg, H. (2000). *Family therapy: An overview* (5th ed.). Belmont, CA: Brooks/Cole.

Greenwald, R. (1999). *Eye movement desensitization and reprocessing (EMDR) in child and adolescent psychotherapy.* Northvale, NJ: Aronson.

Hiebert-Murphy, D. (1998). Emotional distress among mothers whose children have been sexually abused: The role of a history of child sexual abuse, social support and coping. *Child Abuse and Neglect, 22,* 423–435.

Jaberghaderi, N., Greenwald, R., Rubin, A., Zand, S. O., & Dolatabadi, S. (2004). A comparison of CBT and EMDR for sexually abused Iranian girls. *Clinical Psychology and Psychotherapy, 11,* 358–368.

Jensen, T. K. (2005). The interpretation of signs of child sexual abuse. *Culture and Psychology, 11,* 469–498.

Kendall-Tackett, K. A., Williams, L. M., & Finkelhor, D. (1993). Impact of sexual abuse on children: A review and synthesis of recent empirical studies. *Psychological Bulletin, 113,* 164–180.

Kendler, K. S., Bulik, C. M., Silberg, J., Hettema, J. M., Myers, J., & Prescott, C. A. (2000). Childhood sexual abuse and adult psychiatric and substance use disorders: An epidemiological and cotwin control analysis. *Archives of General Psychiatry, 57,* 953–959.

King, N. J., Tonge, B., Mullen, P., Myerson, N., Heyne, D., Rollings, S., et al. (2000). Treating sexually abused children with posttraumatic stress symptoms: A randomized clinical trial. *Journal of the American Academy of Child and Adolescent Psychiatry, 39,* 1347–1355.

London, K., Bruck, M., Ceci, S. J., & Shuman, D. W. (2005). Disclosure of child sexual abuse: What does the research tell us about the ways that children tell? *Psychology, Public Policy, and Law, 11,* 194–226.

Lovett, J. (1999). *Small wonders: Healing childhood trauma with EMDR.* New York: Free Press.

Madanes, C. (1990). *Sex, love, and violence.* New York: Norton.

Manion, I. G., McIntyre, J., Firestone, P., Ligezinska, M., Ensom, R., & Wells, G. (1996). Secondary traumatization in parents following the disclosure of extrafamilial child sexual abuse: Initial effects. *Child Abuse and Neglect, 20,* 1095–1109.

Maxfield, L. (1988). *Working with victims and their families* (Training material for professional training programs). Vernon, British Columbia, Canada: Author.

Maxfield, L., & Hyer, L. A. (2002). The relationship between efficacy and methodology in studies investigating EMDR treatment of PTSD. *Journal of Clinical Psychology, 58,* 23–41.

McCauley, J., Kern, D. E., Kolonder, K., Dill, L., Schroeder, A. F., DeChant, H. K., et al. (1997). Clinical characteristics of women with a history of childhood abuse: Unhealed wounds. *Journal of the American Medical Association, 277*(17), 1362–1368.

Minuchin, S. (1974). *Families and family therapy.* Cambridge, MA: Harvard University Press.

Minuchin, S., Montalvo, B., Guerney, B. G., Jr., Rosman, B., & Schumer, F. (1967). *Families of the slums.* New York: Basic Books.

Molnar, B. E., Buka, S. L., & Kessler, R. C. (2001). Child sexual abuse and subsequent psychopathology: Results from the National Comorbidity Survey. *American Journal of Public Health, 91,* 743–760.

National Clearinghouse on Child Abuse and Neglect. (2005). *Child maltreatment 2003: Reports from the States to the National Child Abuse and Neglect Data Systems—National statistics on child abuse and neglect.* Retrieved July 31, 2005, from http://www.acf.dhhs.gov/programs/cb/publications/cm03/index.htm.

Nichols, M. P., & Schwartz, R. C. (1995). *Family therapy: Concepts and methods* (3rd ed.). Boston: Allyn & Bacon.

Romans, S., Martin, J., Anderson, J., O'Shea, M. L., & Mullen, P. E. (1995). Factors that mediate between child sexual abuse and adult psychological outcome. *Psychological Medicine, 25,* 127–142.

Sachs-Ericsson, N., Blazer, D., Plant, E. A., & Arnow, B. (2005). Childhood sexual and physical abuse and the 1-year prevalence of medical problems in the National Comorbidity Survey. *Health Psychology, 24,* 32–40.

Shapiro, F. (1991). Stray thoughts. *EMDR Network Newsletter, 1,* 1–3.

Shapiro, F. (1995). *Eye movement desensitization and reprocessing: Basic principles, protocols and procedures.* New York: Guilford Press.

Shapiro, F. (2001). *Eye movement desensitization and reprocessing: Basic principles, protocols and procedures* (2nd ed.). New York: Guilford Press.

Soberman, G. B., Greenwald, R., & Rule, D. L. (2002). A controlled study of eye movement desensitization and reprocessing (EMDR) for boys with conduct problems. *Journal of Aggression, Maltreatment, and Trauma, 6,* 217–236.

Spaccarelli, S., & Kim, S. (1995). Resilience criteria and factors associated with resilience in sexually abused girls. *Child Abuse and Neglect, 19,* 1171–1182.

Tinker, R. H., & Wilson, S. A. (1999). *Through the eyes of a child: EMDR with children.* New York: Norton.

Trocme, N., & Wolfe, D. (2001). *Child maltreatment in Canada: Selected results from the Canadian Incidence Study of Reported Child Abuse and Neglect.* Ottawa, Ontario, Canada: Minister of Public Works and Government Services.

Wakefield, J., & Maxfield, L. (1991). *Training manual for the Sexual Abuse Intervention Project: Levels one and two.* Vernon, British Columbia, Canada: Author.

Walker, J. L., Carey, P. D., Mohr, N., Stein, D. J., & Seedat, S. (2004). Gender differences in the prevalence of childhood sexual abuse and in the development of pediatric PTSD. *Archives of Women's Mental Health, 7,* 111–121.

Whiffen, V. E., & MacIntosh, H. B. (2005). Mediators of the link between childhood sexual abuse and emotional distress: A critical review. *Trauma, Violence, and Abuse: A Review Journal, 6,* 24–39.

CHAPTER 18

Medical Family Therapy

Margaret (Peggy) V. Moore

The reciprocal relationship between physical and mental health is well documented. Research has shown that physical illness can result in depression and anxiety and that depression and anxiety can exacerbate medical illness. Accordingly, the provision of mental health services has become a frequent practice on hospital wards treating patients with life-threatening or chronic diseases (Wise & Rundell, 2002).

> In the narrative of every human life and every family, illness is a prominent character. Even if we have avoided serious illness ourselves, we cannot escape its reach into our family lives and our friendship circles. Illness brings us closer to one another in caregiving, and it separates us through disability and death. It moves us to make sense of our lives, and it creates confusion and doubt. It inspires courage and fear, hope and despair, serenity and anxiety. (McDaniel, Hepworth, & Baird, 1992, p. 1)

In recent years, there has been recognition of the role that the family plays in the course of medical illness. For example, the recovery of patients with chronic pain appears to be strongly influenced by their spouse's attitudes and the quality of the marital relationship (Turk, Kerns, & Rosenberg, 1992). Similarly patients' recovery from a cardiac arrest is impacted by their spouse's related anxiety and depression (Moser & Dracup, 2004). Studies with children suffering from asthma have found that children with a criticizing mother had more frequent attacks of asthma than did children with a noncriticizing mother (Campbell, 1993; Schobinger, Florin, Zimmer, Lindemann, & Winter, 1992).

The illness of an individual can have a deleterious impact on his or her family members. When a loved one is unexpectedly diagnosed with a serious or terminal disorder, family members may develop Posttraumatic Stress Disorder (PTSD) and have difficulty providing an appropriate level of support to the infirm member. Further, children often develop emotional problems when a parent is diagnosed with cancer (Visser et al., 2005). Caregivers of those with chronic disorders, such as Alzheimer's disease, have been found to have higher rates of both physical and mental disorders (Pruchno & Potashnik, 1989).

Don Bloch (1992, p. xii), a pioneer in the field of family therapy and family medicine, described the struggles faced by families coping with illness:

> Severe and chronic illness acts like a magnifying glass for families. Everything is exaggerated, is seen in bold relief, in high intensity, so that those issues that families are dealing with, in the normal developmental process, can become part of an amplifying distortion—in a word, become pathological.

When individuals struggle with a serious or chronic medical problem, their recovery is influenced by their role in the family and the reactions of the family to their illness. For example, Joan, a single mother of two grown children, was diagnosed with an enlarged heart, high blood pressure, and dangerous levels of HDL cholesterol. It was clear to her friends that the unrelenting stress of caring for her numerous grandchildren and alcoholic son played a contributing role in her illness. She was in a position where the choices that she made would impact her health: She could create appropriate boundaries with her son and refuse to enable his drinking, thereby reducing stress and providing the opportunity for her health to improve, or she could continue to be used as a caretaker when he was unemployed and homeless, consequently placing her own life at risk.

When medical family therapists encounter an individual who is ill, they appreciate that the patient is part of a family system and that the whole group has been affected by the medical challenge. Families facing serious or chronic medical issues, or the death of a family member, can be traumatized by the experiences they encounter during this difficult time in their lives. They also can be exhausted by the caregiving that they are providing to their loved one. Daily routines are upended; roles can be suddenly reversed. Cooking, child care, bill paying, and other household tasks may have to be performed by a different family member. Family members may struggle with guilt, depression, and the fear of losing the infirm individual. In addition, the illness of one member may cause old unresolved conflicts to surface among other members.

The crisis that illness and death creates can be a window of opportunity for the family, where members make choices that create meaningful change in their lives; or the crisis can become a roadblock where members tighten their grip on patterns and choices that are destructive.

Working with Families of Patients with Medical Problems

The concept of treating the whole family spread into the medical field in the late 1960s, when William Doherty, a family therapist, and Macaran Baird, a family physician, developed a model for integrating family therapy practices with family medical care. They explained that their model grew out of a frustration with the "fragmented, individually oriented treatment of children's psychiatric disturbances" and stated that they created family therapy medicine as a response to this problem (Doherty & Baird, 1983, p. 1). This chapter discusses the work of medical doctors who apply the principles of psychosocial medicine and the work of psychotherapists who practice medical family therapy.

Psychosocial Medicine

The past 40 years have seen an increase in knowledge regarding the practice of primary care medicine and an understanding of the value of integrating psychosocial treatment to maximize physical healing. Today the family medicine literature emphasizes the importance of looking at the effects that the illness has on the entire family, not just the ill individual. The primary physician who recognizes the effects of emotion on healing can be more effective than one who does not (Doherty & Baird, 1983). Additionally, those who work in family medicine, pediatrics, or internal medicine state unequivocally that the health of the patient is directly related to the functioning of the family.

The integration of family therapy principles into the daily practice of a medical doctor can be challenging. To assist with this process, Braulio Montalvo, Margaret Moore, and colleagues (Montalvo, Moore, & Schor, 1987; Moore, Cohen, & Montalvo, 1998) taught family therapy concepts in a pediatric residency program. Their goal was to sensitize the pediatric residents to the dynamics of the patients' families so that the pediatrician could identify and utilize opportunities for addressing family issues. The premise was that psychosocial medicine is best taught in the hospital setting, where technical and emotional support can be provided. Residents were encouraged to bring family problems immediately to the teaching team, and these real-life complexities were used as teaching opportunities. Psychosocial medicine becomes more meaningful and useful when taught in this context, as opposed to an academic presentation in a separate curriculum.

Although Minuchin's (1974) family therapy model is stressed in the training of physicians, it is not practical for most doctors in their everyday practice. In their discussion about the types of interventions available to family physicians, Doherty and Baird (1983) distinguished between counseling and family therapy and suggested that counseling, as opposed to family therapy, is an activity the physician can do with greater ease. They asserted, "Therapy interventions differ from counseling interventions in that the former are more intrusive, more suited to dealing with resistance, more potentially destabilizing, and more far-reaching in intent" (p. 89).

Physicians are faced with the lack of time and support when they delve into family issues and consequently cannot usually conduct comprehensive family therapy. Instead, they are taught to be alert to family dynamics and are instructed in simple and practical counseling interventions. An example of this is the case of a psychosomatic family. The 13-year-old boy had undergone extensive medical testing and evaluation for elusive physical problems, including a brief period of paralysis, asthma, chronic constipation, and a multitude of other complaints. He was not attending school and appeared to be enmeshed with his mother. The pediatrician intervened by taking charge of the boy's allergy management and making decisions about his school attendance; the doctor also put the stepfather in charge of the boy's diet. This intervention resulted in a complete turnaround in the boy's health and the interactional patterns in his family. The authority represented by the doctor and his restructuring of interactions allowed change to occur.

Medical Family Therapy

Whereas psychosocial medicine is practiced by medical doctors, medical family therapy is provided by psychotherapists from various disciplines. The roots of medical family therapy are embedded in the theories developed at the Philadelphia Child Guidance Clinic by Minuchin, Montalvo, and Haley in the 1960 and 1970s. This model emphasized the therapeutic system as the unit of treatment and viewed the therapist as a participant rather than just an observer in the therapy (Doherty & Baird, 1983); the clinician is encouraged to "join with the family" to assist them in changing their interactions. Minuchin's (1974) model viewed the family structure in four basic ways: their transactional patterns (how they interact with each other), their adaptability (ability to change), the relationships between subsystems (e.g., parental subsystem, sibling subsystem), and the nature of the boundaries between subsystems. The focus of treatment is on changing interactions to change the family structure.

Recently, medical family therapy has taken an eclectic approach to theory (Doherty & Baird, 1983; Fraenkel, 2005), drawing from the work of Bowen (1978), Minuchin (1974), Satir (1964, 1972, 1988), and Haley (1987), as well as Rolland (1994), and Baird, McDaniel, Hepworth, and Doherty (Doherty & Baird, 1983; McDaniel, Hepworth, & Doherty, 1997). Since leaving Philadelphia in 1985, Montalvo has consulted and taught in the southwestern United States. Two of the therapists involved in the cases described here were his students (Moore and Vinajeras). Just as his approach has not remained static, so medical family therapy has continued to evolve. There is no rigid school of thought about how medical family therapy should be conducted.

Generically, it is important that the psychotherapist recognize the effects of the illness on the family. Nichols and Schwartz (2001) described the use of family therapy in the treatment of chronic illnesses and emphasized the importance of addressing the impact that all medical problems have on the whole family. They recommended the use of psychoeducational and medical family therapy approaches as ways to help families "reorganize their beliefs and resources to keep the illness from dominating them" (p. 335). They also emphasized that family therapy in a medical setting is a collaborative process, involving not only the family therapist but the entire medical team.

Some of the roles of the medical family therapist include:

- Educating the family about the illness: its symptoms, course, and prognosis
- Helping the family cope with the member's illness and the changes in family roles
- Helping the family improve communication with doctors and other medical professionals
- Reducing conflict over medication and treatment issues

- Advocating family lifestyle changes where appropriate (e.g., diet, exercise)
- Addressing family issues that interfere with the member's recovery
- Identifying and addressing the psychiatric contributors to the illness and family reactions
- Identifying and addressing the interpersonal contributors to the illness

Research Evaluating Medical Family Therapy

Research done by Law and colleagues (Law, Crane, & Berge, 2003) demonstrated that family therapy has a positive effect on physical health care usage. They concluded that individual, marital, or family therapy for high usage individuals (those who utilize health care services twice as much as the average person) reduced the use of health care significantly. Conjoint therapy had the effect of reducing care by 57%. Similarly, in a review (Campbell, 1993) of studies of families with children who had chronic lung diseases, more frequent use of child health care was predicted by the parents' own frequent use of health care services, parents' poor mental health, high maternal distress, and high family stress. Campbell concluded that psychosocial factors predicted the use of health care service usage and found that interventions that addressed these family problems dramatically reduced the number of times children were hospitalized or brought into the clinic.

Eye Movement Desensitization and Reprocessing

Some of the goals of the medical family therapist involve addressing the individual psychiatric problems of the patient and/or family members. For example, George was having a difficult time supporting his wife in her cancer treatment. He had recently lost his mother to cancer and was struggling with grief and the fear that he would also lose his wife; every time he entered the hospital he became overwhelmed with anxiety. Eye Movement Desensitization and Reprocessing (EMDR) resolved these issues, so that George was able to actively participate in his wife's treatment.

EMDR (Shapiro, 2001, 2002) is used to process memories of distressing incidents that contribute to current problems. Shapiro's Adaptive Information Processing model posits that when individuals have an unresolved past traumatic incident, current situations may trigger reactions, emotions, and cognitions related to that original incident. Consequently, the individuals are unable to respond adaptively in the current situation. Many families dealing with medical crises have had previous experiences with illness and death that have been emotionally challenging and have not been adequately processed. These individuals may have many symptoms of PTSD, anxiety disorders, and depression. As a result, they are not able to respond appropriately to the current crisis.

EMDR has been used very effectively in processing past traumas, and multiple treatment studies have revealed its efficacy in this approach (Maxfield & Hyer, 2002). The American Psychiatric Association (2004) recommends EMDR for the treatment of PTSD. It is also thought to be very effective in the treatment of traumatic phobias (De Jongh, Ten Broeke, & Renssen, 1999). Further, case studies by Kleinknecht (1993) and Lohr, Tolin, and Kleinknecht (1995) investigated the effectiveness of EMDR in the treatment of medical phobias (e.g., needle phobia and blood-injury-injection phobia). After treatment, the patients were able to tolerate these medical procedures with minimal anxiety.

EMDR has also been used to improve physical complaints, such as pain. Shapiro (2001) has outlined a specific protocol for the use of EMDR with illness and somatic disorders to address the psychological and physical challenges that clients face. An EMDR protocol for chronic pain developed by Mark Grant (1999) combines pain management techniques with trauma resolution. Using this protocol, Grant and Threlfo (2002) conducted a case study investigation with three patients who all reported a decrease in pain levels and negative affect, combined with an increased ability to control pain (see also Ray & Zbik, 2001).

THERAPY PROCESS

When therapeutic work with families with medical issues happens in a medical setting, psychotherapy can be untidy. Although therapy can occasionally be structured and clearly planned, the therapist must often be flexible enough to take advantage of a situation as it presents itself. The therapist's time with a family may be limited, and follow-up after immediate crises may not always be possible. In treatment planning, the therapist must consider how many treatment sessions will be possible. In some instances, the patient and family are available for only one or two sessions. At other times, the therapist is able to engage the family in a more comprehensive treatment program. Given this needed flexibility, the integration of EMDR and family therapy for families with medical problems may involve individual EMDR sessions, family therapy sessions, and sessions in which EMDR is used with several family members present. Nevertheless, the therapist should seek to follow the treatment protocol as rigorously as possible to maximize treatment outcome (Maxfield & Hyer, 2002).

Although the interventions described here occurred in a hospital setting, practitioners in a variety of settings find themselves working with clients who have medical problems or have a family member with a medical problem. An understanding of the patient as a member of a family, no matter how sparse or unconventional that family may be, is essential for assessment, conceptualization, and treatment.

One of the first steps in medical family therapy is determining who the family members are. Defining the family impacted by a patient's illness can be difficult. Doherty and Baird (1983) divided the term into two categories: "structural" family, which refers to the legal categories of membership (e.g., marriage, parenthood, in-laws), and "functional" family, which refers to the everyday interdependence among people. Bloch (as cited in Rolland, 1994, p. x) described family as "the problem-defined system," meaning an assemblage of persons affected by the problem or having an affect on it, either in terms of maintaining (causing) it or changing (treating) it. Family can thus be understood as a group of people who have a significant emotional and/or legal relationship with the patient. They may be supportive, or they may emotionally drain the person seeking medical care.

An example of a functional family is the constellation that makes up Jimmy's circle. Judy and her partner, Martha, adopted Jimmy when he was an infant. Judy and Martha separated and each began a new relationship, but they continued to share parenting. Jimmy developed severe asthma. The constellation of caregivers included Martha, her mother and father, Judy, and her current partner. Judy was living in an intentional community (a group of people who live in close proximity to each other for the purpose of providing support), and this group also was involved intimately in Jimmy's life. Jimmy had a large functional family. Another example is Joyce, whose functional family consisted of her close friend and neighbor, who cared for her in her old age after she was widowed and estranged from her stepchildren.

Phase 1: History Taking

The practice of talking to patients about their family and collecting a thorough family history is strongly recommended by McDaniel et al. (1992; see also Doherty & Baird, 1983; McDaniel, Lusterman, & Philpot, 2001). Shellenberger (cited in McDaniel et al., 1997) illustrated the technique of asking patients to tie the physical issue they are struggling with to the emotional issues in their family. She described the case of a woman named Marjorie who had been seriously injured on the job. Marjorie had chronic pain and felt that no one cared about her, not her doctors, her employer, nor the people on the site where she was injured. When Shellenberger began discussing her family, a similar theme of lack of caring was discovered. Her twin brother was critical of Marjorie's relationship with her son and ignored her health problems. The physical symptoms were seen as a reflection of the family issues. Other important issues included estrangement from family members, roles within the family, and the family's past history of coping with the disease.

It is also critical to identify the family's priorities. When a family's' primary concern is the health of their family member, the therapist must remember to focus on the expressed goals and needs. The medical problem is the priority. McDaniel et al. (1997) warned that the therapist must recognize the impact that chronic illness has on the family. An example of the error of not focusing on the family's priority was the case of a woman with multiple sclerosis. She was hospitalized for depression and was seen by a family therapist in sessions with her husband and their three daughters. The family therapist ignored the critical issue of the woman's multiple sclerosis and focused on what she decreed was the true underlying problem: the overinvolvement of the patient's daughters with their mother (McDaniel et al., 1992). The result of this misguided intervention was that two of the daughters withdrew their support, leaving the already overwhelmed third daughter as the sole support of the parents (Nichols & Schwarz, 2001).

The history-taking process alerts the therapist to areas where EMDR may be helpful and to the relationships in the family that are creating roadblocks to change. Constructing a multigenerational family genogram (Guerin & Pendergast, 1976; McGoldrick, Pearce, & Giordano, 1982; Nichols & Schwartz, 2001) can provide information about the family's history and identify targets for EMDR. When several family members are present during the history taking and genogram construction, the therapist and the members gain a multidimensional view of the family. This also helps to dilute the blame they may be placing on one member. For example, seeing that grandparents and aunts and uncles also struggled with cancer or heart attacks puts these issues in a different perspective.

In addition to evaluating the family's past experience with this disease and determining how that is influencing their current approach to the crisis, history taking can identify the patient's role within the family and the illness-related shifts in that role. The role of other family members may also be important to the status quo or the shift toward change. Issues of estrangement and isolation are also relevant, as these may affect the patient's ability to heal.

An example of this is the case of a middle-aged woman who frequently came into the emergency room. She complained of chest pain and had heartbeat irregularities that led to hospital stays. Finally, a doctor asked her who in her family caused her heart to ache. A flood of emotion followed as she spoke of her estrangement from her children. She described her husband as emotionally withdrawn and unavailable. The team was astounded by the amount and quality of information they received by asking a simple question related to the woman's place in her family.

Phase 2: Preparation

During Phase 2, the therapist introduces EMDR and family therapy to the family as treatment options. The therapist makes decisions with the family about the work to be done and the therapeutic method to be used. (They may not want to do EMDR.) The therapy can then proceed with informed consent.

Considerations in Treatment Planning

In consultation with the family, the therapist must decide which therapy will be most beneficial and when to provide it. Factors to consider are the physical and emotional strengths possessed by the patient and family, the severity of the stressors facing them, and the availability of a strong support system. For example, a couple facing life-threatening surgery for the wife and whose adult children are argumentative and nonsupportive may not be ready to deal with the intensity of EMDR therapy. They may benefit most from family therapy that provides psychoeducation and helps the couple problem-solve regarding their current situation.

Assessing Family Interactions and Planning Family Interventions

The therapist attends to the interactions between and statements made by family members, noting the multiple levels of communication. The therapist uses this information to plan appropriate interventions in the family system. As was stated earlier, there are important pieces of information the therapist needs to elicit: Which family member administers treatments or medications? Who is in charge? Is there a grandmother or other important person in the extended family whose advice the family seeks before taking action? Is this an enmeshed or a disengaged family, and how does that affect the way the family deals with the medical problem? To identify possible targets for EMDR treatment, the therapist is also listening and watching for descriptions of traumatic events and beliefs that may be blocking the solutions: Has the family recently experienced the death of a family member or close friend? Have there been other serious illnesses or hospitalizations in the past? Have family members had interactions with medical personnel that have been unpleasant or traumatic?

Phases 3 through 7: Assessment and Processing

Using Shapiro's (2001) protocol for EMDR with Illness, the therapist should start with the family member who is ill, if his or her condition allows it. Other family members can be seen individually for EMDR sessions as their personal issues about the illness are identified. With young children, it is advisable to have parents present during an EMDR session. In her text on the use of EMDR with children, Joan Lovett (1999), a behavioral pediatrician, discussed those who present with trauma-related somatic complaints. Lovett recommended that family therapists include parents as an important part of the treatment process because children's behaviors are often the entrée into a family problem. For example, children who are experiencing EMDR therapy often turn to a parent and say something like "You are the one who is scared." It is also possible to do EMDR with a couple when both spouses are present. Family sessions can be interspersed as appropriate. If the need arises during a family session, the therapist can provide EMDR to one family member while the others observe and provide support.

As an issue is processed and cleared, the therapist checks in with the family and asks what changes, if any, they have seen in the individual's behavior. The change in one member's behavior has an effect on the entire family system. Other issues can emerge. For example, a family member with a needle phobia may be excused from giving blood for an ill member. If the phobia is resolved, what change does that bring about in the balance of relationships in the family? Perhaps the member with the needle phobia was always marginalized by the family and now can come to the aid of the ill person, thus taking on a different role in the family. At this point, the therapist would want to conduct a conjoint family session to explore what is currently happening in the family.

The therapist follows the EMDR model for assessment and processing when EMDR is identified as the method to be used and uses family therapy for issues that require discussion among family members. For example, an individual may be anxious about an upcoming surgery; his wife is equally anxious but also feeling overwhelmed by the amount of home care she may need to give. The couple may be in disagreement about the role their adult children should take during and after the surgery. Family therapy sessions are recommended for sorting out the roles of the children and the stresses on the wife as caretaker. EMDR can be helpful for the patient and his wife in reducing anxiety about the surgery, which may be conducive to a more positive attitude about the surgical procedure. If time allows, and if medically appropriate, EMDR could also be used to address any unresolved feelings about the children's involvement. Using EMDR for future projection about the surgery can be very helpful. As in all EMDR sessions, there should be appropriate closure at the end and reevaluation at the beginning of the next session. The family therapist may also prescribe homework for the family between sessions. For example, the therapist may ask the family to plan an evening together before the next session.

Additional Aspects

It is essential that family therapists recognize the family's culture and the impact of this on their response to the sick or dying family member. It is also important that therapists monitor their own countertransference.

Cultural Aspects

The family therapist working in a medical setting, a mental health clinic, or private practice may encounter families from a variety of cultural backgrounds who are coping with the illness of a family member. Understanding the different perceptions of physical and mental illness and beliefs about illness, health, and death is challenging but necessary. For example, a traditional Navajo family appeared to abandon their hospitalized child who was dying of leukemia. The staff understood that Navajos avoid death and death sites and that the family was acting in a rational way based on their belief system. If therapists are not knowledgeable about the culture of their clients, they can ask the family to provide information about their culture.

Therapists who work with medical illness need to form a picture of the family and determine where the patient fits into that system, because this will affect the ongoing care and the outcome of the therapy. Regardless of the family systems theory one uses, it is essential to see the family as a living organic system that may be stuck and thus unable to access thoughts and behaviors that will allow them to grow and thrive. Old beliefs and past traumas may drive current behaviors. For example, a pediatric resident was struggling with a Native American mother who was refusing a treatment that would help her child recover from a life-threatening illness. When he asked her about her fears and beliefs, he learned that other family members had experienced dreadful outcomes from similar treatment. She also revealed that she could not make decisions about treatment without consulting an influential family member. With this information, and a new and stronger bond with the mother, the resident was able to provide better medical care. The extended family came to the hospital and discussed the treatment, and the influential elder gave his consent and support to the doctor and the mother. The child made a complete recovery. If the doctor had not been able to see this child and mother in the context of their family and culture, the outcome may not have been so successful. This example also illustrates how families experience medical traumas. The way they cope with the current crisis is related to past traumas and how the family and its members handled those experiences (Montalvo, 1986, personal communication).

Countertransference

Awareness of how a family's problems may trigger the therapist's own unresolved family issues is also helpful. Not only do illness and death affect the family, but the therapist brings his or her own family of origin into the consulting room (Doherty & Baird, 1983; McDaniel et al., 1997). When medical family therapists are alert to their own issues that are triggered by the medical problems their patients are facing, they can work more effectively and sensitively. Awareness of this phenomenon and the willingness to use it as an agent of change is the challenge presented to the therapist. Doherty and Baird (1983, p. 88) explained it well: "It is uncanny how families in one's professional practice bring up issues not successfully resolved in one's own personal life. Such a professional confrontation carries the opportunity for personal development for the counselor." If these factors are openly examined, they can be transformed into doors toward healing for all parties involved. For example, Jan, a family therapist who had experienced the death of her mother as a result of an ill-conceived medical procedure, was faced with the challenge of working with a family who had had a similar experience. She realized that her own unresolved anger was interfering with her ability to help this family. When she was able to resolve her own issue, the work with the family progressed much more easily.

CASE EXAMPLES

Case 1: Needle Phobia When Staying Alive Is All about Needles

Jonathan was a 12-year-old boy who was struggling with T-cell leukemia. He had a long list of presenting problems: intense fear, helplessness, loss of control, nightmares, sleep disturbance, psychological distress, moodiness, irritability, deterioration of academic interest, excessive fear of needles, palpitations, pounding heart, hyperventilation, feelings of inadequacy, and low self-esteem. He had been diagnosed with PTSD due to his medical condition as well as Generalized Anxiety Disorder and Panic Disorder without Agoraphobia.

Jonathan transferred his fear and anger about his disease to medical personnel during the painful procedures he had to undergo, resulting in a wrestling match during every procedure. Everyone was exhausted after each chemotherapy treatment. The needle, not the treatment itself, was the source of his fear: Thinking about or seeing needles triggered an acute and dramatic response. As a result, heavy sedation and restraint became necessary for every procedure. It was hard on him, the staff, and his mother, Susan. She, especially, suffered from feelings of guilt and helplessness. Jonathan was Susan's only child. His father had long since disappeared from their lives, and Susan worked full time to support them. Because of this, she was often unable to go with Jonathan to his appointments. Susan's mother, who was coping with a reoccurrence of bladder cancer, stepped in for Susan on these occasions.

Jonathan's pediatric oncology social worker was concerned about the deteriorating relationship between the staff and the family, the practical real-life problems that this serious illness created for Jonathan's mother and grandmother, and the trauma that Jonathan experienced with each painful procedure. Because she had worked with this family for months, she knew their psychosocial history and had a good working relationship with them.

The social worker developed a treatment plan for Jonathan and his mother that included family therapy, art therapy, EMDR, and case management interventions. In conceptualizing this treatment plan, the social worker and the EMDR consultant focused on the family network, looking at the issues the members faced over time. The therapist used several family therapy approaches in treating this family. From a structural perspective, she realized that Jonathan's illness had elevated him into the adult arena and his mother was having difficulty being in charge. Jonathan's illness had also brought up many old unresolved issues for his mother from her family of origin, such as her abandonment by Jonathan's father and the death of her father from a blood clot. The therapist also had to bring about change in the systems that were impacting the family, such as the mother's workplace and the oncology clinic staff. The social worker advocated with Susan's employer, and she gained more release time from her job so that she could be with Jonathan; the social worker also provided consultation to the clinic staff, who perceived Jonathan as a problem patient.

Jonathan's EMDR Sessions

The social worker began the EMDR phase by educating the mother and Jonathan about the effects of EMDR treatment. Both Jonathan and his mother agreed to make use of EMDR. The EMDR work included addressing past, present, and future problems. In working with the needle phobia, the therapist looked for and processed all past and present experiences related to the fear. She then helped Jonathan to create a future template, imagining how he wanted to behave during the upcoming procedures.

Their first EMDR session was on a Saturday, when other children in the cancer treatment program were going to a local amusement park. Jonathan's mood was so low that he did not feel like making the trip. He was pale, with a greenish tint to his complexion. The therapist began the session with family therapy by having Jonathan and his mother discuss the ordeal of anesthesia for the cancer treatments. It became clear that his anxiety began well in advance of the procedure, with Jonathan experiencing nausea and tension before each treatment. With this information in hand, the therapist identified this anticipatory anxiety as the target for the first EMDR session. After the session, Jonathan's appearance had changed, his energy returned, his cheeks were flush and glowing, and he was hungry and eager to join the children at the amusement park. Jonathan's mother could not believe the physical change she saw in his face. The response that Jonathan and his mother experienced that day changed both of them. A problem that had created great distress for the staff and family began to resolve.

The next time he came in, Jonathan reported that his anxiety about receiving chemotherapy treatment had disappeared. He was not nauseated and he felt relaxed. He now wanted to target the moment of pain when the needle was injected. This was the worst part of the procedure because he had no control. His *Positive Cognition* was that he wanted to feel in control. When asked to rate the validity of his cognition on the Validity of Cognition (VOC) scale, where 1 is completely untrue and 7 is completely true, his VOC was 3, and he felt fearful and anxious. He rated his distress at 8 on the Subjective Units of Disturbance (SUD) scale, where 0 is no distress and 10 is overwhelming distress. He said he felt it all over his body. At the end of the session he reported a SUD level of 0 and a VOC of 7. He said he felt relaxed and in control.

The use of EMDR and family therapy enabled Jonathan to go through his next medical procedures with courage and poise. His mother was relieved and proud. The staff were grateful and surprised. He said, "My mother feels better and so do I." He went on to say of his mother, "Her father had died of a blood clot, and I have a blood clot, so I know this worries her." Now that he felt calm and relaxed, the experience of going in for chemotherapy was easier for everyone. The social worker reported that Jonathan "showed considerable improvement," with the changes evident on the psychometric measures. Both the Impact of Events Scale and Child Report of Post-traumatic Symptoms showed a decrease in post-traumatic symptoms after the EMDR treatments (Vinajeras, 1999).

Susan's EMDR Sessions

The therapist worked individually with Jonathan's mother, using EMDR to help her process her guilt, frustration, and grief. Susan had suffered many losses in her life and was facing the possible loss of her only child. The therapy sessions with Susan allowed her to work swiftly through many old traumas, such as the abandonment by her husband, the death of her father, and the reoccurrence of cancer in her mother. These losses were coloring her reactions to Jonathan, and she came to realize that her interactions with him tended toward overcompensation. Susan used EMDR to process the triggers that led her to give in to his demands and to process templates that allowed her to imagine more adaptive future functioning. Setting age-appropriate boundaries was difficult for her because of her guilt about his illness, and family therapy was used with Susan to help her set better boundaries with Jonathan.

Family Therapy

Family therapy with Jonathan and his mother focused on helping Susan regain her role as executive in the family. The social worker helped her connect with other families experiencing the same medical problems. This provided other adult support and role modeling for her efforts to continue to parent Jonathan in as normal a way as possible. For instance, previously Jonathan had insisted on having his own way and Susan capitulated to his demands. In family therapy, Susan learned how to establish better boundaries with Jonathan and to assert herself. Now, instead of automatically giving in to Jonathan's demands, she was coached to offer several reasonable alternatives and to set limits on what she would and would not do. One family session was devoted to working out the problem presented by Jonathan's fear about leaving his cat behind when he and his mother were traveling out of state for treatment. He was essentially holding his mother hostage by his demands and fear regarding the cat. The therapist helped Susan to take charge of the situation by setting boundaries about the cat's care. She insisted that they could not take the cat with them, and she located a family friend who would care for the cat. The therapist supported the mother's plans for the cat's care, while empathizing with Jonathan's fears about leaving his pet behind. By doing this she presented a united adult position.

Susan's employers were not always helpful or supportive in allowing her time off to accompany Jonathan to his appointments. The resolution of old traumas helped Susan be more self-assured and assertive with her employers. The social worker was able to intervene and helped her arrange for an extended leave of absence and financial support so that Susan could accompany Jonathan to a medical center in a distant city, where he had a bone marrow transplant.

Jonathan did not win his battle with leukemia. His mother grieved over her loss but was not devastated beyond repair. She continued therapy after Jonathan's death and she went on with her life. Healing is not always about curing a disease; it is about reestablishing balance in a system. The therapist's work with this family involved the mother, son, and grandmother, as well as the social and medical system. From a systemic perspective:

> Human life is a seamless cloth spun from biological, psychosocial, social, and cultural threads . . . patient and families come with bodies as well as minds, feelings, interaction patterns, and belief systems . . . there are no biological problems without psychosocial implications, and no psychosocial problems without biological implications. (McDaniel et al., 1992, pp. 1–2)

Case 2: The Frightened Sister and Doña Sebastiana

Combining medical social work and family therapy in the same session is often necessary when working with children and their families in the pediatric oncology program. Often it becomes clear to the social worker that some family members are having more difficulty dealing with the illness than the patient is. As part of the healing process, the therapist listens for subtle calls for help from family members. He or she is on the alert for the opportunity to bring them into the consulting room to address the distress that the family is experiencing. This provides the entry point where change can be stimulated. When the therapist uses EMDR, the symptoms enter the room in full force. The following case is an example of an intervention in a conjoint session with a mother and an older sister around their fears.

In this case, there was also an unspoken cultural metaphor of which the therapist was aware. In the southwestern United States among the Hispanic population, death is referred to as Doña Sebastiana; she is depicted as a skeleton riding in a cart with a bow and arrow. Stories and songs relate the inevitable encounter with this figure. This folk art image is prominent in the community where Mary and her family lived.

Mary, a 13-year-old with leukemia, was offered EMDR treatment and made good use of this therapy during her visits to the oncology clinic for chemotherapy. She traveled to a regional medical center with her family from a town about 120 miles away. Her mother and older sister frequently accompanied her and stayed at the Ronald McDonald House near the hospital. Mary's father came, too, but often he did not stay for the whole session because of his work demands.

During one of their family therapy sessions, they agreed to have an EMDR session that would include the whole family. Just before the time to meet, Mary's father suddenly left, saying he had to get back to work. Although his departure was abrupt, the other family members saw this exit as normal. Mary, her mother, and her older sister remained for the session.

They initially indicated that they rarely talked about Mary's illness. The two daughters insisted that the mother would benefit from EMDR treatment and strongly urged her to try it, so the therapist began with the mother, asking her about the stresses in her life. After exploring various stories about Mary's illness, the therapist decided to target with EMDR the memory of the day they were given the diagnosis. The mother recounted the frantic drive to the medical center, trying to meet up with the father along the way. The daughters listened with rapt attention. At the end of the EMDR session, the mother reported that she felt as light as a feather. Mary and her sister were smiling. All of them felt relieved that their mother was able to talk more openly about Mary.

During this session, it became apparent that the older sister had a paralyzing fear about death. She said she worried all the time that someone in her family was going to die. Her fear, she said, centered on her father, because his job of gathering and selling landscaping materials seemed hazardous to her. If her father was late getting home she would call everyone, asking for him. The therapist targeted this fear. After the session, her fear subsided and she no longer felt anxiety that her father would be injured or hurt while traveling "out in the wilds," and she reported that she felt relaxed and at ease. The mother seemed relieved. Mary's sister could no longer displace her fear of death on to her father and she was able to acknowledge that Mary was the one dancing with Doña Sebastiana.

This family addressed two issues during this session. The mother was able to resolve the unpleasant memory of the day of diagnosis, and her older daughter coped with an almost crippling anxiety. *Having family members witness another member resolve an old troubling issue can be a very powerful experience for everyone.* This family tapped into their adaptive processing capacities to help them move through a difficult time in their lives. Sometimes small shifts can bring about major trait changes in a family. This family appeared to have triangulated the ill child with the mother and sister. The mother, Mary, and her sister were aligned (i.e., closely connected). Thus, the parental executive position in the family was disrupted by the alliance of the mother and daughters to the exclusion of the father. On the other hand, Mary's father saw his role as that of provider of financial support to the family and was resistant to the efforts of the social worker to include him in family therapy sessions. His resistance may have been due to cultural beliefs about his role and Mary's mother's role as caretaker. Because he attended only a few of the family therapy sessions, his motives and beliefs were never clear. It is not always possible to induce important family members to participate in the therapy sessions. However, working with what is available can still bring about important changes in the way families interact and support each other. Structural and Strategic Family Therapies (Minuchin, 1974;

Watzlawick, Weakland, & Fisch, 1965) posit that small changes in the behavior of one or more family members create change that ripples through the family. The crisis created by the diagnosis of cancer provided the opportunity for change to occur. The goal was to move the family in the direction of healthier emotional interactions. However, in this case, the changes appeared to affect only those participating in the therapy. Getting the father to be more emotionally available did not happen.

Mary had a complete remission and returned to her school and normal life at home. The social worker continued to work with the family to help with Mary's reentry into her home, family, and school. Mary's identity as the sick or vulnerable child was no longer valid. When possible, the therapist provided individual EMDR sessions for Mary to address her readjustment to her peer group and her role in the family. As Mary's treatment visits decreased, the family therapy and EMDR sessions also came to a close.

Case 3: The Drowning

The pastor of a family whose 1-year-old son had almost drowned in a swimming pool called an EMDR therapist. Bobby had survived but was in a vegetative state when his parents brought him home from the hospital. He showed no eye contact, his limbs were stiff and contracted, and he was unresponsive to his surroundings. The therapy began with the parents. During the first few EMDR sessions, which occurred during the first week, the therapist focused on the grief and trauma that the parents had experienced.

To work with Bobby, the therapist had his mother hold him in her lap and tap as she told the story of the drowning. (The process of having the mother tap bilaterally on the child provided stimulation not only to the child but also to the mother—two for one.) When she got to the place in the story recounting the emergency personnel pulling Bobby from the water and working to revive him, the child stiffened. His whole body reacted to the story as if he were reliving the experience. At the conclusion of the narrative, and for the first time since the accident, his arm dropped from its bent, stiff position. He fell asleep in his mother's arms.

The therapist followed up with another session the following day. She repeated the same treatment. At the end of that EMDR session, Bobby made eye contact with his mother for the first time since the accident. It appeared that his body had let go of the trauma. His parents were now able to move on to the challenge of helping him function at as high a level as possible. They were not held back by their unresolved trauma; nor, apparently, was Bobby.

The therapist checked in with the family months later and asked them if the original event still had any charge for them. Both parents dismissed the event as history and wanted to talk about the progress their son was making and the new challenges they faced with a brain-injured child. This case illustrates a brief intervention around a recent trauma. The therapist recognized that all family members needed trauma resolution. By immediately addressing the issues, she prevented pathological responses in the future and assisted the parents in moving on so that they could provide for the current needs of their son.

DISCUSSION

These cases illustrate the importance of addressing the traumatic experiences of individual family members while working with the family as a whole. This approach recognizes that the entire family is affected by and in turn affects the outcome of the medical problem with which the identified patient is struggling. The therapist in each case began with family therapy and interspersed the EMDR treatments as the issues and triggers became clear. Family treatment can become stuck because of unprocessed individual factors. Processing the issues that block individual family members can pave the way for effective family therapy. Also, individuals who have experienced successful EMDR treatment react differently in their family. This may result in nudging the family out of a cycle of interaction that has not been healthy. For example, EMDR was used with a mother whose 17-year-old son had recently been diagnosed with Schizophrenia. She was overcome with depression and unable to function in her key role as the glue for the family. After two EMDR sessions, she was willing to consider trying an antidepressant and was able to resume her family position. This opened the door for the therapist to work with the other family members. This strategic and structural intervention helped the mother reestablish her function, and the family was able to achieve homeostasis again. Bowen's (1978) approach to family therapy promotes differentiation from one's family of origin as the fulcrum for changing an entire family system; this perspective is useful to the EMDR family therapist treating only one family member (Nichols & Schwartz, 2001).

The three case illustrations discussed in this chapter all required different approaches. Jonathan's case required Structural and Strategic Family Therapy approaches. He and his mother were enmeshed to the point that she had lost some of her ability as the executive, and her authority had to be reestablished. This was made easier after his EMDR sessions freed him from the needle phobia and her EMDR sessions eased the trauma of witnessing his overly anxious behavior during medical procedures and her guilt over her inability to always be there with him. EMDR became the strategic tool in this case.

EMDR enabled Jonathan to change a behavior that had defined him as a problem patient. Jonathan's beliefs about himself as a victim who had no control in his medical treatment shifted quickly. Family therapy gave his mother the opportunity to be in charge again. EMDR allowed her to move through her grief in a healthier manner. The conjoint session with Jonathan and his mother allowed her to witness the transformation her son experienced in the EMDR session and it gave her hope.

Mary's family members were not all present in the Conjoint Family Therapy session described. However, from a systemic perspective, change in one member will impact the entire family, so therapists can have confidence about continuing to work with available members. This crucial impact on the family is also seen with EMDR treatment, even if that is not the original intent. In this conjoint session, Mary's family witnessed the resolution of issues in one another. The process of this witnessing and support can strengthen family ties. Mary's sister could no longer displace her fear of death on to her father, as she recognized that Mary was the one dancing with Doña Sebastiana. Mary's father's absence was diagnostic of a core family issue that the therapist tried to pursue further.

Bobby's case was very straightforward. Because the therapist understood the importance of addressing the issues of everyone in the family, she provided a healing experience for them. They were not seeking family therapy, but they benefited because the therapist recognized that each member needed treatment. The EMDR treatments quickly accessed the family's internal Adaptive Information Processing system and moved on to the problem at hand, dodging the bullet of unresolved trauma.

These cases illustrate how the integration of family therapy and EMDR can bring about swift and lasting change for families in a medical crisis. Too often in medical cases, only the identified patient is treated and the rest of the family is left to fend for themselves. This approach can stifle the rate at which an individual recovers, for it leaves other problems in the family system untreated. The combination of EMDR and family therapy can provide a swift exit out of this dilemma. EMDR enhances and enriches the quality of family therapy.

For nearly 40 years now, family therapists have realized that great strides in healing occur when we recognize that what happens to one family member happens to all. Early medical family therapists used the ideas developed by Minuchin (1974) as the basis for their work with patients and families. As with any theory, once it is planted in an area, it grows and evolves according to the environment. Just as the family that is not too rigid nor too flexible is more successful at coping with change, so psychotherapy theories that can stretch and bend and grow can serve their clients better. Family therapy has been practiced for nearly 50 years and many schools of thought have sprung up along the way. The therapist who can approach a family with a solid knowledge base and good clinical family skills and choose an eclectic approach that enhances the basic application of family therapy theory will probably be reasonably successful in most cases. Maintaining an integrative approach to family therapy is essential, and the situation of each client will often determine the direction therapy will take. The old adage "Start where the client is" should always be foremost in the therapist's mind, whether doing EMDR or family therapy or both.

REFERENCES

American Psychiatric Association. (2004). *Practice guideline for the treatment of patients with acute stress disorder and posttraumatic stress disorder.* Arlington, VA: American Psychiatric Association Practice Guidelines.

Bloch, D. (1992). Foreword. In S. McDaniel, J. Hepworth, & M. Baird (Eds.), *Medical family therapy* (p. vii). New York: Basic Books.

Bowen, M. (1978). *Family therapy in clinical practice.* New York: Aronson.

Campbell, T. L. (1993). Research reports: Impact of family factors on childhood illness. *Family Systems Medicine, 11,* 433–440.

De Jongh, A., Ten Broeke, E., & Renssen, M. R. (1999). Treatment of specific phobias with eye movement desensitization and reprocessing (EMDR): Protocol, empirical status, and conceptual issues. *Journal of Anxiety Disorders, 13,* 69–85.

Doherty, W. J., & Baird, M. A. (1983). *Family therapy and family medicine.* New York: Guilford Press.

Fraenkel, P. (2005). What ever happened to family therapy? *Psychotherapy Networker, 29*(3), 31–39, 70.

Grant, M. (1999). *Pain control with EMDR.* Pacific Grove, CA: EMDR Humanitarian Assistance Programs.

Grant, M., & Threlfo, C. (2002). EMDR in the treatment of chronic pain. *Journal of Clinical Psychology, 58,* 1505–1520.

Guerin, P., & Pendergast, E. (1976). Evaluations of the family system and the genogram. In P. Guerin (Ed.), *Family therapy: Theory and practice* (pp. 450–479). New York: Gardner Press.

Haley, J. (1987). *Problem solving therapy* (2nd ed.). San Francisco: Jossey-Bass.

Kleinknecht, R. A. (1993). Rapid treatment of blood and injection phobias with eye movement desensitization. *Journal of Behavior Therapy and Experimental Psychiatry, 24,* 211–217.

Law, D. D., Crane, D. R., & Berge, J. M. (2003). The influence of individual, marital, and family therapy on high utilizers of health care. *Journal of Marital and Family Therapy, 29,* 353–363.

Lohr, J., Tolin, D., & Kleinknecht, R. A. (1995). An intensive investigation of eye movement desensitization of medical phobias. *Journal of Behavior Therapy and Experimental Psychiatry, 26,* 141–151.

Lovett, J. (1999). *Small wonders: Healing childhood trauma with EMDR.* New York: Free Press.

Maxfield, L., & Hyer, L. A. (2002). The relationship between efficacy and methodology in studies investigating EMDR treatment of PTSD. *Journal of Clinical Psychology, 58,* 23–41.

McDaniel, S., Hepworth, J., & Baird, M. (1992). *Medical family therapy.* New York: Basic Books.

McDaniel, S., Hepworth, J., & Doherty, W. J. (1997). *The shared experience of illness: Stories of patients, families, and their therapists.* New York: Basic Books.

McDaniel, S., Lusterman, D., & Philpot, C. L. (2001). *Casebook for integrating family therapy: An ecosystems approach.* Washington, DC: American Psychological Association.

McGoldrick, M., Pearce, J. K., & Giordano, J. (1982). *Ethnicity and family therapy.* New York: Guilford Press.

Minuchin, S. (1974). *Families and family therapy.* Cambridge, MA: Harvard University Press.

Montalvo, B., Moore, M., & Schor, E. L. (1987). Psychosocial aspects of pediatrics: Middle level theory building. *Family Systems Medicine, 5*(1), 65–77.

Moore, M., Cohen, S., & Montalvo, B. (1998). Sensitizing medical residents to fantasies and alignments in the family: Mastering psychosocial skills in medical encounter. *Contemporary Family Therapy,* 416–433.

Moser, D. K., & Dracup, K. (2004). Role of spousal anxiety and depression in patients' psychosocial recovery after a cardiac event. *Psychosomatic Medicine, 66,* 527–532.

Nichols, M. P., & Schwartz, R. P. (2001). *Family therapy: Concepts and methods.* Boston: Allyn & Bacon.

Pruchno, R. A., & Potashnik, S. L. (1989). Caregiving spouses: Physical and mental health in perspective. *Journal of the American Geriatrics Society, 37,* 697–705.

Ray, A. L., & Zbik, A. (2001). Cognitive behavioral therapies and beyond. In C. D. Tollison, J. R. Satterthwaite, & J. W. Tollison (Eds.), *Practical pain management* (3rd ed., pp. 189–208). Philadelphia, PA: Lippincott Williams & Wilkins.

Rolland, J. S. (1994). *Families, illness and disability: An integrative treatment model.* New York: Basic Books.

Satir, V. (1964). *Conjoint Family Therapy.* Palo Alto, CA: Science and Behavior Books.

Satir, V. (1972). *Peoplemaking.* Palo Alto, CA: Science and Behavior Books.

Satir, V. (1988). *The New People Making.* Palo Alto, CA: Science and Behavior Books.

Schobinger, R., Florin, I., Zimmer, C., Lindemann, H., & Winter, H. (1992). Childhood asthma: Paternal critical attitude and father-child interaction. *Journal of Psychosomatic Research, 37,* 743–750.

Shapiro, F. (2001). *Eye movement desensitization and reprocessing: Basic principles, protocols and procedures* (2nd ed.). New York: Guilford Press.

Shapiro, F. (Ed.). (2002). *EMDR as an integrative psychotherapy approach.* New York: Guilford Press

Turk, D. C., Kerns, R. D., & Rosenberg, R. (1992). Effects of marital interaction on chronic pain and disability: Examining the down side of social support. *Rehabilitation Psychology, 37,* 259–274.

Vinajeras, Y. (1999). *Life isn't always a day in the sun: A case presentation.* Unpublished master's thesis, Highlands University, Las Vegas, NM, School of Social Work, Integrated Project.

Visser, A., Huizinga, G. A., Hoekstra, H. J., Van Der Graaf, W. T. A., Klip, E. C., Pras, E., et al. (2005). Emotional and behavioral functioning of children of a parent diagnosed with cancer: A cross-informant perspective. *Psycho-Oncology, 14,* 746–758.

Watzlawick, P., Weakland, J., & Fisch, R. (1965). *Change.* New York: Norton.

Wise, M. G., & Rundell, J. R. (2002). *American Psychiatric Press textbook of consultation-liaison psychiatry: Psychiatry in the medically ill.* Washington, DC: American Psychiatric Press Inc.

PART V

Community Disasters

CHAPTER 19

Disaster Response: EMDR and Family Systems Therapy under Communitywide Stress

Robert A. Gelbach and Katherine E. B. Davis

Disaster is commonly understood as an overwhelming misfortune that is not easily overcome or set right. Though our lives may go on after a disaster, it is virtually certain that they will have been transformed in some profound way. Nevertheless, it is very clear that not all who live through a disaster will be traumatized by it and that only a fraction of survivors will develop trauma-related disorders such as Posttraumatic Stress Disorder (PTSD).

Disasters, in the sense used here, often befall small groups, such as a family unit, or even individuals, without affecting others directly. This chapter, however, considers disasters that radically disturb and disrupt the context in which a community lives its life. The disaster may be a physical event or process, such as an earthquake or hurricane, or a social upheaval, such as a war or revolution. Here, whole communities, regions, or even nations are disrupted and overwhelmed by great misfortune. The fabric of normal life for great numbers of people is simultaneously shredded so that they simply cannot go on with business as usual but must find a way to cope with adversity and retrieve what they can of their past lives and future hopes. The shared nature of their misfortune is a critical component of the disaster; it affects them as individuals but also as members of society, a status that is often mediated by their more intimate membership in a family system (Erikson, 1976).

PTSD is conceptualized as having three symptom clusters: intrusive memories or reexperiencing, avoidance and numbing, and hyperarousal. The consensus of opinion among researchers is that PTSD is a universal phenomenon, although specific expression of symptoms may be culture-bound (e.g., Marsella, Friedman, Gerrity, & Scurfield, 2001). Symptoms of hyperarousal and reexperiencing are universally reported in the literature, whereas avoidance and numbing are less reliably reported. The reasons for this may be culturally mediated or

This chapter describes the work of the EMDR Humanitarian Assistance Programs (HAP). HAP was formed in 1995 by clinicians responding to the Oklahoma City bombing. Since then, HAP has worked worldwide to serve traumatized communities by providing clinical training in EMDR to local therapists.

may represent a difference in the way that different populations experience trauma. For example, after the tsunami in India, the EMDR Humanitarian Assistance Program volunteers (HAP; 2005) reported that symptoms of reexperiencing and hyperarousal were common. However, the experience of emotional numbing, which occurred in the same individuals, was sometimes described as "transcending" the trauma and therefore viewed as a positive event, with no perception or awareness that there might be a related cost.

PTSD is reported in 15% to 25% of the population in postdisaster situations (van der Kolk & McFarlane, 1996). First responders and vulnerable segments of the population (e.g., children, or those with preexisting medical conditions) may experience much higher levels of PTSD. Within the whole population experiencing the same catastrophe, there will be variations in incidence of PTSD, partially related to the degree of exposure. For example, people will encounter different numbers or qualities of incidents, such as greater or lesser lethality. Each impacted person experiences the same disaster differently. When the community infrastructure (water, food, shelter, civil order) is destroyed, the incidence of PTSD rises. Man-made disasters can be equally overwhelming and can add intensifying elements of felt betrayal and malevolence.

Societies that have resources and choose to use them to shore up the infrastructure quickly and effectively will buffer their populations from increasing levels of PTSD. For children, the family *is* the infrastructure. Therefore, when the family is intact and can access the resources essential to meet the needs of the child, the incidence of PTSD for children will be lower.

Impact of Disasters on Family and Societal Function

Although a full PTSD diagnosis may not be applicable to all survivors, disaster-related trauma often produces symptoms that impair the functioning of individuals in their families and societies. Levels of anxiety and depression may increase; adults may be unable to work or to parent; rates of chemical dependency, abuse, and suicide increase (McFarlane & Yehuda, 1996, p. 163). Children also suffer the impact of trauma, which may be reflected in behavior problems, nightmares, or impaired school performance.

Disaster typically disrupts the availability of basic resources, such as food, water, shelter, and medical care. The sudden death or serious injury of individuals not only affects those who love them, but also undermines the services that they provided in the community. Housing and physical infrastructure, communication and transport systems, hospitals, schools, and places of employment and economic production may all be damaged or destroyed. Many people may be forced to flee from their home community and separated from family members. Their continuing traumatization may be lived out in the insecure environs of refugee camps. Then, too, disasters may extend over long stretches of time, such as the AIDS epidemic and periodic famines in Africa.

Intervention Priorities

The modern world has periodically "rediscovered" psychological trauma after major wars, but this understanding was also substantially modified during the last third of the twentieth century through advances in neuroscience and psychotherapy (van der Kolk & McFarlane, 1996). At the same time, technologies of transportation and communication have made rapid response to disaster a new possibility, while also making it increasingly likely that any major natural disaster will become the focus of world attention. This was evident in the tsunami that struck South Asia at the end of 2004, the hurricanes on the U.S. Gulf coast in 2005, and the devastating earthquake in Pakistan that same year.

By contrast, disasters that are man-made or are less tied to a single dramatic event may elicit less concern or evoke less generous and practical responses. Cases in point are the politically charged disasters in Rwanda and Kosovo in the 1990s, the pandemic of AIDS in sub-Saharan Africa, and the low-intensity warfare and terrorism that have afflicted such disparate societies as Northern Ireland, Sri Lanka, parts of Indonesia and Timor, Sudan, and Haiti. Counterexamples—where supportive intervention was more substantial—include the response in the United States to the politically motivated Oklahoma City bombing of 1995 and the terrorist attacks of September 11, 2001, in New York and Washington.

Although there is undeniable psychological stress for those who live through disaster and for many who come to their aid, psychotherapy in the initial period of disaster response is often contraindicated as a relief strategy (Litz, Gray, Bryant, & Adler, 2002). A governing question is: Which of many human needs should be addressed in what order? The need to prioritize grows out of three considerations. First, resources are scarce, and premature efforts at some forms of aid will make other, more valuable efforts more costly or impossible. Second is a variant of Maslow's hierarchy of needs: Some forms of assistance are simply not usable until other needs have been met. Until people have been treated for life-threatening injuries, provided with food and shelter, and safeguarded from physical attack, they usually are not accessible in any meaningful sense for psychotherapy. Well-intentioned mental health volunteers who rush to disaster settings may simply add to the cost and confusion of restoring order, and careless efforts to get survivors to talk about their trauma may result in painful retriggering without resolution. Third, physical and material stabilization are in themselves powerful means to reduce traumatization.

Report of the Task Force of the International Society for Traumatic Stress Studies

Emerging standards for intervention are being shaped and tested in practice. The underlying premise is that psychosocial intervention should, first, do no harm and, second, should provide timely and relevant support, in cooperation with that provided by indigenous agencies, to strengthen the affected community's capacity to care for itself. An influential statement of the issues is contained in the

Task Force (2002) report of the International Society for Traumatic Stress Studies and is summarized next.

Disaster Relief Standard 1

The emerging international disaster relief standard holds that *basic physical and material stabilization of conditions for disaster survivors must take priority.* As survivors locate their missing loved ones and find a roof or tent over their heads, medical treatment for their injuries and illnesses, and food for themselves and their children, their psychological stress typically declines to a more functional level where it can support and motivate self-help efforts. Simple human warmth and support from all helpers add to the positive effects. Individuals so disabled by shock that they cannot access services are in a special category and may benefit from psychological first aid. As public services are restored and schools and employment resume functioning, stress is further reduced for the majority of people, who will be able to resume normal lives and may never develop persistent PTSD.

For a certain percentage of survivors, however, psychological problems, including PTSD, anxiety, and depression, will remain. Motivation for psychological help emerges at different times for different individuals. Mothers, for example, will often get help for their children or highly distressed loved ones before they will seek it for themselves.

Disaster Relief Standard 2

Interventions should be based on an assessment of locally defined and locally felt needs in the specific setting of the disaster. Capacity for needs assessment varies with the prior state of mental health services in the affected region. For example, where local assessments are not available, HAP works with partner agencies to determine needs before designing and implementing relief projects.

Disaster Relief Standard 3

A third emerging standard for intervention is that *the format and effects of mental health services should be documented.* There is still not widespread consensus in relief agencies on which therapies are effective and useful for survivors of disaster traumas. Consequently, in all its disaster-related training projects, and despite often challenging circumstances, HAP attempts to gather data to contribute to an expanding body of research. This includes information about the traumatized population and evaluations of the efficacy of the Eye Movement Desensitization and Reprocessing (EMDR) treatment conducted by the local clinicians (Errebo, Knipe, & Altayli, 2005; Jarero, Artigas, & Hartung, 2006; Konuk, Knipe, Eke, Yusek, Yurtsever, & Ostep, 2006; Silver, Rogers, Knipe, & Colelli, 2005).

Disaster Relief Standards 4 and 5

Psychosocial interventions should be conducted only at the invitation of two or more governmental or health agencies from the affected community. The particular interventions employed should be capable of integration into the primary

health care system of the country. For example, HAP teaches EMDR to local clinicians and psychological stabilization methods to nonclinical caregivers, but
only at the invitation of local health leaders.

Disaster Relief Standard 6

*Avoid teaching powerful mental health interventions to individuals who lack
the requisite training to make safe and effective use of them.* This can be a
tricky issue in societies that have less developed clinical licensure systems, or
where the more highly credentialed professionals are often not engaged in
clinical practice. Two judgments may need to be made in the field: Will the
highly credentialed professionals actually do clinical work in the disaster area
if trained in EMDR, are the less credentialed caregivers who usually provide
mental health services sufficiently skilled to learn and use EMDR? A great
advantage of training local clinicians who meet these tests is that they are already attuned to cultural issues relevant to psychotherapy practice in their
country. They make appropriate accommodations more quickly and effectively than foreign therapists could. Most important, by training local clinicians, mental health volunteers multiply their impact both immediately and in
the long term by leaving behind an enhanced local capacity to serve mental
health needs.

Psychotherapy as a Response to Disaster

While avoiding premature interventions and efforts that are poorly coordinated
with the local health care system, therapists can make a powerful contribution
to relief and recovery. Failure to plan for and provide effective treatment to the
15% to 25% of the exposed population who present with PTSD symptoms after
3 months places a significant constraint on subsequent efforts for community recovery. Beyond the distress visited directly on traumatized individuals and their
families, the community is impacted by the loss of up to one quarter of its work-
force. The impaired productivity, the loss of community services, including
school services for large percentages of children, and rising rates of addiction
and suicide further inhibit social recovery.

Although it may appear that the treatment of psychologically distressed individuals and families would expedite community recovery, the provision of effective and affordable psychotherapy is not yet a priority among the major
international disaster relief organizations. There is some debate about the utility
of psychotherapy for trauma as a postdisaster response. Some researchers have
argued that sociocultural interventions other than psychotherapy should be favored. For example, Miller and Rasco (2004) took this view, although their focus
appeared to be aimed at the cultural and practical disadvantages of "talk" therapies rather than EMDR. There are also questions regarding the allocation of
scarce resources among competing mental health options. How much response
time should be devoted to training local providers? How much time should be al-
located to direct service? Should resources support individual or group treatment, focus on children or adults, stress clinical care or nonclinical stabilization
procedures? Is it too early to work on trauma, or are there benefits to addressing

PTSD as soon as it emerges? Though we have good working understandings of these issues, there is insufficient research to answer these questions definitively, and suggestive studies sometimes pull in different directions (Litz et al., 2002).

One recurrent worry, especially in non-Western societies, is whether psychotherapy is a culturally biased intervention with negative consequences. Particularly in the case of refugees and populations traumatized in the context of long-term interethnic conflicts, some writers view therapy itself as stigmatizing—carrying the implication that trauma survivors are mentally ill, thus pathologizing a normal response to an abnormal situation (e.g., Miller & Rasco, 2004). In highly politicized situations, partisans sometimes fear that therapy might undermine an understanding of distress as caused by the political adversary. In HAP's experience, clinicians trained in EMDR and traumatology have been able to get beyond these worries and embrace a post-disaster treatment method that focuses on supporting the brain's natural capacity to reprocess disturbing information to an adaptive resolution (HAP Volunteers, 2005).

After a Disaster, Psychotherapy Is Different

Clinicians in any culture typically conduct their work against an assumed background of normal cultural and societal realities. Disaster may rupture those realities. Nonetheless, the underlying cultural and societal inheritance filters and structures the effort of survivors to give meaning to their disaster. This section describes two approaches to postdisaster psychotherapy that have adapted well in diverse cultural environments.

Eye Movement Desensitization and Reprocessing

EMDR (Shapiro, 2001) has proved to be well adapted across cultures. EMDR is a psychotherapy approach provided to an individual to assist him or her in successfully processing distressing and traumatic memories. Several studies have evaluated the efficacy of EMDR in postdisaster contexts, with children and adults, in various countries and cultures.

In a controlled study, Chemtob, Nakashima, and Carlson (2002) found EMDR to be an effective treatment for children who had chronic disaster-related PTSD 3 years after Hurricane Iniki in Hawaii. These children had not responded to a previous intervention. EMDR treatment gains were maintained at 6-month follow-up, and health visits to the school nurse were significantly reduced following treatment. Positive results with EMDR were also found with children from Italy. Fernandez, Gallinari, and Lorenzetti (2004) described a school-based EMDR intervention for children who had witnessed an airplane crash in Milan, Italy. Here, a group intervention was provided to 236 schoolchildren exhibiting PTSD symptoms 30 days postincident. At 4-month follow-up, teachers disclosed that all but two children evinced a return to normal functioning after treatment.

Treatment efficacy with 9/11 survivors shortly postevent was documented by Silver et al. (2005), who reported on a HAP community-based intervention project in New York City. Clients made highly significant positive gains after brief treatment (no more than five sessions) on a range of outcome variables, including validated psychometric tests and self-report scales. Analyses of the data indicated that EMDR was a useful treatment intervention both in the immediate aftermath of disaster and later.

In a study of Hurricane Andrew survivors that compared EMDR recipients and nontreated individuals, Grainger, Levin, Allen-Byrd, Doctor, and Lee (1997) found significant differences on the Impact of Event Scale (Horowitz, Wilner, & Alvarez, 1979) and subjective distress. Positive outcomes of treatment with earthquake survivors in Turkey have been documented by Konuk and colleagues (2006). Similarly positive outcome data from EMDR treatment of tsunami survivors in Sri Lanka was described by Errebo et al. (2005).

Family Systsems Approaches

A clinical focus on family systems after disaster is important for several reasons. In many developing countries, the family is the most important social context and support for individuals. The family also mediates broader cultural values and orientations (McGoldrick, 1998; McGoldrick & Giordano, 1996). When disaster disrupts other social supports, family ties assume increased importance. Moreover, when the family itself is the locus of loss, the place of family in the survivor's identity may well become the focal point of trauma.

Disasters often destroy communal infrastructures, including family structures and functions. Family members die or are injured; other family members experience consequent upheavals in their own family status, which in turn may redefine their wider societal status in often devastating ways. Women who were widowed by the tsunami in some parts of South Asia, for example, lost their entire network of social safeguards. It is not surprising that many of the traumas reported by clients receiving postdisaster therapy related to family issues.

Family systems theory helps to elucidate these issues and employs several constructs and tools that can be particularly useful in treatment planning, assessment, and intervention. Chief among these are the genogram to rapidly chart the constellation of relationships in a client's history (Carter & McGoldrick, 1980; Shellenberger, Chapter 3); family therapy's focus on the intersection of traumatic events with major family development issues (Carter & McGoldrick, 1980); and sensitivity to past, present, and future transmission of trauma consequences between generations (Guerin, 1976). When family units are broken or roles are transformed by disaster, therapy can help the new, postdisaster family to become a resource for surviving family members, enhancing a sense of control and definition of self.

Family systems therapies view the individual in his or her familial context. Not all of the family members may be physically present in the session with the therapist and the individual client. It is a tenet of family systems approaches that any change in one person will provoke a change in all others in the family system (Guerin, 1976). It is as though all family members are connected by large imaginary rubber bands (Wynne, 1978): A tug on one person will show up as movement in another. Therefore, any problem in one member is also a family problem. Recognizing this contextual reality, HAP volunteers have often incorporated elements of family theory in the treatment approach that is taught to local clinicians. For example, after the 1999 earthquake in Turkey, Turkish clinicians were trained by HAP to provide EMDR to residents of a refugee camp. A mother brought her child for treatment of PTSD symptoms; when the child improved, the mother also sought treatment. Finally, the father, who had not ventured out of the shelter for weeks, came for treatment and was also helped. Clinicians in such shelter communities become attuned to this pattern and recognize that care extended to one family member may be the means to drawing others into treatment.

THERAPY PROCESS

The EMDR Humanitarian Assistance Programs (HAP) has had more than 10 years of experience responding to communitywide disasters. HAP's primary focus is on training local therapists to treat trauma using EMDR. These therapists are culturally attuned clinicians from the affected society. HAP also trains paraprofessionals in traumatology and stabilization methods so they can supplement the efforts of scarce clinicians. HAP also helps local therapists and organizations set up infrastructures to support ongoing direct service to their communities. HAP trainers have learned to emphasize sensitivity to family and culture because they recognize that the community members' most painful traumas are most often linked to the clients' predisaster family system and to the impact of the disaster on the family's current status and future prospects.

Sometimes, the events of a disaster trigger past traumas. When this occurs, EMDR, with its emphasis on past, present, and future material, has proven especially helpful in processing those events to a neutral state no longer capable of being triggered. Two such examples were reported in work with first responder clients after Hurricane Katrina. One client, who had been shot in an encounter with a criminal well before the hurricane, was exposed to danger and emotional turmoil associated with rescue and recovery work. He had intrusive thoughts and dreams of the earlier shooting, exaggerated fear and uncertainty during the rescue work, and sensations at the site of his prior gunshot wound. The shooting was targeted for EMDR and symptoms remitted after two sessions. The client had no hurricane-related targets to process. A second client had had a seemingly mild experience prehurricane that caused him to call his own professional judgment into question. During rescue activities, he kept flashing on the previous mistake and questioning his current judgment, which hindered his performance and raised his fear that this would happen again and again in his professional life. One EMDR session targeting the past event processed it to neutral; a subsequent session processed events during the rescue work (HAP Volunteers, 2005).

Treatment Structure

Time and circumstances limit disaster practice; there may be many people who need treatment in situations that are not conducive to therapy. Various triage methods have been used in HAP projects. Group meetings with affinity groups (work settings, villages, classrooms) are held in which education about trauma and EMDR are offered, sometimes including techniques for stabilizing internal states (e.g., relaxation, breathing). The Impact of Events scale (Horowitz et al., 1979) may be administered as a screening device. In this way the first two phases of EMDR are begun: first, History Taking and Treatment Planning and second, Preparation. When individual EMDR therapy is offered, these phases are expanded as time permits to better define suitability for treatment, sometimes including administering other measures.

Early Phases and Stabilization

Both family systems therapy and EMDR respect the need to stabilize the client and his or her family by determining that needs for food, shelter, and safety are met first. Indeed, any effective psychotherapy will assess whether these needs are met before undertaking possibly stressful treatment. Noting and strengthening clients' strategies and skills to self-regulate are normal preparation for EMDR. They are critical elements of disaster relief work. People in panic over unmet basic needs cannot use psychotherapy well. In the first stage of EMDR (Client History and Treatment Planning) the client's stability is evaluated; in the second stage (Preparation), stability is enhanced, if necessary. In the immediate postdisaster period, clients with complex presentations and prior trauma histories may be unable to benefit from more than enhanced stabilization, but that in itself often brings about a significant increase in functional behavior and is a central goal of therapy.

The genogram, a tool developed by family therapists, is particularly useful in the first and second stages of EMDR to quickly place individuals presenting for therapy in their social and family settings (see Shellenberger, Chapter 3). "The genogram is a map that provides a graphic picture of family structure and emotional process over time" (Carter & McGoldrick, 1980, p. xxiii). It reveals at a glance much information that will impact the ongoing situation of any given person: What family resources can be counted on? Where are people that are important to the individual? What position does this person have in relation to family and to the developmental challenges facing the family? In the midst of disaster work, not all information can be or should be gathered, but the format allows for information to be collected quickly and used at a glance.

Processing Phases

Family systems work also focuses on the intersection of traumatic events with major family development issues (Carter & McGoldrick, 1980), an emphasis that helpfully informs the choice of targets for EMDR. If the wrong targets are used, positive treatment effects are minimized. Culture, as mediated by the family, defines the meaning of events and therefore defines the contours and connections of what is traumatic, which leads directly to the target to be processed. The following case illustrates the cultural mandates and the family strains experienced when the culturally normative development of roles is disrupted by disaster. Family, culture, and personal pain are considered when establishing a good target for intervention:

> An adolescent son watched his fisherman father washed away in the tsunami. He was unable to hold on to his father's arm as the waves crashed over the boat where both of them worked.

This boy chose two distinct incidents to target for treatment. The scene on the boat was the boy's first target, receiving a rating of 10 on the Subjective Units of Disturbance (SUD) scale, where 0 = No distress and 10 = Extreme distress. It might be expected that the second target would be another "awful" scene or experience, and in some cases, it would be. For this boy, however, his second target was a family one, culturally defined, with a SUD rating of 9. This was his felt inadequacy to replace his father as the primary support of his family, which was the cultural expectation. Although he had come to that role abruptly and prematurely, he expected himself to assume the tasks with no uncertainty, an expectation that most would see as irrational. Indeed, he was able to process this target to an adaptive resolution. He processed his memory of his father teaching him everything he knew about fishing, and therefore realized that he actually was prepared. He also recognized that it was natural to experience some uncertainty when an unfamiliar role was being assumed. Along the way, the boy processed his more unconscious worry that he somehow "profited" in status from his father's death.

Culturally Appropriate Cognitive Interweaves

At any time during treatment, the boy's processing could have been blocked. For example, he may not have accessed the memory of his father teaching him how to fish. In such a situation, the therapist could have used the strategy of the *Cognitive Interweave* (for parameters, see Shapiro, 2001). Knowing the family and cultural settings helps to construct appropriate Cognitive Interweaves. In this example, the clinician could have asked, "Where did you learn how to fish?" to prompt access of this adaptive memory. Likewise, if the client had not felt comfortable talking about his "selfish" increase in status, the clinician could have said, "Some people may have worried that they were achieving an increase in status from the misfortune of their father. Did that happen at all for you?" This construct would obviously require knowledge of the family and culture.

Culturally Sensitive Language

EMDR is culturally adaptable in all eight phases of the therapy. For example, in the assessment and reprocessing stages, scales designate the subjective level of disturbance using the SUD scale (0 = Neutral, and 10 = Highest disturbance imaginable) and the validity of positive statements (Validity of Cognition scale, or VOC, 1 = Completely false and 7 = Completely true). These scales almost automatically reflect the cultural orientation of the subject, but cultural norms can sometimes require adaptations. When HAP was training clinicians in northern Europe, for example, trainers were told, "We are European; we don't do extremes," so SUD scores rarely approached 10; in upstate New York, with Oneida tribe member clinicians, trainers were told, "I can't express extremes with you, because you are not in my clan." The trainer simply adjusted the scale to fit the culture.

Assessment language can also be adapted. In some Muslim countries, the language that is usually used in EMDR Assessment (Phase 3) has no meaning or the wrong meaning when translated. In the assessment "What words go best with that image (event) to describe your negative belief about yourself now?," the word "belief" connotes religious belief only and is too global. Clinicians might ask, as they did in Turkey, "When you think about that image (event), how do you negatively define yourself?" This wording has specificity for the event and gets to the client's negative identity state vis-à-vis the traumatic event. Likewise in the trauma processing or desensitization stage, the words "What do you get now?" have no meaning, whereas "What comes into your mind?" has meaning and will evoke the same material that the former statement would have in another culture.

Important Family and Cultural Considerations

Even good changes will require some accommodation by other family members, which may be challenging. For example, if treatment eliminates an individual's avoidance of the ocean after a tsunami, it may mean that he can fish again and thereby support his family and take his position in the family setting. Doing so is systemically congruent. If, on the other hand, the individual presenting for therapy is the oldest son of an able-bodied but traumatized fisherman father who cannot yet go back to the water, it may not be systemically congruent for that son to fish before the father is able to do so. This might signal the displacement of the father in the family hierarchy, a loss of face for the father. In that case, the son's EMDR therapy may be doomed to failure until this contextual reality issue is addressed.

In Vietnam, Cambodia, and Indonesia, saving face for the family and emphasis on the honor of the family is important. The age of a person, his or her place in the family configuration, and even birth order defines how one responds to situations and other people. Children are seen as subordinate, but as the focus of parental (and often extended family) responsibility; family is more important than any individual. These facts frame any discussion of trauma disorder in these settings because what may be metabolized as traumatic in the West is not the same as that in the East.

Consider the example of some tsunami widows in Indonesia. Women who lost their husband also lost their social status in their culture. Not only did they have the practical issues of how to provide food, shelter, and other resources without their husband, but they could not assume that their standing in the community would help with these matters. Choosing treatment targets for EMDR must take these elements into consideration. Loss of status would be an expected target for clinicians who understood the social context.

Clinicians working in disaster settings have noted that mothers will often bring their symptomatic child to be treated first. Family system theory hypothesizes that the symptom is carried by the family member who can most afford to experience it (Guerin, 1976). Also, one family member, often a child, may express symptoms in order to bring another into treatment. If the child gets therapy first, several things happen. The child's improvement demonstrates for the mother that one can recover from PTSD symptoms, reduces the drain on the resources of the mother (and therefore the whole family), and ratifies the mother's function, showing her to be effective in the role of caring for her child (a primary value in many cultures, most notably in areas hit by the tsunami). This intervention reduces PTSD in the individual and has great ramifications for the family, reinforcing the mother's strengths.

Disaster is indeed a stressor, yet it does not always result in a less healthy family or individual. Sometimes the family discovers strengths that had lain dormant, or develops a new appreciation of the abilities of one of its members. These changes can result in a more resilient family. Disaster also sometimes changes the boundaries of a family. This may happen in many ways, such as through loss of members, inclusion of others in a close bond, or literally through aid that is available to a family that has always been self-sufficient. These "boundary breaches" can be positive, negative, or neutral, but in any case need to be considered in treating disaster victims.

Group Treatment

Although it is often appropriate in disaster settings to employ the standard EMDR protocol, three other protocols are frequently applicable: the Recent Event Protocol and Single Event Protocol are each discussed in Shapiro's (2001) classic text. The EMDR Group Protocol for children, using a procedure called the "Butterfly Hug," has evolved specifically out of the disaster-related work by EMDR clinicians. All protocols include the past, present, and future template and eight phases of EMDR.

The EMDR group protocol, discussed further later in the chapter (for detailed description, see Fernandez et al., 2004), is offered to children as young as 4 (and sometimes, with modifications, to adults) who have been through the same disaster and have reported trauma symptoms as a result. A typical group will consist of eight or fewer participants who have been prescreened. Although one-session treatment has been successfully used (Fernandez et al., 2004; Jarero et al., 2006), at least three sessions separated by days or weeks are recommended for the group participants. Distress levels and cognitions are not usually measured with numbers in younger children, but with gestures of size ("This big"), descriptive words, such as "worst bad" used by one boy, or a Faces scale that gives the range of positive to negative emotions with changes of expression. Body Scan (Phase 6) is sometimes omitted because the rapid processing in children does not generally leave a body residue.

Family members can be involved in a continuum of passive to active roles. The family member can be asked simply to be present and to witness, which has a powerful effect, or to perform a function. Such active help might involve holding the child, telling the narrative of the trauma, helping with bilateral stimulation, or picture drawing. This allows the parent to know what transpired and to support changes later. When parents administer bilateral stimulation, they appear to get therapeutic results themselves.

Group treatment can be used in nonprivate settings, such as a tent or open-air clinic. Group members can aid in maintaining individual gains. The parents can also talk to each other while their children draw, which offers them the same community support, thus helping to solidify gains. Clients in the group do not have to verbalize information about the trauma. Therapy can be done on subsequent days; there is no need for a week of homework between sessions.

Fernandez et al. (2004) reported sustained reduction of symptoms for over 90% of children after group treatment following a disaster at their school in Italy. Anecdotal reports in other situations are consistent with these results. The group method is easily taught to both new and experienced therapists. Its efficacy has been documented in Italy (Fernandez et al., 2004) and South America (Jarero et al., 2006), it seems to be equally effective cross-culturally, and it has the advantage of reaching more people more quickly, involving larger segments of the community. Paraprofessionals can be taught to lead the groups under supervision of a clinician, which allows wide application in societies that have few clinicians. For instance, in Gujarat, India, after a major earthquake, newly trained clinicians conducted group sessions that reached thousands of symptomatic children. In Chennai, India, after the tsunami, HAP-trained clinicians treated 5,000 children in these groups in 1 year (HAP Volunteers, 2005).

CASE EXAMPLES

Two case examples, out of dozens that might have served as well, illustrate the manner in which culture and prior life circumstances shape how disaster-engendered trauma is expressed. At the same time, they demonstrate the powerful benefits of timely and effective therapy.

Case 1: Group Work with Children

On the coast of Thailand, Aiton Birnbaum (2005, personal communication) devised an intervention in which adults were asked to attend a group session with their children, who were experiencing varied trauma symptoms. Usually one or more children from a family attended along with their mother. A short explanation of trauma and EMDR was offered, paper and crayons were distributed, and parents were asked to stand behind their children as they drew pictures. With younger children, parents often facilitated their children's drawing efforts, and some parents talked among themselves as the drawings were made. First the children were asked to draw a picture of something that made them feel safe and happier. They were then asked to look at the picture and the parents were instructed to pat each shoulder alternately. The children were told that they could take their "safe place" pictures home and use this method whenever they needed to feel better. The children were also taught the butterfly hug, a method of bilateral self-stimulation by alternately tapping their shoulders with arms crossed.

The parents' involvement may have provided soothing contact between parent and child and reinforced the parent's role as caretaker and a sense of competence in this role. Their involvement may also have helped them to process their own tsunami experiences. The mothers simultaneously gave bilateral stimulation and received it as they were exposed to their own and their children's trauma experiences, and they were able to talk with other mothers in the group who had had similar experiences. Some mothers participated by drawing their own pictures.

Next, the children were asked to place the "happy picture" face down and to draw a picture of the traumatic experience and indicate their SUD level. When that was completed, parents again patted each shoulder alternately. These sets of stimulation were repeated several times. The clinician monitored reactions in the children, most particularly when their attention seemed to drift off the picture. The stimulation was repeated until it appeared that the child's distress about the event in that picture had been desensitized. Then the child was asked to draw another picture and give another SUD rating, and the bilateral stimulation was again administered. This procedure was followed for a series of pictures; usually the first picture depicted the worst event, and subsequent pictures were of events perceived as less negative. Some Cognitive Interweaves were offered during the desensitization if processing appeared blocked. Typically these were devised to emphasize family roles and the children's connection to their parents in a concerted effort to reconnect to the natural strengths in the system, with emphasis on continuity despite the traumatic event.

When about four pictures had been made and the events depicted were reprocessed to a more neutral state, parent and child were told that processing might continue after the session. Parents were reminded that they could provide soothing by suggesting that the children look at the happy picture while the parent tapped their shoulders alternately or while the child did the butterfly hug.

In each session, and over the course of therapy, a past, present, and future template was followed. Pictures of the trauma evoked the past event and present triggers. Connection of the child and parent also reflected the present, whereas the future focused on planning with the parent and child for continued processing, or other possible distress and ways to sooth the child, if necessary. Further sessions were offered, again with family involvement and with a focus on any remaining difficulties, including present-day issues. The children's descriptions of present-day distress involved the sea; they expressed a desire to play in the water as they had done in the past. The fear of the sea was targeted in pictures and desensitized.

In addition, an excursion to the beach with the children was planned; this was designed as a systemic intervention for the family and community. Even when the parents refused permission for a child's participation, the seed was planted that people might choose to go back to the sea. If the child was allowed to go, the family and surrounding community awaited the result. Were the children able to enter the water? When they did enter the water, this provided a model and inspiration for others in the community, including siblings and parents. The family members also reacted to this new development. Some were mildly shamed into confronting their own fears. After all, if a child can go back to the sea, should not a parent be able to do so?

Case 2: Family Impact of Parental Traumatization

Forty children in Sri Lanka were treated in one community using the EMDR group protocol for children while parents watched and helped. In one group, a

4-year-old child reported a variety of stress symptoms, including severe nightmares. His Sri Lankan therapist noted his difficulty identifying a "safe place" to draw. Later, in an individual discussion with the mother, it became clear that the child could not find a safe place because his mother had been very angry and had hit him many times since the tsunami. HAP volunteer Karen Forte (2005, personal communication) reported what followed.

The mother agreed to EMDR therapy for herself. Her presenting issue was intense grief and anger at the loss of two of her children, who had died in the tsunami. She had also taken in a motherless 1-year-old baby after her own 1-month-old baby died. The family had lost their home, all their belongings, and their source of income. The adopted baby constantly cried as this mother held him in a tight, angry grip. Her own mother, her 4-year-old child, and the 1-year-old baby accompanied the mother to her first EMDR session. She could not refrain from yelling angrily at her 4-year-old son as the session started. The child was offered some distraction with crayons and paper. The supervising therapist held the baby as the Sri Lankan trainee worked with the mother in her first EMDR session. The grandmother anxiously watched her grief-stricken daughter. The focus of the first session was the manner of death of the two children, using the single event protocol.

The atmosphere became more relaxed as the session progressed, and both the 4-year-old and the baby fell asleep. The mother's SUD decreased substantially for this single issue. The mother and a now beaming grandmother expressed gratitude for the mother's progress. Although further treatment was indicated, the mother and her family had gained a large measure of relief from trauma symptoms, allowing a return to functioning more typical of the family pretsunami.

Additional Aspects

The overwhelming nature of disaster, and the many heartrending situations encountered, makes it necessary to protect clinicians from secondary traumatization. In HAP projects, built-in debriefing and frequent consultations with senior-level therapists mitigate this possibility. But the nature of EMDR therapy also helps to reduce the dose of traumatic detail that a therapist experiences, because it is unnecessary, indeed often contraindicated, for the client to articulate all the details of the trauma. Clinicians can also self-administer bilateral stimulation or rely on team members to desensitize aspects of the encountered trauma that threaten to stick. Realizing the potent ability of EMDR to reduce pain for clients is also an antidote to secondary traumatization. As one clinician trainee in Sri Lanka put it, "Sometimes abreactions shook me with terror. But 'go with it' worked out beautifully" (HAP Volunteers, 2005).

DISCUSSION

PTSD is a cross-cultural phenomenon highly prevalent in the wake of disaster. EMDR is an evidence-based psychotherapy, able to accommodate cultural variations in the expression of symptoms. Clinicians in both Western and non-Western settings have found that EMDR is well structured to accommodate their cultures and the imperatives of postdisaster treatment of PTSD.

Complementing EMDR in disaster relief settings, family systems theory focuses on a universal social construct: the family. Family systems theory has the capacity to illuminate the stresses that disaster exacerbates, to focus attention on areas needing therapeutic attention, and to support the clinician's need to adapt EMDR to the cultural context of the client. Clinicians can use the culturally informed "meaning" of traumatic memories to process traumatically encoded information that presents a barrier to functional living in the present for the individual and the family. Family "talk" gives clinicians entry into culturally diverse settings because the family plays a central role in all human cultures.

Complicating treatment in the postdisaster setting is the fact that the infrastructure for meeting basic human needs, such as food, shelter, and emergency medical care, is frequently in disarray. If, in addition, predisaster mental health care was sparse or nonexistent, time and resources must be spent on capacity building among local caregivers before they can employ effective therapies.

In the cases presented, use of family therapy conceptualizations and resources supported astute treatment planning, optimized the supportive resources of family members, and impacted the extended family system along with the identified subject of treatment. There were no discernible disadvantages to integrating EMDR and family therapy in these cases.

Clinicians who are newly trained in EMDR provide most of the clinical treatment of trauma promoted by HAP in disaster settings. Giving them substantial additional training in family systems therapy would be impractical in the short run. However, the clinicians are sensitized during EMDR training to be aware of the needs of the clients within their extended family, community, and culture. As an adjunct, distilling out of family systems theory those elements that could be taught quickly and effectively along with EMDR may be a useful challenge for the future.

In the meantime, EMDR training teams that are sensitive to family system issues would appear to have a definite advantage in teaching EMDR across cultural divides, and reliance on local clinicians to deliver EMDR to their own compatriots increases the likelihood that family issues and sensitivities raised by disaster will be attended to in treatment. By positively supporting the health of family systems, postdisaster treatment can promote more rapid recovery of communities and forestall intergenerational transmission of traumatic effects.

REFERENCES

Carter, E., & McGoldrick, M. (1980). The family life cycle and family therapy: An overview. In E. Carter & M. McGoldrick (Eds.), *The family life cycle: A framework for family therapy* (pp. 3–20). New York: Gardner Press.

Chemtob, C., Nakashima, J., & Carlson, J. (2002). Brief-treatment for elementary school children with disaster-related PTSD: A field study. *Journal of Clinical Psychology, 58,* 99–112.

Erickson, K. (1976). *Everything in its path.* New York: Simon & Schuster.

Errebo, N., Knipe, J., & Altayli, B. (2005). *Preliminary program evaluation, Sri Lanka tsunami response/traumatology and EMDR training* (Unpublished internal report). Hamden, CT: EMDR Humanitarian Assistance Program.

Fernandez, I., Gallinari, E., & Lorenzetti, A. (2004). A school-based EMDR intervention for children who witnessed the Pirelli Building airplane crash in Milan, Italy. *Journal of Brief Therapy, 2,* 129–136.

Grainger, R., Levin, C., Allen-Byrd, L., Doctor, R., & Lee, H. (1997). An empirical evaluation of eye movement desensitization and reprocessing (EMDR) with survivors of a natural catastrophe. *Journal of Traumatic Stress, 10,* 665–671.

Guerin, P. (1976). *Family therapy: Theory and practice.* New York: Garden Press.

HAP Volunteers. (2005). *Informal reports of EMDR Humanitarian Assistance Program volunteers in India, Sri Lanka, Thailand and the U.S. Gulf Coast.* Available from: http://www.emdrhap.org.

Horowitz, M. J., Wilner, N., & Alvarez, W. (1979). The Impact of Event Scale: A measure of subjective stress. *Psychosomatic Medicine, 41,* 209–218.

Jarero, I., Artigas, L., & Hartung, J. (2006). EMDR integrative group treatment protocol: A post-disaster trauma intervention for children and adults. *Traumatology, 12*(2).

Konuk, E., Knipe, J., Eke, I., Yusek, H., Yurtsever, A., & Ostep, S. (2006). Effects of EMDR therapy on post-traumatic stress disorder in survivors of the 1999 Marmara, Turkey earthquake. *International Journal of Stress Management, 13,* 291–308.

Litz, B. T., Gray, M. J., Bryant, R. A., & Adler, A. B. (2002). Early intervention for trauma: Current status and future directions. *Clinical Psychology: Science and Practice, 9,* 112–134.

Marsella, A., Friedman, M., Gerrity, E., & Scurfield, R. (2001). Ethnocultural considerations in the treatment of PTSD: Therapy and service delivery. In A. Marsella, M. Friedman, E. Gerrity, & R. Scurfield (Eds.), *Ethnocultural aspects of posttraumatic stress disorder* (pp. 529–538). Washington, DC: American Psychological Association.

McFarlane, A., & Yehuda, R. (1996). Resilience, vulnerability, and the course of post-traumatic reactions. In B. A. van der Kolk, A. C. McFarlane, & L. Weisaeth (Eds.), *Traumatic stress* (pp. 155–181). New York: Guilford Press.

McGoldrick, M. (1998). Introduction: Re-visioning family through a cultural lens. In M. McGoldrick (Ed.), *Re-visioning family therapy* (pp. 3–19). New York: Guilford Press.

McGoldrick, M., & Giordano, J. (1996). Overview: Ethnicity and family therapy. In M. McGoldrick, J. Giordano, & J. Pearce (Eds.), *Ethnicity and family therapy* (pp. 1–30). New York: Guilford Press.

Miller, K., & Rasco, L. (2004). An ecological framework for addressing the mental health needs of refugee communities. In K. Miller & L. Rasco (Eds.), *The mental health of refugees* (pp. 1–66). Mahwah, NJ: Erlbaum.

Shapiro, F. (2001). *Eye movement desensitization and reprocessing: Basic principles, protocols, and procedures* (2nd ed.). New York: Guldford Press.

Silver, S. M., Rogers, S., Knipe, J., & Colelli, G. (2005). EMDR therapy following the 9/11 terrorist attacks: A community-based intervention project in New York City. *International Journal of Stress Management, 12,* 29–42.

Task Force on International Trauma Training of the International Society for Traumatic Stress Studies. (2002). Guidelines for international training in mental health and psychosocial interventions for trauma exposed populations in clinical and community settings. *Psychiatry, 65,* 156–164.

van der Kolk, B., & McFarlane, A. (1996). The black hole of trauma. In B. A. van der Kolk, A. C. McFarlane, & L. Weisaeth (Eds.), *Traumatic stress* (pp. 3–23). New York: Guilford Press.

Wynne, L. C. (1978). Knotted relationships, communication deviances, and meta-binding. In M. M. Berger (Ed.), *Beyond the double bind* (pp. 177–188). New York: Brunner/Mazel.

PART VI

Conclusion

CHAPTER 20

The Integration of EMDR and Family Systems Therapies

Louise Maxfield, Florence W. Kaslow, and Francine Shapiro

A fundamental tenet of systems theory is that the whole is greater than the sum of its parts (von Bertalanaffy, 1968). Clearly, this basic principle can be applied to the integration of Eye Movement Desensitization and Reprocessing (EMDR) and family systems therapy (FST): The combined approach has a synergistic effect, with each of the two treatment components intertwining to maximize the individual effects of the other. This integrative treatment approach can result in profound changes for both the individual and the family.

EMDR AND FAMILY SYSTEMS THERAPIES

The approaches of EMDR and FST are generally very different. They differ in theory, identification of the patient, focus, temporal view, and desired outcomes. Nevertheless, the majority of FST therapists would agree with Shapiro's (Chapter 1, p. 5) statement that the "primary goal is to address the entire clinical picture to bring about the most comprehensive treatment effects."

Theories

The concept of "circular causality" is a basic tenet of systems theory; this is a departure from the position of "linear causality" espoused by medical models. Linear causality posits that one event causes the next, in what Goldenberg and Goldenberg (2000) refer to as the "billiard ball model": A causes B, B causes C, C causes D. From this perspective, exposure to a virus causes the flu; the flu causes symptoms; symptoms cause distress. Although linear models recognize inherent vulnerabilities that may make one person more likely to succumb to the flu than another, the direction is linear. This model has been applied by some to the assessment of families, for example, by those who posit that bad parenting causes disturbed children. In his Foreword to this book, Siegel discusses how parents' emotional styles are thought to produce various types of attachment problems in their children. This expression of causality is consistent with a linear model.

On the other hand, most FST theories postulate circular causality. This is the chicken-and-egg model of causality, wherein each element is seen as a contributing factor to the other: A causes B, B causes A, A causes B, ad infinitum. There is a recursive process within the system. An individual's symptoms are viewed as a product of the system and as serving a function within the system. Seeking to understand the origin of A outside of A's role in the current system is considered "pointless" (Goldenberg & Goldenberg, 2000, p. 14), as the meaning is to be found within the system. For example, a wife's demanding, clingy behavior results in her husband's distancing himself; his withdrawal increases her intrusive demanding behavior, which in turn causes further distancing by the husband. In this framework, pathology is viewed as a systemic problem. While some FST therapies see pathology as residing in an individual (e.g., feminist therapies perceive violent and abusive behavior as an individual pathology), all view the system as maintaining the pathology. All FST treatments are designed to address and change the pattern of interactions within the system, that is, the interpersonal dynamics, although a small number also address the intrapsychic dynamics and pay attention to the impact of the individual and vice versa.

To some extent, the Adaptive Information Processing (AIP) model, which explains EMDR, can be seen as endorsing linear causality (Shapiro, 2001; Chapter 1, this book). In simplistic terms, unprocessed trauma is said to cause pathology. Specifically, Shapiro has argued that when traumatic or distressing events are inadequately processed, they result in a wide range of pathological symptoms and diagnosable disorders. Current symptoms are understood to be the manifestation of unprocessed disturbing memories. Shapiro has clarified that symptomatic behavior often results from an interaction between the unprocessed memories and the current situation. For example, a wife's clinginess is elicited by her perceptions of her husband's actions and influenced by his reactions; nevertheless, the essential cause of her chronic misperceptions and inappropriate behaviors is understood to be the unprocessed material. In the AIP model, present triggers and the incorporations of new behaviors need to be addressed; however, chronic and resistant interactional systems are viewed as based on pathological responses within the individual; therefore, the "problematic relationship is simply another symptom of a wounded inner world" (Shapiro, Chapter 1, p. 28).

Identification of the Patient

The AIP model perceives the problem as residing primarily within the individual, and EMDR treatment is provided to the individual, even though family members may sometimes be present in the session. FST therapists view the family or one of its subsystems (e.g., marital couple) as the patient, although some individual sessions may be provided. In the integrated models described in the chapters of this book, there is a balance between the individual approach of EMDR and the systemic approach of FST. However, most chapter authors designated the family or couple as the patient and recommended bringing the material from any individual sessions back into the couple or family sessions to assist in changing the systemic dynamics.

Temporal View

In EMDR, the distress elicited by current situations is understood to arise from the unprocessed past material. The goal of EMDR treatment is to assist individuals in processing the past disturbing events and "to liberate clients . . . from the experiential contributors that set the foundation for the current pathology" (Shapiro, Chapter 1, p. 28). Consequently, the focus is on identifying and processing those past events that are "experiential contributors" before moving on to present triggers and future templates. In contrast, many FST therapists focus on present-day interactions among family members or subsystems. Nonetheless, some FST therapies address past issues (e.g., Psychodynamic/Object Relations, Bowen Theory, Emotionally Focused Therapy, Contextual Therapy; see Chapters 2, 7, 8, 9, 10, 15). In the integrative treatment described in this book, the authors outline the advantages of understanding and addressing precursors of current dysfunctions. When an individual family member resolves painful memories and their heritage, he or she is liberated to interact in a healthier, more loving, and authentic way. Family therapy can then help to consolidate these changes and to create new and healthier patterns of relationship behavior within the system.

Focus and Goals

EMDR is an individual therapy that transforms disturbing memories and brings them to an adaptive resolution, eliminating inappropriate negative affects and physical sensations and reformulating related cognitions. It is assumed that these intrapersonal transmutations will be reflected in positive changes in the individuals' behavior and relationships. Consequently, the focus of treatment is the identification and processing of prior events, along with the current triggers that reactivate them, before introducing new behaviors with future templates.

In FST, assessment and intervention are focused on issues related to family structure, dynamics, patterns of interaction, boundaries, roles, rules, myths, expectations, and communications. The primary purposes of treatment are to change the family's dysfunctional interactional patterns and expectations. Other goals "include the development of role flexibility and adaptability; a balancing of power, particularly in marital therapy; the establishment of individuality within the family collectivity; and greater clarity and specificity of communication" (Kaslow, Chapter 2, p. 38). Most FST theorists posit that individual change will occur as a result of systemic change (Sander, 1979).

In this book, the authors describe the integration of systemic and individual goals. Their chapters illustrate the balance between working on an individual's distressing memories and the couple or family interactions. Although some authors (e.g., Koedam, Chapter 11) recommend completing the individual work before engaging in couple or family therapy, most incorporate the two approaches by alternating sessions (see Tofani, Chapter 13, for a thorough description) or by utilizing conjoint sessions with the other member(s) present (e.g., Moses, Chapter 7). The integrative approach requires flexibility from the therapist and an ability to shift purposefully and knowledgably from the individual to the systemic, from past events to current circular interactions, and to consider a multiplicity of goals.

FAMILY SYSTEMS THERAPIES USED IN THE INTEGRATIVE APPROACHES

The authors in this book describe the integrative treatment of many problems commonly faced by individuals and families, including but not limited to marital distress, parenting problems, attachment injuries, divorce, abuse, and health difficulties. In all cases, they describe how the past experiences of a family member cause distress for that individual and his or her family, and they detail an approach that addresses both the individual and systemic aspects of the problem.

These chapters describe the integration of EMDR with various types of family systems therapies (see Kaslow, Chapter 2, for detailed descriptions). Many authors describe the use of Structural Family Therapy in their integrative approaches (Bardin, Comet, & Porten, Chapter 16; Klaff, Chapter 14; Koedam, Chapter 11; Maxfield, Chapter 17; Tofani, Chapter 13; Wesselman, Chapter 5). Others chronicle the use of Bowen Theory (Knudsen, Chapter 8), Contextual Therapy (Litt, Chapter 15), Emotionally Focused Therapy (Moses, Chapter 7; Errebo & Sommers-Flanagan, Chapter 10), Experiential Family Therapy (Tofani, Chapter 13), Medical Family Therapy (Moore, Chapter 18), Imago Relationship Therapy (Talan, Chapter 9), and Therapy of Social Action (Stowasser, Chapter 12). Many authors also use various FST techniques derived from Strategic, Narrative, Bowenian, Experiential, Object Relations, and Communications Family Therapy models. Two chapters describe innovative approaches, one for maternal-infant bonding failures (Madrid, Chapter 6) and the other for community disasters (Gelbach & Davis, Chapter 19).

CASE EXAMPLE

In Chapter 1, Dr. Shapiro described the EMDR treatment of Tara, a 15-year-old girl, who was treated successfully with EMDR (for details, refer to Chapter 1). This case is summarized here to serve as a foundation for a discussion of similarities and differences among the various FST models, as well as to provide an overview of an integrative FST and EMDR treatment.

Tara lived with her mother and father. Therapy was requested by the mother to treat Tara's excessive anxiety, panic attacks, and pronounced school phobia. Tara presented with extremely low self-esteem, social anxiety, extreme self-consciousness (with a hunched-over posture), and suicidal thoughts. After successful EMDR, Tara lost both her social and school phobias. Her posture, appearance, and demeanor improved markedly, and she developed new friendships with peers, who even gave her a surprise party for her birthday.

Unfortunately, Tara's parents, who consistently treated her in ways that caused her to feel defective, prematurely withdrew her from therapy. In the following section, we revisit this case and discuss how some of the integrative approaches described in this book could be applied to Tara's family if the parents had been willing to engage in the treatment process. We begin with a summary of Tara's family history and interactive patterns within the family.

Tara's premature birth was a critical event. She weighed only 2 pounds and was in the Pediatric Inpatient Care Unit for 4 months on a respirator. After leaving the hospital, her health continued to be poor, and her parents spent hours a day watching over her. This was a traumatic experience for her mother, whose memory about this continued to elicit distress. Her mother also reported a history of anxiety and depression.

The marital relationship had been conflictual when Tara was younger, but her mother and father no longer argued. The father was preoccupied with business affairs and rarely home. When home, he was emotionally detached from his wife and daughter and assumed a patriarchal role; his primary interactions with Tara were dismissive and derogatory.

The mother eventually gave up trying to involve the father in the family life and devoted herself completely to Tara. She was very overprotective of Tara and was not supportive of her growing independence as a young woman. For example, when Tara wanted to cut her hair, her mother would not allow it, saying she "liked it that way." Tara was not allowed to individuate or take on more mature responsibilities. She felt like a burden to her parents, although her parents denied this. Tara also felt responsible for her parents' emotional well-being and wondered, "If I leave for college, who will hold the family together?"

APPLICATIONS OF VARIOUS INTEGRATIVE APPROACHES

In this section, we suggest how the various integrative treatment approaches described in this book could have been used if the parents had been willing to engage in family therapy with Tara. This commitment would have involved discussion about treatment goals and an agreement by the family members to address and change relational problems, and perhaps to address their own individual issues and family histories.

The following describes the conceptualization of the family problem from the perspective of the specific approaches and suggests treatment targets, possible interventions, and desired outcomes. It is hoped that these examples will provide a practical illustration of the application of these approaches as well as contrasting similarities and differences among them.

Structural Family Therapy

Many authors in this book employed Structural Family Therapy (Minuchin, 1974) in their integrative treatment approaches (Bardin et al., Chapter 16; Klaff, Chapter 14; Koedam, Chapter 11; Maxfield, Chapter 17; Moore, Chapter 18; Tofani, Chapter 13; Wesselman, Chapter 5). This FST conceptualizes the family as a hierarchical organization in which the parents are the executors in the system. It contains various subsystems (e.g., marital dyad, parental subsystem, parent-child dyads, sibling subsystem) separated by individual and generational boundaries (see Kaslow, Chapter 2, for detailed description). Treatment focuses on readjusting the structure of the family and the nature of the boundaries so that the members can individuate appropriately and grow emotionally. Goals are achieved by altering roles, rules, and the nature of interactions and transactional patterns, for example, helping parents assume appropriate authority and deparentifying children.

An assessment of Tara's family from a Structural Family Therapy perspective identifies a number of problems. The disengagement between the mother and father is evident in the marital dyad. The parental subsystem lacks clear definition, the parents do not function as a unit, there is no joint decision making, and parental authority is inconsistent. The mother functions as a single parent when the father is absent, and when he returns home, he usurps her authority and makes arbitrary decisions. The mother-daughter dyad is an enmeshed relationship, with the mother and daughter overly involved with each other's emotions. They are also aligned in a coalition against the father, with both complaining about him when he is not present. The father-daughter subsystem is marked by distance and disengagement.

With this family, a structural family therapist probably would use many of the techniques outlined by Kaslow (Chapter 2). Some of the goals would include strengthening the parental coalition's authority so that the parents would function together more as a unit, with more sharing of decision making and parenting activities. The enmeshed relationship in the mother-daughter subsystem and related coalition would be addressed by creating more appropriate personal boundaries between Tara and her mother, helping the mother see Tara no longer as her premature baby but as an adolescent ready for independence, and by establishing new transactional patterns. The disengagement in the marital dyad would be broached, just as the distance between father and daughter would be addressed as a focus of treatment. Homework assignments might include family activities planned by all three members, father helping Tara with homework, the parents going out without Tara one night a week, and mother getting involved in a vocational pursuit or with friends so that she is less dependent on Tara.

Integration of EMDR and Structural Family Therapy

The expected outcome of the integration of EMDR and structural family treatment is increased differentiation of all members and clearer boundaries between subsystems, with Tara free to individuate, grow, and develop; with mother developing interests outside the family and becoming her own person; and with father becoming more emotionally connected to his wife and daughter. The approaches outlined in this book, which describe the integration of this FST and EMDR, tend to utilize both approaches simultaneously, interspersing family and individual sessions.

In Chapter 1, Dr. Shapiro described successful EMDR treatment for Tara. This therapy would have been more comprehensive if it had included the family therapy component, and the mother and father also would have benefited from their own EMDR sessions to address the trauma of Tara's birth and difficult infancy. From an AIP perspective, this pivotal experience was probably inadequately processed, with the mother becoming anxious and overprotective and the father becoming distant and disengaged. Depending on readiness and safety factors, such as the ability of each member of the couple to be supportive to the other (see Shapiro, 2001), it potentially would be most helpful if EMDR sessions addressing this issue were conducted in a conjoint manner (see Moses, Chapter 7), with mother and father present during each other's processing. Given the father's adherence to a patriarchal structure, such conjoint work might not have been possible because of his fear of emotional disclosure and of appearing weak to his wife. Therefore, the decision for individual or conjoint processing would need to be carefully assessed.

In addition, each of the parent's own histories would be explored to identify earlier experiences that laid the groundwork for their differential responses to the same trauma. For instance, what childhood experiences caused the mother's history of anxiety, depression, and emotional dependence? What experiences set the groundwork for the father's dismissive behaviors and his separation from his more tender emotions? It would be anticipated that resolving these issues, along with the trauma of Tara's premature birth, while simultaneously working on the family transactional patterns should effect a very significant change for this family.

Experiential Therapy

In Chapter 13, Laura Rocchietta Tofani describes the treatment of an anxious young woman who is struggling to individuate and separate from her family, using an approach that integrates Experiential Therapy with EMDR. There are clear parallels between this case and that of Tara and her family. Tofani argues that experiential therapy (Giat Roberto, 1992; Napier & Whitaker, 1978) facilitates individuation processes because it "emphasizes the importance of personal choices and awareness of the ongoing process of individuation and the young person's responsibility and competence" (Tofani, Chapter 13, p. 268). Treatment techniques include direct emotional expression and self-disclosure among family members to "break rigid cycles of automatic behaviors and to change the family myth about family unity" (p. 268).

If Tofani's integrative approach were applied with Tara and her parents, the experiential therapy would assist the family in understanding their own epistemology, or philosophy of life. Questions that could be used to assist the father in expressing his epistemology include What does he want for his family? How does he view his daughter? What does he think about her relationship with her mother? What are his hopes and dreams for his future? Similar questions would be asked of each member as well as questions about what they value most in life. Experiential therapy would focus on family rules and communication patterns and why the parents have restricted Tara's development; family themes such as opposing fears of longing for closeness and distance, for security, and for independence would be identified. The family members would be encouraged and coached in emotional expression and self-disclosure and in a larger range of appropriate responses to one another.

In this integrative approach, EMDR would be used to address Tara's anxieties and increase her self-awareness. It could also be used to process the experiences at the root of each parent's fears and anxieties, as well as the triggers and templates for appropriate communication. The expected outcome would be enhanced self-understanding for each member, a greater sense of freedom, and self-confidence, as well as support for Tara in her development, growth, and individuation.

Contextual Therapy

Contextual Therapy is described by Barry Litt (Chapter 15) and illustrated with a case example that has many similarities to Tara's family. Contextual Therapy (Boszormenyi-Nagy, 1987) focuses on the legacies and loyalties within families. These lead family members "to accrue and maintain an invisible ledger of merit and indebtedness, a multigenerational account system of investments and obligations in each relationship" (Kaslow, Chapter 2, p. 46). When there is an imbalance in these ledgers, issues related to trust, entitlement, and indebtedness arise, and a family member is often selected as the scapegoat. The goal of treatment is the rebalancing of the individual's obligations in family relationships.

The application of Contextual Therapy constructs would reveal that Tara's filial loyalty caused her "to become the captive object" of her mother's dependency needs (Litt, Chapter 15, p. 320). As a result, Tara was parentified and believed that it was her responsibility to hold the family together. The mother's need to possess Tara in a captive object role prevented Tara from differentiating and developing a sense of her own entitlement and merit. Contextual Therapy would assist Tara's parents to change the pathogenic family processes. Treatment would involve family members becoming aware of and communicating their personal loyalties and ledgers of merit and indebtedness and engaging in a process to address and adjust imbalances. In particular, the mother and father would be encouraged to acknowledge Tara's contributions to them and to the family and to recognize her earned entitlement.

In Contextual Therapy, the parents are encouraged to understand the impact of their childhood experiences within their family of origin and to comprehend how this has affected their sense of loyalty, their legacy, and the balancing of indebtedness and entitlement. EMDR can be effectively employed to address painful past memories and to assist the individual in rebalancing the ledger. The result of treatment is expected to include "improvements in mood, attributional style, self-worth, adaptive self-referencing beliefs, and overall psychosocial functioning, plus improved communication and boundary maintenance in the family" (Litt, Chapter 15, p. 319). By the end of treatment Tara's desire to go away to college would be acknowledged as a tribute to all of them, and their progress, and should be celebrated.

Maternal-Infant Bonding Therapy

Tara was born prematurely, weighed only 2 pounds at birth, and was unwell during infancy. In Chapter 6, Antonio Madrid discusses maternal-infant bonding failures, which can occur after a birth like Tara's. He defines maternal-infant bonding (MIB) as "a set of primitive and instinctual emotions and behaviors that exist in the mother" (p. 133) and explains that this differs from the concept of attachment, which is understood as the child's experience. The biological, psychological, and emotional bond between mother and child can be damaged when the child is separated from the mother at birth, or when the mother is emotionally distressed during pregnancy, birth, or early infancy. In his chapter, Madrid provides thorough information about the assessment of maternal-infant bonding failures and the related treatment of the mother.

The experience of Tara's birth, with immediate and prolonged separation while she was being monitored and treated in the Intensive Care Nursery, suggests the possibility of MIB problems. It is not apparent from the information about this case whether such a failure actually occurred. For example, Tara's mother did not describe feeling emotionally disconnected from Tara and did not say, "I don't have any maternal feelings for this child." However, she did describe Tara as hard to soothe, fussy, colicky, and demanding, and it was evident in the mother-daughter relationship that Tara's mother was often dissatisfied with her. To extrapolate the theory, the distant and dismissive behaviors and attitudes that characterized Tara's father may indicate that paternal bonding did not take place.

Assuming that there had been a bonding failure, Tara's parents could have been provided with the MIB Therapy described in Chapter 6. This approach involves four steps: (1) identifying the original impediment to bonding, (2) processing the event, (3) installing an alternative birth, and (4) following up. EMDR is used throughout the process and is integrated with a form of Narrative Therapy (White & Epston, 1990). In this process, Tara's parents could have developed and adopted a new positive birthing story. The expected outcome is that they would then bond with their daughter and experience positive, appropriate feelings toward her. The changed relationship would reduce many of the stressors between Tara and her parents. Even in the absence of a bonding failure, the MIB protocol could be a useful adjunct to the standard EMDR procedures that the therapist would use to treat the trauma of Tara's premature birth and fragility during infancy. In addition, as previously indicated, EMDR processing would still be valuable to address the experiences underlying the mother's previous history of overreacting, anxiety, and depression, as well as the impact the restrictive parenting has had on Tara. Optimally, the father's distant and demeaning attitude to both mother and daughter would also be addressed.

Bowenian Theory

In Chapter 8, Nancy Knudsen outlines the components of Bowen Theory (Bowen, 1978) and describes its integration with EMDR. Bowenian therapy could be applied to assist Tara's parents in differentiating from their respective families of origin, decreasing their emotional fusion, and allowing Tara to pursue her developmental maturation. Currently it appears that Tara is triangulated into her parents' relationship as a way to diffuse their anxiety, lack of closeness, and conflict and that she is the object of the "family projection process" (Bowen, 1978, p. 477) onto which her parents have projected their own anxieties. To adequately assess this family, the therapist would need further information about the parents' relationships with their families of origin to evaluate the multigenerational transmission process.

A skilled Bowenian therapist might engage in genogramming with each of the parents, asking them some of the questions delineated by Shellenberger (Chapter 3) to ascertain more about their family of origin loyalties, attachments, cutoffs, and resentments to determine what unresolved issues from the past need to be revisited and resolved. EMDR could then be used to process the contributory experiences. This would further their own individuation from their respective families of origin, thus freeing up their emotional and psychic energy. They would then be able to foster and enjoy their daughter's striving to differentiate while still remaining connected to her as their adult child. The present experiences that have contributed to the dysfunctional dynamics could be processed with EMDR, along with templates for appropriate future communication and behaviors.

Marital Therapy

Although it is most likely that Tara's family might achieve the greatest benefit from one of the family therapies mentioned here, had her parents been willing, it is possible that the mother and father might be referred for marital therapy. Two specific models of marital therapy are discussed in chapters in this book: Emotionally Focused Therapy (Johnson, 2002, 2004) and Imago Relationship Therapy (Hendrix, 1996, 2001). Both provide treatment to couples with trauma and attachment injuries and seek to facilitate the expression of emotion and self-disclosure and to increase intimacy and compassion. Errebo and Sommers-Flanagan (Chapter 10), Moses (Chapter 7), and Talan (Chapter 9) illustrate how the integration of EMDR with these therapies allows for the resolution of past traumas while repairing injuries and strengthening the current relationship. A specialized form of marital therapy, Therapy of Social Action (Madanes, 1990), is described by Julie Stowasser (Chapter 12) for the treatment of couples in which a partner has been physically violent. Her detailed description emphasizes the importance of safety and accountability.

If Tara's mother and father were to engage in marital therapy in which the therapist utilized Hendrix's (1996, 2001) Imago Relationship Therapy, the sessions would focus on increasing connection, communication, and intimacy. The treatment techniques would involve identification and sharing of the early wounds of childhood while the therapist maintained a safe environment. The pair would engage in the Couples' Dialogue, a strategic communication technique designed to assist the couple in expressing emotions and vulnerabilities. The goal of the therapy is to resolve marital conflict and eliminate criticism and to assist them in becoming an "intentional couple," making conscious and deliberate choices rather than being reactive. The integration of this approach with EMDR is described by Talan (Chapter 9, p. 199), who suggests that the combined treatment approach may result in "faster and deeper resolution of early childhood wounds and trauma" as well as "increased compassion and intimacy."

Emotionally Focused Therapy is an experiential therapy (see Kaslow, Chapter 2) in which couples develop a more secure attachment within the safety of the therapy session. The focus is on the emotional experience of each partner and his or her interpersonal dynamics. The therapist helps the pair to identify and express their experiences "by noticing, reflecting, and validating the affect of each partner and actively restructuring their interpersonal enactment" (Errebo & Sommers-Flanagan, Chapter 10, p. 207). When integrated with EMDR, treatment also focuses on resolving attachment issues from early childhood and attachment injuries in the relationship (Moses, Chapter 7).

Integrative Family Therapy

Like the chapter authors in this book, many other seasoned, well-trained FST clinicians over time increasingly adopt an integrative perspective (Kaslow & Lebow, 2002; Pinsof, 1995), believing that being bound by the parameters of one model, in a doctrinaire manner, does not permit them to offer what might constitute the treatment of choice to a specific couple or family. They expand their repertoire of knowledge and skills and generally include new empirically validated FST approaches such as functional family therapy (Alexander & Sexton, 2002), incorporating the models and associated techniques selectively into their practices. Once they have assessed the presenting problem, the situation, and the clients/patients, they then try to determine the theory (or theories) that has the greatest explanatory power for illuminating this case and tailor their approach accordingly. They may combine several approaches, moving back and forth as needed in any given session, or integrate approaches sequentially, as Pinsof has recommended. In Pinsof's integrative paradigm, one begins (Phase 1) with the presenting problem and tries to deal with it using here-and-now techniques drawn from such theoretical schools as narrative, cognitive-behavioral, communication, structural, strategic, solution-focused, and systemic (see Chapters 2, 5, 11, 13, 14, 16, 17, 18, and Appendix D).

If Tara's family were to receive integrative family therapy, treatment might begin with the therapist contacting the father and telling him it is important that he attend several family sessions if he wants his daughter's emotional state to improve. Once he comes, a contract for three to six family sessions might be negotiated and goals set for the family as a unit. Each member might be asked to tell his or her story about the family's history, emphasizing the family's problems and strong points, and what each would like to see changed. Some initial questions might be directed to the father to emphasize his importance in the family and make his role more central. The therapist might comment that if one member of the family is in pain, all are in pain, and then each could be asked to describe how and where he or she feels or is affected by the pain. The miracle question ("Suppose that one night there is a miracle and while you are sleeping the problem that brought you to therapy is solved. How would you know?") taken from solution-focused therapy might be raised with Tara (de Shazer, 1985; Kaslow, Chapter 2). Her answer might break through the impasse that was engulfing them.

However, if none of these types of intervention worked, separately or in combination, then in Phase 2 the therapist could introduce family of origin work and explore the family's past. Here the integrative family therapist might turn to Bowenian therapy and engage in genogram interviewing (see Chapter 3) to help Tara's parents get in touch with information about and connections to and in their past that are relevant to current thoughts, feelings, and patterns of behavior. Accordingly, the therapist may suggest they make a "voyage home" to visit their families of origin, see how they react, and try to finish unfinished business from the past so they no longer have to project cognitive distortions and overreactivity from the past into the present and onto the next generation—in this instance, Tara.

If the therapist chose to incorporate contextual therapy, he or she might suggest that one or two three-generation sessions be held with Tara, her parents, and members of both parents' families of origin attending. This would allow their legacies and invisible loyalties to be explored in vivo and the ledger of balances redressed so that Tara is freed of obligations that do not rightfully belong to her and all can feel that their entitlements are recognized and honored. All family members could be helped to acknowledge their reciprocal and mutual loyalty and indebtedness and to recognize their shared history of sorrow and joy. They would be encouraged to express their emotions, and the therapist might support each in turn through siding with each, using the strategy of multilateral partiality (Boszormenyi-Nagy & Spark, 1973), so that each voice would be strengthened and heard as separate, yet as part of the family.

If this still does not get to the crux of the problem, the clinician would shift into Phase 3 and undertake psychodynamic, intrapsychic work with the individuals involved, using psychodynamic, object relations, or some aspects of experiential and existential therapies. The therapist in this case might see only Tara and decide it was important to refer each parent to a different therapist so that they would feel they had someone uniquely empathic to turn to. Insight-oriented personal exploration of affects, "repressed" memories, and long ago events could be undertaken and the material brought back to conscious awareness and reinterpreted. For example, with Tara, one might focus on what such continuous themes as lack of bonding with her father, not being liked or accepted by her peers, and smothering by her mother meant to her.

After each had dealt with their own deep-seated dilemmas and sufficient healing had occurred, Phase 4 would be initiated, bringing the family back together to share their new insights, improved self-confidence, and increased ability to empathize and reach out to one another and to accept each other as individuals while also enjoying belonging to their ongoing, dynamically evolving family unit.

Incorporating EMDR and Integrative FST

From an AIP perspective (Shapiro, 2001, 2002; Chapter 1, this book), chronic dysfunctional responses may be the product of insufficient education and modeling (i.e., positive information is not present in the memory networks) or may be caused by unprocessed disturbing experiences that have configured the client's personality and characteristic responses and get triggered by present situations. These unprocessed experiences result in the inappropriate affects, attitudes, and behaviors that inhibit personal happiness and preclude loving and intimate connections, including nurturing family lives. In one approach, EMDR would be incorporated into the integrative FST paradigm after Phase 1 has investigated whether education and opportunities for guided communication can heal the family ruptures and dislocations. As with any clinical situation, it is important not to pathologize reactions that are caused by a simple lack of understanding or opportunity for spontaneous healing.

Assuming that Phase 1 has been unsuccessful, EMDR could be integrated into Phases 2 and 3 to process the experiences that are identified through the genogram, the use of other individual assessment instruments, including a time line, and the clinical interviews, in which there is an identification of negative beliefs, affects, and symptoms (see Shapiro, Chapter 1). Present situations that are distressing for each family member would be explored and EMDR techniques used to identify the earliest memories that set the groundwork for the disturbance. These memories would be processed, along with the current situations that are triggering disturbance. In each instance, positive templates would be constructed that incorporate FST suggestions regarding appropriate communication, boundaries, and hierarchies.

If in Phase 2 the therapist recommended that the parents travel to visit with their own families of origin to complete unfinished business, EMDR would first be used to process the primary disturbing past experiences, any present or anticipatory anxiety, and templates for useful and adaptive encounters. EMDR would also be used to inoculate the clients against potential failures due to the intransigence or dysfunction of their own parents or siblings. Every attempt would be made to ensure that the client would be able to remain stable, resilient, and self-assured regardless of the results of any communication or confrontation. A skillful marital or family therapist of any theoretical orientation who uses this strategy would also do similar preparation for a visit. However, the EMDR processing of these earlier experiences can often make such real-world encounters optional, as the "business" is "finished" internally.

Essentially, all of the themes and potential disturbances mentioned in the previous section would be addressed through incorporating FST procedures with the EMDR three-pronged protocol (i.e., processing of past, present, and future; see Shapiro, Chapter 1) to foster new attitudes, positive affects, and adaptive behaviors. As indicated throughout this book, the integration of EMDR can allow the transformation of the individual family members to take place at an accelerated rate, while family stability is maintained and healthy interactions are enhanced through processing the triggers and templates needed to incorporate adaptive responses and behaviors. Phase 4 would then allow a sharing of achievements, the celebration of common goals, and an opportunity to observe real-world interactions that may be in need of additional attention then or at a future date.

AN INFORMATION PROCESSING FRAMEWORK: SYNERGY IN INTERACTION

It is a tenet of the AIP model that dysfunctional reactions in the present are symptoms of the unprocessed experiences stored within the individual (see

Shapiro, Chapter 1). From this perspective, family dysfunction is viewed as only one symptom of the individual's psychic wounds that will generally be manifested in myriad ways throughout his or her lifetime. Attending directly to these wounds can set the groundwork for a reorganization of the family structure and a transformation of the individual in ways that transcend family boundaries. Within this framework, the FST techniques and models are used to identify targets for individual growth as well as family change. For instance, the genogram would be used to point out how each member could benefit from personal therapy to undo the damage caused by childhood traumas, loyalties, and other dysfunctional patterns. Therapists would explore with the clients ways they are being driven in other social or work environments by the same forces that are causing the anxieties, fears, and unhappiness in the family. The family problems would become a doorway of opportunity to optimize functioning and personal development for all family members in all aspects of life. EMDR therapy for the parents could open the family system so that new and more satisfying interactional skills may take root and also undo the damage caused by their own poor parenting. This can have a far-reaching and profound effect on their own self-image and societal functioning.

The synthesis of EMDR and FST allows clinicians to view the entire spectrum of possibilities and decide on the therapeutic goals with family members who are educated about the effects of previous experiences on every facet of their lives. The therapy contract would decide whether the emphasis is to remain on family interactions or attend to the comprehensive clinical picture. Certainly, attending only to the experiences that are impacting the family directly can liberate the system and stop the cycle of abuse in current and future generations. Alternatively, one can simultaneously focus on comprehensive personal development and process targets that fully liberate the clients as well. The goals of such therapy would be a well-functioning and harmonious family and individual members who have reached their full potential, able to establish nurturing and beneficial relations with peers and other members of society.

CONCLUSIONS

Some FST theorists, therapists, and integrationists use approaches that address intrapsychic issues in an interpersonal context (e.g., Emotionally Focused Therapy, Imago Relationship Therapy, and psychodynamic, attachment, and object relations approaches). These treatments are similar to EMDR in their focus and goals of resolving the problems and healing the wounds that have contributed to causing the dysfunctional behaviors and the individual personality constellations. As Talan (Chapter 9, p. 199) states, "Both practices assist clients in processing unconscious or implicit memories that hold unfulfilled needs of childhood, defenses related to early childhood wounds and trauma, and past experiences that appear to have an effect on current and future relationships." The combination of EMDR and these family systems therapies appears to result in faster and deeper resolution, more comprehensive change, and increased compassion and intimacy.

Other FST theorists and therapists focus primarily on the interpersonal and transactional aspects of the problem and view individuals primarily in the context of their family. They differ from EMDR in their view of pathology, and they provide diverse treatment approaches in an attempt to change the family's dysfunctional interactional patterns and expectations. Perhaps it is this difference in focus and perspective that allows for such an impressive integration at the clinical level. EMDR is primarily intrapersonal, whereas these FST approaches utilize an interpersonal approach. EMDR works at the individual level and transforms the roots of individual pathology, whereas FST treats the family system and focuses on changing interactional patterns. Together these two broad treatment approaches provide a comprehensive approach that addresses all aspects of the individual and systemic dysregulation and dysfunction. As Errebo and Sommers-Flanagan (Chapter 10, p. 220) point out, in integrated marital therapy, "blending the two treatments increases the comprehensiveness of therapy by reducing the reactivity of both partners to current triggers of past traumas while simultaneously increasing the emotional safety and stability of the relationship itself."

Used separately, both FST and EMDR are vibrant, viable, fine approaches to different arrays of problems. When indicated, they may be used in tandem, concurrently, or sequentially, and their combined strength provides a powerful overall intervention modality. As complementary approaches, the combination can support the therapeutic practice of both individual and family therapists to help ease turbulent life situations, foster the development of nurturing families, and enhance individual growth. This synergistic potential has many implications, both personally and globally. To return to the quotation that opened this book:

To put the world right in order, we must first put the nation in order; to put the nation in order, we must first put the family in order; to put the family in order, we must first cultivate our personal life; we must first set our hearts right.

—Confucius

REFERENCES

Alexander, J. F., & Sexton, T. L. (2002). Functional family therapy: A model for treating high-risk, acting out youth. In F. Kaslow & J. Lebow (Eds.), *Comprehensive handbook of psychotherapy: Vol. 4. Integrative/eclectic,* (pp. 111–132). Hoboken, NJ: Wiley.

Boszormenyi-Nagy, I. (1987). *Foundations of contextual therapy: Collected papers of Ivan Boszormenyi-Nagy, MD.* New York: Brunner/Mazel.

Boszormenyi-Nagy, I., & Spark, G. (1973). *Invisible loyalties: Reciprocity in intergenerational family therapy.* New York: Harper & Row.

Bowen, M. (1978). *Family therapy in clinical practice.* New York: Aronson.

de Shazer, S. (1985). *Keys to solution in brief therapy.* New York: Norton.

Giat Roberto, L. (1992). *Transgenerational family therapies.* New York: Guilford Press.

Goldenberg, I., & Goldenberg, H. (2000). *Family therapy: An overview* (5th ed.). Belmont, CA: Brooks/Cole.

Hendrix, H. (1996). The evolution of imago relationship therapy: A personal and professional journey. *Journal of Imago Relationship Therapy, 1*(1), 1–17.

Hendrix, H. (2001). *Getting the love you want: A guide for couples.* New York: First Owl Books. (Original work published 1988)

Johnson, S. M. (2002). *Emotionally focused couple therapy with trauma survivors: Strengthening attachment bonds.* New York: Guilford Press.

Johnson, S. M. (2004). *The practice of emotionally focused couple therapy: Creating connection* (2nd ed.). New York: Brunner-Routledge.

Kaslow, F. W., & Lebow, J. (Eds.). (2002). *Comprehensive handbook of psychotherapy: Vol. 4. Integrative/eclectic.* Hoboken, NJ: Wiley.

Madanes, C. (1990). *Sex, love, and violence.* New York: Norton.

Napier, A. Y., & Whitaker, C. (1978). *The family crucible.* New York: Harper & Row.

Pinsof, W. M. (1995). *Integrative problem centered therapy.* New York: Basic Books.

Sander, F. M. (1979). *Individual and family therapy: Toward an integration.* New York: Aronson.

Shapiro, F. (2001). *Eye movement desensitization and reprocessing: Basic principles, protocols and procedures* (2nd ed.). New York: Guilford Press.

Shapiro, F. (2002). Paradigms, processing, and personality development. In F. Shapiro (Ed.), *EMDR as an integrative psychotherapy approach: Experts of diverse orientations explore the paradigm prism* (pp. 3–26). Washington, DC: American Psychological Association Books.

von Bertalanaffy, L. (1968). *General system theory.* New York: George Braziller.

White, M., & Epston, D. (1990). *Narrative means to therapeutic ends.* New York: Norton.

Appendixes

EMDR Resources

EMDR Network: http://www.emdrnetwork.org
This web site provides access to information important for clients and clinicians. Links are provided to updated research and clinical information. The organizations listed are well established and professionally scrutinized to uphold the highest standards.

EMDR Humanitarian Assistance Programs: http://emdrhap.org
EMDR Humanitarian Assistance Programs (HAP), a 501(c)(3) nonprofit organization, can be described as the mental health equivalent of Doctors Without Borders: a global network of clinicians who travel anywhere there is a need to stop suffering and prevent the aftereffects of trauma and violence. It provides low-cost training to nonprofit agencies and the U.S. Department of Veterans Affairs. HAP also provides a traumatology workshop to educate helping professionals and the general public about trauma and its effects.

HAP's Trauma Recovery Network coordinates clinicians to treat victims and emergency service workers after crises such as the Oklahoma City bombing, the 9/11 terrorist attacks, and Hurricane Katrina. HAP is supported by tax-deductible contributions from the general public and by volunteer services of clinicians and others. Clinical aids and manuals are also available. For more information, contact

EMDR Humanitarian Assistance Programs
P.O. Box 6505 Hamden, CT 06517
Phone: (203) 288-4450
Fax: (203) 288-4060
E-mail: contact@emdrhap.org
Web site: http://emdrhap.org

EMDR International Association: http://www.emdria.org
The EMDR International Association is a professional organization of EMDR-trained therapists and researchers devoted to promoting the highest standards of excellence and integrity in EMDR practice, research, and education for the public good.

EMDRIA provides educational materials, publications, and an annual conference. In addition, EMDRIA evaluates and sets standards for EMDR trainings and specialty programs and certifies EMDR-trained clinicians, consultants, and instructors of the basic training of EMDR. For more information about EMDRIA, contact:

EMDR International Association
5806 Mesa Drive, Suite 360, Austin, TX 78731
Phone: (512) 451-5200
E-mail: info@emdria.org
Web site: http://www.emdria.org

EMDR Europe Association: http://www.emdr-europe.org
With 14 member nations, the EMDR Europe Association is the governing body for all the national European EMDR Associations and Israel. It works in close cooperation with EMDRIA and performs a similar function as the overseeing professional organization of European EMDR-trained therapists and researchers. It is also devoted to promoting the highest possible standard of excellence and integrity in EMDR practice, research, and education. The web site contains an overview of EMDR, research, clinician resources, and training opportunities. Further details can be found on their web site:

http://www.emdr-europe.org
E-mail: info@emdr-europe.org

EMDR Institute: http://www.emdr.com
Dr. Shapiro, the originator of EMDR, founded the EMDR Institute in 1990 and has trained all workshop leaders. Trainings are conducted worldwide in strict adherence to the researched protocols. The EMDR Institute also provides access to 63,000 graduates of its programs for client referrals. Its web site contains a list of commonly asked questions, latest research, and published clinical applications.

The EMDR Institute is one of the many training organizations certified by EMDRIA (see above). Trainings authorized by the Institute display the EMDR Institute logo.

For further information on training or referral:

EMDR Institute
P.O. Box 750, Watsonville, CA 95077
Phone: (831) 761-1040
Fax: (831) 761-1204
E-mail: inst@emdr.com
Web site: http://www.EMDR.com

EMDR Trauma Research Findings and Further Reading

INTERNATIONAL TREATMENT GUIDELINES

American Psychiatric Association. (2004). *Practice guideline for the treatment of patients with acute stress disorder and posttraumatic stress disorder.* Arlington, VA: American Psychiatric Association Practice Guidelines.

    EMDR given the highest level of recommendation (category for robust empirical support and demonstrated effectiveness) in the treatment of trauma.

Bleich, A., Kotler, M., Kutz, I., & Shalev, A. (2002). *Guidelines for the assessment and professional intervention with terror victims in the hospital and in the community.* A position paper of the (Israeli) National Council for Mental Health, Jerusalem, Israel.

    EMDR is one of only three methods recommended for treatment of terror victims.

Chambless, D. L., Baker, M. J., Baucom, D. H., Calhoun, K. S., Crits-Christoph, P., Daiuto, A., et al. (1998). Update on empirically validated therapies: II. *Clinical Psychologist, 51*(1), 3–16.

    According to a task force of the Clinical Division of the American Psychological Association, the only methods empirically supported for the treatment of any Posttraumatic Stress Disorder (PTSD) population were EMDR, exposure therapy, and stress inoculation therapy.

CREST. (2003). *The management of post traumatic stress disorder in adults.* A publication of the Clinical Resource Efficiency Support Team of the Northern Ireland Department of Health, Social Services and Public Safety, Belfast.

    Of all the psychotherapies, EMDR and cognitive-behavioral therapy (CBT) were stated to be the treatments of choice.

Department of Veterans Affairs & Department of Defense. (2004). *VA/DoD clinical practice guideline for the management of post-traumatic stress.* Washington, DC: Author. Available from http://www.oqp.med.va.gov/cpg/PTSD/PTSD_cpg/frameset.htm.

    EMDR was placed in the "A" category as "strongly recommended" for the treatment of trauma.

Dutch National Steering Committee Guidelines Mental Health Care. (2003). *Multidisciplinary guideline: Anxiety disorders.* Utrecht, The Netherlands: Quality Institute Heath Care CBO/ Trimbos Institute.

    EMDR and CBT are both treatments of choice for PTSD.

Foa, E. B., Keane, T. M., & Friedman, M. J. (2000). *Effective treatments for PTSD: Practice guidelines of the International Society for Traumatic Stress Studies.* New York: Guilford Press.

    EMDR is listed as an efficacious treatment for PTSD.

INSERM. (2004). *Psychotherapy: An evaluation of three approaches.* Paris: French National Institute of Health and Medical Research.

>   Of the different psychotherapies, EMDR and CBT were stated to be the treatments of choice for trauma victims.

National Institute for Clinical Excellence. (2005). *Post traumatic stress disorder (PTSD): The management of adults and children in primary and secondary care.* London: NICE Guidelines.

>   Trauma-focused CBT and EMDR were stated to be empirically supported treatments for adult PTSD.

Sjöblom, P. O., Andréewitch, S., Bejerot, S., Mörtberg, E., Brinck, U., Ruck, C., et al. (2003). *Regional treatment recommendation for anxiety disorders.* Stockholm, Sweden: Medical Program Committee/Stockholm City Council.

>   Of all psychotherapies, CBT and EMDR are recommended as treatments of choice for PTSD.

Therapy Advisor. (2004). Available from http://www.therapyadvisor.com.

>   This web site, sponsored by the National Institute of Mental Health (NIMH), lists empirically supported methods for a variety of disorders. EMDR is one of three treatments listed for PTSD.

United Kingdom Department of Health. (2001). *Treatment choice in psychological therapies and counseling evidence based clinical practice guideline.* London: Author.

>   Best evidence of efficacy was reported for EMDR, exposure, and stress inoculation therapies.

META-ANALYSES

Bradley, R., Greene, J., Russ, E., Dutra, L., & Westen, D. (2005). A multidimensional meta-analysis of psychotherapy for PTSD. *American Journal of Psychiatry, 162,* 214–227.

>   EMDR is equivalent to exposure and other cognitive-behavioral treatments. It should be noted that exposure therapy uses 1 to 2 hours of daily homework and EMDR uses none.

Davidson, P. R., & Parker, K. C. H. (2001). Eye movement desensitization and reprocessing (EMDR): A meta-analysis. *Journal of Consulting and Clinical Psychology, 69,* 305–316.

>   EMDR is equivalent to exposure and other cognitive-behavioral treatments. It should be noted that exposure therapy uses 1 to 2 hours of daily homework and EMDR uses none.

Maxfield, L., & Hyer, L. A. (2002). The relationship between efficacy and methodology in studies investigating EMDR treatment of PTSD. *Journal of Clinical Psychology, 58,* 23–41.

>   A comprehensive meta-analysis reported that the more rigorous the study, the larger the effect.

Van Etten, M., & Taylor, S. (1998). Comparative efficacy of treatments for posttraumatic stress disorder: A meta-analysis. *Clinical Psychology and Psychotherapy, 5,* 126–144.

>   This meta-analysis determined that EMDR and behavior therapy were superior to psychopharmaceuticals. EMDR was more efficient than behavior therapy, with results obtained in one-third the time.

RANDOMIZED CLINICAL TRIALS

Carlson, J., Chemtob, C. M., Rusnak, K., Hedlund, N. L., & Muraoka, M. Y. (1998). Eye movement desensitization and reprocessing (EMDR): Treatment for combat-related posttraumatic stress disorder. *Journal of Traumatic Stress, 11,* 3–24.

>   Twelve sessions of EMDR eliminated PTSD in 77% of the multiply traumatized combat veterans studied. Effects were maintained at follow-up. This is the only randomized

study to provide a full course of treatment with combat veterans. Other studies (e.g., Pitman et al., 1996; Macklin et al., 2000) evaluated treatment of only one or two memories, which, according to the International Society for Traumatic Stress Studies Practice Guidelines, is inappropriate for multiple-trauma survivors. The VA/DoD Practice Guideline also indicates that these studies (often with only two sessions) offered insufficient treatment doses for veterans.

Chemtob, C. M., Nakashima, J., & Carlson, J. G. (2002). Brief-treatment for elementary school children with disaster-related PTSD: A field study. *Journal of Clinical Psychology, 58,* 99–112. EMDR was found to be an effective treatment for children with disaster-related PTSD who had not responded to another intervention. This is the first controlled study for disaster-related PTSD and the first controlled study examining the treatment of children with PTSD.

Edmond, T., Rubin, A., & Wambach, K. (1999). The effectiveness of EMDR with adult female survivors of childhood sexual abuse. *Social Work Research, 23,* 103–116. EMDR treatment resulted in lower scores (fewer clinical symptoms) on all four of the outcome measures at the 3-month follow-up, compared to those in the routine treatment condition. The EMDR group also improved on all standardized measures at 18 months follow-up (Edmond & Rubin, 2004).

Edmond, T., Sloan, L., & McCarty, D. (2004). Sexual abuse survivors' perceptions of the effectiveness of EMDR and eclectic therapy: A mixed-methods study. *Research on Social Work Practice, 14,* 259–272. Combination of qualitative and quantitative analyses of treatment outcomes with important implications for future rigorous research. Survivors' narratives indicate that EMDR produces greater trauma resolution, whereas in eclectic therapy, survivors value more highly their relationship with their therapist, through whom they learn effective coping strategies.

Ironson, G. I., Freund, B., Strauss, J. L., & Williams, J. (2002). Comparison of two treatments for traumatic stress: A community-based study of EMDR and prolonged exposure. *Journal of Clinical Psychology, 58,* 113–128. Both EMDR and prolonged exposure produced a significant reduction in PTSD and depression symptoms. This study found that 70% of EMDR participants achieved a good outcome in three active treatment sessions, compared to 29% of persons in the prolonged exposure condition. EMDR also had fewer dropouts.

Jaberghaderi, N., Greenwald, R., Rubin, A., Dolatabadim, S., & Zand, S. O. (2004). A comparison of CBT and EMDR for sexually abused Iranian girls. *Clinical Psychology and Psychotherapy, 11,* 358–368. Both EMDR and CBT produced significant reduction in PTSD and behavior problems. EMDR was significantly more efficient, using approximately half the number of sessions to achieve results.

Lee, C., Gavriel, H., Drummond, P., Richards, J., & Greenwald, R. (2002). Treatment of posttraumatic stress disorder: A comparison of stress inoculation training with prolonged exposure and eye movement desensitization and reprocessing. *Journal of Clinical Psychology, 58,* 1071–1089. Both EMDR and stress inoculation therapy plus prolonged exposure (SITPE) produced significant improvement, with EMDR achieving greater improvement on PTSD intrusive symptoms. Participants in the EMDR condition showed greater gains at 3-month follow-up. EMDR required 3 hours of homework compared to 28 hours for SITPE.

Marcus, S., Marquis, P., & Sakai, C. (1997). Controlled study of treatment of PTSD using EMDR in an HMO setting. *Psychotherapy, 34,* 307–315. Funded by Kaiser Permanente. Results show that 100% of single-trauma and 80% of multiple-trauma survivors were no longer diagnosed with PTSD after six 50-minute sessions.

Marcus, S., Marquis, P., & Sakai, C. (2004). Three- and 6-month follow-up of EMDR treatment of PTSD in an HMO setting. *International Journal of Stress Management, 11,* 195–208.

>Funded by Kaiser Permanente. Follow-up evaluation indicates that a relatively small number of EMDR sessions result in substantial benefits that are maintained over time.

Power, K. G., McGoldrick, T., Brown, K., Buchanan, R., Sharp, D., Swanson, V., & Karatzias, A. (2002). A controlled comparison of eye movement desensitization and reprocessing versus exposure plus cognitive restructuring, versus waiting list in the treatment of posttraumatic stress disorder. *Journal of Clinical Psychology and Psychotherapy, 9,* 299–318.

>Both EMDR and exposure therapy plus cognitive restructuring (with daily homework) produced significant improvement. EMDR was more beneficial for depression and required fewer treatment sessions.

Rothbaum, B. (1997). A controlled study of eye movement desensitization and reprocessing in the treatment of posttraumatic stress disordered sexual assault victims. *Bulletin of the Menninger Clinic, 61,* 317–334.

>Three 90-minute sessions of EMDR eliminated PTSD in 90% of rape victims.

Rothbaum, B. O., Astin, M. C., & Marsteller, F. (2005). Prolonged exposure versus eye movement desensitization (EMDR) for PTSD rape victims. *Journal of Traumatic Stress, 18,* 607–616.

>In this NIMH-funded study, both treatments did equally well, although EMDR utilized no homework and less exposure time.

Scheck, M., Schaeffer, J. A., & Gillette, C. (1998). Brief psychological intervention with traumatized young women: The efficacy of eye movement desensitization and reprocessing. *Journal of Traumatic Stress, 11,* 25–44.

>Two sessions of EMDR reduced psychological distress scores in traumatized young women and brought scores within 1 standard deviation of the norm.

Shapiro, F. (1989). Efficacy of the eye movement desensitization procedure in the treatment of traumatic memories. *Journal of Traumatic Stress Studies, 2,* 199–223.

>This seminal study appeared the same year as the first controlled studies of CBT treatments. Three-month follow-up indicated substantial effects on distress and behavioral reports. Marred by lack of standardized measures and the originator serving as sole therapist.

Soberman, G. B., Greenwald, R., & Rule, D. L. (2002). A controlled study of eye movement desensitization and reprocessing (EMDR) for boys with conduct problems. *Journal of Aggression, Maltreatment, and Trauma, 6,* 217–236.

>The addition of three sessions of EMDR resulted in large and significant reductions of memory-related distress and problem behaviors by 2-month follow-up.

Taylor, S., Thordarson, D. S., Maxfield, L., Fedoroff, I. C., Lovell, K., & Ogrodniczuk, J. (2003). Comparative efficacy, speed, and adverse effects of three PTSD treatments: Exposure therapy, EMDR, and relaxation training. *Journal of Consulting and Clinical Psychology, 71,* 330–338.

>The only randomized study to show exposure therapy to be statistically superior to EMDR on two subscales (out of 10). This study used therapist-assisted in vivo exposure, (where the therapist takes the person to previously avoided areas), in addition to imaginal exposure and 1 hour of daily homework (@ 50 hours). The EMDR group used only standard sessions and no homework.

Van der Kolk, B., Spinazzola, J., Blaustein, M., Hopper, J., Hopper, E., Korn, D., et al. (in press). A randomized clinical trial of EMDR, fluoxetine and pill placebo in the treatment of PTSD: Treatment effects and long-term maintenance. *Journal of Clinical Psychiatry.*

>EMDR was superior to both control conditions in the amelioration of both PTSD symptoms and depression. Upon termination of therapy, the EMDR group continued to improve while the Floxetine participants again became symptomatic.

Vaughan, K., Armstrong, M. F., Gold, R., O'Connor, N., Jenneke, W., & Tarrier, N. (1994). A trial of eye movement desensitization compared to image habituation training and applied muscle relaxation in posttraumatic stress disorder. *Journal of Behavior Therapy and Experimental Psychiatry, 25,* 283–291.

> All treatments led to significant decreases in PTSD symptoms for subjects in the treatment groups as compared to those on a waiting list, with a greater reduction in the EMDR group, particularly with respect to intrusive symptoms. In the 2 to 3 weeks of the study, 40 to 60 additional minutes of daily homework were part of the treatment in the other two conditions.

Wilson, S., Becker, L. A., & Tinker, R. H. (1995). Eye movement desensitization and reprocessing (EMDR): Treatment for psychologically traumatized individuals. *Journal of Consulting and Clinical Psychology, 63,* 928–937.

> Three sessions of EMDR produced clinically significant change in traumatized civilians on multiple measures.

Wilson, S., Becker, L. A., & Tinker, R. H. (1997). Fifteen-month follow-up of eye movement desensitization and reprocessing (EMDR) treatment of posttraumatic stress disorder and psychological trauma. *Journal of Consulting and Clinical Psychology, 65,* 1047–1056.

> Follow-up at 15 months showed maintenance of positive treatment effects with 84% remission of PTSD diagnosis.

NONRANDOMIZED STUDIES

Devilly, G. J., & Spence, S. H. (1999). The relative efficacy and treatment distress of EMDR and a cognitive behavioral trauma treatment protocol in the amelioration of posttraumatic stress disorder. *Journal of Anxiety Disorders, 13,* 131–157.

> The only EMDR research study that found CBT superior to EMDR. The study is marred by poor treatment delivery and higher expectations in the CBT condition. Treatment was delivered in both conditions by the developer of the CBT protocol.

Fernandez, I., Gallinari, E., & Lorenzetti, A. (2004). A school-based EMDR intervention for children who witnessed the Pirelli Building airplane crash in Milan, Italy. *Journal of Brief Therapy, 2,* 129–136.

> A group intervention of EMDR was provided to 236 schoolchildren exhibiting PTSD symptoms 30 days post-incident. At 4-month follow-up, teachers reported that all but two children evinced a return to normal functioning after treatment.

Grainger, R. D., Levin, C., Allen-Byrd, L., Doctor, R. M., & Lee, H. (1997). An empirical evaluation of eye movement desensitization and reprocessing (EMDR) with survivors of a natural catastrophe. *Journal of Traumatic Stress, 10,* 665–671.

> A study of Hurricane Andrew survivors found significant differences on the Impact of Events scale and subjective distress in a comparison of EMDR and a nontreatment condition.

Jarero, I., Artigas, L., & Hartung, J. (2006). EMDR integrative group treatment protocol: A post-disaster trauma intervention for children and adults. *Traumatology, 12*(2).

> A study of 200 children treated with a group protocol after a flood in Mexico indicates that one session of treatment reduced trauma symptoms from the severe range to low (subclinical) levels of distress. Data from successful treatment at other disaster sites are also reported.

Konuk, E., Knipe, J., Eke, I., Yuksek, H., Yurtsever, A., & Ostep, S. (2006). The effects of EMDR therapy on post-traumatic stress disorder in survivors of the 1999 Marmara, Turkey, earthquake. *International Journal of Stress Management, 13,* 291–308.

Data reported on a representative sample of 1500 earthquake victims indicated that five sessions of EMDR successfully eliminated PTSD in 92.7% of those treated, with a reduction of symptoms in the remaining participants.

Puffer, M., Greenwald, R., & Elrod, D. (1997). A single session EMDR study with 20 traumatized children and adolescents. *Traumatology, 3*(2).

In this delayed treatment comparison, over half of the participants moved from clinical to normal levels on the Impact of Events scale, and all but 3 showed at least partial symptom relief on several measures at 1 to 3 months following a single EMDR session.

Silver, S. M., Brooks, A., & Obenchain, J. (1995). Eye movement desensitization and reprocessing treatment of Vietnam War veterans with PTSD: Comparative effects with biofeedback and relaxation training. *Journal of Traumatic Stress, 8,* 337–342.

One of only two EMDR research studies that evaluated a clinically relevant course of EMDR treatment with combat veterans (e.g., more than one or two memories; see Carlson et al., 1998). The analysis of an inpatient veterans' PTSD program ($N = 100$) found EMDR to be vastly superior to biofeedback and relaxation training on seven of eight measures.

Silver, S. M., Rogers, S., Knipe, J., & Colelli, G. (2005). EMDR therapy following the 9/11 terrorist attacks: A community-based intervention project in New York City. *International Journal of Stress Management, 12,* 29–42.

Clients made highly significant positive gains on a range of outcome variables, including validated psychometrics and self-report scales. Analyses of the data indicate that EMDR is a useful treatment intervention in the immediate aftermath of disaster as well as later.

Solomon, R. M., & Kaufman, T. E. (2002). A peer support workshop for the treatment of traumatic stress of railroad personnel: Contributions of eye movement desensitization and reprocessing (EMDR). *Journal of Brief Therapy, 2,* 27–33.

Sixty railroad employees who had experienced fatal grade-crossing accidents were evaluated for workshop outcomes and for the additive effects of EMDR treatment. Although the workshop was successful, in this setting, the addition of a short session of EMDR (5–40 minutes) led to significantly lower, subclinical scores that further decreased at follow-up.

Sprang, G. (2001). The use of eye movement desensitization and reprocessing (EMDR) in the treatment of traumatic stress and complicated mourning: Psychological and behavioral outcomes. *Research on Social Work Practice, 11,* 300–320.

In a multisite study, EMDR significantly reduced symptoms more than the CBT treatment on behavioral measures and on four of five psychosocial measures. EMDR was more efficient, inducing change at an earlier stage and requiring fewer sessions.

INFORMATION PROCESSING, PROCEDURES, AND MECHANISM OF ACTION

EMDR contains many procedures and elements that contribute to treatment effects. Although the methodology used in EMDR has been extensively validated (see previous sources), questions still remain regarding mechanism of action. An information processing model (Shapiro, 2001, 2002) is used to explain EMDR's clinical effects and guide clinical practice. This model is not linked to any specific neurobiological mechanism because the field of neurobiology is as yet unable to determine the neurobiological concomitants of any form of psychotherapy (nor of many medications). However, because EMDR achieves clinical effects without the need for homework or the prolonged focus used in exposure therapies, attention has been paid to the possible neurobiological processes that might be evoked. Although the eye movements (and other dual attention stimulations) are only one procedural element, this aspect has come under greatest scrutiny. Controlled studies evaluating mechanism of action of the eye movement component follow this section.

Lee, C., Taylor, G., & Drummond, P. D. (in press). The active ingredient in EMDR: Is it traditional exposure or dual focus of attention? *Clinical Psychology and Psychotherapy.*
This study tested whether the content of participants' responses during EMDR is similar to that thought to be effective for traditional exposure treatments (reliving), or is more consistent with distancing, which would be expected given Shapiro's proposal of dual process of attention. Greatest improvement on a measure of PTSD symptoms occurred when the participant processed the trauma in a more detached manner.

MacCulloch, M. J., & Feldman, P. (1996). Eye movement desensitization treatment utilizes the positive visceral element of the investigatory reflex to inhibit the memories of posttraumatic stress disorder: A theoretical analysis. *British Journal of Psychiatry, 169,* 571–579.
One of a variety of articles positing an orienting response as a contributing element (see Shapiro, 2001, for comprehensive examination of theories and suggested research parameters). This theory has received controlled research support (Barrowcliff et al., 2003, 2004).

Perkins, B. R., & Rouanzoin, C. C. (2002). A critical evaluation of current views regarding eye movement desensitization and reprocessing (EMDR): Clarifying points of confusion. *Journal of Clinical Psychology, 58,* 77–97.
Reviews common errors and misperceptions of the procedures, research, and theory.

Raboni, M.R., Tufik, S., and Suchecki, D. (2006). Treatment of PTSD by eye movement desensitization and reprocessing improves sleep quality, quality of life and perception of stress. *Annals of the New York Academy of Science, 1071,* 508-513.
Specifically citing the hypothesis that EMDR induces processing effects similar to REM sleep (see also Stickgold, 2002), polysomnograms indicated a change in sleep patterns post treatment, and improvement on all measures including anxiety, depression, and quality of life after a mean of five sessions.

Ray, A. L., & Zbik, A. (2001). Cognitive behavioral therapies and beyond. In C. D. Tollison, J. R. Satterhwaite, & J. W. Tollison (Eds.) *Practical pain management* (3rd ed., pp. 189–208). Philadelphia: Lippincott.
Note that the application of EMDR guided by its information processing model appears to afford benefits to chronic pain patients not found in other treatments.

Ricci, R. J., Clayton, C. A., & Shapiro, F. (2006). Some effects of EMDR treatment with previously abused child molesters: Theoretical reviews and preliminary findings. *Journal of Forensic Psychiatry and Psychology, 17,* 538–562.
As predicted by the Adaptive Information Processing model the EMDR treatment of the molesters' own childhood victimization resulted in a decrease in deviant arousal as measured by the plethysmograph, a decrease in sexual thoughts, and increased victim empathy.

Rogers, S., & Silver, S. M. (2002). Is EMDR an exposure therapy? A review of trauma protocols. *Journal of Clinical Psychology, 58,* 43–59.
Theoretical, clinical, and procedural differences referencing 2 decades of CBT and EMDR research.

Servan-Schreiber, D., Schooler, J., Dew, M. A., Carter, C., & Bartone, P. (2006). EMDR for PTSD: A pilot blinded, randomized study of stimulation type. *Psychotherapy and Psychosomatics, 75,* 290–297.
Twenty-one patients with single-event PTSD (average score on the Impact of Events scale: 49.5) received three consecutive sessions of EMDR with three different types of

auditory and kinesthetic stimulation. All were clinically useful. However, alternating stimulation appeared to confer an additional benefit to the EMDR procedure.

Shapiro, F. (2001). *Eye movement desensitization and reprocessing: Basic principles, protocols and procedures* (2nd ed.). New York: Guilford Press.

> EMDR is an eight-phase psychotherapy with standardized procedures and protocols that are all believed to contribute to therapeutic effect. This text provides descriptions and clinical transcripts.

Shapiro, F. (2002). (Ed.). *EMDR as an integrative psychotherapy approach: Experts of diverse orientations explore the paradigm prism.* Washington, DC: American Psychological Association Books.

> EMDR is an integrative approach distinct from other forms of psychotherapy. Experts of the major psychotherapy orientations identify and highlight various procedural elements.

Stickgold, R. (2002). EMDR: A putative neurobiological mechanism of action. *Journal of Clinical Psychology, 58,* 61–75.

> Comprehensive explanation of the potential links to the processes that occur in REM sleep. Controlled studies have evaluated and supported these theories (see next section; Christman et al., 2003; Kuiken et al., 2001–2002).

RANDOMIZED STUDIES OF HYPOTHESES REGARDING EYE MOVEMENTS

A number of International Practice Guideline committees have reported that the clinical component analyses reviewed by Davidson and Parker (2001) are not well designed (International Society for Traumatic Stress Studies/ISTSS, 2000; DoD/DVA, 2004). Davidson and Parker note that there is a trend toward significance for eye movements when the studies conducted with clinical populations are examined separately. Unfortunately, even these studies are flawed. As noted in the ISTSS guidelines (Chemtob et al., 2000), because these clinical populations received insufficient treatment doses to obtain substantial main effects, they are inappropriate for component analyses. However, as noted in the DoD/DVA guidelines, the eye movements used in EMDR have been separately evaluated by numerous memory researchers. These studies have found a direct effect on emotional arousal, imagery vividness, attentional flexibility, and memory association.

Andrade, J., Kavanagh, D., & Baddeley, A. (1997). Eye-movements and visual imagery: A working memory approach to the treatment of posttraumatic stress disorder. *British Journal of Clinical Psychology, 36,* 209–223.

> Tested the working memory theory. Eye movements were superior to control conditions in reducing image vividness and emotionality.

Barrowcliff, A. L., Gray, N. S., Freeman, T. C. A., & MacCulloch, M. J. (2004). Eye-movements reduce the vividness, emotional valence and electrodermal arousal associated with negative autobiographical memories. *Journal of Forensic Psychiatry and Psychology, 15,* 325–345.

> Tested the reassurance reflex model. Eye movements were superior to control conditions in reducing image vividness and emotionality.

Barrowcliff, A. L., Gray, N. S., MacCulloch, S., Freeman, T. C. A., & MacCulloch, M. J. (2003). Horizontal rhythmical eye-movements consistently diminish the arousal provoked by auditory stimuli. *British Journal of Clinical Psychology, 42,* 289–302.

Tested the reassurance reflex model. Eye movements were superior to control conditions in reducing arousal provoked by auditory stimuli.

Christman, S. D., Garvey, K. J., Propper, R. E., & Phaneuf, K. A. (2003). Bilateral eye movements enhance the retrieval of episodic memories. *Neuropsychology, 17,* 221–229.

Tested cortical activation theories. Results provide indirect support for the orienting response/REM theories suggested by Stickgold (2002). Saccadic eye movements, but not tracking eye movements, were superior to control conditions in episodic retrieval.

Kavanagh, D. J., Freese, S., Andrade, J., & May, J. (2001). Effects of visuospatial tasks on desensitization to emotive memories. *British Journal of Clinical Psychology, 40,* 267–280.

Tested the working memory theory. Eye movements were superior to control conditions in reducing within-session image vividness and emotionality. There was no difference 1-week post.

Kuiken, D., Bears, M., Miall, D., & Smith, L. (2001–2002). Eye movement desensitization reprocessing facilitates attentional orienting. *Imagination, Cognition and Personality, 21*(1), 3–20.

Tested the orienting response theory related to REM-type mechanisms. Indicated that the eye movement condition was correlated with increased attentional flexibility. Eye movements were superior to control conditions.

Sharpley, C. F., Montgomery, I. M., & Scalzo, L. A. (1996). Comparative efficacy of EMDR and alternative procedures in reducing the vividness of mental images. *Scandinavian Journal of Behavior Therapy, 25,* 37–42.

Results suggest support for the working memory theory. Eye movements were superior to control conditions in reducing image vividness.

Van den Hout, M., Muris, P., Salemink, E., & Kindt, M. (2001). Autobiographical memories become less vivid and emotional after eye movements. *British Journal of Clinical Psychology, 40,* 121–130.

Tested their theory that eye movements change the somatic perceptions accompanying retrieval, leading to decreased affect, and therefore decreasing vividness. Eye movements were superior to control conditions in reducing image vividness. Unlike control conditions, eye movements also decreased emotionality.

ADDITIONAL NEUROBIOLOGICAL EVALUATIONS

Lamprecht, F., Kohnke, C., Lempa, W., Sack, M., Matzke, M., & Munte, T. (2004). Event-related potentials and EMDR treatment of posttraumatic stress disorder. *Neuroscience Research, 49,* 267–272.

Lansing, K., Amen, D. G., Hanks, C., & Rudy, L. (2005). High resolution brain SPECT imaging and EMDR in police officers with PTSD. *Journal of Neuropsychiatry and Clinical Neurosciences, 17,* 526–532.

Levin, P., Lazrove, S., & van der Kolk, B. A. (1999). What psychological testing and neuroimaging tell us about the treatment of posttraumatic stress disorder (PTSD) by eye movement desensitization and reprocessing (EMDR). *Journal of Anxiety Disorders, 13,* 159–172.

Oh, D.-H., & Choi, J. (2004). Changes in the regional cerebral perfusion after eye movement desensitization and reprocessing: A SPECT study of two cases. *Korean Journal of Biological Psychiatry, 11,* 173–180.

van der Kolk, B., Burbridge, J., & Suzuki, J. (1997). The psychobiology of traumatic memory: Clinical implications of neuroimaging studies. *Annals of the New York Academy of Sciences, 821,* 99–113.

APPENDIX C

Family Systems Resources

PART I—FAMILY THERAPY/PSYCHOLOGY ORGANIZATIONS AND RESOURCES

American Association for Marriage and Family Therapy
112 South Alfred Street
Alexandria, VA 22314
Phone: (703) 838-9808
Fax: (703) 838-9805

American Board of Family Psychologists (National certifying organization)
c/o American Board of Professional Psychology
300 Drayton Street, 3rd Floor
Savannah, GA 31401
Phone and Fax: (800) 255-7792

American Family Therapy Academy
1608 Twentieth Street, NW
4th Floor
Washington, DC 20009
Phone: (202) 483-8001
Fax: (202) 483-8002
E-mail: afta@afta.org

American Psychological Association
Division of Family Psychology (#43)
c/o Division Services Office
750 First St., NE
Washington, DC, 20002-4242
Phone: (800) 374-2721
E-mail: KCooke@apa.org

International Academy of Family Psychology
Gregory J. Jurkovic, PhD, President (2006–2010)
Department of Psychology
Georgia State University
University Plaza
Atlanta, GA 30303
Phone: Office (404) 651-2283
        University (404) 651-3271
        Cell (404) 401-1778
Fax: (404) 651-1391
E-mail: gjurkovic@gsu.edu

International Family Therapy Association
c/o William J. Hiebert, STM, Central Office Director
1800 Third Avenue
Suite 512
Rock Island, IL 61201-8000
Phone: (309) 786-4491
Fax: (309) 786-0205
E-mail: iftanews@aol.com

PART II—GENOGRAM COMPUTER PROGRAMS

Genogram-Maker Millennium (computer software, version 1.1.6), 2005
GenoWare, Inc.
http://www.genogram.org

Relativity (computer software, version 3.0), 2003
WonderWare, Inc.
http://www.interpersonaluniverse.net

A Brief History of the Field of Family Psychology and Therapy

Florence W. Kaslow

This appendix briefly highlights the emergence of *some* of the major schools of family therapy to provide the background for the theories discussed in Chapter 2 and to show the concurrent and continuous evolution of many theories. Not all can be covered, but hopefully enough have been to illustrate how the first generation of leaders emerged and new theorists continue to come to the fore. (For a fuller history of family therapy in the United States and around the world, see Guerin, 1976; F. Kaslow, 1990c, 2000a, 2000b.)

The emergence of the field of family therapy dates from the early 1960s and is marked historically by the appearance of a special literature in the form of books (see, e.g., groundbreaking early books by pioneers like Ackerman, 1961; Boszormenyi-Nagy & Framo, 1965/1985; Bowen, 1959, 1988; Satir, 1964, 1967, 1972; Whitaker, 1975, 1976) and journal articles that first appeared in omnibus journals, followed by the inauguration of a separate journal, *Family Process,* in 1966. This development and presentations by these and other early pioneers at various professional conferences were followed by the formation of some Family Institutes, where the therapeutic techniques that accompanied the evolving theories were being used in clinical practice. Apprentice models of teaching became popular as trainees clamored to learn these new theories and techniques from those who emerged quickly as the masters. Viewing through one-way mirrors, sitting in as cotherapists, and later call-in techniques and the use of split teams all became strategies used to teach and learn family therapy. These techniques swiftly changed extant views about how confidentiality is perceived and definitions of who is the patient.

In the ensuing 55 years, the theories and methodologies of these mavericks have been expanded, taught at the numerous Family Institutes established by the progenitors of the different models and, increasingly, also taught in graduate departments of psychology and social work, as well as in psychiatry (and psychology) internship and residency programs. Graduate programs in marital and family therapy (MFT) have been established in some colleges and universities, and those that meet the curriculum and other established criteria have become accredited by the American Association of Marriage and Family Therapists

(AAMFT), which is authorized by the U.S. Department of Education as the official accrediting body for MFT programs.

BOWENIAN SYSTEMS THEORY

Murray Bowen, the progenitor of this school, presented a seminal professional paper in 1967 on his own process of differentiation from his family of origin. This laid the groundwork for his focus on the awareness of, and disengagement from, toxic triangles in one's family of origin (also applied to his supervision with trainees). He believed that therapists in training who undertook personal family of origin work became more effective psychotherapists and had more satisfying personal relationships than those who did not (Roberto, 1992).

Guerin and Fogarty (1972) elaborated Bowen's intriguing work on genograms, dimensions of self (Fogarty, 1976), and the multigenerational model of family therapy (Guerin & Guerin, 1976). McGoldrick and Gerson (1985), later joined by Shellenberger (McGoldrick, Gerson, & Shellenberger, 1999), further illuminated the language and technique of genograms (see Chapter 3).

CONTEXTUAL/RELATIONAL THERAPY

The originator and leading proponent of contextual family therapy was Ivan Boszormenyi-Nagy. In one of his early works, coauthored with colleague James Framo, *Intensive Family Therapy* (Boszormenyi-Nagy & Framo, 1965/1985), they attempted to integrate British Object Relations Theory (particularly that of Fairbairn), European existentialism as discussed by Buber, and the interpersonal model of psychiatry articulated by Sullivan, Fromm-Reichmann, and Searles (Roberto, 1992). In *Invisible Loyalties: Reciprocity in Intergenerational Family Therapy,* coauthored with colleague and cotherapist Geraldine Spark (Boszormenyi-Nagy & Spark, 1973), the concepts of legacy, loyalty, indebtedness to one's family of origin, ledger of balances, the continuing profound influence of one's biological relatedness (even if unknown or disowned), and the value of an ethical-existential framework in conceptualizing family relationships were brought to the forefront. Following the publication of this classic book, Boszormenyi-Nagy renamed this approach, shifting from intergenerational family therapy to Contextual Therapy, reflecting the dual focus on multigenerational relational dynamics and individual personality dynamics.

SYMBOLIC-EXPERIENTIAL FAMILY THERAPY

Whitaker and colleagues Warkenten and Malone, working at Emory University's Department of Psychiatry, focused on deciphering the symbolic meaning of psychotic communications. They treated inpatients in conjunction with their significant others, as this increased everyone's awareness of family dynamics and the identified patients' symptomatology. They eventually explicated their seminal approach in *The Roots of Psychotherapy* (Whitaker & Malone, 1953).

In the early 1960s, Whitaker moved from Atlanta to the University of Wisconsin Medical School to teach family theory and therapy. There he further elaborated and articulated the symbolic-experiential model of family therapy (Whitaker & Keith, 1981). In *The Family Crucible,* Napier and Whitaker (1978) eloquently described the process of Symbolic-Experiential Family Therapy by offering vignettes of a prototypical family in therapy.

Whitaker's personal warmth, playfulness, sense of humor, genuine compassion, intuitive giftedness, keen knowledge of people, and grounding in the conventional theories of therapy (which he publicly eschewed as inadequate and restrictive) attracted many students and established professionals to his courses and workshops. He discouraged all from becoming anyone's disciples, encouraging them not to be "carbon copies of the master."

COMMUNICATION MODEL

The Mental Research Institute (MRI) interactional school originated in Palo Alto, California, in the late 1950s, when Gregory Bateson, Don Jackson, John Weakland, and Jay Haley, who all shared an interest in the nature of the communication process, engaged in a research collaboration. They applied anthropological methods of participant observation and objective scrutiny, as well as social systems theory, to their work with families of schizophrenics. The MRI still continues to serve as a major center for training, research, and therapy.

Based on their careful research on communication patterns in schizophrenic families, the Palo Alto group posited that all behavior is communication, occurring both at the *surface or content level* and the *metacommunication or intent level* (a communication that adds meaning to the content-level communication). Bateson, Jackson, Haley, and Weakland (1956) conceptualized double bind communications, a form of paradoxical communication, as those in which contradictory and logically inconsistent messages are communicated concurrent with a third message that the recipient of the contradictory communication not make explicit the logical inconsistencies in the message received. Once the receiver perceives the world in these contradictory "damned if you do and damned if you don't" messages, any portion of the sequence is sufficient to precipitate confusion.

Several other concepts contributed to family systems theory by members of this group merit inclusion here. Jackson (1957) developed the construct of family homeostasis, referring to attempts of the family unit to maintain its status quo and resist internal and external threats to its equilibrium. Thus, therapists' efforts at change may stir up family mistrust, making a shrewd and accurate comprehension of the family's dynamics essential. The therapist must be able to decode the family's verbal and nonverbal messages and utilize subtle intervention strategies.

Virginia Satir joined the MRI group several years after its inception and rapidly moved into the limelight of family therapy pioneers. In her early primer, *Conjoint Family Therapy,* Satir (1967) spelled out the core ideas of the communications school of family systems theory and therapy. Her clearly distilled publications and her charismatic presentations induced many clinicians to obtain training in family therapy.

Satir (1967) asserted that if one family member is troubled and in pain, then all the members are, in some way, in pain. Leverage for gaining entrée can be found in recognizing this shared, reciprocal pain and indicating that all can find ways of having their own needs met and improving family functioning at the same time, as well as reducing the pain through Conjoint Family Therapy. Because of her great sensitivity to the nuances of nonverbal communication and her realization of its cogency, Satir developed such techniques as family sculpting, a means of depicting each member's view of the family without using words filtered through secondary-process thinking. Sculpting has been elaborated further by Constantine (1978), Duhl (1983), and Papp (1976).

Weakland and other, newer colleagues at MRI later fashioned brief family intervention and crisis techniques, combining communications, strategic, and structural theory and techniques (Bodin, 1981). Rapid problem resolution conducive to positive change is pursued in this approach (Watzlawick, Weakland, & Fisch, 1974; Weakland, 1977).

In 1978, Steve deShazer, Insoo Berg, and colleagues established the Brief Family Therapy Center in Milwaukee, where solution-focused brief therapy was developed and practiced (de Shazer, 1985); it has become influential in shaping the form and nature of some contemporary family therapy. This model assumes that family dysfunction reflects ineffective problem-solving efforts and that families inherently possess the knowledge and motivation necessary for problem resolution. Thus, therapy helps families initiate the solution process. The therapist works with the family to develop blueprints for change, referred to as "skeleton keys," enabling the family to unlock doors to enhanced problem resolution and associated family satisfaction. This approach draws heavily from the Ericksonian tradition and has many similarities to Milan systemic therapy.

STRUCTURAL FAMILY THERAPY

Minuchin's experiences in his native Argentina, as a physician in the Israeli Armed Forces, and with displaced Jewish and Arab children sparked his interest in working with families and were the precursors to his view of the *therapist as expert* needing to intervene quickly.

Back in the United States, Minuchin became involved in a research project at Wiltwyck School for Boys in New York, studying the structure and process of interactions in low socioeconomic status families with delinquent children. This research focused on the family environment that produced and supported the child's style of coping, which, when in conflict with the external environment, was labeled "delinquent." The researchers identified a family structure in these family units characterized by invisible walls that separated individuals and groups of individuals and prevented closeness, an absence of intergenerational boundaries, and definable patterns of communication and behavior maintained by the lack of structure and rules. By restructuring family subsystems and boundaries, new patterns of interaction were fostered, which facilitated change. Other work at Wiltwyck led to recognition of the importance of the family's communication system (who related to whom: the splits, schisms, and alliances) and of a disengagement-enmeshment continuum (Minuchin, Montalvo, Guerney, Rosman, & Schumer, 1967). From these studies and clinical observations, the basic tenets of structural theory took shape, and concrete, action-oriented techniques emerged that have proven successful in treating this category of families.

The theory continued to evolve at the Philadelphia Child Guidance Clinic (PCGC), where Minuchin served as director from 1965 to 1981. Montalvo and Rosman accompanied him there from Wiltwyck. Haley joined them in 1967 and became a leading proponent of Structural Family Therapy. Together they turned a small, urban clinic into the largest facility of its kind in the country, which served primarily low-income families. For several decades PCGC was an internationally recognized center for training professionals and paraprofessionals in Structural Family Therapy. This approach has been adapted for use with African American populations, as it incorporates an ecostructural perspective wherein family transactions with external social systems are a locus of concern (Boyd-Franklin, 1989).

STRATEGIC FAMILY THERAPY

Strategic Family Therapy, a model that came into prominence during the 1970s and 1980s, was widely acclaimed by many who read *Uncommon Therapy* (Haley, 1973), *Problem-Solving Therapy* (Haley, 1976), *Ordeal Therapy* (Haley, 1984), and *Strategic Family Therapy* (Madanes, 1981). While with the Palo Alto group, Haley interwove ideas from communications and cybernetic systems theory with the hypnotic and unorthodox metacognitive therapeutic techniques of Milton Erickson. Out of this synthesis he fashioned his *Strategies of Psychotherapy* (Haley, 1963), the approach that has been labeled Strategic Family Therapy. He articulated this model during his time at the PCGC with Minuchin, and subsequently at the Family Therapy Institute of Washington, DC, which he cofounded with Cloe Madanes. Haley (1971) and Madanes (1981), like Whitaker, became intrigued with the power inherent in the use of paradox to disrupt rigid relational and communication patterns. They exemplified the communication theorists' absorption in strategic interventions based on evaluation of the current structure and functioning of the family unit.

Another bastion of Strategic Family Therapy was in Texas, where Robert MacGregor, Harry Goolishian, and Alberto Serrano devised multiple-impact family therapy (Beels & Ferber, 1972). They brought families who lived a distance from their therapy center into Galveston for several days of marathon evaluation and treatment (MacGregor, 1990). They recognized that potent strategic maneuvers were needed to dislodge existing inflexible patterns and structures. Later Goolishian and colleagues were captivated by the use of paradoxes and metaphors and incorporated these into their treatment model. In the late 1970s, the Galveston Family Institute emerged as a major training and treatment site for this theory and methodology. Leading figures included Goolishian, Harlene Anderson, George Pulliam, and Paul Dell (Goolishian & Anderson, 1990). The Galveston group also became intrigued by and involved in epistemology, cybernetics, recursiveness, and the work of Humberto Maturana (Dell, 1981).

In Norway, Tom Andersen's (1991) work with a reflecting team, who join the interviewer and family and share their observations, added another compelling component to the spreading social constructionist, postmodern wing of family therapy. The team's reflections are tied directly to the content of the therapeutic dialogue; they do not use any negative connotations in describing events. The reflecting process provides the participants the option to shift between listening and talking about the issues. This approach assumes that there is not one right way to construe any given situation or problem. For Andersen, language is the vehicle through which the clinician and family cocreate a description and understanding of the presenting issues; to him, *"Language is not innocent"* (Andersen, 1996, p. 119).

SYSTEMIC FAMILY THERAPY

Initially led by Mara Selvini Palazzoli, this model has been adopted internationally by strategic and systemic theoreticians and clinicians. Selvini Palazzoli, an Italian psychiatrist who also studied in the United States, came into contact with researchers and therapists primarily at MRI and the Philadelphia Child Guidance Clinic. Influenced by their ideas, most notably Bateson's writings on circular epistemology, she returned to Milan and incorporated family systems theory into the Milan model of brief systemic therapy.

The Milan approach was applied first to disturbed children and their parents (Selvini Palazzoli, Boscolo, Cecchin, & Prata, 1978), including families with an anorexic member (Selvini Palazzoli, 1974). Some of their work also focused on the role of the referring person in the therapy and the use of paradox and counterparadox (Selvini Palazzoli et al., 1978). The Milan team devised treatment methods for families who lived long distances from the Center and could attend therapy only monthly (Selvini Palazzoli et al., 1978), just as the Galveston team had done.

The Milan treatment methods (e.g., use of therapeutic team as consultants, symptom prescription and ritualized prescriptions) influenced many European (Andolfi, 1979), Canadian (Tomm, 1984a, 1984b), and U.S. family therapists, including some then at Ackerman Institute, among them, Lynn Hoffman, Peggy Papp, and Olga Silverstein.

The Milan team split into two autonomous groups in 1980, with Selvini Palazzoli and Giuliana Prata turning their efforts to research and clinical endeavors aimed at finding an *invariant prescription* applicable to all families. In 1985, Selvini Palazzoli and a group of research collaborators enunciated a systemic model of psychotic processes in families (Selvini Palazzoli, Cirillo, Selvini, & Sorrentino, 1989). Luigi Boscolo and Gianfranco Cecchin (Boscolo, Cecchin,

Hoffman, & Penn, 1987) formed their own treatment and training center (Milan Associates) and focused on clinical work, positing that interventions should be tailored to each family's unique dynamics and not be ritually prescribed.

BEHAVIORAL AND COGNITIVE-BEHAVIORAL THERAPIES

Behavioral Marital Therapy (BMT), originated by Richard Stuart (1969, 1980) and Robert Liberman (1970), was further articulated by Jacobson and Margolin (1979). It incorporates principles from both social learning and social exchange theory and teaches couples to use skills that enhance their relationship, thus increasing marital satisfaction.

Behavioral techniques have been applied to the treatment of sexual dysfunction in couples (see Heiman, LoPiccolo, & LoPiccolo, 1981; Kaplan, 1974, 1979, 1987; Masters & Johnson, 1970; Masters, Johnson, & Kolodny, 1986). Many sex therapists believe that sexual dysfunction is a primary contributor to relationship problems. Although the various sex therapy approaches differ, they share certain elements, including sex education and reeducation, communication and skills training in sexual techniques, reduction of performance anxiety, and attitude change strategies.

A huge body of literature has accumulated regarding the efficacy of behavioral parent training programs for children. Parent training (Gordon & Davidson, 1981), drawing on principles of social learning theory, teaches parents about behavioral concepts and techniques that may be applied to dealing with problematic child behavior. This work emanates from the application of behavior modification techniques to severely disturbed (e.g., schizophrenic) and organically impaired (mentally retarded, autistic) children. As it became apparent that the most effective and rapid way to alter children's behavior was to teach their parents intervention techniques, behavioral parent training was practiced with parents of children and adolescents exhibiting numerous emotional difficulties. The goal of behavioral parent skills training is to modify parents' responses to undesirable child actions to reduce and control such behaviors (G. Patterson, Reid, Jones, & Conger, 1975).

After determining a baseline of the problem behavior and conducting a functional analysis of the child's problem behaviors, the therapist helps the family develop an alternative set of reinforcement contingencies that will lead to new, more adaptive child behaviors. Strategies such as time-out procedures and contingency contracts are adopted. Parent training programs have become popular because they empower parents, who are the ones with the potential to be the most significant change agents in their child's life.

Epstein and colleagues (Epstein, Bishop, & Levin, 1978) developed the McMaster model of family functioning, now termed problem-centered systems therapy (Epstein & Bishop, 1981), which uses general systems theory to describe the structure, organization, and transactional patterns of the family unit in the following domains of family functioning: problem solving, communication, roles, affective responsiveness, affective involvement, and behavioral control. Elements of this treatment approach include defining the problems and prioritizing them, outlining feasible treatment options, negotiating expectations for change, implementing tasks germane to addressing the issues, evaluating task completion, summarizing treatment progress, and future planning for problem management.

PSYCHOEDUCATIONAL FAMILY THERAPY

The family psychoeducation work that has gained the most prominence is the work with families in whom one member manifests severe psychopathology, such as Schizophrenia (Anderson, Reiss, & Hogarty, 1986; Falloon, Boyd, & McGill, 1984), and more recently, affective disorders (Clarkin, Hass, & Glick, 1988). In the past 3 decades, in response to the challenges of deinstitutionalization and substantially increased use of medication, many psychosocial researchers turned their attention away from the etiology of severe psychopathology to understanding the communication patterns (e.g., communication deviance) and social processes (e.g., expressed emotion, affective style) that shape the course of Schizophrenia Spectrum Disorders (Doane, Falloon, Goldstein, & Mintz, 1985; Leff & Vaughn, 1981; Miklowitz, Goldstein, Falloon, & Doane, 1984; Wynne, Cromwell, & Matthysee, 1978).

Findings from this research led to the development of a family-based treatment aimed at prevention of symptomatic relapse in families with a schizophrenic member (Anderson, Griffin, et al., 1986). Proponents adhere to a medical model that conceptualizes Schizophrenia as a severely debilitating functional brain impairment. A core assumption is that families can be educated to create an environment that minimizes stressors that exacerbate the patient's psychiatric condition and improve his or her adaptive functioning. A minority view is that this intervention genre is not a form of family therapy in the traditional sense, but rather a methodology for working with families with an individual suffering from a biologically based disorder.

Some authors selectively have combined a limited number of perspectives (Alexander & Parsons, 1982; Anderson, Griffin, et al., 1986; Epstein, Schlesinger, & Dryden, 1988; Greenberg & Elliott, 2002; Greenberg & Johnson, 1988; F. Kaslow & Lebow, 2002). Other scholars have advocated broad integration of a spectrum of marital and family therapy models (Duhl & Duhl, 1981; Gurman, 1981; F. Kaslow, 1981; D. Kirschner & Kirschner, 1986; Moultrup, 1986; Textor, 1988).

RECENT TRENDS

Noteworthy changes and trends have emerged in the 1980s and 1990s that have significantly altered this field (Broderick & Schrader, 1991; F. Kaslow, 1990a, 1990b, 1990c; N. Kaslow & Celano, 1993). These are elucidated next.

Promulgation of Ethical Guidelines

The establishment, teaching, and enforcement of ethical guidelines for the practice of family therapy (AAMFT, 1988; Doherty & Boss, 1991) and family research (N. Kaslow & Gurman, 1985) have had a significant impact. Critical issues have been addressed, such as how to handle the situation when the therapist has contact with various members of the family separately, as subsystems, and related questions about the confidentiality of information received on such hot button issues as HIV and other medical conditions, incest, affairs, and finances, which is not consciously known by or shared with all family members. A corollary trend has been the quest for increased consistency between ethical guidelines and legal mandates for reporting such behaviors as sexual and physical abuse of minors, elder abuse, and imminent risk of suicide or homicide. These trends have precipitated great controversy regarding identified patient (IP) status in instances of suicidality and homicidality and culpability in cases of abuse. To pure systems theorists, these problems are symptoms reflective of family dysfunction. The idea of a perpetrator being held responsible for his or her behavior, or a psychiatrically impaired family member or the therapist being subject to legal mandates for reporting and for hospitalizing are antithetical. Conversely, to the multitude of nonpurist family therapists today, the idea that an individual's dysfunctional behavior may need to be addressed individually, as well as in the transactional system, is not only logical but even essential. Thus, in cases of parent-child incest, nonpurist therapists believe that the adult is the perpetrator and must be held accountable for his or her behavior, even if years earlier this adult also was an abused child (S. Kirschner, Kirschner, & Rappaport, 1993; Trepper & Barrett, 1989).

Increasing Shift of Training into Graduate School Programs

In the past 30 years, more and more psychology graduate programs have added family psychology courses, tracks, and specializations. These programs teach psychological testing and other forms of assessment as part of the evaluation to be conducted with patients, which is one of the aspects of training that differentiates psychology programs from MFT programs. Research methodology is taught also. Consonant with the traditional emphasis of psychology on the importance of methodological rigor and testing of hypotheses about theoretical assumptions, intervention techniques, and replicability of findings, both process and outcome research have been conducted and quantitative and qualitative studies have received the attention of family psychology researchers.

Licensure and Certification Laws

Almost all states now have separate licensure or certification laws for marriage and family therapists. The rationale for this runs the gamut from consumer protection through augmenting the status of marriage and family therapy as a distinct mental health specialty whose practitioners may be eligible for insurance reimbursement. This focus on ethics, law, and licensure or certification has increased the level of accountability of members of this profession.

Family Assessment Devices

The past 25 years have seen the development of an increasing number of family assessment devices (N. Kaslow, F. Kaslow, & Farber, 1999; Nurse, 1999), including self-report measures of marital satisfaction and family function and micro- and macro-analytic coding schemas for family interaction (Markman & Notarius, 1987). Self-report measures of overall marital adjustment include the Locke-Wallace (Locke & Wallace, 1959) and the Dyadic Adjustment Scale (Spanier, 1976). Commonly used self-report measures of family adjustment include such psychometrically sound instruments as the Family Environment Scale (Moos & Moos, 1981), the Family Adaptability and Cohesion Evaluation Scale (Olson et al., 1983), and the McMaster Family Assessment Device (Epstein, Baldwin, & Bishop, 1983). Various other self-report instruments tap marital communication and intimacy, quality of family life, and family life cycle events, all of which may be used by therapists of different theoretical orientations (T. Patterson, 1999).

Gender-Sensitive Paradigms

Paralleling the developments in American psychology in which feminist theorists and therapists underscored the power imbalances between men and women and highlighted gender differences in various domains of functioning, feminist family therapists brought the same issues to the fore, focusing . . . on marital, parent-child, and larger family relationships. (N. Kaslow et al., 1999, p. 768; see also Goodrich, Rampage, Ellman, & Halstead, 1988; Hare-Mustin, 1978; McGoldrick, Anderson, & Walsh, 1989; Walters, Carter, Papp, & Silverstein, 1988)

The *Journal of Feminist Family Therapy,* first published in the mid-1980s, provided a vehicle for articulation of dilemmas that many feminists wanted to catapult to the attention of the broader field. Feminist family therapy seeks to alter the social conditions contributing to the maintenance of gender-prescribed behaviors and to modify the social structures that perpetuate an oppressive, hierarchical, and male-dominated society in ways detrimental to the well-being of women. They posit that by stressing the importance of egalitarianism in relationships, individuals are free to reach their fullest potential in the realms of power and intimacy and to enjoy the numerous roles they live interpersonally as parents, partners, and children.

Subsequently, the men's movement sprouted (Bly, 1990; Meth & Pasick, 1990; Pittman, 1993), partially in reaction to the women's movement. It also simultaneously evolved from the internal needs men were experiencing about wanting to communicate with one another on deeper, more personal levels. Key concerns of the men's movement have been to validate the multiplicity of images, behaviors, and lifestyles of men and to support them in valuing feelings and relationships with their partner, children, and members of their family of origin. For some, there has been a decreased overemphasis on the competitive, power-driven pursuit of work and money.

The overpowering phenomenon of these two movements ultimately caused considerable disruption and controversy in the field (and in many marriages). This in turn prompted a reevaluation of some of the basic tenets of family therapy and necessitated the formulation of new, more gender-sensitive models of assessment and intervention (Philpot, Brooks, Lusterman, & Nutt, 1997).

Diversity

Beginning in the 1980s and continuing unabated in the new millennium, the new waves of immigrants from myriad countries who did not want to forsake their original identities made it impossible to continue to promulgate a melting pot assimilationist theory of a culturally unidimensional society. Thus, there has been substantial pressure to accept ethnic, racial, religious, and socioeconomic diversity and for therapists who treat clients with diverse cultural traditions and beliefs to do so sensitively and respectfully (Boyd-Franklin, 1989; Ho, 1987; McGoldrick, Giordano, & Garcia-Preto, 2005). This trend reflects a heightened emphasis on recognition of all kinds of diversity and the need for cultural sensitivity and competence (or the willingness to make appropriate referrals when the task exceeds one's areas of competence).

Multiplicity of Family Forms

As the composition of families in the United States has become more variegated, clinicians have enlarged their repertoire for dealing with the current multiplicity of family forms, which can now be categorized as including single-parent families by choice or circumstances; heterosexual, gay, and lesbian couples living together; married couples without children; married couples with children; three- and four-generation families living together; divorced binuclear families; remarried and stepfamilies; adoptive families; foster families; and groups of individuals choosing to live together as a family unit (Ahrons & Rodgers, 1987; Bray & Berger, 1993; F. Kaslow & Schwartz, 1987; Nichols, Pace-Nichols, Becvar, & Napier, 2000; Visher & Visher, 1991; Wallerstein & Kelly, 1980).

Internationalization of the Field

This trend, begun slowly in the 1970s, picked up momentum and was formalized in the 1980s. It resulted in the formation of the International Family Therapy Association (IFTA) in 1987 in Prague, Czechoslovakia, and of the International Academy of Family Psychologists (IAFP) in Tokyo, Japan, in 1990 (see F. Kaslow, 1990a, 1990b, 1991). Family therapy journals and books are now published in many countries and many languages. Family therapists throughout the world turn not only to leading teachers, theoreticians, researchers, and practitioners from the United States for tutelage, but also to those from Australia, Germany, Israel, Italy, Norway, and the United Kingdom, and other countries. These influences are reflected in chapters in this book where authors talk about the Milan Systemic Model (Italy) and Narrative Therapy (Australia). Some form of family therapy is practiced in the majority of nations of the world.

Research

Recognition and acknowledgment of the importance of firmly grounding theory and practice in the findings of quantitative and qualitative research has grown. Increasingly, empirical research has been conducted to enable better description of family processes and to ascertain the efficacy of various family intervention approaches for various types of problems and families. Members of the major organizations in the field are occasionally involved in these endeavors collaboratively, and some portions of professional conferences and publications are being devoted to the integration of family research, theory, and practice.

CONCLUDING COMMENTS

The future of practice, research, and training in marital and family therapy and psychology will incorporate the trends and theoretical approaches presented here and will evolve in response to the emergence of new academic, clinical, professional, sociocultural, and political influences. Consistent with the burgeoning integrative family therapy approaches, it is probable that the fields of family therapy and psychology will witness a decreasing emphasis on rigid adherence to particular schools of thought and clinical methods and a concurrent shift to increasing flexibility in combining treatment models and associated techniques, just as this book elaborates how EMDR and family systems approaches are combined in ways that increase the synergistic impact of each. As a result, marital and family therapists will become more effective in treating couples and families presenting with a broad range of biopsychosocial problems and dysfunctions, perhaps with more utilizing EMDR, and will do so in a manner that focuses increasingly on the therapist-family relationship.

Despite the proliferation of research on family interactional processes, limited empirical data exist on family therapy process and outcome. Future research will be enriched by better cooperation between clinicians and researchers and strengthened by attention to theory-based evaluations and the integration of quantitative and qualitative research efforts. Hopefully, gains and advances in empirical investigations, combined with the trend toward theory integration, will influence positively the nature of clinical practice and enhance its efficacy.

REFERENCES

Ackerman, N. W. (1961). A dynamic frame for the clinical approach to family conflict. In N. W. Ackerman, F. L. Beatman, & S. N. Sherman (Eds.), *Exploring the base for family therapy* (pp. 52–67). New York: Family Service Association of America.

Ahrons, C. R., & Rodgers, R. H. (1987). *Divorced families: A multidisciplinary developmental view.* New York: Norton.

Alexander, J. F., & Parsons, B. V. (1982). *Functional family therapy.* Monterey, CA: Brooks/Cole.

American Association for Marriage and Family Therapy. (1988). *AAMFT code of ethical principles for marriage and family therapists.* Washington, DC: Author.

Andersen, T. (1991). *The reflecting team: Dialogues and dialogues about the dialogues.* New York: Norton.

Andersen, T. (1996). Language is not innocent. In F. W. Kaslow (Ed.), *Handbook of relational diagnosis and dysfunctional family patterns* (pp. 119–125). New York: Wiley.

Anderson, C. M., Griffin, S., Rossi, A., Pagonis, I., Holder, D. P., & Treiber, R. (1986). A comparative study of the impact of education versus process groups for families of patients with affective disorders. *Family Process, 25,* 185–206.

Anderson, C. M., Reiss, D. J., & Hogarty, G. E. (1986). *Schizophrenia and the family.* New York: Guilford Press.

Andolfi, M. (1979). *Family therapy: An interactional approach.* New York: Plenum Press.

Bateson, G., Jackson, D. D., Haley, J. E., & Weakland, J. (1956). Toward a theory of schizophrenia. *Behavioral Science, 1,* 251–264.

Beels, C., & Ferber, A. (1972). What family therapists do. In A. Ferber, M. Mendelsohn, & A. Napier (Eds.), *The book of family therapy* (pp. 168–232). New York: Science House.

Bly, R. (1990). *Iron John.* Reading, MA: Addison-Wesley.

Bodin, A. M. (1981). The interactional view: Family therapy approaches of the Mental Research Institute. In A. S. Gurman & D. P. Kniskern (Eds.), *Handbook of family therapy* (pp. 267–309). New York: Brunner/Mazel.

Boscolo, L., Cecchin, G., Hoffman, L., & Penn, P. (1987). *Milan systemic family therapy.* New York: Norton.

Boszormenyi-Nagy, I., & Framo, J. L. (1985). *Intensive family therapy.* New York: Brunner/Mazel. (Original work published 1965)

Boszormenyi-Nagy, I., & Spark, G. (1973). *Invisible loyalties.* New York: Harper & Row.

Bowen, M. (1959). Family relationships in schizophrenia. In A. Auerbach (Ed.), *Schizophrenia: An integrated approach* (pp. 147–178). New York: Ronald.

Bowen, M. (1967). Toward the differentiation of self in one's own family. In J. L. Framo (Ed.), *Family interaction: A dialogue between family researchers and family therapists* (pp. 111–173). New York: Springer-Verlag.

Bowen, M. (1988). *Family therapy in clinical practice* (2nd ed.). Northvale, NJ: Aronson.

Boyd-Franklin, N. (1989). *Black families in therapy: A multisystems approach.* New York: Guilford Press.

Bray, J. H., & Berger, S. H. (1993). Developmental issues in stepfamilies research project: Family relationships and parent-child interactions. *Journal of Family Psychology, 7*(1), 76–90.

Broderick, C. B., & Schrader, S. S. (1991). The history of professional marriage and family therapy. In A. S. Gurman & D. P. Kniskern (Eds.), *Handbook of family therapy* (Vol. 2, pp. 3–40). New York: Brunner/Mazel.

Clarkin, J. K., Haas, G. L., & Glick, I. D. (Eds.). (1988). *Affective disorders and the family: Assessment and treatment.* New York: Guilford Press.

Constantine, L. L. (1978). Family sculpture and relationship mapping techniques. *Journal of Marriage and Family Counseling, 4,* 13–24.

Dell, P. (1981). Paradox redux. *Journal of Marital and Family Therapy, 7*(2), 127–134.

de Shazer, S. (1985). *Keys to solution in brief therapy.* New York: Norton.

Doane, J. A., Falloon, I., Goldstein, M. J., & Mintz, J. (1985). Parental affective style and the treatment of schizophrenia: Predicting course of illness and social functioning. *Archives of General Psychiatry, 43,* 34–42.

Doherty, W. J., & Boss, P. G. (1991). Values and ethics in family therapy. In A. S. Gurman & D. P. Kniskern (Eds.), *Handbook of family therapy* (Vol. 2, pp. 606–637). New York: Brunner/Mazel.

Duhl, B. S. (1983). *From the inside out and other metaphors: Creative and integrative approaches to training in systems thinking.* New York: Brunner/Mazel.

Duhl, B. S., & Duhl, F. J. (1981). Integrative family therapy. In A. S. Gurman & D. P. Kniskern (Eds.), *Handbook of family therapy* (pp. 483–516). New York: Brunner/Mazel.

Epstein, N. B., Baldwin, L., & Bishop, D. S. (1983). The McMaster family assessment device. *Journal of Marital and Family Therapy, 9,* 171–180.

Epstein, N. B., & Bishop, D. S. (1981). Problem centered systems therapy of the family. In A. S. Gurman & D. P. Kniskern (Eds.), *Handbook of family therapy.* New York: Brunner/Mazel.

Epstein, N. B., Bishop, D. S., & Levin, S. (1978). The McMaster model of family functioning. *Journal of Marital and Family Counseling, 4,* 19–32.

Epstein, N. B., Schlesinger, S. E., & Dryden, W. (Eds.). (1988). *Cognitive-behavioral therapy with families.* New York: Brunner/Mazel.

Falloon, I., Boyd, J., & McGill, C. (1984). *Family care of schizophrenia.* New York: Guilford Press.

Fogarty, T. (1976). Systems concepts and the dimensions of self. In P. J. Guerin (Ed.), *Family therapy: Theory and practice* (pp. 144–153). New York: Gardner Press.

Goodrich, T. J., Rampage, C., Ellman, B., & Halstead, K. (1988). *Feminist family therapy: A casebook.* New York: Norton.

Goolishian, H. A., & Anderson, H. (1990). Understanding the therapeutic process: From individuals and families to systems and language. In F. W. Kaslow (Ed.), *Voices in family psychology* (Vol. 1, pp. 91–113). Newbury Park, CA: Sage.

Gordon, S. B., & Davidson, N. (1981). Behavioral parent training. In A. S. Gurman & D. P. Kniskern (Eds.), *Handbook of family therapy* (pp. 517–555). New York: Brunner/Mazel.

Greenberg, L. S., & Elliot, R. (2002). Emotion focused therapy. In F. W. Kaslow & J. Lebow (Eds.), *Comprehensive handbook of psychotherapy: Vol. 4. Integrative/eclectic* (pp. 213–240). Hoboken, NJ: Wiley.

Greenberg, L. S., & Johnson, S. M. (1988). *Emotionally focused therapy for couples.* New York: Guilford Press.

Guerin, P. J. (1976). Family therapy: The first 25 years. In P. J. Guerin (Ed.), *Family therapy and practice* (pp. 2–22). New York: Gardner Press.

Guerin, P. J., & Fogarty, T. (1972). Study your own family. In A. Ferber, M. Mendelsohn, & A. Y. Napier (Eds.), *The book of family therapy* (pp. 445–467). New York: Science House.

Guerin, P. J., & Guerin, K. B. (1976). Theoretical aspects and clinical relevance of the multigenerational model of family therapy. In P. J. Guerin (Ed.), *Family therapy: Theory and practice* (pp. 91–110). New York: Gardner.

Gurman, A. S. (1981). Integrative marital therapy: Toward the development of an interpersonal approach. In S. Budman (Ed.), *Forms of brief psychotherapy* (pp. 415–457). New York: Guilford Press.

Haley, J. (1963). *Strategies of psychotherapy.* New York: Grune & Stratton.

Haley, J. (1971). *Changing families.* New York: Grune & Stratton.

Haley, J. (1973). *Uncommon therapy: The psychiatric techniques of Milton H. Erickson, MD.* New York: Norton.

Haley, J. (1976). *Problem-solving therapy.* San Francisco: Jossey-Bass.

Haley, J. (1984). *Ordeal therapy: Unusual ways to change behavior.* San Francisco: Jossey-Bass.

Hare-Mustin, R. T. (1978). A feminist approach to family therapy. *Family Process, 17,* 181–194.

Heiman, J. R., LoPiccolo, L., & LoPiccolo, J. (1981). The treatment of sexual dysfunction. In A. S. Gurman & D. P. Kniskern (Eds.), *Handbook of family therapy* (pp. 592–630). New York: Brunner/Mazel.

Ho, M. K. (1987). *Family therapy with ethnic minorities.* Newbury Park, CA: Sage.

Jackson, D. D. (1957). The question of family homeostasis. *Psychiatric Quarterly Supplement, 31,* 79–90.

Jacobson, N. S., & Margolin, G. (1979). *Marital therapy: Strategies based on social learning and behavior exchange principles.* New York: Brunner/Mazel.

Kaplan, H. S. (1974). *The new sex therapy: Active treatment of sexual dysfunction.* New York: Brunner/Mazel.

Kaplan, H. S. (1979). *Disorders of sexual desire.* New York: Brunner/Mazel.

Kaplan, H. S. (1987). *Sexual aversion, sexual phobias, and panic disorder.* New York: Brunner/Mazel.

Kaslow, F. W. (1981). A dialectic approach to family therapy and practice: Selectivity and synthesis. *Journal of Marital and Family Therapy, 7,* 345–351.

Kaslow, F. W. (Ed.). (1990a, August). Part I: First World Conference of Family Therapy [Special issue]. *Contemporary Family Therapy, 12*(4).

Kaslow, F. W. (Ed.). (1990b, October). Part II: First World Conference of Family Therapy [Special issue]. *Contemporary Family Therapy, 12*(5).

Kaslow, F. W. (Ed.). (1990c). *Voices in family psychology* (Vols. 1 & 2). Newbury Park, CA: Sage.

Kaslow, F. W. (Ed.). (1991, December). Second World Conference of Family Therapy [Special issue]. *Contemporary Family Therapy, 13*(6).

Kaslow, F. W. (2000a). Continued evolution of family therapy: The last 25 years. *Contemporary Family Therapy, 22*(4), 357–386.

Kaslow, F. W. (2000b). History of family therapy: Developments outside of the USA. *Journal of Family Psychotherapy, 11*(4), 1–35.

Kaslow, F. W., & Lebow, J. (Eds.). (2002). *Comprehensive handbook of psychotherapy: Vol. 4. Integrative/eclectic.* Hoboken, NJ: Wiley.

Kaslow, F. W., & Schwartz, L. (1987). *The dynamics of divorce: A life cycle perspective.* New York: Brunner/Mazel.

Kaslow, N. J., & Celano, M. (1993). The family therapies. In A. S. Gurman & S. B. Messer (Eds.), *Modern psychotherapies: Theory and practice* (pp. 343–402). New York: Guilford Press.

Kaslow, N. J., & Gurman, A. S. (1985). Ethical considerations in family therapy research. *Counseling and Values, 30,* 47–61.

Kaslow, N. J., Kaslow, F. W., & Farber, E. W. (1999). Theories and techniques of marital and family therapy. In M. B. Sussman, S. K. Steinmetz, & G. W. Peterson (Eds.), *Handbook of marriage and the family* (2nd ed., pp. 767–793). New York: Plenum Press.

Kirschner, D. A., & Kirschner, S. (1986). *Comprehensive family therapy: An integration of systemic and psychodynamic treatment models.* New York: Brunner/Mazel.

Kirschner, S., Kirschner, D. A., & Rappaport, R. L. (1993). *Working with adult incest survivors: The healing journey.* New York: Brunner/Mazel.

Leff, J., & Vaughn, C. (1981). The role of maintenance therapy and relatives' expressed emotion in relapse of schizophrenia: A 2-year follow-up. *British Journal of Psychiatry, 139,* 102–104.

Liberman, R. (1970). Behavioral approaches to family and couple therapy. *American Journal of Orthopsychiatry, 40,* 106–118.

Locke, H. J., & Wallace, K. M. (1959). Short marital adjustment and prediction tests: Their reliability and validity. *Marriage and Family Living, 21,* 251–255.

MacGregor, R. (1990). Team family methods in the public sector. In F. W. Kaslow (Ed.), *Voices in family psychology* (Vol. 1, pp. 156–170). Newbury Park, CA: Sage.

Madanes, C. (1981). *Strategic family therapy.* San Francisco: Jossey Bass.

Markman, H. J., & Notarius, C. I. (1987). Coding marital and family interaction: Current status. In T. Jacob (Eds.), *Family interaction and psychopathology: Theories, methods, and findings* (pp. 329–390). New York: Plenum Press.

Masters, W. H., & Johnson, V. E. (1970). *Human sexual inadequacy.* Boston: Little, Brown.

Masters, W. H., Johnson, V. E., & Kolodny, R. (1986). *On sex and human loving.* Boston: Little, Brown.

McGoldrick, M., Anderson, C. M., & Walsh, F. (Eds.). (1989). *Women in families: A framework for family therapy.* New York: Norton.

McGoldrick, M., & Gerson, R. (1985). *Genograms in family assessment.* New York: Norton.

McGoldrick, M., Gerson, R., & Shellenberger, S. (1999). *Genograms: Assessment and intervention* (2nd ed.). New York: Norton.

McGoldrick, M., Giordano, J., & Garcia-Preto, N. (Eds.). (2005). *Ethnicity and family therapy* (3rd ed.). New York: Guilford Press.

Meth, R. L., & Pasick, R. S. (1990). *Men in therapy: The challenge of change.* New York: Guilford Press.

Miklowitz, D. J., Goldstein, M. J., Falloon, I. R. H., & Doane, J. A. (1984). Interactional correlates of expressed emotion in the families of schizophrenics. *British Journal of Psychiatry, 144,* 482–487.

Minuchin, S., Montalvo, B., Guerney, B. G., Jr., Rosman, B., & Schumer, F. (1967). *Families of the slums.* New York: Basic Books.

Moos, R. H., & Moos, B. S. (1981). *Family Environment Scale manual.* Palo Alto, CA: Consulting Psychologists Press.

Moultrup, D. (1986). Integration: A coming of age. *Contemporary Family Therapy: An International Journal, 8,* 157–167.

Napier, A. Y., & Whitaker, C. A. (1978). *The family crucible.* New York: Harper & Row.

Nichols, W. C., Pace-Nichols, M. A., Becvar, D. C., & Napier, A. Y. (2000). *Family development and intervention.* New York: Wiley.

Nurse, A. R. (1999). *Family assessment: Effective uses of personality tests with couples and families.* New York: Wiley.

Olson, D. H., McCubbin, H. I., Barnes, H., Larsen, A., Muxen, M., & Wilson, M. (1983). *Families: What makes them work.* Beverly Hills, CA: Sage.

Papp, P. (1976). Family choreography. In P. J. Guerin (Ed.), *Family therapy: Theory and practice* (pp. 465–479). New York: Gardner Press.

Patterson, G. R., Reid, R. B., Jones, R. R., & Conger, R. E. (1975). *A social learning approach to family intervention: Vol. 1. Families with aggressive children.* Eugene, OR: Castalia.

Patterson, T. (1999). *Couple and family clinical documentation sourcebook.* New York: Wiley.

Philpot, C. L., Brooks, G. R., Lusterman, D. D., & Nutt, R. L. (1997). *Bridging separate gender worlds.* Washington, DC: American Psychological Association.

Pittman, F. (1993). *Man enough: Fathers, sons, and the search for masculinity*. East Rutherford, NJ: Putnam.

Roberto, L. G. (1992). *Transgenerational family therapies*. New York: Guilford Press.

Satir, V. (1964). *Conjoint family therapy*. Palo Alto, CA: Science & Behavior Books.

Satir, V. (1967). *Conjoint family therapy* (2nd ed.). Palo Alto, CA: Science & Behavior Books.

Satir, V. (1972). *People-making*. Palo Alto, CA: Science & Behavior Books.

Selvini Palazzoli, M. (1974). *Self starvation*. London: Human Context Books.

Selvini Palazzoli, M., Boscolo, L., Cecchin, G., & Prata, G. (1978). *Paradox and counterparadox*. Northvale, NJ: Aronson.

Selvini Palazzoli, M., Cirillo, S., Selvini, M., & Sorrentino, A. M. (1989). *Family games: General models of psychotic processes in the family*. New York: Norton.

Spanier, G. B. (1976). Measuring dyadic adjustment: New scales for assessing the quality of marriage and similar dyads. *Journal of Marriage and the Family, 38,* 15–28.

Stuart, R. B. (1969). Operant-interpersonal treatment of marital discord. *Journal of Consulting and Clinical Psychology, 33,* 675–682.

Stuart, R. B. (1980). *Helping couples change: A social learning approach to marital therapy*. New York: Guilford Press.

Textor, M. R. (1988). Integrative family therapy. *International Journal of Family Psychiatry, 9,* 93–105.

Tomm, K. (1984a). One perspective on the Milan approach: Pt. I. *Journal of Marital and Family Therapy, 10,* 113–125.

Tomm, K. (1984b). One perspective on the Milan approach: Pt. II. *Journal of Marital and Family Therapy, 10,* 253–271.

Trepper, T. S., & Barrett, M. J. (1989). *Systemic family treatment of incest*. New York: Brunner/Mazel.

Visher, E. B., & Visher, J. S. (1991). *How to win as a stepfamily* (2nd ed.). New York: Brunner/Mazel.

Wallerstein, J. S., & Kelly, J. B. (1980). *Surviving the breakup: How children and parents cope with divorce*. New York: Basic Books.

Walters, M., Carter, B., Papp, P., & Silverstein, O. (1988). *The invisible web: Gender patterns in family relationships*. New York: Guilford Press.

Watzlawick, P., Weakland, J., & Fisch, R. (1974). *Change: Principles of problem formation and problem resolution*. New York: Norton.

Weakland, J. H. (1977). Family somatics: A neglected edge. *Family Process, 16,* 263–272.

Whitaker, C. A. (1975). Psychotherapy of the absurd: With a special emphasis on the psychotherapy of aggression. *Family Process, 14,* 1–16.

Whitaker, C. A. (1976). The hindrance of theory in clinical work. In P. J. Guerin (Ed.), *Family therapy: Theory and practice* (pp. 154–164). New York: Gardner Press.

Whitaker, C. A., & Keith, D. V. (1981). Symbolic-experiential family therapy. In A. S. Gurman & D. P. Kniskern (Eds.), *Handbook of family therapy* (pp. 187–225). New York: Brunner/Mazel.

Whitaker, C. A., & Malone, T. P. (1953). *The roots of psychotherapy*. New York: Blakiston.

Wynne, L. C., Cromwell, R. L., & Matthysee, S. (1978). *The nature of schizophrenia: New approaches to research and treatment*. New York: Wiley.

Author Index

Subject Index